THE
COLUMBIA
HISTORY OF
EASTERN
EUROPE
IN THE
TWENTIETH
CENTURY

EDITED BY
Joseph Held

Columbia University Press
New York

Columbia University Press
New York   Chichester, West Sussex
Copyright © 1992 Columbia University Press
All rights reserved

Library of Congress Cataloging-in-Publication Data

The Columbia history of Eastern Europe in the twentieth
century / edited by Joseph Held.
    p.   cm.
  Includes bibliographical references and index.
  ISBN 0–231–07696–7 (alk. paper)
  ISBN 0–231–07697–5 (pbk.)
  1. Europe, Eastern—History—20th century.   I. Held,
Joseph.
DJK42.C65   1991
909'.09717082—dc20   91-29132
                                                         CIP

Printed in the United States of America

c   10   9   8   7   6   5   4   3   2   1
p   10   9   8   7   6   5   4   3   2   1

The Columbia History of Eastern Europe in the Twentieth Century

This volume is dedicated to
Stephen Fischer-Galati,
whose untiring labors in the vineyards of
scholarship kept Eastern European studies alive
even in hard times.

Contents

Acknowledgments

This volume originated in a conference held at Rutgers University's Camden Campus in February 1990. The participants at this conference submitted the papers that comprise the individual studies in the book. As is usual in such matters, they all considered the task important: we gathered at a time when Eastern Europe was, once again, in flux, when new political and social structures were emerging and the future seemed somewhat brighter than the past.

The conference was supported, first of all, by a grant from Rutgers University–Camden's dean and provost, Walter K. Gordon, and we all owe him gratitude. The staff of the dean's office did everything they could to make our venture successful, and we thank them for their efforts. Professors Peter Pastor of Montclair State College, Ellison Katz of Temple University, and Sidney Katz of Rutgers University–Camden provided sage advice that helped the success of the conference and, ultimately, of our joint undertaking. Dr. Andrew Lees of Rutgers University–Camden provided support when it was most needed.

Above all, Kate Wittenberg, our editor at Columbia University Press, has done more to have this volume put into shape than anyone. Her patience and understanding were most needed and are greatly appreciated. We also thank John Moore, the director of Columbia

University Press, who took time out of his busy schedule to attend the first day of the conference and encouraged us to proceed with the project.

Finally, I must express my deep appreciation for the scholars who came to Rutgers University–Camden to hear each other's thoughts on the troubled history of Eastern Europe and who eventually—though not without coaxing—submitted their papers for publication in this volume. We all became friends in a short time and can only hope that the peoples of Eastern Europe follow our example and bury old antagonisms in a new age.

Joseph Held

Chronology of Events in Eastern Europe, 1918–1990

1918   *May 7*: In signing the Treaty of Bucharest, Romania obligates itself to reenter the war on the side of the Allies. On November 10, Romanian troops enter Transylvania, promised by the Allies to the Romanian state.

October 14: The Czechoslovak national council declares its independence.

October 17: The Hungarian parliament declares the country independent of Austria. The monarchy, however, is retained.

October 19: The national council at Zagreb proclaims the Yugoslav union.

October 30: The Slovak national council votes for Czechoslovak unity.

October 31: Revolution breaks out in Hungary; the new government is headed by Count Mihaly Károlyi.

November 3: The independent Polish Republic is proclaimed. The new Polish army advances into Ukrainian Galicia, and takes Lemberg twenty days later.

November 16: A Hungarian republic is proclaimed in Budapest.

1918 *(continued)* *December 1*: The kingdom of Serbs, Croats, and Slovenes is formally declared. Prince Alexander of Serbia accepts the regency of the new state.

December 25: Albania is attacked by Yugoslavia in the north and by Italy on the Adriatic coast.

December 27: Polish troops occupy Poznan.

1919 *January 17*: Ignace Jan Paderewski forms a coalition government and General Joseph Pilsudski is named president of the new Polish state.

March 21: Károlyi resigns as Hungarian premier in protest for the Allies giving Transylvania (with 2.5 million Hungarians) to Romania. The same day a communist government takes power in Hungary. Alexander Garbai, a Social Democrat, is named president, but the real power is in the hands of Béla Kun, a communist.

April 10: Romanian troops advance into Hungary. By August 1, they reach and occupy Budapest; looting is heavy and widespread.

May 15: In the ongoing Greek-Turkish dispute, which will not be resolved until late 1922, the Greek army, with Allied assistance, invades Anatolia.

May 28: Romania's Jews are allowed to apply for Romanian citizenship.

June 13: The Allies decide that the territory of Banat with its mixed population, formerly belonging to Hungary, will be divided between Romania and Yugoslavia. The territory's 550,000 ethnic Hungarians will come under Yugoslav control.

June 28: Germany and the Allies sign the Peace Treaty of Versailles. The treaty establishes the League of Nations and the International Labor Organization (ILO). It also specifies the conditions imposed on Germany by the Allies. These conditions include losses of German territories and colonies, military restrictions, and, most controversial, reparations payments for "all the loss and damage" to the Allies caused by German aggression.

The Treaty of Versailles creates a new Polish western frontier, and Poland receives a corridor along the Vistula River to the Baltic Sea. Danzig is to be a free city.

Newly independent Poland and Lithuania go to undeclared war over the city of Vilnius.

Poland and Czechoslovakia dispute the city of Teschen, and battles occur between armies of the two states.

August 1: Béla Kun's regime in Hungary falls after an unsuccessful offensive against Romania. Kun flees to Vienna.

August 17: In Bulgarian elections the Peasant party wins an overwhelming victory.

September 14: Romania is admitted to the League of Nations.

October 6: Alexander Stamboliiski becomes the first prime minister of Bulgaria from the Peasant party.

November 19: The U.S. Senate fails to ratify the Treaty of Versailles.

1920   *January 10*: The League of Nations convenes. The first meeting of its assembly will be held on November 15.

February 25: Romanian troops leave Hungary after extensive pillaging and looting.

February 29: A Czechoslovak constitution based on the French model is adopted.

March 1: Admiral Miklós Horthy, commander in chief of the army, is named regent of Hungary.

April 18: The first regular, relatively free elections are held in Czechoslovakia. Various coalition governments will rule, since no single party is able to garner a majority.

April 25–October 12: The Polish-Soviet war begins with Soviet successes, but ends (after France provides extensive military equipment and advice to Poland) with a Polish victory.

June 4: The Treaty of Trianon is signed. Hungary loses two-thirds of its former territory and about four million ethnic Hungarians through the operation of Wilsonian principles of national self-determination.

August 2: Italy agrees to evacuate the Albanian city of Valona, but retains the island of Saseno.

August 14: Czechoslovakia signs a treaty with Yugoslavia—the first step toward the establishment of the Little Entente. The purpose is, first, to establish a *cordon sanitaire* on the western borders of the Soviet Union and, second, to prevent Hungary from regaining lost territories and ethnic Hungarian population from the successor states and Romania.

December 16: Bulgaria is admitted to the League of Nations.

1921   *January 1*: A new constitution is proclaimed in the kingdom of Serbs, Croats, and Slovenes, creating a centralized government dominated by Serbs.

February 19: A French-Polish treaty for mutual aid and military cooperation is executed. By this treaty France attempts to bring Poland into the French alliance system in Eastern Europe. The Polish-Czech conflict over Teschen, however, will prevent this from becoming reality.

March 3: Romania concludes a defensive alliance with Hungary and Poland against the Soviet Union. Romanian troops, taking advantage of the weakened state of the Soviet Union, occupy and annex Bessarabia.

March 8: Claiming nonfulfillment of German treaty obligations, the French occupy some German cities.

March 17: A constitution is accepted by Poland.

March 20: A plebiscite in Silesia decides in favor of Germany; "unofficial" Polish troops occupy the disputed area. The League of Nations partitions the territory between Poland and Germany.

March 21: King Charles of Habsburg makes an unsuccessful attempt to regain the Hungarian throne.

April 14: Count Istvan Bethlen forms a cabinet, beginning the stabilization of Hungary.

April 23: Romania and Czechoslovakia sign a mutual aid treaty (the Little Entente) directed against Hungary.

April 27: The reparations commission declares German reparation obligations to be an amount equivalent to 132 billion gold marks.

June 7: Yugoslavia and Romania conclude a mutual aid pact, directed against Hungary, thus completing the formation of the Little Entente, supported by the French.

August 19: Alexander is named King of the Serbs, Croats and Slovenes.

October 20: The former emperor King Charles makes a second attempt to regain his throne in Hungary. Czechoslovakia and Yugoslavia mobilize their armies, and Hungary expels the former king.

1922   *January 8*: Following a plebiscite, Poland receives the Lithuanian city of Vilnius. This creates years of bad relations between the two countries.

April 16: Weimar Germany and the Soviet Union sign the Rapallo Treaty. It denounces reparations and proposes friendly relations between the two powers.

August 1: The Balfour note is delivered. Great Britain states its willingness to abandon claims for German reparations if the U.S. cancels the war debt of its European allies.

September 18: Hungary is admitted to the League of Nations.

October 11: As part of the Treaty of Lausanne the Greek-Turkish war, a disaster for Greece, is officially ended. Istanbul and most of Asia Minor is in Turkish hands.

October 28: The Italian Fascists seize power in Rome.

1923   *January 9*: Germany is declared to be in default of reparations. Two days later French and Belgian troops occupy the Ruhr valley, Germany's industrial heartland. Germany resorts to passive resistance and increases the money supply to pay the striking workers.

June 9: In Bulgaria, Stamboliiski is overthrown by a group of officers and is killed a week later.

September 26: The Germans cease passive resistance. Inflation is ravaging the German and French economies, and the Ruhr occupation is a failure.

December 19: Ladislaw Grabski forms a new cabinet of experts that succeeds in stabilizing Poland's internal situation.

December 20: The League of Nations accepts a plan for the economic reorganization of Hungary.

1924   *January 25*: France and Czechoslovakia sign a treaty for mutual aid and defense.

April 9: The Dawes Plan reduces German reparations and grants a loan to Germany to help stabilize its currency.

August 16: A conference of European statesmen in London accepts the Dawes Plan and provides for the evacuation of French and Belgian troops from the Ruhr.

1925   *January 21*: Albania is proclaimed a republic. Ahmed Zogu is named its first president.

April 16: Communist terrorists explode a bomb in Sofia Cathedral, killing 124 and maiming many others.

May 4: In response to the outrage the communists are outlawed in Bulgaria.

August 25: French and Belgian troops cease to occupy the major cities of the Ruhr valley.

October 16: The Locarno Conference concludes with a series of agreements intended to secure peace in Europe. The frontiers of Germany, France, and Belgium are declared secured. Germany, Poland, and Czechoslovakia agree to the arbitration of their disputes. French-Polish and French-Czechoslovak treaties for mutual aid in case of German attack are also approved. The French eventually strengthen their ties with the Little Entente and build the Maginot line.

October 22: Greek-Bulgarian clashes are settled by the League.

December 28: Land reform legislation is introduced in Poland distributing 500,000 acres of land a year among the peasants for a period of ten years.

December 28: Prince Carol abdicates his right to the kingship of Romania and goes into exile.

1926   *March 26*: A treaty of alliance is concluded between Romania and Poland, to be followed in June by a similar treaty between Romania and France. In September, Romania will sign a treaty of friendship with Italy.

May 12: A military revolt against the Polish government is led by General Pilsudski. It brings into power Ignace Moseicki, a friend of Pilsudski.

October 12: Pilsudski is named president of Poland.

November 27: A treaty is signed between Italy and Albania wherein they promise to maintain their borders, and Italy agrees to refrain from interfering in the internal affairs of Albania.

1927   *April 5*: Mussolini signs a treaty of friendship and cooperation with the Hungarian government, thus breaking the diplomatic isolation of Hungary enforced by the Little Entente.

June 7: After frequent frontier incidents Albania and Yugoslovia break off diplomatic relations.

July 20: King Ferdinand of Romania dies and is succeeded by his nephew Michael, six years of age. Regent is Prince Nicolae, the late king's father.

September 8: Germany is admitted to the League of Nations and receives a permanent seat on its Supreme Council.

November 22: The Second Treaty of Tirana includes a defensive alliance between Italy and Albania. Its duration is to be twenty-five years and it provides for military cooperation.

1928   *August 27*: The Kellogg-Briand pact, renouncing aggressive war (without proposing sanctions), is signed in Paris by the major powers.

September 1: Ahmed Bey Zogu is proclaimed Zog I, King of Albania.

September 3–26: The League of Nations include the Kellogg-Briand pact in a general act.

November 9: Julius Maniu, head of the reconstructed Peasant party in Romania, is named prime minister.

1929   *January 5*: In Yugoslavia, after a series of twenty-three governments between 1918 and 1928, King Alexander proclaims his dictatorship.

March 6: Bulgaria and Turkey sign a friendship treaty.

June 7: American Howard Young, head of a new League committee, introduces yet another plan dealing with German reparations. The Young Plan reduces the reparations to be paid by Germany and establishes the Bank for International Settlements in Basel, Switzerland.

August 3–31: At a conference at the Hague Germany accepts the Young Plan. France terminates its presence in the Rhineland.

October 3: The name of the Kingdom of Serbs, Croats and Slovenes is officially changed to Yugoslavia.

October 28: The New York Stock Exchange suffers its biggest one-day drop and signals the beginning of a worldwide recession.

1930   *June 6*: Prince Carol returns to Romania to assume the throne. (King Michael was deposed in his favor.)

October 5–12: The First Conference of Balkan States is held in Athens. This is the beginning of the Balkan version of the Little Entente.

1931   *March 20*: Germany and Austria announce a customs union to widespread Western criticism. France recalls its loans to both countries.

April 18: Prince Carol appoints a coalition government for Romania under the premiership of his former tutor, the historian Nicolae Jorga.

May 11: The largest Eastern European bank, Austrian Creditanstalt, fails. This precipitates a general financial crisis, which turns the worldwide recession into the Great Depression. Foreign investments are withdrawn from Germany, creating further panic and unemployment.

June 17: An Italian loan is extended to Albania that includes provisions for Italian supervision of Albanian economic life. Albania becomes an Italian colony in the Balkans.

June 20: President Hoover proposes a moratorium on all intergovernmental debts; the French, however, oppose this for fear that the Germans will stop paying reparations altogether.

June 21: In elections in Bulgaria, the Peasant party wins an overwhelming victory.

September 3: King Alexander declares the end of the dictatorship. A new Yugoslav constitution creates a quasi-parliamentary system subordinate to the king.

September 23: The Japanese attack China.

November 9: Elections—with most candidates named by the king—are held in Yugoslavia. The opposition boycotts the proceedings.

1932   *February 8*: Bulgaria refuses to make further reparation payments.

May 31: Jorga resigns the premiership of Romania after failing to obtain a loan from France.

June 16–July 9: At a conference in Lausanne, France, Great Britain, Japan, Belgium, Italy, and Germany agree to cancel Germany's reparations debt in exchange for 5% bonds in the amount of three billion marks to be deposited with the Bank for International Settlements for fifteen years. But the U.S. Senate, whose agreement is necessary, balks. This is the end of German reparation payments.

July 17: The Peasant party again wins overwhelmingly the elections in Romania. Maniu is reappointed premier.

October 4: Gyula Gömbös, a deactivated military officer, is appointed prime minister of Hungary by Regent Horthy. He is determined to establish close relations with fascist Italy.

1933   *January 31*: Hitler is appointed German chancellor.

February 14–16: The governments of the Little Entente attempt to create a standing council and secretariat in order to strengthen the alliance in response to the new government in Germany.

June 17: Hungarian prime minister Gömbös visits Hitler; in July he will visit Mussolini, his aim being to gain the two countries' support for Hungary's revisionist aims.

June 24: A Bulgarian government roundup nets over one thousand communists and other subversives.

October 14: Germany withdraws from the League of Nations.

1934   *January 26*: The Polish government accepts Hitler's offer of a nonaggression treaty. This signals the first breach in the alliance system that France has built around Germany.

February 9: Turkey, Greece, Romania, and Yugoslavia conclude the Balkan Pact. The purpose of the pact is to contain Bulgaria, which is acting as Mussolini's puppet.

March 17: The Rome protocols are signed. They result in close cooperation among Hungary, Italy, and Germany.

July 25: Austrian Chancellor Dollfuss is assassinated by Austrian Nazis.

August 2: German President Hindenburg dies, and Hitler becomes dictator.

September 18: The Soviet Union joins the League of Nations.

October 9: Yugoslav King Alexander (together with Louis Barthou, French foreign minister) is assassinated while on a visit to Marseilles. Peter II, son of Alexander, becomes the new king.

1935   *January 13*: A plebiscite in the Saar valley calls for unification of the province with Germany.

March 16: Hitler declares the disarmament clauses of the
Versailles treaty null and void. Germany reintroduces a universal draft and increases its peacetime army to thirty-six
divisions.

April 17: The League of Nations condemns Germany's
rearmament.

April 23: Poland adopts a new constitution.

May 2: The Soviet Union and France conclude a five-year
pact for mutual defense in case of unprovoked aggression.

May 12: General Joseph Pilsudski dies. His successor to the
presidency of Poland is Edward Smigly-Rydz.

May 16: An agreement for mutual assistance is reached by
Prague and Moscow.

October 6: Hungarian prime minister Gyula Gömbös dies;
his successor is Kálmán Darányi.

November 5: Milan Hodza, a Slovak nationalist, becomes
Czechoslovak prime minister and forms a new government
following an election which gave the Sudeten Germans forty-
four parliamentary seats.

December 13: Thomas G. Masaryk resigns the presidency of
Czechoslovakia; his successor is Eduard Beneš.

1936   *March 7*: The German army unexpectedly reoccupies the
demilitarized Rhineland. The British and French protest this
repudiation of the Locarno Pact but do not act.

March 17: The Military League, which engineered the 1934
military takeover of Bulgaria, is dissolved.

May 11: Germany and Yugoslavia reach a trade agreement,
opening the Balkans to German commercial and political
penetration.

July 18: The Spanish Civil War begins.

October 25: The German-Italian Axis is established.

November 25: Italy, Germany, and Japan agree to stop communist expansionism and to curtail the underground activities of the communist International.

1937   *January 2*: Italy and Great Britain agree to respect each other's interests in the Mediterranean.

January 24: Bulgaria and Yugoslavia sign a treaty of friendship and cooperation.

March 25: Italy and Yugoslavia sign a nonaggression and neutrality agreement.

September 14: Masaryk, national hero of Czechoslovakia, dies.

October 16: Various extreme rightwing groups unite to form the Hungarian National Socialist party ("Arrow Cross") under the leadership of former army major Ferenc Szálasi.

December 21: The government of Romania suffers a resounding defeat in the elections.

December 28: The new Romanian government, headed by Octavian Goga, introduces a series of anti-Jewish laws.

1938   *February 10*: King Carol of Romania dismisses Goga and announces his own dictatorship.

March 7: Relatively free elections bring victory to many opponents of the Bulgarian government. However, parliament's role is merely consultative to King Boris.

March 10: The Austrian *Anschluss* begins. German troops march into Austria, and Hitler declares the unification of the two German-speaking countries.

May 3–9: Hitler visits Mussolini in Rome.

May 13: A new cabinet is formed in Hungary. Béla Imrédy is named prime minister.

May 19–20: Germany instigates a crisis in Czechoslovakia by encouraging the ethnic German population of the Sudeten region to demand autonomy.

August 21–23: The Little Entente recognizes Hungary's right to rearm.

September 7–19: The German diplomatic offensive begins, coupled with threats of military action against Czechoslovakia.

September 15: British prime minister Chamberlain visits Hitler at Berchtesgaden. Hitler states his demand for the annexation of German-populated regions of Czechoslovakia. After Chamberlain's return, he consults with the French government, and both advise the Czechs to concede to Germany. Poland and Hungary announce their own claims.

1938 *(continued)* *September 29*: The Munich conference opens; the Western governments concede everything Hitler demands. The will for peace is so strong that the returning British and French statesmen are greeted by jubilant crowds.

A Polish note is sent to beleaguered Czechoslovakia demanding the territory of Teschen. The Czechs yield.

October 5: President Beneš of Czechoslovakia resigns. The next day, the long-standing demand of Slovak nationalists for full autonomy is granted. A Roman Catholic priest, Joseph Tiso, becomes Slovak prime minister.

October 20: The Communist party is outlawed in Czechoslovakia; many of its leaders eventually receive asylum in the Soviet Union.

November 2: Hungary regains its former northern highlands from Czechoslovakia. Of the one million inhabitants, 750,000 are ethnic Hungarians.

November 26: The Soviet Union and Poland renew their mutual aid and nonaggression agreements.

November 30: While in jail the head of the Romanian Iron Guard, Corneliu Codreanu, is killed by his guards, as are thirteen of his supporters. The right-wing extremists thereby lose their most important leader.

1939 *March–April*: The Polish-German crisis intensifies.

March 16: Bohemia and Moravia are proclaimed German protectorates.

March 28: The German press begins an anti-Polish campaign.

March 31: An Anglo-French guarantee of Poland's territorial integrity signals the repudiation of the policy of appeasement.

April 1: The Spanish Civil War ends after the Fascists overpower the Republic.

April 7: Italy invades Albania and overruns the country. King Zog flees to Greece, then to Turkey.

May 3: Drastic anti-Jewish laws are introduced in Hungary, limiting Jewish participation in the professions, business, and government.

May 22: Germany and Italy establish a military alliance.

June–August: Great Britain, the Soviet Union, and France begin negotiations for a possible alliance against Germany.

The Soviet Union conducts secret talks with Nazi Germany as well.

August 23: Nazi Germany and Soviet Russia conclude a nonaggression pact. In a secret protocol they divide their spheres of influence in Eastern Europe and agree to the partition of Poland and the annexation of Romanian Bessarabia, Estonia, Lithuania, and Latvia by the Soviet Union. In exchange the Soviet government promises to supply Nazi Germany with essential raw materials and food.

September 1: Germany invades Poland; the Second World War begins.

September 3: Britain and France declare war on Germany.

September 1–October 16: Poland is swiftly defeated by the German army. After three weeks of war, the Soviet Union sends the Red Army into eastern Poland and occupies the area that Poland took from the Soviet state after 1919. For the rest of the war, Poland is under foreign occupation; Czechoslovakia is under German occupation during most of that time.

December 14: The Soviet Union is expelled from the League of Nations after the Soviet invasion of Finland.

1940   *May 11*: Winston Churchill forms a coalition government in Britain.

June 5: Hitler proclaims a war of total annihilation against his enemies.

June 15: The Soviet Red Army occupies the Baltic republics of Estonia, Latvia, and Lithuania.

June 22: France accepts an armistice.

September 6: The Romanian Iron Guards force King Carol to abdicate in favor of his son Michael.

October 7: German troops enter Romania.

November 1: Greece repels Italian attacks launched from Albania.

November 20: The Hungarian government endorses the Rome-Berlin-Tokyo Axis and joins it against the Allies.

November 22: Greek forces capture the Albanian town of Koritza.

1941   *March 25*: Yugoslavia joins the Axis under the directions of the regent, Prince Paul.

1941 *(continued)*   *March 27*: The Yugoslav government is overthrown and Peter II is declared king.

April 6: Germany, in alliance with Hungary and Bulgaria, attacks and swiftly defeats Yugoslavia. Belgrade is occupied on April 11. The guerrilla movement comprises both the communist Partisans, led by Josip Broz (Tito), and the četniks, who oppose communism. The war against the Germans will be waged by this divided resistance.

June 22: Germany attacks the Soviet Union.

October 16: The Soviet government evacuates Moscow.

November 25: Bulgaria joins the Axis. (Romania had already joined the Axis.)

December 4: The German attack on Moscow is halted.

December 7: Japan attacks the U.S. naval base at Pearl Harbor.

December 12: Romania declares war on the United States.

1942   *June 3–7*: The American naval victory in the battle of Midway Island turns the tide in the Pacific.

August 1942–February 1943: The Soviet defense at the battle of Stalingrad forces the Germans to retreat.

December 2: The first self-sustaining controlled nuclear chain reaction is achieved in Chicago by a team of scientists led by Enrico Fermi.

1943   *May 5*: The Hungarian parliament is adjourned indefinitely.

May 22: The Soviets dissolve the Comintern.

July 25: Mussolini is overthrown; three days later the Italian Fascist party is dissolved.

September 10: The Germans occupy Rome three days after Italy surrenders.

November 28: Churchill, Roosevelt, and Stalin meet in Teheran for strategic discussions. They agree that Britain and the United States will attack Germany through France and the Benelux countries, while the Soviet Union will attack through Poland and the Danube countries.

1944   *March 19*: The German army occupies Hungary and begins the systematic extermination of its last Jewish enclave.

August 1: As the Red Army nears Warsaw, it broadcasts radio appeals to the Polish home army to rise against the

Germans. The Poles, assuming the Soviets
on their occupiers only to see the Red Army
The U.S. and Britain air drop supplies to the
two months the home army surrenders; War
leveled.

August 15: King Michael of Romania overthro
ernment of Ion Antonescu and declares Romania ̲ ̲̲di-
tional surrender.

August 31: The Red Army occupies Bucharest.

September 5: The Soviets declare war on Bulgaria. Bulgaria
asks for an armistice and, on September 7, declares war on
Germany.

October 14: The Allies occupy Athens.

October 15: Hungary asks for armistice terms.

December 26: The Red Army encircles Budapest.

1945   *January 17*: Soviet troops capture Warsaw.

February 4–11: Churchill, Roosevelt, and Stalin meet at Yalta
on the Black Sea to discuss military and postwar issues. They
agree to a concerted push by the Western Allies in Italy and
along the western front, while the Soviet Union attacks Japan. They also agree on the postwar division of Germany
into four occupation zones. The United States and Britain
complain that communist regimes are already being installed
in Bulgaria and Romania. No real decision is reached on
Poland, where the Western Allies continue to support the
Polish government-in-exile in London while the Soviets now
back the pro-Moscow "Lublin committee" provisional government. The Yalta conference recognizes Marshal Tito's rule
in Yugoslavia.

March 6: Petru Groza establishes a government in Romania
with the participation of the Communists.

March 8: A Yugoslav government is established under Tito.
The members of the cabinet are mostly Tito's Partisans, but
five former exiles are also included.

April 5: Klement Gottwald, vice prime minister of Czechoslovakia and a leader of the Czechoslovak Communist party,
declares that the new Czechoslovak state will be based on the
equality of Czechs and Slovaks.

April 11: The Red Army enters Vienna after a seven-day
battle.

1945 *(continued)*   *April 12*: Franklin Delano Roosevelt dies at the age of sixty-three. His vice president, Harry Truman, succeeds him.

April 21: A Soviet-Polish treaty of friendship and postwar cooperation is signed in Moscow by the Lublin committee provisional government.

April 27: Soviet, American, and British forces finally meet in the Elbe River town of Torgau, signaling the end of Nazi Germany.

April 28: Italian partisans shoot Mussolini.

April 30: Hitler kills himself.

May 2: Berlin is occupied by the Red Army. The German armies in Italy surrender.

May 8: The Second World War in Europe ends.

June 5: The Allied Control Commission is established by the United States, the Soviet Union, Britain, and France to decide all questions concerning defeated Germany. Four occupational zones are established; Berlin is placed under four-power control.

June 6: Edvard Beneš, president of Czechoslovakia, declares that the German and Hungarian minorities must be expelled from his country.

June 26: In San Francisco, Britain, China, the Soviet Union, and the United States sign the United Nations charter.

June 28: A Provisional Government of National Union is formed in liberated Poland. It consists of twenty-one ministers, of whom sixteen come from the so-called Committee for National Liberation, formed under Communist and Soviet auspices, and five from the exiled government in London.

July 17–August 2: Churchill (replaced by Clement Atlee after the British elections), Truman, and Stalin attend the last Allied conference of the war, at Potsdam. At U.S. insistence they establish a conference of foreign ministers (of the U.S., Soviet Union, Britain, France, and China) to draft peace treaties and resolve international disputes. German reparations are to be divided by the Allies; the procedure for war trials is agreed upon. The Western Allies accede to the Polish occupation of the territory between the Oder and the western Neisse. Ethnically German populations from Poland, Czechoslovakia, and Hungary would be transferred to Germany. Most major contentious issues are deferred.

August 6: The U.S. drops an atomic bomb on Hiroshima.

August 8: The Soviet Union declares war on Japan. The United States drops a second atomic bomb on Nagasaki.

August 14: Japan surrenders unconditionally to the Allies.

September 2: The Second World War ends.

September 11–October 2: The first session is held of the conference of foreign ministers. The U.S. secretary of state demands the dismantling of dictatorial governments in Hungary, Bulgaria, and Romania without success.

November 4: National elections take place in Hungary. Zoltán Tildy is elected president and Ferenc Nagy prime minister. The government comprises a coalition of five parties, and the Communists gain the ministries of the interior and justice, thus controlling the secret police forces.

November 11: The rigged Yugoslav elections produce 80.06 and 90.84 percent absolute majorities for Tito's Communist government in the two houses of parliament.

November 18: In Bulgaria, the Communist-dominated National Front receives 90 percent of the vote in rigged elections. The U.S. government declares that it will not recognize the election results as valid.

November 20: The Nuremberg war crime trials begin.

November 25: Elections are held in occupied Austria, with socialist Karl Renner elected president of the republic.

November 30: The Allied Control Commission notifies the Hungarian government that it accedes to the Hungarian request to expel 500,000 ethnic Germans from Hungary. These people are to be resettled in the American zone of occupied Germany. During 1946 about 150,000 ethnic Germans are expelled with great barbarity, and in 1947 another 100,000 are expelled. The latter are sent to the Soviet occupied zone (later to become East Germany).

December 16–26: The second session of the conference of foreign ministers reaches agreement about future peace treaties. Korea is to be occupied by Soviet and American forces.

1946   *January 10*: The first meeting of the newly formed United Nations general assembly is held.

1946 *(continued)* *January 11*: The newly "elected" parliament, which receives 95 percent of the vote, declares Albania the first People's Republic in Eastern Europe.

February 1: The Hungarian parliament declares the country a republic.

February 27: The Czechoslovak and Hungarian governments agree that ethnic Slovaks from Hungary and ethnic Hungarians from Czechoslovakia who volunteer to return to their native countries will be exchanged in equal numbers.

March 5: Winston Churchill delivers a speech at Westminster College in Fulton, Missouri, in which he declares that an "iron curtain" has descended upon Eastern Europe from the Baltic to the Adriatic.

April 21–22: The forced merger of the German Communist party and the Social Democratic party in the Soviet zone of occupation establishes the German Socialist Unity party.

May 26: In Czechoslovak elections the Communist party receives 38 percent of the vote and thus becomes the strongest party in the parliament.

July 29–October 15: Twenty-one nations participate in the Paris Peace Conference, in which discussions cannot solve fundamental differences between the Western Allies and the Soviet Union.

October 1: The International Court sitting at Nuremberg issues its war crimes verdicts on twenty-four former Nazi leaders: twelve death sentences, three life-terms, and nine acquittals.

October 27: Terror and intimidation reign over the national elections in Bulgaria. The Communist party gains 277 seats in the National Assembly. Stalinist Georgi Dimitrov is named prime minister.

November 9: In the Romanian national elections 91 percent of the vote goes to the bloc of democratic parties dominated by the Communists. As elsewhere in Eastern Europe, the electorate is terrorized and intimidated.

1947 *January 1*: The occupational zones of Britain and the United States in Germany unite into one economic unit.

January 5: The Communist-dominated Hungarian Ministry of the Interior accuses several parliamentarians of the anti-Communist Smallholders party of antistate conspiracy. Prime Minister Ferenc Nagy becomes a target of trumped-up charges. On May 30, while in Switzerland, he resigns, and the Communist party soon wins complete control over the country.

January 19: In another rigged election the Polish Socialist Workers (Communist) party, leading the so-called Democratic Bloc, "wins" 384 seats in the 444-member parliament. In September Stanislaw Mikolajczik is forced to resign and flees to London.

February 10: The victorious Allies sign peace treaties with Italy, Finland, Hungary, Romania, and Bulgaria. Germany and Japan are conspicuously absent.

March 12: Proclamation of the Truman Doctrine for the containment of communism.

May 30: In the Soviet-occupied zone of Germany all mines are nationalized without compensation to owners.

June 5: Proclamation of the Marshall Plan to help rebuild war-torn Europe. The Soviet Union refuses to participate and forces the countries under its occupation to follow its lead.

August 6: The show trial of opposition statesman Petkov begins in Sofia, Bulgaria. The verdict: death by hanging.

August 31: Rigged elections in Hungary. Through coercion the Communist party receives 27 percent of the vote. The so-called Leftist Bloc gains 60.8 percent of the total vote. Thus the Hungarian Communist party establishes a one-party dictatorship.

October 6: A new international organization, the Communist Information Bureau (the Cominform) is established in Belgrade.

November 12: Ion Maniu, the leader of the Romanian Peasant party, is sentenced to life imprisonment for alleged anti-state activities.

November 21: The Hungarian Communist government nationalizes all banks.

December 26: Bulgaria nationalizes all banks, mines, and industry.

1947 *(continued)*   *December 30*: King Michael of Romania is forced to abdicate; in April 1948 the Communist dictatorship will declare Romania a People's Democracy.

1948   *February 13*: A Soviet-Hungarian treaty of cooperation and mutual aid is signed.

February 25: Klement Gottwald forms a government clearly dominated by the Communist party in Czechoslovakia.

March 1: Tito's Yugoslav government rejects Soviet proposals for a Yugoslav-Bulgarian federation.

March 10: All industrial firms, banks, and retail trade companies are nationalized in Czechoslovakia. In addition, all estates of more than 50 hectares are confiscated without compensation to the owners.

March 17: Five countries (Great Britain, France, Holland, Belgium, and Luxembourg) sign an agreement for economic and cultural cooperation that becomes the seed for NATO.

March 20: The Allied Control Commission ceases operating because of irreconcilable differences between the Soviet Union and the Western powers.

June 12: The Hungarian Communist leadership coerces the Hungarian Social Democratic party to merge with the Communists. The new party takes the name Hungarian Workers' party.

June 23: The Berlin blockade begins. Soviet armed forces close all roads between West Berlin and Western countries.

June 27: The Czechoslovak Social Democratic party is forced to merge with the Communist party.

June 28: Yugoslavia is expelled from the Cominform.

July 1: The Berlin Airlift begins supplying the British, French, and American zones with food and fuel.

August 11: The Bulgarian Social Democratic party and the Communist party declare their merger under the name Bulgarian Communist party.

December 21: The Polish Socialist party and the Communist party merge into the Polish United Workers' party.

1949   *January 25*: Six countries (the Soviet Union, Bulgaria, Czechoslovakia, Poland, Hungary, and Romania) establish the Council of Mutual Economic Assistance (Comecon).

April 4: The North Atlantic Treaty Organization (NATO) basic agreement is signed in Washington, by Britain, France, Italy, Portugal, Denmark, Norway, Iceland, Canada, and the United States. The Soviet Union protests the pact.

May 3: A ten-nation conference of Western European states establishes the Council of Europe.

May 12: The Berlin blockade is lifted by the Soviet Union, but the city remains divided.

May 23: The Federal Republic of Germany (FRG or, before 1990, West Germany) is established in Bonn.

May 30: In the Soviet-occupied zone of Germany the constitution of the German Democratic Republic is proclaimed.

September 12: Konrad Adenauer, a Christian Democrat, is elected chancellor of the FRG, and Theodor Heuss is elected president.

September 24: In Hungary the show trial of László Rajk and his accomplices ends with seven death sentences.

October 1: The Peoples' Republic of China is proclaimed.

October 7: The German Democratic Republic (GDR or, before 1990, East Germany) is proclaimed. Wilhelm Pieck, a veteran communist, is installed as president.

October 16: The Greek civil war ends with the defeat of the Communist insurgency.

December 7: The show trial of Todor Kostov, former assistant prime minister of Bulgaria, ends in a sentence of death.

1950   *February 14*: Mao Zedong and Stalin sign a thirty-year alliance between China and the Soviet Union.

April 13: The first shipment of military aid to France under the NATO pact is unloaded at Cherbourg.

May 23: Rigged elections in Albania result in 98.18 percent of the vote being cast for the Albanian Communist party candidates.

June 25: North Korea attacks South Korea: the Korean war begins.

July 6: Poland and East Germany sign an agreement in which the Oder-Neisse line will be the permanent border between the two countries. East Germany formally renounces its claim to German territories annexed by Poland and the Soviet Union.

August 9: The Council of Europe proclaims the need for a

European army, including German units. Thus the rearmament of West Germany is broached for the first time since the end of World War II.

1951 *April 8*: France, the Benelux countries, Italy, and West Germany sign an agreement establishing the European Coal and Steel Union.

May 1: Radio Free Europe and Radio Liberty start broadcasts from Munich. Soviet jamming begins almost immediately.

July 9: Great Britain, France, and the United States declare the end of the state of belligerence with Germany.

September 8: Forty-nine countries sign a peace treaty with Japan. China, the Soviet Union, North Korea, and East Germany refuse to participate. On the same day Japan and the United States sign a security agreement in which the United States promises to aid Japan in case of unprovoked aggression.

November 9: Yugoslavia lodges an official complaint at the United Nations about the openly hostile attitude of the Soviet Union toward it.

1952 *March 10*: A Soviet note is sent to the three Western Allied powers expressing concern over their signing of a German peace treaty.

May 26: An agreement accepting the West German state as a sovereign and equal partner is signed by West Germany, France, Great Britain, and the United States. Allied troops stationed in West Germany are declared to be there in order to protect it against aggression.

October 3: Britain tests its first atomic bomb off the coast of Australia.

November 1: The first American hydrogen bomb is exploded in the Marshall Islands.

November 20–27: The show trial of Rudolf Slansky and Vladimir Clementis occurs; both are former high-ranking officials of the Communist party and the Czechoslovak government. Both are sentenced to death. A host of show trials of lesser officials follows.

1953 *March 5*: Stalin dies. Nine days later Nikita Khrushchev becomes first secretary of the Communist party of the Soviet Union (CPSU).

June 17: A treaty of friendship and cooperation is signed between West Germany and the United States. Construction workers in East Berlin protest the imposition of increased work quotas. Soviet tanks are called in to crush the demonstrations—twenty-one people are killed and 187 are seriously wounded. In the aftermath more than 1,200 East Germans are jailed or sent to concentration camps.

July 10: Lavrentii P. Beria, former chief of the Soviet secret police, is arrested. He and six of his associates are executed on December 23.

August 8: Soviet Prime Minister Malenkov announces the explosion of the first Soviet hydrogen bomb.

September 8: The head of the Polish Roman Catholic church, Cardinal Wyszynski, is arrested for alleged conspiracy against the state. He is interned in a monastery and held incomunicado for years.

1954   *January 17*: Milovan Djilas is relieved of his state and party offices but, for the time being, not expelled from the Yugoslav Communist party. Charges against him include slandering the party in several of his articles.

May 7: The French fortress in Vietnam, Dien Bien Phu, falls to the North Vietnamese Communists, supplied by the Soviet Union and China.

June 27: The Soviet Union opens the world's first nuclear-generated power plant.

June 28: Jou Enlai and Nehru sign the Five Principles of International Relations, intended to be the basis for peaceful coexistence.

December 4: Establishment of the Atomic Energy Agency of the United Nations.

December 16: The Soviet Union notifies France that if the Paris agreements for the West European Union are accepted, the Soviet Union will consider its treaties with France and England null and void.

1955   *January 25*: The Supreme Soviet of the USSR declares the end of the state of belligerence with Germany as a whole.

1955 *(continued)* *May 5*: France, Great Britain, and the United States declare that the occupation of Germany is over. West Germany attains full sovereignty. West Germany, under the name of the Federal Republic of Germany, joins NATO. The Western European Union comes into being. On May 7 the Soviet Union renounces its treaties with France and Great Britain.

May 14: The Soviet Union signs the Warsaw Pact treaty with its satellites in Eastern Europe. The organization is under tight Soviet control, and the commander in chief and chief of staff of the united armed forces is always a Soviet general.

May 15: The four occupying powers sign the Austrian State Treaty, ending the occupation of the country and neutralizing it, in the first significant withdrawal of Soviet power in Europe.

May 26–June 2: Khrushchev and Bulganin visit Yugoslavia. Tito wins recognition of Yugoslavia's independence in domestic and international affairs. The long-range consequences of the visit include the replacement of Mátyás Rákosi of Hungary, who led the Stalinist campaign against Tito in the 1940s and 1950s.

July 18–23: The foreign ministers of Britain, France, the United States, and the Soviet Union meet in Geneva to lessen tensions between the Western powers and the Soviet Union.

September 9–13: German Chancellor Adenauer visits Moscow. Agreement is reached on the repatriation of over ten thousand German soldiers still detained in Soviet prisoner-of-war camps.

December 14: Albania, Bulgaria, Hungary, and Romania are admitted to membership in the United Nations.

1956 *February 14–25*: The Twentieth Congress of the Soviet Communist party approves the concepts of peaceful coexistence and "different roads to socialism." Khrushchev, in a secret speech, denounces Stalin's crimes against the Soviet people.

April 10: Polish Communist leader Wladislaw Gomulka, arrested in 1951 on false charges, is "rehabilitated."

April 17: The Soviets announce the disbanding of the Cominform.

June 2: Yugoslav President Tito visits the Soviet Union.

June 28: In Poland, beginning in the city of Poznan, rioting breaks out over sudden consumer price increases. Workers demonstrate in the streets, and Polish Communist leaders order the army to fire on the demonstrators. More than fifty workers die, and about three hundred people are wounded.

July 18: The Hungarian Workers party removes first secretary Mátyás Rákosi from office. His successor is his longtime collaborator Ernő Gerő. János Kádár is made a member of the Political Committee.

October 6: Former Hungarian foreign minister László Rajk, executed in 1949, is posthumously rehabilitated and two hundred thousand people attend his funeral.

October 19: In spite of Soviet reservations, Wladislaw Gomulka is elected first secretary of the Polish Communist party, and the central committee adopts a liberalized policy.

October 23: Revolution breaks out in Hungary. The people demand the replacement of the Communist monopoly on power with a multiparty parliamentary system. Within days the Communist *apparat* and the secret police are swept away, and the Soviet tanks are defeated. Hungary brings to power Imre Nagy, a Muscovite Communist who broke with Mátyás Rákosi early in the 1950s over the Soviet exploitation of Hungary.

October 28–November 2: Three months after Colonel Nasser of Egypt nationalizes the Suez Canal, President Eisenhower publicly calls upon Israel not to "endanger the peace." The following day Israeli forces invade Egypt and, after five-days' fighting, gain control of the Sinai peninsula. On October 30 Britain and France veto a U.N. security council resolution calling for an Israeli withdrawal; the following day they launch a joint offensive against Egyptian military targets. On November 2 the U.N. general assembly called for an immediate ceasefire in Egypt.

October 30: The Soviet government declares its willingness to review its relations with the Socialist countries on the basis of equality and sovereignty.

November 1: The Hungarian prime minister declares Hungary's neutrality and its withdrawal from the Warsaw Pact alliance. On the same day János Kádár appears in the city of

Szolnok under Soviet guard and begins to organize a puppet government.

November 4: A massive Soviet military intervention of 2,000 tanks and 150,000 soldiers succeeds in suppressing the revolution in Hungary. Although sporadic fighting continues, the revolution ends. More than 200,000 Hungarians flee to the West through Austria. János Kádár becomes the new Hungarian prime minister. His premiership begins with bloody retribution. Imre Nagy and some of his ministers flee to the Yugoslav embassy in Budapest. After being promised safe passage, they are betrayed by both the Yugoslav government and the Soviet authorities in Hungary. Nagy and his entourage emerge from the embassy and are arrested and taken to Romania. Held prisoner until 1958, Nagy and his collaborators are tried under false charges and executed by order of János Kádár.

November 6–7: Anglo-French and Egyptian forces accept a U.N. ceasefire.

1957   *March 25:* The European Economic Community's founding document, the Treaty of Rome, is signed. Members are France, Italy, the Federal Republic of Germany, and the Benelux states, who also establish the European Atomic Energy Union.

May 30: CBS TV interviews Nikita Khrushchev, who predicts that the grandchildren of the reporters will eventually live under a socialist system in the United States. His famous quip, "We will bury you," makes headlines and is considered an open challenge to American society.

October 4: The Soviet Union's *Sputnik 1* becomes the first man-made earth satellite.

1958   *March 31:* Khrushchev declares that the Soviet Union has unilaterally stopped nuclear testing.

May 24: The Warsaw Pact announces the withdrawal of Soviet troops from Romania and the lowering of troop levels in Hungary.

October 28: Pius XII dies; his successor is Pope John XXIII.

December 10: Boris Pasternak, the Soviet author of *Doctor Zhivago* who was thrown out of the Writers Union, receives the Nobel Prize for literature. Pasternak, afraid that if he travels to Stockholm he would not be permitted to return home, declines to accept.

1959   *January 1–2*: A revolution in Cuba, led by Fidel Castro, succeeds in overthrowing the dictatorship of Batista. Six weeks later Castro becomes prime minister.

August 23: The Soviet Union announces plans for an oil-pipeline network between the Soviet Union and Eastern European countries, expected completion date 1963.

September 13: The Soviets launch *Lunik II*, the first man-made object to land on the moon.

December 28: Yugoslavia unveils its first nuclear reactor.

1960   *January–March*: A half million peasants in East Germany lose their land to forcible collectivization of agriculture.

February 13: France explodes its first atomic bomb in the Sahara desert in Algerian territory.

May 1: An American U-2 piloted by Gary Powers is shot down while engaged in military reconnaissance over Soviet territory.

May 7: Leonid Brezhnev replaces Marshal Vorosilov as president of the Soviet Union.

May 16: The Paris summit between Khrushchev and Eisenhower collapses over the U-2 incident.

May 25: The U.S. ends foreign aid to Cuba.

September 25: Khrushchev leads the Soviet delegation to the U.N. general assembly and criticizes U.N. peace-keeping operations in the Congo. He is photographed during one session banging his shoe on his desk.

November 8: In the American elections John F. Kennedy is elected president over Vice President Nixon by a tiny margin.

1961   *April 12*: Soviet Major Yuri Gagarin becomes the first person to orbit earth.

April 17–20: The Bay of Pigs invasion of Cuba: about 1,400 Cuban expatriates land on the island, but President Kennedy refuses to provide air support, and the invasion fails.

June 3–4: President Kennedy and Soviet premier Khrushchev meet in Vienna.

August 13: East German workers build the Berlin wall (under the supervision of Soviet KGB officers and military personnel) to stop the flood of East Germans fleeing to the West.

August 31: The Soviet Union resumes nuclear testing.

1961 *(continued)* *October 31*: Stalin's body is removed from Lenin's Tomb in Red Square.

December 10: The Soviet Union severs diplomatic relations with Albania, whose leaders accuse the Soviet leadership of abandoning Marxist-Leninist principles.

1962 *January 13*: Beijing signs a treaty of mutual help with Albania.

March 14: A seventeen-nation disarmament conference opens in Geneva.

May 31: Adolph Eichmann is executed in Israel after being found guilty of crimes against humanity.

September 3: A Cuban delegation visits the Soviet Union.

October 24: President Kennedy orders a naval quarantine of Cuba after the discovery of missile bases built by Soviet advisers.

October 28: The Soviet Union agrees to dismantle the bases and to cease providing offensive weapons to Cuba.

November 20: The United States ends the Cuban blockade.

1963 *June 14*: An open letter from the Chinese Communist party is presented to the Soviet leadership, accusing them of deviations from the Marxist-Leninist line.

June 20: The British House of Commons censures Juhn Profumo who, as secretary of state for war, unwittingly shared a girlfriend with the Soviet military attaché in London.

July 20: Negotiations conducted in Moscow between the Chinese and Soviet Communists to eliminate ideological differences fail.

August 5: In Moscow the foreign ministers of Great Britain, the United States, and the Soviet Union sign the first partial nuclear test ban treaty, rejected by France.

August 15: The Chinese rail against the Soviet Union for signing the partial ban on nuclear testing.

August 31: The hot-line link between the Kremlin and the White House goes into service.

November 16: Greece begins to release Communist prisoners taken during the 1947–49 civil war.

November 22: President Kennedy is assassinated in Dallas. Conspiracy theories abound but are never proven.

1964   *August 2*: In the Tonkin Gulf North Vietnamese patrol boats fire on American warships. This incident leads to congressional authorization of the use of American troops in Vietnam.

October 15: Khrushchev is ousted from the Soviet Politburo. Leonid Brezhnev becomes first secretary of the CPSU, and Alexei Kosygin becomes prime minister.

October 16: China explodes its first atomic device.

November 3: Lyndon B. Johnson, Kennedy's vice president, wins an overwhelming victory in the U.S. presidential election.

1965   *March 7*: The first of a group of 3,500 American marines land in South Vietnam.

March 19: Romanian Communist leader G. Georghiu-Dej dies; his successor is Nicolae Ceauşescu.

1966   *March 29–April 8*: The Twenty-third Congress of the Soviet Communist Party meets. The Chinese refuse to participate.

March 30: France proclaims her exit from the integrated command system of NATO.

April 14: The Polish government refuses visas to foreign visitors intending to participate in the celebration of one thousand years of Polish Christianity.

April 30: China announces a "cultural revolution" to wipe out "bourgeois ideology."

June 20–July 1: President De Gaulle visits the Soviet Union.

August 15: A contract is signed between the Soviet Union and the Italian automobile manufacturer Fiat for the production of 600,000 automobiles in the USSR.

August 21: There are large demonstrations in Beijing by the Red Guard, during which the Soviet and East German embassies are attacked. The cadres carry placards declaring war on the world.

October 27: China announces a successful test of an atomic warhead.

November 28–December 3: The Ninth Congress of the Hungarian Socialist Workers Party meets. The main topic is economic reform.

1967   *January 4–5*: European Socialist parties meet in Rome.

1967 *(continued)* *February 15*: Chinese authorities order the dissolution of all "revolutionary organizations" and the return of their members to their home provinces.

February 27: An international treaty banning nuclear weapons in outer space (and prohibiting military use of the moon and other celestial bodies) is signed in London, Moscow, and Washington.

March 12: Svetlana Alliluieva, Stalin's daughter, arrives in Switzerland and requests permanent resident status.

April 21: The military accomplishes a coup d'état in Greece.

April 24: Twenty-four European Communist and Socialist parties meet in Karlovy Vary. Leonid Brezhnev seeks to reassert the leading role of the Soviet Union in the affairs of these parties but does not succeed.

June 17: China explodes its first hydrogen bomb.

September 3: The Chinese again order the Red Guards to cease their violent activities.

September 13: The United States announces its antiballistic missile system is targeted at China.

October 9: Che Guevara, Cuban revolutionary and political leader, is killed in Bolvian guerrilla fighting.

October 22: Massive demonstrations in opposition to the Vietnam war take place in Washington, London, and other Western capitals.

1968 *January 1*: Hungary introduces a set of economic reforms called the New Economic Mechanism (NEM) to provide incentives for increased agricultural production.

January 5: First secretary of the Czechoslovak Communist party, Antonín Novotný, is ousted. His successor is a Slovak reform-Communist, Alexander Dubček. Novotný retains the presidency, a largely meaningless position from which he will be removed in March.

April 4: The Reverend Martin Luther King, Jr., is assassinated in Memphis, Tennessee.

April 8: A new cabinet takes office in Czechoslovakia. Prime minister is Otto Cernik, his assistant is Ota Šik, and foreign minister is Jiry Hajek.

May 10: Violent clashes begin between rioting students and police in Paris.

May 17: French workers occupy their factories. President de Gaulle cuts short his Romanian trip.

June 5–6: Senator Robert Kennedy is shot and dies in Los Angeles.

June 15: The Warsaw Pact holds its maneuvers in Czechoslovakia.

June 27: Seventy Czechoslovak intellectuals criticize the Czechoslovak Communist party's policies in an open letter entitled "Two Thousand Words."

July 14–15: Five members of the Warsaw Pact admonish the Czechoslovak Communist leadership to adhere to the ideals and policies inspired by Marxism-Leninism.

August 20: Soviet troops, tanks, and planes (and nominal contingents from other Warsaw Pact countries) invade Czechoslovakia to crush the "Prague Spring." The pretext is the defense of socialism. Dubček remains first secretary of the Czechoslovak Communist party for the time being, but Gustáv Husák, a rigid, old-line Communist, becomes the real authority in Czechoslovakia.

September 11: Soviet troops leave Prague.

September 12: Albania, in protest against the intervention in Czechoslovakia, withdraws from the Warsaw Pact.

October 16: A treaty is signed, providing for the permanent stationing of Soviet troops in Czechoslovakia.

October 30: Czechoslovak President Svoboda signs a law creating a two-state federation of Slovakia and the Czech lands (Silezia, Moravia, and Bohemia). In Bratislava (Pressburg and Pozsony) a Slovak Socialist Republic is proclaimed.

November 5: Richard M. Nixon is elected president of the United States.

November 12: The Brezhnev Doctrine is advanced in a speech before the Polish party congress: "a threat to a Socialist country is a threat to all Socialist countries."

1969   *March 2 and 5*: Sino-Soviet border clashes on the Ussuri River claim the lives of several soldiers on both sides.

April 17: Alexander Dubček is replaced as first secretary of the Czechoslovak Communist party by Gustáv Husák.

May 27: Hungary ratifies the Nuclear Non-Proliferation Treaty.

1969 *(continued)* *June 5–17*: A meeting of seventy-five Communist parties is held in Moscow. The Soviet leaders hope for a condemnation of the Chinese but fail to receive such a mandate.

July 14: The first major contingent of U.S. troops begins withdrawing from Vietnam.

July 21: Neil Armstrong becomes the first person to walk on the moon.

September 27: Alexander Dubček is expelled from the central committee of the Czechoslovak Communist party.

October 15: Dubček resigns as president of the Czechoslovak Federal Assembly.

November 24: The United States and the Soviet Union ratify the Nuclear Non-Proliferation Treaty.

1970 *March 19*: West German Chancellor Willy Brandt meets for the first time with Willi Stoph, the prime minister of East Germany, but the discussions do not lead to agreement.

June 26: Alexander Dubček is expelled from the Czechoslovak Communist party. He is demoted to work in a forestry office in Slovakia.

August 13: Chancellor Brandt and Prime Minister Kosygin sign a nonaggression treaty in Moscow.

October 6–13: The French president, Pompidou, visits the Soviet Union.

November 21: The United States resumes bombing North Vietnam after a two-year halt.

November 23–28: The Tenth Congress of the Hungarian Socialist Workers Party convenes. The congress declares its complete agreement with the foreign policies of the Soviet Union and pledges the continuation of economic reforms.

December 6–8: Chancellor Brandt visits Poland and signs a treaty recognizing the Oder-Neisse border.

December 16: In response to new price increases, rioting breaks out in the Gdansk shipyards. As a consequence, Wladyslaw Gomulka is replaced as leader of the Polish Communist party by Edward Gierek. The first act of the new government is to raise wages and freeze prices.

1971 *March 30–April 9*: The Twenty-fourth Congress of the CPSU is held in Moscow. Communists from ninety-one countries send representatives.

April 10–17: An American table tennis team visits Beijing; the visit signals a rapprochement between China and the United States.

May 3: Walter Ulbricht, first secretary of the East German Socialist Unity Party (SED), resigns his posts. His successor is Erich Honecker.

May 6: Albania and Greece agree to resume diplomatic relations, which were broken off in 1940.

June 10: The United States lifts a twenty-one-year-old embargo on trade with China.

July 9–11: Henry Kissinger, national security adviser to President Nixon, visits Beijing. Agreement is reached for a personal visit by the president to China.

August 9: The Soviet Union and India sign a twenty-year treaty of friendship and mutual cooperation.

October 26: The United Nations general assembly expels Taiwan and recognizes Communist China as the sole representative of the Chinese people.

October: Chancellor Willy Brandt is awarded the Nobel Peace Prize.

1972   *February 21–28*: President Nixon visits China.

February 24–26: János Kádár, first secretary of the Hungarian Communist party, visits Romania and signs a mutual aid and cooperation agreement with Nicolae Ceauşescu.

March 29: For the first time in six years, West Germans are allowed through the Berlin Wall to visit relatives in the East.

May 22–29: President Nixon visits the Soviet Union. He and Premier Brezhnev sign the Strategic Arms Limitation Treaty (SALT I) agreement.

June 2: The leaders of the Bader-Meinhof terrorist gang are captured in Frankfurt.

June 16: In Washington, five burglars are caught breaking into the national Democratic campaign headquarters in the Watergate office building.

July 18: Anwar Sadat, president of Egypt, expels all Soviet advisers.

December 21: In East Berlin both Germanies conclude a basic agreement establishing formal relations and clearing the way for their entry (as two states) into the United Nations.

1973   *January 1*: Britain, Denmark, and Ireland become members of the European Common Market.

January 27: North Vietnam and the United States sign a ceasefire agreement.

February 9: Great Britain and France recognize East Germany as a separate state.

May 18–22: Leonid Brezhnev visits the Federal Republic of Germany. An agreement is signed between the USSR and the FRG for economic and technical cooperation.

June 18–25: Brezhnev visits the United States. Several agreements providing for economic and technological cooperation are signed. No agreement is reached on SALT II.

June 25–26: Brezhnev visits France where he tries to create dissension between France and the United States.

October 6: Syria and Egypt launch simultaneous sneak attacks on Israel on Yom Kippur. This fourth Arab-Israeli war sees the beginning of the Arab oil producers' attempt to use oil supply (and later price) as a weapon to weaken international support for Israel. An indirect effect is to increase the hard-currency earnings of the world's largest oil producer—the Soviet Union.

December 6: Gerald Ford, speaker of the House of Representatives, becomes vice president after Spiro Agnew resigns under criminal investigation.

December 11–12: West Germany's Chancellor Brandt visits Czechoslovakia. He signs a treaty normalizing relations between the two countries.

1974   *January 26–28*: A conference of twenty Western Communist parties takes place in Brussels. They agree on a general statement of principles.

March 17–18: OPEC ends the oil embargo against the United States.

April 25: Günther Guillaume, a close adviser of Chancellor Brandt, is arrested for spying for East Germany. The ensuing scandal forces Brandt's resignation. His successor is Helmut Schmidt.

May 16: India explodes its first atomic bomb.

June 24: President Nixon visits the Soviet Union. He and the

Soviet president sign the agreement for limitations on underground nuclear testing.

July 15: After an attempted coup by the Greek officers of the National Guard in Cyprus, Turkish contingents· invade the island and establish a separate enclave for Turkish nationals. Turkish troops control 40 percent of the island's territory.

July 23: The government of the Greek generals is overthrown. The new premier is Constantine Karamanlis who declares a general amnesty for political prisoners.

August 8: Following the Watergate scandal, Nixon resigns the presidency of the United States in order to avoid impeachment.

September 4: Diplomatic relations are established between the United States and East Germany.

November 17: Greece holds general elections for the first time since 1967.

1975   *February 13–17*: British prime minister Harold Wilson visits Moscow and signs several agreements with the USSR on economic and political cooperation.

April 30: The Vietnam war ends after the North Vietnamese march into Saigon.

July 30–August 1: The "Helsinki accords" are signed by thirty-three European countries, Canada, and the United States at the first summit meeting of the Conference on Security and Cooperation in Europe (CSCE). The accords finalize the borders of the European signatory states and guarantee human rights in Europe by committing the signatory states to follow-up conferences on compliance.

October 9: Dr. Andrei Sakharov receives the Nobel Peace Prize.

November 22: Juan Carlos is crowned King of Spain two days after the death of Generalissimo Franco.

1976   *January 8*: Jou Enlai, Chinese prime minister and one of the founders of the Chinese Communist party, dies.

February 24–March 5: The Twenty-fifth Congress of the Soviet Communist party is held in Moscow. China and Albania refuse to send representatives.

May 9: Ulrike Meinhof, one of the leaders of the Bader-

Meinhof terrorist gang, commits suicide in her prison cell in Stuttgart.

June 29–30: European Communist and Socialist parties confer in Berlin. (Albania refuses to send delegates.) The conference rejects Moscow's bidding and does not condemn the Chinese party. Nor does it accept further Moscow domination of the European communist movements.

September 9: Mao Zedong dies. His immediate successor is Hua Guofeng.

October 7: The "Gang of Four," including the former wife of Mao Zedong, Jiang Qing, is arrested in Beijing and accused of planning a coup d'état.

November 2: Jimmy Carter is elected president of the United States.

1977   *January 7*: Two hundred and fifty-seven Czechoslovak intellectuals issue "Charter 77," a document demanding the observation of human rights in the country. The government declares the document to be against the social and political order.

April 1: The Spanish government orders the dissolution of the Falangist (Francoist) party.

July 5: Ali Bhutto is overthrown in a coup d'etat in Pakistan.

October 7: The "Stalin" constitution of 1936 is replaced by a new Soviet constitution.

November 2: On the sixtieth anniversary of the Russian Revolution, Brezhnev offers to halt testing and production of nuclear weapons.

1978   *January 6*: Secretary of State Cyrus Vance heads a U.S. delegation to Budapest. The visitors return the Holy Crown of St. Stephen to Hungary.

April 7: President Carter announces that the U.S. will not put the neutron bomb into production.

October 15: Cardinal Karol Wojtyla of Cracow becomes the first non-Italian pope in 450 years. The new pope takes the name John Paul II.

1979   *January 1*: The United States restores full diplomatic relations with China.

January 16: Muhammad Reza Shah Pahlevi, the shah of Iran, flees the country.

March 26: Egyptian President Sadat and Israeli Prime Minister Begin sign a peace treaty in Washington. Eighteen Arab countries reject this agreement.

April 3: The Chinese government notifies the Soviet Union that it will not renew the Soviet-Chinese agreement for mutual aid and cooperation when it expires in 1980.

May 28: Greece joins the European Common Market.

June 2: John Paul II visits Poland for the first time since his election to the papacy. Hundreds of thousands of Poles turn out to see him.

June 15: Brezhnev and Carter sign the SALT II treaty, limiting the number of strategic missiles each country is allowed to possess.

November 4: A crowd of "students" attacks and occupies the U.S. embassy in Teheran. Seventy diplomatic officials are captured and held hostage until January 20, 1981. In retaliation the United States freezes all Iranian assets in the U.S. and breaks off diplomatic relations with the Ayatollah's regime.

December 12: In response to the introduction of new offensive rockets into Eastern Europe by the Soviet Union, NATO approves the deployment in Europe of American cruise and Pershing ballistic missiles.

December 20: The foreign policy subcommittee of the United States Senate fails to ratify the SALT II treaty in its current form. Nevertheless, the U.S. and the USSR continue to observe its conditions.

December 27: Soviet troops march into Afghanistan. President Carter orders an immediate embargo of all food deliveries to the Soviet Union and stops the previously arranged delivery of heavy equipment for oil exploration. Soon Carter will declare that the United States will not send athletes to the Moscow Olympic games. At the same time, the United States begins aiding the Muhajeddin, the Muslim armed resistance. The president also withdraws the SALT II treaty from Senate consideration.

1980   *January 10*: A Turkish-American mutual defense agreement is signed in Ankara. Four U.S. bases continue to operate in the country.

January 22: The Presidium of the Soviet Union orders the withdrawal of all state awards and benefits given to Andrei

Sakharov. It orders the banishment of Sakharov and his wife, Elena Bonner, to the city of Gorki as a punishment for his outspoken criticism of the Afghan invasion.

January 24: Israel and Egypt exchange ambassadors.

May 4: Tito dies at the age of eighty-eight. A collective leadership rules Yugoslavia in his place.

July 19–August 3: The Olympic games are held in Moscow. Sixty-two countries refuse to attend, mostly because of Soviet aggression against Afghanistan.

July 27: Shah Pahlevi dies of cancer in Cairo.

August 14: A wave of strikes hits Poland in response to sudden price increases on consumer goods ordered by the Communist government of Gierek. In the shipyards of Gdansk, 17,000 workers go on strike. Their numbers increased to 120,000 by August 20. Lech Walesa, a worker in the shipyard, begins organizing a trade union called "Solidarity."

August 31: The Polish government agrees to the establishment of independent trade unions, and it recognizes the right to strike. On September 1 the strikers return to work.

September 6: Edward Gierek, first secretary of the Polish Workers' party, is replaced by Stanislaw Kania.

September 14: The Soviet Union provides a loan of $260 million to Poland and consents to the postponement of repayment of a previous $280 million loan. The United States provides a $670 million loan for food for Poland.

September 20: Iraq attacks Iranian targets; the Iran-Iraq war begins.

September 21: Polish radio broadcasts Mass for the first time in thirty-five years.

October 24: The Polish government officially recognizes Solidarity as an independent trade union.

November 4: Ronald Reagan is elected president of the United States.

December 5: The Warsaw Pact renounces the use of force in Poland.

December 19: Resignations from the Polish parliament include that of Edward Gierek.

1981   *January 30–31*: Pinkowski, the prime minister of Poland, has successful talks with the leaders of Solidarity. They establish a 41½-hour work-week and approve the publication of a Solidarity-sponsored daily newspaper and its nationwide distribution.

February 9: Pinkowski resigns and is replaced by General Wojciech Jaruzelski.

February 23: King Juan Carlos defends democracy and foils a military coup in Spain.

April 17: The Polish government concedes the right of farmers to form independent trade unions.

May 13: Pope John Paul II is shot by Mehmet Ali Agca, a Turk with Bulgarian connections; the surgery to remove the bullets lasts over four hours.

June 8: Israeli warplanes destroy a nuclear reactor under construction in Iraq.

June 10: Kania survives an attempt by hard-liners to oust him.

July 23: The Polish government announces food price hikes and cuts in rations. Protests lead to a general strike on August 5.

August 8: The Reagan administration, reversing the Carter administration policy, decides to build and stockpile neutron bombs.

August 30: In Poland the price of bread and cereals triples.

September 4: The Soviet Union begins massive military exercises.

September 5–10: Solidarity holds its first national congress in Gdansk. The independent union now has nine million members.

September 17: The Soviet Union delivers an ultimatum to the Polish leadership to act against Solidarity.

October 6: At a military review mutinous soldiers murder Anwar Sadat, the president of Egypt. His successor is Hosni Mubarak, former vice president.

October 9: In Romania draconian orders are issued against citizens who hoard food. Groceries may be bought only at designated stores.

October 18: Stanislaw Kania is replaced by General Jaruzelski as first secretary of the Polish Communist party. Three days later street riots break out over food shortages.

1981 *(continued)* *November 30*: Disarmament talks begin in Geneva between the United States and the Soviet Union. They continue for two years.

December 9: After Soviet authorities issue his daughter-in-law an exit visa, Andrei Sakharov ends the hunger strike he began on November 22.

December 13: General Jaruzelski seizes emergency powers in Poland and declares martial law. Solidarity leaders and other prominent dissidents are interned. Solidarity is outlawed. For the first time in Eastern Europe, power is taken away from a ruling Communist party by the country's military. The United States suspends all economic aid projects.

1982 *January 4*: The foreign secretaries of the nations of the Common Market agree to institute restrictions in their dealings with the Soviet Union and Poland in response to the emergency measures of Jaruzelski. On January 11 the NATO member states declare their intention to introduce sanctions against the Soviet Union, if the emergency decrees are not rescinded in Poland.

April 25: Israel withdraws from the Sinai peninsula, handing over control to Egyptian authorities as prescribed by the Israeli-Egyptian peace treaty.

May 3–4: After huge demonstrations in Warsaw, the Polish government makes mass arrests of adults and children participating in the action.

July 7–9: Francois Mitterand visits Budapest and negotiates with János Kádár over French-Hungarian relations.

October 1: The West German parliament votes "no confidence" in Helmut Schmidt's government. The new government is headed by Helmut Kohl, head of the Christian Democratic party.

October 8: The Jaruzelski regime dissolves all trade unions, including rural Solidarity. A new law forbids strikes for political reasons and regulates strikes for economic benefits. In response the United States withdraws most-favored-nation status for Polish exports.

November 10: Leonid Brezhnev dies at age seventy-six. His replacement is Yuri Andropov, former head of the KGB.

November 13: Lech Walesa is released from detention.

The U.S. lifts sanctions on companies working on Soviet oil and gas pipelines.

December 21: Andropov offers to reduce the number of Soviet medium-range nuclear missiles by two-thirds if NATO cancels the deployment of cruise and Pershing missiles in Europe; Western leaders reject the proposal.

December 30: General Jaruzelski suspends martial law in Poland.

1983   *January 4–5*: Meeting in Prague, the Warsaw Pact offers to sign a nonaggression pact with NATO.

March 30: President Reagan announces the introduction of a Strategic Defense Initiative (quickly nicknamed "star wars") to develop a viable space-based defense against intercontinental ballistic missiles.

April 24: Parliamentary elections in Austria result in victory for the Socialist party, but the party must form a coalition government. Bruno Kreisky refuses to serve in the new government. His successor is Franz Sinowatz.

June 16: Pope John Paul II makes his second visit to Poland. The pontiff receives Lech Walesa and confers twice with General Jaruzelski.

July 21: President Jablonski declares the end of the emergency in Poland, and introduces an amnesty proposal in parliament. Members of Solidarity and the Social Self-Defense Committee, however, are excluded from the amnesty.

October 5: Lech Walesa is awarded the Nobel Peace Prize.

October 25: The Soviet government announces the establishment of new missile bases in Czechoslovakia and Poland.

November 22: The West German parliament approves the placing of new Pershing II missiles in that country. In retaliation, the Soviet Union suspends negotiations over the proposed START II treaty with the U.S.

1984   *January 1*: The Common Market and the European Free Trade Association abolish all tariffs on industrial goods. The total number of people affected: 312,000,000.

February 2–4: Margaret Thatcher, British prime minister, visits Hungary.

1984 *(continued)* *February 9*: Andropov dies. His successor is Konstantin Chernenko, seventy-three-year-old secretary of the Central Committee of the Soviet Communist party.

May 8: The Soviet Union boycotts the Olympic games in Los Angeles in retaliation for the boycott of the Moscow games of 1980.

June 21–23: Helmut Kohl visits Hungary.

July 21: The Polish government announces that 652 political prisoners will be granted amnesty on the eve of the fortieth anniversary of communist rule.

July 25: West Germany approves $330 million in private bank credits to East Germany in exchange for eased restrictions on travel and immigration.

September 4: Erich Honecker cancels his planned visit to West Germany after Soviet attacks on his perceived willingness to improve relations with West Germany. Five days later Todor Zhivkov of Bulgaria also announces that he will not be visiting West Germany as planned.

October 19: Jerzy Popieluszko, a Catholic priest in Warsaw who supports Solidarity, is kidnapped and murdered.

October 20: China approves economic reforms that liberalize small urban businesses and allow factory managers autonomy to compete for customers. The ownership of the means of production still vests in the state. Central planning had been partially abandoned in rural areas in 1978, and the changes proved highly successful.

October 27: Poland's minister of the interior announces that a member of his agency has confessed to killing Father Popieluszko. In December four suspects go on public trial.

November 6: Ronald Reagan scores an overwhelming victory in the U.S. presidential elections.

November 22: New negotiations begin in Geneva between the United States and the USSR over limiting the number of nuclear warheads and offensive missiles.

December 15: Mikhail Gorbachev makes his first visit to London. He has replaced Chernenko as first secretary of the Soviet Communist party.

1985 *February 7*: In Poland a secret police colonel and captain receive jail sentences of twenty-five years (two lieutenants each receive fifteen years) for the murder of Jerzy Popie-luszko.

March 12: In Geneva negotiations between the U.S. and USSR for limiting the number of strategic armaments are once again renewed.

April 26: The party secretaries of the Warsaw Pact nations sign a ten-year extension of the Pact.

June 8: In Hungary municipal elections are held in which two or more candidates run for each office. This is the first such election since the Communist takeover in 1947.

June 12: Portugal and Spain are admitted to the Common Market.

July 1: Andrei Gromyko is elected president of the Supreme Soviet. His replacement as foreign minister is Eduard Shevardnadze, a confidant of Gorbachev.

November 6: General Jaruzelski is replaced by Zbigniew Messner, an economics professor, as Polish prime minister. While retaining his position as first secretary of the Polish Communist party, Jaruzelski is the new president.

November 19–20: Ronald Reagan and Mikhail Gorbachev meet in Geneva.

1986   *January 3*: General Jaruzelski replaces the Polish ambassador to the Soviet Union with a career diplomat as part of his campaign against hard-liners in the government.

February 25–March 6: In his keynote address to the Twenty-Seventh Congress of the CPSU, Gorbachev calls for sweeping economic reforms. Moscow party boss Boris Yeltsin causes a furor with his speech, which lambasts party privileges and abuses of power. The congress votes 124 new members into the 307-member central committee.

April 26: The world's worst nuclear accident occurs in one of the four reactors of the Chernobyl power plant in the western Ukraine. Radioactivity spreads throughout Eastern and Western Europe. Large areas of Belorussia and the Ukraine are permanently evacuated.

June 27: The Soviet Union announces that Glavlit, the agency that censors all print media, will be disbanded. Its ten thousand employees will be reassigned.

September 2: In a return to cultural repression, seven leaders of the Czechoslovak Musician's Union Jazz Section are arrested, and their papers are searched and confiscated.

September 10: In the small village of Lakitelek Hungarian dissidents, including environmentalists, meet. Presiding at the meeting is Imre Pozsgay, a member of the Political Committee of the Hungarian Socialist Workers party. The group issues a statement mildly critical of the Hungarian government's cultural policies. It also criticizes the government for its refusal to raise its voice over the plight of Hungarian minorities in Romania and Czechoslovakia.

September 14: Imre Pozsgay publishes an article in the official journal *Magyar Nemzet* in which he declares that the 1956 "events" were a popular uprising against oppression, not a counterrevolution.

1987   *February 19:* President Reagan lifts the last remaining economic sanctions imposed on Poland in the wake of the imposition of martial law.

June 25: The Hungarian government announces that Károly Grosz, the Budapest district party secretary, will replace György Lázár as prime minister.

July 12: Eight Soviet diplomats arrive in Tel Aviv.

November 11: Boris Yeltsin is dismissed as boss of the Moscow Communist party after criticizing Gorbachev for the slow pace of reforms.

November 15: In the first violent demonstrations in Romania in ten years, several thousand workers ransack the Brasov city hall during protests against wage cuts and a likely third consecutive winter of food and energy shortages. Since 1981 Ceauşescu has halved Romania's external debt at the people's expense.

November 29: Poles are asked to vote in a referendum for severe economic austerity and moderate political changes. Solidarity, still outlawed, urges Poles to abstain from voting; the referendum is defeated.

December 17: Miloš Jakeš replaces Gustáv Husák as head of the Czechoslovak Communist party.

1988   *January 30:* The Polish government announces substantial price increases to "limit state subsidies and to accelerate the transition to a market economy." The higher prices are to be partially offset by wage increases of nearly 40 percent.

February 23: The Soviet news media reports unrest in Nagorno-Karabakh, a region within Azerbaijan whose population (some 135,000 people) is 80 percent ethnically Armenian.

April 8: Agreement is reached under United Nations auspices in Geneva for the full withdrawal of 115,000 Soviet troops from Afghanistan within nine months.

April 25: Transportation workers in the Polish city of Bydgoszcz negotiate a 63 percent wage increase after staging a twelve-hour wildcat strike that cripples the city. The strike is apparently organized by local leaders of the government-endorsed union that supplanted Solidarity. By April 29 labor unrest has spread throughout Poland.

May 15: The Soviet Union begins withdrawing its troops from Afghanistan at the end of its unsuccessful eight-and-one-half-year effort to defend the communist Kabul government against U.S.- and Muslim-supported guerrillas. More than 13,300 Soviet soldiers are dead, with some 35,000 wounded. The civil war has claimed over one million Afghan casualties and left some five million homeless.

May 16: Yugoslavia imposes wage controls as one of the conditions of an IMF (International Monetary Fund) pledge of $430 million in credits and a rescheduling of some $21 billion in loans from Western creditors.

May 17: Some 100,000 protesters in Yerevan, the capital of the Armenian Soviet Socialist Republic, are dispersed by Soviet troops after demonstrating for annexation of Nagorno-Karabakh.

May 20: The Fourteenth Congress of the Hungarian Socialist Workers party convenes. János Kádár is replaced as first secretary by Károly Grósz, who had been prime minister. Kádár is given the meaningless post of president of the party. The reformists Rezső Nyers, Imre Pozsgay, and Miklós Németh are elected members of the party's Central Committe.

May 29: The Moscow Reagan-Gorbachev summit begins. On June 1 they sign the formal ratification of the Intermediate-Range Nuclear Forces (INF) treaty, limiting European-based U.S. missiles that can reach the USSR and Soviet missiles that can strike Western Europe.

June 28: At a special party conference Gorbachev calls for a new type of Soviet presidency, to be elected by a new, broadly-based Congress of People's Deputies. He also proposes pop-ularly elected republican legislatures with sufficient powers to carry out reforms. On July 1 the delegates approve most of the proposed changes.

July 20: Iran accepts a U.N. security council ceasefire reso-lution, thereby calling a halt to the eight-year Iran-Iraq war. Human losses are estimated at one million dead, 1.7 million wounded, and 1.5 million refugees. The cost of the war is estimated at $400 billion.

August 16: Thousands of Polish miners in upper Silesia strike for higher pay and the restoration of Solidarity. On August 23 Lech Walesa calls for dialogue with the government to diffuse the growing tension. After discussions with the gov-ernment, on August 31 Walesa calls for an end to the now nationwide strikes. By September 3 most workers are back on the job.

August 23: Tens of thousands of demonstrators march in the capital cities of Estonia, Latvia, and Lithuania on the anniver-sary of the 1939 Ribbentrop-Molotov secret protocols, which led to the annexation of the Baltic republics by the Soviets in 1940.

September 21: Soviet authorities declare a state of emer-gency in Nagorno-Karabakh. A curfew is imposed in Stepan-akert, the capital, after shots are fired, cars set ablaze and unknown numbers killed and wounded.

October 10: Lubomir Strougal, Czechoslovak premier for eighteen years, resigns, followed by his entire cabinet of min-isters the next day. Party chief Milos Jakes names Ladislav Adamec premier. Adamec is expected to promote change at a more gradual pace than Strougal.

November 23: In the autonomous Yugoslav province of Ko-sovo, Serbian authorities ban all public assemblies and dem-onstrations to curb protests by ethnic Albanians, who consti-tute a majority in the province, and who oppose proposed changes in local party leadership and in the province's consti-tutional status.

Milkos Németh is appointed Hungarian prime minister. Reportedly Rezső Nyers, an advocate of economic change, turned down the post; he is nominated to a new post as minister for economic affairs.

December 7: In an address to the United Nations general

assembly President Gorbachev pledges unilateral Soviet reductions in men and tanks in Europe and on the Sino-Soviet border. After his speech he curtails his trip after an earthquake virtually destroys several cities in the Armenian republic, killing about twenty-five thousand.

1989   *February 2:* More than a thousand Czechoslovak artists demand the release of all political prisoners in the country.

February 3: North Korea recalls its ambassador to Budapest in protest over Hungary's recognition of South Korea, and expels the Hungarian ambassador from North Korea.

February 8: The long-postponed talks between Solidarity and the government begin in Warsaw.

February 9: Miloš Jakeš, secretary-general of the Czechoslovak Communist party, declares that the government will not discuss matters with "antisocialist" groups.

February 10–11: An extraordinary meeting of the Central Committee of the Hungarian Socialist Workers party is held to discuss member Imre Pozsgay's statement that the 1956 "events" in Hungary represented a popular uprising.

February 15: The Polish opposition journal *Odrodzanie,* publishes a report on the Katyn massacre, originally issued in 1943 according to which Polish officers were murdered by Soviet secret police troops.

February 23: The Czechoslovak Communist party's daily newspaper prints a long article condemning Václav Havel as a subversive of Czechoslovak social order.

February 24: Over thirteen thousand Romanian refugees are allowed to enter Hungary.

February 25: Sayed Ali Khameini, president of Iran, visits Romania. A joint communiqué announcing cooperation is signed. Bilateral trade between the two countries is expected to reach one billion dollars a year.

February 26: Prime Minister Mieczyslaw Rakowski attends the performance of a Havel play in Warsaw and expresses his disapproval of the playright's imprisonment for political activity.

February 27: The East German Communist party daily issues a statement that the party will pursue its own road to socialism, maintaining the party's monopoly in politics, state control of industry, and subsidies for necessary goods.

1989 *(continued)* *February 28*: The Hungarian government announces that the security and alarm systems along the Austrian border will be dismantled.

March 12: East German authorities refuse to permit distribution of the German-language version of *Novoie Vremia*
because it published an interview with Lech Walesa.

March 17: *Scinteia,* the daily newspaper of the Romanian
Communist party, declares in an editorial that whoever criticizes the internal situation of the country commits espionage
and treason.

Dimitar and Diana Boyadzhiev, two founders of the independent Bulgarian trade union *Podkrepa,* are expelled from
the country.

April 4: The West German government recalls its ambassador to Romania in protest against the human rights violations
of the Ceauşescu regime.

April 12: The Central Committee of the Hungarian Socialist
Workers party expels four conservative members, including
the chief ideologist, János Berecz, who is the main opponent
of reform.

April 13: Ceauşescu declares that Romania can produce nuclear weapons and use them if threatened.

April 24: The European Community formally suspends talks
on a new economic agreement with Romania until its government improves the conditions of minorities.

May 5: Central Committee member and historian Mária Or-
mos, in a speech delivered at the Hungarian Academy of
Sciences, calls Kádár's government a Soviet puppet. Three
days later the Hungarian Socialist Workers party relieves
János Kádár of his posts as a member of the Central Committee and as party president.

May 10: Lech Walesa receives the Council of Europe's Human Rights Prize for 1989.

May 17: Václav Havel is released from a Czechoslovak prison
after serving half his eight-month sentence for dissident activities.

Romania proposes that an emergency meeting of the Warsaw Pact countries be held in June in order to reestablish
unity within the alliance.

June 5: The daily party newspaper of East Germany supports China's shooting of dissident students in Tiananmen Square.

The first round of elections for the Polish parliament is held. Only about 62 percent of eligible voters turn out, but they vote overwhelmingly for the candidates supported by Solidarity and other dissident groups.

June 6: Election results in Poland show that Solidarity-supported candidates won 92 of 100 seats in the Senate and 160 of 161 seats in the Sejm (the lower house).

June 7: Thousands of ethnic Turks in Bulgaria are expelled from the country.

June 8: Minister of Culture and Education, Ferenc Glatz, announces in Budapest that, as of September, the Russian language will no longer be a required subject in Hungarian schools and universities.

June 14: The Czechoslovak Communist party daily declares its support for the shooting of students in Beijing.

June 16: An estimated 200,000 people file by in Budapest's Hero's Square, paying last tribute to the exhumed corpses of Imre Nagy, Hungary's Prime Minister in 1956, and his martyred companions, executed on Kádár's orders in 1958.

June 27: Albanian leader Ramiz Alia announces that the reforms in the Soviet Union, China, Poland and Hungary are tantamount to the restoration of capitalism.

July 12: President George Bush arrives in Warsaw on a trip to Poland and Hungary. He visits with Lech Walesa and addresses a huge crowd at the monument commemorating workers killed during the strikes of 1970. Radio Bucharest calls Bush's news conference on the eve of his departure for Eastern Europe an effort to destabilize the socialist countries of the region.

In Poland, the Citizens' Parliamentary Caucus decides not to join a Communist-led government. Solidarity members also refuse cabinet posts in such a government.

August 8: Mesut Yilmaz, Turkish foreign minister, announces that over 250,000 refugees from Bulgaria have entered Turkey.

August 9: After giving an interview to Canadian television in which he openly criticized the Ceauşescu government for oppressing the Hungarian minority in Romania, László Tőkés, a Calvinist minister in Transylvania, is arrested but released the following day.

August 14: The homes of four leading Slovakian human rights activists are searched, and two of the activists are detained by the Czechoslovak police.

August 16: The Hungarian government sets up tents at a campsite near Budapest for East Germans wishing to go to the West. Since opening its western border in May, East Germans have been streaming into Hungary to get to West Germany.

The Polish Senate unanimously adopts a resolution condemning the Warsaw Pact members' invasion of Czechoslovakia in 1968.

Lech Walesa tells the Polish press that Solidarity is prepared to form a coalition government without the Communists.

August 22: Turkey closes its borders with Bulgaria after 310,000 ethnic Turkish refugees arrive from Bulgaria.

President Jaruzelski nominates Tadeusz Mazowiecki as the new prime minister of Poland. Two days later, the Polish Sejm approves Mazowiecki as prime minister by an overwhelming majority.

August 27: Czechoslovak radio calls Lech Walesa a threat to socialism everywhere. Albanian radio declares Mazowiecki's premiership an act of bourgeois counterrevolution.

September 10: Gyula Horn, speaking for the Hungarian government, announces that East Germans who desire to go to the West through Hungary are free to do so and that Hungary is temporarily suspending its 1969 agreement with East Germany that prohibited such a step. The decision brings a vehement denunciation by the East German government. Chancellor Kohl of West Germany expresses his thanks to Hungary for this humanitarian gesture.

October 9: Two days after the official celebration of the fortieth anniversary of the GDR, a massive prodemocracy demonstration in Leipzig is allowed to proceed.

November 9: East Germany opens its borders to West Germany and the Berlin Wall to West Berlin.

November 17: End of one-party rule in Czechoslovakia, where the Communist regime collapses. In December, Václav Havel is elected the new president.

December 21: A revolution in Romania overthrows the Ceauşescu clan. Nicolas and Elena Ceauşescu are executed December 25.

1990 *January 1*: President Havel declares an amnesty for a large group of common prisoners. As a consequence, the Skoda automobile plant near Prague has to stop most production, since most workers are inmates.

January 2: A decree abolishes the secret police department in the Ministry of Internal Affairs in Bulgaria.

New economic measures are introduced in Yugoslavia in order to stop the downward spiral of production and the growth of inflation.

January 5: The Hungarian parliament adopts a resolution calling for the withdrawal of Soviet troops from Hungary by the end of December 1991.

January 7: The new Romanian government issues a decree permitting citizens to acquire passports and to travel abroad.

January 10: After a heated two-day Comecon summit in Sofia, the Soviet-bloc trading organization agrees to gradually adopt a free market approach; to turn to hard currency dealings at world market prices; and to replace long-term multilateral barter with bilateral trade.

January 12: Romania becomes the first East European country to outlaw its Communist party; the move is forced on the provisional government of the National Salvation Front by popular demand.

January 15: Thousands of angry protesters storm the East Berlin headquarters of the *Stasi* (state security service) causing extensive damage.

Bulgaria revokes the Communist party's constitutionally guaranteed monopoly on power when the National Assembly votes to revoke the party's dominant role.

January 18: The Bulgarian state news agency reports that former leader Todor Zhivkov is under house arrest on charges of inciting ethnic hostility, misuse of government property and money, and malfeasance in office.

January 23: An extraordinary congress of the Yugoslav League of Communists adjourns one day after delegates vote to relinquish the party's political monopoly. The congress collapses when the Slovenian delegation walks out after demanding greater autonomy for the republics.

The Hungarian Democratic Forum calls for an investigation into the continuing activities of Hungary's secret service, such as monitoring the telephone conversations and the mail of opposition party figures.

January 27: The Romanian Front for National Salvation declares that it will run candidates in the May 20 elections. Thousands of young people demonstrate in Bucharest against the Front, accusing its leaders of continuing the communist policies of the Ceauşescus.

January 29: The Polish United Workers (Communist) party votes itself out of existence and re-forms as the Social Democratic party.

January 30: The Czechoslovak Communist party loses more than 100 seats in the Federal Assembly when a total of 120 new deputies are sworn in, only 9 of them Communists.

February 2: The Bulgarian Communist party names Alexander Lilov to the new post of party chairman, replacing Petar Mladenov who was secretary general of the party; Mladenov remains head of state. The premier is replaced by Andrei Lukanov.

February 4: The Slovenian League of Communists declares its independence from the Yugoslav Communist party.

February 11: U.S. secretary of state James Baker visits Romania. He announces food aid in the amount of eighty million dollars but also says that long-term improvement in relations depend upon free elections in Romania.

February 17: Representatives of Czechoslovak radio and television meet a delegation of Radio Free Europe to discuss possible sharing of information, exchanges of programs, and joint projects.

February 26: The Red Army begins phased withdrawals of its 73,500 troops in Czechoslovakia. The troops have been there since 1968; the withdrawal is expected to be complete by July 1, 1991.

March 1: The Polish government reports that inflation dropped from 78 percent in January to 10 percent in February. Similar conditions are expected for March.

March 13: Bulgaria and Albania sign a treaty on culture,

aviation, and health care. This is the first visit of an Albanian minister to Bulgaria.

West German Chancellor Kohl, campaigning for right-wing candidates in East Germany, promises to exchange East German deutsch marks one-for-one for West German deutsch marks when the country is reunified. (Economists are horrified by the cost and inflationary pressures of this move.)

March 14: More than five thousand Romanians cross into Austria via Hungary seeking political asylum before a scheduled tightening of Austrian immigration regulations.

March 18: The Alliance for Germany, a three-party conservative coalition backed by Kohl, wins 48.1 percent of the vote in East Germany's first general election. The Social Democratic Union places second with 21.8 percent of the vote.

March 19–20: After a celebration of Hungarian National Day by local ethnic Hungarans and visiting Hungarian citizens, ethnic violence errupts in the Romanian city of Tirgu Mures, leaving three dead and hundreds injured.

March 24: Hungary and West Germany agree to permit their citizens to travel between countries without visas. The first free elections in Hungary proceed smoothly.

March 29: A new name, the Czech and Slovak Federative Republic is adopted for Czechoslovakia. In addition, in written Slovak, the name may be hyphenated: Czecho-Slovakia.

April 3: Bulgaria's Communist party renames itself the Bulgarian Socialist party.

April 5: Bulgaria announces the dismantling of fortifications on the Yugoslav border.

April 8: In Hungarian run-off elections the center-right Democratic Forum and its allies win nearly 60 percent of the seats in parliament and agree to a conservative coalition government.

April 11: The Polish parliament abolishes all censorship.

May 9: In an interview in Gdansk, Lech Walesa indicates a growing rift between Solidarity's leftist blue-collar base and the free market intellectual wing embodied by the Polish prime minister, Tadeus Mazowiecki.

May 20: In Romanian general elections, Ion Iliescu and the National Salvation Front win the vote for president and parliament.

1990 *(continued)* *May 23*: The Hungarian parliament approves the cabinet of a coalition of three parties, led by the Hungarian Democratic Forum. The prime minister is József Antall.

The Romanian National Salvation Front and Ion Iliescu are the winners of the Romanian elections.

In the Bulgarian elections the Bulgarian Socialist party receives the largest number of votes.

May 29: The parliament of the Russian Republic elects Boris Yeltsin president of the Russian Republic.

June 7: Meeting in Moscow, the leaders of the Warsaw Pact proclaim the end of the idea of the West as an "ideological enemy."

June 8–9: In Czechoslovakia's first free elections in more than forty years, Civic Forum and its Slovak sister party, Public Against Violence, capture 46.3 percent of the vote and 170 seats in the 300-member Federal Assembly. The communists place second with 13.6 percent and 47 seats.

June 13–15: Student-led antigovernment protests in Bucharest are brutally put down by ten thousand miners from the north who virtually take over the city. The police do not interfere as the miners beat anyone they suspect of opposing the government; they also ransack and destroy headquarters and apartments of opposition party leaders.

June 17: The ruling Bulgarian Socialist party wins a solid majority in parliamentary run-off elections marred by reports of voter intimidation and irregularities.

June 20: Ion Iliescu is sworn in as Romanian president; the U.S. ambassador boycotts the ceremony.

June 21: The East and West German parliaments ratify the treaty reunifying the nation.

June 26: The Hungarian parliament votes for a negotiated withdrawal from the Warsaw Pact.

June 28: The Conference on Security and Cooperation in Europe (CSCE) concludes a four-week human rights conference in Copenhagen with the adoption of a resolution committing its members to multiparty free elections; the separation of political parties from the state; independent judiciaries; respect for minority rights; and the freedoms of expression, organization, and assembly. This marks the first time that the Soviet Union signs a document pledging a multiparty system.

June 28–July 6: Thousands of Albanians take refuge in foreign embassies in Tirana. After preventing food deliveries to the embassies, the communist government bows to international pressure and orders evacuation to begin.

July 1: German monetary union is established with parity between East and West German marks.

July 3: The parliament of Slovenia declares that its laws and constitution take precedence over those of the Yugoslav federal government.

July 5: Serbia dissolves the parliament and government of the autonomous province of Kosovo; police under Serbian direction seize television and radio stations in the provincial capital, Pristina.

July 10: The CSCE accords Albania observer status in return for Albania's pledge to improve its human rights record. Albania was the only European country not a member of the CSCE.

July 12: Boris Yeltsin resigns from the Communist party during the Twenty-eighth Congress of the CPSU.

July 16: Chancellor Kohl meets with President Gorbachev in Zheleznovodsk, near Stavropol. Gorbachev accepts a reunified Germany retaining NATO membership as long as NATO troops are not stationed in eastern Germany. Kohl agrees that Germany will pay the costs of withdrawing and rehousing Soviet troops by 1994. In addition to extensive German credits to the Soviet Union, the FRG will assume all the GDR's commercial obligations to the USSR.

July 19: General Jaruzelski expresses his willingness to resign as Polish president before the end of the year, to allow for an elected successor.

July 22: The Hungarian governing coalition agrees to the reprivatization of farmlands.

July 25: The Polish government reports that Soviet oil deliveries are down by 30 percent. Similar shortages are recorded in the other Eastern European countries.

July 30: Albania and the Soviet Union restore diplomatic relations, which were broken off in 1961.

1990 *(continued)* *August 3*: The Hungarian parliament elects acting president Árpád Göncz, writer and former dissident, president.

August 5: Zhelyu Zhelev, the new Bulgarian president announces the abolition of all anticonstitutional laws and the creation of a consultative body that will confer with all political parties.

August 6: Skoda, the giant Czechoslovak auto-manufacturing firm, announces its interest in becoming partners with either Renault or Volkswagen.

Bulgaria and Czechoslovakia condemn Iraq's invasion of Kuwait.

August 18: Amid roadblocks, street clashes, and mounting tension, the Serbian minority (11 percent of the population) in the Yugoslav republic of Croatia begin voting on an unofficial referendum on political autonomy. The ballot initiative is declared illegal by the republic's government.

August 23: After bitter debate on the date, the East German *Volkskammer* votes for reunification with West Germany on October 3.

August 26: Antigovernment protesters in Sofia storm, loot, and set fire to the headquarters of the ruling Bulgarian Socialist party.

August 31: East and West Germany sign the reunification treaty, with October 3 as the date for unity. In Moscow on September 12 the four Allied powers and the two Germanies officially verify the Treaty on the Final Settlement with Respect to Germany.

September 19: General Jaruzelski effectively resigns by asking parliament to set a date to end his term in office. He had been named Polish president by parliament in 1989 with a six-year term.

September 27: The Council of Europe denies Romania observer status because the human rights situation in the country has not improved.

October 3: Germany is reunified as the former GDR becomes five eastern *Länder* (states) of the FRG.

Croatian and Slovenian presidents meet in Zagreb in order to plan their moves to obtain full autonomy from Yugoslavia.

October 14: Soviet troop withdrawals from Czechoslovakia

are ahead of schedule. The commanding Soviet general announces that complete withdrawal is planned for April 1991, two months early.

The Hungarian opposition gains victory in municipal elections.

October 15: President Gorbachev is awarded the Nobel Peace Prize.

October 17: The European Community offers $7.7 million in emergency assistance for Romanian orphans. As part of Ceaușescu's plan to increase Romania's population from 22 million in 1988 to 30 million in the year 2000, abortions and contraception had been banned, and each woman was expected to bear five children. The result is at least 100,000 parentless children in squalid state orphanages. Earlier in the year, the World Health Organization responded to a report of at least 500 AIDS-infected babies in Romanian hospitals and institutions.

October 23: The Hungarian parliament declares this day, the anniversary of the revolution of 1956, a national holiday. Ceremonies are held nationwide commemorating the victims of the revolution and of the reprisals by the Kádár regime.

Tensions within Yugoslavia increase. The Croatians and Slovenes adamantly demand the revision of the form of the state and threaten secession. The Serbs, on the other hand, hope the army will maintain the unity of the state.

October 25: The Slovak parliament approves a law declaring Slovak the official language of the state. The law allows minorities to use their own language in official matters in areas where they make up 20 percent or more of the population.

October 30: Slovenia, in response to an earlier Serbian tariff, imposes customs duties on Serbian goods. This effectively means the end of a unified Yugoslav internal market.

November 14: The foreign ministers of Germany and Poland sign an agreement in Warsaw confirming existing borders between the two states. A second treaty on bilateral relations is to be submitted for ratification to the Reichstag.

November 18: The Romanian communist party is reborn under the name Socialist Labor party.

November 19–21: The leaders of the CSCE hold their second summit in Paris, marking the formal end to the Cold War. (The first CSCE summit was in 1975 in Helsinki.) The members, represented by 11 presidents, 22 premiers, one Vatican representative and many foreign ministers sign a treaty drastically reducing conventional weapons in Europe. The leaders also sign a Charter of Paris for the New Europe, proclaiming an end to the "era of conflict and division in Europe" and vowing a "new era of democracy, peace, and unity."

November 25: In Polish elections for president, Walesa wins with a plurality over Tyminski (an enigmatic expatriate businessman), with Mazowiecki coming in last. Run-offs would be held December 9.

November 29: Bulgaria's acting president Andrei Lukanov resigns amid a general strike.

December 1: The Yugoslav defense secretary, General Kadijević, warns that the military is prepared to counter "highly aggressive anti-Yugoslav and antisocialist forces" undermining national unity. The general is a Serb, as are 60 percent of military officers. On December 3, Croatian president Franjo Tudjman responds that "the army can't decide what is democratic and what is not, what is in the interest of progress and what is not."

December 7: Bulgaria's Grand National Assembly elects an independent politician, Dimiter Popov, as prime minister.

December 9: Lech Walesa wins Poland's run-off election for president.

The Czechoslovak government chooses Volkswagen as the Western partner of Skoda.

December 11: Hungary signs a trade agreement with the Soviet Union. The Soviet partner now owes more than one billion dollars to Hungary.

Lech Walesa wins the Polish presidential election. Former president Wojciech Jaruzelski apologizes to all Poles for the wrongs committed against them by the Communists during four decades of dictatorial rule.

December 12: The Czechoslovak Federal Assembly approves legislation that will lead to power sharing between the central government and the Czech and Slovak republics.

December 13–14: The Albanian government deploys security forces in several cities to halt an unprecedented wave of anticommunist unrest; the mobs display no identifiable political leaning other than a hatred for the hardline represented by Hoxha.

December 20: Soviet foreign minister Eduard Shevardnadze resigns, warning that the nation is heading toward a dictatorship.

The Bulgarian Grand National Assembly confirms the first multiparty government in forty years; eight Socialist party ministers; three Union of Democratic Forces ministers; and two Agrarian Union ministers.

December 23: The Yugoslav republic of Slovenia votes overwhelmingly for a referendum to have the republic secede should efforts at confederation fail.

December 25: Romania expels King Michael less than twelve hours after his arrival in the country, on the first anniversary of the Ceauşescu execution.

December 29: President Walesa choses thirty-nine-year-old economist Jan Krzysztof Bielecki as his prime minister, subject to parliamentary confirmation.

December 30–31: More than three thousand Albanians, mostly ethnic Greeks, flee over the Greek border, seeking political asylum.

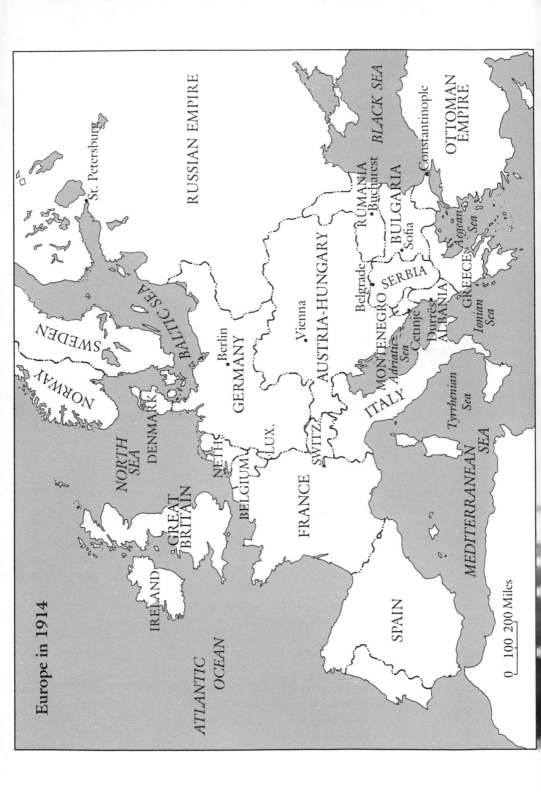

Europe in 1914

ATLANTIC OCEAN

IRELAND

GREAT BRITAIN

NORTH SEA

NORWAY

SWEDEN

St. Petersburg

RUSSIAN EMPIRE

BALTIC SEA

DENMARK

NETH.

BELGIUM

LUX.

GERMANY

Berlin

FRANCE

SWITZ.

Vienna

AUSTRIA-HUNGARY

ITALY

SPAIN

MEDITERRANEAN SEA

Tyrrhenian Sea

Adriatic Sea

MONTENEGRO

Cetinje

ALBANIA

Durrës

Ionian Sea

GREECE

Aegean Sea

SERBIA

Belgrade

BULGARIA

Sofia

RUMANIA

Bucharest

BLACK SEA

Constantinople

OTTOMAN EMPIRE

0   100   200 Miles

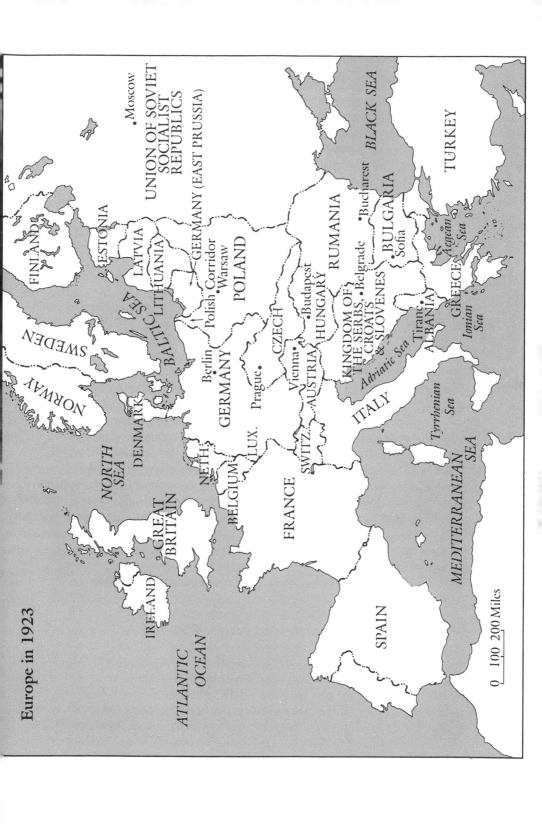

Europe in 1923

NORWAY

SWEDEN

FINLAND

ESTONIA

LATVIA

LITHUANIA

UNION OF SOVIET
SOCIALIST
REPUBLICS

• Moscow

GERMANY (EAST PRUSSIA)

Polish Corridor

• Warsaw

POLAND

Berlin •

GERMANY

Prague •

CZECH

Vienna •

AUSTRIA

• Budapest

HUNGARY

RUMANIA

• Bucharest

BLACK SEA

KINGDOM OF
THE SERBS,
CROATS
& SLOVENES

• Belgrade

BULGARIA

• Sofia

Tiranë •

ALBANIA

GREECE

TURKEY

Aegean
Sea

Ionian
Sea

Adriatic Sea

ITALY

Tyrrhenian
Sea

MEDITERRANEAN
SEA

SWITZ.

FRANCE

BELGIUM

LUX.

NETH.

DENMARK

NORTH
SEA

BALTIC SEA

GREAT
BRITAIN

IRELAND

ATLANTIC
OCEAN

SPAIN

0   100   200 Miles

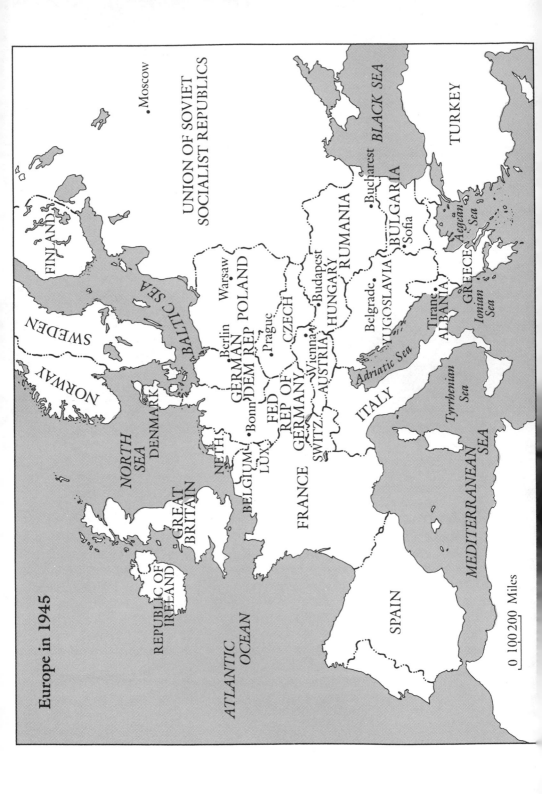

Europe in 1945

MOSCOW

UNION OF SOVIET
SOCIALIST REPUBLICS

FINLAND

SWEDEN

NORWAY

BALTIC SEA

NORTH
SEA

DENMARK

GREAT
BRITAIN

REPUBLIC OF
IRELAND

ATLANTIC
OCEAN

NETHS.

BELGIUM

LUX.

FRANCE

Warsaw

Berlin

GERMAN
DEM REP

•Bonn

FED
REP OF
GERMANY

SWITZ.

POLAND

Prague

CZECH

•Vienna

AUSTRIA

Budapest

HUNGARY

RUMANIA

Bucharest•

•Sofia

BULGARIA

Belgrade•

YUGOSLAVIA

Adriatic Sea

Tirane•

ALBANIA

Ionian
Sea

GREECE

Aegean
Sea

BLACK SEA

TURKEY

ITALY

Tyrrhenian
Sea

MEDITERRANEAN
SEA

SPAIN

0 100 200 Miles

The Columbia History
of Eastern Europe in
the Twentieth Century

1 Eastern Europe in the Twentieth Century: "Old Wine in New Bottles"

Stephen Fischer-Galati

Three times during the twentieth century—in 1918, 1945, and 1989—Eastern Europe was to be made "safe for democracy." The dismantling of the empires of the Habsburgs, Ottoman sultans, Russian tsars, Hitler's Germany, and that of the Soviet Union in the face of the irresistible force of the oppressed nations' quest for democracy has fulfilled the axiomatic ideological position of Western champions of the principle of self-determination of nationalities. Yet even after the overthrow of the most pernicious forms of totalitarianism democracy remains illusory. It may well be asked what factors mitigated against the triumph of democracy after the world wars and to what extent these factors remain relevant today.

The failure of democracy to take root or to develop in the way that Woodrow Wilson, Franklin Delano Roosevelt, and others expected has been attributed, in rather simplistic terms, to a variety of external and internal developments that are presumably becoming irrelevant. The rise of totalitarianism in Italy, Germany, and the Soviet Union in the interwar years taken in conjunction with French and British appeasement and American isolationism, as well as the economic devastation caused by the Great Depression, had a negative impact on the democratic evolution of Eastern Europe. Similarly, Western errors at Yalta, reflecting political naïveté with respect to Stalin's aggressive imperialism, made possible the conquest of Eastern Europe by the Soviet Union. According to the proponents of such explanations, the forces of democracy that have prevailed in Germany since World War II are making headway in the Soviet Union itself under Mikhail Gorbachev. These forces are being supplemented and reinforced by Japan, the United States, and a European community vocally committed to the promotion of human rights, tolerance of ethnic and religious diversity, political pluralism, a market economy, and a new world order. These factors are likely to further and facilitate the democratic revolution and evolution of Eastern Europe in the future.

Internal factors, designed to explain the retardation of the democratic evolution of the nations of Eastern Europe, range over a wide area. They include the standard lack of democratic experience in the face of fascist aggression in the 1930s and the more realistic assessment of nationalist excesses and internecine conflicts between diverse ethnic, nationalistic, and religious groups. In addition, we must consider the failure of ruling elites to address social and economic inequities, with a corresponding exacerbation of class conflicts leading to the eventual failure of fledgling democratic experiments of the interwar period. Western analysts routinely attribute the inability of democratic forces to assert themselves after World War II to Stalinism and neo-Stalinism. However, with the removal of the barriers to democracy following the collapse of the communist regimes of Eastern Europe in 1989, the democratic inclinations of the peoples of Eastern Europe, inflamed by decades of totalitarian repression, are assumed to have been unleashed and to be bound to triumph in the age of *perestroika* and *glasnost.*

As appealing as these premises may be for interested parties and well-wishers, it may be well worth assessing their validity in the light of the historic realities of the twentieth century. It is indisputable that external factors played a major role in the destabilization of Eastern Europe in the interwar years, yet the failure of the democratic experiments might more reasonably be attributed primarily to internal factors in all the Eastern bloc countries (except perhaps Czechoslovakia).

The presumption that the principle of self-determination of nationalities represented the ultimate expression of the oppressed nations' search for and commitment to Wilsonian democracy and peaceful coexistence among the peoples of Eastern Europe on both intra- and international bases was erroneous from its inception. It simply ignored prevailing political, cultural, and socioeconomic realities. By the end of World War I, social, economic, and political retardation were characteristic of most of the region. The largely agrarian, semi-literate societies were politically immature; they were certainly un-committed to—and in most cases, unfamiliar with—democracy. The political culture, such as it was, had its roots in ecclesiastical and monarchical paternalism. This was most evident in the Orthodox and Catholic communities which comprised the majority of the inhabitants of the successor states. State armies, with their inherent stratifications that cut across some nationalist, religious, and class lines, provided points of identification, but little in the way of political organization. It seems fair to surmise that church, monarchy, and army were no more committed to Wilsonian democracy than were the majority of political organizations striving for leadership in the struggle for national independence and self-determination. National self-determination presupposed the total elimination of the imperial orders and the creation of the largest national states from the remnants of empires and competing national states. Nationalism, often virulent, became the standard for all political groups seeking the support of the masses and the ear of the peacemakers committed to the dissolution of the empires and creation of democratic states. This brand of nationalism, however, was generally intolerant of religious and ethnic diversity and focused most explicitly on territorial issues. Disputes over the borders of the successor states tended to exacerbate conflicts among various ethnic and religious groups. In this respect most inflammatory was the singling out of Jews—outcasts both on religious and ethnic grounds—as not only unidentifiable with national causes but also as overt opponents of national states by virtue of their presumed affiliation with Bolshevism.

The extent of political negativism and intolerance varied from country to country. It was least evident in urbanized and industrialized Bohemia and Moravia in present day Czechoslovakia. It was most striking in Hungary and Romania, albeit for different reasons. The Hungarians resented the loss of Transylvania to Romania more than any other territorial loss they suffered at the end of World War I. The revolution that brought to power the communist regime of Béla Kun contained the roots of an identification of Hungarian Jews with Bolshevism. In turn, the leaders of Greater Romania fearful of Hungarian irredentism and, even more so, of the Bolsheviks' rejection of the annexation of Bessarabia by Romania in 1918, made the defense of the country's national and territorial integrity against Hungarians and "Judeo-Communists" a sine qua non for political success.

This is not to say that the masses of Eastern Europe were swayed by such political arguments or that they were committed to nationalist doctrine. Nor can it be said that all political organizations rejected democratic principles. In a few instances, they even attempted to establish truly democratic political institutions and practices. However, the traditional conservative forces—church, monarchy, and army—favored and supported nationalist, anticommunist, anti-Semitic, and essentially nondemocratic and antidemocratic organizations that, at least in the 1920s, were willing to support the traditional pillars of the political culture of their underdeveloped societies.

The political dynamics of the successor states were relatively simple. In the absence of historical models of pluralism and representative government, the various political parties founded at the beginning of the century and, with increasing frequency, after World War I, did not necessarily command the confidence of their constituents. Conservative as well as liberal political organizations, often headed by the landed gentry, urban businessmen, industrialists, and intellectuals, generally failed to gain the allegiance of the masses. The socialist and social-democratic organizations, which functioned primarily in Czechoslovakia and Hungary, and, to a lesser extent, in Romania and Poland, were vulnerable because of their popular identification with communist and Jewish influences.

The principal target in most of Eastern Europe was the peasant, not because most politicians identified with rural society and its interests or, for that matter, were of peasant origin themselves but rather because the key socioeconomic issues of the successor states revolved around the redistribution of land and attendant problems. Land reform, redistribution of wealth, industrialization, urbanization, social dislocation, and modernization in general all involved, in one way or another, the peasantry. The peasant concerns were most acute in Romania, Bulgaria, Hungary, and Poland and, to a lesser degree, in certain parts of Yugoslavia and Czechoslovakia. Peasant parties by a variety of names—Agrarian, Smallholder, National Peasant—all championed vaguely defined interests of the rural masses: more often than not, however, ineffectually and for the benefit of the leadership. With the most notable exception of the Bulgarian Agrarian party, headed by Alexander Stamboliiski, the peasant parties failed to meet the expectations of their constituents, which were ultimately grounded in the unhindered possession and exploitation of the land. The radicalism of Stamboliiski's reforms and securing of political power for the peasants' benefit revealed the peasantry's great intolerance toward urban society and governmental bureaucracies. It also revealed the peasants' distinctly anti-intellectual, parochial, antimodern, and antinationalist attitudes. All this scared not only the conservative elites but also liberals, socialists, communists, and even many of the leaders of Eastern European agrarian organizations. These in general favored compromises that would assure economic progress for the peasantry while subordinating the peasants' interests to those of urban politicians, businessmen, industrialists, and intellectuals.

Political activity, therefore, focused initially on the adaptation of underdeveloped agrarian societies to the social and economic problems of the interwar years. But land reforms were usually insufficiently generous to provide a base for a profitable agricultural economy and industrialization. With few exceptions, these economies were slow and not competitive in European markets. Thus the economic viability of most of the successor states soon became questionable. Instead of seeking meaningful solutions to their countries' economic and related social problems, political parties tended to direct their activities at narrow confrontational issues mostly concerned with ethnic and religious diversity, communism, territorial revisionism, nepotism, and corruption. By the end of the 1920s the democratic structures mandated by the victorious Allies at the end of World War I had been seriously compromised in Poland, Albania, Bulgaria, and Yugoslavia (where de facto dictatorships were in place), were limping along in Hungary, and showed signs of discomfiture in Romania. Czechoslovakia alone, by virtue of its successful urban and industrial traditions and policies, was true to its commitment to pluralistic, parliamentary democracy.

What is noteworthy in this diminution, if not outright failure, of the democratic experiment is that it occurred at a time of relative international peace and prosperity. Indeed, in the 1920s none of the later revisionist or aggressive European powers or their client states posed serious threats to the beneficiaries of the territorial awards made at the end of World War I. The Russo-Polish war ended in Poland's favor; Russian revisionism could be ignored also by Romania; and Mussolini's attempted subversion of Yugoslavia's territorial and political integrity was largely ineffectual. Hungarian irredentism, in the absence of external support, posed no threat to Romania, Yugoslavia, or Czechoslovakia, while Bulgarian agitation over Macedonia and the Dobrudja caused little alarm in Yugoslavia and Romania. Nevertheless, such revisionist activities could be—and were— used to foment xenophobic agitation by political organizations and ruling elites seeking legitimacy and/or the furthering of their political standing within various segments of the respective populations. This was true equally of winners and losers. The fact remains, however, that international issues and territorial disputes were only marginally responsible for the waning of democracy on the eve of the crises of the 1930s.

The political turmoil in Romania, for instance, erupted from the challenge of the moderate National Peasant party to the authoritarian and virtually monopolistic hold on power by the National Liberal party as well as from the gradual evolution of the populist, anti-Semitic, and protofascist Legion of the Archangel Michael. In Hungary, the consolidation of power by Admiral Horthy's authoritarian regime was realized through legitimation of resistance to communism, following the fall of Béla Kun's communist republic, and through invoking the need for a strong regime to secure the historic territorial rights of the Hungarians. In Yugoslavia the political crisis centered on the challenge to Serbian power by Croatia. In Bulgaria the army and urban establishment assumed power after Stamboliiski's assassination in the name of protecting the national interest against subversion by the communists on the left and by the extremist Internal Macedonian Revolutionary Organization (IMRO) on the right. For similar reasons, related to political instability caused by interparty conflicts and perceived threats to Polish integrity, General Joseph Pilsudski established his dictatorship, following a coup d'état, in 1926. Finally, political restiveness in tribal Albania, provoked largely by left-wing intellectuals in confrontation with ultraconservative landowners, made short shrift of democratic procedures as Ahmed Bey Zog established a de facto dictatorship in 1925.

In the absence of solid foundations for the establishment of the practices of Western-style democracy, given the general acceptance by the population and conservative pillars of society of authoritarian rule, the few truly democratic forces of Eastern Europe were fighting a losing battle against the impact of the Great Depression and the corollary rise of aggressive totalitarianism of the right in the 1930s.

Yet it would be difficult to account for the gradual demise of democracy in the decade before World War II only in terms of economic adversity and external subversion by Mussolini's Italy and Hitler's Germany. The economic crisis of the 1930s affected underdeveloped Eastern Europe much less dramatically than the industrial West. It is true that the economies were generally stagnant, but the internal political crises were largely unrelated to economic factors. The assassination of King Alexander of Yugoslavia by extremists belonging to IMRO in 1934, for instance, had little to do with economics. For that matter, the subsequent intensification of internecine conflicts (most notably the Serbian-Croatian one) was only marginally connected with the deterioration of the Yugoslav economy. Nor can it be argued that the extraordinary rise in power of the virulently anti-Semitic Romanian Iron Guard was due to mass resentment over alleged economic exploitation of the Romanian worker and peasant by Jewish entrepreneurs. The assumption of power in Poland by the "colonels" was unrelated to the economic woes of the impoverished Polish peasantry. The political turmoil of the 1930s can be better explained by Italian and German interference in the internal affairs of the successor states. The fascists' and Nazis' influence exacerbated internal and international frictions and conflicts and eventually subverted all political orders and activities within Eastern Europe.

Mussolini's support of the IMRO and of Bulgarian irredentism toward Yugoslavia clearly destabilized Alexander's royal dictatorship. Also, Italian support of Croatian separatism, which became reality in 1939, undermined the precarious stability of the authoritarian regency headed by Alexander's brother, Prince Paul, and facilitated the eventual dissolution of the entire kingdom. However, even without Mussolini's work, the Serbo-Croatian confrontation was reaching the crisis stage by the mid-1930s, propelled, on the one hand, by Catholic Croatian leaders and, on the other, by the Serbian political establishment, both engaged in a struggle for political power within Yugoslavia. It would be fair to say that neither protagonist was thinking in terms of democratic alternatives, compromises, and solutions. Moreover, when Nazi Germany destroyed Yugoslavia after crushing Serbian resistance in 1941, it should be remembered that the Serbs fought the Germans not for the preservation of democracy but in defense of the Serbian nation.

Nor was Mussolini's influence of paramount importance in strengthening Horthy's authoritarianism in Hungary. Fascist Italy did support Hungarian irredentism, in part to undermine the antirevisionist Little Entente of Yugoslavia, Czechoslovakia, and Romania. But the movement to the right in Hungary, manifested in its extremist forms by the actions of the xenophobic and anti-Semitic Arrow Cross movement, was closely related to the antiurbanism and anti-intellectualism of the proletariat, peasantry, and clergy all united against Jewish enclaves in Budapest and other urban centers. Mussolini's influence was evident in Poland, yet the homespun military rule of the colonels was based on the traditional invocation of the threat posed to the Polish nation by German and Russian imperialism and by Jewish economic power and influence.

Mussolini's activities are generally agreed to have been less pernicious and significant in affecting the history of pre–World War II

Eastern Europe than Hitler's. It is incontestable that Nazi Germany's moves against Poland (starting with the Danzig crisis) and against Czechoslovakia (first via the Sudetenland), when combined with economic penetration and extension of support to extremist organizations, threatened political stability and encouraged antidemocratic forces throughout Eastern Europe. But Hitler exploited, rather than created, conditions favorable for the destabilization of political systems. The nationality question in Czechoslovakia, for instance, was not as relaxed as suggested by contemporary and later champions of the merits of Czechoslovak democracy. The Sudeten Germans' resentment over the monopoly of power enjoyed by Prague largely accounted for their susceptibility to German revisionist propaganda. The Slovaks, strongly Catholic and subject to clerical influence, were jealous of Czech economic and political power and Prague's apparent disdain for the country's "second-class" Slovak citizens. It is not that they were pro-Hitler, but rather that certain elements of fascist doctrine and practices were acceptable to and, in some cases, embraced by the Slovak political leadership. In fact, "clerico-fascism," which became so overt later in Slovakia, has its roots in the political culture of interwar Czechoslovakia. What was true of clerico-fascism in Slovakia was also true in Catholic Croatia and Slovenia and, more than anywhere else, in the Romanian Iron Guard's legionary movement.

The Iron Guardist movement was the ultimate expression of unbridled nationalism, populism, and anti-Semitism in Eastern Europe. The movement paralleled Nazism in its origins and development, differing mainly in terms of the political culture and societal structures of the countries in which it flourished. As a product of traditional Romanian nationalism and anti-Semitism adapted to post–World War I conditions, it was an expression of the rejection by young men and women, mostly of peasant origin, of modernization. Identifying all the evils of modernization with Jewish or pro-Jewish values and ideologies, the "legionnaires of the Archangel Michael," with the blessing of much of the clergy, preached a variant of Christian populism that sought the extirpation of Judeo-communist influences and a return to neo-medieval "Autocracy, Orthodoxy, Nationality." It is important to recognize, however, that the Iron Guard had little, if any, direct financial and only limited political support from Nazi Germany.

There is thus insufficient merit in the theory that the crises and de facto abandonment of democratic rule in Eastern Europe prior to the *Anschluss* of March 1938 were ascribable primarily to external factors. Rather, the factors that accounted for the decline and later abandonment of democratic practices were primarily of internal origin, related as they were to confrontational situations involving immature political organizations tending to encourage and exploit prejudices held by the politically immature masses. Most of the political parties of Eastern Europe were essentially forged in defiance of a group or regime rather than evolving from positive common aims, such as reform, change, or adaptation to conditions that could have promoted economic viability, resolution of social problems, modernization, democratization, international reconciliation, and toleration of diversity. In the absence of positive programs and solutions, conservative, antidemocratic, nationalistic forces at the grassroot and governmental levels steered the internal forces of the countries of Eastern Europe, with the partial exception of Czechoslovakia, toward a generally stagnant course.

External factors became decisive after the annexation of Austria by Hitler and the ensuing Nazi moves to dismember Czechoslovakia. The growing evidence of French and British abandonment of Eastern Europe combined with the rekindling of Stalin's interest in preventing the expansionist moves of the Axis powers into Russia's own *cordon sanitaire* made meaningful democratic opposition to authoritarian rule—ostensibly designed to safeguard national interests against foreign and domestic threats—virtually impossible. Instead, even before the absorption of Czechoslovakia in 1939, the struggle for power in Eastern Europe involved, both internally and internationally, confrontations between radical and moderate antidemocratic forces all jockeying for support from Hitler and/or Mussolini. The irredentism of Poland and Hungary, for instance, with respect to what was left of Czechoslovakia, of Hungary and Bulgaria to what was left of Romania following the Soviet seizure of Bessarabia and northern Bukovina in early 1940, was indicative not only of the mentalities and modus operandi of the leaders but also, of the significance of virulent nationalism as a determinant of political attitudes. The bloody confrontations between Romanians and Hungarians following the partitioning of Transylvania in 1940, the mutual extermination of Serbs and Croats in partitioned Yugoslavia, and the brutal treatment of Jews in Romania, Poland, and Slovakia were not ordered by Nazi Germany or Fascist Italy; rather, they were initiated or approved by those nations' rulers themselves with the consent of most of their subjects.

Militant nationalism determined the actions of Eastern Europe in World War II. Romania voluntarily joined Nazi Germany in war against the Soviet Union for liberation of the territories seized by Stalin in 1940, for the incorporation of Transnistria, populated by people of Romanian origin, and for the destruction of Judeo-communism. Hungary, which had joined the Axis before Romania—to further its territorial claims against its neighbors—also fought against the Soviet Union. Bulgaria secured the support of the Axis for its territorial demands and joined it formally, however, without participating in the war against the Soviet Union. Anti-Czech and anti-Semitic sentiments characterized Slovakia's pro-Nazi regime, led by Bishop Hlinka.

Nationalism was also a source of opposition to Nazi Germany in Poland (which also opposed the Soviet Union) and parts of occupied Yugoslavia. Still, nationalists seldom were committed to reconciliation of ethnic or religious divisions. It should be noted that even those who opposed the occupying forces and native dictatorial regimes held out few prospects for democracy. That was true of Mihailović's Četniks and Tito's Partisans, of the small Eastern European communist or procommunist underground, and even of the anticommunist and anti-Nazi Polish freedom fighters who could not resolve their differences on the political organization of a restored postwar Poland. Moreover, even when the defeat of Nazi Germany became imminent and the formulation of postwar political patterns could be entertained, the predominant issues were still related to territorial matters. The only democratic solutions to the problems of Eastern Europe toward the end of the war were propounded by the Czech and Polish governments-in-exile and by a handful of political leaders in areas "liberated" by the Soviet armed forces. Their views and legitimacy were, however, unacceptable to the Soviet Union and given only token support by the Western Allies. The aims of this tiny minority were also questioned by at least some of their own compatriots.

The defeat of Hitler, while clearly welcomed by the vast majority of the peoples of Eastern Europe, was not a source of jubilation, since the alternative of communist rule enforced by Stalin's armies and agents was dreaded by most of the politically conscious elements of the population. Few pinned their hopes on the Western Allies' supporting democratic alternatives despite the rhetoric of Washington and London. Under the circumstances, the political leadership representing organizations that had been active in the interwar years and had not cooperated with the Nazis or native dictatorships thought primarily in terms of accommodation with the communists and leftist groups supported or tolerated by Moscow rather than of championing Western democracy. Only the naive or the foolhardy were willing to assume great risks in the forlorn hope of meaningful American, or even British, support. As collaboration with the communists became essential for survival, issues related to the democratization of the political and social order in a manner contrary to communist plans for modernization on Stalinist patterns were all but forgotten and the very meaning of democracy was altered. By 1947 "people's democracy," a euphemism for communism, had for all intents and purposes replaced "bourgeois democracy," by then a euphemism for fascism and other varieties of anticommunism embodied by the capitalist West.

The evolution of political attitudes after the end of World War II remains unclear. There are no blanket answers because, in fact, not everyone had been against right-wing authoritarianism or against communism or, for that matter, in favor of democratic alternatives. There was no overriding desire among the peoples to bring war criminals to justice or for reconciliation of outstanding ethnic or religious differences, for toleration of diversity, for market economies, for restoration of multiparty systems. Even in Yugoslavia, which was "liberated from fascism" by Tito's Partisans rather than by the Soviet armies, enthusiasm for "Yugoslavism" was limited. Serbian nationalists forgave neither the destruction of the Četniks nor the atrocities committed by the Croatian Ustaši. However, Tito's opposition to Stalinist imperialism made Yugoslavism a principal element of Titoism and, as such, at least palatable to the inhabitants of the country.

Elsewhere in Eastern Europe, where Soviet armies were present and Stalin's agents active, the masses reacted according to their own political experience. For example, in Romania, with a small industrial working class and a large peasantry, the communists and their allies had little support. Whatever following they enjoyed was the result of land reform and the restitution of northern Transylvania, on Stalin's dictate, to Romania. However, the predominance of Jews and Hungarians in the communist movement and the presence of Russian forces in the country revived nationalism and anti-Semitism to wartime levels. In Hungary, the loss of part of Transylvania together with Jewish visibility in the communist movement made support for the communists scarce and exacerbated the traditional anti-Semitism and anti-Romanianism of the population. In Poland the communists who had been associated with resistance to the Nazis during the war were initially identified with Polish nationalist interests and, as such, had popular support as nationalists. Anticommunism became significant only after the communist movement had lost its Polish flavor. In Czechoslovakia, on the other hand, the communists enjoyed at least as much popular support as the members of the government in exile who returned after the war. The Czechoslovak Communist party had been active before the war and had opposed Nazis and collaborators during the war. It preached national unity and exploited opposition to political leaders who had spent the war years abroad and who, rightly or wrongly, were identified both with the surrender at Munich and indifference toward the needs of the working class. Thus the coalition governments established after the war became ever more vulnerable to communist pressure and could not ultimately resist the outright communist takeover, ordered by Stalin, in 1948. Finally, in Bulgaria and Albania democracy was never an issue after World War II. The majority of the Bulgarian people had been traditionally pro-Russian and knew little about their Soviet "liberators." In Albania, democracy was an unknown phenomenon since the 1930s, first under King Zog and later under Italian occupation. Enver Hoxha, the dogmatic Stalinist who assumed power in 1944, had opposition only from a few intellectuals whose relations with the Albanian masses were frail at best.

It is a matter of pure speculation under what conditions the countries of Eastern Europe would have been able to evolve democratic political and social orders after World War II. Had the Marshall Plan been extended to all Europe, which might have occurred had Stalin adopted a different course, there might have been a possibility of gradual transition from authoritarianism and/or totalitarianism to democracy. It is possible to ascertain, however, the reasons for opposition to communist totalitarianism during the forty years of its existence and the impact of that totalitarianism on the political and socioeconomic culture of Eastern Europe.

The prevailing opposition to totalitarian communism of the Stalinist or neo-Stalinist varieties was motivated primarily by the elimination and/or limitation of private property rights and the corresponding pauperization of the populations at large. These factors, at least among the peasant and working classes, were more important than the severe restriction of personal liberty and abuse of human rights that characterized the communist regimes. Whereas the imposition of ideological conformity and consequent abrogation of freedom of expression were major determinants of the urban intellectuals' opposition to communism, the attack on religion, particularly in Orthodox and Catholic regions, precluded the ideological legitimation of communism with the rural masses.

From as early as 1951 Stalin and ethnic communist leaders sought to nationalize the communist regimes of Eastern Europe in an effort to seek identification of communism with the historic traditions of their respective states. Yet "socialist patriotism" never equaled historic nationalism. The communist leaders' attempts to claim legitimacy as executors of the national historic legacies and socioeconomic desiderata of the peoples were never persuasive to the vast majority of their citizens. Even in such extreme interpretations as those propounded by Nicolae Ceauşescu in Romania—who adopted the same heroes and identified the same enemies of the Romanians as did his fascist predecessors—communist nationalism was not regarded as representative of the national political culture. On the other hand, the leaders' identification with historic traditions kept alive, perhaps even regenerated, intra- and international confrontations and ethnic and religious conflicts suppressed in the early years of communist rule.

Such phenomena were most evident in Romania where systematic anti-Russian and anti-Hungarian propaganda on matters related to territorial rights in Bessarabia and Transylvania, respectively, and overt discrimination against ethnic minorities assumed major proportions in the later years of the Ceauşescu regime. They were also evident in Bulgaria, where the Macedonian question and the persecution of the Turkish minority inflamed the spirits of nationalists, as well as in Yugoslavia where ethnic or religious questions focusing on Serbo-Albanian and Serbo-Croat relations assumed crisis proportions after Tito's death. Anti-Romanian propaganda in Hungary and uneasy relations between Czechs and Slovaks in Czechoslovakia surfaced periodically, as well. In all Eastern European countries where nationalism was linked to Jewish questions, anti-Semitism was tolerated, if not encouraged, by communist rulers.

Other deleterious aspects of communist governance appear to have affected the reaction of the masses to their governments to a lesser degree. The destruction of the old ruling elites and bourgeoisie was generally taken in stride by the overwhelmingly agrarian and proletarian societies. The expansion of the bureaucracy, the creation of new privileged groups, the corruption of functionaries, excessive nepotism—all familiar phenomena of authoritarian rule—became intolerable only because the communists generally failed to undertake reforms that would have resulted in "socialism with a human face." Indeed, where such reforms were implemented, in Kádár's Hungary and Tito's Yugoslavia, "reformist" communism was found acceptable, at least for a while.

In view of these considerations it is necessary to address the question raised at the beginning of this essay: Is Eastern Europe ready, willing, or able to be made safe for democracy as totalitarianism of the left has collapsed or is disintegrating?

The free use, or rather misuse, of the term *democracy* by parties involved in shaping the course of Eastern Europe in the post-totalitarian period renders a simple answer impossible. The contention that the various revolutions that removed neo-Stalinist, oppressive, and even moderate communist regimes were an expression of the people's quest for democracy is basically fallacious. Anticommunism was clearly the motivating force in people's actions, but anticommunism does not necessary represent a commitment to Western-style democracy.

After nearly a half century of communist rule political pluralism has no solid bases in the countries in question. The elites that evolved under communism, chiefly the bureaucratic state machine, the *apparat* and *nomenklatura,* resemble the precommunist bureaucracy in subservience to authority and lack of sympathy for Western democratic procedures and ideas. Nor are the armed forces, so important in the events of 1989, committed to democracy. The intellectuals who, together with students, played a leading role in overthrowing communist rule are not necessarily tolerant of diversity, and seem to support nationalism. Except in Czechoslovakia, urban intellectuals who were leaders or active participants in the movements that undermined and eventually removed the communists from power do not appear to enjoy the confidence of the masses. The link between the intellectuals and the masses tends to be anticommunist nationalism that, in many an instance, is assuming a xenophobic and/or anti-Semitic character. If the elections held in Eastern Europe in 1990 serve as a guide, it would appear that the working class and the peasantry are not enthusiastic about Western-style democratization. Their reasons are pragmatic and directly related to economic factors. Oppressive as communism may have been, it at least provided, albeit in a miserly manner, economic security. The introduction of a market economy, it is feared, would lead to massive unemployment and higher prices. Political pluralism is no substitute for perceived economic catastrophe for the traditionally apolitical and uneducated masses, never mind the assurances of eventual prosperity given by economists, political leaders, and entrepreneurs favoring free economies.

All these caveats are largely dismissed as irrelevant by interpreters of the historic evolution of Eastern Europe in the twentieth century who believe that communist totalitarianism had such a negative impact on Eastern Europe that its peoples would be willing to face new hardships and uncertainties inherent in political and economic restructuring to secure a democratic order. Realistically, however, the historic legacy of the twentieth century in general and of the communist period in particular, mitigate against such optimism.

Taking stock of Eastern Europe in 1991, we find economically bankrupt states burdened by enormous foreign debts, inefficient and outdated industrial and agricultural systems, grave environmental problems, and a restless working class. Moreover, political instability related to problems of transition from entrenched communist totalitarianism to a pluralistic system appears to be more complex than assumed in the euphoria created by the events of 1989. The lack of experience of the newly formed or reactivated pretotalitarian political organizations is probably less significant in this respect than matters related to their ability to secure the confidence of the population. The brutalizing of the peoples of Eastern Europe by communist totalitarianism has frightened the electorate and brought out its immediate self-interest. Under the circumstances, people voted on the basis of personal fears and prejudices for those whom they believed most likely to be able to remedy existing evils. For democracy to succeed it would have to remove fears and alleviate prejudices. In other words, it would have to alter the political and socioeconomic order and culture. That would be a monumental task given the circumstances in contemporary Eastern Europe.

Present conditions are no better for making Eastern Europe safe for democracy than they were at the end of World War I. If economic prosperity, presumably assured by a market economy, is essential for democracy, the prospects are grim. The highly competitive capitalist economies of Western Europe, the United States, and Japan are only marginally interested in providing economic assistance or in developing markets in heavily indebted countries with worthless currencies, inefficient work forces, and obsolete industrial plants. And even if for reasons unrelated to the furthering of democracy they would decide to penetrate the markets of Eastern Europe, it would take a long time before the economies of those countries would be able to ensure the well-being ostensibly guaranteed by market economies. It seems fair to say that economic solutions provided by means other than free economic systems are likely to be adopted, or continued, in most of Eastern Europe.

It could be argued, of course, that a socialist economy is not necessarily an impediment to the attainment of political democracy. In fact, socialism and democracy are compatible. Functional socialist economies may be to the liking of East Europeans. Still, transition from communist-style planning and economic development to socialism would require a greater financial input by the major capitalist countries of the world than those countries probably can or will assure.

Even if we were to assume that the prospect of slow advancement toward free market or socialist economies would be a price the peoples of Eastern Europe would be willing to pay for democracy, we should ask ourselves whether the accompanying changes in these peoples' political and social cultures are likely to occur in the foreseeable future.

The answer is: probably not. The anticommunism of the East Europeans has, if anything, strengthened the traditional role played by religion and religious institutions in their lives. Since the view that heathen communism in association with anti-Christian Judaism were responsible for the evils that befell Eastern Europe after World War I has resurfaced and is being promoted by anticommunist and nationalist politicians, intellectuals, and often emigrés, anti-Semitism is on the rise. This, in conjunction with the nationalism engendered by the communists and later by the labeling of the movements that led to the collapse of the communist regimes as "national revolutions," has not advanced the spirit of toleration of ethnic or religious diversity so essential for the promotion of democracy.

Finally, in a period of economic uncertainty, of getting even with previous oppressors, of social readjustment, and of general nervousness and insecurity, national and international reconciliation and political stability in general are not likely to be recorded soon. It is doubtful that totalitarianism of the communist variety would recur, but authoritarianism, paternalistic or even militaristic, cannot be excluded as an alternative to (potential) democracy should economic conditions deteriorate. Only if the economies of Eastern Europe gradually improve and eventually even prosper could democracy—socialist or laissez-faire capitalist—take root before the end of the century. In the meantime, it is not enough to use the slogan "We shall overcome"; rather we should address the ever-pertinent question "What's to be done?"

2 Albania

Nicholas C. Pano

Albania is the smallest and least-developed state in Eastern Europe. It has, however, at various times in the twentieth century enjoyed a prominence disproportionate to its size and power. Much of the attention Albania has attracted stems from the efforts of its leaders and people to preserve the country's independence and territorial integrity and to transform it into a viable nation-state.

Albania was the last of the Balkan countries to achieve independence. After some 450 years of Ottoman domination, Albania's independence was proclaimed on November 28, 1912, at a hastily convened assembly of Albanian notables. The alacrity with which the Albanians acted to sever their ties with the Ottoman Empire—and to abandon their earlier goal of autonomous status within the empire—was occasioned by the outbreak of the First Balkan War during the summer of 1912 and the subsequent success of the allied Balkan countries against the Turks. These developments had caused the more politically astute Albanian patriotic leaders to fear their homeland would be partitioned among its immediate neighbors—Greece, Serbia, and Montenegro—which had long coveted portions of Albania and whose troops were engaged in combat on Albanian soil.

The conference of ambassadors of the Great Powers of Europe

(Austria-Hungary, France, Germany, Great Britain, Italy, and Russia) held in London on December 20, 1912, recognized the autonomy and neutrality of Albania and appointed commissions to demarcate the boundaries of the new state. In July of the following year the conference proclaimed Albania an independent principality. Subsequently the Great Powers selected William, Prince of Wied, a German army officer who lacked both political and diplomatic experience, as Albania's first ruler. Prince William assumed his duties in March 1914.

Although the growth of Albanian national consciousness during the late nineteenth and early twentieth centuries, as well as during the uprisings against the Turks (especially on the eve of and during the First Balkan War [1912–13]), was a necessary precondition to Albanian independence, the decisive factor in this eventuality was the stance of the European powers.[1] Albania's independence was ensured by the divergent positions of the powers on the "Albanian question," and by their determination to avoid plunging Europe into a major war over the issue. The Albanians also benefited from their neighbors' conflicting territorial designs on the new state. Albania's leaders and a growing number of its people had become aware since the turn of the century of the extent to which external forces had shaped the origins of their nation and might continue to influence its development. They also came to resent this reality as it emerged as a persistent factor in Albania's history.

Albania's relations with Greece, Serbia, and Montenegro remained strained, even after the plans of these states to expand by partitioning the lands inhabited by Albanians had been frustrated. Greece continued to pursue its claim to southern Albania (northern Epirus) on the basis of its assertion that all Orthodox Christian inhabitants of the region were Greek. (This issue would remain a major irritant in Greek-Albanian relations until the late 1980s.) Serbia was disappointed that it had not received access to the Adriatic Sea through Albania, while Montenegro resented its inability to expand its boundaries into northern Albania.

For their part, the Albanians were unhappy that only about 740,000 of the approximately 1,330,000 of their compatriots who lived in areas contiguous to independent Albania were included in the boundaries of the new state.[2] They especially resented the decision of the European powers to award the predominantly Albanian-inhabited district of Kosovo to Serbia. This marked the beginning of "the Kosovo question" in Albanian politics and diplomacy.

The independent Albanian state, however, was among the most ethnically homogenous countries in Europe, with Albanians comprising 95 percent of its population. Greeks, Vlachs (Romanians), and Macedonians constituted the largest minority groups. Despite the new country's ethnic cohesiveness, the task of building a viable Albanian nation-state would prove to be difficult. Along with the external threats to Albania's sovereignty and territorial integrity, its new government was faced with a host of internal challenges that would have to be overcome to ensure the nation's survival.

Although most Albanians in 1912 had a strong sense of their national identity, Albanian national consciousness—the nineteenth century Albanian patriot Pashko Vasa (1825–92) had termed it "Albanianism"—had not fully matured. Albanians were aware and proud of their descent from the ancient Illyrians and of the differences between them and their Greek, Slav, and Turkish neighbors. The Albanians were bound together by the common history they shared and had preserved and by their pride in the exploits of their fifteenth-century national hero Skanderbeg. They had managed to keep their spoken language and, during the nineteenth century, had sought to develop a common written alphabet, a goal finally realized in 1908. During the latter half of the nineteenth century, the first Albanian-language schools and presses were established. These Albanian initiatives were remarkable when one takes into account the efforts of the Ottoman authorities, supported by the Patriarch of Constantinople and the governments of Greece, Montenegro, and Serbia, to suppress the development of Albanian nationalism by scattering the Albanians among four provinces of the empire, by seeking to accentuate religious and regional differences among the Albanians, and by opposing the establishment of Albanian-language schools.

The Albanians are, in fact, divided into two subgroups: the Gegs, who are found north of the Shkumbi River; and the Tosks, who live to its south. The two groups differ but slightly in their physical appearance and speak distinct but mutually intelligible dialects of Albanian. The Gegs, who resided mainly in the mountainous districts of the country, managed during the period of Ottoman rule to preserve their clan-structured, essentially egalitarian social system and continued to be governed by their tribal chiefs. On the other hand the Tosks resided in southern Albania, where the terrain was less rugged. Consequently, they had been subject to a greater degree of political and economic control by the Ottoman authorities and were more susceptible to the foreign influences that penetrated Albania. Contacts between Gegs and Tosks had been limited before the country's independence, but they had cooperated during the nineteenth-century Albanian national renaissance and in the armed struggle against the

Ottoman Empire. While patriotic, the Gegs were less than enthusiastic about the establishment of a strong central government that would threaten their traditional freedoms.

There were also religious divisions among the Albanians. The Gegs comprised primarily Sunni Muslims and a Catholic minority. The majority of the Tosks were Muslim, too, but their community included both Sunnis and Bektashis. The latter group was more mystical and tolerant in its teachings than were the Sunnis. The remainder of the Tosks were Eastern Orthodox Christians who, for the most part, shared the patriotic sentiments of their Muslim compatriots. Since most Albanians, as a rule, were not fanatical in their religious beliefs, tensions in this area were less divisive than those arising from regional, tribal, or class differences.

In 1912, Albania had the least-developed economy in Europe. The country relied on primitive, self-sufficient agriculture and the raising of livestock. There was no industry worthy of mention, and interregional and international trade were nonexistent. The primary road network, in a country with an area of approximately 28,000 square kilometers, comprised only some 300 kilometers, of which just 185 kilometers was paved. Prospects for economic development appeared bleak owing to Albania's lack of capital, limited attraction for foreign investors, and internal instability.

Approximately 88 percent of the Albanian population in 1912 lived in rural areas. There were only three cities in the country with a population over 10,000, Shkoder in northern Albania being the largest, with 25,000 inhabitants. Tension was acute in southern Albania, where the Greek minority, egged on by Athens, agitated for incorporation into Greece or for autonomous status within Albania. There was unrest in parts of central Albania stemming from the hostility of the peasantry toward the landed aristocracy. Furthermore, illiteracy was rampant with only about 10 percent of the Albanian people able to read and write their national language. The estimated 250 private primary schools enrolled at most 7,500 pupils, and the few secondary schools an additional 200, with instruction principally in Greek, Italian, or Turkish.

The Albanian governments that exercised authority between 1912 and 1914 never really had the opportunity to deal constructively with the problems confronting the country.[3] During the brief reign of Prince William (March–September 1914), for example, the government was paralyzed by the bickering between Austria-Hungary and Italy over strategy to keep Serbian influence out of Albania, the unpopularity of the cabinet with the peasantry, the political and military interference of Albania's neighbors, the hostility of Muslim religious leaders toward the prince, and, finally, the outbreak of World War I. With his position in Albania becoming increasingly untenable, Prince William left the country on September 3, 1914.

With the departure of the Albanian ruler all semblance of central authority in the country ceased to exist. Albania between 1914 and 1920 was invaded and occupied at various times by the armies of its Balkan neighbors as well as those of Italy, Austria-Hungary, and France. The major concern of Albanian patriots both within and outside the country was to protect its territorial integrity and restore its sovereignty. The small Albanian colony in the United States raised $150,000 in June 1917 to underwrite lobbying efforts in Washington, London, Paris, and Rome, as well as to ensure that there would be adequate funding to maintain an Albanian delegation at the postwar peace conference.

The publication by the Bolshevik regime in November 1917 of the World War I secret treaties revealed that, according to the provisions of the April 1915 secret treaty of London, Albania was slated to be partitioned among Greece, Italy, Montenegro, and Serbia. This revelation served to intensify the efforts of Albanian activists to influence world public opinion. By early 1918 they had found a new ally in the president of the United States, Woodrow Wilson.

During the lengthy discussion of the Albanian question at the Paris peace conference, the British, French, and Italian delegations reiterated their support for the partition of Albania as envisaged by the secret treaty of London and subsequent similar arrangements such as those agreed to by the prime ministers of France, Great Britain, and Italy in January 1920. Although President Wilson was not averse to some modification of the 1913 Albanian-Greek boundary, he was unequivocally opposed to the dismemberment of Albania. Owing mainly to Wilson's position on this issue, Albania emerged from the peace conference with its independence and territorial integrity intact. The Albanians also helped their own cause when, in January 1920, they convened a national Council at Lushnja that proclaimed Albania's determination to protect its independence and to drive all foreign troops from its territory. By September 1920 the combination of Albanian military pressure and the waning of domestic support for the occupation of Albania had caused the Italians to withdraw.

Albania's international position was enhanced by its admission to the League of Nations in December 1920 and by the reaffirmation the following November of its 1913 boundaries by the conference of ambassadors. Although the last Italian troops left Albania in September 1920, Greece and Yugoslavia maintained a military presence there until 1922. Albania's relations with those two neighbors remained tense as they continued to withhold recognition of their frontiers with Albania until 1926.

As Albania's international status was being normalized, the national unity and resolve demonstrated at the Council of Lushnja dissolved, and the country between 1921 and 1924 experienced a period of political instability. Aside from the conflicting personal ambitions of various Albanian leaders, the political battles of this period revolved around what could be termed "national development strategies." They were conducted by two loose groupings of parliamentarians known as "populists" and "progressives." By 1922 Fan Noli (1882–1965), a Harvard-educated Eastern Orthodox clergyman, had emerged as the spokesperson for the reform-oriented "populists." Noli and his followers maintained that Albania could not embark upon a program of modernization until the power of the former Ottoman bureaucrats—and the landowning aristocracy which had dominated Albanian politics since independence—was broken. Ahmet Zogu (1895–1961), who served as prime minister or minister of the interior in several of the governments of this period, reflected the views of the "progressives" that the establishment of law and order throughout Albania was a prerequisite to social and economic reforms. The Noli faction emerged victorious in the first stage of the power struggle in June 1924 when it seized control of the government following a short-lived uprising.

Upon assuming office, Noli issued a twenty-point program of economic, social, and legal reforms. Among other things he promised the distribution of land to the peasants, the dismantling of the power of the landowners, the establishment of national legal and educational systems, and the honest administration of the state.

The Noli regime managed, however, to remain in office for only six months, as a result both of factors beyond the control of the prime minister and of his own mistakes. Recognizing Albania's need for disinterested foreign assistance, Noli sought aid from the League of Nations but was unsuccessful. This meant that Noli would have to turn to a foreign power, a predicament he had hoped to avoid. Noli alienated several members of his cabinet and many of his liberal partisans by refusing to call elections to legitimatize his position, by establishing a political court to condemn his most prominent enemies and confiscate their property, and by failing to implement his promised reforms. The conservatives were repelled by Noli's proposed "radical reforms" and by his recognition in July 1924 of the Soviet

Union. His subsequent decision to exchange diplomatic missions with the Soviet Union produced anxiety in Balkan capitals and London that Albania might become a base for Soviet propaganda and subversive activities in southeastern Europe. In December 1924, with the blessings of the British and the military backing of the Yugoslavs, Zogu returned to Albania and forced Noli into exile. With the overthrow of the Noli regime, prospects for the establishment of a democratic parliamentary system in Albania dimmed. Furthermore, Albania's failure to obtain economic aid from the League suggested it would have to become a client of a major European state to survive.

Ahmet Zogu emerged as the dominant political personality in Albania after the ouster of Noli. The son of a Geg tribal chieftain of the Mat district, Zogu had attended military schools in Monastir and Constantinople and had spent part of World War I in Vienna as an Austro-Hungarian prisoner of war. Upon his return to his homeland at the conclusion of the war, Zogu impressed his countrymen with his organizational skills and determination to rid Albania of foreign troops. In December 1922, at the age of 31, Zogu became prime minister. Three years later he was named president and in September 1928, he transformed the country into a monarchy, assuming the title "Zog I, King of the Albanians," much to the consternation of the Yugoslavs, who erroneously viewed this gesture as an attempt on the part of the new monarch to claim jurisdiction over the Albanians of Yugoslavia. As it evolved between 1928 and 1939, the new Albanian regime took on many of the characteristics of the dictatorial monarchies of southeastern Europe.

Within Albania, the opposition to Zog was manifested in a series of narrowly based antigovernment uprisings in 1925, 1926, 1935, 1936, and 1937. Zog managed to put these down without difficulty, but he was sensitive to his unpopularity among some segments of the population and feared assassination. During the 1930s the internal opposition to the regime was most pronounced among the nation's few intellectuals as well as among students and workers who variously espoused democratic, fascist, or communist alternatives to Zog's pragmatic conservatism. Outside Albania the principal threat to the regime between 1925 and 1930 came from Fan Noli's National Liberation Committee (KONARE), which was subsidized by the Comintern. By the mid-1930s, however, Noli ended his public opposition to Zog, and the few external antiregime groups posed no serious threat to the monarchy.

As had been the case during his tenure as prime minister, Zog accorded highest priority to establishing order within the country by creating a national bureaucracy and police force, by disarming the northern tribesmen—except for his Mati tribesmen—and by eliminating to a large extent the practice of the blood feud. Between 1928 and 1931 he also promulgated civil, commercial, and criminal law codes based on Western European models.

Although Zog succeeded in laying the foundation for the achievement of political unity and enhancing the authority of the central government, he was less successful, apparently intentionally so, in encouraging popular participation in the political process. By 1938 there were no organized political parties in the country, and the manipulation of elections by the king and his associates fostered political apathy and alienated the younger and better-educated Albanians. Furthermore, sectionalist antagonisms continued to exist. There was considerable resentment toward the regime on the part of the Tosks who resented paying a disproportionately large percentage of taxes, while the Gegs appeared to be the beneficiaries of the lion's share of state expenditures.

With only about 15 percent of its inhabitants residing in urban areas, Albania in the late 1930s was still a predominantly rural society.[4] The number of cities with a population above 10,000 had doubled (to six), and the national population in 1938 had risen to 1,046,000. Reflecting the primitive state of Albania's medical services, the average life expectancy in 1938 was thirty-eight years. There had been some progress in the development of a national education system, which by 1938 consisted of 654 schools with an enrollment of 56,283 students. But on the eve of World War II there were only 380 university graduates in the country, and 80 percent of its population was still illiterate.

Zog succeeded in limiting foreign influences in the Muslim and Albanian Orthodox religious communities and bringing them under effective state control. The Sunni Muslims had in 1923 severed their ties with the Caliphate. Two years later the Bektashi moved their headquarters to Albania. Both groups were governed by state charters and recognized the primacy of secular law. Zog also supported the efforts of the Albanian Orthodox church to obtain recognition of the autocephalous status it had sought since 1922. This goal, despite the opposition of the Greek government, was realized in April 1937 by decree of the Patriarch of Constantinople. Only the Catholic church was not fully subordinated to the state, owing to its ties with the Vatican and the backing it enjoyed from Italy, but its school system was subjected to state regulation. Zog's policies toward the religious bodies weakened their independence and contributed to the deepening of secular nationalistic attitudes during the interwar period.

Between 1912 and 1938 there was progress in several sectors of the Albanian economy, but it remained the least developed in Europe. There was no fundamental change in its structure or character. The low level of agricultural output necessitated the import of breadgrains and other foodstuffs to meet domestic requirements. This situation contributed in turn to the country's chronic trade deficit. Industrial development was still in its infancy and limited mainly to small factories engaged in food processing or the production of consumer goods. Between May 1925 and March 1938 Albania and Italy concluded a series of economic agreements that resulted in Italian domination of Albania's banking system, oil and mineral resources, overseas shipping, and other sectors of the economy in return for economic and technical development assistance and subsidies to offset Tirana's chronic budget and trade deficits. Despite these initiatives Albania's economy in 1938 was still predominantly agricultural, with industrial production accounting for only 4.4 percent of the national income. The Italians did make a significant contribution to the development of the Albanian infrastructure by nearly doubling the length of the road network to 2,200 kilometers, upgrading the facilities at Durres, Albania's major port, and modernizing portions of the capital, Tirana.

Albania's pressing need for economic assistance served as the impetus for its evolving relationship with Italy during the Zog era. Since neither the League of Nations nor any of the European powers save Italy were interested in taking on Albania as a client, Zog's list of potential patrons was limited to Yugoslavia and Italy. He rejected Belgrade's overture on the grounds that its capacity to furnish Albania with the aid it required could not match that of Rome. Additionally, the Albanian ruler feared that Yugoslavia might capitalize upon any special position it might enjoy and seek a boundary "adjustment" or attempt to replace him with a more pliant leader. In addition to its economic advantages, the connection with Italy would also discourage Greece and Yugoslavia from pressing their territorial claims against Albania.

Not surprisingly, Italy and Albania were soon drawn into a closer political relationship. Against the background of what he viewed as a serious Yugoslav-inspired conspiracy against his regime, and in response to Italian demands for a closer alignment of Tirana's economic and foreign policies with Rome, on November 26, 1926, Zog authorized the signing of the First Italo-Albanian Tirana Pact. By the terms of this treaty the signatories pledged to cooperate in maintaining the political, juridical, and territorial status quo in Albania. A year later, on November 22, 1927, in the Second Tirana Pact, the partners transformed the relationship into a twenty-year defense alliance. Italy subsequently assumed responsibility for the training and equipping of the Albanian army.

During the 1930s Zog attempted on several occasions to loosen the Italian grip on Albania. He enjoyed some success at times when Mussolini was preoccupied with more important undertakings, such as his Ethiopian campaign and the Spanish Civil War. But in April 1939, angered by Zog's refusal to transform Albania into an Italian protectorate and military base and jealous of Hitler's occupation of Czechoslovakia, Mussolini authorized the invasion of Albania. The Albanians were able to offer only limited resistance, and King Zog fled the country with his wife and newborn son. On April 12, 1939, an assembly of Albanian leaders convened by the Italians voted to rescind the 1928 constitution and to offer the crown to Victor Emmanuel III, who would rule Albania and Italy in a personal union.

The reign of King Zog ended in the tragic loss of Albania's independence. In this respect Zog was a failure. He had lost the support of a considerable number of his subjects during the 1930s as Italy's influence in Albania increased. Zog's reluctance to arm the people to resist the Italian invasion coupled with his flight from the country upon the landing of the Italian forces further undermined his popularity both in Albania and in Albanian communities abroad. This situation contributed to the refusal of the World War II Allies to recognize an Albanian government in exile headed by Zog. The king's legitimacy was thus further undermined, and it appeared that Albania's future would once again be decided by the results of a great war and the attitudes of the victorious powers toward Albania.

Zog's critics, with justification, note that he ruled as a royal dictator, combining the administrative styles of an Albanian tribal chieftain and an Ottoman pasha. The Zog regime was characterized by widespread corruption, the practice of terror and intimidation, and a low regard for the human and legal rights of citizens. A not insignificant portion of the economic assistance obtained from Italy was diverted to the king for his personal use or employed to offset the foreign trade and budget deficits. The Albanian ruler has been further faulted for not implementing a land reform program and for selecting the majority of his ministers more for their loyalty to him than for their competence.

On the other hand, Zog had in 1925 inherited an Albania with a weak and ineffective central government, a semifeudal society, and an undeveloped economy. Even Zog's critics acknowledge his policies brought law and order to most of Albania and initiated the process of economic development. There should be added to this list of accomplishments the improvement in the transportation and communications systems that helped to weaken sectional sentiments and tribalism, and the expansion of the national school system that served as an important agency in the political socialization of Albanians born during the 1920s and early 1930s. In short, Zog did succeed in laying the foundations for the modern Albanian state. And while it is apparent that the changes that occurred in the economic and social sectors were modest, it should be noted that the Zog era lasted only fourteen years and that the human and material resources available to the king were limited compared to the magnitude of the problems confronting the nation.

World War II and the Triumph of Communism in Albania[5]

The Italian invasion and occupation of Albania marked the end of the Zog regime and ushered in the brief but significant transitional period between the prewar monarchy and the communist regime. During the period of the Italian occupation (April 1939–September 1943), a series of five puppet governments headed by members of the landowning aristocracy and other political opponents of Zog exercised nominal control in Albania. Under this arrangement Italy conducted Albania's foreign relations; the Albanian army was incorporated into that of Italy; and Albania's economy was aligned more closely with that of its suzerain.

From its Albanian base Italy in October 1940 launched its invasion of Greece. The Albanians, however, showed little enthusiasm for a venture they viewed as a struggle between two nations that had designs on their independence and territorial integrity. These fears were realized when the Greeks reaffirmed their claim to southern Albania as they pursued the retreating Italian forces into that region in early 1941. Following the German intervention in Yugoslavia and Greece in April of the same year, the Italians reestablished their control in all Albania. Sensitive to the irredentist sentiment within Albania and wanting to strengthen Albanian allegiance to the occupation regime, Germany and Italy in August 1941 incorporated the Albanian-inhabited Kosovo region of Yugoslavia into Albania.

After the Italian surrender in September 1943, the Germans occupied Albania and sanctioned the establishment of a new Albanian government which proclaimed the country's independence and neutrality. Albania was also permitted to retain its 1941 frontiers. In general, Berlin pursued a conciliatory line toward Albania that served to undercut the noncommunist opposition to the Germans.

Neither the Italian nor the German collaborationist regimes enjoyed much popular support, and the opposition to their rule increased with each year of the Axis occupation. For the most part, the Albanians who cooperated with the Italians and Germans came from the ranks of the prewar political and economic elites, from a group of Zog's exiled political opponents who had been invited to return to their homeland, and from the Catholic clergy and intelligentsia. Their wartime collaboration discredited these groups in the eyes of a large segment of the Albanian population and thus paved the way for the emergence of a new ruling class. The Albanian communists would fill this power vacuum.

Before World War II communism was an insignificant factor in Albanian politics. During the early 1920s a few Albanian students, intellectuals, and workers developed an interest in Marxism and the new Soviet state. At this time the Kosovo Committee, an organization that advocated the union of the Albanian-inhabited Yugoslav territories with Albania, established ties with the Comintern and the Balkan Communist Federation movement. Following the demise in December 1924 of the Fan Noli regime, about two dozen young communist sympathizers went to the Soviet Union for ideological and political training. Several of these Moscow-trained Albanian communists returned to their homeland during the 1930s, but were able to attract few recruits to the movement. At the time of the Italian occupation there were no more than two hundred communists in the country. The movement lacked leadership and discipline, enjoyed little popular support, and was split into four major contending factions. Given these circumstances, it is not surprising that the Comintern had not yet authorized the formation of an Albanian Communist party. Thus Albania, alone among the former Eastern European party states, did not have an established communist party at the outbreak of World War II. Furthermore, the ties of the Albanian communists to the Comintern were limited.

In retrospect, it is apparent that the formation of the Albanian Communist party (ACP) in November 1941 represents a major turning point in Albania's history. Although several of the communist factions had sought to form a unified party between 1939 and 1941, the Nazi invasion of the Soviet Union provided a new impetus to this effort. With the assistance of two emissaries of the Yugoslav Communist party with which the Albanian communists had maintained a loose relationship, representatives of three of these Albanian groups met clandestinely in Tirana, where, on November 8, 1941, the Albanian Communist party was formed. The delegates elected an eleven-person Central Committee and chose Enver Hoxha, a thirty-three-year old former school teacher, as provisional secretary. The majority of the party leadership and the bulk of the 130 original party members were young intellectuals and students of middle-class origins. The remainder were laborers or artisans. With only a few exceptions, they had neither been trained in the Soviet Union nor been associated with the Comintern.

One of the most important decisions to emerge from the organizational meeting of the ACP was the selection of Enver Hoxha (1908–85) as provisional secretary. Hoxha would be the dominant political personality in Albania for over four decades and would shape the nature of Albanian communism.

Enver Hoxha was born into a middle-class Muslim family in the southern Albanian city of Gjirokastra, which had been one of the objects of Greek expansionist aspirations. Like most of his contemporaries, Hoxha was raised with a strong sense of patriotism and an appreciation of the threats to Albania's independence and territorial integrity posed by the policies of its Balkan neighbors. By 1930 he had completed his studies at the Korca lycée, one of the most prestigious secondary schools in pre–World War II Albania. At Korca he was first exposed to Marxist doctrines and developed what were termed "progressive tendencies."

Hoxha received a state scholarship to study natural sciences at the University of Montpellier, despite his expressed preferences to pursue a degree in history or political science. He found it difficult to maintain an interest in his studies, preferring instead to spend his time in cafés discussing politics and literature. He made so little progress toward his degree that the government revoked his scholarship in March 1934. Hoxha now took up residence in Paris where he established contacts with Albanian political émigrés and members of the French Communist party. Hoxha left Paris in December 1935 and spent the next six months in Brussels in the employ of the Albanian consul. Here too he developed associations with Marxist groups, connections that continued until he lost his position because of his "revolutionary" views.

At that point Hoxha returned to Albania without a university degree but as a confirmed Marxist. He had come to view Marxism as both a revolutionary and modernizing ideology that could play a positive role in the development of Albania.

Hoxha's academic qualifications and his family's political connections enabled him in April 1937 to secure a position as an instructor in French at his alma mater, the Korca lycée. In Korca Hoxha joined the local communist group, but maintained a low profile—confining most of his activity to café discussions of Marxist theory and political issues. Following the Italian invasion and occupation, Hoxha became more visible in anti-Italian and procommunist agitation. These activities resulted in the loss of his teaching position in December 1939 for "subversive activities."

Hoxha next went to Tirana where he operated a tobacco shop that served as a meeting place for political dissidents. Once again he ran afoul of the law and went underground following the issuance of a warrant for his arrest.

Up to this time Hoxha had not distinguished himself as a political leader. Nevertheless, he appeared to have enjoyed the respect of his communist colleagues both in Korca and Tirana for his knowledge of Marxist doctrine, his dedication to the goal of establishing a unified Albanian Communist party, and his patriotism.

Hoxha's rise to power was facilitated by the decision of the ACP's founders to select their new secretary from outside the ranks of the leadership of the existing communist groups. Their choice possessed intelligence, a knowledge of Marxist-Leninist doctrines, unblemished credentials as a patriot, oratorical skills, a pleasing personality, and an attractive appearance. These served him well as he gradually consolidated his position within the party hierarchy.

Hoxha's attitudes and outlook would be shaped by his experiences during this formative phase of his political career.[6] Between 1941 and 1945 the novice Albanian leader was confronted by factionalism within his party, egged on by the ACP's Yugoslav advisors who wished to enhance their influence within Albania and replace Hoxha with a more pliant leader. Hoxha developed a distrust toward the United States and Great Britain, both of which he feared were set on installing a noncommunist regime in the country, or at least on requiring the communists to share power with their political rivals. Greece, by persisting in its claims to northern Epirus, not only solidified Hoxha's antagonism toward Athens but also raised the possibility that Albania's territorial integrity might be violated with the full approval of the Western democracies. Only Stalin's Soviet Union, which never established a presence in Albania during the war years, seemed to be a genuine source of friendship and moral support. The victories of the Red Army on the Eastern Front, the success of Tito's Partisans in Yugoslavia, and the presence of a strong procommunist resistance movement in Greece also served indirectly to strengthen the communist position in Albania.

Under Hoxha's leadership the Albanian communists between 1942 and 1944 assumed a dominant role in the wartime resistance movement. In September 1942 they convened the Peza Conference attended by representatives from most of the active anti-Fascist forces in the country. The conference established the National Liberation Movement (NLM) to coordinate the war effort and authorized the formation of popularly elected national liberation councils to exercise local political control over the liberated areas of Albania. As the only organized political party in the NLM, the communists were able to dominate this organization—and its affiliate, the Albanian Army of National Liberation—by placing their members in key leadership positions. The communists were aided in their quest for power by the weakness and ineptitude of their political rivals, the Balli Kombetar (BK) and the pro-Zog Legality Organization.

Formally organized in November 1942 and headed by veteran Albanian patriot Midhat Frasheri, the BK comprised mainly moderate to liberal Albanian nationalists who advocated the establishment of a republican regime, the enactment of social and economic reforms, and the preservation of the ethnic Albanian state created in 1941 by the Axis occupiers. During the first half of 1943 the NLM and BK waged war both with the Italians and with each other. At that time the BK forces were larger, but the NLM appears to have been more effective in fighting the enemy and publicizing its successes. Furthermore, the BK's decision to reduce its military operations against the Italians during the summer of 1943 (both to lessen the loss of life and property in Albania and to conserve the strength of its forces for a showdown with the communists) weakened the organization's support among the masses and distressed the British military advisors then present in Albania seeking to expand the scope of the Albanian resistance effort.

At the behest of the British military mission and patriotic non-collaborationist Albanian politicians, the representatives of the BK and NLM met at Mukja on August 1–3, 1943, in an effort to establish a united front. Hoxha, against the advice of the Yugoslav advisors attached to the ACP, had agreed to participate in this venture in the hope of incorporating the BK into the National Liberation Movement and eliminating the armed conflict between the two groups, thus enabling them to concentrate their efforts on driving the Italians from Albania. The ACP leader, however, refused to approve the agreement presented by his emissaries since it provided for scrapping the NLM and creating a new resistance organization in which power would be shared equally by the two groups. This would have seriously diminished the prospect for a communist takeover following the liberation of Albania. Furthermore, Hoxha's Yugoslav advisors objected to the agreement since it endorsed the Albanian retention of Kosovo, a stance unacceptable to the Yugoslav communists who were attempting to enhance their domestic position.

Following the Mukja conference, Hoxha's relations with the Yugoslavs became more strained. Hoxha's repudiation of the Mukja agreement led to the defection of Abas Kupi, one of the few remaining noncommunists in the NLM leadership. Kupi, an ardent monarchist, formed the Legality Organization, which favored the restoration of King Zog. Hoxha's decision also led to the resumption of hostilities between the BK and the NLM. As 1943 drew to a close the NLM found itself opposed by the combined forces of the German army (which had occupied Albania following the capitulation of Italy in September), the new pro-German Albanian puppet government, the BK, and the Legality Organization.

The Albanian wartime power struggle was decided during the winter of 1943–44 when the NLM succeeded in holding the opposition at bay until it launched a successful counteroffensive during the spring of 1944. Although the British military mission made repeated efforts to arrange a truce among the contending Albanian factions and bring the noncommunist forces into the war against the Germans, they were unsuccessful in realizing these objectives. The popular support for the noncommunists markedly diminished in southern and central Albania.

In May 1944, when most of southern Albania had been freed from Nazi control, the NLM convened a congress in Permet. At this meeting the NLM was renamed the National Liberation Front (NLF). Hoxha was appointed supreme commander of the Albanian National Liberation Army, King Zog was formally deposed and forbidden to return to Albania, and the treaties concluded by the Albanian government before 1939 that were deemed to be "contrary to the interest of the Albanian state" were repudiated. The Congress of Permet also created the Anti-Fascist Council of National Liberation and declared that this body was "the repository of the sovereignty of the Albanian people." Additionally, the Congress elected an eleven-member cabinet, nine of whom were communists. In October 1944, when the NLF had established its control over most of Albania, it convoked a congress at Berat. The Congress of Berat established a provisional government headed by Hoxha and dominated by communists. It also issued a Declaration of the Rights of the Albanian People, pledged to hold free elections for a constituent assembly, and expressed its intention to maintain close ties with "the great allies, Great Britain, the Soviet Union, and the United States."

Although the communist victory in the wartime power struggle was decisive in ensuring the establishment of the Albanian communist regime, it was also facilitated by a series of external factors. First in importance of these was the decision of the Allies not to recognize the Zog government or an alternative regime-in-exile. This situation stemmed from the opposition to Zog within Albania and the split in the Albanian communities outside the country into pro- and anti-Zog factions. Furthermore, the Greek government strongly opposed the recognition of an Albanian government-in-exile in order to strengthen its hand in its efforts to "rectify" the Greek-Albanian boundary. Second, the Albanian communists profited from the organizational and military advice they received from the Yugoslav advisors stationed in the country during the war as well as from the example of the communists' success in Yugoslavia. Third, the military assistance and the propaganda support through radio broadcasts beamed to Albania by Great Britain and the United States proved valuable to the NLF as it consolidated its position in the country in 1944–45. Finally, a series of military and strategic decisions by the Allies ensured that there would be no U.S. or British troops in Albania at the conclusion of hostilities. These included the decision of the Teheran Conference in November 1943 not to support Churchill's plan to open a second front in the Balkans; the agreement between Roosevelt and Churchill at the Second Quebec Conference in September 1944 to forbid the use of the military forces assigned to Italy in any country but Greece; and the August 1944 recommendations of the U.S. Joint Chiefs of Staff that American troops be deployed in Albania solely for the purpose of relief and rehabilitation operations.

By late November 1944 the last units of the German army withdrew from Albania, and the communist-dominated provisional government was installed in Tirana. The new regime found itself with considerable popular support within most of Albania and appeared to have the backing of three major wartime Allies because of its contribution to the war effort. Thus, even before the end of World War II in Europe, communism had triumphed in Albania, and Albania had the distinction of being the only country in Eastern Europe where the communists had come to power without direct Soviet assistance and without the presence of Soviet troops on its soil. The young, ambitious, inexperienced, patriotic, indigenous communist leadership that had emerged during the war now turned its attention to the task of consolidating its authority and establishing its legitimacy.

The Hoxha Era, 1944–1985

When the Communists assumed control in Albania in late 1944, they faced many of the same problems that had confronted the nation's founding fathers in 1912. The economy was in a shambles, and much of the progress that had been made in upgrading the infrastructure had been negated by the actions of the anti-Axis guerrilla forces and the retreating German army. There was considerable opposition to the new Tosk-dominated regime in northern Albania, especially among the Catholic population of the region and some die-hard supporters of King Zog. Within the Communist party the Yugoslavs encouraged the activities of an anti-Hoxha faction that Belgrade hoped would result in the replacement of the Albanian wartime leader with his openly pro-Yugoslav deputy, Koci Xoxe. Belgrade, furthermore, left no doubt of its intention to reincorporate Kosovo into Yugoslavia once the region had been liberated. Greece, which refused to recognize Albania as a member of the World War II anti-Axis coalition and maintained that a state of war existed between the two countries because of the Italian invasion of Greece from occupied Albania, renewed its claims to northern Epirus. There was also the problem of Hoxha's deteriorating relationships with the United States and Great Britain. After initially expressing interest in establishing diplomatic ties with Albania in 1945, Washington and London reversed their position owing to their growing disenchantment with Albania's domestic and foreign policies. For his part Hoxha was disappointed by the opposition of the two Western powers to Albania's admission to the United Nations and what he construed to be their support of the Greek position on the northern Epirus issue.

In this context Enver Hoxha formulated his program for Albania: to maintain himself and the Communist party in power; to establish effective party control over all aspects of Albanian life; to modernize the country and construct socialism in accordance with the Leninist-Stalinist Soviet model; and to protect the independence and territorial integrity of Albania. Hoxha's persistence in pursuing these goals during the four decades of his rule brought him, at various times, into conflict with elements of his own party as well as with Yugoslavia, the Soviet Union, China, and the majority of the world's Communist parties.

Political Trends

The immediate task of the new regime was to consolidate its position and secure its legitimacy. After eliminating virtually all their actual and suspected political opponents during 1945 and 1946 through purges and "war crimes" trials, the Communists transformed the NLF into the Democratic Front (DF) and in its name ran a slate of candidates composed of party members and their sympathizers in the December 1945 elections for the constituent assembly that would establish the new political order in Albania. The DF slate polled 93 percent of the ballots cast, and on January 11, 1946, the newly elected constituent assembly formally abolished the monarchy and proclaimed Albania a "people's republic." Two months later the new constitution of the People's Republic of Albania was promulgated, the first of three during the Hoxha era. Since the socialist revolution was in its initial stages and since the Communists at this time preferred to exercise their power behind the facade of the DF, the 1946 constitution did not include any references to such matters as the special role of the Communist party, the collectivization of agriculture, the nationalization of trade, or other aspects of the new socialist order. But by the spring of 1946 the Communists had legitimized their position in Albania. Outwardly, at least, Enver Hoxha was the leading personality in the new regime serving simultaneously as secretary-general of the ACP, president of the DF, prime minister, foreign minister, defense minister, and commander in chief of the nation's armed forces.

The new Albanian ruling elite was almost exclusively made up of members of the Communist party who were veterans of the Albanian National Liberation Army, as well as members of mass organizations such as the DF, the women's trade union, and youth organizations. For the most part Albania's new rulers were young, with the average age in 1948 of the party Politburo and Central Committee membership being thirty-five and thirty-two, respectively. At age forty in 1948, Hoxha was among the oldest of the party leaders. A review of the available biographical data for government and party leaders of the late 1940s and early 1950s reveals that about half this group either studied at the university level or possessed a university degree. They were thus better educated than the typical Albanian of the period. In contrast to the pre–World War II period, the new Albanian leadership was dominated by Tosks. Given the opposition of the Catholics to the new regime, it is not surprising that they were under-represented in its upper echelons and that the Eastern Orthodox Tosks held a disproportionately high number of key positions.

Although there was considerable popular support between 1944 and 1946 for the government's announced program of economic and social reforms and for its expressed preference to pursue an even-handed relationship with the countries of both Eastern and Western Europe as well as with the United States, the Communists nevertheless sought to consolidate their position by relying on the army and recently established security forces to discourage popular opposition. Throughout the Hoxha era the army and the security forces, along with the penal and labor camp systems, served as mainstays of the Communist regime.

The political history of Albania during the Hoxha era is dominated by a series of challenges to the primacy and policies of the Albanian leader both from within the ranks of the ruling elite and from abroad. Hoxha was successful in rebuffing these threats to his position, and his responses to these challenges served to define the nature of Albanian communism.

Hoxha's first challenge came from Koci Xoxe, his powerful deputy, who since World War II had been the Yugoslav choice to replace Hoxha. During late 1945 and early 1946, as the Cold War was intensifying, Xoxe advocated accelerating the pace of the socialist revolution in Albania, closer alignment of Tirana's foreign policy with those of the USSR and Yugoslavia, and the complete integration of the Albanian and Yugoslav economies as a preliminary step to their political union. Hoxha had initially endorsed this program in an effort to placate Belgrade, but when he recognized that his acquiescence did not cause the Yugoslavs to abandon Xoxe, he exploited the 1948 Soviet-Yugoslav rift to keep himself in power, to strengthen his credentials as the guardian of Albania's sovereignty and territorial integrity, and to unleash a purge of Xoxe and his followers at the First Congress of the Albanian Party of Labor (APL) in November 1948.

The next major threat to Hoxha's leadership came during the early 1950s, when a faction within the APL headed by Politburo members Bedri Spahiu and Tuk Jakova began to argue for a slowdown in the industrialization program, a delay in the collectivization of agriculture, a more tolerant attitude toward religion, the "democratization" of party governance, and, after 1953, the initiation of a program of de-Stalinization. Hoxha, who had enthusiastically embraced Stalinism during the late 1940s, strongly opposed most of these initiatives on the grounds they would undermine the successful construction of socialism. He did, however, agree to implement the concept of collective leadership in Albania by relinquishing during 1953 and 1954 all his government positions while retaining his leadership of the party and Democratic Front. Mehmet Shehu (1913–81) assumed the office of prime minister and became a member of Hoxha's inner circle, which at this time included Politburo members Hysni Kapo (1915–79), Gogo Nushi (1913–70), and Liri Belishova (b. 1923).

Although Jakova and Spahiu and their leading supporters were ousted from their positions, their ideas continued to enjoy the sympathy of middle- and low-level party and state bureaucrats. Following the Twentieth Congress of the Communist Party of the Soviet Union (CPSU) in 1956, a large and vocal group of delegates at the Tirana city party conference in April made a final effort to obtain backing for a program of de-Stalinization in Albania. Hoxha, however, was able to assert his authority and quash this effort, and again the dissidents were subjected to a broad range of punishments.

Hoxha's success between 1948 and 1956 in defeating his rivals and establishing his control over the APL resulted from several factors: the opposition's lack of effective leadership and organization as well as its inability to win over the armed forces or security organs, its failure to attract grass-roots support, and its appearance of being pro-Yugoslav. Up to this time Hoxha also had the advantage of enjoying at least the nominal public backing of the Soviet leaders.

The Third APL Congress (May 25–June 3, 1956) marked the point at which Hoxha fully consolidated his hold on the party. The Politburo and Central Committee elected by the Congress were composed of staunch Hoxha loyalists. There would be no further significant challenges to his leadership until the 1970s. The Third Congress also witnessed Hoxha's first public defiance of the Soviet Union when he refused to rehabilitate Xoxe, Jakova, and other "victims" of the Albanian "Titoist purges." Hoxha also appears to have acted contrary to the wishes of Moscow in announcing his intention to accelerate the pace of industrialization and the collectivization of agriculture.

The experiences of Poland and Hungary during 1956 seemed to confirm that any substantial deviation from the Stalinist model would disrupt the process of economic development, produce internal unrest, and, possibly, result in rebellion; this, in turn, would provide the USSR and Yugoslavia with an excuse to intervene in Albania and impose a regime more to their liking. This view appears to have been shared by the Albanian leadership during the late 1950s and early 1960s and served to strengthen Hoxha's internal position as Soviet-Albanian relations deteriorated.

Tirana's refusal to abandon Stalinism and its unwillingness to align its foreign and economic policies more closely with those of the USSR culminated in the Soviet-Albanian ideological and diplomatic break in December 1961. Albania's successful defiance of the USSR is largely attributable to the intensification of the Sino-Soviet rift and the consequent diplomatic and economic backing Tirana obtained from Beijing, the unity of the Albanian leadership and its ironhanded control over the country, and Albania's geographic location, which made difficult a Soviet intervention to force Hoxha and his associates into line or depose them.

Between 1961 and 1964 the most pressing concern of the Albanian leadership was to avert an economic collapse following the termination of Soviet and East European aid programs. In 1964, when Chinese aid began to flow into Albania and the economic situation had been somewhat stabilized, Hoxha moved to implement what has become known as Albania's "Ideological and Cultural Revolution," the main features of which he had outlined at the Fourth APL Congress (February 13–20, 1961).

As conceived by Hoxha, the Ideological and Cultural Revolution was intended to destroy those attitudes, traditions, practices, and institutions that up to the mid-1960s had, in his view, impeded the regime's efforts to build a modern nation-state grounded in Marxist-Leninist principles. Specifically, this movement aimed to eliminate the influence of religion, "excessive" family and sectional loyalties, "bourgeois" economic and social outlooks, poor labor discipline, and indifference to political authority in Albania. During its main phase (1966–69), the Ideological and Cultural Revolution featured a campaign to reduce the size of the bureaucracy in order to prevent the rise of a "new class" of civilian and military specialists who might be tempted to undermine the party leadership in the management of the economy and other key sectors of Albanian life. The women's emancipation campaign sought to eliminate socially conservative attitudes, which the party viewed as an obstacle to the socialization process, and to promote a greater female presence in the labor force. Unique aspects of this "revolutionization" process were the abolition of the institutional church in 1967 and the proclamation of Albania as an atheist state. A year earlier the Ministry of Justice had been done away with on the grounds that the establishment of "socialist legality" in Albania was complete. Other noteworthy results of the Ideological and Cultural Revolution included the strengthening of the ideological component of instruction at all levels of the educational system, the achievement of the total collectivization of agriculture, a reduction in the allowable size of a collective farmer's private plot, and a narrowing of the range of the nation's wage structure.

Although contemporaneous with China's Great Proletarian Cultural Revolution, the Albanian Ideological and Cultural Revolution does not appear to have been significantly influenced by its Chinese counterpart. In fact, there were significant differences between the two movements. The Albanian version, unlike that of China, did not result in an intense power struggle within the party, a weakening of the party and its mass organizations, considerable violence and economic disruption, the repudiation of the Western cultural heritage, or its diplomatic isolation.

It was during this period that Hoxha seems to have begun to regard himself as an important Marxist-Leninist ideologue. Tirana at this time began to publish and distribute his speeches widely, and in 1968 the first volume of Hoxha's *Works* appeared.

When China phased out its cultural revolution during 1969, there was sentiment both within the ranks of the APL leadership and among the masses that Albania should follow suit. Although Hoxha recognized that not all the objectives of the Ideological and Cultural Revolution had been met, he did realize that the people needed a respite from the demands made on them constantly since 1966. Between 1970 and 1973, Albania enjoyed a period of somewhat relaxed party controls, and Tirana flirted with cultural and economic reforms.

These reforms in many respects resembled those that would be proposed by the party leadership in the late 1980s and early 1990s, but they aroused the strong opposition of such Politburo conservatives as Hysni Kapo, Hoxha's closest associate, and Minister of the Interior Kadri Hasbiu (1920–83). The conservatives resented the popularity enjoyed by Albanian novels and plays produced during the early 1970s that focused on exposing the perceived shortcomings in Albanian society. In addition, they were angered by the suggestion that the Union of Albanian Labor Youth (UALY) be transformed from a party-controlled mass organization to a national nonpolitical cultural and sports club.

By March 1973 Hoxha had become sufficiently alarmed by reports of flagrant breaches of discipline by young Albanians at work and school, and by the open repudiation of "socialist realism" by some of the country's prominent writers and artists, to reinstitute strict controls on the nation's youth and intellectuals. There were major leadership changes in the League of Albanian Writers and Artists and the Union of Albanian Labor Youth. The three Central Committee members—Fadil Pacrami, Todi Lubonja, and Agim Mero—who had strongly championed the moderate line toward youth and culture were purged. The political demise and subsequent punishment of this trio who enjoyed the respect and confidence of the majority of Albania's intellectuals had a chilling effect on Albania's cultural life for more than a decade.

The purge that reduced Albania's cultural establishment to submission was extended to other critical areas between 1974 and 1976. This process seemed to take on a new urgency after Hoxha suffered a heart attack in October 1973.

Following the crackdown on the nation's youth and intellectuals, Hoxha next turned his attention to the military establishment. Under the leadership since 1953 of Defense Minister Beqir Balluku (1917–77), the fourth-ranking member of the APL hierarchy, the Albanian armed forces had been one of the mainstays of the regime since its inception. By the early 1970s tensions appear to have developed in the relationship between the party leadership and the military over the latter's desire to decrease party influence in the armed forces, to downgrade Hoxha's concept of "people's war"—the mobilization of the masses and reliance on guerrilla tactics to resist foreign aggression—in defense strategy, and to lessen Albania's dependence on China for assistance. Balluku seems also to have advocated that Albania improve its relations with one or more of the superpowers and reduce its support for the anti-Moscow "Marxist-Leninist" splinter parties (such as those in India and Indonesia) as Beijing had done.

Hoxha appears to have been unsympathetic to both the domestic and international positions of the military leadership. Furthermore, he feared the emergence of a professional army dominated by a career officer class with only loose ties to the party. Under these conditions, the Albanian leader believed, the military would have a sufficiently strong and independent power base to be able to overthrow the regime. To Hoxha such a situation was unacceptable, and consequently he orchestrated the removal of Balluku and the top echelons of the defense establishment. No evidence has been uncovered to demonstrate convincingly that the military leadership was engaged in a conspiracy against Hoxha. Instead, the growing paranoia of the Albanian leader seems to have contributed to his decision to purge Balluku and his associates.

During the early 1970s differences also arose between Hoxha and his Politburo colleagues and ministers entrusted with managing the economy. Hoxha was especially critical of the introduction of various "experiments" that provided workers with bonuses of cash and consumer goods to stimulate production, established special marketing divisions within economic enterprises, and encouraged local initiatives in economic planning. The Ministry of Foreign Trade advocated reducing Albania's dependence on China, expanding trade with Western Europe, and accepting credits from capitalist countries to finance necessary economic development projects. There were also differences over priorities for the 1976–80 five-year plan. Hoxha responded to this situation by initiating a massive purge of the nation's economic and managerial elite. Once again the reforms proposed to address the ills of the economy were premature. Hoxha, who during the last decade of his life often asserted that Albania was the sole remaining center of "Marxist-Leninist purity," was in no mood to compromise with capitalism. The purge of his economic advisors also provided him with convenient scapegoats for Albania's failure to realize the goals of its 1971–75 five-year plan.

The purges of the mid-1970s were accompanied by the dismissals of numerous party and state bureaucrats and their replacement with individuals elevated to these positions primarily for their ideologically and politically correct views rather than for their professional qualifications. This development served to stifle opposition to Hoxha's policies and to discourage creative approaches to the problems confronting Albania during the final years of the Hoxha era.

As a consequence of the purges, seven members of the Politburo— 41 percent of the membership of this body—lost their positions between 1971 and 1976. During this same period twenty-eight of the seventy-one Central Committee members were dismissed and an additional seven demoted to candidate (nonvoting) status. Of the twenty-six district party first secretaries, twenty-four were either fired or transferred to new posts. There were, in addition, seventeen cabinet changes between 1972 and 1977. Hoxha had prevailed over his opposition because of the tight control he exercised over the nation's formidable internal security forces and the loyalty he commanded from such longtime Politburo colleagues as Prime Minister Mehmet Shehu, Hysni Kapo (the party secretary for organizational affairs), and Ramiz Alia (the party secretary for ideology and propaganda).

As Hoxha began to rebuild the party and state leadership, in a departure from past practice, he turned to district party officials and successful farm and factory managers. For the most part these new appointees to top party and state posts were relatively young and unquestionably loyal to Hoxha, to whom they owed their promotions. Most, however, lacked the background and ability to address the challenges of the positions to which they had been appointed, and they did not enjoy the respect and confidence of the masses.

In an effort to discourage further opposition to his policies and to bind his successors to them, in December 1976 Hoxha promulgated a new constitution for the country. Although the 1976 constitution did not significantly alter the structure of the political system, it did change the name of the country to the People's Socialist Republic of Albania to underscore Hoxha's contention that Albania, alone among the European communist states, was building socialism in accordance with Marxist-Leninist doctrine. The constitution emphasized the leading role of the party in all aspects of Albanian life. Specifically, the document proclaimed Marxism-Leninism as the nation's official ideology (Article 3); committed Albania to support "revolutionary" national and social liberation struggles (Article 15); abolished private property except for personal residences and articles for personal or family use (Articles 16 and 23); prohibited the granting of concessions to, or the receipt of credits from, foreign companies or states (Article 28); forbade the practice of religion (Article 37); and stipulated that the armed forces were under the control of the party while designating the party first secretary as commander in chief of the armed forces (Articles 88 and 89).

Following the death in September 1979 of Hysni Kapo, who at that time appears to have been the most trusted of his associates, Hoxha, who was not in the best of health, became increasingly preoccupied with the task of designating his successor. The Albanian leader had expressed his unhappiness with the consequences of the Soviets' failure to determine who would succeed Stalin, and he was apparently determined that Albania be spared this fate.

As he began to plan for the transfer of power to follow his death, Hoxha seems to have concluded that Prime Minister Mehmet Shehu, who had health problems of his own, was not the logical person to succeed him. Aside from the issues of his age and health, Shehu was disliked and feared by many party members and officials. There was also animosity between Hoxha's wife and Shehu's spouse who headed the V. I. Lenin Higher Party School in Tirana. Finally, Hoxha appears to have lacked confidence in Shehu's ability to oversee the administration of the bureaucracy and the nation's problem-plagued economy. Indeed, during the late 1970s and early 1980s First Deputy Prime Minister Adil Carcani had been given increased responsibility for managing the government. After apparently failing to convince Shehu to step aside voluntarily in favor of Ramiz Alia, the candidate favored by Hoxha and his wife, the Albanian leader bitterly denounced Shehu at the meeting of the Politburo on December 17, 1981.

The following day the Albanian media announced that Shehu had committed suicide "in a moment of nervous crisis." Subsequently, Hoxha accused his longtime associate of having been a "foreign intelligence agent" who had taken his own life when he feared his subversive activities, including his alleged involvement in a "Yugoslav-inspired conspiracy" to assassinate the Albanian leader, had been uncovered.

While Hoxha's sensationalistic charges against Shehu were probably not true, it does appear that Shehu's death was related to major differences between the two Albanian leaders over succession. Also awaiting definitive resolution is the question as to whether Shehu committed suicide or whether he was killed at the order of Hoxha.

Following Shehu's death, Hoxha initiated a purge of the late prime minister's allies and protégés in the party and government hierarchy. The regime also unleashed a propaganda campaign designed to vilify Shehu, his family, and his associates.

During 1982 Hoxha began the transition to the new leadership. In January Adil Carcani was named prime minister. In November, Ramiz Alia assumed, in addition to his party duties, the post of chairman of the Presidium of the People's Assembly (the Albanian head of state), which provided him with broader domestic and international exposure. As Hoxha's health continued to decline during the early 1980s and as the Albanian leader began to devote much of his time to writing his memoirs, Alia gradually assumed more of his mentor's duties. The two Albanian leaders also developed during this time a close personal relationship. Upon Hoxha's death in April 1985, Alia was unanimously elected party first secretary by the Central Committee.

Socioeconomic and Cultural Trends[7]

During the four decades he ruled Albania, Enver Hoxha devoted considerable attention to the task of addressing the economic problems confronting the country. When the Communists assumed power in late 1944, Albania was a war-ravaged, underdeveloped agricultural nation. After focusing its initial efforts on undoing the damage Albania had suffered during World War II, the new regime formulated its long-range development strategy, which was designed to transform Albania from a backward agrarian nation to a modern industrial-agricultural state. In pursuing this goal the Albanian leaders eagerly embraced the Stalinist centralized economic planning and management system, which they believed was best-suited, given the conditions they had inherited, to building socialism and achieving modernization. Albania's economic policies between 1945 and 1985 emphasized rapid industrialization, the collectivization of agriculture, the expansion of farm output, and the upgrading of social services.

Although Hoxha recognized that Albania could not realize its economic and social goals without foreign assistance, he was determined, in light of the country's pre–World War II experiences, to make the economy as self-sufficient as possible in order to insulate his homeland from external economic and political pressures. Albania's unswerving pursuit of this objective throughout the Hoxha era contributed to the development of tensions in its relations with successive economic patrons: Yugoslavia, the Soviet Union, and China. In turn, Belgrade, Moscow, and Beijing came to view Albania's development strategy as unrealistic, uneconomic, and even inimical to their respective interests.

Albania inaugurated its program of long-range economic planning in 1950. In addition to emphasizing the rapid development of industry, the leadership gave high priority to the exploitation of the country's natural resources such as oil, chrome, copper, iron and nickel ore, and hydropower. During the first two five-year-plan periods (1951–60), the industrial sector grew at a rate of close to 20 percent per year, primarily because of the minuscule base on which it was built.

Both Stalin and, initially, Khrushchev had been sympathetic to the Albanian industrialization effort. But by the late 1950s the Soviet leadership reversed its position and urged the Albanians to emphasize the development of agriculture in accordance with the doctrine of the "international socialist division of labor" within the communist commonwealth. Under this scheme, Albania was to be relegated to supplying the USSR and communist Eastern Europe with foodstuffs and raw materials. Hoxha balked at abandoning his economic strategy for Albania and rejected the Soviet scheme on the grounds that it would preclude the balanced economic development of the country; restrict the growth of the industrial proletariat, which he regarded as a prerequisite to the building of socialism; and subject his homeland to a permanent dependency on the Soviet Union, thus making it vulnerable to coercion from Moscow. This situation contributed to the 1961 Soviet-Albanian break and the formation of the Chinese-Albanian alliance.

After a temporary disruption caused by the loss of Soviet and

Eastern European aid, the Albanians, with generous assistance from the Chinese, were able to continue their industrialization drive during the Fourth and Fifth Five-Year Plans (1966–75). During this period Albania extended its hydropower network, constructed oil refineries and ore-processing plants, developed its chemical and machine tool industries, expanded its consumer-goods and food-processing industries, and embarked on the construction of a steel mill.

By the early 1970s, however, as China ended its self-imposed isolation, effected a rapprochement with Western Europe and the United States, and began to focus on resolving its accumulated domestic problems, Beijing decided to reduce its economic support of its Balkan ally. These developments produced serious tensions in the Sino-Albanian relationship that, in 1978, culminated in the termination of China's economic and military assistance programs in Albania.

With the loss of Chinese aid Albania, for the first time in its postwar history, found itself without an economic patron. Since the Albanians were barred by the provisions of the 1976 constitution from seeking foreign loans or credits, and since Hoxha was unwilling to compromise his ideological principles by turning to the Soviet Union and Eastern Europe for assistance, Albania after 1978 attempted to underwrite its ambitious industrialization program through its own resources and export earnings. These, however, were insufficient to sustain the 10 percent average annual growth rate in industrial output that had been achieved between 1961 and 1975. During the Seventh Five-Year Plan (1981–85), the last over which Hoxha would preside, the average annual growth rate for industry fell to 4 percent, and this sector was increasingly plagued with problems as it grew in size and complexity.

As was the case in other communist nations, the Albanian leaders encountered serious problems in their efforts to collectivize and modernize agriculture. After abandoning his initial collectivization drive in 1954 at the request of Khrushchev, Hoxha resumed it two years later in a display of independence from Moscow. By 1960 approximately 86 percent of the nation's farmland was incorporated into the socialist sector. However, the collectivization drive produced considerable negative reaction in the countryside between 1956 and 1960 and resulted in a temporary decline in farm output. Full collectivization was achieved in 1967, and subsequently the size of a farmer's private plot was reduced to about one-quarter to three-quarters of an acre in an effort to eliminate all vestiges of capitalism from agriculture. During the 1960s and 1970s Albanian agriculture consistently realized only about 50 percent of its assigned goals.

Beginning in the 1970s, Hoxha advocated the combination of smaller collective farms into larger units to increase productivity. This initiative—along with a program to combine the private herds of livestock of the collective farmers into "brigades" to improve the quality and quantity of the meat supply—failed to achieve the desired results and further alienated the peasantry. Nevertheless, in 1976 the regime claimed that Albania had achieved self-sufficiency in the production of breadgrains and that by 1980 it would be able to meet virtually all its food requirements from domestic production. Despite increased mechanization of farm operations, expanded use of chemical fertilizers, a growth in the number of agricultural specialists, and a rise in investment in the agricultural sector, Albania does not appear to have been successful in reducing its imports of foodstuffs during the 1980s.

In addition to the apathy of the peasants, other factors made it difficult for the Albanian government to raise food production to the point where it could keep pace with the country's rapidly growing population. For example, much of the increase in agricultural output during the Hoxha era resulted from additional land being brought under cultivation or from improvements made in existing cultivated areas. By the beginning of the 1980s the maximum benefits from both these practices had been realized. Furthermore, adverse weather conditions also contributed to the lower-than-expected levels of farm output. During the Seventh Five-Year Plan the average annual increase in agricultural production declined to 2 percent, barely above the 1.9 percent annual population growth rate for this period.

Between 1945 and 1985 there were notable improvements in Albania's infrastructure. The country's highway system was greatly expanded and by 1985 consisted of 6,900 kilometers of roads capable of carrying motor vehicle traffic. This network linked the nation's major cities and its important centers of economic activity. Its significance was underscored by the fact that approximately 66 percent of the goods shipped within the country were transported by truck. Since 1945 the Albanians have constructed, from scratch, a small railroad network that in 1985 totaled 603 kilometers. In 1986 it became linked with the European rail system. Notwithstanding the constraints of government policies regulating the movement of people within the country, the improvements in the transportation system also served to weaken regionalism. The port facilities at Durres have been continually expanded and modernized, although they are still inadequate to efficiently handle the growing volume of Albania's foreign trade. While warehouses, distribution centers, and motor parks have been established in key areas of the country, these are not sufficient to meet the needs of the expanding economy and consumer expectations.

Although Albania made considerable economic progress under Hoxha, it remained the least-developed country in Europe with an estimated per capita gross national product of $930 in 1986.[8] By the mid-1980s the economy was clearly the most pressing problem for the regime. The dimensions of Albania's economic difficulties were revealed in the report of the results of the Seventh Five-Year Plan (1981–85). Industrial production targeted to rise 36–38 percent had gone up 27 percent. Agricultural output scheduled to increase 30–32 percent had grown by only 13 percent. There were serious production shortfalls in the oil, gas, mining, and machine tool industries upon which the regime relied for exports. Consequently, exports, which had been planned to increase 58–60 percent, grew just 29 percent. As a result by 1985 Albania had a serious balance-of-payments deficit.

Aside from the loss of Chinese aid and the occurrence of several natural disasters, Albania's economic difficulties in the mid-1980s also stemmed from its highly centralized economic planning and management structures, a shortage of well-trained management and technical personnel, poor worker morale and discipline, and an inability to produce export goods of the quality necessary to compete in some foreign markets. During the late 1970s and early 1980s Hoxha attempted to deal with these problems by leadership changes in the ministries charged with administering the economy. But this tactic was insufficient to cure the ills afflicting Albania. Since Hoxha was unwilling, on the grounds of ideological orthodoxy, to make the systemic changes needed to improve the country's economy, he created serious difficulties for his successors.

There were also significant social changes in Albania during the Hoxha era. Between 1944 and 1985 the country's population increased from 1,122,000 to 2,962,000. Throughout this period Albania had the highest population growth rate in Europe, and as recently as 1980, the population was continuing to grow by 2 percent per year. More than two-thirds of the people alive in 1985 had grown up during the period of communist rule. In demographic terms the population was young, with about 35 percent under the age of fifteen. Owing to Hoxha's isolationist policy, few Albanians had direct contact with foreigners or the outside world.

With the diversification of the economy, the composition of the social structure began to change. By 1985, 51 percent of the working-age population was classified as farmers, 30 percent as industrial laborers, and 19 percent as white-collar workers. Albania in the mid-1980s had eighteen cities with a population of more than ten thousand, and 34 percent of the population resided in cities. Reflecting the improvements in health services, sanitation, and diet, the average life expectancy had risen to seventy-one years.

In its development program for Albania, the Hoxha regime accorded a high priority to education. The schools were viewed as institutions to inculcate loyalty to the Communist party, the nation, and the doctrines of Marxism-Leninism as interpreted by Hoxha and to provide the trained personnel required for the nation's economy and society. In the mid-1980s Albania's educational system comprised 1,641 eight-year primary schools, 370 (mostly vocational) secondary schools, and 8 institutions of higher education, including its only university, the State University of Tirana, established in 1957. This system in 1985 enrolled 744,000 students. In marked contrast to the pre–World War II period, there were at this time 61,256 university or postsecondary school graduates in the country. By the end of the Hoxha era illiteracy in the country had been eradicated.

The growth of an educated, literate population was accompanied by an increase in literary and artistic activity and by the emergence of an Albanian intelligentsia. This development was reflected in the growth of the Albanian League of Artists and Writers, whose membership increased from 70 in 1945 to 1,300 in 1980. By the early 1980s approximately one thousand books were being published annually, and the country's thirty newspapers and fifty journals and magazines provided outlets for the work of the nation's writers and scholars. On the surface it appeared that Albanian culture was flourishing under communism. However, the creativity of the nation's intellectual community was stifled by the rigorous ideological and political controls exercised by party and government censors. Despite these strictures several Albanian writers, such as Ismail Kadare (b. 1936), managed to produce works of high quality that attracted international attention and acclaim.

Albania's entrance into the age of television in 1971 had a profound impact on its people. By 1985 there were about 200,000 television receivers in the country. Many Albanians were able to receive telecasts from Italy, Greece, and Yugoslavia. Ignoring official admonitions concerning the dangers of the "harmful" foreign influences transmitted through these programs, these viewers were able to gain some insight into life beyond their homeland. And as they learned more about the outside world, they developed a stronger sense of the material and spiritual poverty of their lives.

International Trends

Albania's international relations during the Hoxha era may be divided into four periods. Between 1944 and 1948 Albania was a Yugoslav dependency, and its foreign policy focused on issues involving the two nations. From 1949 to 1960 Albania was a Soviet satellite and maintained close ties with the USSR and the Eastern European communist states. From 1961 to 1978 Albania was allied with China. Since its break with China in 1978 Albania has followed an independent course in its international relations.

The Yugoslav Communists had enjoyed a special position in Albania since 1941, when they assisted in the organization of the ACP. They continued to exert considerable influence in the country, with the apparent approval of Stalin, following World War II. Between 1944 and 1948 Albania was, in effect, a Yugoslav subsatellite.

During this period the Yugoslavs directly and through their closest ally in the Albanian leadership, Koci Xoxe, sought to discourage Albania from establishing diplomatic and economic ties with Western Europe and the United States. Albania was required to assent to the restoration of Kosovo to Yugoslavia. At the same time a series of agreements concluded during 1946 integrated the economies of the two countries, a preliminary step to Yugoslavia's annexation of Albania. The 1948 Soviet-Yugoslav break enabled Albania to end the special relationship with Yugoslavia and to preserve its independence.

Following the break with Yugoslavia, Albania became, like the other Eastern European communist states, a full-fledged satellite of the Soviet Union. Although there was some desire within the Albanian leadership to normalize relations with the United States and Great Britain, Hoxha had been angered by their refusal to recognize his regime, their opposition to Albania's admission to the United Nations, and their perceived support of the Greek claims to portions of southern Albania. What appears to have finally confirmed Hoxha in his decision to align Albania totally with the Soviet Union was the existence, between 1949 and 1983, of a series of joint Anglo-American–sponsored clandestine operations intended to overthrow his government. These ventures failed because of poor planning and their betrayal to Moscow and Tirana by a Soviet agent within British intelligence, H. A. R. (Kim) Philby.[9]

As a full-fledged member of the Soviet camp, Albania was admitted to the Council of Mutual Economic Aid (Comecon) in 1949 and was one of the signatories to the Warsaw Pact in 1955. During the 1950s approximately 90 percent of Albania's trade was with the Soviet Union and its Comecon partners, and the USSR was the country's main foreign aid donor. The assistance that Albania received from the Soviet Union and its Eastern European allies helped ensure the success of the first and second five-year plans.

By the mid-1950s, however, serious differences had arisen between the USSR and Albania. Hoxha was unnerved by the Soviet-Yugoslav rapprochement following Stalin's death in 1953. This, he feared, might set the stage for a new Yugoslav move to annex Albania. Albanian leaders opposed Khrushchev's de-Stalinization campaign and resisted Moscow's efforts to implement these policies in their homeland out of fear they might lead to internal unrest, Soviet intervention, and their eventual removal from power. Soviet-Albanian relations were further strained by the differences over economic policy that had emerged between the two countries.[10]

These were the major factors that contributed to the 1961 Soviet-Albanian break. The Albanians might not have been as aggressive in pressing their quarrel with the Soviets without assurances of Chinese support. As in 1948 it was a development within the Soviet camp—in this instance, the Sino-Soviet rift—that enabled the Albanian leadership to remain in power and to continue to pursue its own line. Although Albania severed its diplomatic and economic relations with the Soviet Union, it did maintain ties in both these areas with the Eastern European communist states. However, Albania ceased to participate in the activities of Comecon and the Warsaw Pact alliance and in September 1968, following the Soviet invasion of Czechoslovakia, renounced its membership in the latter organization.

At the February 1961 Fourth Congress of the ruling Albanian Party of Labor, Hoxha proclaimed his "dual adversary" theory, which held that the world communist movement was confronted with the twin dangers of "imperialism" and "Soviet-led . . . modern revisionism." Consequently, it was necessary for all "true Marxist-Leninists" (China, Albania, and their allies) to wage a two-front war against both these enemies of socialism. To accomplish this goal, Tirana strongly endorsed Beijing's efforts to form anti-Soviet Marxist-Leninist parties. Thus, following the Soviet-Albanian break, Albania was cut off from the main body of world communism, and as Hoxha became increasingly obsessed with insulating his homeland from "alien ideologies," Albania's isolation became more pronounced.

China's economic and military aid contributed significantly to Albania's survival following the Moscow-Tirana split. Outwardly the relationship seemed cordial and equal, especially during the 1960s.

However, there were problems between the two allies.[11] From the outset the Albanians feared that the periodic Sino-Soviet meetings intended to resolve their quarrel would result in a settlement that would leave Albania totally isolated. Hoxha had misgivings about China's Great Proletarian Cultural Revolution and feared it would lead to the destruction of the Communist party's authority. Another sore point was Tirana's unhappiness at being kept in the dark about developments in China. Finally, the Albanians were disappointed by the nature of the Chinese support they received following the Soviet invasion of Czechoslovakia.

Sino-Albanian relations further deteriorated during the 1970s when Beijing phased out its cultural revolution, improved its relations with Western Europe and the United States, abandoned its support of the Marxist-Leninist parties, and informed Tirana of the proposed reductions in Chinese aid programs for the 1976–80 five-year-plan period. When the post–Mao Zedong Chinese leadership opted for a more moderate domestic course and continued to improve relations with a variety of nations, including "revisionist" Yugoslavia, Tirana viewed these developments as a "betrayal" of Marxism-Leninism and inimical to Albania's national interest.

In July 1978 the Chinese responded to the continuing and escalating Albanian attacks on their policies and leaders by halting their economic and military assistance programs. This action marked the end of the Sino-Albanian alliance. The two countries did not sever their diplomatic ties, however, and in 1982 the erstwhile allies effected a reconciliation.

Following the break with China, Albania was left without a protector. Ironically, Yugoslavia came closest to playing this role during 1978–80. But relations between the two countries soured following Belgrade's use of what Tirana termed "excess force" to restore order in Kosovo following demonstrations by the province's Albanian population in March 1981.

Albania's deepening economic problems, which had become apparent by the early 1980s, prompted the regime to adopt a more pragmatic stance in the conduct of foreign policy. With the apparent approval of Hoxha, Tirana moved to ease its isolation somewhat by strengthening its ties with such states as Greece, Turkey, Italy, and Austria. In an obvious effort to improve their external image, the Albanians also reduced their ties with the Marxist-Leninist parties and muted their ideological polemics. Hoxha refused to consider the restoration of relations with the United States or the Soviet Union, however.

The Hoxha Legacy

Enver Hoxha had ruled Albania for some forty years when he died on April 11, 1985, at the age of seventy-six. His influence and the imprint of his policies were evident in every aspect of Albanian life and they had shaped the nation's external image. For the country's three million inhabitants—most of whom had not known or lived under another leader—Hoxha's passing was a traumatic (to some) and momentous (to all) event.

Hoxha's eulogists and Communist party historians have emphasized that during his lifetime the long-time Albanian leader realized the goals he had established for himself and his party. Albania's independence and territorial integrity were preserved. The country lived under a socialist system constructed according to the Leninist-Stalinist model of the early 1950s and made discernible progress in its quest for economic development and social transformation. The Communists succeeded in retaining power and preserving Marxist-Leninist ideological orthodoxy, and Enver Hoxha managed to survive despite the internal and external challenges to his leadership.

The Hoxha legacy is, however, more complex and less positive than his admirers and Communist party historians have claimed. With the end of the political monopoly of the Communist party and the onset of the "democratization" movement in Albania in the early 1990s, Albanian and other scholars have the opportunity to reappraise the Hoxha epoch in a freer intellectual environment.

Undeniably, there were positive changes and progress in some aspects of Albanian life by the end of the Hoxha era. The gains in health, education, and cultural activity were especially notable, and the standard of living of virtually the entire population had improved in comparison to that of the pre–World War II period. It seems that the regime was also largely successful in its efforts to complete the process of nation- and state-building initiated by King Zog. The authority of the central government was established in all parts of the country, and the divisive forces that had hindered the achievement of national unity—such as regional loyalties, Geg-Tosk rivalry, and religious differences—had been rendered insignificant.

These advances, however, were offset by Hoxha's insistence on ideological conformity. As a consequence of his unwillingness to introduce much-needed systemic changes in the management of the economy, his successors have had to deal with the mess he created in this area. By 1985 most of the nation's intellectuals and youth were alienated from the regime, owing to the rigid controls it exercised in the cultural sector. The pervasive violations of human rights used to discourage opposition to party and state policies produced much resentment, and consequently the regime enjoyed only the superficial and forced allegiance of the vast majority of the Albanian people.[12]

Although Hoxha skillfully exploited conflicts within the global communist movement to preserve Albania's independence, his policies of isolation and self-sufficiency aggravated the country's economic plight. Albania's image was tarnished by its support for the radical Marxist-Leninist splinter parties, its refusal to sign the 1975 Helsinki agreements, and its repressive domestic policies. It was not until the final years of his life that Hoxha recognized the need to adopt a more pragmatic approach in conducting the nation's international relations, and even then his initiatives in this area were limited.

Albania in the Post-Hoxha Era[13]

Although Hoxha can be faulted for his shortsightedness and errors during his lengthy tenure, he appears to have made a sound choice in his selection of Alia as his successor. Alia was born on October 18, 1925, in the northern Albanian city of Shkoder and was one of the relatively few Gegs in the inner circle of the Albanian leadership. He joined the Communist party in 1943 and the following year was appointed political commissar, with the rank of lieutenant colonel, of the Albanian division which was dispatched to Yugoslavia to assist in the liberation of Kosovo. After World War II Alia held leadership posts in the Communist Youth Organization and in 1948 was elected to the party's Central Committee. The following year Alia became president of the Communist Youth Organization, a post he held until 1955. In 1954 he was sent to the Soviet Union to study Marxist-Leninist theory.

Upon his return to Albania, Alia began his rapid ascent within the communist establishment. By 1955 he became minister of education and the following year joined the Politburo as a candidate (non-voting) member. In 1958 Alia relinquished his post as minister of education to become the Central Committee's director of propaganda and agitation, a position he held until his appointment as Central Committee secretary for ideology and culture. At the fourth party congress in February 1961 he was promoted to full membership in the Politburo. Alia's rise to the inner circle of the leadership occurred during the period when Soviet-Albanian relations were deteriorating, and he was staunchly loyal to Hoxha during the critical period that culminated in the rupture of Soviet-Albanian ideological and diplomatic ties. Subsequently he played a prominent role in Albania's Ideological and Cultural Revolution and coordinated the party's domestic and international propaganda campaigns against Soviet, Yugoslav, and Chinese "revisionism."

Alia was in many respects the logical choice to succeed Hoxha. Aside from his demonstrated loyalty to the aging Albanian leader, he was probably the most enlightened and competent member of the party secretariat and the Politburo. He also appears to have been the most widely respected member of Hoxha's inner circle and, in contrast to most of his colleagues, seems to have appreciated the gravity of the problems confronting Albania as the Hoxha era was drawing to a close.

The precarious state of the economy was clearly the most pressing problem which Alia had to address when he assumed power. It was apparent by 1985 that the Seventh Five-Year Plan (1981–85) would fail, as had its predecessors, to meet its assigned goals. And the prospects for the Eighth Five-Year Plan (1986–90) would be equally bleak if the problems that plagued the economic sector were not corrected. The weakness of the economy caused the Albanian masses to endure the lowest standard of living in Europe and resulted in their growing alienation from or indifference to the regime.

Alia was also sensitive to the disaffection of Albania's youth, the most numerically significant group in a country where the average age of the population in 1989 was twenty-seven. The small but growing intellectual community in the country was also increasingly resentful of the restrictions to which it was subjected. In addition Alia was aware of the need to strengthen the quality and appeal of the nation's cultural output for its expanding and increasingly sophisticated domestic audience.

Finally, the Albanian leader wanted to expand the country's international contacts in order to promote stronger commercial and cultural relations with both Western Europe and Albania's Balkan neighbors. He abandoned the regime's long-standing opposition to participation in multilateral diplomatic activities. He was especially intent on changing the image of Albania as an isolated, dogmatic, and repressive nation.

Alia sought to deal with these issues by undertaking a series of initiatives, beginning in 1985. It is important to note in this respect that Alia had a relatively modest and limited agenda for reform. His primary concern was to strengthen the stability of the communist regime through a program of controlled administrative change from above. In this context, Alia's initiatives of 1985–89 should be viewed more as a series of efforts to maintain the existing system than as a program of comprehensive reforms.

Between April 1985 and August 1989 Alia sought to revitalize the Albanian economy by introducing wage incentives for workers, by permitting plant managers more autonomy in fulfilling plan directives, and by encouraging peasants to market the produce from their private plots. He also placed heavier emphasis on providing consumer goods and services and sought to improve worker discipline and productivity. These and other related measures failed to effect the turnaround of the economy that Alia had anticipated. In addition to being harmed by worker apathy and bureaucratic footdragging, Alia's economic reforms were further hampered by unfavorable weather conditions and a lack of investment capital.

Similarly, the efforts to win over the nation's youth by providing them with additional recreational facilities, special radio programming, improved employment opportunities, and promises of educational reform met with only limited success, as did a spirited campaign to upgrade the quality of the country's literary, artistic, and musical productions and to ease somewhat the party's control over the nation's cultural and intellectual life.

It was in this context that one of the most important cultural events of the 1985–89 period occurred—the publication in August 1989 of Neshat Tozaj's novel, *Thikat* (The Knives). In this work Tozaj, a veteran Albanian writer and an employee of the Ministry of the Interior, provided a moving account of the lack of respect for truth and for basic human rights by the Albanian secret police. Ismail Kadare, the nation's most distinguished writer, subsequently published a strongly positive review of the novel in the October 15, 1989 issue of *Drita,* the weekly newspaper of the League of Writers and Artists. This review attracted considerable attention within Albania owing to its pleas for a more just society based on the rule of law, for greater respect for the rights of the individual, and for increased freedom of expression for writers and artists.

During the last half of the 1980s, Albania made considerable progress in strengthening its ties with the outside world. Relations with Greece were fully normalized with the ending of the state of war between the two nations in 1987. That same year Albania resumed diplomatic relations with West Germany and Canada. Albania participated in the 1988 Conference of the Foreign Ministers of the Balkan States, hosted a meeting of the region's deputy foreign ministers the following year, and agreed to host the second foreign ministers meeting in October 1990. Additionally, there were numerous exchange visits by Albanian and Western European diplomatic and economic delegations during this period. A major motivation for the opening of diplomatic relations with Western Europe and with Albania's Balkan neighbors was economic—the need for markets for Albanian exports and for foreign capital and technical expertise to modernize and diversify the nation's economy.

While it is significant that Alia sought to bring about changes in key sectors of Albanian life prior to the overthrow of the Eastern European communist regimes, it should be noted that he did not develop a well-defined program for reform. It is also important to recognize that there probably was not a consensus among the leadership regarding the appropriateness of the changes advocated by Alia and his supporters. There is little doubt that there was a lack of enthusiasm for Alia's initiatives within the ranks of the middle and lower levels of the bureaucracy. The workers, too, seem to have been generally indifferent. Their major interest lay in the improvement of their living standards, and some feared they would have to work harder or receive lower wages if they failed to meet their productivity quotas. In sum, the intellectuals, the smallest segment of Albanian society, appeared to be the most supportive of Alia's policies. And among the intellectuals, there were many who were dissatisfied with the pace of reform.

The reform process in Albania began to accelerate with the demise of the Eastern European communist regimes and the intensified level of discontent within Albania during the autumn of 1989. This development was spurred by the widespread ownership of radios and television sets that enabled the masses to follow events in Eastern Europe as reported by a variety of foreign sources. The reforms promised and promulgated during the first half of 1990 represented an extension, in many areas, of the policies initiated by Alia since 1985. As the leadership sensed the dissatisfaction of the masses with the pace of change, it accelerated its timetable for reform. However, this produced discomfort in the top echelons of both the party and the government and created difficulties and confusion in the implementation of change.

The initial phase of Alia's comprehensive reform program was announced in stages at the Eighth (September 1989), Ninth (January 1990), Tenth (April 1990), and Eleventh (July 1990) meetings of the party Central Committee, and at the May 1990 session of the People's Assembly. It focused on such areas as the economy, the political system, the legal system and human rights, freedom of discussion, education, and foreign relations.

The Albanian regime designated the economic program it sought to implement "The New Economic Mechanism," a term borrowed from the Hungarian reforms of the late 1960s and early 1970s. While revolutionary in the context of the Albanian experience, the economic changes were modest compared to the transformations of the Soviet and Eastern European economic systems during the late 1980s.

In essence the Albanian reform retained the structure and many of the features of the centralized economic planning system. However, individual economic enterprises and district-level governments were given greater input into the planning process and the authority to implement plan directives. Enterprise managers were given greater freedom in decision-making, but were held to higher standards of accountability. Subsidies for inefficient or unprofitable industrial, service, and agricultural units were to be phased out and replaced by long-term credits, which would be withdrawn if the units continued to operate at a loss. The size of private plots on collective farms was doubled and farmers were encouraged to sell their produce at free markets that were established throughout the country. Ownership of livestock from the herds of the collective farms was transferred to the peasants. Artisans, craftsmen, and individual retailers were granted permission to carry on trade in a newly created private sector. Wages for the lowest categories of workers were increased, and workers were guaranteed 80 percent of their wages if laid off because of conditions beyond their control. The government also indicated its intention to ease control over prices and to allow market forces to determine the prices of "nonessential" items. To satisfy the unfilled popular demand for consumer goods, the regime promised to increase imports of these items.

In an effort to stimulate the flagging economy, the regime promulgated, despite the proscriptions of the 1976 constitution, legislation permitting foreign investment in Albania and sanctioning joint ventures between Albanian and foreign firms. To upgrade the skills of management personnel in such areas as marketing and administration, the Albanians invited European businessmen to conduct seminars of limited duration in Tirana.

Alia's economic reforms came too late to have any impact on the Eighth Five-Year Plan (1986–90). Indeed, they appear to have contributed to the nation's economic woes. Furthermore, they were regarded as insufficient to remedy the ills of the ailing economy by many of the country's most prominent economists, who advocated scrapping the existing system totally and embracing a market economy. In addition, economic performance during 1990 was hindered by bureaucratic snafus, strikes and other work stoppages, increased worker absenteeism, and unfavorable weather.

At year's end the economy was in chaos. It was subsequently disclosed that national income during 1990 declined by 10 percent from that of 1989 and that the country's accumulated trade deficit rose to $350 million. The government acknowledged that inflation had become a serious problem and that fifty thousand workers were unemployed.[14] It was apparent that the resolution of the nation's economic difficulties would be a long and painful process.

Alia's proposals for political reform indicated he was unwilling to permit significant changes in this area. Up until December 1990, he repeatedly and emphatically stated that the Communist party would not surrender its monopoly on power and that it would continue to play a leading role in all aspects of the nation's life. Alia's proposed political reforms provided for contested elections for party and state offices, with the exception of those at the highest level. Party and state officials would ordinarily be limited to two terms. The Democratic Front and other mass organizations, such as women's, youth, and trade organizations—all controlled by the Communist party—were encouraged to play a more active role in Albanian politics. Alia further promised to call a constitutional convention to revise the 1976 constitution in a manner that would reflect the "changing conditions" within the country and embody the principle of the rule of law. As a sop to Albanian public opinion, in July 1990 he removed from the Politburo several of Hoxha's longtime cronies and hardliners, who had become objects of public scorn and ridicule. Several cabinet changes were also announced at this time.

But these measures did not appease public opinion; dissatisfaction was most pronounced among students, intellectuals, and young workers, who favored the establishment of a full-fledged multiparty political system. The promotion of a despised hardliner, Xhelil Gjoni, to the secretariat of the party Central Committee and the Politburo caused many Albanians to question the commitment of Alia to genuine political reform. The disappointment of many Albanians, especially the intellectuals, with the scope and pace of the leadership's efforts was underscored by the decision of the eminent writer Ismail Kadare to seek political asylum in France.

Alia, in fact, was forced to modify his position regarding the preservation of the Communist party's monopoly on power following a student strike at the State University of Tirana (December 8–12, 1990) and the outbreak of violent demonstrations in such industrial centers as Durres, Elbasan, Kavaja, and Shkoder. On December 18, the Presidium of the People's Assembly approved a decree establishing a multiparty system. The next day the Democratic party (DP), the first alternative political party to be founded in communist Albania, was legalized. Subsequently, opposition political groups were permitted to publish newspapers.

In an obvious effort to forestall the defection of communist moderates to the new party and to others that were in the process of being formed, as well as to improve the image of the Communist party within the country, Alia continued to remove unpopular leaders from their positions. Additionally, Nexhmije Hoxha, the late dictator's wife, announced her retirement from the presidency of the Democratic Front. To dramatize Albania's break with its Stalinist past, all statues of the late Soviet leader were removed and all memorials to him renamed. The Communist party also prepared a new reform platform intended to enhance its stature with the public.

The final significant political development of the year was the publication of the draft of a new constitution on December 31. The document sanctioned the multiparty political system, guaranteed extensive civil liberties to the people, and incorporated many of the economic reforms that had previously been enacted into law. There was considerable opposition, however, to some of the provisions of the document, including the investment of vast powers in the president; the portions of the preamble that lauded the role of the Communist party in Albania's post–World War II history; and the retained designation of Albania as a "People's Socialist Republic."

In contrast to the relatively limited scope of the political changes proposed by Alia, the legal reforms promulgated by the regime during 1990 were significant. The Ministry of Justice, which had been abolished in 1966, was reestablished and mandated to protect the civil rights of the nation's citizens and to ensure that government agencies and officials observed the laws of the land. The number of capital crimes was reduced from thirty-four to eleven, and penalties for other criminal violations were lessened. The prohibition against the private practice of religion was lifted. And, while the law was unclear as to the reopening of churches and the official status of the clergy, public religious services were being conducted in various parts of Albania by late 1990. One of the most eagerly awaited of the legal reforms was the proclamation of the new passport law that granted citizens the right to request and receive a passport for foreign travel. Initially the

Passport Office of the Ministry of the Interior was slow in processing passport requests. Confusion over the interpretation and implementation of this law contributed in part to the exodus in July 1990 of some 4,500 Albanians who had taken refuge in foreign embassies in Tirana. They were the first of approximately 50,000 Albanians who fled the country between July 1990 and April 1991. The majority of this group apparently left Albania for economic reasons; i.e., they hoped to start a new life for themselves and their families. Although some 57,000 passports were issued between January and November 1990, relatively few Albanians were able to use them, owing to lack of funds for travel.

In July 1990, the government announced a series of education reforms designed to result in compulsory ten-year schooling, a restructuring and redefinition of the secondary school system, and greater opportunities for secondary education in rural areas. In addition, university entrance examinations are to be revised and the number of students admitted to the nation's institutions of higher education to be increased. The curricula, textbooks, and instructional methodology for the entire spectrum of higher education are to be reviewed and changed to reflect "the new conditions" in the country. All these matters have been of great concern to students.

There was also a relaxation of restrictions on the press and other communications media during 1990. This resulted in an extensive and largely unfettered exchange of views, especially in the press. As in the case of Gorbachev in the USSR, Alia has sought to use the freer press to mobilize support for his policies. The discussions in the press, however, generated a variety of perspectives on contemporary issues and provided a useful forum for the expression of the accumulated grievances of the people.

The more relaxed atmosphere that prevailed in Albania contributed to the growth of tourism. Between 1987 and 1989 the number of foreign tourists visiting Albania grew from 7,000 to 14,435, and this figure was expected to rise to some 25,000 to 30,000 for 1990. In March 1990 Albania's contacts with the outside world were enhanced by the inauguration of direct-dial international telephone service. Albanians made extensive use of this service to call relatives and friends abroad. Both these developments have contributed to the breakdown of Albania's isolation.

The pronouncements of Albania's leaders during 1990 left no doubt that they had abandoned Hoxha's dogmatism in the conduct of the nation's foreign policy and that they were making a conscious effort to shed Albania's image as Europe's most isolated country. It was also apparent that the regime's domestic reform program was intended to improve the country's image. Throughout the year a lengthy procession of foreign journalists, statesmen, and businessmen visited Albania. This included U.S. legislators and United Nations Secretary General Pérez de Cuéllar. Tirana signaled its readiness to restore diplomatic relations with the United States and the Soviet Union. Relations were reestablished with the USSR in July 1990 and with the United States in March 1991. Tirana, however, was less successful in its quest for membership in the Conference on Security and Cooperation in Europe (CSCE). This organization continued in 1990 to have reservations about the degree to which the Albanian government was, despite its reforms, respecting the civil rights of its citizens.

During the year Tirana signed the Nuclear Non-Proliferation Treaty and expanded its participation in the activities of the United Nations and its various agencies, and by year's end Albania had shown interest in developing affiliations with the World Bank and the International Monetary Fund in the hope of benefiting from the advice and resources of these agencies.

Alia during 1990 found it necessary to expand the scope of his reforms and accelerate the pace of their implementation owing to the intense pressure from the masses. He was able to remain in power and avert a possible civil war by granting concessions to the dissidents at several critical points, especially during December. He clearly would have preferred to move more cautiously in the hope of avoiding the disruptions that had previously occurred in virtually every area of Albanian life.

The pattern established during the closing months of 1990 persisted into early 1991. As economic conditions worsened Albanians continued to flee to Greece, Italy, and Yugoslavia to escape the uncertainties they faced at home. A major bone of contention between Alia and the new opposition parties was the timing of elections for the People's Assembly. Following a wave of strikes, demonstrations, and heated debates, the elections were postponed until March 31, 1991. During the unrest that swept Albania in late February, the statue of Hoxha that had stood in a place of honor in Tirana's Skenderbeg Square was toppled and decapitated. Growing popular opposition to Prime Minister Adil Carcani led to Alia's decision to oust him. Carcani's replacement, Fatos Nano (b. 1952), was an economist by training and a moderate. The new prime minister's cabinet comprised, for the most part, individuals with backgrounds and outlooks similar to his. The changes in the government and party leadership during 1990 and early 1991 resulted in the elimination from positions of influence of Hoxha's "old guard" and cronies.

On March 31, 1991, Albania held its first free elections since the 1920s. According to the official tally, 98.9 percent of eligible voters cast ballots. The Communists polled 56 percent of the vote and won 68 percent of the seats in the People's Assembly. The opposition DP received 39 percent of the vote and 30 percent of the seats. The remaining seats went to candidates from other political parties and groups. It appears the elections were honestly conducted, but it is clear that the Communists exploited their favored position in Albanian society to obtain greater media coverage, recruit campaign workers, and fund their partisan activities.

Albania was again plunged into turmoil following an outbreak of violence in the aftermath of the elections. The unexplained deaths of several young DP workers in April and the subsequent investigation, apparently bungled by the state police, became a major issue in the debates of the newly elected People's Assembly, where Fatos Nano was reelected prime minister. On May 1, 1991, Ramiz Alia, who had been defeated in his bid for a seat in the Assembly, was nonetheless elected president. To accept this position Alia was required to relinquish his post as first secretary of the Communist party. The country was now called the Republic of Albania. It appeared that Albania had passed into a new era.

In June 1991, however, after less than two months in office, Prime Minister Nano resigned. The pronounced differences between the two major parties in the Assembly over such issues as the postelection deaths, the approval of the constitution, and strategies to deal with the nation's economic crisis had produced an impasse. Ylli Bufi, Nano's minister of nutrition and a competent administrator, was appointed prime minister in a "government of national salvation" whose main responsibility was to address the problems confronting the economy and to make arrangements for a new election.

Albania in early 1991 is at another critical juncture. As has been the case throughout its history as an independent state, the country faces serious economic difficulties. It has yet to formulate a strategy for scrapping its command economy and adopting a new economic structure. In the short run, however, its most pressing problem is the need to restore productivity in all sectors of the economy.

With only limited experience in parliamentary government, the Albanian leadership is faced with the challenge of fashioning a viable political system within a multiparty environment. As the number of political parties continues to increase, the Albanians must seek to avoid excessive partisanship that could lead to parliamentary deadlock.

Albania will have to compete with the Soviet Union and the (former) Eastern European Communist party states for the development funding and technical expertise it requires. Except in the case of Yugoslavia, there are no serious tensions in Tirana's relations with its neighbors and major trading partners; the Albanian-Yugoslav relationship will continue to be influenced by Belgrade's policies toward the Albanians of Kosovo.

NOTES

1. For a comprehensive discussion and analysis of the Albanian national renaissance of the nineteenth and twentieth centuries, see Stavro Skendi, *The Albanian National Awakening, 1878–1912* (Princeton: Princeton University Press, 1967). For a detailed treatment of this important movement reflecting the consensus of Albanian scholarship at the end of the Hoxha era, see Stefanaq Pollo et al., eds., *Historia e Shqipërisë,* vol. 2 (Tirana: Akademia e Shkencave e RPS të Shqipërisë, 1984). For a summary version of this movement from the perspective of Albanian communist historiography, see Stefanaq Polio and Arben Puto, *The History of Albania,* trans. Carol Wiseman and Ginnie Hole (London: Routledge & Kegan Paul, 1981).

2. See Pollo et al., eds., *Historia e Shqipërisë,* 2:49–52.

3. Two useful accounts of Albania's history between 1912 and 1939 are Bernd Jurgen Fischer, *King Zog and the Struggle for Stability in Albania* (Boulder and New York: East European Monographs/Columbia University Press, 1984); and Michael Schmidt-Neke, *Entstehung und Ausbau der Königsdiktatur in Albanien (1912–1939)* (Munich: R. Oldenbourg Verlag, 1987). For the detailed Albanian version, see Pollo et al., eds., *Historia e Shqipërisë,* 3:7–477. Pollo and Puto, *History of Albania,* 146–223, provide a good summary.

4. For information on economic, social, and cultural developments in Albania between 1912 and 1939, see *Albania,* Geographic Handbook Series (Oxford: H. M. Stationery Office, 1945); also helpful are the relevant sections of Stavro Skendi's *Albania* (New York: Praeger, 1956) and Pollo et al., eds., *Historia e Shqipërisë,* vol. 3.

5. For a more extensive treatment of the establishment of the Communist regime in Albania and its policies into the 1970s, see Anton Logoreci, *The Albanians: Europe's Forgotten Survivors* (Boulder: Westview Press, 1978); Ramadan Marmullaku, *Albania and the Albanians* (Hamden, Conn.: Archon Books, 1975); Nicholas C. Pano, *The People's Republic of Albania* (Balti-

more: Johns Hopkins University Press, 1968); and Peter R. Prifti, *Socialist Albania Since 1944* (Cambridge: MIT Press, 1978). For Albanian perspectives on these developments, see Institute of Marxist-Leninist Studies, *History of the Albanian Party of Labor,* 2d ed. (Tirana: "8 Nentori" Publishing House, 1982); and Luan Omari and Stefanaq Pollo, *The History of the Socialist Construction of Albania* (Tirana: "8 Nentori" Publishing House, 1988).

6. For some useful insights into the influences that helped shape Hoxha's attitudes and policies, consult Jon Halliday, ed., *The Artful Albanian: The Memoirs of Enver Hoxha* (London: Chatto and Windus, 1986); and Bernhard Tönnes, *Sonderfall Albanien: Enver Hoxhas "eigener Weg" und die historischen Ursprünge seine ideologie* (Munich: R. Oldenburg Verlag, 1980).

7. The data used to illustrate developments in the economy, society, and culture have been derived from *40 Years of Socialist Albania: Statistical Data on the Development of the Economy and Culture* (Tirana: Directory of Statistics, State Planning Commission, 1984); and the Statistical Yearbooks of the People's Socialist Republic of Albania for 1988, 1989, and 1990, issued by the State Planning Commission.

8. World Resources Institute, *World Resources, 1990–91* (New York: Oxford University Press, 1990), 245.

9. The best available extensive account of this episode is Nicholas Bethell's *The Great Betrayal: The Untold Story of Kim Philby's Biggest Coup* (London: Hodder and Stoughton, 1984).

10. Despite its 1963 publication date William E. Griffith's *Albania and the Sino-Soviet Rift* (Cambridge: MIT Press) is a reliable guide to the Soviet-Albanian relationship.

11. The Sino-Albanian relationship is perceptively analyzed in Elez Biberaj's *Albania and China: A Study of an Unequal Alliance* (Boulder: Westview Press, 1986).

12. For an examination of Albanian human and civil rights violations under Communism, see *Albania: Political Imprisonment and the Law* (London: Amnesty International, 1984); and *Human Rights in the People's Socialist Republic of Albania* (Minneapolis: Minnesota Lawyers International Human Rights Committee, 1990).

13. Two useful accounts of developments in Albania between 1985 and 1989 can be found in Elez Biberaj, *Albania: A Socialist Maverick* (Boulder: Westview Press, 1990); and Franz-Lothar Altman, ed., *Albanien im Umbruch: Eine Bestandsaufnahme* (Munich: R. Oldenburg Verlag, 1990). Some interesting perspectives on post-Hoxha developments and an appraisal of Ramiz Alia's policies through 1990 are found in Ismail Kadare's *Nga një dhjetor në tjetrin: Kronikë, këmbim letrash, persiatje* (Paris: Fayard, 1991).

14. Albanian Telegraphic Agency, *News Bulletin,* May 10, 1991, 6–7.

3 Bulgaria

Marin Pundeff

As the century opened, Bulgaria was, in its modern form, barely coming of age. Less than twenty-one years earlier, in the spring of 1879, an assembly of notables stipulated by the Treaty of Berlin had met at Turnovo, the medieval capital, to resurrect a Bulgarian state after nearly five centuries of Ottoman rule. According to the will of the European powers, the new state, a principality, remained in the Ottoman empire as a vassal, along with other parts of the nation's territory in Thrace (eastern Rumelia) and Macedonia, which the preliminary Russo-Turkish Treaty of San Stefano had defined as Bulgarian.

The constitution worked out at Turnovo complied with the treaty stipulation that there be freedom of religion for all citizens as well as foreign residents in Bulgaria, and no discrimination on the basis of religion in the exercise of civil, political, and economic rights, nor impediments to the internal organization of the religious communities and their relations with superiors abroad. With respect to the system of government, the constitution was largely a victory of the Liberals (the "Young") over the Conservatives in the assembly. One of the most democratic documents of its time, it provided for the franchise of all male citizens over twenty-one, eligibility for elective office for those over thirty and literate, a unicameral parliament, freedom of speech, press, and assembly, broad local self-government, and free elementary education.

However, it invested the ruler not only with the functions of head of state and commander in chief but also with powers to approve and promulgate the laws and to control the executive branch of government without bearing responsibility for its decisions. These powers created a permanent tension between the advocates of popular sovereignty and those who saw the ruler as the ultimate arbiter and authority.[1]

Politically, the two decades before 1900 were stormy. The first prince, Alexander von Battenberg, a twenty-two-year-old lieutenant of the Prussian Guards in Berlin, qualified for the job only because he was a favorite nephew of Alexander II, the Russian tsar, and was related to nearly all the reigning houses of Europe. Even before he arrived in Sofia, he was convinced that he could not rule on the basis of such a constitution. Following the assassination of Alexander II and the return to reaction under Alexander III, he managed to suspend the constitution and run a "personal regime" with Russian backing until 1883. This cost him Liberal as well as Conservative support, and in his personal crisis with Alexander III—he had been forced by the Bulgarian nationalists into accepting the union of eastern Rumelia with the principality in 1885 without the prior approval of the Russian autocrat—he found himself without a political base for survival in Bulgaria. His abdication brought to the fore Liberals and Russophobe nationalists led by Stefan Stambolov, who frustrated Alexander III to the point of his breaking off all relations with Bulgaria in 1886.[2]

The second prince, whom the Stambolov regency hurriedly found in Vienna to stabilize the situation, was another inexperienced young officer, Ferdinand of Saxe-Coburg-Gotha, whose dynastic ties extended even to the French house of Orléans. Happy to have a throne, he went to Bulgaria despite the relentless hostility of the Russian emperor, who declared him a usurper and blocked his international recognition. The country, seething with Russophile- and Russian-inspired plots as well as agitation by the Orthodox hierarchy against Ferdinand, a Catholic, was kept in line by Stambolov who, as prime minister until 1894, was not loath to using strong-arm methods against the threats to stability from the right or the left.

The opportunity for Ferdinand to appease Russia and normalize his position came in 1894 when Alexander III died and the new emperor, Nicholas II, showed himself receptive, on the condition that

Ferdinand baptize his heir, Boris, in the Orthodox faith. In the process, Ferdinand also rid himself of Stambolov and turned to more pliant politicians such as Konstantin Stoilov, who formed a new conservative People's party and served as prime minister until 1899. With his new-found security, Ferdinand began to build his own personal regime, particularly through his control of the ministers of war, always army officers, who were directly subordinate to him. Unlike Alexander von Battenberg, however, he did not go so far as to suspend the Turnovo constitution and preferred foxier ways of ruling.[3]

Economically, Bulgaria emerged from Ottoman rule a poor agricultural country, with most of the land owned by smallholders. Handicrafts and nascent manufacture, largely stimulated by the demands of the Turkish army and domestic markets, were marginal but promising components of the economy. In a population of 3,774,000 in 1900, over 80 percent were peasants, with most families (433,714) owning their land.[4] The methods of cultivation were traditional and primitive; for example, only 6.8 percent of the households had metal plows. Industry was at first slow to grow, although protectionist legislation was enacted to encourage certain branches. An index was the fact that by 1900 there were less than 8,000 workers employed in industrial establishments, as distinct from handicrafts workshops that employed 129,000 workers. Railroads expanded somewhat faster after the closing of the Bulgarian gap in the Vienna-Constantinople route—the famous Orient Express—and the building of lines to ports on the Danube and the Black Sea. In education, a key to progress, the country had a good network of elementary and secondary schools, but no university. Before the liberation in 1878, the small number of Bulgarians who had some higher education were mainly products of Russian universities and theological academies, although a significant portion of those who attained leading positions after 1878, including Konstantin Stoilov, came from the American Robert College in Constantinople or from institutions of French- or German-speaking countries. After 1878, a veritable flight to universities in the West took place, in pursuit of modern education which the new country needed and which Russia was generally unable to supply.[5] This trend gave rise to concerns that Bulgarians trained abroad would lack the national and patriotic components in their education that only a native university could provide. The result was the establishment of a Higher School in 1888, renamed the University of Sofia in 1904, to produce teachers, civil servants, and jurists in three faculties: history and philology, physics and mathematics, and law. For the vast array of other disciplines (e.g., medicine, dentistry, engineering, economics) as well as for advanced training, Bulgarian students by the thousands continued to head west.

What the country lacked in wealth, it made up in a general thrust toward progress. Time and again foreign visitors remarked that the newest and best building in a Bulgarian village was the school. When in 1901 the United States finally established diplomatic relations with Bulgaria, Charles M. Dickinson, the first "diplomatic agent," toured the country to survey economic conditions and the opportunities for trade. "It is a fine diversified country," he reported, "and has made remarkable progress in view of the fact that but little more than twenty years ago nearly every substantial thing upon it was laid waste by devastating armies. In general intelligence, progressive ideas and a readiness to examine and seize upon new things, Bulgaria is already far in advance of Turkey and considerably in advance of southern Russia. Here [Dickinson was writing from Constantinople] the fact that a thing or method is new excites suspicion and distrust; there the fact that it is recommended by modern nations commands immediate confidence and respect."[6]

The twelve years before the Balkan wars were a time of unprecedented progress. Swept up into the general trends in the West prior to World War I, Bulgaria responded with such youthful enthusiasm and energy that she began to be held up as an example of rapid and dynamic development. One of the notable accolades came from Theodore Roosevelt, vice president and president when U.S.-Bulgarian diplomatic relations began. Writing in 1912 as the special contributing editor of *The Outlook,* he compared Bulgaria's progress with Japan's: "No other nation has traveled so far and so fast as Bulgaria has traveled in the last third of a century. Americans have a just cause to feel proud that Robert College gave to many of the leading Bulgarian citizens their education, so that it has played a peculiar part in the making of the Bulgarian nation. Not the rise of Japan itself has been more striking and unexpected than the rise of Bulgaria."[7]

A closer look at the conditions of the broad masses, however, might have prompted a less sanguine assessment. Much of the material progress was financed by borrowing heavily abroad, mainly in France, as was the military buildup in anticipation of war with Turkey over the territories the Treaty of Berlin had returned to Turkish rule. By 1912 the nation's foreign debt was nearly 1.3 billion leva, requiring periodic tax increases and the establishment of special state monopolies over goods of general use to service it.[8] The tax burden was acutely felt by the peasantry who, in addition, labored under a mounting indebtedness to local moneylenders. Since the existing parties were not prone to look after the peasants' interests, rural teachers and intellectuals formed a Peasant Union in 1900 that in a few years became a major political force under the sway of the young editor of its newspaper and fiery orator, Alexander Stamboliiski.

Urban conditions also showed the underside of progress. The processes of industrialization and urbanization drew workers from the villages to the cities in search of alternative employment and a better life. A case in point was Sofia, the capital, which grew in population from 20,000 in 1878 to 120,000 in 1912 through the influx of peasants-turned-laborers or -tradesmen as well as office-seekers, bureaucrats, and refugees from Turkish Macedonia and Thrace, Romanian Dobrudja, and other Bulgarian areas. The newcomers' living conditions at the edge of town were miserable and periodic unemployment made them worse. Socialists, organized as a party in 1891, sought to speak for this "proletariat," but they were divided over doctrines and tactics and their efforts to organize a following were largely ineffective. In 1903, they split into a "Broad" Social Democratic party, led by Ianko Sakuzov, and a "Narrow" party of revolutionary Marxists, led by Dimitur Blagoev. As of 1912 there was only one Socialist deputy (Sakuzov) in the National Assembly.[9]

The era of progress was cut short by two wars in five years, both ending in debacle. The cause of both was the so-called Macedonian question. Macedonia first became the object of ethnic claims by Bulgarians and Greeks in 1870, when the Ottoman government restored religious autonomy to the Bulgarians under an Exarchate and set in motion a process of defining its territory by plebiscites in contested areas. After 1878 the struggle became triangular with the entry of Serbia, which came to see Macedonia as an area for expansion. Each of the three Christian countries employed its religious and educational resources to establish a hold on the parts of Macedonia it coveted in anticipation of the eventual end of Ottoman rule.

The Macedonian population was an ethnic amalgam containing, in addition to the Turks, Greeks, and Bulgarians, large numbers of Albanians, Vlachs, Gypsies, Armenians, Jews, and marginally, Serbs. *Macédoine* even moved into the French language as a synonym of mixture. In the absence of usable Ottoman statistics, it defied consensus even among scholars as to the size of each nationality, although it appeared that the "Slavophone" population predominated in the northern and central parts of the region.[10] At any rate, it was Bulgarian Macedonians who created in 1894 the well-known Internal Ma-

cedonian Revolutionary Organization (IMRO) to seek either autonomy within the Ottoman empire or annexation by Bulgaria. Strapped
for funds, the IMRO sought support from the Macedonian refugees
in Bulgaria and the "Supreme Macedonian Committee" in Sofia,
which had ties to the Bulgarian court and army, and had even kidnapped an American missionary, Ellen Stone, for a huge ransom and
publicity.[11] In 1903, it launched in Bulgarian areas of Turkey an ill-
planned and ill-prepared uprising that ended in bloody suppression
and the flight of tens of thousands of additional refugees to Bulgaria.
To deal with the Macedonian problem, the European powers dele-
gated Russia and Austria, the two empires most directly concerned,
but the so-called Mürzsteg reforms soon proved unworkable.

In the prevailing climate of irredentism, nationalism, and militarism, it was easy to embrace war as the solution. An alliance was,
however, needed to take on the Ottoman empire in the Balkans.
Although they were rivals in Macedonia, Bulgarians and Serbs began
to band together through their racial, linguistic, and religious similarities, as well as by the inducements of Russia, which always saw the
Balkan Slavs as useful tools against both Turkey and Austria. The
first attempt to build an alliance was a treaty in 1904, which also
provided for a customs union, but it bore no results. The Young Turk
revolution in 1908 gave Austria the opportunity to annex Bosnia and
Herzegovina, thus injuring Serbian and Russian interests, while Bulgaria proclaimed its independence from the Ottoman empire and
invested Ferdinand with the medieval title of tsar (Caesar[12]) of all
Bulgarians regardless of where they lived.

Russia, nevertheless, supported Bulgaria in its quest for international recognition of its independence and continued to foster an
understanding between Serbia and Bulgaria. By 1912, the pieces fell
into place. In Sofia, the cabinet of Ivan E. Geshov, an Anglophile,
Russophile, and Americanophile,[13] rushed to an agreement with Serbia when the Italo-Turkish war created the dangerous possibility that
Italy and Austria would move into Albania and Macedonia, as well
as an opportunity to exploit Turkey's predicament. The alliance provided for partitioning northern and central Macedonia, with Serbia
taking the region north and west of the Shar Mountain, and Bulgaria
the area south and east of a line from Mount Golem on the Bulgarian
border to Lake Ohrid. The "contested zone" in-between was to be
divided after the war or, in case of deadlock, at the discretion of the
Russian emperor acting as arbiter. Hastily, Bulgaria also concluded
an alliance with Greece that omitted the question of their future
frontier in Macedonia and Thrace, and undertook to finance much of

the war effort of Montenegro, the fourth member of the Balkan League.[14]

In the war that began in October 1912, geography determined who fought where. It fell to Bulgaria to take on the main Turkish forces in eastern Thrace, whereas Serbia, Greece, and Montenegro moved to subdue the Turkish garrisons in Macedonia. Seized by a spirit of proving its mettle and avenging five centuries of oppression, the Bulgarian army scored spectacular victories in a few weeks on the way to Constantinople, which Ferdinand—like Bulgarian medieval tsars—dreamed of conquering. However, Macedonia, the main prize for which the war was fought, fell into Serbian and Greek hands. When some Bulgarian units reached Salonika, they found the city firmly under Greek control. The peace conference in London (May 1913) became deadlocked, with Bulgaria insisting on observance of the treaties, including arbitration by the Russian emperor, while Serbia and Greece demanded that occupation should determine possession. The Treaty of London thus incorporated only one point of agreement: that the boundary of Turkey in Europe should run from Enos on the Aegean Sea to Midia on the Black Sea and, therefore, give Adrianople to Bulgaria.

Since the Concert of Europe, then drawing its last breath in the face of a general war, refused to mediate, Bulgaria had three choices: swallowing the loss of most of Macedonia, pressing for Russian arbitration, or cutting the proverbial Gordian knot by the sword. The new cabinet of Stoian Danev, a Russophile, favored the second choice, but with Serbia and Greece signing an alliance against Bulgaria and the army becoming increasingly restive, Ferdinand and his deputy as commander in chief, General Mikhail Savov, turned to the third. When Russia finally summoned the Balkan allies to St. Petersburg, Ferdinand and Savov ordered (June 29) an attack on the Serbian and Greek positions without a declaration of war to make, as Savov later claimed, a "political demonstration" with an "educational meaning."[15] Within a month this "criminal folly," as Geshov characterized it, led to utter disaster. Seizing the opportunity to gain territory, Romania invaded from the north and threatened to take Sofia, while Turkey reopened hostilities and quickly took Adrianople. Embattled on all sides, Bulgaria surrendered to her Christian enemies in Bucharest and to Turkey in Constantinople.

To secure justice for Bulgaria, American missionaries led by James F. Clarke, a "missionary for fifty-four years," addressed a memorandum to Sir Edward Grey and other leaders of the Concert of Europe, indicating that "after years of acquaintance with Macedonia, either through residence or travel or both, mingling with the people and living in their homes," they were convinced that "the great bulk of the population in the region which we have indicated as the Macedonian field of our work, is Bulgarian in origin, language, and customs, and forms an integral part of the Bulgarian nation."[16] The missionaries also requested that provision be made "to guarantee full religious liberty for all . . . and to insure the same freedom to carry on religious and educational work which has been enjoyed in the past," since Serbia and especially Greece had records of hostility toward the missionaries' activities. The request, backed by a note of the American government,[17] was practically identical with the position Bulgaria took that the peace treaty should bind all parties to "recognize in their newly-annexed territory the autonomy of religious communities and the freedom of schools."[18]

The peace treaty of Bucharest (August 10, 1913) ignored these pleas and divided most of Macedonia between Serbia and Greece, while Bulgaria received only a small adjacent part known as the Pirin region. On the argument of territorial balance in the peninsula, Romania took Bulgaria's southern Dobrudja, while Bulgaria was allowed to annex Aegean (western) Thrace from the Mesta estuary to a line east to be determined by the Bulgarian-Turkish peace treaty. The latter restored the old boundary and used the lower Maritsa River as the boundary of western Thrace.

The nation was stunned. Within a month, triumphs and world acclaim had turned into utter defeat and humiliation. Macedonia, as Bulgarians thought of it, was no longer under a disintegrating empire but in the hands of assertive states bent on driving Bulgarian influence from the parts they had seized. In southern Dobrudja and eastern Thrace, Romania and Turkey had the same objective, and the gain of the coastline on the Aegean with an undeveloped port at Dedeagach and mixed population could hardly be seen as compensation for the 66,000 lives Bulgaria lost in the wars. Internationally, Bulgaria had ended up friendless, despite the injustices it had suffered;[19] even Russia, the liberator of 1878, had sided with Romania and Serbia.

Ferdinand, defeated and discredited as master diplomat and strategist, muttered on occasion: "my vengeance shall be terrible" and demobilized the army with the ominous words that it must "fold the flags for better times." The Agrarians and the Socialists, who gained new support for opposing Ferdinand, called for the National Assembly to investigate him and the wartime cabinets and bring those responsible for "the national catastrophe" to trial, but the constitutional provision making the ministers, not the monarch, responsible for all decisions saved Ferdinand from investigation. Others, mostly nationalists, chauvinists and refugees from Macedonia, Dobrudja and Thrace, clamored for retaliation against the treacherous neighbors at the first opportunity.

Ferdinand's choice of a new prime minister was Vasil Radoslavov, an admirer of Austria and Germany, where he had received his education in law. The two set out to secure a parliamentary majority, repair the damage to the economy (Bulgaria had mobilized 598,000 men, or almost all of its productive work force), re-equip the army, and refurbish Ferdinand's image. One of the gambits they pursued involved the United States.

When a decade earlier Ferdinand first received an American diplomat accredited to him,[20] he stressed the "great importance" of the new contacts "to advance commercial and industrial relations between the two countries."[21] In 1904, Bulgaria made a major effort at the World Exposition in St. Louis, Missouri, to show what it could sell America. Trade, consisting largely of Bulgarian rose oil and tobacco for American farm implements, grew to the point of exceeding Bulgaria's trade with Russia or neighboring Serbia, but Bulgaria was initially disinclined to open a legation or a consulate, presumably for reasons of economy, and Bulgarian-American trade never reached its full potential.

In the wake of the debacle in 1913, however, the opportunities America presented took hold of Ferdinand's imagination. When he announced the opening of a legation in Washington, Ferdinand spoke grandly of "the noble and generous United States" and "its constant philanthropy." His choice of minister could not have been more pleasing to Americans. Stefan Panaretov was one of the early graduates of Robert College and had a prestigious career there as professor of Bulgarian language and literature. The president of the board of trustees, Cleveland H. Dodge, a classmate of President Wilson at Princeton, introduced him to Wilson and to his Secretary of State, William Jennings Bryan, in glowing terms, and throughout his eleven years in Washington Panaretov enjoyed singular respect.

Ferdinand's second wife, Queen Eleanora, was a Protestant with close ties to the American missionaries—especially the Clarke family—and an abiding commitment to charitable work. One of her projects was to train nurses under the auspices of the Red Cross, and she wished to visit the United States for that purpose. Ferdinand turned her project into a grand scheme to restore his image as the astute diplomat. Its centerpiece was to be an imposing visit by the couple and their sons, Boris and Kiril, with a large entourage of "notables," to establish political, financial, commercial, and cultural contacts.

The planned visit, however, was declined by the United States since American interests did not warrant it. Ferdinand also hoped to visit the world exposition in San Francisco, which was to mark the completion of the Panama Canal, but the outbreak of World War I led to cancellation. A proposal to link Dedeagach and New York by steamship service also fell through. Feelers to obtain a large loan in the United States, which would have been free from the political strings usually attached to loans from European countries, were slow to produce results, and when parallel negotiations with a consortium of European banks led by the German Disconto-Gesellschaft ended in agreement on July 12, 1914, Bulgaria took a loan of 500 million francs tying her to Germany.[22]

The outbreak of World War I, beginning in effect as a third Balkan war between Serbia and Austria, raised for Bulgarian nationalists the prospect of a *revanche* over Macedonia, but Bulgaria was in no condition to attack Serbia and the government proclaimed "strict neutrality" in the conflict. The involvement of Turkey in the war against Russia, France, and Britain created a different prospect of evening the score in Thrace. It was this possibility and its attendant problems that Bulgaria faced in 1915.

Bulgaria's hand was first forced by the Dardanelles campaign, Winston Churchill's pet project as First Lord of the Admiralty. Launched in February 1915 by British and French naval forces, it aimed at opening the Black Sea Straits to deliver aid to their flagging Russian ally, knock Turkey out of the war, and keep the other Balkan states from joining the Central Powers. It was a brilliant strategy lacking the military power necessary to see it through. As the naval operation bogged down, it was realized that land forces were needed to reach Constantinople and assure the success of the campaign. Only Bulgaria could provide them.

Even before the failure of the naval operation, Britain began courting Bulgaria by offering Turkish Thrace and Serbian Macedonia beyond the contested zone if Bulgaria would join the Allies. The pressure and the bidding mounted in the summer of 1915—"the Bulgarian summer," as a French author called it. In July, Churchill himself argued that the Allies must win Bulgaria over immediately since she was strong, her army was ready, and her territorial claims were just.[23] However, beyond Turkish Thrace the Allies had to be circumspect about promises at the expense of Serbia, whom they were fighting to protect, or Greece and Romania, whom they wanted to woo to the Allied camp. The Central Powers, on the other hand, were in a position to offer Bulgaria all of Serbian-held Macedonia, the territories Bulgaria wanted from Greece and Romania if and when they went over to the Allies, and even border rectifications in Turkish Thrace.

It was this array of factors—the nationalist obsession with Macedonia and the so-called San Stefano Bulgaria, Ferdinand's ties to Germany and Austria, Radoslavov's orientation, and the pressure from the IMRO and other irredentist refugee organizations in Sofia— that was behind the secret decision of Ferdinand and Radoslavov to ally Bulgaria with the Central Powers. The secret treaties were signed on September 6, 1915, committing Bulgaria to attack Serbia within thirty-five days.[24]

Since the mobilization could not be kept secret, on September 17 Ferdinand met with leaders of the opposition including Geshov, Danev, the head of the Democratic party, Alexander Malinov, and Stamboliiski. Stamboliiski, the peasant tribune, minced no words. Demanding adherence to strict neutrality, he warned Ferdinand that his people's faith in him had been shaken and destroyed and that he had been fortunate to escape punishment for the debacle in 1913. "If this criminal act is repeated," Stamboliiski said, "we, the members of the Agrarian Union, will not stand between you and the people's wrath. We will become its instrument to execute its severe but just decision." The exchange, long and sharp, was ended by Ferdinand, saying "Don't worry about my head. I am old. Think of your own which is still young."[25] Stamboliiski promptly published the exchange, leading to his trial by a military court and a death sentence, commuted by Ferdinand to life imprisonment.

Bulgaria's intervention doomed Serbia as well as the Dardanelles campaign. Churchill resigned in disgrace and it was no wonder that later, in his account *The World Crisis* (1923–1929), he blamed Bulgaria not only for that fiasco but also for the Russian revolution— which he thought Allied assistance to Russia through the Straits might have prevented—and for the consequences of that revolution. In December 1915, the Allies began evacuating their forces to Salonika, which became the base for opening a front in Macedonia.

The defeat of Serbia was swift. Caught in a vise, the Serbian army retreated to Kosovo and across the snow-covered mountains of Montenegro and Albania to Adriatic ports from which the Allies helped its remnants reach Corfu. The Bulgarian army overran eastern Serbia and Macedonia to the Greek border: its troops, feeling that their job was done, settled at the frontline to wait for the end of the war. The war, however, kept expanding and the Allies kept building up their forces in Greek Macedonia.

In August 1916, Romania joined the Allies on the prospect of gaining Transylvania and other parts of Austria-Hungary. The defeat of Romania would take longer. Bulgaria had to transfer forces from Macedonia and, entering across the border in Dobrudja and the Danube, the Bulgarians, converging with the Austrians and the Germans, reached Bucharest and the delta of the Danube in December. Along the way in Dobrudja they had to fight, for the first time, Russian units coming to help the Romanians.

The regime which the Germans imposed in Dobrudja aroused deep resentment even among Bulgarian Germanophiles. To Bulgarians Dobrudja was the cradle of the nation since Khan Asparukh founded a state there in the seventh century. In 1870 it was acknowledged without question to be part of the nation's religious domain. The Germans, ignoring these sensibilities, declared it a condominium (joint possession) and even let Romanian religious and civil authorities function in some areas. Radoslavov's government strongly objected, but the condominium remained in place, and under the terms of the peace treaty which Romania accepted in May 1918, Bulgaria received only the part of Dobrudja which Romania had taken in 1913, with minor additions, while the rest to the delta formally became a German-Austrian-Turkish-Bulgarian possession.[26]

The decisive turn in the war was America's entry in 1917. Its declaration of war on April 6 was limited to Germany, the only Central Power the United States had clashed with (over submarine warfare in the Atlantic). The U.S. government thus expected to fight only on the western front. Debates in and out of Congress about expanding the war to Germany's allies continued throughout the year, but the issue did not reach the point of decision until the beginning of December when it appeared that American troops might have to fight Austrians on Italy's flagging front. Germany pressed its allies to declare war on the United States or at least to sever relations, but while Austria and Turkey did withdraw their diplomats from Washington, Bulgaria refused to do so on the ground that its treaty with Germany required it to render assistance only if Germany were attacked by a country adjoining Bulgaria.[27]

From the time they allied Bulgaria to Germany, Ferdinand and Radoslavov had made a consistent effort to assure the United States that "the relations of perfect friendship" would be kept intact. The channels of communication, however, presented increasing difficulties. The American minister to Bulgaria, Charles J. Vopicka, was also minister to Serbia and Romania. He resided in Bucharest, and when Romania collapsed he became isolated from Sofia. In Sofia the United States had only a consul-general, Dominic I. Murphy, a veteran diplomat, who communicated with Washington via Switzerland. In Washington, Panaretov surrendered his code book to the Department of State to avoid charges of being a spy for Germany and communicated with Sofia only through official American channels. He was nevertheless the object of charges of espionage by Serbian and Greek propagandists as well as by American critics of Wilson's policies, especially after he published a brochure in 1917, under the pseudonym "Historicus," entitled *Bulgaria and Her Neighbors*, explaining Bulgaria's claims and concluding that she had a stronger claim to Macedonia than France did to Alsace-Lorraine.[28]

In preparing his message to Congress to declare war on Austria, President Wilson also included the "Teutonic allies," Turkey and Bulgaria, in response to demands from his own party as well as from leading Republicans, such as Senator Henry Cabot Lodge and Theodore Roosevelt. Particularly influential was Roosevelt who declared in one of his editorials: "I was formerly a staunch champion of Bulgaria, and would be again if she returned to her senses. But she now serves the devil, and shame be upon us if we do not treat her accordingly. No one can doubt that the Bulgarian Legation is an agency for German spies in this country."[29]

The prospect of war with Turkey and Bulgaria, however, aroused strong opposition from the leaders of missionary and educational organizations in Boston and Washington. They felt that the achievements of decades of work might be dissipated unnecessarily, particularly since American forces were not likely to be used in those areas. It was Cleveland Dodge who privately approached Wilson, and the missionaries' arguments changed Wilson's mind. His message to Congress requested a declaration of war only on Austria, indicating that Turkey and Bulgaria did not "yet stand in the direct path of our necessary action" and that "we should go only where immediate and practical considerations lead us and not heed any others."

In support, the secretary of state, Robert Lansing, submitted a lengthy memorandum pointing out with respect to Bulgaria that the "wisdom of a declaration of war" was "even more doubtful" than taking such a step against Turkey. The Bulgarians had "always been extremely friendly toward the United States. Robert College at Constantinople is often referred to by Bulgarians as 'the cradle of Bulgarian Liberty.' The Bulgarian interest in this war is a purely local one, the Bulgarians are merely fighting out their old feud with the Serbians. The Bulgarians not only have no interest in the German plans for world conquests but, on the contrary, they are already beginning to appreciate the danger of German domination." As to the charges that Panaretov served as a spy for Germany, Lansing stressed that he had "no communication whatsoever with his own Government nor with any of the Bulgarian representatives in neutral countries. He has no pouch service, and cipher messages are not permitted to be exchanged by him with anyone."[30]

In Bulgaria, Ferdinand and Radoslavov continued to resist German and Austrian pressure to declare war on the United States or, as Turkey had done, at least sever relations. Radoslavov adamantly linked the issue to Germany's imposition of the condominium in Dobrudja and even raised the threat that Bulgaria might leave the alliance. His last success in the alliance was the participation in the conclusion of the Brest-Litovsk peace treaty with Soviet Russia in March 1918, which opened the possibility of Bulgaria becoming a partner in another quadripartite condominium in the Caucasus.[31]

The replacement of Radoslavov by Alexander Malinov as head and foreign minister of an Entente-oriented cabinet in June 1918, showed that even Ferdinand was willing to make a separate peace. The Wilsonian program of peace without victors and vanquished, based on the principles of justice and self-determination in the Fourteen Points, raised the hope that Bulgaria could secure recognition of her just claims in advance of the general peace conference. The military collapse, however, came first. Ill-supplied and demoralized, the troops on the Macedonian front faced a massive Allied concentration of men and materiel, and when the expected offensive began on September 15, the result was a wide breakthrough at Dobro Pole within three days. Within another three to four days the troops were in general retreat, in fact a rout, many of them becoming prisoners of war, others fleeing toward Kiustendil, the army's general headquarters which they seized, and Sofia.

On September 25 in Sofia, Ferdinand and Malinov's government decided to seek an armistice with the Allies. As preparations were being made to defend the capital, Stamboliiski and his associate, Raiko Daskalov, were released from prison in the hope that they would control the mutinous peasant soldiers. Stamboliiski was taken to see Ferdinand who, now a supplicant, asked him to use his prestige to stop the disintegration of the army, and expressed fear for his own safety. Before going to the rebellious troops Stamboliiski also saw Blagoev in order to gain the cooperation of the Narrow Socialists, whose influence had grown markedly. He offered to accept their program and to form a joint government with the only proviso being that the peasants should retain the right of private property. Blagoev, adhering to the party line that the class struggle was against all other classes and that the property-minded peasantry was in effect bourgeois, categorically refused.[32]

Daskalov joined the troops and at Radomir, proclaiming the so-called Radomir Republic, prepared to march on Sofia. From Kiustendil Stamboliiski agreed and returned to the capital to persuade the government to yield power peacefully but, when threatened again with imprisonment, he went into hiding. Daskalov's force of about 8,000 soldiers was repulsed at the Vladaia pass south of Sofia by General Alexander Protogerov, a leader of the IMRO, commanding elements of the Sofia garrison, IMRO volunteers, and German troops being transferred from the Crimea to the Macedonian front. By October 2, the Radomir Republic was no more.

In the meantime, Malinov's government, persuading the American consul-general Murphy to act as intermediary, arranged an armistice with the Allies. Enjoying great popularity not only as representative of America but also as a kindhearted man, *diado* (grandfather) Murphy, as he was affectionately called, agreed to lead the Bulgarian emissaries across the Allied frontline to Salonika at some risk to his person as well as to his position, since he undertook the mission without prior authorization.[33]

The terms of the armistice on December 29, dictated by the French and the British, were harsh: Bulgaria was required to withdraw at once from the Greek and Serbian territories it held; the army was to be demobilized except for units needed for defense against Turkey and the German-Austrian forces in Dobrudja; all units west of the Skoplje meridian were to surrender as prisoners of war, to be used as laborers until peace was concluded; and German and Austrian troops, diplomats, and civilians were to leave Bulgaria within four weeks. Secret clauses provided for temporary Allied occupation of Bulgarian areas, except Sofia, as well as for use of Bulgaria's railroads, ports, and communications.

The second military debacle, longer in the making than the first, was much more devastating in both its immediate and its longterm consequences. It deeply affected the nation's morale and self-confidence, discredited the so-called national ideals and the goal of "San Stefano Bulgaria" among broad segments of the people, and radicalized political life. The economy was on the brink of collapse, brought there by the mobilization of nearly 850,000 men, deliveries of foodstuffs to Germany and Austria, profiteering, and rampant inflation. Hundreds of thousands of war casualties and refugees from the areas Bulgaria lost were simply beyond help. As the winter of 1918 approached, the country faced starvation, narrowly averted by food shipments from the American Relief Administration and paid for by credits against Bulgaria's gold reserves.

His life at risk and the Allies set against him, Ferdinand abdicated on October 3 in favor of his son Boris and left for Germany by train, guarded by German troops. A new government of national unity headed by Teodor Teodorov of the People's party included Stamboliiski and other Agrarians, as well as Broad Socialists. In August 1919 it held parliamentary elections to determine the will of the nation. The vote was overwhelmingly in favor of the radical parties. The Agrarians won eighty-five seats (180,648 votes), the Narrow Socialists ("Communists" since joining Lenin's Communist International, or Comintern, in March) forty-seven seats (118,671 votes), and the Broad Socialists thirty-six seats (82,826 votes). The strongest of the so-called bourgeois parties, the Democrats, gained only twenty-eight seats (65,267 votes).

Stamboliiski, commanding only 85 seats out of 233 in the National Assembly, needed a coalition to govern. The communists, viewing the situation through the prism of the events in Russia, saw Stamboliiski as a Bulgarian Kerensky. The Broad Socialists, on the other hand, demanded such a high price for joining the coalition (control of the army, police, and other departments) that Stamboliiski turned to the parties on the right. As the prime minister of a shaky coalition he left for France to sign the peace treaty the Allies had formulated for Bulgaria.

The American position on post-war Europe was first formulated by the Inquiry, the group of experts who produced the basis for the Fourteen Points and advised Wilson at the Paris peace conference.[34] With regard to the Balkans, the Fourteen Points stipulated that the arbitrary treaty of Bucharest should be set aside and Bulgaria should receive southern Dobrudja, eastern Thrace to the Enos-Midia line, and western Thrace including the developed port of Kavalla and the mouth of the Struma River, while the question of frontiers in Macedonia should be further studied. This was the thinking behind Point Eleven, which declared in a general formula that Balkan borders should be determined "by friendly counsel along historically established lines of allegiance and nationality." The Balkan allies of the

Entente attacked it for its implications, but Bulgaria welcomed it and asked that the American president "be the arbiter of the Balkans."[35]

The course the Paris peace conference took, however, stymied Bulgarian hopes and aspirations. It took up first the most important and the most difficult treaty with Germany, which was to set the pattern for the remaining treaties, and in the negotiating battles of the Council of Four Wilson was blocked by the leaders of France, Britain, and Italy who wanted a punitive peace and all the gains of victory for themselves and their friends. The resulting harsh *Diktat,* as the German representatives at Versailles called it, was repudiated, together with the plan for a League of Nations, by the American Senate. The United States slid into isolationism. So, by November 1919, when Stamboliiski signed the Treaty of Neuilly, the United States, the only power that Bulgarians felt could secure justice for their claims, had dropped out of the peacemaking process.

The treaty that resulted was punitive: in addition to the territories lost in 1913, Bulgaria ceded western Thrace to the Allies (who assigned it in 1923 to Greece, despite their promise to secure to Bulgaria an economic outlet to the Aegean Sea). Bulgaria also lost areas along the Serbian border. Reparations were set at 2.25 billion gold francs, an amount astronomical if not absurd for a small and ruined country, to be paid in thirty-seven years at five percent interest; thousands of head of livestock and a huge amount of coal, Bulgaria's only natural resource, were to be delivered to Serbia (now part of the Serb-Croat-Slovene kingdom, later called Yugoslavia), Greece, and Romania; and the Bulgarian army was to be limited to 20,000 volunteers. The treaty further required Bulgaria to accept any Allied terms for "mutual and voluntary emigration of minorities" as an obvious substitute for drawing the borders on the basis of ethnic self-determination, with a Greek-Bulgarian convention ready for signature.[36] Stamboliiski, having no say or choice, signed both. Convinced that such a treaty could not escape revision, he declared that Bulgaria intended to be a trustworthy partner for peace. He then quickly returned home to face staggering domestic problems.

To say that the problems were staggering is to understate them, but Stamboliiski had little doubt that he could handle them. At forty, his physical and mental powers were yet to be tapped. He had begun in 1909 to formulate an indigenous ideology of "Agrarianism" as a third way between capitalism and Marxism with his *Politicheski partii ili suslovni organizatsii?* (Political parties or estatist organizations?) and other writings. He was proud that it was a "homegrown" product and stressed time and again that its essence was *narodovlastie* (democracy) as developed in "the revolutions in England, America, France, and Russia."[37] However, he was adamantly opposed to Lenin's policies and the views of the Bulgarian Communists, particularly on the "peasant question." In foreign policy he was for a "Green" (peasant) International to counter Lenin's Red International and for the closest possible ties with Yugoslavia, a Balkan federation, and orientation to the European democracies, as well as to the United States, which he and the king wished to visit.[38]

Stamboliiski's ideas and policies gained him powerful enemies on the left and on the right. First the Communists went on the attack, launching a series of strikes that climaxed in a massive one-week walkout of transport and communications workers in December. Stamboliiski responded by militarizing the facilities, ordering his minister of internal affairs (police), Alexander Dimitrov, to use force when necessary, and bringing out the Agrarian Orange Guard, peasant units armed with clubs (*tsepenitsi*) and controlled by the local Agrarian organizations (*druzhbi*), to meet any threat to his government. The strike was defeated, but the Communists remained locked in a political war with the Agrarians. Their younger leaders, Vasil Kolarov (a lawyer educated in Switzerland and groomed by Blagoev as his successor), Georgi Dimitrov (a printer who rose in the labor movement in Sofia),[39] and others viciously assailed Stamboliiski in their press and the National Assembly, while he threatened mockingly on occasion to ship them to the workers' paradise. Their ties to Soviet Russia, it should be noted, were not simply ideological; emissaries traveled regularly and clandestinely to Moscow, and in 1922 the Bolsheviks entrusted Kolarov with the crucial job of general secretary of the Comintern, while Dimitrov was appointed member of the Executive Bureau of the Profintern, the Comintern's arm for the international labor movement.

To put through his program serving the peasants' interests Stamboliiski held new elections in March 1920, in the hope of receiving a mandate to form a purely Agrarian government. The results came close to what he wanted. The Agrarians won 110 seats (349,212 votes) out of the total of 229, with the Communists coming second (fifty-one seats and 184,616 votes) and the Democrats third (twenty-three seats and 91,177 votes). Invalidation of thirteen seats on the basis of a strict interpretation of the election law gave him the majority he needed to govern.

The dozens of reforms Stamboliiski proposed were mainly intended to modernize the countryside and make Bulgaria a "model agricultural state" in a projected twenty years of Agrarian rule. The cities, which he sometimes denounced as inhabited by "parasites," had a marginal place in his vision; in a memorable utterance he described Sofia as a "Sodom and Gomorrah" of wickedness and corruption. He wanted the bureaucracy—including the diplomatic service—cut to a minimum, government pensions reduced or eliminated, and the taxation system altered to free the peasants from supporting the town folk. His ideas for changes even extended to the alphabet and spelling, which he wanted simplified in order to promote literacy. This attempt brought him into a nasty fight with traditionalist scholars at the University of Sofia and the Bulgarian Academy of Sciences. Politically, he envisaged an end of the existing party system and a democratic rule of the majority of the nation—the peasantry—allied with other strata such as the workers and the artisans. He remained in favor of a republic; but since in this as in other matters the views of the Allies had to be considered, he left Boris on the throne. The young, timid, and uneducated monarch seemed content with the role of a figurehead. In the political system Stamboliiski planned, Boris would be unable to build the personal regime Ferdinand had, and the Agrarians would have the power to defang the "poisonous snake" which by nature, he was convinced, the king was.[40]

Since Stamboliiski ruled not twenty but only three more years, most of his reforms were aborted. He was violently overthrown in 1923. One of those reforms that endured was an ingenious compulsory labor service that circumvented the limitations of the peace treaty and was adopted later for the same purposes by Hitler in Germany. In foreign affairs, he undertook a one-hundred-day tour of European capitals to break Bulgaria's diplomatic isolation, but the results were meager. He had little success obtaining relief on the reparations question or organizing an effective "Green International" in Eastern Europe. Improvement of Bulgarian-Serbian relations being his top priority, he sent his closest associate and minister of police, Alexander Dimitrov, to Belgrade to assure the prime minister, Nikola Pašić, that Bulgaria was not behind the terrorist activities in "South Serbia" (Serbian Macedonia) and would take strong measures against IMRO leaders and elements in Bulgaria. As a result Dimitrov received a death sentence from the IMRO's triumvirate (Todor Alexandrov, General Protogerov, and Petur Chaulev) operating underground, and was assassinated in October 1921, near Kiustendil. Undeterred, Stamboliiski pressed on with his efforts toward a Serbian-Bulgarian reconciliation and in 1922 paid an official visit to Belgrade; for the resulting agreement signed at Niš in March 1923, he, too, received a death sentence from the IMRO. His last trip abroad was to attend the Lausanne conference called to settle the Greek-Turkish war and issues left unresolved by the aborted peace treaty with Turkey in 1920. He argued strenuously for the Allies to honor their promise of an economic outlet for Bulgaria to the Aegean, but they gave western Thrace to Greece.

Returning empty-handed, Stamboliiski faced a formidable array of enemies on both sides of the political spectrum, but boldly moved to secure Agrarian rule and carry out his program to remake Bulgaria. Changes in the electoral system to end proportional representation and reintroduce single constituency slates in the new parliamentary elections in April 1923 gave the Agrarians 212 seats (52.7 percent of the vote), the Communists 16 (18.9 percent), and the rightist Constitutional Bloc 14 (15.5 percent of the vote). With such a majority he laid out plans to change the constitution, end the party system, and, as rumor had it, abolish the monarchy.

On the left, beaten in the transport strike and outmaneuvered in the elections, the Communists were actually the lesser threat, especially since they were still led by the aged Blagoev (who had never planned a revolution). On the right, however, a diverse assortment of forces had emerged, united by the will to overthrow the hated Agrarians: the IMRO and the refugees from the "lost territories"; a Military League of officers still in the army or retired under the requirements of the peace treaty; nationalists, and royalists from other social strata; urban classes threatened in their interests; and the leaders of opposition parties threatened with extinction. A large number of them were in fact under investigation as members of the 1912 through 1918 war cabinets responsible for the two debacles; the trial of the Radoslavov cabinet had ended on March 31, 1923, with prison sentences from ten years to life, and the trials of the Geshov, Danev, and Malinov cabinets were imminent. Last but not least, there were some 36,000 Russian refugees from the civil war in the Ukraine, most of them armed, who also saw Stamboliiski as another Kerensky and plotted to overthrow him.

The country was rife with rumors of plots, particularly in the army; Stamboliiski still felt secure because of his broad peasant base of support. He took inadequate and ill-advised steps to muster the forces needed to deal with the far-flung network of enemies. He called on the Orange Guard to be ready for local action and, reshuffling his cabinet, appointed two young and inexperienced men, Khristo Stoianov and Konstantin Muraviev (thirty-one and thirty years old, respectively), to head the crucial ministries of the interior (police) and the army.

The fatal blow to Stamboliiski and the Agrarian regime came from the right in 1923. The plotters struck in the early hours of June 9 and promptly were made secure on the left, as the Communists proclaimed neutrality in the looming civil war between their class enemies. Army units, IMRO elements, and armed civilians took Sofia without resistance. Stamboliiski, then in his home village near Pazardzhik, tried to organize a local force but was captured, tortured—his right hand was hacked off "for signing the Niš agreement"—and stabbed repeatedly. His head was cut off, allegedly to present to King Boris. Sporadic peasant resistance was overcome within a week, and liquidations and murders of Stamboliiski supporters continued long thereafter.

The bloody overthrow of the peasant government and the vicious killing of Stamboliiski dug a chasm in Bulgarian political life that remained unbridged, some seventy years later. It also squelched the authentic native effort, generated and shaped by Stamboliiski, to develop a new political, economic, and social system better suited to the interests of the peasants, the majority of the nation, than were the alternative systems of the time—"bourgeois" democracy cum unchecked private enterprise, Bolshevism, or fascism. The responsibility for this radical turn in the nation's life with the bloodshed that accompanied it was quite clear, except for the role of the king. The chief plotters were the leaders of the Military League, Damian Velchev, Kimon Georgiev, Ivan Vulkov, and others, acting in conjunction with IMRO elements and the civilian politicians who made up the new government of Alexander Tsankov. Threatened by the constitutional changes Stamboliiski planned for the monarchy, Boris obviously had a stake in the outcome of the political struggle. It seemed clear in the view of Agrarians and others, that his part in the plot— played out through officers in his entourage connected with the Military League and the IMRO—was crucial.

The Tsankov government, a coalition calling itself the "Democratic Alliance," was an odd mixture. Tsankov himself was a professor of political economy and an early advocate of the Bulgarian-Serbian customs union, but like many socialists after World War I, had evolved from socialism toward fascism and nationalism. He and his foreign minister, Khristo Kalfov, an officer from the king's entourage, turned to Mussolini's Italy, which was in search of partners to isolate and dismantle Yugoslavia. General Ivan Vulkov, a confidant of Boris as well as of IMRO leaders, took the ministry of war. The most intriguing personality was the minister of communications, Dimo Kazasov, an agile politician with a facile pen who had also moved from socialism toward fascism.

The bloody overthrow of the Agrarian regime and the wave of terror that followed it created a situation which the leaders of the Comintern in Moscow decided to exploit in their pursuit of world revolution. An added impetus was the fact that Vasil Kolarov, general secretary of the Comintern and heir-apparent to Blagoev in the leadership of the Bulgarian Communist party, was in an ideal position to direct the venture. He was swiftly dispatched to Bulgaria to change Blagoev's line of neutrality and passivity in the struggle between the Agrarians and their enemies and to launch an uprising as soon as possible, based on an alliance (a "united front," in Lenin's formulation) of workers and peasants, for the purpose of establishing a Bolshevik regime in the country. It was a tall order, given the antagonism between the Communists and Agrarians and the lack of planning for an insurrection. Party leaders, particularly the secretary, Todor Lukanov, opposed the Comintern line as promising only failure and destruction of the party, but Kolarov, aided by Georgi Dimitrov and others, prevailed with a decision in August to launch the uprising the following month.[41] The government, anticipating what was to come, enacted a draconian Law on the Defense of the State, which provided for stern measures against any form of subversion.

Ill-prepared, the September uprising sputtered without coordination in several areas even before the appointed time. It was more effective in northwest Bulgaria, near the Yugoslav border, where Kolarov and Dimitrov took charge in the hope of converging with insurgents on Sofia. The capital and other major urban centers, however, remained quiet, despite the Communists' claims of strength in the cities. Within four days the uprising was over and Kolarov and Dimitrov fled, with hundreds of followers, to Yugoslavia. Casualties were never confirmed, but the Communists accepted the figure of 5,000 for the uprising and the mop-up operations after it.[42] The shoddy venture shattered the organizational structure and the morale of the party and left it torn by the questions of who bore the blame and which course it was to take after the fiasco. The government, invoking the Law on the Defense of the State, had the party judicially declared outside the law in January 1924. It remained in legal limbo until 1944.

The idea of a united front of Agrarians and Communists against Tsankov's "Fascist" regime was pursued for a while by their leaders abroad. Since the Communists commanded Soviet resources and the Agrarians had no such backing, Dimitrov and Kolarov sought to dictate the conditions for such collaboration, including Communist control of the ministries of internal affairs (police), war, and communications in a future government of workers and peasants. In negotiations at Vienna and Moscow in January 1924, however, the Agrarians turned these conditions down, and the idea of collaboration was not revived until World War II.[43]

With the idea of Communist-Agrarian revolution in Bulgaria ending in failure, the Comintern turned to the IMRO in search of allies in the Balkans. After World War I the IMRO entered a period of crisis that ended in its disintegration in 1934. Its objective of liberating Macedonia from foreign rule no longer meant fighting against a decayed Ottoman empire condemned by the West; now it meant fighting against two vigorous Balkan states determined to keep the fruits of their victories and backed by the international coalition of the Western powers. Moreover, the broad mass of the Bulgarian people had become alienated from "the cause of Macedonia" in the wake of the catastrophes of 1913 and 1918, and was even hostile to the restless refugees and the risks and burdens they put on the country. Even Tsankov's government found it necessary to reaffirm Stamboliiski's pledge at Niš that Bulgaria would keep IMRO guerrillas from crossing the border to commit terrorist activities in Yugoslav Macedonia.

Stymied and increasingly divided by what direction to take, the IMRO's leaders agreed for a brief period in 1924 to tie the cause of Macedonia to the chariot of world revolution driven by the Comintern. The agreement was negotiated in Vienna by Chaulev and others from the IMRO's left wing, signed by Alexandrov and Protogerov, and publicized in the so-called May Manifesto setting forth the IMRO's new direction and goals. In essence, the Macedonian problem was to be resolved by the revolutionary establishment of a Balkan federation of communist states, including Macedonia.[44] With such means and ends adopted by the IMRO, even the Tsankov government could not feel safe. Upon their return from Vienna Alexandrov and Protogerov were pressured to repudiate the May Manifesto, which they did, blaming Chaulev for acting on his own and forging their signatures.

In the unfolding play for high stakes, the first to pay with his life was Alexandrov, gunned down in the Pirin region in August 1924. The assassins were known, but who had sent them became a matter of speculation when they themselves were killed. Next to die was Chaulev, hunted down in Milan. Alexandrov's place on the triumvirate went to his secretary, Ivan Mikhailov, a ruthless and ambitious young man, who tested his future wife by sending her to kill another left-wing leader, Todor Panitsa, in Vienna. The assassinations set a pattern of internecine warfare—some of it gangster-style—which claimed dozens of victims. Most of them fell opposing Mikhailov's drive to assume control of the IMRO.

Outlawed and disoriented, the communists also contributed to the state of tension and violence. Apart from assassinations, local brigandage, and an attempt on the king's life, their "Military Center" conceived and carried out a grandiose scheme to assassinate a prominent leader and use his funeral service to blow up the Cathedral of Sofia and kill Boris, Tsankov, and the political and military elite that were certain to attend. The choice fell on a retired general, Kosta Georgiev; the explosion set at the start of his funeral on April 16, 1925, missed Boris, who was probably tipped off and did not arrive on time, but killed some 150 persons and wounded about 500. Tsankov and members of his cabinet escaped with minor injuries.[45]

The reprisals by the police and the army, termed "white terror" by the communists, further escalated the violence at a time when the Tsankov government required a better image to negotiate a loan in the West to finance the resettlement of refugees and other needs. Unable to achieve domestic peace, which Britain in particular demanded as a precondition for the loan, Tsankov resigned in January 1926. The new cabinet was formed by another leader of the governing coalition, Andrei Liapchev, a Macedonian known for his soft touch. His slogan was the Bulgarian equivalent of "easy does it."

In line with his stated objective of internal pacification, Liapchev relaxed repressive measures, enacted an amnesty for persons convicted under the Law on the Defense of the State, and allowed the communists to reenter political life under the guise of a Workers' party formed in February 1927. With these moves he had no difficulty in obtaining a "refugee loan" as well as a second "stabilization loan" to shore up the country's financial structure and economy. However, Liapchev was unable—his critics said unwilling—to deal with the paroxysm of IMRO murders, many in the streets of Sofia, after Mikhailov ordered the assassination of Protogerov in 1928 for alleged complicity in the death of Todor Alexandrov. Without interference from Liapchev and with assistance from fascist Italy, Mikhailov decimated the Protogerovists with gunmen recruited among the villagers in the Pirin region. There he also ran, without obstruction, a state-within-a-state, including labs for production of drugs that drew the attention of League of Nations agencies.[46]

Liapchev's five years in power witnessed new downward trends in the economy as the effects of the Great Depression began to reach Bulgaria. First to be affected by falling prices were the peasants, but in the urban centers unemployment started to parallel the mounting distress in the countryside. Under these conditions, the marriage of Boris to Giovanna ("Ioanna" in Bulgarian), one of the daughters of the Italian king, in 1930 gave Bulgarians something to cheer about.[47]

From the point of view of democratic and constitutional government, Liapchev's notable legacy was to move to free elections in June 1931, which his coalition massively lost. The winner was the "People's Bloc," composed of the Democratic party (led by Alexander Malinov and Nikola Mushanov), centrist Agrarians (led by Dimitur Gichev, Konstantin Muraviev, and Vergil Dimov and known as "Vrabcha 1," their street address in Sofia), Radicals (led by Stoian Kosturkov), Liberals, and others. As economic conditions worsened, the communist Workers' party gained thirty-one seats in the National Assembly and a majority on the city council of Sofia in 1932. The new government was headed at first by Malinov, but he yielded to Mushanov and took the speakership of the Assembly.

The economic crisis stimulated radicalism on the left and on the right, with National Socialism in Germany providing yet another model of an authoritarian approach to the deepening problems. The most noteworthy of the new rightist organizations was Tsankov's "People's Social Movement," that leaned to Nazism. An additional stimulus for rightist activism was the prospect of revision of Europe's frontiers, a plan on resurgent Germany's agenda. In the Balkans the prospect ended a promising trend of regional cooperation expressed in numerous conferences and much talk of a "Balkan Union."[48] To protect themselves against Bulgarian revisionism, Romania, Yugoslavia, Greece, and Turkey formed a Balkan pact in 1934, guaranteeing the interwar frontiers.

A curious phenomenon of this period of searching for new ways was a political circle formed by Dimo Kazasov and called *Zveno* (Link). Placing itself above partisan politics, it sought to link across party lines people from the political, intellectual, and professional elites fed up with the sterility of partisan struggles and the failure to deal with the economic and moral crises. It acquired strong support from the Military League which, taking advantage of a cabinet crisis, carried out a bloodless coup on May 19, 1934, and installed a government under Kimon Georgiev. Damian Velchev, the moving spirit behind it, stayed out of sight in order not to appear to grasp for power, and urged austerity and self-sacrifice at all levels of the new administration.

The "Nineteenth of May Government," as it was called, proclaimed a program of "social renewal" to be achieved by authoritarian rule based on Article 47 of the Turnovo constitution, which provided that in case of external or internal threat the king could issue decrees (with the cabinet taking responsibility) having the force of law. It dissolved the National Assembly, banned all political parties and activities, and surprisingly enough had no trouble disarming and liquidating the IMRO.[49] Velchev and others were in favor of establishing a republic, having come around to Stamboliiski's negative view of the king. In foreign policy "the men of May Nineteenth," despite their authoritarianism, oriented themselves toward the Western democracies, opened diplomatic contacts with the Soviet Union, and intended to pursue good relations with all Balkan neighbors.

Their rule, however, was brief. Under pressure from royalist officers in the Military League, many of whom favored alignment with Italy and Germany, Kimon Georgiev resigned in January 1935, directly playing into King Boris's plan to achieve what had eluded his father: a personal government administered through pliant officers and civilian nonentities without a political base of their own. It was a turning point in Bulgaria's twentieth-century political history.

Boris chose as prime minister the minister of war, General Pencho Zlatev, who declared in his policy statement that he was an "enemy of republicanism," that the monarchy was the only form of government suited to the Bulgarian people, and that the Bulgarian monarchy was a "state above classes and parties" maintained for "social peace."[50] To avoid the appearance of a military regime (the cabinet also had four other army officers), Boris replaced Zlatev three months later with a civilian, Andrei Toshev, who ill-advisedly announced plans for a new constitution—a political Pandora's box—that, among other reasons, led to his replacement seven months later.

Boris's new choice was his chief of staff at the palace and Toshev's foreign minister, Georgi Kioseivanov. A career diplomat intimately attuned to the ways and interests of the palace, Kioseivanov carried out the king's will for more than four years (November 1935 through February 1940), the period of the rapid reshaping of Europe by resurgent Nazi Germany. Notable events during his tenure were the trial of Velchev and other republican-minded officers, the Bulgarian-Yugoslav Pact of Eternal Friendship in 1937, and the 1938 agreement at Salonika with Bulgaria's neighbors that allowed Bulgaria to rearm. The rearmament program, largely achieved through deals with Germany, was in the hands of the minister of war (until 1938) General Khrusto Lukov, a strong-willed right-winger with political ambitions, and Prince Kiril, the king's brother.

Boris (who died in August 1943) had several meetings with Hitler—more, in fact, than any other European leader. They got along very well from the start, given Boris's ingratiating ways, his family background, and his fluency in German. Hitler afforded the king what he preferred: one-on-one discussions and commitments without interpreters or record keepers. On occasion Hitler spoke very highly of him to associates, and even after some strains developed during the war, he had nothing worse to say than that Boris had been well-schooled by his father, foxy Ferdinand, whom Hitler admired, and was a consummate fox himself.[51]

To avoid the appearance as well as the responsibility of personal rule, Boris agreed to schedule elections for parliament in 1938 which the leaders of the banned parties urged in order to normalize political life and protect the country against the kind of adventurist policies and secret commitments Boris's father perpetrated in 1913 and 1915. The elections, however, were held entirely on his terms and preserved his free hand: no one identified with the banned parties was allowed to run; the candidates, screened by the courts and faced with tight censorship, presented themselves solely as individuals; women of presumably conservative categories were enfranchised; and the 274 seats of the old parliament were reduced to the more manageable size of 160. With a dependable majority of about a hundred, made up of nationalists, jingoists, and admirers of fascist Italy and Nazi Germany, Kioseivanov continued in office.[52]

With war approaching, in July 1939, Kioseivanov paid a much-touted visit to Berlin where he assured Hitler and his foreign minister Ribbentrop that "Bulgaria was Germany's natural ally" despite the absence of formal commitments, since both had suffered injustices after the World War and sought to right the wrongs inflicted on them. Bulgaria, he said, was surrounded by neighbors who all had annexed Bulgarian territories and would attack her in the event of war. For that she needed further rearmament to fight them off until Germany could render effective aid. Hitler and Ribbentrop agreed with the need to rearm but remained aloof with regard to formal ties and territorial changes, probably in order not to complicate the negotiations for the Nazi-Soviet pact then under way. The German-Russian partnership, made public the following month, was welcomed with relief in Bulgaria since growing ties with Germany presumably could not injure Russian interests.

As Kioseivanov returned from Berlin, the president of the National Assembly, Stoicho Moshanov, left for London and Paris on what was later explained to be a private visit. Known for his leanings to the West, he became the object of special attention in both capitals and was received at the highest levels, which gave rise to speculation concerning policy clashes in Sofia. To rid himself of such personalities in parliament and strengthen the pliant majority, Boris scheduled new elections which produced, under much the same rules, the desired results. The new cabinet formed in February 1940, was headed by Professor Bogdan Filov, a renowned archaeologist and art historian, whose special qualifications were his love for Germany—where he had been educated—and his connections with German academic circles. As fate had it, Filov presided over Bulgaria's affairs until September 9, 1944, first as Boris's prime minister and, after the king's death, as the key regent.

The summer of 1940 brought the first of the territorial gains Bulgaria was to make under Germany's aegis. Acting under the terms of the secret protocol to the Nazi-Soviet pact, the Soviet Union pressed Romania to cede Bessarabia and other areas, and in the ensuing collapse of Romania its other borders were redrawn in the so-called Vienna Award to satisfy Hungary's claim to Transylvania and Bulgaria's claim to southern Dobrudja. Germany's entry into Romania to safeguard the oilfields for itself, however, brought the war to the Balkans, and when Italy launched a campaign in Greece to match Germany's latest acquisition, Bulgaria acquired an importance in the winter of 1940–1941 similar to what it had been in the summer of 1915.

The first to press Boris was Mussolini, who required help with his ill-conceived campaign through the Albanian mountains. He urged Boris to intervene and seize western Thrace, but Boris declined, citing adverse public opinion in the country. Next was Hitler, who was thrown off course by his ally's blunder and had to intervene not only to save the Axis powers from ignominy but also to protect his southern flank, including the vital Romanian oilfields, for the projected Operation Barbarossa, the invasion of Russia. Realizing that the British could soon threaten the oilfields from air bases in Greece, he ordered the planning of Operation Marita, the invasion of Greece via Romania and Bulgaria, on November 12, the very day he and Ribbentrop conferred with Soviet foreign minister Molotov in Berlin regarding the adherence of the USSR to the Tripartite Pact of Germany, Italy, and Japan.

The conference, essentially a charade by Hitler (who had made up his mind to invade the USSR), focused among other areas on Bulgaria where the Soviet Union wanted a position like that Germany had acquired in Romania and, more specifically, naval bases for eventual action against Turkey and the Bosphorus Straits. Hitler testily countered that Bulgaria and Italy would have to agree to all that beforehand. On November 17 he received Boris to tell him what had transpired and what was expected of him for the execution of Operation Marita. Boris called attention to the weather and road conditions in the Bulgarian mountains that would not permit full deployment until March and declared it of greatest importance not to be burdened by German preparations in Bulgaria until the last moment, leaving the question of the collaboration of the Bulgarian army open.

Following up on the terms for joining the Tripartite Pact, the Soviets sent Molotov's deputy, Arkadii Sobolev, to Sofia with a twelve-point proposal. Its essence was that in exchange for a mutual assistance pact, which in no way would affect "the internal regime, the sovereignty, or the independence of Bulgaria," the Soviet Union would help Bulgaria obtain Greek as well as Turkish Thrace, whereas Bulgaria would render assistance "in case there should arise a real threat to the interests of the Soviet Union in the Black Sea or in the Straits." It was "entirely possible that the Soviet Union will in this case adhere to the Three Power Pact." [53]

The Soviet hope of swaying Boris was ill-founded, given his ties to Germany, his fears of Bolshevism, and the agitation by Bulgarian communists and leftists which the "Sobolev action" set off. The offer also gave Boris an easy way out. The Bulgarian reply on November 30 indicated that Bulgaria's interests were not directly involved in the Straits question and that the pact would create a sense of "an ever present danger of war." [54] In fact, within three months Bulgaria concluded a nonaggression agreement with Turkey.

The last to press Boris was the United States. On behalf of President Roosevelt, William J. Donovan, later head of the OSS, visited Balkan capitals in early 1941. In Sofia he told Boris that America intended to see Great Britain victorious and warned him of the consequences of collaborating with the Nazis. Boris gave him the impression that things were still not settled with Germany but declined to say whether he would let Germany come through or would participate in the German operation against Greece.

The relationship with Germany was already cemented in a number of ways. Economically, Bulgaria had become, especially after the annexation of Austria, a German satellite. Cultural ties, strong since before World War I, were vastly expanded by German programs in

Bulgaria, scholarships, and visits by cultural personalities, as the celebration of the fiftieth anniversary of the establishment of the University of Sofia in particular illustrated. Nazi-like activities centered on
Professor Tsankov and General Lukov, while others had a free rein,
although Boris was not willing to share power with any of them. To
please Hitler, measures against the Jews based on the Nuremberg
laws had been officially under consideration since July 1940. In January 1941, the parliament passed and Boris promulgated a Law on the
Protection of the Nation, which was expanded and worsened by
subsequent regulations and placed the Bulgarian Jews under much the
same disabilities as had been imposed by the Nazis in Germany. The
law aroused wide protest; among other bodies, the Synod of the
Bulgarian Orthodox church declared that "we are all sons of a heav-
enly Father" and that if there were dangers to the nation, measures
should be taken against individuals and not against ethnic and religious groups.[55]

With the invasion of the Soviet Union set for May 15, Hitler rushed
to start deploying for Operation Marita. As Filov signed the Tripartite
Pact in Vienna, the German army began crossing the Danube on
March 1. As a reward Bulgaria was to receive Greek Thrace between
the Struma and Maritsa rivers after the German army overran it.
Cajoled and pressured, Yugoslavia also signed the pact on March 25,
but two days later a military coup reversed the decision, enraging
Hitler and causing him to add the destruction of Yugoslavia to Operation Marita. Attacked from several sides, Yugoslavia caved in quickly,
but in Greece it took the Germans until May 31 to overcome the last
British resistance in Crete.

By prior agreement most of the Bulgarian army was deployed on
the Turkish border to keep the German left flank safe, and Bulgarian
units did not take part in the German assault operations. On April 19
Boris went to see Hitler in Vienna, maps in hand, to receive his verdict
on what part of Yugoslavia Bulgaria was to get. Yugoslav Macedonia
was the minimum, and for good measure Hitler threw in an area on
the Morava River where Bulgaria also had claims. In Greece, beyond
western Thrace Boris wanted Salonika and parts of Greek Macedonia,
but the Germans kept the city as their Balkan headquarters and
demurred on areas west of the Struma River.[56] As their invasion
of the Soviet Union bogged down, however, they became increasingly
willing to let Bulgaria occupy additional regions in order to release
German troops for the Eastern Front.

The entry of Bulgarian forces and administrators into the "newly
liberated territories" understandably created elation at home, espe-

cially since at first no Bulgarian blood was shed. The official propaganda proclaimed the ideal of national unification to have been achieved by Boris, dubbed the "Tsar-Unifier." Trouble, however, was apparent from the start. In western Macedonia the Italians, first on the spot from Albania, claimed some areas and towns as Albanian, and relations with "the in-laws," so called because of Boris's marriage, soured. The Germans regarded the Bulgarian presence in the territories they had conquered solely as carrying out the functions of administration and policing—they retained the upper hand everywhere with regard to resources. Bulgaria's possession of these lands would be subject to the decisions of a final peace conference. As the war became global later in 1941, the analogy to what happened to Bulgaria as an ally of Germany in World War I emerged ever more threateningly.

The German failure to defeat the Soviet Union in five months as planned raised the question of help from Germany's allies. In Bulgaria's case Boris succeeded in convincing Hitler that the Bulgarian army was best used in the Balkans, to protect the Turkish flank and suppress the rising guerrilla activity in Yugoslavia and Greece. Traditional Russophilia was strong. Moreover, Bulgarians as soldiers would fight well in the Balkans where they were at home and understood the issues, but were apt to become disoriented on a faraway front. Bulgarian-Soviet diplomatic relations were thus preserved, but on November 25 Bulgaria joined the Anti-Comintern Pact which Germany regarded as a pledge to the crusade against the Soviet Union, although Japan—about to attack the United States—played down its military implications.

Pearl Harbor led Boris and Filov to commit the utter folly, which Ferdinand and Radoslavov, their predecessors as German allies, had taken care to avoid. In solidarity with Japan, Germany and Italy declared war on the United States and asked the other members of the Tripartite Pact to follow suit, although the pact provided for no such obligation. For greater effect the Bulgarian decision to declare war on America as well as Britain was submitted on December 13 to the National Assembly where a solid majority passed it without debate. To allay public concern, the declaration of war was said to be "symbolic" and without military effect, ignoring the long arm of air power that would later devastate Sofia with heavy casualties and break the nation's morale. Apologists of Boris cite German pressure, but his father was also pressured, and their evidence consists of statements of interested courtiers and ministers. In any event, he committed Bulgaria to war against "the arsenal of democracy," and at a time when Germany suffered its first and portentous defeat outside Moscow.

The end of Boris came unexpectedly in August 1943, at the age of forty-nine. The new and decisive German loss at·Stalingrad and the advance of the Allies into Italy made Bulgaria's position increasingly precarious. Stalingrad stimulated the Communists to launch an organized guerrilla movement and to establish the "Fatherland Front" coalition, which Georgi Dimitrov urged from Moscow as a wider framework. The term was simply a variant of the Popular Front against Fascism, which Dimitrov (general secretary of the Comintern after his acquittal at the Reichstag fire trial) proclaimed in 1935. The movement was gradually joined by left-wing Agrarians (led by Nikola Petkov), Social Democrats, members of Zveno and the Military League, and others who agreed to work with the communists. By September 1944, when the Red Army reached Bulgaria, the resistance movement peaked at about 10,000 members, with an additional 5,000 killed in action.[57] Compared to the Yugoslav resistance, as Tito and other Yugoslav communists pointed out, it was puny.

The Nazi plans for a final solution of the "Jewish question" extended to Bulgaria in late 1942. First to be delivered to ships at ports on the Danube were the Jews from the "new territories" in Greece and Macedonia. The operation—involving some 11,400 persons—was carried out in March 1943, without much difficulty, but the plans for deportations from the "old kingdom" aroused waves of public protest much wider and stronger than those at the enactment of the anti-Semitic law in 1941. As a result Boris sanctioned the alternative of expelling the Sofia Jews (more than half of the country's Jewish population of 48,000) to the provinces and confiscating their properties. Beset by much greater problems, the Germans did not challenge this less-than-final solution, and at the end of the war Bulgaria could say that her Jews had been saved from the Holocaust.[58]

The last time Boris met with Hitler was on August 14–15, 1943 at his headquarters in East Prussia, amid rumors that the Allies planned to land in the Balkans and that, with Italy about to surrender, Germany's satellites had begun to seek their way out of the war. As at previous meetings, no record was kept. Accounts that the meeting was stormy because Hitler suspected Boris of collusion with his father-in-law or because Boris refused to send troops to the Eastern Front have no basis in evidence.[59] Nine days after his return Boris fell ill; after four more days he died. The death certificate cited natural causes, but even though he was not known for robust health, conspiracy theories abounded that he had been poisoned by the Germans, the Soviets, the Italians, or others.

The Germans arranged through a special envoy for a smooth transition with personalities around Boris. Since his son, Simeon, was only six, a regency, consisting of Prince Kiril, Filov, and the war minister, General Nikola Mikhov, took over. The new cabinet under the minister of finance, Dobri Bozhilov, also consisted of conservative loyalists who harbored no thoughts of abandoning Germany.

Allied air raids from bases in Italy soon changed the situation in Sofia. The Bulgarian capital had little military importance, and the Allied decision to bomb it was mainly to show that the war was real, not symbolic, and to stimulate moves for surrender. Particularly shattering were the raids of January 10 and March 29–30, 1944. After the first, the government ceased to function for about a week as officials scrambled, along with tens of thousands of civilians, out of the capital for safety in villages and small towns. The second raid set the city ablaze with incendiary bombs and presaged the horrors that lay ahead if the country did not change course. However, still clinging to the hope of keeping the "new territories" and fearful of German reprisals, the regents were slow to move, appointing a new cabinet under a right-wing Agrarian, Ivan Bagrianov, only on June 1 and authorizing contacts with Americans in Istanbul.

The time to sign an armistice rapidly ran out. To save Greece from the communists, in May Churchill had proposed a division of "military responsibility" whereby the Soviet Union would, for symmetry, deal with Romania. In early June he added Bulgaria to Romania and Yugoslavia to Greece. Roosevelt reluctantly agreed, apprehensive about the emergence of postwar spheres of influence, and asked for a review of the arrangement by the three powers after a trial period of three months.[60] The division of military responsibility was disclosed by Churchill on August 2 in a statement to the House of Commons: "It seems to me that Romania must primarily make its terms with Russia whom they have so outrageously assaulted and at whose mercy they will soon lie. The same applies to Bulgaria. Thrice thrown into wars on the wrong side by a miserable set of criminal politicians, who seem to be available for their country's ruin generation after generation, three times in my life has this wretched Bulgaria subjected a peasant population to all the pangs of war and chastisement of defeat. For them also, the moment of repentance has not passed, but it is passing swiftly." He was obviously speaking with the memory of 1915 in mind.

Nevertheless, the peace talks, conducted on the Bulgarian side by Stoicho Moshanov, continued at Ankara and Cairo. Bagrianov tried to get results by proclaiming strict neutrality, determination to disarm the Germans in Bulgaria, and withdrawal of the Bulgarian army from the "new territories," but to no avail. On September 2 he gave way to another cabinet still farther to the left, headed by Konstantin Muraviev, Stamboliiski's minister of war, but before it could do anything the Soviet Union, with its army poised on the Bulgarian-Romanian border, declared war on September 5. In the early hours of September 9, before the Red Army reached Sofia, a coup organized by members of the Military League and communists arrested without difficulty the ministers and the regents and installed a government of the Fatherland Front coalition.

The new government headed by Kimon Georgiev included members from the Communist party, the Agrarian Union, Zveno, the Social Democrats, and the Independents, but the real foundation of power came from a deal Churchill struck with Stalin in Moscow on October 9. Known as the Percentage Agreement, it extended the earlier arrangement, presumably only for the duration of the war, and specified that in Bulgaria the Soviet Union would have a 75–25 percent preponderance, raised the following day to an 80–20 ratio. The agreement came to light only much later, but the fact that Bulgaria had to sign the armistice agreement in Moscow and that it provided for a three-power Allied Control Commission (ACC) chaired by the Soviet representative evidenced the Soviet preponderance. The chairman, General S. S. Biriuzov, acted from the start as a Soviet viceroy, restricting even the movements of his British and American counterparts and adding to the frictions that grew into the Cold War.[61] The stage was thus set for the inclusion of the country in the Soviet empire, but due to the resistance of democratic forces and the complex international situation, the process took more than two years to complete.

The original program of the coalition government was a democratic call for restoration of the Turnovo constitution and revealed practically nothing of the communist plans except the "right of the Macedonian population to self-determination," that is, to join, in conformity with Comintern decisions, the Macedonian "nation" in the Yugoslav federation proclaimed in 1943.[62] The first aim of the communists was to liquidate their actual or potential enemies, whom they labeled fascists, by outright executions and "disappearances" as well as arrests for trial as war criminals as the program stipulated. Controlling the ministries of internal affairs and justice—and directed by Soviet security personnel—they launched a wave of terror: the trials alone meted out 2,138 death sentences and some 10,000 prison terms (by official figures) to the regents, ministers, members of the National Assembly, courtiers, and various officials who had been in office since March 1, 1941. The total number of victims of the terror has remained unknown, but since the collapse of the communist regime in November 1989, estimates in the Bulgarian press have ranged as high as 180,000 for 1944–1989.

Within the coalition, the first to oppose the communists were the Agrarians. Upon his return from wartime exile in Cairo, Dr. G. M. Dimitrov (called "GeMeto" by his detractors), a left-wing Agrarian opposed to Boris's pro-German policy, assumed the leadership of the Agrarians and immediately questioned the range of communist and coalition policies, from the terror to the commitment of the inexperienced Bulgarian army to fight under Soviet command. Drawing his inspiration from Stamboliiski, he saw the Agrarians, not the communists, as entitled by their numbers to lead postwar Bulgaria and establish the peasant-based democracy Stamboliiski had sought. Sensing the popular mood at Agrarian rallies, he attacked communist policies across the board. This marked him for quick elimination. In January 1945, Biriuzov himself demanded his removal as general secretary of the Agrarian Union and threatened to dissolve the union itself. Under virtual house arrest, Dimitrov yielded the post to Nikola Petkov and, fearing for his life, took refuge in the American political mission. Its chief, Maynard B. Barnes, faced the threat of Soviet troops entering his residence to seize Dr. Dimitrov, but stood his ground and eventually received Soviet assent to transport Dr. Dimitrov to exile in the United States.[63]

Far from collapsing, the Agrarian opposition grew stronger with support from Social Democrats and others in the coalition. The basis for hope that democracy could be established came with the Yalta agreement of February 1945. Whatever the secret Churchill-Stalin agreements were or were guessed to be, the Yalta Declaration openly and emphatically affirmed "the right of all peoples to choose the form of government under which they will live" and the *joint* responsibility of the Three Powers "to foster the conditions in which the liberated people may exercise these rights" and to "jointly assist" them "to form interim governmental authorities broadly representative of all democratic elements in the population and pledged to the earliest possible establishment through free elections of governments responsive to the will of the people; and . . . to facilitate where necessary the holding of such elections." The Americans, who wrote this text, even proposed a tripartite commission in Sofia, independent of the ACC, to watch over the preparations for elections, but the Soviets turned down their proposal.[64]

The elections, scheduled for August 26, became a critical issue within the coalition as well as in the ACC. The opposition wanted them postponed in order to have time to organize, and Barnes vigorously supported postponement in the ACC. The communists held rallies chanting slogans (e.g., "We are not afraid of the atom bomb," and "We have taken power by shedding blood and will give it up only by shedding blood."). Biriuzov held out until the last minute but, after referring the matter to Moscow, agreed to postpone the elections. The victory of the opposition, plainly achieved with American and British support, heightened hopes that real democracy had a chance in Bulgaria.

To shore up the communist position, Stalin sent Georgi Dimitrov, even though his health was less than good, to Bulgaria in time for the elections now scheduled for November. The opposition refused to take part, since it had neither the time nor the resources to organize, and the communists with some new allies in the coalition gained a hollow victory. In September 1946, Dimitrov orchestrated a referendum on the abolition of the monarchy and the vote came in overwhelmingly in favor of a republic. The following month elections for a Grand National Assembly, required by the Turnovo constitution for constitutional changes, were scheduled and the opposition, despite the lack of democratic freedoms, decided to participate. The 1,200,000 votes it received (twenty-eight percent of the total) were a remarkable assertion of democracy, given the conditions in which they were cast. The opposition entered the final phase of the battle with ninety-nine members of the assembly, eighty-nine of whom were Agrarians led by Petkov and nine Socialists (Social Democrats) led by Kosta Lulchev.

The destruction of the opposition in the assembly by Dimitrov was brutal, but carefully timed to take advantage of the peace treaty and demonstrate the powerlessness of the United States in relation to Bulgaria. The treaty, negotiated and signed in Paris on February 10, 1947, recognized Bulgaria's acquisition of southern Dobrudja and burdened her only with relatively light reparations to Greece and Yugoslavia. In Sofia a scheme was already underway to implicate Petkov and others in the opposition in a conspiracy with army officers to overthrow the government. In sharp exchanges with Dimitrov, Petkov pointed out that he had never owed allegiance to a foreign country, whereas Dimitrov had been a Soviet citizen for years. Aware that he faced death, he remained undaunted, having in his family two examples of political courage, his father and his brother (who were assassinated for their convictions in 1907 and 1924 respectively). On June 5, the day the United States Senate ratified the peace treaty, Petkov was stripped of his parliamentary immunity and arrested inside the assembly. Brought up on predictable charges, he was sentenced to death on September 23. A week after his execution the United States took the last step implied by the peace treaty and extended diplomatic recognition to Dimitrov's government.[65] The liquidation of the parliamentary opposition made it easier to adopt a constitution in December patterned quite closely on the Stalin constitution of 1936. It came to be known as the Dimitrov constitution.

The peace treaty also freed Dimitrov's hands on the Balkan federation question. Moves were initiated with Yugoslavia in October 1944, but the British, opposed to the scheme, argued that as a defeated country Bulgaria could not conclude treaties. In 1945 and 1946 the population of Bulgaria's part of Macedonia (the Pirin region), however, was subjected to intense efforts, some of them by teachers and propagandists from Yugoslav Macedonia, to make it feel a part of the Macedonian "nation." The effort included a push to join the core within the Yugoslav federation with Greek Macedonians after the communists prevailed in the Greek civil war. As a result, the Bulgarian census of 1946 recorded some seventy percent of the population of the Pirin region as Macedonian, thus constituting a new ethnic minority in Bulgaria. The federation talks between Dimitrov and Tito in 1947, however, bogged down on the issue whether Bulgaria and Yugoslavia would be coequal members or Bulgaria would be the seventh member of the Yugoslav federation, with Dimitrov declaring that Bulgarian Macedonia would join Yugoslav Macedonia only after the larger federation was established.[66] The federation idea died in 1948 when Stalin vetoed it and broke off relations with Tito.

Among Dimitrov's last "achievements" in applying the Soviet model to Bulgaria were the liquidation of private business (industry, commerce, banking, etc.) by means of a nationalization law in December 1947,[67] and the reduction of the Bulgarian Orthodox church and other churches and religious communities to impotence. Resistance in the Orthodox church to communist policies of keeping it from influencing the young and from performing charitable work among the old and the needy was strongly voiced by its primate, Exarch Stefan, who was forced to resign in September 1948 and lived out his days banished to a monastery. The Jewish religious community was neutralized by providing the opportunity to emigrate to Israel, which the vast majority of the Bulgarian Jews took. Legal and extralegal measures based on the Criminal Code and a new law on religious denominations, passed in early 1949, were taken against the small Catholic and Protestant communities, accused as foreign agents and spies, and the tribunals meted out death and long prison sentences.[68] All Western schools, affiliated with churches or not, were closed. Only the Muslims, by far the largest religious and ethnic community in Bulgaria with the status of a national minority under the Dimitrov constitution and thus entitled to their own culture and language, were spared harsh repressive measures at this stage. Their turn came later under Dimitrov's successors, Vulko Chervenkov (Dimitrov's brother-in-law) and Todor Zhivkov.

Before he died in July 1949, Dimitrov became enmeshed in the so-called Traicho Kostov affair. After Stalin's conflict with Tito escalated, the Soviet leader began to see Titoist sympathizers and conspirators throughout Eastern Europe. In Bulgaria the chief culprit in his eyes was Kostov, a party secretary under Dimitrov in charge of economic affairs. In discussions with Soviet representatives Kostov had sought to protect Bulgarian economic interests. This marked him as a dangerous nationalist. In the hunt for Titoists he was singled out as the leader of a supposed plot to detach Bulgaria, with Yugoslav and American help, from the socialist camp and was branded by Dimitrov himself as "a devious, refined, and well-versed scoundrel" scheming to surface at the right time. The trial in December 1949, resulted in his execution and prison terms for a number of alleged co-conspirators. The trial charged the American minister, Donald R. Heath, with a role in the conspiracy. The Bulgarian government declared him persona non grata, and the United States severed diplomatic relations with Bulgaria in February 1950.

Dimitrov's natural successor was Vasil Kolarov, but he died six months after Dimitrov and the post went to Vulko Chervenkov, who not only had the inside track as Dimitrov's relative but also was a replica of Stalin. Emigrating to the Soviet Union as a young man in 1925, he showed aptitude for ideological work and was trained at the Marx-Engels Institute in Moscow, teaching in programs for foreign communists and working in the Comintern. During the war he served as head of the Soviet radio station broadcasting to Bulgaria. Steeped in Stalin's ideas and methods, he was the man to secure the situation in Bulgaria and complete the Sovietization of the country.

Chervenkov's first task was to purge the party from top to bottom of unreliable elements. He charged "lack of vigilance" against "Trai-cho-Kostovites" and other enemies and eliminated within a few months 92,500 (or more than 20 percent) of the party members. With equal zeal, he undertook to complete the collectivization of agriculture begun earlier and, at the fastest pace in Eastern Europe, collectivized land jumped to 61 percent in 1952, 77 percent in 1956, and 92 percent in 1958. The Turkish ethnic and religious minority proved particularly resistant to collectivization, as well as to atheistic communist indoctrination, and Chervenkov turned to the Stalinist method of thinning out opposition to his policies by deporting vast numbers of Turks. In August 1950, he announced that 250,000 (more than one-third of the minority) would be at the border within three months for emigration to Turkey. By November 1951, when Turkey closed its border, some 155,000 Bulgarian Turks had been expelled.[69] In the case of the Orthodox church, he again adopted the Stalinist solution of granting it the status of a patriarchate in exchange for strict subservience to communist policies at home and abroad.

The death of Stalin, however, cut short the career of Bulgaria's "Little Stalin." The chief beneficiary was a young *aparatchik*, Todor Zhivkov, whom Chervenkov, looking for new men during the party purge, had brought into the Politburo in 1951. Born in the village of Pravets, northeast of Sofia, in 1911, Zhivkov migrated to Sofia, working as a printer and joining the party in 1932. During the war he was the liaison between the party leadership in Sofia and the "Chavdar" guerrilla brigade commanded by Dobri Dzhurov and based in the Pravets region. His official biographies have credited him with directing and carrying out the coup of September 9, 1944, in Sofia, but since his fall on November 10, 1989, new testimony of participants has come out, rendering suspect what was published during his regime.

In the coup Zhivkov and the guerrillas converged on Sofia and became the new police (militia), securing the new regime at the capital and carrying out the liquidations and arrests discussed above. As the militia's political chief of staff, Zhivkov obviously did his job well, for he rose rapidly in the party hierarchy: in 1945 he was made a candidate (non-voting) member of the Central Committee; in 1948—a regular member; and in 1950—a candidate member of the Politburo and secretary of the Central Committee. At the same time he served as first secretary of the party's committees for the city and region of Sofia, in effect as mayor and boss of the capital and its environs. In elevating him to the Politburo, Chervenkov might have felt that the uneducated provincial *aparatchik*, no matter how effective a pragmatist he was, would need and respect the leadership of the ideologist with the Soviet credentials. If so, events proved Chervenkov wrong.

In line with the changes in Moscow, in 1954 Chervenkov yielded the post of general secretary to Zhivkov who, like Khrushchev, was now styled first secretary of the party. Khrushchev's policy of reconciliation with Tito and his broadside attack on Stalin's crimes and personality cult made Chervenkov's position untenable, and he relinquished the premiership to an old enemy and Zhivkov's chief in the militia, Anton Yugov. It was Zhivkov, however, who articulated in April 1956 the policies coming down from Moscow and formulated the "April Line," that served as the guideline for the next thirty-three years of his regime. In 1962, he rid himself of Yugov as well and, like Khrushchev, took control of both the government and the party. Dabbling in structural changes and innovations, he enacted a new constitution in 1971, the main feature of which was the creation of a State Council as the top policy-making body. As its president Zhivkov became the head of state, relieved from day-to-day responsibilities of running the country, but setting the general policies nevertheless. The execution of these policies fell to the Council of Ministers headed by a series of pliant prime ministers.

The essence of Zhivkov's policies was to make Bulgaria an inseparable part of the Soviet Union, or as he liked to put it, to make them share a "common circulatory system." Within a general framework provided by the Council of Mutual Economic Assistance (Comecon), the bilateral economic relationship turned Bulgaria into a miniature of the Soviet model, complete with giant ore-processing plants, iron and steel works, cement factories, and hydroelectric stations, built on Soviet know-how and technology of the 1930s. As in the USSR, impact on the environment and threats to food production were simply not considered. Light industry, also built largely on Soviet models, produced goods which, because of their inferior quality, could only be absorbed by the Soviet Union and other Comecon members or peddled to Third World countries. The official propaganda, which did have an impact on the outside world, presented a picture of incessant progress in all spheres of life.[70]

As stagnation and downward trends hit the Soviet economy, the "common circulatory system" carried the ills to Bulgaria, and Zhivkov resorted to heavy borrowing in the West to stave off decline and maintain the image of progress. Hard currency apparently also came from trafficking in arms, drugs, and terrorism under the guise of such companies as Kinteks (or "Kintex," the Bulgarian acronym for dry goods and textiles) and others. These activities, like everything else that took place in Bulgaria after 1944, require reexamination in the new conditions of openness in order for the true picture to emerge. Western experts, dependent on official sources and misled by doctored statistics, failed to uncover, for example, Bulgaria's staggering foreign debt of some eleven billion dollars until it was officially acknowledged after Zhivkov's fall. Critical faults in the "umbilical cord" system, especially with regard to the supply of Soviet oil, as well as Bulgaria's current economic collapse, are further proof that Western scholarship failed to provide much important information about Bulgaria.

Domestic and international politics provides other examples of concealed developments in the Zhivkov era that are now coming to light and require revision of its history. His slavish submission to Soviet wishes in international politics was always evident, as for example in committing Bulgarian troops to the invasion of Czechoslovakia in 1968. What has not been known until recently is that on his own initiative he twice offered, to Khrushchev and to Brezhnev, to formally end his country's independence by making it the sixteenth member of the Union of Soviet Socialist Republics and that only a Soviet veto prevented him from reaching his ultimate objective.

In line with the rehabilitation and release of victims of Soviet Stalinism, in Bulgaria Kostov was posthumously rehabilitated in 1956 (clearing the way to resumption of U.S.-Bulgarian relations in 1960) and thousands of victims of Chervenkov's purge of the party were restored to good standing. Infighting at the leadership level, however, continued before and after Zhivkov defeated Yugov and his confederates in 1962. According to recent revelations, there were eight or nine plots against him, some of them involving the military, of which only one—in 1965—became public. The false image of tranquillity and stability that Zhivkov's propaganda cultivated took hold in Western analyses and media which failed, in particular, to see and assess the crucial alienation from communism as an ideology and a system of the younger generations.

The evidence revealed so far does not indicate the nature and degree of Soviet participation in the formulation of Zhivkov's policies toward the Macedonian and Turkish minorities, cutting across the spheres of domestic and international affairs. In the early stages of the communist regime, Moscow through the Comintern was in fact the author of the policy of the Bulgarian communists on the Macedonian question, with Georgi Dimitrov acting as its executor in Bulgaria. Following the Stalin-Tito break, Moscow and Sofia preferred to see it languish, but Skoplje and Belgrade insisted that there was a Macedonian minority in Bulgaria as evidenced by the Bulgarian census of 1946 and that it was entitled to its own language, culture, and ultimate self-determination. Heavily involved in Macedonian nation-building, which included creation of a full-fledged national language, history, and even a Macedonian Orthodox church, Skoplje of necessity invaded what Bulgarians regard as the history of their western regions and appropriated events and personalities to weave into the history of the Macedonian nation. Under Zhivkov Sofia's response was that there was no Macedonian nation or language and that most of Macedonia, throughout its history, had been part of the Bulgarian ethnic, linguistic, and cultural domain. The clash of these views produced violent encounters at scholarly conferences, not to mention exchanges in the mass media, as well as piles of publications on each side. It is not likely to abate in the post-Zhivkov era.

The Turkish policy on the other hand can be labeled, on existing evidence, as "Made in Bulgaria." Despite the Dimitrov constitution, which provided that "the national minorities are entitled to be taught in their mother's tongue and to develop their national culture," actual policies since the early 1950s aimed at reducing the Turkish population (numbering 675,500 out of a total population of 7,029,349 in 1946) by pressure to emigrate or assimilate. Forced emigration occurred under Chervenkov, and the schools for the Turkish minority were closed in 1958. Religious life was severely curtailed, as evidenced by the precipitous drop in the number of imams (prayer leaders, authorities on Islamic law) from 2,715 in 1956 to 570 in 1982 and 400 in 1987.[71] The change of policy from recognizing ethnic and religious minorities to creating an amalgamated Bulgarian nation was also indicated by the fact that the national censuses after 1965 provided no counts of such groups. In the early 1970s the Bulgarian-speaking Muslims, known as "Pomaks" (estimated at 170,000 and thus the second-largest minority in the country), were forced to change their Turkish-Arabic names to Slavic "equivalents" and the term *Pomak* itself was banned. The main minority, the ethnic Turks, were further thinned out by emigration in 1968–1978 of some 130,000 under an agreement with Turkey. Significantly, the Zhivkov constitution of 1971 dropped all references to minorities.

The decision to solve the Turkish question once and for all came in late 1984. The official rationale behind it has not surfaced yet, but the need for a "final solution" was given various explanations by its advocates in the Bulgarian media before Zhivkov's fall, ranging from the plausible to the grotesque. Historians were enlisted to show that the Turks were simply Bulgarians who in the centuries of Turkish rule had lost their national consciousness even though, until 1984, it had been a central tenet of Bulgarian historiography that the Turks were descendants of colonists after the conquest of the Bulgarian lands in the fourteenth century. Political commentators argued that eventual Turkish separatism would turn Bulgaria into another Cyprus and provide an excuse for Turkey to intervene unless preventive measures were taken. Still others painted a picture of the eventual demographic extinction of the Bulgarians who, given the higher birth rate of the Turks, would become in the foreseeable future an ever-shrinking minority in their own country.

Zhivkov's measures were characteristically brutal. In addition to forcing the Turks, like the Pomaks, to change their names to Slavic ones, the use of the Turkish language in public was prohibited, and circumcision (required by Islamic law) was banned. Enforcement by special troops led to confrontations, clashes, and casualties as well as trials and imprisonment of leaders of the minority. International condemnation for violating the Helsinki accords of 1975 and other covenants on human rights Bulgaria had signed did not deter Zhivkov from intensifying the campaign in May 1989. Recalcitrant Turks were forced or induced to leave their homes—with only the possessions they could carry in trains, buses, or cars—and move to Turkey. Under these circumstances Turkey declared that all Turks who wished to emigrate would be taken in, with the result that by August some 310,000 had relocated in Turkey or were awaiting relocation in makeshift camps on either side of the border. The size of the exodus exceeded Zhivkov's expectations and, embarrassed by such a vast number of "Turkicized Bulgarians" declaring themselves Turks, he called them "tourists" who would soon return to their Bulgarian homeland. Internationally, this policy was condemned and even the Soviet Union, a supporter Zhivkov was accustomed to count upon, showed disapproval.

Zhivkov's relationship with the Soviet Union under Gorbachev was difficult from the start. In part the difficulty was generational: twenty years the senior of the young Soviet leader, Zhivkov thought Gorbachev had much to learn whereas Gorbachev saw Zhivkov as a remnant of an age that was coming to an end. The main difficulty stemmed of course from Gorbachev's policies. Zhivkov viewed *perestroika* at best as irrelevant in Bulgaria, and when pressed about it he declared that Bulgaria's restructuring had been under way since 1956 under the April Line. As to *glasnost,* he publicly ignored it, undoubt-edly hoping that Gorbachev's experiment with it would be shortlived and that the controls he had in place would keep Bulgaria safely orthodox.

However, the "common circulatory system" brought the Soviet infection in and spread it widely. Under the system the Bulgarians' daily mental diet concerning developments abroad came almost exclu-sively from the Soviet print and electronic media and, for the intelli-gentsia in particular, from Western radio stations such as the Voice of America, BBC, Radio Free Europe, Deutsche Welle, and others. While Zhivkov could jam the Western broadcasts, he could do prac-tically nothing about the Soviet media reaching Bulgarians. Fired up by what *Moscow News, Ogonyok,* and other Soviet publications were printing and advocating, writers began to speak up at Writers' Union meetings, and informal groups began to spring up, as in the Soviet Union, around seemingly nonpolitical issues such as protection of the environment. The first major manifestation of unrest was the 1988 ecological demonstration in Ruse, Bulgaria's main port on the Dan-ube, whose air was dangerously polluted by Romanian plants across the river at Giurgiu. The demonstration and a meeting in Sofia in its support were violently suppressed and leaders who were communists in good standing, including the wife of the president of the National Assembly and Stanko Todorov, a Zhivkov associate since before 1944, were expelled from the party.

The thrust for change, however, could not be halted. By late 1988 and early 1989 a number of "informal organizations" began to prolif-erate: writers' groups in Plovdiv and Sofia; a committee for religious rights, freedom of conscience, and spiritual values in Veliko Turnovo led by a young churchman, Khristofor Subev; an ecological associa-tion in Sofia calling itself *Ekoglasnost* and led by Petur Slabakov, Petur Beron, and Alexander Karakachanov; a club for support of *glasnost* and *perestroika* in Bulgaria at the University of Sofia, later renamed "Club for Glasnost and Democracy" and chaired by Dr. Zheliu Zhelev and others; an independent federation of labor like Poland's Solidarity calling itself *Podkrepa* (Support), headquartered in Sofia and led by Dr. Konstantin Trenchev; and numerous other "informals," a term adopted, as in the Soviet Union, to avoid scrutiny by the authorities. Zhivkov's regime responded with arrests and de-portations of some of the leaders, but the "informals" were too numerous and amorphous to eliminate.

To improve the regime's international image Zhivkov and Petur Mladenov (his foreign minister since 1971) decided to host in October

1989 a conference on ecological issues (EcoForum) sponsored by the Conference on Security and Cooperation in Europe (CSCE), carrying forward the Helsinki process. The conference was a singular opportunity for Ekoglasnost to present an unvarnished picture of the country's many ecological problems and to voice its grievances, but the police effectively kept its spokesmen from reaching the conference or individual delegates as well as from talking to representatives of the Western media. A small demonstration held on October 26 at a central square in Sofia was brutally suppressed, with dozens of people beaten and hauled off in police vans in full view of conference delegates and foreign journalists. The publicity and the outrage it produced abroad at a time of momentous changes in other Eastern European countries added to the growing mood among party leaders that Zhivkov was a millstone around their necks and had to go.

The leader of the move to oust Zhivkov was Mladenov. As foreign minister for nearly two decades, Mladenov was more fully cognizant than anyone around Zhivkov of the disastrous international consequences of his policies and Bulgaria's virtually total isolation which had the effect, among others, of making Bulgaria less and less able to obtain financial credits. His personal relations with Zhivkov were at the breaking point, since on October 24 he had submitted a lengthy letter of resignation, subsequently published in the Bulgarian press, citing their differences. On November 5–6 he went to China on a visit that had been scheduled well in advance and on the way back stopped over in Moscow. Whether he received a "go ahead" signal there Mladenov has not denied. Upon his return the preparations were completed on November 9 (the day the Berlin Wall was breached) with the help of Dobri Dzhurov, Stanko Todorov, and other Zhivkov confederates. The following day a meeting of the party's central committee confronted Zhivkov with their decision and he yielded without a fight. His posts as the party's general secretary and president of the republic went to Mladenov.[72]

The fall of the dictator ignited a fever of demonstrations, with thousands, at times hundreds of thousands converging in Sofia's central squares to taste freedom and demand the end of totalitarianism and communist rule. Mladenov pledged no police interference with the activities of the opposition, respect for political pluralism, and elimination of the Bulgarian equivalent of the KGB for domestic security. Violence was thus avoided, giving rise to the notion of a "gentle revolution," although at a demonstration on December 14, when the crowd was on the verge of seizing the National Assembly while it was in session, Mladenov called for tanks to be brought out.

A major factor in the avoidance of violence was the *Suiuz na demokratichnite sili* (Union of Democratic Forces, or UDF), formed on December 7 to coordinate the activities of the existing organizations and others mushrooming after November 10 and willing to join it, such as the Social Democratic party, the Green party, the Democratic party, the Radical Democratic party, the Federation of Independent Student Associations, and others. By January 1990, UDF had become an umbrella organization representing sixteen affiliates under a coordinating council chaired by Dr. Zheliu Zhelev, a Marxist philosopher persecuted for unorthodox views since the 1960s and a representative of what was by then a Federation of Clubs for Glasnost and Democracy.[73] Under his leadership UDF committed itself to the peaceful dismantling of the totalitarian system and transition to democracy and a market economy. To reach the necessary agreements with the communists, it proposed a Polish-style round table.

The communists did their utmost to divorce themselves from Zhivkov and his "circle," numbering fewer than twenty, and declared that he and others would be brought to trial. The policy toward the Turks was totally reversed and at a hastily convened congress the party changed its name to the Bulgarian Socialist party, with a reformist, Alexander Lilov, as president of its supreme council and slogans like "democratic socialism" and "Bulgaria above all" as the new buzzwords for political survival. The congress revealed serious splits and factions, some calling themselves Alternative Socialist party, Alternative Socialist Union, and even Bulgaria's Road to Europe, while others demanded preservation of the old Stalinist orthodoxy. The BSP took all of the BCP's property, including the huge headquarters (called "Bulgaria's Bastille" by UDF supporters) in the heart of Sofia, that continued to fly the Soviet hammer-and-sickle flag and flaunt a Soviet red star high above the city. Moreover, the power structure (*nomenklatura*) of the BCP at the center and in the provinces remained intact.

The round-table negotiations produced, after months of wrangling, agreements concerning distribution of newsprint, access to state television and radio stations, principles of the future political system, and procedures for holding elections for a Grand National Assembly—a term taken from the Turnovo constitution and meaning twice the size of the regular assembly with competence over especially important questions—to work out the country's new democratic constitution. A central electoral commission was entrusted with supervising the elections, and provisions were made for foreign observers. The 400 seats were to be filled on June 10 and 17, allowing for runoffs where there was no majority.

The elections produced mixed results. BSP received 47.15 percent of the popular vote but 211 seats. The rest of the votes were scattered among thirty-nine parties and associations of which only three obtained sizeable numbers of seats: the UDF coalition received 144; the Movement for Rights and Freedom organized by the Turks, 23; and the Agrarian Union, a former ally of BCP but independent after Zhivkov's fall, 16.[74] Given this mix of numbers, an immediate reaction was that neither the Reds won nor were the Blues (UDF's color) defeated. Analysis of the voting patterns showed that BSP swayed mainly the countryside, while UDF's strength lay in Sofia and other urban areas where fear, by which BCP had kept itself in power, was much less a factor. What apparently also worked for the BSP was the fear, particularly among the vast numbers of pensioners, that the change to a market economy would be to their detriment.

Although the elections were declared free and fair in general, protests against voter manipulation and violations of voting procedures poured in. Most vocal and effective were students at the University of Sofia affiliated with the UDF who went on strike, charging election fraud, information blackout on the state television and radio, and cover-up of BSP crimes, and demanding the resignation of Mladenov for wanting to use tanks against the people in the demonstration of December 14. The students' determination forced Mladenov out on July 6, 1990; on August 1, after prolonged wrangling, BSP accepted the leader of UDF, Dr. Zhelev, as head of state (president), with one of its own reformist leaders, General Atanas Semerdzhiev, as vice-president.

BSP's acceptance of Zhelev as head of state, over the opposition of its hardline wing, was recognition that it could not govern alone. Its parliamentary majority was threatened by secessions and by demands that BSP deputies implicated in Zhivkov's policies should resign; its public support as reflected in opinion polls was in sharp decline. On August 26, the party's headquarters, "the Bastille," was torched during a demonstration (in circumstances which some observers saw as paralleling the Reichstag fire in 1933 that the Nazis used to crush their opponents), and as a result the offensive red star was finally taken down. When demonstrators "desecrated" Dimitrov's mausoleum, a replica of Lenin's in Moscow, the party yielded to the demands for removal of "the mummy" and slipped the corpse out to relatives for cremation. Such minor concessions raised other demands that the party's properties be disclosed and nationalized, the cover-up of the effects of the Chernobyl disaster on Bulgaria be investigated, and the full range of the party's responsibility for the national crisis—

increasingly called the third national catastrophe—be admitted and individuals involved punished. The efforts of President Zhelev, an activist with an able team and definite plans for peaceful dismantling of the totalitarian system, could not lessen the tensions.

The survival strategy of BSP's government headed by Andrei Lukanov, a third-generation communist bigwig, was to urge the UDF to join it as a junior partner in a coalition of national consensus needed to put through the unpalatable policies of transition to a market economy. UDF steadfastly refused unless it dominated the coalition, since otherwise BSP would emasculate the opposition, cover up the responsibilities and crimes of "the vandals," as Zhivkov himself called his former associates in a remarkable interview,[75] and further retard the changes UDF was committed to bring about.

A year after Zhivkov and communism, which he has now declared wrong, were toppled, Bulgarians stood amidst the political, economic, ecological, social, and moral wreckage, facing a crisis of unprecedented dimensions in their twentieth-century history. It was only the prospect of linking their country once again with the West, and more specifically with the United States, as Zhivkov emphatically urged in the interview, that provided the hope needed to sustain life.

NOTES

1. Cyril E. Black, *The Establishment of Constitutional Government in Bulgaria* (Princeton: Princeton University Press, 1943).

2. Charles Jelavich, *Tsarist Russia and Balkan Nationalism: Russian Influence in the Internal Affairs of Bulgaria and Serbia, 1879–1886* (Berkeley: University of California Press, 1958); A. Hulme Beaman, *M. Stambuloff* (New York: Varne, 1895).

3. Stephen Constant, *Foxy Ferdinand, 1861–1948: Tsar of Bulgaria* (London: Sigdwick & Jackson, 1979); Ivan Iovkov, *Koburgut* (Sofia: Partizdat, 1983).

4. These and other statistics in the text are from the official Bulgarian *Statisticheski godishnik* and other abstracts reflecting the censuses since 1881. See also *Ikonomikata na Bulgariia do sotsialisticheskata revolitsiia*, vol. 1 of *Ikonomika na Bulgariia*, Zhak Natan et al., eds. (Sofia: Nauka i izkustvo, 1969).

5. For details see Marin Pundeff, "Bulgaria's Cultural Reorientation after 1878," *Papers for the V. Congress of Southeast European Studies, Belgrade, September 1984*, K. K. Shangriladze and E. W. Townsend, eds. (Columbus: Slavica, 1984), 300–320.

6. Marin Pundeff, "Charles M. Dickinson and U.S.–Bulgarian Relations," *Dokladi* [of the Second International Congress of Bulgarian Studies], *Bulgariia sled osvobozhdenieto (1878)* (Sofia: Bulgarska akademiia na naukite, 1988), 8:76–88. Establishment of relations with Bulgaria had been urged since the 1880s by Eugene Schuyler, the distinguished American diplomat in Russia, Turkey, and the Balkans, who played a key role in Bulgaria's liberation. On the early history of American presence in Bulgaria, see James F. Clarke, *Bible Societies, American Missionaries, and the National Revival of Bulgaria* (Ph.D. dissertation, Harvard University, 1937; reprinted, New York: Arno Press, 1971); and William W. Hall, *Puritans in the Balkans: The American Board Mission in Bulgaria, 1878–1918* (Sofia: Cultura, 1938).

7. *The Outlook*, November 23, 1912.

8. Tsvetana Todorova, *Diplomaticheska istoriia na vunshnite zaemi na Bulgariia, 1888–1912* (Sofia: Nauka i izkustvo, 1971), 460.

9. John D. Bell, *The Bulgarian Communist Party from Blagoev to Zhivkov* (Stanford: Hoover Institution Press, 1986), 16.

10. The Bulgarian claims were best documented by Vasil Kunchov, *Makedoniia: Etnografiia i Statistika* (Sofia: Bulgarsko knizovno druzhestvo, 1900).

11. Miss Stone, a veteran of missionary work in Bulgaria and Macedonia, was kidnapped in September 1901 by guerrilla Iane Sandanski, a left-wing leader of IMRO. She and a Bulgarian companion were released the following February after the ransom was reduced to $66,000. Interestingly, Stone went on to publish and lecture in the United States in terms favorable to her captors; see Laura B. Sherman, *Fires on the Mountain: The Macedonian Revolutionary Movement and the Kidnapping of Ellen Stone* (East European Monographs, Boulder, Colo., distributed by Columbia University Press, New York, 1980); and Konstantin Pandev and Maia Vaptsarova, *Aferata "Mis Stoun"; spomeni, dokumenti i materiali* (Sofia: OF, 1983).

12. *Tsar*, a Slavic contraction of Caesar, was first used in Bulgaria in the tenth century. The term migrated to Russia and was first assumed as a title by Ivan the Terrible in 1547.

13. Geshov, scion of a wealthy Plovdiv family, was educated in Manchester, England, and was named the first honorary American consul in a Bulgarian community in 1876, a post which the events of 1876–78 prevented him from assuming. After Stoilov's death he became the leader of the People's party.

14. Ivan E. Geshov, *The Balkan League* (London: Murray, 1915); E. C. Helmreich, *The Diplomacy of the Balkan Wars, 1912–1913* (Cambridge: Harvard University Press, 1938).

15. Richard C. Hall, "Civil-Military Conflict in Bulgaria During the Balkan Wars," *East European Quarterly* (September 1989), 293–303.

16. Reprinted in Vladimir A. Tsanoff, *Reports and Letters of American Missionaries Referring to the Distribution of Nationalities in the Former Provinces of European Turkey, 1858–1918* (Sofia, 1919), 71–73.

17. Helmreich, *The Diplomacy of the Balkan Wars*, 395.

18. Quoted in Viktor A. Zhebokritskii, *Bolgariia vo vremia balkanskikh voin 1912–1913 gg.* (Kiev, 1961), 243.

19. Writing in 1925, Lord Grey described the Bucharest settlement as being "not one of justice but of force. It left Bulgaria sore, injured, and despoiled and deprived of what she believed should belong to her. Any future Balkan peace was impossible so long as the Treaty of Bucharest remained. To make peace secure for the future, it would have been necessary for the Great Powers to have intervened to make the settlement of Bucharest a just one. This they did not do. They dared not do it, being too afraid of trouble between themselves." Edward Grey, *Twenty-five Years, 1892–1916* (New York: Stokes, 1925), 1:253–54.

20. The diplomat was John B. Jackson, minister to Greece, Romania, and Serbia. He resided in Athens.

21. *Foreign Relations of the United States 1902–1903* (hereafter *FRUS*), 21–23.

22. For further details of Ferdinand's American policy, drawn from U.S. archives, see Marin Pundeff, "Stefan Panaretov and Bulgarian-American Relations," *Bulgarian Historical Review* (1989) 3:18–41.

23. Ivan Ilchev, "Kazhi kakvo stana s Dardanelite," in Georgi Gunev and Ivan Ilchev, eds., *Uinstun Churchil i Balkanite* (Sofia, 1989), 78–81, quoting a memorandum by Churchill.

24. Texts in B. D. Kesiakov, *Prinos kum diplomaticheskata istoriia na Bulgariia, 1878–1925* (Sofia: Rodopi, 1925), 71–74.

25. Text in Aleksandur Stamboliiski, *Dvete mi sreshti s tsar Ferdinand* (Sofia: BZNS, 1919), and Nikola D. Petkov, *Aleksandur Stamboliiski; lichnost i idei* (Sofia, 1946). English translation of the exchange in John D. Bell, *Peasants in Power: Alexander Stamboliski and the Bulgarian Agrarian National Union, 1899–1923* (Princeton: Princeton University Press, 1977), 119–20.

26. F. I. Notovich, *Bukharestskii mir 1918 g.* (Moscow: Izdatel'stvo sotsial'no-ekonomicheskoy literatury, 1959), 111, 123–26, 210–11.

27. Vasil Radoslawoff, *Bulgarien und die Weltkrise* (Berlin: Ullstein, 1923), 247–48; Victor S. Mamatey, "The United States and Bulgaria in World War I," *The American Slavic and East European Review* (April 1953), 233–57.

28. Pundeff, "Stefan Panaretov and Bulgarian-American Relations," 30–31.

29. Theodore Roosevelt, *Roosevelt in the Kansas City Star: War-time Editorials* (Boston: Houghton Mifflin, 1921), 54–55.

30. *FRUS*, 1917, Supplement 2, 1:448–54.

31. Ministerstvo na vunshnite raboti i na izpovedaniiata, *Diplomaticheski dokumenti po namesata na Bulgariia v Evropeiskata voina* (Sofia, 1921), 984.

32. *Istoriia na Bulgariia*, Dimitur Kosev et al., eds. (Sofia: Nauka i iz-kustvo, 1961–1964; 3 vols), 3:25–28.

33. In fact, Murphy fell ill on the way to Salonika. The British objected to his role on behalf of the Bulgarians, and the State Department eventually transferred him from Sofia, for being too deeply involved in Bulgarian politics. Nevertheless, he remained in touch with Bulgarian friends and politics until the end of his life. "The heaviest disappointment of my life from which I have not yet recovered," he wrote in 1926, was that Americans had not secured justice for "poor Bulgaria." See Pundeff, "Stefan Panaretov and American-Bulgarian Relations," 36–37.

34. Bulgaria set up its own group of experts in Switzerland to prepare documentation for propaganda and for the defense of Bulgarian claims at the coming peace conference.

35. *FRUS*, 1918, Supplement 1, 1:326–27. Further details in Andrei L. Pantev and Petko Petkov, *SASht i Bulgariia po vreme na purvata svetovna voina* (Sofia: Nauka i izkustvo, 1983).

36. Texts in Kesiakov, *Prinos kum diplomaticheskata* (Sofia, 1926), 1:84–87, of the convention, and vols. 2 and 3 of the treaty. American delegates did sign the treaty.

37. Evgeni Tanchev, *Durzhavno-pravnite vuzgledi na Aleksandur Stamboliiski* (Sofia: BZNS, 1984), 8, 22.

38. Pundeff, "Stefan Panaretov and Bulgarian-American Relations," 39. For further elaboration on Stamboliiski's ideas and policies, see Bell, *Peasants in Power*, 57–73.

39. Dimitrov was the son of Protestant refugees from Macedonia who eventually settled in Sofia. For a while in 1903 he was employed as a printer at the American schools in Samokov. See V. Khadzhinikolov et al., *Georgi Dimitrov: biografiia* (Sofia: Partizdat, 1972), 14–35.

40. For a detailed and balanced account of Stamboliiski's reforms, see Bell, *Peasants in Power*, 154–83, and for a Bulgarian perspective, see Dimitrina V. Petrova, *Samostoiatelnoto upravlenie na BZNS, 1920–1923* (Sofia: Nauka i izkustvo, 1988).

41. Bell, *The Bulgarian Communist Party*, 35–37.

42. *Entsiklopediia Bulgariia* (Sofia: BAN, 1988), 6:162–67.

43. For details, see the memoirs of the Agrarian negotiator, Kosta Todorov, *Balkan Firebrand: The Autobiography of a Rebel, Soldier and Statesman* (Chicago: Ziff-Davis, 1943). Todorov, a close associate of Stamboliiski, and Alexander Obbov were the Agrarian leaders in exile after the assassination of Raiko Daskalov in Prague by IMRO in August 1923.

44. Extensive details are provided by Joseph Rothschild, *The Communist Party of Bulgaria: Origins and Development, 1883–1936* (New York: Columbia University Press, 1959), 170–90.

45. Georgi Naumov, *Atentatut v katedralata "Sv. Nedelia," 16 April 1925 g.* (Sofia: Partizdat, 1989), 128–53.

46. Stefan Troebst, *Mussolini, Makedonien und die Machte, 1922–1930* (Cologne-Vienna: Bohlau, 1987), 491–520.

47. Stephane Groueff, *Crown of Thorns: The Reign of King Boris III of Bulgaria, 1918–1943* (Lanham, Md.: Madison Books, 1987), 163–78. The author is the son of Pavel Gruev, a leading figure in the king's entourage.

48. T. I. Geshkoff, *Balkan Union: A Road to Peace in Southeastern Europe* (New York: Columbia University Press, 1940).

49. The Protogerovists dissolved their ties of their own accord. Ivan Mikhailov fled to Turkey, masterminded the murder of the Yugoslav king in Marseilles, spent the war years in the fascist state of Croatia, and after the war lived in secrecy in Italy, where he died in 1990. He was supported financially by the so-called Macedonian Political Organizations (formed in the United States in 1922 and headquartered in Indianapolis), where he published propaganda tracts and four volumes of memoirs that end in 1934.

50. Kosev et al., eds., *Istoriia na Bulgariia*, 3:96–97.

51. Adolf Hitler, *Secret Conversations, 1941–1944* (New York: Farrar, Straus and Young, 1953), 370–71, 396.

52. For details and documentation, see Marin Pundeff, "Bulgaria's Place in Axis Policy, 1936–1944," Ph.D. dissertation, University of Southern California, 1958; and Marshall Lee Miller, *Bulgaria During the Second World War* (Stanford: Stanford University Press, 1975).

53. Text in Marin Pundeff, "Two Documents on Soviet-Bulgarian Relations in November, 1940," *Journal of Central European Affairs* (January 1956), 375–76.

54. Pundeff, "Two Documents on Soviet-Bulgarian Relations," 377–78.

55. Quoted in Marin Pundeff, "Churches and Religious Communities," *Bulgarien*, Klaus Getler Grothusen, ed. (Gottingen: Vandenhoeck & Ruprecht, 1990), 549. For details, see Frederick B. Chary, *The Bulgarian Jews and the Final Solution, 1940–1944* (Pittsburgh: University of Pittsburgh Press, 1972).

56. Vitka Toshkova, *Bulgariia i tretiiat raikh (1941–1944): politicheski otnosheniia* (Sofia: Nauka i izkustvo, 1975), 53–55.

57. Nissan Oren, *Bulgarian Communism: The Road to Power, 1934–1944* (New York: Columbia University Press, 1971), 214–18.

58. Albert Cohen and Anri Assa, *Saving of the Jews in Bulgaria, 1941–1944* (Sofia: Septemvri, 1977).

59. Groueff, *Crown of Thorns*, 355–61.

60. Herbert Feis, *Churchill-Roosevelt-Stalin: The War They Waged and the Peace They Sought* (Princeton: Princeton University Press, 1957), 338–41.

61. Cyril E. Black, "The View from Bulgaria," *Witnesses to the Origins of the Cold War*, Thomas T. Hammond, ed. (Seattle: University of Washington Press, 1982), 60–97.

62. Text of the program in *Ustanoviavane i ukrepvane na narodno-*

demokratichnata vlast, Septemvri 1944–mai 1945: sbornik dokumenti, Voin Bozhinov et al., eds. (Sofia: BKP, 1969), 133–36.

63. For extensive details, see Charles A. Moser, *Dimitrov of Bulgaria: A Political Biography of Dr. Georgi M. Dimitrov* (Ottawa, Ill.: Caroline House, 1979).

64. Black, "The View from Bulgaria," 74–75.

65. Michael Padev, *Dimitrov Wastes No Bullets: Nikola Petkov: The Test Case* (London: Eyre & Spottiswoode, 1948). The official record of the trial is in *The Trial of Nikola D. Petkov* (Sofia: Ministry of Information and Arts, 1947). For the diplomacy surrounding it, see Michael M. Boll, *Cold War in the Balkans: American Foreign Policy and the Emergence of Communist Bulgaria, 1943–1947* (Lexington: University Press of Kentucky, 1984) and its companion volume, edited by Boll, *The American Military Mission in the Allied Control Commission for Bulgaria, 1944–1947: History and Transcripts* (Boulder: Westview Press, 1985).

66. Stephen E. Palmer and Robert R. King, *Yugoslav Communism and the Macedonian Question* (Hamden, Conn.: Archon Books, 1971), 117–30.

67. For details see John R. Lampe, *The Bulgarian Economy in the Twentieth Century* (London: Croomhelm, 1986).

68. For details, see Pundeff, "Churches and Religious Communities." It is of interest to note that Dimitrov's mother was a devout Christian who was converted to Protestantism by American missionaries.

69. Huey L. Kostanick, *Turkish Resettlement of Bulgarian Turks, 1950–1953* (Berkeley: University of California Press, 1957).

70. For a sample of the propagandistic impact of this image, see *Modern Bulgaria: History, Policy, Economy, Culture,* Georgi Bokov, ed. (Sofia: Sofia Press, 1981).

71. Pundeff, "Churches and Religious Communities," 562–63; see also the related chapters on national minorities by Stefan Troebst and the school system by Peter Bachmaier as well as the chapter on domestic politics by John D. Bell.

72. For an account of Zhivkov's last days in power, see Kostadin Chakurov, "Vtoriiat etazh," Supplement to *Plamuk* (1990), 9–110. Chakurov was a close aide of Zhivkov until his ouster.

73. For the leaders of the UDF affiliates and their views, see the guide, in Bulgarian, to "Who is What in the UDF" in *ABV* (Sofia), February 20, 1990; and Emiliia Antova-Konstantinova, *Liderite na suiuza na demokratichnite sili ili "zimata na nasheto nedovolstvo"* (Sofia, 1990). Zhelev's reputation was based on his book *Fashizmut,* which appeared in 1982 as a mutilated version of his original work on the totalitarian state. The book equated communism with fascism and was promptly banned. For a reprint complete with a new introduction and postscript by Zhelev, as well as a preface in English and Bulgarian by Marin Pundeff, see Zheliu Zhelev, *Fashizmut* (Social Science Monographs, Boulder, distributed by Columbia University Press, New York, 1990).

74. *Demokratsiia* (UDF's daily), June 15 and 20, 1990; *Elections in Central and Eastern Europe: A Compendium of Reports on the Elections Held from March Through June 1990,* compiled by the Staff of the U.S. Commission on Security and Cooperation in Europe (Washington: CSCE, 1990), 135–57.

75. *The New York Times,* November 28, 1990, A4.

4 Czechoslovakia

Sharon L. Wolchik

Czechoslovakia's history, as that of other countries in Eastern Europe in this century, has been characterized by discontinuities. Czech and Slovak leaders and citizens faced many of the same issues and experienced many of the same problems as others in the region. Among the most important of these were the founding of a new state in the aftermath of the breakup of the Austro-Hungarian empire in the course of World War I, the destruction of the interwar system, the experience of World War II, and the imposition of communist rule after World War II. More recently, Czechoslovakia's citizens experienced an attempt to reform socialism from within that was ended by outside force in 1968. In November 1989 the country underwent another rapid change in regime when, as the result of the peaceful mass demonstrations that came to be known as the "Velvet Revolution," Czechoslovakia joined other Eastern European states in ousting Communism and began to reinstitute a democratic political system and a market economy. The history of the country has also been shaped in important ways by its position at the heart of Europe and the resulting need to take the actions of larger powers and developments in the broader international environment into account.

At the same time, there are a number of ways Czechoslovakia differed from its neighbors and from other countries that came to be ruled by communist leaders. The twentieth-century history of Czechoslovakia and the common experiences noted above have been mediated by these differences. The account that follows traces the impact of three of the most important of these: the country's advanced level of economic development, its diverse ethnic composition, and its particular blend of political attitudes and values.

The Interwar Republic

As most accounts of political and economic developments in Eastern Europe note, Czechoslovakia was in many ways the exception to the rule in the interwar period. The result of the work of Czech and Slovak leaders at home and abroad during World War I and the Allies' desire to create a system of independent nation-states to replace the Austro-Hungarian empire in the region, the new state brought political independence to the Czechs and Slovaks who had been part of larger empires for centuries. It also brought together ethnic groups that differed from each other in many important ways, in part as the result of their very different experiences under foreign rule. These differences, which were a persistent source of conflict during the interwar period and also left their imprint on socialist Czechoslovakia during the communist period, spanned many areas, including levels of economic development, religious and cultural traditions, and political experiences.[1]

The many ways in which Czechoslovakia differed from its neighbors were evident in each of these realms. In contrast to other Eastern European states after World War I, which were largely agrarian, Czechoslovakia had a relatively highly developed economy from the outset of its existence as an independent state.[2] Thus, while most of the other newly independent states in the region had to begin programs of industrialization, the process was well underway in Czechoslovakia before the creation of an independent political state. Levels of urbanization and the social structure, particularly in the Czech Lands, were more similar to those of the industrialized Western European countries than to those of most other countries in the region. Approximately 48 percent of the population was urban (lived in towns or cities with populations of five thousand or more) in 1930, for example. The literacy rate was also very high. In contrast to the situation in Yugoslavia, Bulgaria, and Romania, where a majority of the population was illiterate, in Czechoslovakia only 4.1 percent of the population ten years of age and older was illiterate in 1930.[3] As I will discuss more fully, these differences were particularly noticeable in the Czech Lands, which were substantially more developed during the interwar period than was Slovakia.

Czechoslovakia also differed from its neighbors in the political realm. The new state structure set up after 1918 had many of the same features—including a multiparty system, proportional representation, and the resulting need for coalition government—that posed a threat to political stability among its neighbors. However, in contrast to the situation in surrounding nation-states, democratic government survived in Czechoslovakia until it was ended by outside forces.

The explanation for why democracy succeeded in Czechoslovakia while it failed elsewhere in the region during this period can be traced in part to the fact that the country had the best preconditions for creating and sustaining democratic government. The country's relatively high level of economic development, its large middle class, the absence of a native aristocracy and its predominantly literate population all played a role. In the Czech Lands in particular the citizenry had a tradition of autonomous, pluralistic group activity and some experience in limited self-government. All these features created better conditions for the maintenance of democracy than existed elsewhere in the region.[4]

The persistence of democracy in Czechoslovakia was also facilitated by the values and actions of many Czech and Slovak political leaders. Personified in the figure of Tomáš G. Masaryk, the first president of the Republic, these values included a deep attachment to and respect for the institutions and procedures of self-government, as well as long-standing ties to Western culture and a commitment to social justice.[5] The influence of these values was reflected in the willingness of party leaders to compromise and cooperate in the coalition governments the electoral system necessitated. It was also evident in the industrial and agrarian reforms begun soon after the establishment of the state, as well as in the decision to enact substantial changes (including land reform and nationalization of certain services) in order to deal with pressing social and economic problems and to defuse popular discontent.[6]

Respect for democratic procedures and awareness of the necessity of compromise in a democracy were also evident in the ability of the leaders of the "Petka," as the five parties that formed the majority of the governments throughout the interwar period—except between March 1926 and November 1929—were called, to maintain party discipline and honor the agreements they made. These values contributed to the continuity of policy and political direction in the new state. They also helped leaders incorporate diverse groups of citizens into the new political system and fostered allegiance to the Republic on the part of ordinary citizens.[7]

Czechoslovak democracy also benefited from the fact that there were fewer severely alienated groups in Czechoslovakia than in many other East European countries. The Czechoslovak Communist party (*Kommunisticka strana Československa* or KSČ) was legal and attracted a sizable following. The large degree of support for the Communist party during the interwar period and the broader consensus concerning certain socialist ideals illustrate the dual political culture that existed in the country. As H. Gordon Skilling has argued, support for the democratic values exemplified by Masaryk and Beneš was balanced by support for the non-democratic values espoused by Communist party leaders and supporters.[8]

Founded in 1921, the KSČ grew out of a longstanding socialist movement that had considerable support before the country gained its independence. Evident in the activities of the Czech-Slav section of the Austrian Social Democratic party under the Dual Monarchy, this support was channeled into the Czechoslovak Social Democratic and Socialist parties that continued to be active after 1918. When Soviet leaders called for the formation of separate communist parties in Europe, the more radical members of the Czechoslovak Social Democratic party, led by Bohumir Šmeral, broke with the right and center of the party and joined with representatives of leftist parties in Slovakia and Ruthenia to establish the KSČ. The conflict between the reality of the situation in Czechoslovakia and Soviet or international considerations that would plague the party throughout its history was evident from the beginning.

The fact that it existed in what was to remain the only functioning democracy in the region was a mixed blessing for the leaders of the KSČ. Because it remained legal until outside actors suspended the activities of all parties, the party had better opportunities to organize its followers and gain popular support than communist parties elsewhere in the region, which were outlawed or suppressed early in the interwar period. At the same time, the necessity of operating in an electoral environment put certain constraints on the party.[9]

Although communist leaders often used nonparliamentary means to further their cause during this period, the party's structure, base and activities were influenced by the need to compete for support in a democratic society. Particularly before 1929, when Klement Gottwald came to head it, the KSČ was a large, mass-based party that bore little resemblance to a standard Leninist cadre party. Although it was not part of the government, its leaders participated in Parliament. The need to compete with other parties for electoral support and the fact that class conflict in Czechoslovakia had been defused to some degree by the government's efforts to promote social justice and progressive social welfare policies also moderated the party's position. These positions changed somewhat after 1929, as Gottwald attempted to follow Soviet desires and Bolshevize the party.[10]

However, even after this change, the activities of the Communist party were less threatening to Czechoslovak democracy in the early years than were problems that arose from other sources. Chief among these were ethnic issues. Challenges arising from the conflicting aims and perspectives of the country's different ethnic groups were less successfully dealt with than those based on economic grounds, and it was ethnic conflict that ultimately provided the pretext for the breakup of the Czechoslovak Republic in 1938. The new Czechoslovak state brought together several ethnic groups in a common state for the first time. The political conflicts that arose from Czech-Slovak differences were complicated in the interwar period by the different interests and activities of several sizeable minorities, including Germans (who comprised 23.4 percent of the population in 1921), Hungarians (5.6 percent), and Ruthenians, Ukrainians, and Russians (3.5 percent).[11]

It was the situation of the Sudeten Germans that ultimately provided Hitler with the excuse to dismember Czechoslovakia. However, Czech and Slovak relations were the more central political issue during most of the interwar period. The roots of this conflict may be found in the disparate experiences of the two groups under foreign rule. As a result of these experiences, Czechs and Slovaks entered the new state with very different levels of economic development, political experiences, national traditions, histories, and cultural lives.

The center of the Austro-Hungarian empire's industrial development, the Czech Lands were far more developed economically and far more urbanized than were Slovakia and Ruthenia. In 1921, for example, 336.4 of every 1,000 inhabitants in the country as a whole were employed in industry, and 395.6 in agriculture. Approximately 406 per 1,000 inhabitants in Bohemia and 378 per 1,000 in Moravia-Silesia worked in industry during that year, but only 175 in Slovakia and 104 in Ruthenia. Much larger proportions of citizens living in Slovakia and Ruthenia worked in agriculture.[12] Literacy rates were also higher in the Czech Lands than in Slovakia and Ruthenia.[13]

The political experiences of the population also differed in the two parts of the country prior to independence. Ruled from Vienna, the Czech Lands benefited from the moderation of Austrian rule that characterized the second half of the nineteenth century. Czech politicians and citizens had an increasing number of opportunities to participate in public life within the framework of imperial and regional institutions. They also benefited from a nationalities policy that exhibited tolerance for the languages and cultures of nondominant nationalities. In Slovakia, on the other hand, there was little room for non-Magyars to play any public role. Slovaks also faced much greater pressure to give up their ethnic identity altogether.

These differences were reflected in the development of national movements among Czechs and Slovaks. In both cases, nationalist leaders first concentrated their efforts on the revival of their respective languages and the development of national literatures. However, the social bases, content, and degree of success of the two movements differed.

Conditions for the development of nationalism were much more favorable for the Czechs than for the Slovaks. In part, this situation reflected the differing strategies for dealing with nationality issues and incorporating diverse national groups in the two halves of the empire. Vienna did not yield to Czech demands for autonomy the way it had to the Hungarians in the compromise of 1867, and Czech-German conflict in Bohemia—as well as in Vienna—grew more acute in the final years of the empire. Nonetheless, the Habsburgs tolerated the formation and activities of nationally oriented groups in Bohemia and, particularly in the late nineteenth century, provided opportunities for participation in limited forms of self-government.[14]

These factors, coupled with the growing industrialization of Bohemia, created favorable conditions for the consolidation of ethnic loyalties among the Czechs and the flowering of Czech culture in the late nineteenth century; they also allowed the development of a mass base for the Czech national movement.[15] The creation of mass political parties after the adoption of universal male suffrage in 1907 increased these opportunities.[16]

In contrast to the situation in the Czech Lands, which allowed a rich associational life to develop and created opportunities for broad segments of the population to participate to some degree in the public life of the nation, in Slovakia the population faced heavy pressure to give up its national identity. The use of Slovak in public life was restricted; there were also severe limitations on nationalist political activity. In addition, Slovak national leaders were handicapped by the low levels of literacy and urbanization in Slovakia. They thus worked under very difficult conditions to prevent the total denationalization of their ethnic group.[17] The Slovak national movement remained weak and relatively small throughout the last years of the Austro-Hungarian empire. Suffrage restrictions also kept most Slovaks from participating in the broader political life of the region.[18]

The Czechs and Slovaks who came together in the interwar republic were separated by religious differences that influenced the political ideals and values of each group. Although the majority of both peoples were nominally Roman Catholic, the nature of Catholicism differed among the two groups, as did the relationship of religion to nationalism, and the impact of religion on politics. Czech culture had become secularized before independence, and the Catholic church played a negligible role in the political life of the Czechs during the interwar period. In addition to Catholic figures Czech national consciousness also came to include a strong Protestant and anticlerical strain. Catholicism was not, then, tied to the sense of Czech national identity that grew out of the efforts of Czech national leaders in the eighteenth and nineteenth centuries in the same way that it was to the development of Slovak national identity. Leaders such as Palacký looked back to the distant past, when Jan Hus, a Bohemian priest, defied the authority of the church and began an early attempt to reform the church. Although Hus was burned at the stake as a heretic in 1415, his teachings provided the spiritual inspiration for the religious and political movement that dominated Bohemian life for much of the next century and brought Bohemia and Moravia into conflict with much of the rest of Europe. The Hussite tradition and Protestant experience remained an important part of the nation's heritage despite the defeat of the Czech nobility in 1620 and the forcible re-Catholicization of the Czech people after the end of the Thirty Years' War in 1648.[19]

Slovakia also developed a Protestant tradition during the Reformation. In contrast to the Czech experience, the Counter Reformation was not as thoroughgoing in Slovakia, since many of the Magyar nobles were Protestant. Protestant intellectuals also played a prominent role in early Slovak efforts to develop a national movement in Slovakia. However, the Roman Catholic church came to exert a much stronger influence on the personal lives, political beliefs, and behavior of Slovaks. Given the lower urbanization and literacy levels in Slovakia, the Catholic clergy were important public figures. Giving voice to mounting Slovak resentment, they became leaders of the movement to promote Slovak national aims.[20]

The consequences of the differences between Czechs and Slovaks became evident soon after the establishment of the new state. Slovak expectations of autonomy in the republic were disappointed by the unitary state structure adopted, as well as by perceived domination of Slovak economic and political life by Prague.[21] Efforts to industrialize Slovakia failed, in part as the result of the world depression. The economy recovered to some degree in the mid-1930s, but Slovakia's level of development remained far below that of Bohemia and Moravia as World War II approached.[22]

The newly established educational system led to a substantial increase in literacy among Slovaks and a vast improvement in their educational levels.[23] The creation of a more urbanized, educated population also provided resources that could be mobilized by Slovak national leaders.[24]

The gains made in Slovakia in these areas, however, were not substantial enough to outweigh the effects of economic hardship and Slovaks' perceptions of injustice. Economic grievances and Prague's continued insistence on centralism provided fertile ground for the action of Slovak nationalists. Influenced by the growing power of Germany and the extremist views of radical nationalist leaders such as Vojtech Tuka, the activities of the People's party (led by Father Andrej Hlinka until his death in 1938 and later by Josef Tiso), paved the way for the establishment of a Slovak state under Nazi tutelage in March 1939. For all practical purposes a puppet of the Third Reich, the new Slovak Republic nonetheless did go a certain way toward satisfying the desires of some Slovaks for their own state. It also created expectations for greater autonomy in the postwar period.[25]

Although Czech-Slovak relations remained problematic throughout the interwar period, the pretext for the break-up of the interwar Czechoslovak state was provided by the grievances of the smaller German minority. Comprising 22.3 percent of the population in 1930, the Sudeten Germans were the descendants of groups that had come to what became Czechoslovakia centuries earlier. Long-term residents of the area for the most part, they were part of the dominant German element of the Austro-Hungarian empire prior to the establishment of independent Czechoslovakia. The conflict that developed between the wars thus had its roots in the interplay of Czech and German culture that had occurred in the region for several centuries. However, two new elements came into the picture during this period. The first to arise was the fact that the Germans, long used to being part of the dominant culture, now found themselves a minority in a Slavic state.

In addition, Czech-German relations came to be tied very closely to events outside the country's border, particularly to the development of Nazism in Germany.[26]

Occupying areas of the country that had substantial resources, the Sudeten Germans shared a number of grievances that were increasingly exploited by militant nationalists and agents of Hitler. Because they were among the wealthiest of the new state's citizens, the Sudeten Germans were disproportionately hit by the land reform and other redistributive policies of the fledgling government.[27] Most of the large estates confiscated for redistribution were German, but most of the land was given to Czechs. Ties to German banks and a heavy export orientation also made industries in this area more vulnerable than those in the rest of the Republic to the impact of the Depression and to the actions of outside powers. Other grievances included banking policies. Security considerations also encouraged the migration of Czechs to traditionally German areas.[28]

These grievances came to outweigh the guarantees of minority rights in the areas of education and culture enjoyed by the Germans and served as issues to mobilize antagonism to the Republic. Although there were democratic German political parties whose representatives took part in Parliament after 1926 and supported the continuation of the Republic, they proved unable to stem the movement toward extremism in the region. Nazi influence grew with Hitler's success in Germany and was reflected in the swell of support for the Sudeten German party, founded by Konrad Henlein, which became an increasingly militant voice for German demands. Coordinating their actions with Hitler's plans, leaders of the German minority provided the excuse for Hitler's dismemberment of the Czechoslovak state. Thus, although outside forces, including Germany's move to take over Czechoslovakia and Western policies of appeasement, ultimately were responsible for the overthrow of democratic government in Czechoslovakia, its heterogenous ethnic composition and policies with regard to ethnic issues created weaknesses that could be exploited by outside actions.[29]

Munich and the Second World War

Abandoned by its Western allies as the result of the Munich Agreement of September 29, 1938, the government of Czechoslovakia submitted to Hitler's demands that it cede the Sudetenland to Germany on September 30 without armed resistance. The capitulation of Presi dent Edvard Beneš and other Czechoslovak leaders to German pressure and this ultimatum was but the first step in the dismantling of the interwar Czechoslovak state. Slovak nationalists under the leadership of the Slovak People's party established an autonomous Slovak government in October 1938 and, under the threat of Hungarian invasion, declared Slovakia an independent republic in March 1939. Ruthenia, which had gained autonomy at the same time as Slovakia, was soon taken over once again by Hungary. Czecho-Slovakia, as the truncated Czechoslovak state was called between October 1938 and March 1939, was further subjected to Hitler's control in March 1939, when Beneš' successor, Emil Hacha, was forced to accept the establishment of a German Protectorate of Bohemia and Moravia, and Germany occupied the country.[30]

The experiences of Czechs and Slovaks during the Second World War differed substantially. These differences reinforced those already evident before the war. They also created new issues and points of contention for the government that came into being once the war was over. In the Czech Lands, German occupation was directed at extinguishing all vestiges of Czech culture and political values. Although human losses among the population as a whole were not on the order of those in countries such as Poland, the Jewish community was virtually destroyed. As occupied regions whose task was to produce industrial products for Germany and the war effort, Bohemia and Moravia also suffered heavy economic losses.[31]

In contrast to the situation in the Czech Lands, in Slovakia the suspension of democratic freedoms and normal cultural life came about as the result of actions by Slovaks. Initially welcomed by certain Slovaks as the realization of their national aims, the Slovak state set up in 1939 emulated Nazi Germany in its policies and organization. Extreme nationalism and anti-Semitism led to the persecution of Czechs and the deportation of Slovak Jews to concentration camps.[32]

At the same time, it was in Slovakia that the most dramatic resistance occurred. (Although some Czechs engaged in passive resistance, there was little open resistance to the occupation.)[33] In Slovakia, on the other hand, opponents of the regime were able to organize more effectively. Democratic and communist forces cooperated in an armed uprising in August 1944. The Germans eventually reasserted their control over the territory freed by resistance forces, but it took them four months to do so. Although the Slovak uprising was not successful, it gave Slovaks who did not support the Slovak state a claim to consideration in the postwar order. The participation of communist leaders in the uprising also provided a basis for later claims by Slovak communists that they had defended Slovakia's honor in a period of national shame.[34]

Czechoslovakia's Development After World War II

Czechoslovakia's level of economic development, distinctive political traditions and values, and ethnic composition have continued to have an important influence after the Second World War. From 1945 (when the country was liberated) to February 1948, Czechoslovakia enjoyed a modified form of pluralism. During this time, which coincided with some Soviet toleration of diversity in political structures and policies throughout Central and Eastern Europe, Czech, Slovak, and other communist leaders talked of the need to take national circumstances into account.[35] In contrast to the situation in many of the countries in the region, which had governments clearly dominated by the Communist party from the time of the end of hostilities on their territories, the Czechoslovak Communist party shared leadership with representatives of other parties. Prominent noncommunist figures, including the prewar president, Edvard Beneš, returned to the country to play a role in public life.

From the beginning of the post–World War II period, however, the Communist party enjoyed certain advantages over its democratic opponents. These included the psychological and other benefits derived from the party's association with the liberating Soviet forces and the presence of the Red Army. The communists were also the beneficiaries of several aspects of the political agreements between Beneš and the Soviets that had preceded his return to Czechoslovakia, and of the provisions of the 1945 Košice Government Program, which became the basis for the newly reconstituted Czechoslovak state. Among the most important of the latter was the agreement to simplify Czechoslovakia's party structure. Justified in part by the argument that parties that had collaborated with the Germans and the puppet Slovak state should be excluded from the new system, the agreement in effect limited the number of legitimate parties to four in Bohemia-Moravia and two in Slovakia. These included, in addition to the Communist party of Czechoslovakia, the National Socialist party, the Czechoslovak People's party, and the Social Democratic party in the Czech Lands and the Communist party of Slovakia and the Slovak Democratic party in Slovakia.[36] According to the provisions of the Košice Government Program, all parties were to be part of the government coalition; there was no true opposition.[37]

The Communist party also benefited from the fact that it controlled key components of the new government, including the ministries of information, the interior, education, and agriculture. The party also sponsored measures, such as efforts to recover from the effects of World War II, which appealed to the patriotism of the population and had genuine popular support.

As a result of these factors, as well as the opportunism of those who saw the communists as the most likely victors in the struggle over the direction of the country's development, the party's membership increased substantially, reaching over a million in 1946.[38] The party also enjoyed a good deal of support from nonmembers, particularly in the Czech Lands. This support was most evident in the 1946 elections, in which the Communist party gained 37.9 percent of the vote, the largest share obtained by any party.[39]

The uneasy truce between the Communist party and other political forces in Czechoslovakia came to an end in February 1948. The immediate catalyst for the institution of a government clearly dominated by the Communist party was a crisis over control of the police, which led to the resignation of the democratic (i.e., noncommunist) cabinet ministers. Designed to force President Beneš to dissolve the government and call for new elections, the resignations backfired as Beneš yielded to the threat of civil unrest posed by communist-organized demonstrations and propaganda.[40] This step, the subject of fierce controversy in Czechoslovakia and elsewhere, opened the way for the formation of a government composed of members of the Communist party and selected sympathizers in other parties. The government was clearly controlled by Klement Gottwald and the Communist party. The May 1948 elections, which offered voters only those candidates approved by the Communist party, reflected the new political realities. The resignation of President Beneš in June—which was followed by his death three months later—further marked the end of the post–World War II coalition period.

Paradoxically, the democratic nature of the interwar political system in Czechoslovakia did not moderate—but rather seemed to intensify—the approach that Czech and Slovak Communist party leaders took to transforming the country once they came to power. Despite the many ways in which their country differed from the Soviet Union, Klement Gottwald and other Communist party leaders began implementing the Stalinist model of political organization, social transformation, and economic development in earnest after February 1948. Their desire to emulate the Soviet experience, even though, or precisely because, it conflicted with the dominant political and cultural values of the country, was evident in the severity of the purges and the terror that accompanied the imposition of communist rule.

In the political realm, earlier efforts to discredit and reduce the power bases of noncommunist actors were stepped up, as were measures designed to strengthen the organizational base of the Communist party and ensure its domination of political life. This process, which began during the coalition period, involved the political use of judicial and propaganda campaigns against leaders of other parties.[41] Political measures were supplemented by economic policies, including further nationalization of industry, severe restrictions on private inheritance, and currency reform, that removed the economic power base of noncommunist elites.[42]

The party leadership also embarked on a renewed campaign to strengthen the Communist party's own organization during this period. Membership in the party expanded greatly and reached two million by the spring of 1948, when the KSČ encompassed approximately one out of five adults in the country. Recruiting campaigns supplemented the influx of members from the former Social Democratic party and diversified the party's social composition by bringing in large numbers of middle-class and white-collar citizens.[43]

The imprint of Soviet experience was soon evident in the institutional structure of Czech and Slovak societies, which were simplified to conform to the Soviet pattern and ensure the political control of the Communist party. It was also reflected in the policies adopted by the post-February government. The formal governmental structure of the country remained relatively unchanged by the new constitution enacted in May 1948. However, governmental organs at every level were effectively subordinated to the corresponding Communist party body. The party structure that had until February 1948 reflected, though in truncated form, the multiparty system from the interwar period, also changed. All political parties with any potential for challenging the communist order were neutralized. The Social Democratic party was forced to merge with the Communist party; the National Socialist and Slovak Democratic parties were disbanded. The Socialist party and the People's party in the Czech Lands, and the Party of Freedom and the Slovak Revival party in Slovakia were allowed to continue only after substantial changes in their leaderships. However, they served largely to mobilize their members to support the aims and policies of the Communist party.[44]

The associational life of the country, which had reflected both the tradition of pluralism and the multiparty nature of the political system in the interwar period, underwent further simplification. Voluntary associations—including trade unions, student groups, and women's associations—had been centralized to some extent since the early post–World War II period as the result of the requirement that they be part of nationwide umbrella organizations and the National Front. After 1948, the noncommunist groups were dissolved, and the unified mass organizations were subordinated to the party.

The Czechoslovak leadership also set up institutions similar to those that existed in the Soviet Union to direct a centrally planned economy. Earlier measures to nationalize large industries were supplemented by policies designed to increase central control over the economy. Eventually, the government passed legislation that eliminated virtually all private ownership.[45]

These measures accompanied the expansion of the central planning mechanism and the adoption of a series of five-year economic plans. As in the Soviet Union and other Eastern European countries, economic planners adopted ambitious programs of rapid industrialization based on the mobilization of all available labor resources. Central officials emphasized heavy industry in particular, to the detriment of agriculture and Czechoslovakia's traditional strength, light industry. The communist government redirected the country's foreign trade, heavily oriented toward Western Europe in the interwar period, to the Soviet Union and other Eastern European countries. They also emulated Soviet practice in agricultural policies. The collectivization drive, which began in earnest in 1950, succeeded in greatly increasing state control over agriculture. By 1960, more than 90 percent of all farm land in Czechoslovakia was collectivized.[46]

The Czechoslovak leadership also followed the Soviet example in attempting to promote social and value change during this period. Party leaders made efforts to restructure the stratification hierarchy and change the status of disadvantaged social groups by manipulating wage policies as well as by controlling access to secondary and higher education. Communist officials used the centrally controlled mass media as well as the newly established system of censorship to discredit members of the old elite and to promote new images of manual laborers, agricultural workers, and women.[47]

They also mounted a concerted campaign against religion, closing seminaries and religious schools, and confiscating church property. Priests were subjected to political controls and their numbers reduced. People known to be believers were harassed, and outward manifestations of religious belief, including church attendance and participation in religious ceremonies such as baptism, marriage, and funerals, declined.[48] Communist leaders also made efforts to socialize Czech and Slovak citizens to accept new political values. The arts and cultural life as well as leisure time activities suffered from these efforts, as political leaders attempted to politicize all aspects of life. In this area, as in others, KSČ leaders took Soviet experience as their guide, disregarding previous links to Western European culture.

As happened in other communist countries, Czech and Slovak leaders increasingly relied on coercion to accomplish their aims. Despite the fact that there had been some genuine support for the Communist party in the interwar and immediate post–World War II period and notwithstanding the lack of any serious challenge to the institutions of the new system after 1948, Czechoslovakia experienced political purges and widespread use of terror as the Stalinist system was consolidated. The purges within the party, which began in 1949 with the wholesale replacement of members of several regional party organizations and soon moved to the upper echelons, were among the most severe in Eastern Europe. The Slovak party was particularly hard hit by the purges, which involved show trials of numerous Slovak communist leaders, including Gustáv Husák (who later led the party), on charges of bourgeois nationalism.[49]

In contrast to the situation in Hungary and Poland, the Stalinist system persisted relatively unchanged in Czechoslovakia after Stalin's death. Workers' riots in Plzen over economic issues in 1953 failed to spread to other areas of the country and were quickly suppressed. Khrushchev's denunciation of Stalin and his crimes in 1956, which ushered in an era of de-Stalinization in the Soviet Union and led to dramatic challenges to the communist system in Hungary and Poland, had a very limited impact in Czechoslovakia. Antonín Novotný, who rose to head the party after Klement Gottwald's death in 1953, continued his predecessor's policies in most areas.

The persistence of Stalinism in Czechoslovakia can be traced to a number of factors that differentiated Czechoslovakia from its neighbors. Because the Czechoslovak economy was not as severely affected by the Stalinist model of development as those of Poland and Hungary by the mid-1950s, the Soviet leadership did not push Czech and Slovak leaders to institute radical changes. The relatively good performance of the economy also meant that economic discontent, one of the primary reasons for mass pressure for change in Poland and Hungary in 1956, was not as pervasive in Czechoslovakia at that time. The Czechoslovak leadership also benefited from a loyal intelligentsia. A reflection of the legality of the Communist party throughout the interwar period and the fact that it enjoyed a fair degree of support in the immediate post–World War II period, there was less pressure for change from communist and nonparty intellectuals than in Hungary and Poland. The party also profited from the fact that there was no strong historical animosity toward Russia or the Soviet Union, neither in the Czech Lands nor in Slovakia.

The severity of the purges and the high level of political control also inhibited change at this time. The harshness of the Stalinist system prevented intellectual opponents of the regime from mounting a political challenge, and the personal involvement of Novotný and his colleagues in the purges strengthened the leadership's resistance to change.

Czechoslovakia's multiethnic composition also contributed to the maintenance of Stalinism. As in later periods, political leaders were able to deflect dissatisfaction with the political system toward other ethnic groups. The differences in the experiences of the Czech Lands and Slovakia also made the development of a unified opposition difficult.

"Socialism with a Human Face"

By the early 1960s, changes in both economic performance and ethnic relations contributed to the movement for reform that culminated in the effort to create "Socialism with a Human Face." Although the overtly political aspects of the reform only came into the open after January 1968, when Alexander Dubček replaced Antonín Novotný as head of the party, the reform movement that came to be known as the Prague Spring was preceded by a lengthy period of debate, discussion, and preparation. To some extent this effort can be seen as a process of delayed de-Stalinization. However, the process was shaped by the particular problems the Stalinist model created in Czechoslovakia. It was also shaped by the different political histories and national traditions of the Czechs and Slovaks.

In Czechoslovakia the original impetus for change came from within the party itself. Ordinary citizens and nonparty intellectuals eventually became involved in the reform process, but it was initiated by the leadership of the party and intellectuals affiliated with the party.

The events that developed into the Prague Spring in 1968 had their roots in several areas of Czech and Slovak life. By the early 1960s the deformations caused by Stalinist economic policies, and the problems associated with central planning and unbalanced investment elsewhere in the region began to be evident in Czechoslovakia. By 1963, the situation had deteriorated to the point that Czechoslovakia had a negative growth rate.

Although it first resisted the idea of economic reform, in 1963 the party leadership appointed a team of economic experts, headed by Ota Šik, to devise a method of improving the economic situation. Šik and his team developed a proposal for economic reform that formed the basis for a program of economic changes approved at the Thirteenth Party Congress in 1966.[50] The incomplete and halting implementation of the reforms over the next two years led some of the economists who supported the reform to argue that it would be impossible to effectively reform Czechoslovakia's economy without change in the political sphere as well.[51]

The spirit of criticism that animated reform economists found echoes in other areas of life. In part a response to Khrushchev's renewed denunciation of Stalin at the Twenty-second Congress of the CPSU in 1962, this attitude also reflected a maturing of the generation of young communists who had joined the party in their early twenties at the close of the war or soon after the party's rise to power in 1948.

Creative communist intellectuals were the first to challenge the regime. Writers and dramatists denounced party control of cultural life and called for greater freedom of expression. Less visible but equally important changes also occurred in other areas as scholars began to question and in many cases renounce established dogmas.[52]

By the late 1960s, the critical tendencies evident in debates and discussions at the elite level spread to other groups in society, including young people, and to the mass organizations. Student radicalism, which arose from concern with student problems, soon came to reflect the new thinking of older intellectuals concerning the need for political change.[53] Reformist tendencies also became evident in the activities of certain mass associations, most notably the women's organizations, during the mid- and late-1960s.[54] For the most part, however, these activities remained confined to intellectuals and members of the political elite. With the exception of new developments in culture and the arts, the public at large had not become involved at this stage of the process.

Slovak desires for greater parity in the Czechoslovak state also contributed to the growing pressure for change in the late 1960s. Slovak leaders and intellectuals resented the broken promises of autonomy for Slovakia made by Czech and Slovak communists after 1945 and the fate of indigenous Slovak communist leaders jailed on charges of "bourgeois nationalism" in 1951. Slovak desires for greater equality within the common state continued to grow during the 1950s and 1960s. In part a reflection of the general intellectual ferment that occurred in the country during this time, Slovak calls for better treatment also expressed continued frustration at the remaining inequalities in living standards and development levels in the two parts of the country, despite investment patterns that gave Slovakia a slight edge in capital investment.[55]

In late 1967, support for political change became evident within the leadership of the party itself. Although the leadership's composition remained relatively stable, divisions developed between those who wanted to preserve the status quo and others, including Alexander Dubček, who supported economic or political change. Opposition to the Novotný leadership came to the fore at the October and December 1967 meetings of the Central Committee. In January 1968, Novotný was forced to relinquish his post as head of the party.[56] His removal signaled the broadening of participation in the debate and discussion about change in Czechoslovakia beyond the elite level. Once censorship effectively ceased to exist in March 1968, the way was open for free expression of a kind unseen in Czechoslovakia since 1948. In the course of eight months, Czechs and Slovaks challenged the shibboleths of the Stalinist system and formulated plans for dramatic changes in public life. A reflection of the rethinking and renewal that had taken place among party intellectuals in the preceding years, this process was aimed at correcting the abuses of the old system. It was also an attempt to devise a form of socialism better suited to Czechoslovakia's democratic traditions, historic links to the rest of Western culture, and relatively advanced level of economic development.

Among the intellectual and political elite, the process focused on several key issues. These included the attempt to come to terms with Stalinism and a reexamination of the purge trials; efforts to prevent future abuses of socialist legality and to institutionalize guarantees of free expression and other civil liberties for citizens; a redefinition of the proper place and role of the Communist party and other political and social organizations; attention to Slovak grievances and the position of Slovakia in the common state; and economic reform. Most succinctly expressed in the Action Program of the party adopted in April 1968, the changes envisioned by the reformers in the party stopped short of a renunciation of one-party rule. As would be the case with Gorbachev's efforts to implement *glasnost* and *perestroika* in the Soviet Union in the 1980s, the 1968 reform movement in Czechoslovakia, which was the precursor of these policies, took as its premise the continuation of socialism in some form.[57]

At first wary of what seemed only another change at the top, the population gradually came to take advantage of the new freedom to criticize past mistakes and discuss public concerns. Free from the restraints of the past two decades, Czech and Slovak citizens aired grievances and called for changes that in many cases went beyond those the party leadership was willing to entertain.[58] Pressure from the general populace for further democratization was most noticeable in the Czech Lands. In Slovakia, national issues took precedence for the population as well as for many party leaders.[59]

Dubček and his supporters in the party leadership thus found themselves caught between the increasingly radical demands from below and the fears of their socialist neighbors. Reluctant to resort to coercion to restrain the activities of their citizens, they also faced mounting pressure from disgruntled conservatives within the party leadership.

In the end, it was the Dubček leadership's inability to reassure Czechoslovakia's external allies that brought about the end of the experiment. Alarmed at what they perceived to be a serious challenge to the leading role of the Communist party and concerned lest the political innovations under discussion spill over into their own countries, the Soviets and conservative Eastern European leaders warned Dubček of the need to change course. When their warnings failed to achieve the desired results, Soviet leaders resorted to military force on August 21, 1968 to bring the Czechs and Slovaks back into line.[60]

Although there was little armed resistance to the invading troops, both the reformists in the leadership and broader groups of Czech and Slovak citizens attempted to preserve as much of the reform momentum as possible. The populace, which had exhibited some skepticism about the proposed reforms in the pre-August period, united behind Dubček, who came to symbolize the country's national pride and hopes for change. The prevailing attitude of passive resistance to the invaders was punctuated by isolated cases of more dramatic opposition throughout the last months of 1968 and early 1969, including the self-immolation of a Czech student, Jan Palach, in Prague in January 1969. The efforts of both the reformist leaders and the population were increasingly hampered, however, by the growing influence of the hardliners within the party leadership.

"Normalization"

The ouster of Dubček as head of the party and his replacement by Gustáv Husák in April 1969 signaled the end of this period of ambivalence. The change in top leaders was soon followed by a concerted effort to stamp out or reverse as many of the changes begun in the reform era as possible.

Of the three factors that influenced Czechoslovakia's history that have been traced so far, the country's ethnic composition and level of economic development appear to be most important in the post-1968 era. As in the period before 1968, Czechoslovakia's ethnic composition meant that Czech and Slovak leaders could deflect part of the population's dissatisfaction with the political system to other targets. Slovak perceptions of inequality continued, despite the fact that the federalization of the country, adopted in October 1968 and put into effect in January 1969, was one of the few aspects of the changes proposed during the reform era that remained after the invasion. They were matched by Czech resentment of the advantages Slovaks were perceived to have gained as the result of the fact that Gustáv Husák was a Slovak, as well as the continued priority given to investment in Slovakia.[61] Ethnic divisions also hampered the development of an effective opposition until the late 1980s.

Czechoslovakia's level of economic development also served to support the status quo in the twenty years after the Soviet invasion. Although the country's economy suffered many of the same distortions as other centrally planned economies, it did not experience the severe crises that occurred in Poland throughout the 1970s and 1980s. In part because the country's economy was less connected to the world economy and as the result of the leadership's refusal to borrow from the West to support further modernization, the oil crisis of the 1970s and the resultant downturn in Western economies did not hurt Czechoslovakia as much as it did some of its socialist neighbors. Although the country experienced chronic economic difficulties in many sectors, economic performance did not really plummet again until 1981. It was not until the 1980s, then, that poor economic performance threatened the leadership's political strategy of gaining popular compliance by improving the standard of living.

Czechoslovakia's ties to the rest of Western culture appeared to be of less importance than the other two characteristics discussed above for much of this period. However, as the development of the dissident movement and the growth of opposition to the communist system in the late 1980s illustrate, many groups in the population continued to hold values at odds with those of the leadership. Czechoslovakia's links to Western culture and contacts with individuals and organizations in democratic countries helped to sustain these values and further undermined support for the system.

The effort to roll back the clock to the pre-1968 period and return Czechoslovakia once again to its position as the Soviet Union's most loyal East European ally intensified after the selection of Husák as top party leader in April 1969. The ability of the Husák leadership to revert to the prereform situation, a process which became known as "normalization," was facilitated by the fact that many of the changes discussed in the first half of 1968 had not been institutionalized when the invasion occurred.

In the political realm, normalization included efforts to reassert the leading role of the party, the reinstitution of control of the media and other forms of information, massive personnel purges, and a change in the political formula. Explicitly disavowing the "post-January course" of the party, the leadership took steps to reduce the influence of nonparty groups and individuals in politics and restore party discipline. Dubček's supporters were removed from positions of influence, to be replaced by people who had either opposed the reform or had remained uninvolved.

Similar changes were made in the leaderships of the mass organizations, whose activities were redirected along more traditional lines, and in the universities and research institutes. The centers of intellectual life were particularly hard hit by the personnel changes made at this time, as many of the most capable experts lost their positions. These changes involved approximately a half-million people during 1969–1970,[62] and were more far-reaching in the Czech Lands than in Slovakia, where many of those who supported Dubček were primarily concerned with national issues. The personnel changes had long-term repercussions in Czechoslovakia, for they depleted the talent the postreform leadership could draw on to formulate public policies in all areas of life. Thus, although the policy of relying more heavily on the input of experts and specialists in policy-making begun in the period leading up to the reform continued, the level of expertise and talent available to the leadership declined.[63]

"Normalization" also involved a change in the political formula. The Husák leadership repudiated the attempt to create citizen support through opportunities for greater involvement by broader groups of people in the political process. Instead, it reverted to the strategy, much more common in communist countries, of gaining citizen compliance through a combination of material rewards and coercion.[64]

This strategy proved to be successful in preventing any open manifestation of dissatisfaction in Czechoslovakia for almost a decade. At the mass level, improvements in the standard of living, as well as increases in social welfare benefits and their extension to previously uncovered groups of the population, such as collective farmers, appeared to have bought the quiescence if not the support of much of the population. The impact of these measures was supplemented in Slovakia by the benefits the Slovaks received from federalization as well as by the perceived increase in Slovak influence in Prague after Husák's elevation to the position of top party leader.[65]

The leadership relied on similar measures, and on the selective use of coercion, to neutralize any overt opposition by intellectuals during this period. More directly affected by the purges and reinstitution of party control than other segments of the population, many Czech and Slovak intellectuals also retreated from the political realm to focus on nonpolitical concerns.[66]

As the emergence of Charter 77 in January 1977 and events in 1988 and 1989 indicate, this strategy did not eliminate all organized opposition and dissent in Czechoslovakia. Despite persistent harassment of those who signed or served as spokespersons of the Charter, the group continued its activities for over a decade. Encompassing ex-reformers from 1968 and dissidents from a variety of other perspectives, the Charter from its inception championed human rights in Czechoslovakia. It also came to serve as the focus of an increasingly vigorous independent or "second" culture and as an alternate source of information and analysis.[67] Important as the Charter was as a symbol of hope and as a focus for nonconformist activity and thought, it did not pose a real threat to political stability in Czechoslovakia until the late 1980s. The persistent risk of arrest or other reprisals for open participation in Charter activities limited the number of people willing to support its activities openly. The Charter's impact was also curtailed by its social and ethnic composition and by the fact that, in contrast to the situation that emerged in Poland in the late 1970s and early 1980s, the Chartists were not successful in forging an alliance with broader groups in society—such as the workers—until external factors changed significantly.[68] However, as the events of November 1989 were to show, the Charter's activities helped to undermine support for the communist regime. While a relatively small number of people (approximately 2,500 by late 1987) signed the Charter, its influence on perceptions of issues and thinking in Czechoslovakia was much wider. Charter activists also played pivotal roles in the Civic Forum, the organization that emerged to lead the revolution in November 1989, and in the noncommunist government that emerged in December of the same year.

The Rise of Gorbachev and the Collapse of Communism

Gorbachev's rise to power in the Soviet Union at first had very little impact in Czechoslovakia. In contrast to the situations in Poland and Hungary, Czechoslovakia appeared to be mired in the aftereffects of normalization during the early years of Gorbachev's rule. As I have argued elsewhere, the picture of Czechoslovakia that prevailed in the West—as a country whose apathetic, alienated population was ruled by an aging coalition of hardline and moderate leaders—was too simplistic.[69] However, from 1985 to 1987, developments in the country seemed to conform to this image. Gustáv Husák and other leaders gave lip service to the positive nature of the changes being attempted in the Soviet Union but they were noticeably less enthusiastic about following the Soviet example than usual. They were particularly hesitant to enact any changes that would signal the dawning of an era of *glasnost* in Czechoslovakia.[70]

Glasnost thus had few echoes in the political realm in Czechoslovakia. Scattered incidents, such as the lenient sentences given the leaders of the Jazz Section who were tried and convicted for their independent cultural activities indicated that there was some degree of division among the leadership and raised hopes that *glasnost* in the Soviet Union would lead to a similar loosening of the reins in the political sphere in Czechoslovakia.

However, as later reprisals against religious believers and other dissidents illustrated, the leadership was not willing to allow any real discussion of political reform. Clearly afraid of a repetition of the events leading up to 1968, when economic reforms spilled over into the political realm, the party leadership continued to set strict limits on political debate. There was also relatively little turnover of personnel in the party or the state until mid-1988, despite perfunctory calls for the elimination of corruption and the rejuvenation of party cadres at all levels.

Prior to 1987, the main area in which Gorbachev's policies in the Soviet Union had an impact in Czechoslovakia was the economy. Prodded by continuing poor economic performance, as well as by the

Soviet emphasis on *perestroika,* the Husák leadership adopted a new approach to economic change in January 1987. The measures adopted by the party leadership included the endorsement in principle of substantial changes in the organization and management of the economy. Thus, the document envisioned a significant reduction in the role and size of the central planning apparatus, with a corresponding increase in the powers of enterprises; greater worker input in the selection of managers; greater use of the profit motive and other incentives; and price reform as well as change in the organization of the foreign trade system.[71] As with earlier efforts to improve economic performance, the leadership approved only broad principles, leaving detailed policy measures to be worked out later. The approach to economic issues adopted in 1987 differed substantially from that which informed efforts to improve economic performance in the early 1980s. In contrast to the earlier efforts that had attempted to make the centralized planning system work more efficiently, the changes proposed in 1987 were similar in many respects to those which economists who eventually came to support the political reform of 1968 formulated in the early 1960s.

The general nature of the principles adopted and the gradual timetable envisioned for the implementation of concrete changes in economic practice raised the possibility that opponents of change would sabotage the reform before it was put into practice. There were also numerous problems with the nature of the proposed reforms themselves. Many economists in Czechoslovakia and abroad expressed serious doubts concerning their efficacy.[72] In any event, few of the proposed changes had been implemented before the communist system was ousted.

The collapse of the communist system in Czechoslovakia in November 1989 was precipitated by events outside the country. The negotiated end of communism in Poland and Hungary and the fall of the hardline Honecker regime in East Germany after mass protests were important catalysts in bringing about the end of communism in Czechoslovakia. But while these developments, which ultimately can be traced to change in Gorbachev's policies toward Eastern Europe were critical, the events of 1989 reflected the underlying crises and widespread dissatisfaction of the people of Czechoslovakia with the communist system. They were also conditioned by important changes at both the mass and elite level between 1987 and 1989.[73] These domestic developments, in turn, are crucial to understanding the dramatic changes that occurred in 1989 and political developments since that time.

Despite the surface stability of the Husák (and later Jakeš) leadership, Czechoslovakia's leaders confronted many of the same political and economic problems that plagued other communist leaders in the final years of communism in the region. In the area of politics, Czech and Slovak leaders faced the continued impact of the legacy of 1968. Evident in the strategy of rule adopted by the leadership, the memory of the reform era was also reflected in the fear of the Husák, and later Jakeš, leadership of any movement toward reform. This uneasiness was also evident in the failure of a reformist faction to materialize within the party leadership itself. The specter of 1968 also overshadowed the leadership's reactions to independent activists and helps to explain why there was so little effort on the part of the Czechoslovak leadership to reach some sort of accommodation with the opposition—as occurred in Hungary and Poland prior to the end of communist rule—despite the spread of opposition.

The leadership also faced serious economic problems. Although economic performance in Czechoslovakia never deteriorated to the level found in Poland during the communist period, by the 1980s, poor economic performance had thrown the leadership's strategy of rule into question.[74] By the end of the 1980s, then, Czech and Slovak leaders faced increasingly serious challenges in both the political and economic realms, despite the surface stability of the system.

The late 1980s also saw a number of changes at both the elite and mass levels that proved to be important in 1989. At the elite level, there were major changes in the composition of the top party bodies. Gustáv Husák's replacement by Miloš Jakeš as head of the party in December 1987 was followed by the resignation of many of the full members of the Presidium. In March 1985, the average tenure of the eleven full members of the Presidium was seventeen years, and four of the full members had been on that body for eighteen to twenty years. By March 1989, by way of contrast, six of the eleven full members had been in their positions for less than two years.[75] The career patterns and social backgrounds of those who were selected to replace them did not differ to a great degree. However, the new members of the party leadership were younger and, therefore, less personally responsible for and, as it turned out, committed to the policies of "normalization." They were also less experienced than their predecessors. The turnover at the top increased the divisions within the leadership. In addition to those who were elevated to their positions in the late 1980s, there was a core of holdovers from the Husák era, many of whom had been in power since the early 1960s. The impact of these divisions at the top manifested itself in the vacillating response of the leadership to the mounting challenge from below, as well as in the differing views that began to emerge concerning the reforms of 1968 and the necessity of opening a dialogue with the opposition.

The period between 1987 and 1989 also saw important changes in the willingness of citizens to challenge the communist system. Numerous new independent organizations were formed. Larger numbers of citizens also began to participate in unauthorized demonstrations and protests. These included religious pilgrimages and processions that came to involve an estimated 600,000 people in 1989. Opposition activists also organized commemorations of important political events—such as the demonstrations on the anniversary of the 1968 invasion of Czechoslovakia—in 1988 and 1989. One of the most important of these was the January 1989 commemoration of the twentieth anniversary of the suicide of Jan Palach. This event was harshly broken up by the police and resulted in the jailing of Václav Havel and an estimated forty other dissidents.

These activities were to some extent a continuation of earlier forms of dissent. But they also marked important changes in the relationship of citizens to the regime and the nature of opposition in Czechoslovakia. Thus, in contrast to the apparent political passivity of most young people in the twenty years after 1968, many of the most energetic of the new activists were young people. The events of 1987 to 1989 were also significant in that dissent began to emerge from the intellectual ghetto to which it had been confined. Increasing numbers of Slovaks also began taking part in unauthorized activities. The letters of support sent by ordinary workers to Václav Havel after his arrest in early 1989 and the willingness of people who remained part of the official world to sign petitions, including "A Few Sentences," which called for political freedom and an end of censorship, indicated the extent of popular dissatisfaction.

The late 1980s also saw an awakening in the official intellectual world. Particularly after 1987, social scientists and creative intellectuals began to challenge accepted dogma in many areas. As in the period that led up to 1968, many used the leadership's ostensible support for Soviet policies to criticize official positions more openly.[76]

Thus, although political developments in Czechoslovakia in the late communist period were not as dramatic as those in Hungary or Poland, changes at both the mass and elite levels in the late 1980s had undermined the stability of the system. They also limited the capacity of the communist leadership to deal with increasing challenges from within and without.

These developments had an important impact on the dramatic events of November 1989 and their aftermath. In Poland and Hungary reformists within the party leadership negotiated the end of communist rule in discussions with the opposition over a period of several months, but the communist system fell in the space of twenty-three days in Czechoslovakia. As it attempted to deal with the spread of protests after the brutal beating of peaceful student demonstrators on November 17, 1989, the Jakeš leadership was hampered by its internal divisions and inexperience. Although certain individuals, including Ladislav Adamec, who replaced Lubomir Štrougal as premier in 1988, attempted to serve as mediators, the party's options were limited by the fact that, in contrast to the situations in Hungary, Poland, and the German Democratic Republic, where communist reformist factions helped ease the transition to multiparty rule, there had been no clearly identifiable reformist factions in the Czechoslovak leadership for over twenty years. Unable to regain the initiative from the opposition once it became clear that Soviet forces could no longer be counted upon, the party leadership quickly acceded to the main demands of the opposition, including the end of one-party rule.

When the police attack on student demonstrators galvanized the nation in November 1989, the links that had been forged between well-known dissident activists, student leaders, and critical intellectuals in the official world allowed them to organize quickly to direct the growing demonstrations and use the momentum generated to press for the end of the communist system. The umbrella organization that emerged to negotiate with the government, Civic Forum and its counterpart in Slovakia, Public Against Violence, thus had their roots in the opposition movement that had developed over the preceding decades. However, opposition leaders and activists were also taken by surprise at the speed with which the old system fell and by the extent of the changes they were able to achieve.

The Transition to Democracy and the Market

Although Czechoslovakia lagged behind some of its Eastern European neighbors in challenging the communist system, once the process of change began, the old system was swept away very quickly. The Velvet Revolution led to the resignation of the conservative communist party leadership of Miloš Jakeš, the renunciation of the party's leading role, and the formation of the country's first noncommunist government in forty-one years. The victory of the revolution was capped by the election of Václav Havel, a dissident playwright, as president of the Republic in late December 1989. Because the old system collapsed so quickly, opposition activists had to take responsibility almost immediately for running the government as well as for instituting fundamental political and economic reforms. The Government of National Understanding, as the new noncommunist government came to be called, thus began the arduous process of restoring multiparty democracy, recreating a market economy, and reorienting the country's external relations. As in earlier periods, the transition to postcommunist institutions and values is being influenced in important ways by Czechoslovakia's precommunist political traditions, level of economic development, and ethnic composition.

Czechoslovakia's new leaders face many of the same political and economic problems that confront other postcommunist leaders. In the political realm they must reestablish the rule of law; find new leaders to replace old officials; reform old institutions and establish new ones; deal with the remnants of the Communist party's power and the legacy of the communist period on popular values and expectations; and find a way of channeling popular desire for change into coherent political directions and policy orientations. They must also reshape the structure of the country to satisfy the national aspirations of Czechs, Slovaks, and other national groups and deal with the accumulated social, environmental, and other problems that are the result of over forty years of communist rule.[77] They must also deal with the economic legacy of communism.

The end of the Communist party's monopoly of power was followed by a rapid repluralization of Czechoslovakia's associational and political life. Most of the official mass organizations that served largely to transmit the directives of the Communist party to their members and the official trade unions were disbanded or lost the majority of their members. These groups have been replaced by a wide variety of interest groups, charitable, patriotic, religious, and professional organizations, and independent unions. Many of these groups are re-creations of pre–World War II groups; others, including several citizen initiatives and ecological movements, have formed around new issues.

The period between November 1989 and June 1990 also saw the proliferation of political parties. As in the interwar period, Czechoslovakia will clearly have a multiparty system in the postcommunist era. Over sixty political parties and nonparty political groupings were registered by late February 1990, and twenty-three fulfilled the conditions necessary to participate in the June 8 and 9 elections. These ranged from the Communist party, which retained the same name, to the Friends of Beer party. The Czechoslovak Socialist party and the Czechoslovak People's party, which had been allowed to exist under the control of the Communist party during the communist period, gained independence. A number of parties with roots in the interwar period; nationalist parties, such as the Slovak National party, and the Movement for Self-Administrative Democracy–Association for Moravia and Silesia; and new political groupings and citizen initiatives formed around new issues, such as the Civic Forum and the Public Against Violence, also competed in the elections.[78]

Many of these parties were winnowed out, at least for the time being, by the results of the June 1990 elections. At the federal level, the Civic Forum–Public Against Violence coalition emerged as the dominant political force and determined the composition of the new government. Civic Forum received 50.0 percent of the vote to the House of Nations and 53.2 percent of the vote to the House of the People of the Federal Assembly. Civic Forum also did well in the elections to the Czech Republic's legislature, receiving 49.5 percent of the vote. Its primary election rival in the Czech Lands, a union of Christian Democratic parties, was badly hurt at the end of the campaign by charges that Josef Bartončík, leader of its main political force, the Czechoslovak People's party, had collaborated with the secret police, and received only 8.7 percent of the vote to the Federal Assembly.

In Slovakia, Public Against Violence did better than expected in the elections to federal bodies, winning 33 percent of the vote for the House of the People and 37 percent for the House of Nations. However, the Christian Democratic party, led by former dissident and current prime minister of Slovakia Ján Čarnogurský, remained a strong political force in Slovakia, where it won 19 percent of the vote to the House of the People and 17 percent to the House of Nations. It received approximately the same proportion of the vote for the Slovak National Council (19.2 percent), compared to 29.3 percent for the Public Against Violence.[79]

The June elections thus validated the policies adopted by the first postcommunist government and legitimized the new government that was formed afterward. At the same time, because the elections took place while the electoral system—as well as the broader political environment—were themselves still very much in flux, the results are not necessarily predictive of future political alignments. Both Civic Forum and Public Against Violence provided umbrellas for a wide variety of groups and individuals with differing political views and policy preferences. Certain groups that originally supported these organizations broke away in 1990, and both groups split further in early 1991 as political views and policy preferences became more differentiated.

As in other political systems in transition,[80] voter preferences and party identification are quite fluid at present. The results of the local elections held in November 1990 illustrate these tendencies. Civic Forum retained its dominant position in the Czech Lands, with 35.4 percent of the vote. However, in Slovakia, Public Against Violence ran second, with 20.4 percent of the vote, to the Christian Democratic Movement, which received 27.4 percent of the vote. The Slovak National party, which public opinion polls indicated was the strongest party in Slovakia during much of the fall of 1990, received a mere 3.2 percent of the vote in November.[81] The fact that support for the Communist party increased in the Czech Lands (to 17.4 percent) and slightly (to 14 percent) in Slovakia is a further indication of the volatility of voter preferences at present.

The Communist party won approximately 13 percent of the vote in both the Czech Lands and Slovakia in the June elections. Representatives of small nationalist parties were also elected to the Federal Assembly from both parts of the country. In the Czech Lands, the Movement for Self-Administrative Democracy—Association for Moravia and Silesia won 7.9 percent of the vote to the House of the People and 9.1 percent for the House of Nations. In Slovakia the separatist Slovak National party, formed in April 1990, won 13 percent and 11 percent of the vote for those houses, respectively. Neither the Social Democrats nor the Greens received enough votes to seat deputies.[82]

Although it is unlikely that the Communist party will play any significant role in Czechoslovak politics in the near future given the dramatic rejection of communism and socialism in all forms evident in the events of the last year, it may continue to play a small role in a democratic Czechoslovakia. The thirteen percent of the vote gained by the party in the June 1990 elections is very similar to its levels of support in the interwar period. Efforts to reform the party have been hampered by the mass defection of party members, as well as by the overall impact of forty years of communist rule. At present, support for the party appears to be drawn largely from older people as well as from those so compromised by their roles in the old system that they have nowhere else to go politically. The party may also gain support as a result of fear of change and the negative impact of economic reforms in the future. But at present it is not a viable alternative to the government in power, and thus, cannot serve as a responsible opposition. The task of creating stable political organizations and orientations remains to be completed in Czechoslovakia as elsewhere in the region.

As they seek to build new institutions and create or resurrect values that will support democratic rule, Czechoslovakia's new leaders continue to struggle with the issue of how to prevent the Communist party from translating its previous advantages into undue power in the new system. Popular resentment over the large number of party members and former party members who remained in important economic and political positions at the local level was reflected in President Havel's call in August 1990 to rout old "mafias" in a number of areas.

The new leadership in Czechoslovakia stated at the outset that there would be no wholesale purges in the governmental or economic sectors. Labor legislation that in effect required that workers and employees receive five-months notice before they were fired and the difficulty of finding qualified replacements further slowed personnel changes. As a result, in many areas new officials comprise only a thin layer at the top of organizations with largely unchanged staffs. Efforts to reform the bureaucracy must include both attempts to reshape the work habits and expectations of employees in these institutions in such a way as to overcome the legacy of their earlier experiences, and more extensive personnel changes.

Czechoslovakia's new leaders are also attempting to counter the impact of the communist period on the political attitudes and values of the population. Czech and Slovak leaders and citizens have turned to their precommunist past as they replace communist political institutions and attempt to create new political values and symbols. In contrast to many of the other formerly communist countries, in Czechoslovakia there are relatively few elements of the precommunist value system and political culture that threaten democracy. As noted earlier in this chapter, there were certain antidemocratic elements in political life in Czechoslovakia, as in other countries in the region, during the interwar period, particularly in Slovakia. A number of actions of the government before and immediately after World War II in regard to members of particular ethnic groups, such as the expulsion of the Sudeten Germans and the Hungarians in Slovakia, also provide grounds for questioning the extent to which democratic values such as tolerance were widespread in the population. The strong support in the twenties and thirties for the Communist party also indicates that the country's political culture at the time was not entirely democratic, but rather a dual one. However, in contrast to the situation in other formerly communist countries, the dominant political culture and traditions were supportive of democracy. The country's twenty-year experience with a functioning democracy, then, at the very least provides a better basis for reconstructing democracy in Czechoslovakia than exists in many other countries in the region.[83] As in the interwar period, when democracy survived in Czechoslovakia while it failed elsewhere in the region in part because the conditions for establishing and maintaining democracy were better in Czechoslovakia than elsewhere, so today the country has many of the prerequisites for successful democratic rule.

Nonetheless, there are several unresolved issues. The first of these is how widespread and deep the attachment to democracy and democratic procedures is in the population at present. In Czechoslovakia there has been a high degree of consensus on the major outlines of the postcommunist order: pluralistic political life and an economic system that will have more elements of the free market. However, it is unclear how the population will respond to the need for day-to-day involvement as the political situation normalizes.

A large sector of the population appears to have become extremely apathetic or cynical about political affairs and alienated from politics. The enthusiastic support for the protests that brought down the communist system, the interest in politics demonstrated by respondents in survey research done in the early part of 1990, and the high levels of voter turnout in the June 1990 elections (ninety-five percent)[84] indicate that this legacy can be overcome. However, certain of the attitudes fostered during the communist period may prove more difficult to eradicate. As the decline in voter turnout for the local elections in November of 1990 and the sharp drop in the number of Czechoslovak citizens who indicated that they were politically involved in mid-1990 compared to January 1990 illustrate,[85] the task of creating a political culture that is based on a view of oneself as an active political subject rather than as an object of politics will be a lengthy one in Czechoslovakia.

Changing public attitudes and values will also be complex in the economic sphere. As in the political realm, although the population clearly rejected much of the official value system, certain aspects appear to have been internalized. For the most part, these do not bode well for the prospects of economic reform and efficiency. Poor worker morale, the lack of individual responsibility in the workplace, and the deep-seated egalitarianism fostered by the communist system[86] will create barriers to efforts to reform the economy and improve economic performance.

Czechoslovakia's new leaders are faced with the economic, as well as political, legacy of forty years of communist rule. The impact of communist policies on the country's economy and the difficulty of the transition to a market economy were expressed succinctly in President Havel's comment in his 1991 New Year's Day address that what they thought was a "neglected house a year ago is, in fact, a ruin."[87] Although there is a general consensus on the need to move toward a market economy, important divisions have occurred among political leaders and experts concerning the pace and extent of economic change that should be enacted. Evident in the differing perspectives of the president's top economic advisors in early 1990, these differences were resolved to some degree by the decision to move ahead more rapidly to liberalize prices, encourage demonopolization, and privatize the economy. A series of laws dealing with private ownership and enterprises, the running of state enterprises, the use of land, joint ventures, foreign exchange, joint stock companies, and foreign trade were adopted in April 1990 to lay the basis for the return to a market economy.[88] Under pressure from numerous political groups, including the Civic Forum, the government adopted a program for economic reform prior to the June elections that has been widely interpreted as a victory for those, including Finance Minister Václav Klaus, who wish to move more quickly. Its key elements are privatization of the economy by use of domestic and foreign capital; a reduction of subsidies and deregulation of prices; and internal convertibility of the crown. Other aspects of the general program of reform adopted by the government include a restrictive monetary policy and institutional changes designed to simplify the economic ministries and planning apparatus and increase the responsibility of enterprise management.[89] The basic tenets of this plan for economic change were reaffirmed in the proposal for economic reform submitted by the federal, Czech, and Slovak governments to the Federal Assembly in early September 1990.[90]

Plans for economic reform also include a substantial reorientation of the country's external economic relations away from the very high level of dependence on the Soviet Union and other Comecon countries toward the West. In 1990, Czechoslovakia rejoined the IMF and World Bank and was granted most-favored-nation status by the United States. The positive responses and promised aid from democratic governments in Western Europe and the United States have been coupled with increased interest on the part of Western investors. At the same time, Czech and Slovak leaders have had to deal with the negative economic impact of changes in Soviet economic policies toward the region and the disruption of its economic relations with many of its other trading partners—including the former GDR—as well as with the impact of the Persian Gulf crisis.[91]

As in the political realm, Czechoslovakia has a number of advantages over some of its Eastern European neighbors that may make the transition to a market economy less painful than it will be elsewhere.[92] These include the country's development level, a skilled labor force that has a high degree of technical training, and a strong industrial tradition that predates the communist period. In addition, the country still has very low levels of external debt, and the standard of living is among the highest in Eastern Europe.

Although these factors may cushion the impact of measures to reintroduce a market economy, they may pose liabilities as well. The fact that Czechoslovakia was one of the most developed countries to become communist means that it also has one of the most outdated physical plants, particularly in Bohemia and Moravia. The low foreign debt that resulted from administrative limitations on imports also meant that the country had to forgo the modernization that the import of Western technologies and processes might have provided. Similarly, although the standard of living provides a buffer that many of the other countries in the region do not have at present, it may also foster resistance to economic change. Public opinion research conducted in 1990 found that the majority of the population favored a conversion to a market economy, even at the expense of a short-term decline in living standards and an increase in unemployment. However, approximately one-third of respondents were somewhat or firmly opposed to such changes. Fears of possible unemployment and of the impact of anticipated increases in rents and the cost of living are also widespread.[93] Resistance to radical reform also continues to be voiced by numerous enterprise managers and economic experts.[94] Differences in the perspectives of the federal and republic level governments regarding economic issues have also emerged. Economic issues will continue to dominate the political agenda in Czechoslovakia in the near future. The success of the government's efforts to reform the economy and deal with the impact of changes in the country's external economic relations without producing a prolonged decline in the standard of living in turn will have important implications for the success of the transition to democracy.

The end of censorship and control of the political agenda by the Communist party has led to the emergence of new political issues and problems and the reemergence in new forms of old issues that could not be dealt with openly during the communist period. These include environmental concerns, crime, and the need to reorient policy in almost all areas of life to remove the distortions created by communist rule.[95]

Ethnic conflicts are among the most important of these issues. Despite the federalization of the country in 1969 and further improvement in the standard of living in Slovakia, tensions between Czechs and Slovaks continued to grow.[96] One of the many issues which have reemerged as the subject of public debate and controversy after the end of one-party rule and the elimination of censorship, ethnic conflicts pervade discussion of most of the critical issues facing the current government. Evident in the prolonged debate over the name of the country, which was changed twice in early 1990, Czech-Slovak conflict increased throughout 1990. In late summer 1990, nine Slovak political parties, led by the nationalist Slovak National party, issued a call for Slovakia to become an independent state. Public opinion polls indicated that support for the Slovak National party grew in the fall of 1990. Many Public Against Violence representatives, as well as those of the Christian Democratic Movement, rejected separatism, but most political parties and groupings in Slovakia want to see an increase in its autonomy. Although the Slovak National party received a very small share of votes in the local elections in November 1990, its actions have increased the salience of ethnic issues and pushed other political forces into more nationalistic positions. Certain leaders of the Christian Democratic Movement, in particular, have begun to push more forcefully for Slovak autonomy. Differences of opinion on the national question thus have strained the coalition between Public Against Violence and the Christian Democratic Movement in Slovakia as well as at the federal level.[97] Differing perspectives on this issue were also one of the factors that led to the ouster of Slovak Prime Minister Vladimir Mečiar in April 1991 and to the formal split between his followers and those of Fedor Gál in Public Against Violence.

Ethnic tensions continue to complicate plans for economic reform as well as the process of constitutional revision now underway. Although the federal, Czech, and Slovak governments issued a joint plan for economic reform in early September 1990, there are important differences in the perspectives of officials of each government concerning the pace of economic change, the priority to be given to environmental issues, and many other aspects of the proposed economic reforms, including structural changes. Because many of the most inefficient large enterprises are in Slovakia, for example, the scheduled end of government subsidies will be particularly painful there. The plan to end Czechoslovakia's production of arms for export would also have been felt disproportionately in Slovakia—where many of the country's armaments plants are located—and was therefore rejected by Slovak leaders.

Disagreement over the division of power between the federal and republic governments proposed in their respective constitutions peaked in December 1990. Renewed disagreements between the republic governments and Czech and Slovak representatives in the Federal Assembly over a draft power-sharing agreement led President Havel to request emergency powers from the national assembly to prevent the breakup of the federation. The crisis was temporarily resolved by a hastily arranged compromise on December 12, 1990, but the two sides continue to disagree on several important issues which are likely to resurface before the new constitutions are adopted. Members of other ethnic groups—such as the Hungarians, Moravians, Ukrainians, and Gypsies—have also begun to organize around ethnic issues and are demanding greater autonomy.[98] As in the interwar period then, the main threat to political stability and the success of Czechoslovakia's transition to democracy comes not from antidemocratic forces, but from ethnic conflict.

As the preceding pages have illustrated, Czechoslovakia's history in the twentieth century has reflected the impact of its particular national traditions, social and ethnic composition, and level of economic development, as well as the impact of events and forces originating beyond its borders. It has also been characterized by important disruptions and changes of regime that have led to discontinuities in the political experiences and values of the country's citizens. As a result of the events of late 1989, the citizens of Czechoslovakia are once again experiencing a fundamental reordering of their economic, social, and political institutions. As in the past, the way in which the country's new leaders deal with the tasks they face in overcoming the legacy of communist rule and creating new economic, political, and social institutions will be determined largely by the country's particular characteristics. At the same time, as has been true throughout the country's history as a political state, developments in Czechoslovakia will continue to be influenced in important ways by events in the country's neighbors and in the broader international environment.

NOTES

1. See Josef Korbel, *Twentieth-Century Czechoslovakia: The Meanings of Its History* (New York: Columbia University Press, 1977), 12–37; Věra Olivová, *The Doomed Democracy: Czechoslovakia in a Disrupted Europe, 1914–1938* (London: Sidgwick and Jackson, 1972), 23–100; Dagmar Perman, *The Shaping of the Czechoslovak State: A Diplomatic History of the Boundaries of Czechoslovakia, 1914–1920* (Leiden: E. J. Brill, 1962); and Victor S. Mamatey, "The Establishment of the Republic," in *A History of the Czechoslovak Republic, 1918–1948*, Victor S. Mamatey and Radomír Luža, eds. (Princeton: Princeton University Press, 1973), 3–38; and Mamatey, "The Birth of Czechoslovakia: Union of Two Peoples," in *Czechoslovakia, the Heritage of Ages Past: Essays in Memory of Josef Korbel*, Hans Brisch and Ivan Volgyes, eds. (New York: Columbia University Press, 1979), 75–88, for discussions of this period. See Sharon L. Wolchik, *Czechoslovakia in Transition: Politics, Economics, and Society in the Post-Communist Period* (London: Pinter, 1991, forthcoming), ch. 1, for a more extensive treatment of many of the arguments made in this chapter.

2. For example, elsewhere in the region, from 52 to approximately 80 percent of the population was engaged in agriculture in 1930. In Czechoslovakia, only 34 percent of the population made a living in agriculture in that year. See Andrew János, "The One-Party State and Social Mobilization: East Europe Between the Wars," in *Authoritarian Politics in Modern Society*, Samuel P. Huntington and Clement Moore, eds. (New York: Basic Books, 1979), 208; and Václav L. Beneš, "Czechoslovak Democracy and Its Problems," in Mamatey and Luža, eds., *A History of the Czechoslovak Republic*, 42–43.

3. Sharon L. Wolchik, "The Precommunist Legacy, Economic Development, Social Transformation, and Women's Roles in Eastern Europe," in *Women, State, and Party in Eastern Europe*, Sharon L. Wolchik and Alfred G. Meyer, eds. (Durham: Duke University Press, 1985), 33.

4. See Beneš, "Czechoslovak Democracy"; Mamatey, "The Establishment of the Republic"; and Josef Anderle, "The First Republic, 1918–1938," in *Czechoslovakia: The Heritage of Ages Past*, Brisch and Volgyes, eds., 89–112, for discussions of these aspects of interwar Czechoslovakia.

5. See Korbel, *Twentieth-Century Czechoslovakia*, 38–40; Beneš, "Czechoslovak Democracy," 87–89; Anderle, "The First Republic," 96–98; and Roman Szporluk, *The Political Thought of Thomas G. Masaryk* (New York: Columbia University Press, 1981), for discussions of Masaryk and his influence.

6. See Beneš, "Czechoslovak Democracy," 89–91; Korbel, *Twentieth-Century Czechoslovakia*, 38–62; and Anderle, "The First Republic."

7. See Mamatey, "The Development of the Czechoslovak Democracy," in Mamatey and Luža, eds., *A History of the Czechoslovak Republic*, 99–166;

Beneš, "Czechoslovak Democracy"; and Anderle, "The First Republic," for detailed discussions of these and other aspects of interwar political developments.

8. H. Gordon Skilling, *Czechoslovakia's Interrupted Revolution* (Princeton: Princeton University Press, 1976), 3–25.

9. See Zdeněk Suda, *Zealots and Rebels: A History of the Ruling Communist Party of Czechoslovakia* (Stanford: Hoover Institution Press, 1980), ch. 2, for a discussion of these factors.

10. See Suda, *Zealots and Rebels,* 1–119; and Korbel, *The Communist Subversion of Czechoslovakia, 1938–1948: The Failure of Coexistence* (Princeton: Princeton University Press, 1959), 1–40, for discussions of the early years of the party.

11. Beneš, "Czechoslovak Democracy," 40.

12. Beneš, "Czechoslovak Democracy," 43; and Owen V. Johnson, *Slovakia, 1918–1938: Education and the Making of a Nation* (New York: Columbia University Press, 1985), 77.

13. Illiteracy rates of the population as a whole approximated those of the more developed West European countries (4.1 percent by 1930). Illiteracy was somewhat higher in Slovakia (8.1 percent of all inhabitants ten years and older) and much higher in Ruthenia, where almost a third of the population in this age group (30.8 percent) were illiterate in 1930. Only 1.2 percent of all persons in Bohemia and 1.5 percent in Moravia were illiterate in that year. From information in "Statní úřad statisticky," *Statistická ročenka Československa* (Prague: Orbis, 1937), 12; and UNESCO, *Literacy Statistics from Available Census Figures* (Paris: Education Clearing House, 1950), 19.

14. See Robert J. Kerner, *Czechoslovakia* (Berkeley: University of California Press, 1949), 43–45; Samuel Harrison Thomson, *Czechoslovakia in European History,* 2d ed. (Princeton: Princeton University Press, 1953), 216–23; and F. Gregory Campbell, *Confrontation in Central Europe: Weimar Germany and Czechoslovakia* (Chicago: University of Chicago Press, 1975), 1–12, for discussions of this period. See Karen J. Freeze, "The Young Progressives: The Czech Student Movement, 1887–1897," Ph.D. dissertation, Columbia University, 1974, for analysis of student activism during this period.

15. See Thomson, *Czechoslovakia in European History,* 222–33; and *The Czech Renaissance of the Nineteenth Century,* Peter Brock and H. Gordon Skilling, eds. (Toronto: University of Toronto Press, 1970).

16. See Kerner, *Czechoslovakia,* 46; Thomson, *Czechoslovakia in European History,* 230–33; and Bruce M. Garver, *The Young Czech Party, 1874–1901, and the Emergence of a Multi-Party System* (New Haven: Yale University Press, 1978).

17. See Johnson, *Slovakia,* 29–31.

18. See Johnson, *Slovakia,* 15–49; Thomson, *Czechoslovakia in European History,* 260–75; and Peter Brock, *The Slovak National Awakening*

(Toronto: University of Toronto Press, 1976), for a more detailed discussion of developments in Slovakia during this period.

19. See Thomson, *Czechoslovakia in European History*, 69–119 and 257–59.

20. Thomson, *Czechoslovakia in European History*, 334–35; and Jorg K. Hoensch, "The Slovak Republic, 1939–1945," in *A History of the Czechoslovak Republic*, Mamatey and Luža, eds., 271–77.

21. See Korbel, *Twentieth-Century Czechoslovakia*, 106.

22. See Zora P. Pryor, "Czechoslovak Economic Development in the Interwar Period," in *A History of the Czechoslovak Republic*, Mamatey and Luža, eds., 188–215. See Alice Teichová, *The Czechoslovak Economy, 1918–1980* (London: Routledge, 1988), 17–86 for an overview of economic conditions during the interwar period.

23. See Johnson, *Slovakia*; and Korbel, *Twentieth-Century Czechoslovakia*, 105–6.

24. See Joseph Rothschild, *Ethnopolitics: A Conceptual Framework* (New York: Columbia University Press, 1981), for an analysis of the impact of these and other factors on the development of nationalism.

25. See Joseph Rothschild, *East Central Europe Between the Two World Wars* (Seattle: University of Washington Press, 1974), 117–21; Yeshayahu Jelinek, *The Parish Republic: Hlinka's Slovak People's Party* (Boulder: East European Monographs, 1976); Korbel, *Twentieth-Century Czechoslovakia*, 153–56; Hoensch, "Slovak Republic"; and Thomson, *Czechoslovakia in European History*, 416–19, for discussions of the Slovak state.

26. See Campbell, *Confrontation in Central Europe*, 1–41; Elizabeth Wiskemann, *Czechs and Germans: A Study of the Struggle in the Historic Provinces of Bohemia and Moravia* (London: Oxford University Press, 1938); and Radomír Luža, *The Transfer of the Sudeten Germans: A Study of Czech-German Relations, 1933–1962* (New York: New York University Press, 1964), 1–46.

27. Korbel, *Twentieth-Century Czechoslovakia*, 116; and Luža, *The Transfer of the Sudeten Germans*, 6–13.

28. Luža, *The Transfer of the Sudeten Germans*, 13–16 and Korbel, *Twentieth-Century Czechoslovakia*, 116.

29. See Rothschild, *East Central Europe*, 122–29; Korbel, *Twentieth-Century Czechoslovakia*, 116–20; Luža, *The Transfer of the Sudeten Germans*, 24–184; and Campbell, *Confrontation in Central Europe*, chs. 3–6.

30. See Korbel, *Twentieth-Century Czechoslovakia*, 121–49; and Rothschild, *East Central Europe*, 129–32, for discussions of the actions of Beneš and other Czechoslovak leaders during this period. See Luža, *Transfer of Sudeten Germans*, chs. 5 and 6; and Anderle, "The First Republic," 107–10 for overviews of this period and references to the vast literature on the Munich Agreement.

31. See Korbel, *Twentieth-Century Czechoslovakia*, 157–60; Luža, *The*

Transfer of the Sudeten Germans, chs. 7–10; Vojtěch Mastný, *The Czechs Under Nazi Rule: The Failure of National Resistance* (New York: Columbia University Press, 1971); and Edward Táborský, "Tragedy, Triumph, and Tragedy: Czechoslovakia 1938–1948," in Brisch and Volgyes, eds., *Czechoslovakia: The Heritage of Ages Past,* 113–34.

32. See Korbel, *Twentieth-Century Czechoslovakia,* 160; Rothschild, *East Central Europe,* 133–34; Eugene Steiner, *The Slovak Dilemma* (London: Cambridge University Press, 1973); and Jelinek, *The Parish Republic,* for discussions of the Slovak state.

33. See Korbel, *Twentieth-Century Czechoslovakia,* 160–64; and Mastný, *The Czechs Under Nazi Rule.*

34. See Anna Josko, "The Slovak Resistance Movement," in Mamatey and Luža, eds., *A History of the Czechoslovak Republic,* 125–28; and Jelinek, *The Lust for Power: Nationalism, Slovakia, and the Communists, 1918– 1948* (Boulder: East European Monographs, 1983), 69–77.

35. See Zbigniew K. Brzezinski, *The Soviet Bloc: Unity and Conflict* (Cambridge: Harvard University Press, 1967), 18–19; and Hugh Seton-Watson, *The East European Revolution* (New York: Praeger, 1956), 339–71, for succinct overviews of this period as a whole. See Paul Zinner, *Communist Strategy and Tactics in Czechoslovakia, 1918–1948* (New York: Praeger, 1963), 106–10; Edward Táborský, *Communism in Czechoslovakia, 1948– 1960* (Princeton: Princeton University Press, 1961), 15–24; and Korbel, *Twentieth-Century Czechoslovakia,* 218–52; and Korbel, *The Communist Subversion,* for more detailed discussions of this period, and the events of 1948 in particular, in Czechoslovakia.

36. See Suda, *Zealots and Rebels,* 178–84, for a more detailed discussion of this aspect of the political structure during this period.

37. See *Košicky vládni program* (Prague: Nakladatelstvi svoboda, 1974).

38. Suda, *Zealots and Rebels,* 195.

39. See Suda, *Zealots and Rebels,* 195–201; and Korbel, *Twentieth-Century Czechoslovakia,* 234–37, for discussions of the circumstances surrounding these elections and an analysis of the vote. See also Richard Voyles Burks, *The Dynamics of Communism in Eastern Europe* (Westport, Conn.: Greenwood Press, 1976), 215.

40. See Korbel, *The Communist Subversion,* 210–20.

41. See Korbel, *Twentieth-Century Czechoslovakia,* 255; and Zinner, *Communist Strategy,* 196–223.

42. See Korbel, *Twentieth-Century Czechoslovakia,* 260–68, for a brief discussion of these policies.

43. Suda, *Zealots and Rebels,* 225–26.

44. See Zinner, *Communist Strategy,* 224–25; and Táborský, *Communism in Czechoslovakia,* 144–45.

45. See Korbel, *Twentieth-Century Czechoslovakia,* 38–41; Teichová, *The Czechoslovak Economy,* 87–100; John N. Stevens, *Czechoslovakia at the Crossroads: The Economic Dilemmas of Communism in Postwar*

Czechoslovakia (Boulder: East European Monographs, 1985), 7–11; Luža, "Czechoslovakia Between Democracy and Communism," in Mamatey and Luža, eds., *History of the Czechoslovak Republic*, 387–415, for brief discussions of social and economic changes enacted between 1945 and 1948. See Zinner, *Communist Strategy*, 226–28; Korbel, *Twentieth-Century Czechoslovakia*, 261–631; and Teichová, *The Czechoslovak Economy*, 101–48 and ch. 4, for further details concerning post-1948 economic policies.

46. Korbel, *Twentieth-Century Czechoslovakia*, 261; Táborský, *Communism in Czechoslovakia*, 382–423; Stevens, *Czechoslovakia at the Crossroads*, 16–57; and Karl-Eugen Wadekin, *Agrarian Policies in Communist Europe: A Critical Introduction* (The Hague/London: Allanheld, Osmun, 1982), for discussion of collectivization and agricultural policy in Czechoslovakia.

47. See Sharon L. Wolchik, "The Status of Women in a Socialist Order: Czechoslovakia, 1948–1978," *Slavic Review* (December 1979), 38(4): 583–603; and "Elite Strategy Toward Women in Czechoslovakia: Liberation or Mobilization?" in *Studies in Comparative Communism* (Summer/Autumn 1981), 14(2/3): 123–42.

48. See Pedro Ramet, "Christianity and National Heritage Among the Czechs and Slovaks," in *Religion and Nationalism in Soviet and East European Politics*, 2d ed., Pedro Ramet, ed. (Durham: Duke University Press, 1989), 277–78.

49. See Jiří Pelikán, *The Czechoslovak Political Trials, 1950–1954* (Stanford: Stanford University Press, 1971), 37–147; Skilling, *Czechoslovakia's Interrupted Revolution*, ch. 13; and Suda, *Zealots and Rebels*, 233–57, for analyses of the trials. See Eugen Loebl, *My Mind on Trial* (New York: Harcourt Brace Jovanovich, 1976), for a more personal account.

50. See Skilling, *Czechoslovakia's Interrupted Revolution*, 58–59.

51. See Skilling, *Czechoslovakia's Interrupted Revolution*, 57–63; Judy Batt, *Economic Reform and Political Change in Eastern Europe: A Comparison of the Czechoslovak and Hungarian Experience* (Houndmills: Macmillan Press, 1988); Martin Myant, *The Czechoslovak Economy, 1948–1988* (Cambridge: Cambridge University Press, 1989), chs. 5–6; Andrzej Korbonski, "Bureaucracy and Interest Groups in Communist Societies: The Case of Czechoslovakia," *Studies in Comparative Communism* (January 1971), 4(1): 57–79; and Wolchik, *Czechoslovakia*, ch. 4, for further information.

52. See Skilling, *Czechoslovakia's Interrupted Revolution*, 62–72; Dušan Hamšík, *Writers Against Rulers* (New York: Random House, 1971), 25–73; Barbara W. Jančár, *Czechoslovakia and the Absolute Monopoly of Power: A Study of Political Power in a Communist System* (New York: Praeger, 1971), 195–201; and Vladimír V. Kusín, *The Intellectual Origins of the Prague Spring: The Development of Reformist Ideas in Czechoslovakia, 1956–1967* (Cambridge: Cambridge University Press, 1971), ch. 5.

53. See Skilling, *Czechoslovakia's Interrupted Revolution*, 72–82; and Kusín, *The Intellectual Origins of the Prague Spring*, 125–42.

54. See Hilda Scott, *Does Socialism Liberate Women?* (Boston: Beacon Press, 1974); Wolchik, "Politics, Ideology, and Equality: The Status of Women in Eastern Europe," Ph.D. dissertation, University of Michigan, 1978, chs. 6 and 7; Wolchik, "Demography, Political Reform, and Women's Issues in Czechoslovakia," in *Women, Power, and Political Systems,* Margherita Rendel, ed. (New York: St. Martin's Press, 1981), 135–50; and Wolchik, "Elite Strategy"; and Alena Heitlinger, *Women and State Socialism: Sex Inequality in the Soviet Union and Czechoslovakia* (Montreal: McGill-Queen's University Press, 1979).

55. See Skilling, *Czechoslovakia's Interrupted Revolution,* 49–56; Kusín, *Political Groupings in the Czechoslovak Reform Movement* (New York: Columbia University Press, 1972), 145–61; Kusín, *Intellectual Origins,* 69–75; and Carol Skalník Leff, *National Conflict in Czechoslovakia: The Making and Remaking of a State, 1918–1987* (Princeton: Princeton University Press, 1988), for more detailed analyses of Slovak issues during this period. See Rothschild, *Ethnopolitics,* for discussion of factors that condition the political expression of national issues.

56. See Skilling, *Czechoslovakia's Interrupted Revolution,* ch. 6, for a discussion of Novotný's downfall.

57. See *Kommunistička strana Československa, 1968,* for a summary of these points.

58. See Skilling, *Czechoslovakia's Interrupted Revolution,* 196–201; Golia Golan, *The Czechoslovak Reform Movement: Communism in Crisis, 1962–1968* (Cambridge: Cambridge University Press, 1971); Jančár, *Czechoslovakia and the Absolute Monopoly of Power;* and Kusín, *Political Groupings.* See Jaroslav Piekalkiewicz, *Public Opinion Polling in Czechoslovakia, 1968–1969: Results and Analysis of Surveys Conducted During the Dubček Era* (New York: Praeger, 1972), for excerpts from public opinion polls taken in Czechoslovakia during this period.

59. See Skilling, *Czechoslovakia's Interrupted Revolution,* ch. 15.

60. See Jiří Valenta, *Soviet Intervention in Czechoslovakia, 1968: Anatomy of a Decision* (Baltimore: Johns Hopkins University Press, 1979); and Grey Hodnett and P. J. Potichny, *The Ukraine and the Czechoslovak Crisis* (Canberra: Australian National University, 1970), for analyses of motivations for the invasion.

61. See Leff, *National Conflict in Czechoslovakia;* and Wolchik, "Regional Inequality in Czechoslovakia," in *The Politics of Inequality,* Daniel J. Nelson, ed. (Lexington, Mass.: Lexington Books, 1983).

62. Kusín, "Husák's Czechoslovakia and Economic Stagnation," *Problems of Communism* (May/June 1982), 31: 29.

63. See Kusín, *Intellectual Origins;* Wolchik, "The Scientific-Technological Revolution and the Role of Specialist Elites in Policy-making in Czechoslovakia," in *Domestic Policy in Eastern Europe in the 1980s: Trends and Prospects,* Michael J. Sodaro and Sharon L. Wolchik, eds. (New York: St. Martin's Press, 1983); and Sharon L. Wolchik and Jane L. Curry, "Specialists

and Professionals in the Policy Process in Czechoslovakia and Poland," report for the National Council for Soviet and East European Research, 1984.

64. See Zvi Gitelman, "Power and Authority in Eastern Europe," in *Change in Communist Systems,* Chalmers Johnson, ed. (Stanford: Stanford University Press, 1970), 235–64, for a discussion of these strategies.

65. See Wolchik, "Regional Inequalities," 249–70; and "Economic Performance and Political Change in Czechoslovakia," in *Prospects for Change in Socialist Systems: Challenges and Responses,* Charles J. Bukowski and Mark A. Cichock, eds. (New York: Praeger, 1987), 35–60.

66. See Otto Ulč, "The Normalization of Post-Invasion Czechoslovakia," *Survey* (1979), 24(3): 201–14, for a more detailed analysis of the retreat to the private sphere.

67. Skilling, "Independent Currents in Czechoslovakia," *Problems of Communism* (January/February 1985), 34: 32–49; and Skilling, *Charter 77 and Human Rights in Czechoslovakia* (Boston: Allen and Unwin, 1981).

68. See Walter D. Connor, "East European Dissent," *Problems of Communism* (January/February 1980), 29: 1–17, for a brief analysis of the dissident-worker alliance in Poland.

69. See Wolchik, "Economic Performance," and "Prospects for Political Change in Czechoslovakia," presented at Midwest Political Science Association, Chicago, April 1989.

70. See Wolchik, "Prospects for Political Change," and "The Roots of Change and the Transition to Democracy in Czechoslovakia," in Trond Gilberg, ed., *Instability in Eastern Europe After Communism* (Boulder: Westview Press, 1991), for further discussion.

71. *Hospodářské noviny,* 1988.

72. See Karel Dyba, *Reforming the Czechoslovak Economy: Past Experience and Present Dilemmas,* 1989; Karel Dyba and Karel Kouba, "Czechoslovak Attempts at Systematic Changes," *Communist Economies* (1989), vol. 1, no. 3; Myant, *The Czechoslovak Economy;* and Wolchik, *Czechoslovakia,* ch. 4.

73. See Wolchik, "Roots of Change," and "Prospects for Political Change," for further discussion.

74. See Dyba, *Reforming the Czechoslovak Economy;* Myant, *The Czechoslovak Economy;* and Wolchik, "Economic Performance."

75. See Wolchik, "Roots of Change," and "Prospects for Political Change," for more information.

76. See Wolchik, "Roots of Change," and *Czechoslovakia,* for further details.

77. See Sharon L. Wolchik, "Central and Eastern Europe in Transition," in *Asia and the Decline of Communism,* Young C. Kim and Gaston Sigur, eds. (New Brunswick, N.J.: Transaction Press, 1991, forthcoming).

78. See "Czechoslovakia Parliamentary Elections on June 8th–9th 1990," *Daily News and Press Survey Bulletin,* Czechoslovak News Agency, Prague, n.d., for a brief summary of the platforms of the individual parties.

79. "Výsledky voleb do FS a ČNR podle jednotlivých krajů," *Svobodné slovo*, June 12, 1990, 4.

80. See Samuel H. Barnes, Peter McDonough, and Antonio Lopez Pina, "The Development of Partisanship in New Democracies: The Case of Spain," *American Journal of Political Science* (November 1985), 29(4): 695–720; Peter McDonough, Antonio Lopez Pina, and Samuel H. Barnes, "The Spanish Republic in Political Transition," *British Journal of Political Science* (January 1981), 11(1): 49–75; Guillermo O'Donnell, Phillippe C. Schmitter, and Laurance Whitehead, eds., *Transitions from Authoritarian Rule: Prospects for Democracy* (Baltimore: Johns Hopkins University Press, 1986); and Laszlo Bruszt, "Without Us but for Us: Political Orientation in Hungary in the Period of Later Paternalism," *Social Research* (Spring/Summer 1988), 55: 43–76.

81. RFE/RL Daily Report, no. 223, November 26, 1990.

82. RFE/RL Daily Report, no. 223.

83. See Wolchik, *Czechoslovakia*, for a fuller discussion of the impact of this legacy.

84. See Marek Boguszak, Ian Gabal, and Vladimír Rak, "Nezaměstnanost u nás," *Mladá fronta*, March 21, 1990, 3.

85. See Boguszak, et al.

86. See Wolchik, *Czechoslovakia*, for citations to studies illustrating these tendencies.

87. Václav Havel, January 1, 1991, as reported in Jiří Pehe, "The Agenda for 1991," *Radio Free Europe Report on Eastern Europe* (January 18, 1991), 2(3): 13.

88. "Právni předpisy pro podnikatele," *Příručka Hospodářských novin* (May 1990); "Zákon o státním podniku," *Příloha Hospodářských novin* (1990), no. 17; "Zákon o soukromém podnikáni občanů," *Příloha Hospodářských novin* (1990), no. 17; "Zákon o akciových společnostech," *Příloha Hospodářských novin* (1990), no. 18; "Novela Hospodářského zákoníku," *Příloha hospodářských novin* (1990), no. 20; and "Zákon o bytovém, spotřebním, výrobním, a jiném družstevnictví," *Příloha Hospodářských novin* (1990), no. 23.

89. Interviews with Vladimír Dlouhý in *Mladá fronta*, April 6, 1990, and June 21, 1990.

90. See "Scénář ekonomické reformy," *Hospodářské noviny*, September 4, 1990, for the latest government proposals on economic reform.

91. See "Suroviny za zboží," *Lidové noviny*, September 3, 1990, 1, 8.

92. See Wolchik, "Central and Eastern Europe in Transition."

93. See research reported in Boguszak, Rak, and Gabal; and Marek Boguszak and Vladimír Rak, *Czechoslovakia—May 1990 Survey Report*, Association for Independent Social Analysis, Prague, July 1990.

94. See Václav Klaus, *Mladá fronta*, June 19, 1990, 1–2; and Karel Hvížďala's interview with Valtr Komárek in *Mladá fronta*, June 20, 1990, 1–2, for example.

95. See, for example, "Kde se v této zemi vzal rasismus?" *Forum* (August 29–September 4, 1990), 31: 2; "Výzva ceskoslovenske vláde," *Lidové noviny*, May 2, 1990, 2; "Konec mnoha fám," *Mladá fronta*, April 28, 1990, 1–2. See also Boris Merhaut, "Udaje dříve 'tabu'," *Svobodné slovo*, March 16, 1990, 6; Věra Pospíšilová, "Kdy bomba vybuchne?" *Lidové noviny*, March 17, 1990, 1–2; František Urban, "Český les," *Přítomnost*, June 4, 1990, 26–27; and Helena Mrázová and Vladka Kučerová, "Brutalita vzrustá," *Mladá fronta*, June 30, 1990, 4.

96. See Leff, *National Conflict in Czechoslovakia*.

97. See for example, Marcela Pecháčková, "Naslouchejme!" *Mladá fronta*, March 24, 1990, 2; Petr Liška, "Toleranci místo sporu," *Lidové noviny*, July 10, 1990, 1; "Nesouhlas s jednou pamětní deskou," *Svobodné slovo*, July 13, 1990, 3; and Pavol Zavarský, "Dozvieme sa pravdu?" *Verejnost*, July 16, 1990, 1–2. See also Marek Boguszak and Vladimír Rak, "Společne, ale každý jinak?" *Lidové noviny*, June 28, 1990, 4; "Kdo chce Slovenský stát?" *Občanský deník*, August 28, 1990, 1–2; see also Karel Staňek, "Devět slovenských stran žádá samostatný stát," *Občanský deník*, August 15, 1990, 1–2; and "Kde konči federace?" *Občanský deník*, August 16, 1990, 1–2.

98. See Ivan Drábek, "List, ktorý rozvířil vášně," *Smena*, May 12, 1990, 1; Adriana Host'ovecka, "Nepripustíme segregáciu," *Verejnost'*, May 8, 1990, 3; and Klára Samková, "Prohlášení Rómské občanske iniciativy," *Respekt* (July 3, 1990), 16: 16.

5 Hungary on a Fixed Course: An Outline of Hungarian History

Péter Hanák and Joseph Held

1918–1945, PÉTER HANÁK

Restoration: Birth of the Horthy Regime

In the final year of the First World War and the subsequent revolutionary period, Hungarian history unfolded at a turbulent pace and abounded in dramatic turns of fate. In June 1919 the troops of the Hungarian Soviet Republic were still on the offensive, a communist republic was set up in Slovakia, and internal disturbances were quelled in Hungary. A month later, however, Romanian interventionist troops inflicted a severe defeat on the Hungarian Red Army along the Tisza River. On August 1, the Revolutionary Governing Council resigned. Three days later, the Romanians occupied Budapest, uprooting the vestiges of the communist revolution. On August 6, a restoration government was formed by István Friedrich, an industrialist of the conservative wing of the Independence party.

However, for months to come, chaos prevailed. The new government lacked power and legitimacy. The Romanian generals in Budapest and the victorious Allies in Paris dictated the rules. Admiral Miklós Horthy, at the head of a hastily recruited army, set up his headquarters at Siofok while gangs of counterrevolutionary officers ravaged the country. This was a period of "white terror," whose chief targets were revolutionaries, socialists, radical democrats, and Jews. The right-wing conservative groups rapidly established themselves.

With unfailing political instincts they cast the blame for military defeat, national devastation, and the general misery that followed on communists and Jews who had played an important part as members of the upper-middle classes in the prewar liberal system, as radical democrats in the so-called aster-revolution of 1918, or as people's commissars in the communist revolutionary government.

The war brought the liberalism of the dualistic era into disrepute and generated hatred against "war millionaires," whereas the two revolutions discredited both pro-Entente (i.e., Wilsonian) democracy and communism. The bulk of the middle class and the peasantry was favorably inclined toward conservative-nationalist change and there was a growing mass of disillusioned working people who secluded themselves from public life and wanted order and consolidation. In mid-November, the Romanians left Budapest. Two days later, Supreme Commander Horthy entered the capital city. His authority, however, rested only on the armed forces and the inertia of the people.

As was often the case with poor gentry males, Horthy chose a military career as a young man. A less usual choice was that he entered the navy. He eventually carved out a fine career for himself and, in the prewar years, became a rear admiral and adjutant to Emperor Francis Joseph. During the war he carried out a series of successful maneuvers (including the suppression of a sailors' revolt in Cattaro in 1918). Although Horthy enjoyed an uncontested reputation, particularly in conservative circles, and was rather well informed in political and diplomatic matters, he lacked a statesman's abilities. At a time when the political elite wanted neither to restore the "discredited" republic nor to abolish the monarchy, his election as regent seemed to be a temporary solution. The various factions were able to arrive at a compromise on this issue, since Horthy alone controlled genuine armed troops in the country. His past promised a strong hand and good connections. Horthy's soldierly appearance, however, disguised a weak and hesitant character, and his good manners concealed inner doubts.

Political consolidation in Hungary began as a result of the interference of the "Big Four," that is, the decision makers at the Paris peace conference. The Allies sent Sir George Clark, a British diplomat, to Budapest. He managed to bring about the establishment of a coalition government consisting of the influential Christian Democratic party, some democrats, and even socialists. The government was headed by Károly Huszár and it was accepted by the Allies as a negotiating party. This government arranged the parliamentary elections for January 1920. When elections came, István Nagyatádi-Szabó's National Smallholder's party and the Christian National Union received the majority of the vote.

The new National Assembly restored the monarchy but in view of the international situation, elected, in the person of Admiral Horthy, a regent instead of a king. The regent continued and legitimized the right-wing, conservative, authoritarian course of the country. His government registered the ultimate triumph of the Christian National (anti-Semitic) tendency. Horthy set up his residence at the royal castle in Buda. He "nationalized" his army by subjecting it to the control of the government and the general staff, though he continued to maintain his position as "supreme warlord" to the very last. A mark of internal consolidation was the participation in the government of the conservative aristocracy, that is, leaders of the landed interests. The country's international status was settled by the signing of the Treaty of Trianon.

The Trianon Peace Treaty

The peace treaty signed with Hungary at Versailles (in the Trianon palace) on June 4, 1920, decisively influenced the fate of Hungary during subsequent decades and into our times as well. At the Trianon conference table the Hungarian nation suffered a blow whose severity can only be compared to the disaster of Mohács in 1526, when the Ottoman army annihilated the Hungarian noble troops, leading to 150 years of Ottoman occupation of the center of the country.

In fact, the infliction of Trianon did not come completely unexpectedly. In the revolution of 1848–1849, the latent hostilities between Hungarians on the one hand and Serbs, Croatians, and Romanians on the other exploded into armed struggle. These enmities left an indelible mark on the consciousness of the Hungarians and their ethnic rivals. One of the organic antecedents of the rearrangement of Eastern European borders at Trianon included the post-1867 policies of Hungarian governments, local authorities, and elites toward the other nationalities. Although these policies were basically liberal in character, assimilation being chiefly characterized by spontaneous integration rather than violence or coercion, the political system of the Age of Dualism was a misshapen one. It included the restriction of national rights and discrimination against national minorities. The Slavic and Romanian peoples of the Hungarian half of the Habsburg empire demanded independence and, later, sovereignty. Hungarian governments also committed the gross political blunder of failing to arrange a compromise with the subject nationalities, either with the Czechs in 1870 or with the Croats and Romanians later on. In addition, the Wilsonian principles of national self-determination were thwarted many times by the bungling of the Great Powers and the nationalist fervor of the victors.

At the end of the First World War, through the dissolution of the Russian and Ottoman empires and of the Habsburg monarchy, favorable conditions were created for the conclusion of a century-old process in European history, namely, the realization of the establishment of sovereignty for the oppressed small nations of Eastern Europe. An opportunity presented itself to reconstitute tripartite Poland as an independent, unified state and to unify the Czechs and Slovaks as well as the South Slavs (Serbs, Croats, and Slovenes) in their own state. However, there were several possible arrangements for the assertion of national sovereignty. Before and during the war, various schemes were put forward for the creation of a Central European or Danubian Confederation; either a coterminous arrangement of political and ethnic boundaries or the settlement of territorial claims by plebiscite or population exchange seemed possible. Yet the Treaty of Trianon concluded this historically mature process without finding an adequate solution for the difficult historical problem of securing the stability of the region—not even temporarily.

The Treaty of Trianon dismembered Hungary, taking away about two-thirds of its territory and population. The non-Hungarian peoples—Slovaks, Romanians, Serbs, and Croats—created their own independent states or were unified with the bulk of their nations, formerly located across the borders. This was an integral part of a large historical transformation the justice and efficacy of which would have been acknowledged by the Hungarian public sooner or later. However, out of the territories of historic Hungary (282,000 square kilometers without Croatia-Slavonia) 124,000 square kilometers were inhabited by non-Magyars; 138,000 square kilometers were settled by Magyars; and only 20,000 square kilometers contained a mixed population. The most serious defect of the Treaty of Trianon was that out of the 138,000 square kilometers of Hungarian-settled lands only 93,000 square kilometers were left for independent Hungary. The rest were distributed among the new states with their Hungarian populations. As a result, there was an ever-growing dissatisfaction and separatism among the Hungarians living in the non-Hungarian states. It was only a question of time and opportunity before this dissatisfaction found an outlet.

Hungary's fixed course were determined by several factors. The first of these was the war itself: it ruined the economies of Austria and Hungary, exhausted the material and psychological reserves of the population and sparked off social and national revolutions. The monarchy's direct war costs amounted to 21 billion U.S. dollars (at the 1914 exchange rate) and, by the end of the war, the crown plummeted to one-third of its prewar value. Agricultural production dropped by the same ratio while industrial output decreased to one-fifth of its prewar level. The loss in human terms was equally painful. Hungary mobilized about 3.8 million men of whom 660,000 were killed and 745,000 were wounded seriously; a similar number fell into enemy hands. Together, they made up 57 percent of all men who were mobilized. This was an enormous loss in terms of population and reserves.

The second factor that fundamentally influenced the postwar situation was the Treaty of Trianon. This rearrangement of territory, sanctioned by international law, was by no means perfect. It has remained highly controversial from its inception. The peacemakers solemnly espoused the ideal of a just settlement, based on principles of ethnic or national self-determination. However, this treaty gave about three million Hungarians to the so-called successor states. (Romania alone annexed 102,000 square kilometers despite the fact that, of these, only 65,000 had a purely Romanian population.)

Contemporary Hungarian society was outraged by such "punishment." Nor could its successors accept the salient injustices of this territorial settlement. Scholarly research has since thrown light on the motives of the committee preparing decisions concerning Hungary. It is obvious from the relevant literature of the past half-century that it was primarily the interests of the French political and military leaders that influenced these decisions. The French intended to use the small states of Eastern Europe as a bulwark first against Soviet Russia, then against defeated Germany. Various historic or strategic grounds were found to deprive Hungary of purely Hungarian-populated territories, as these had to be surrendered to Slovakia, Romania, and Yugoslavia. (The Csallóköz, the lands southeast of the Nagyvárad-Arad line, South Bácska with Szabadka, among others, were all in this category.) Military reasons, such as Polish and Romanian mobilization against Soviet Russia or the openness of Slovakia's southern frontiers, were also determining factors. Finally, in relation to Austria (which otherwise shared the fate of Hungary) the treaty provided that in order to prevent an *Anschluss* with Germany, Austria should be given the Burgenland ("Őrség" in Hungarian) from Hungary.

It is now also apparent from the documents that the British occasionally questioned the soundness of these decisions but for the sake of accord, and in return for compensation elsewhere, they ultimately acquiesced to the French proposals. The American delegates, sometimes President Wilson himself, protested on several occasions against violations of the proclaimed democratic principles but they could rarely win acceptance of their more equitable position. In every single issue debated at Paris the French decided in favor of Romania or the Czechs and Slovaks. The views of the British and American delegates were greatly influenced by their limited knowledge of the small countries and nations of the region. They often took positions under the influence of dubious information and subjective emotions.

This is the way Sir Harold Nicolson, a member of the British delegation, described in his memoirs the information upon which he formed his opinions: "I confess that I regarded ... that Turanian tribe (the Hungarians) with acute distaste. Like their cousins, the Turks, they had destroyed much and created nothing. Buda Pest was a city devoid of any autochthonous reality. For centuries the Magyars had oppressed their subject nationalities. The hour of liberation and retribution was at hand!"

In all these decisions neither the actual extension of the ethnic boundaries of Hungary nor the just claims of Hungarian self-determination and demands for plebiscites were taken into consideration. Even the fact that, in July 1914, the Hungarian government was alone in objecting to the sending of an ultimatum to Serbia and against the starting of the war were ignored. Hungary was undoubtedly very seriously afflicted by the peace treaty, not only physically but politically and psychologically as well.

However, we do not wish to evaluate Trianon from a one-sided, Hungarian point of view. The gravest international consequence of the peace settlement was that it disrupted the region of Eastern Europe as an economic and political unit. Historical scholarship had long ago discarded the propaganda slogan according to which the Habsburg monarchy was a state created and held together by sheer violence, "a prison of the peoples." In fact, the monarchy was from the eighteenth century on bound together by ever more intensifying economic links and, from the mid-nineteenth century, by institutions of economic integration, especially a well-functioning free market.

In the Austro-Hungarian empire the pace of economic modernization and growth was formidable, almost as rapid as in Germany or Sweden. The provinces had become specialized according to the principle of comparative advantages, sending 70–75 percent of their exports to other provinces within the empire. It was under this economic system that the Bohemian (Czech) textile and glass industries, the Austrian engineering industries, and the Hungarian milling industry became large-scale European institutions. The peace treaties sliced up this efficient economic unit, blocked centuries-old commercial routes, and broke off time-tested and fruitful economic relations. These changes were intensified by the postwar chaos, the disintegration of the empire, the sharp decline in production, and unprecedented inflation.

The setback, however, need not have lasted. Everything depended upon the economic strategies that the successor states adopted in the postconsolidation period. As it turned out, the states in question chose the worst possible option: isolation from one another in the effort to achieve the highest possible level of autarky. They dissociated themselves from their former partners, imposing bans on exports and imports, applying high protectionist customs tariffs, and from 1931 on, strict state controls on foreign exchange transactions. By the mid-1930s, Czechoslovakia doubled its wheat-crop production compared to the last prewar year, while Hungarian wheat sales to Czechoslovakia skidded to a mere 5 percent of previous levels. At the same time, Hungary made frantic efforts to develop its textile industry, frequently using obsolete machinery and producing poor-quality goods. As a result, not only did the previously efficient regional distribution of labor collapse, but the economic strategies of development used by the successor states missed the mark as well. It is quite understandable, therefore, that in the 1930s Hungary, hard-hit by permanent unemployment and the marketing crisis, was attracted to the *Lebensraum* (economic breathing space) of Hitler's Germany.

The political disintegration of the region was just as harmful, even fatal, as the disruption of economic unity. The Habsburg monarchy, however imperfect its political structure had been, for centuries had played the role of a counterpoise in Europe that Britain not only respected but strongly supported until the First World War. The monarchy maintained the balance, on the one hand, against the hegemonic aspirations of any continental power (that is, expansion either east or west) and, on the other, between the rival nations in the Danubian Basin. Its destruction created a political vacuum in the region which France was the first to attempt to fill with its power-policy interference. This was the motive behind the favors and territories which the French secured for their small allies, the states of the later Little Entente, at the expense of Hungary. This was the reason behind the reduction of the Hungarian army to a minimal size and other measures that restricted Hungarian sovereignty in the Treaty of Trianon.

It soon became quite clear that France was too weak to assert her hegemony in Eastern Europe, to restore the normal economic relations of the region, or to mitigate its multifarious political conflicts. Other powers came to dominate the region until, in the mid-1930s, its states fell easy prey to Hitler's Germany.

Immediately after the conclusion of the peace treaties Lloyd George foretold their fatal consequences, although he did not take any effective steps to prevent these results. Harold Nicolson also expressed his disappointment: "We arrived [in Paris] determined that a peace of justice and wisdom should be negotiated. We left it conscious that the treaties imposed upon our enemies were neither just nor wise."

Political Consolidation

The signing of the Treaty of Trianon was an important step towards the consolidation of the new Hungarian regime, instantly followed by the next, namely, the appointment of a government led by Prime Minister Count Pál Teleki. Teleki came from a prestigious Transylvanian aristocratic family and was an excellent geographer and an eminent conservative politician. Legality was the *leitmotif* of his activities starting with the elimination and suppression of the roving officer-gangs. At the same time, he tried to reconcile anti-Semitism with "lawfulness," introducing the so-called *numerus clausus* in university admissions. This law restricted the number of Jewish students in higher educational institutions. However, the most important measure introduced by his government was a long-awaited land reform.

According to this law, 750,000 hectares of land were distributed among 400,000 landless peasant families. The obvious purpose of the reform was to create a layer of dwarfholders, bound to their tiny plots of land, and inevitably forced to undertake labor of tenancy. The effects of the reform were reinforced by the fact that it also allotted about 250,000 building lots (one-quarter hectare each) to the poor of the villages. Although the acute tensions that existed in the countryside over land possession were somewhat eased by the reform, it was insufficient to solve the land question and the problem of poverty among the peasantry.

The Teleki government's chance to achieve a stable situation was seriously impaired by the uncertainty about Hungary's form of government. At the fulcrum of this issue was the question of the future of the house of Habsburg. King Charles, adopting a wait-and-see attitude at his refuge in Switzerland, concluded from the initial success of the consolidation that the time had come to regain his inheritance. He considered a coup d'état to be the most effective means to accomplish his goal. He was confident that his sudden appearance in Hungary would draw considerable attention. However, in the face of vehement protests from the two governing parties, the opposition, the Great Powers protecting the treaty system, and especially the neighboring states, both his attempts failed. Teleki and his Legitimist government were compelled to step down as the result of the royal adventure.

Teleki's successor, István Bethlen, also came from a Transylvanian family of long lineage. He was a career politician of outstanding stature, the best politician Hungary produced during the interwar years. From 1901, he belonged to the conservative wing of the governing Liberal* party and was regarded as the chief spokesman of landed interests and an expert on Transylvanian politics. In 1918, Bethlen became the leader of the political organization of the counter-revolution. In the 1920s, he was able to combine the Liberal tradition with conservative ideas and authoritarian governing techniques.

Bethlen considered his main task to be the creation of a powerful but manageable governing party. In this endeavor the attempted royal coup (as a result of which the Legitimists seceded from the governing party) played into his hands as did the breakdown of the Christian Nationalist coalition. Displaying great tactical skill Bethlen joined the Smallholder's party instead of the conservatives. Before long, he turned the Smallholders into the basis of the governing bloc (the United party) by winning over moderate Christian Nationalists and representatives of landed interests as well as Liberal capitalists. In the 1922 election the new party gained an absolute majority with 58 percent of the ballots cast; the extreme right and the Christian parties lost support, and the liberal and socialist left made gains (the Liberals received 8 percent and the Social Democrats 10 percent of the total vote).

The prime minister decided to balance the leftist gains by concluding an agreement with the Social Democrats. The result, the so-called Bethlen-Peyer pact, legalized but at the same time curtailed the activities of the socialists. Beyond the capital, Budapest, the Social Democrats also had supporters in other cities and in the mining districts.

* Terms such as *conservative* or *liberal* applied to Eastern European societies have meanings different from those in the Western political tradition.

Relying on the working class and the democratically inclined intelligentsia, the Social Democratic party managed to preserve its left-wing opposition character during the interwar years.

In the interest of consolidation Bethlen had to constrain the residual influence of officer-gangs and secret racist associations. He was interested mainly in restoring the country's battered reputation and gaining the confidence of the liberal upper middle class. His efforts succeeded; in September 1922, Hungary was admitted into the League of Nations. Bethlen was also able to elicit sympathy for Hungary among British conservative circles and to win Italy's support. In April 1927 Italy concluded a treaty of friendship with Hungary, lending financial and diplomatic support for Bethlen's revisionist endeavors.

Financial stabilization made political consolidation complete. The Hungarian National Bank was established and a new currency, the *pengő*, was issued. A loan from the League of Nations facilitated these actions in the spring of 1924. Bethlen's political talent and unusual tactical skills undoubtedly contributed to the fairly rapid success of the consolidation. However, the process was certainly buttressed by the restoration of the normal functioning of the Hungarian economy and by the realignment of power relations within the country.

The defeat and subsequent revolutions had overthrown the bloc of Liberal magnates and bourgeoisie. They destroyed the Liberal party which had been in office for the last two decades of the Dual Monarchy and destroyed the alliance of radicals and socialists. This created an internal political vacuum. It was filled at first by the agrarian group of conservative landowners and gentry organizations which were formerly condemned to play secondary political roles. The leaders of the gentry organizations came from conservative landowners, civil servants, officers, and right-wing intellectuals. Their number and weight were significantly increased by the masses of unemployed former officers, unable to find lucrative employment, and refugee government officials from neighboring countries.

This new right-wing was imbued with gentry attitudes; it wanted not merely restoration, but redistribution, that is, a share in political power and positions in the top ranks of the Hungarian army. Its members also wanted leading positions in the civil service and yearned to dominate the professions. They clamored for the imposition of high taxes on "plutocrats" and the supervision of laissez-faire policies by the state. They intended to implement statist, authoritarian rule in order to sustain the dominance of a parasitic gentrified elite. The extreme right wing of this new movement consisted of former leaders of officers' gangs and members of secret racist associations including paramilitary pressure groups. They were strongly supported by an antiliberal, anti-Semitic middle class and petty bourgeoisie. These were the most important partisans of statist authoritarianism, a Christian Nationalist ideology, and the redistribution of power, wealth, and influence.

During the Bethlen consolidation, these extremists were ousted from conspicuous political positions but their influence was by no means eliminated; they retained their press organs as well as their leading role in the army, where their supreme warlord, Horthy, lent them undisguised support. This was a system in which the executive branch of government and the armed forces gained the upper hand over the liberal forms of traditional parliamentarianism and the democratic strivings of a civil society. Thus, the conservative gentry continued to thrive throughout the period of consolidation, only to add to their strength and power during the 1930s, when fascism triumphed in Hungary.

Nevertheless, during the consolidation period both internal and international conditions favored the growth of the economic and political power of the bourgeoisie; the main tendency of restoration was moving toward liberalization. Bethlen was determined to revive the prewar alliance between magnates and the bourgeoisie on the level of the government as well as the administration. Organizations safeguarding the interests of capitalists were filled with fresh vigor and their influence over the economic ministry increased. Banks and entrepreneurs played a leading role by investing the huge loans acquired by the state. Thus, the trust of Hungarian and international monied circles, and economic prosperity in general, were among the firm bases of consolidation.

The ideology and propaganda of the new regime were also modified. When the revolutions were suppressed, the efforts to end the prevailing chaos had begun under the banner of militant antiliberalism and anti-Semitism. The adjective "Christian" was not used in a religious sense, as a slogan for moral revival, but with a distinctively anti-Semitic, discriminatory edge. Furthermore, the emphasis on "national character" unambiguously implied total territorial revision to prewar boundaries, while internally it meant racism. However, the suppression of the institutions, open activities, and propaganda of the white terror brought about a shift in the meaning of the adjective "Christian-national," at least among the conservative-liberal circles of the governing party and the elite.

In the dominant ideology, militant anti-Semitism was on the decline: the Bethlen government, for instance, repealed the *numerus clausus* law and encouraged the Jewish middle class to participate in public life. Racism was also eliminated from the interpretation of national character, and the sense of the nation as a political unit was brought back into use. From the mid-1920s on, this concept came to mean the partial or total revision of the Trianon peace treaty. On this point a full national consensus was achieved. Growing professionalism in the techniques of government, authoritarian paternalism, revival of religiosity, patronage of the arts and sciences, and parliamentarianism after the European model were the features with which the system were endowed. As Gyula Szekfü, an eminent historian of the age observed, this was a peculiar, "neobaroque" style of government. At this time the following verse became an obligatory "national prayer" in Hungarian schools: "I believe in one God; I believe in one fatherland; I believe in one eternal godly justice; I believe in the resurrection of Hungary."

On the whole, there is little doubt that the adjectives *fascist* or *semifascist,* which the Communist party used to describe the era, were nothing but political slogans in the service of propaganda and were simply not true.

The Recovery of the National Economy

The crippling effects of the war and the Trianon peace treaty were felt most immediately in the decline of living standards and miseries of everyday life. Farming and especially stock raising suffered. In addition, industries were severely affected: about 60 percent of the prewar output of mining and 45 percent of other industries came from the territories that were separated from Hungary. There was an immediate and significant shortage of mining products (iron ore and salt), as well as wood and paper. Only 40 percent (or 8,000 kilometers) of the country's railroad lines were still within the boundaries of the new Hungary. The crisis created by the blocking of communications was aggravated by the fact that the new frontiers divided and sealed off many thousands of kilometers of branch lines and important paved roads. Blind alleys proliferated along Hungary's borders, often cutting districts or even villages to pieces. Isolation was the main trend in the new economic policies of the shattered region.

When the common market of the Austro-Hungarian Monarchy ceased to exist the successor states first tried to protect themselves against the competition of their neighbors by export-import prohibitions. In the course of 1924–25, new tariffs introduced everywhere in the region laid an average tax of 30 percent on exports and imports. This was three times as high as the customs tariffs under the system used by the Monarchy. As a result, the value of goods brought to Hungary from what had been other parts of a unified market of the Monarchy in 1913, dropped by 68 percent in 1928 and by 80–90 percent in the 1930s. Austria and Czechoslovakia obtained part of their grain and flour supply from America while Hungary made vigorous efforts to develop its textile industry—with obsolete technology and consequent high production costs.

This utter seclusion, the striving for a complete autarky was—especially in the case of the successor states that had inherited open-market economies—by no means inevitable. It resulted from nationalistic political strategies. As early as the 1920s, this phenomenon already foreshadowed the economic surrender to a Central European great power, seizing hegemony over the region.

Temporary difficulties were aggravated by soaring inflation after the war. A gold crown from the "happy times of peace" was worth, in 1919, ten paper crowns; in the spring of 1924, it was worth 18,000. At last, relying on foreign loans, financial stability was achieved. During the following years imported capital aided production. It was in these years that the iron works of Rimamurány were reconstructed, the electrification of railway lines began, and the former owners of estates distributed during the land reform received compensation. Counties and rural towns were able to obtain credit worth 230 million pengős and agriculture received 200 million pengős. Capital imports to Hungary between 1924 and 1931 amounted to 4.3 billion pengős (about 700 million U.S. dollars).

Loans, government subsidies, and commodity credits had a revivifying effect on Hungarian economic life. Agricultural output of the country was, in 1919, one-third and, in 1920, half of the prewar level, and industrial production was 15 and 35 percent of the 1913 production. The gross national product equalled the prewar level by 1927, and by 1929 surpassed it by 12 percent. The textile industry made a great leap and tripled its prewar production.

In the second half of the 1920s capital accumulation facilitated improvements in social policies and education. The Bethlen government broadened considerably the areas of compulsory accident and health insurance and raised the duration and amount of sickness benefits. Old age, disability, and widows' pensions were introduced. Over a million workers were included in insurance systems. The government spent as much on cultural endeavors as all its predecessors in the age of Dualism combined. Minister of Culture Kunó Klébelsberg was, in many ways, a follower of the reformers of the *Ausgleich* (The Compromise of 1867), such as József Eötvös. He concentrated his efforts on improving primary education, a theretofore neglected area of learning. During his ten-year tenure, 5,000 new classrooms were built and the number of both students and teachers increased considerably. Literacy increased to 90 percent, a ratio that was high for Eastern Europe, and came close to Austrian and Czech levels.

The government also paid close attention to university education. The unfriendly atmosphere in the successor states forced the moving of the Universities of Kolozsvár (Cluj) and Pozsony (Bratislava) to Szeged and Pécs respectively. The government provided buildings and equipment as it also did for the University of Debrecen, established during the war. While prior to World War I, a country that was three times the size of Trianon Hungary had only two universities, now there were four. The support of sciences and studies abroad followed directly from Klébelsberg's concept of higher education. He was instrumental in establishing *Collegia Hungarica* (Hungarian Institutes) in Rome, Berlin, and Vienna. His generous efforts were undoubtedly motivated by nationalistic considerations, namely, to demonstrate Hungarian cultural "superiority" over the successor states. Nevertheless, this sort of nationalism was the mildest and most beneficial aspect of the rivalry of the small nations of the region.

The Bethlen government restored the upper house in the national assembly; instead of being appointed by virtue of their titles, the majority of this house were now elected. Moderate reforms were introduced in the election process for municipal governments. All these factors suggested that during the tenure of the Bethlen government Hungary's political system was on the way towards the rule of law and limited parliamentarianism and had indeed consolidated itself.

It was in the midst of this process that the Great Depression hit Hungary.

The Great Depression and Its Consequences

It is most likely that Hungary would have recovered from the serious afflictions she suffered after the war—the economy would have been stabilized and the authoritarian political system could have been liberalized—but for the terrible worldwide epidemic of the Great

Depression. The first waves of this crisis hit in 1930 and they over-whelmed Hungarian agriculture. Having adjusted to agricultural ex-ports that had gone unsold, the country was unable to adjust to the large surpluses and the ensuing plummeting of prices. Between 1924 and 1928, wheat prices declined by 36 percent and livestock exports fell by 48 percent. With agriculture tipping the balance, average prices declined by 50 percent. Although the government tried its best by providing some price supports and helping out with exports, these measures were ineffective. By 1933, agricultural production as well as profits were at a minimum level. By 1931, the depression reached industry. It affected the construction and machine industries and reached light industry as well.

The most serious consequence was the withholding of investments. In the summer of 1931, the collapse of the international credit system began to have its impact on Hungary. Precious metal and foreign currency reserves were drained and the country was on the verge of bankruptcy. The Bethlen government, however, was able to avert this calamity by declaring a moratorium on foreign loans and currency transfers. It also introduced restrictions on foreign exchange transac-tions. In spite of this, the government still lost ground as a result of the social and political effects of the depression.

Agricultural workers were affected by the crisis more than any other social group, their salaries dropping by as much as 56–60 percent. Small peasant landholders did not fare much better; their debts grew threefold on the average in five years' time. Over one-third of industrial workers were unemployed while the rest saw their wages decline by 25–30 percent below 1929 averages. The crisis also reached professionals and civil servants, who lost not only some of their real income but often their jobs. With legions of out-of-work younger people and suddenly dismissed older workers, the political atmo-sphere was tense.

During the depression social conflicts repeatedly erupted. Strikes by industrial workers were matched by mass demonstrations in Bu-dapest on September 1, 1930. The Communists made their first re-appearance since 1919 in these struggles. The Social Democratic party also gained strength and the opposition to the government resurfaced. The Smallholders who had been integrated into the government party began to organize separately once again and their former leaders reestablished the Independent Smallholders party. As the left was reinvigorated, those on the other extreme of the political spectrum also began to mass their forces. Repressed after the White Terror, the extreme right was now reactivated. Frustrated by the misery and the crisis in which they found themselves, many of the lower middle-class and unemployed joined these extremists.

The new extreme right differed from the commandos of 1919 in two significant respects. While the latter's "program" of brutal racism consisted mainly of persecuting Jews and communists, the new extreme right, taking advantage of the misery brought on by the depression, championed social reform and used "national socialist" slogans to buttress its anti-Semitism. The right-wing movements could also look to Italy and Hitler's emerging movement in Germany for support.

The Bethlen government was able to fend off financial problems by extraparliamentary methods. It proclaimed martial law against the communists but was unable to curb the advances made by the middle-class right, in part because Regent Horthy himself was sympathetic to the right wing. In the face of this assault, Bethlen proved powerless. In August 1931, he gave his resignation to Horthy, although not until he had secured a loan of five million pounds sterling from Britain.

The Shift to the Right Under the Gömbös Government

After the fall of a brief interim government Gyula Gömbös was named prime minister by the regent in October 1932. Gömbös was a commoner from a family of teachers. During the war, he was a captain attached to the general staff, but his career took an upward turn during the counterrevolution. As chairman of the right-wing Hungarian National Military Association, he became a minister in Horthy's government in exile in 1919. During the consolidation he removed himself from government and served in various racist organizations. In 1927, he rejoined the government. Following the defeat of Bethlen's semiliberal course, Horthy turned to Gömbös, his close friend and supporter, to carry out a shift to the right.

Gömbös did not break immediately with Bethlen's policies, and he retained some members of the former government in his cabinet. He had learned from bitter experience that politics was a game of compromises. At first he had to concentrate on providing relief and a way out of the depression. His government increased protection against foreign competition for industry, provided subsidies for farmers and agricultural exporters, and secured new markets and loans for enterprises. Gömbös announced a ninety-five-point "national unity program." Its points included reestablishing material well-being and security for the population, restricting the "harmful growth of capitalism," establishing safety in the workplace, and restructuring land ownership in a more equitable way. Gömbös' scheme envisioned a unity of labor, capital, and intellectual talent. One important organizational element in his scheme was the *corporation* à la Mussolini in which workers and employers would reconcile their interests in disputed matters with the state serving as mediator. The plan failed because of the resistance of capitalists and strong labor unions alike.

The internal policy of the Gömbös government based on compromises was matched by a foreign policy based on the notion of "peaceful revision" of Hungary's Trianon borders. For years Gömbös had kept in touch with Mussolini, and he was quick to visit Chancellor Hitler after his rise to power in January 1933. The visit took place the following July. Gömbös was able to reach agreements with Hitler only on economic matters. Hungarian agriculture could certainly benefit from Hitler's grandiose plans for building up German industrial and arms production. But from the beginning it was evident that Hitler would support Hungarian revisionist aims only insofar as they were in line with German national interests in pursuit of European hegemony. At that time it meant taking a stand against Czechoslovakia.

Following the conclusion of the Trianon treaty and the establishment of the Little Entente (the alliance between Czechoslovakia, Romania, and Yugoslavia), Hungary had little room for conducting its foreign policy. Realistically, the choices were to join Italy or Germany. Bethlen himself chose Italy, as noted above, if only for the fact that Weimar Germany was too weak and was not an adequate partner for revisionism. However, with Hitler's emergence, matters took a different turn. Germany was visibly gaining power and influence and was in the process of shaking off the shackles of the Versailles rearrangement of Europe's borders. Hungarian foreign policy was now geared to promote the coming together of its two potential allies. This policy had little success at first. The Rome Protocols of 1934 did buttress the alliance among Italy, Austria, and Hungary, but Gömbös carefully avoided giving the alliance an anti-German character.

Italy looked toward France for support in its imperialistic plans for northern Africa. It concluded an agreement with the French government in January 1935. This agreement also covered central Europe. The main purpose of the treaty was to preserve the European status quo and provide a basis for achieving accords in foreign policy matters. Obviously, such an agreement did not suit the Hungarian revisionist plans. The Gömbös government was also upset by the plan advanced by the Slovak politician, Milan Hodza, which called for close cooperation among Czechoslovakia, Hungary, and Austria. The Hungarians rightly perceived that this plan was created in order to strengthen the border arrangements of the Treaty of Trianon.

Tensions between the states of the Little Entente on the one hand and Hungary on the other increased when, in October 1934, the Croatian Ustaši assassinated King Alexander of Yugoslavia and the French foreign minister Barthou in Marseilles. The preparations and arrangements for the murders were traced back to Hungary. This caused great alarm in Europe especially among the member states of the Little Entente.

In September 1935, Gömbös once again went to Berlin. Although this meeting failed to answer all of Hungary's expectations, it did bring Hungary and Germany closer together. After the meeting, Hungary's foreign policy definitely tilted toward Germany. Two vital national interests set Hungary on this course. The Hungarians saw in Germany a power that could right the wrongs committed in the peace treaty that took away Hungarian territories and their ethnically Hungarian populations. At the same time, Germany seemed capable of revitalizing the Hungarian agriculture and food industries. While large landowners and the gentry elite were contemptuous of the Nazis, the majority of Hungarians were willing to make a pact with the devil himself in the interest of securing border revisions and economic recovery.

In the matter of Hungary's later turn to the right and its government becoming fascist we must examine Gömbös' internal policies. Gömbös undoubtedly leaned toward authoritarian rule, and he felt a special affinity for Mussolini's governmental system. He frequently called for the establishment of a corporate state as Hungary's way to unity. After taking office, he was instrumental in renaming his party the Party of National Unity. This party gained not only a new name but also a new structure and new leadership. The more liberal politicians such as Bethlen and his supporters went into internal opposition and eventually left the party. Gömbös, in order to strengthen his hand, declared early parliamentary elections. The elections were held in April 1935. The authorities openly intervened in the process and the governing party was eminently successful. It won 70 percent of the vote against the the Smallholders, the Social Democrats, and the Socialists. This "success" encouraged Gömbös to launch a comprehensive social and cultural movement. He wanted to draw everything and everyone into national youth, social, and athletic associations,

182 · PÉTER HANÁK

paramilitary organizations, and the new right-wing intellectual trends. A few agile writers were willing to oblige: they started the New Intellectual Front.

In the 1930s a new force appeared among middle-class intellectuals. The new group called itself *népiek* (the most common translation is "populist"). This group was made up of intellectuals of peasant background who sympathized with the plight of the rural poor. They were also concerned about the difficulties facing the middle class of peasant origin. Sociographers such as Zoltán Szabó, Géza Féja, and Ferenc Erdei, the fine poet Gyula Illyés (himself of leftist orientation), the teacher and essayist László Németh, as well as Imre Kovács and József Darvas were the leading personalities of this progressive, literary, and sociopolitical movement. They referred to themselves as the populist writers.

The Hungarian populists differed from the Russian and other Eastern European *narodniks* in that they did not have a messianic, social-revolutionary creed; they were also different from the romantic German *völkisch* intellectuals who identified with fascism. The Hungarian populists were, first and foremost, antifeudal and anticapitalist in their ideology. Their primary goal was to elevate the peasantry to a higher status, because they considered it to be the backbone of the Hungarian nation. They wished to rejuvenate the national ideal advanced by the gentry injecting it with the fresh vigor of the peasantry. Their ideology was based on the notion of the "third road": a peculiar Hungarian version of socialism that was national but not fascist, socialist but not Soviet communist, and one that would bring about "cooperative socialism."

In addition to their strong antifeudal outlook, the new populists were open to the ideas coming from the democratic left. However, they were also willing to listen to the anticapitalist tendencies and anti-Semitism of the right. When Gömbös flirted with the idea of the New Intellectual Front, these tendencies were quite visible. The populist writers were quick to realize what Gömbös was up to and broke off their relations with the governing party. In the following year part of the group began to lean toward the left, while another segment moved over to the right.

The Hungarian fascist movement began to take shape during the first half of the 1930s. By 1935, the various racist and chauvinistic groups were drawn together by Ferenc Szálasi, a staff officer of the army and an extreme right-wing politician. In that year Szálasi left the army and founded the party of Hungarian Will, which, two years later, took the name Hungarian National Socialist party. Its symbol became two arrows forming a cross, lending it the popular title of Arrow Cross party. Its leading elite was composed of déclassé petty-bourgeois individuals, although there were a handful of eccentric aristocrats and chauvinist gentry scions among the members. For some time, the gentry elite of Hungary did not take the Arrow Cross party seriously. Its members were not admitted to the casinos frequented by the upper class. The elite was contemptuous of the masses even more than of the socialist workers.

Gömbös himself rejected any open contact with the Arrow Cross party. This partly explains his failure to broaden the basis of the governing party. In spite of his inclination toward authoritarianism and his pleasure in being called "the Leader," Gömbös was not willing to be considered a sympathizer with the Arrow Cross. A metamorphosis of this type would have been paradoxical: a gentry elite party could not be made into a fascist party of the masses.

Shift to the Right Under Germany's Shadow

Gömbös died in 1936. His place was taken by his minister of agriculture, Kálmán Darányi, a descendant of an old gentry landowning family. At the outset, he was one of Bethlen's men who, in line with Bethlen's conservative policies, was determined to block an excessive shift to the right. He banned the Arrow Cross party, put Szálasi on trial, and attempted to reestablish the norms of a constitutional state. But Hungary was establishing ever closer economic and political ties with Nazi Germany and the newly formed Berlin-Rome axis. Enjoying the covert support of Germany, Szálasi's party was reinstituted and quickly gained influence. By late 1937, Darányi's government was becoming more tolerant toward the activities of the extreme right: it was focusing on the great opportunity that was at hand, namely, the revision of Hungary's borders. The government adjusted its plans to accommodate Germany's efforts and was preparing to confront Czechoslovakia.

In March 1938, the Darányi government introduced a program for rearmament known as the "Győr program," for the city where it was announced. The plan called for one billion pengős to be invested in armament production over a period of five years. Money was to come from taxes levied on large capitalist firms. The war was approaching so fast that the program was actually completed in a shorter time and was financed through bank credits and an inflationary economic policy. By the time the program was accepted, Germany had already annexed Austria. Thus, Germany had become Hungary's next-door neighbor. Budapest began to react to the German moves with increasing compliance. In a short time, Darányi installed conspicuously pro-German men in several ministerial posts. In April, he submitted the first openly anti-Jewish law since the *numerus clausus,* which limited the number of Jews permitted to participate in economic and cultural life in Hungary.

But Darányi was a bit too quick to act. The ruling elite wanted to slow down the shift to the right, so Darányi was replaced by his minister of finance, Béla Imrédy. The scion of a wealthy and prestigious merchant family, the Heinrichs, he came from a branch of the family that was granted a title in the 1820s and subsequently changed its name to Imrédy. For many years before he became prime minister, Béla Imrédy was president of the Hungarian National Bank and then minister of finance. He was considered an outstanding financial expert and a sober and moderate politician. His initial moves fulfilled the antifascist expectations of the elite. He appointed Ferenc Keresztes Fischer, a stern man who believed in strict constitutionality, as his minister of the interior. Imrédy's minister of education was Pál Teleki, an equally respected conservative professor. The Arrow Cross leader Szálasi was brought to trial once again and sentenced to three years in prison. In addition, the government prohibited civil servants from joining any fascist party or organization.

But Imrédy's government was as incapable of stemming the dynamic tide of right-wing forces as his predecessor. Imrédy visited Germany, which was feverishly preparing for war. What he saw there convinced him that Hungary had to seek Hitler's favor and construct a totalitarian internal system if it wanted to recover its lost territories. He was strengthened in this conviction by the Munich accord of September 1938 in which the two major Western powers, Britain and France, gave Hitler a free hand to move against Czechoslovakia. Now the Hungarian government openly supported German aggression. On November 2, 1938, Hitler rewarded Hungary with southern Slovakia, an area of some 12,000 square kilometers with an ethnically Hungarian population of 750,000 and 300,000 mainly Slovak minorities. The Hungarian government was also able to obtain Ruthenia (today's Carpatho-Ukraine) with another 12,000 square kilometers of territory and a mixed Hungarian and Ruthenian population.

The partial revision of Hungary's borders was hailed by everyone in the country. Most people felt that the shackles placed on Hungary by the Treaty of Trianon were finally falling off and the road was opening for a complete return of the lost territories. In the months of euphoria, most people did not think about the price that would have to be paid immediately, or of the even greater price in the future.

The Imrédy government went further in trying to gain German favor. Pro-German ministers were brought into the government and the anti-German minister of foreign affairs, Kálmán Kánya, was ousted. The post of chief of staff of the armed forces went to Henrik Wirth, widely known for his pro-Nazi sentiments. Imrédy also permitted pro-Hitler ethnic Germans living in Hungary to organize a *Volksbund der Deutschen in Ungarn,* a group encouraged by the Nazis. Before Christmas, another anti-Jewish law was proposed in parliament in which the criterion for being considered Jewish was no longer religion but racial background, and which restricted Jewish participation in the professions and the civil service to 5 percent. The Arrow Cross movement also gained momentum, and the government not only tolerated but even encouraged it. Imrédy, however, believed that the best defense against the extremists was to have the government organize its own extreme right-wing movement after the liberal-conservative members of the government party joined Bethlen's moderate opposition.

In early January 1939, the prime minister proclaimed the establishment of a new group, called the Hungarian Life Movement. Its slogans included "national unity," "discipline," "land reform," and "defense of the race." The movement promised a "new life for Hungarians based on ancient Magyar will." Territorial revisionism was thus united with the promise of internal revival, all with a racist undercurrent. When the movement began to stall and the masses were no longer bedazzled by the "wonder stag" borrowed from Hungarian mythology, the governing party changed its name to the Hungarian Life party.

All these gestures adopted from fascism did not help Imrédy. He was unseated by the moderates. Regent Horthy then reached for his old friend, the respected and experienced politician-scholar Pál Teleki, and appointed him prime minister. The "new" scenario opened with the usual moves. All fascist parties were banned, and many members of the Arrow Cross party were placed in detention camps. These steps, however, no longer harmed the Arrow Cross movement. In the elections held in May 1939 the party gained forty deputies and thus became the strongest parliamentary opposition party.

In the face of growing Nazi influence and Arrow Cross threats, Teleki proved to be a brave defender of Hungary's independence. He kept open a narrow channel of diplomacy that still connected Hungary with Great Britain. Teleki was especially apprehensive about making a full commitment to either side in the gathering storm. In September 1939, Germany overran Poland; subsequently, France and Great Britain declared war on Nazi Germany. Teleki moved to refuse permission for the German army to pass through Hungary. He also permitted the movement of 130,000 Polish soldiers into Hungary as refugees, including some who were threatened by prosecution after the collapse of their country. Hitler made his chagrin with the Hungarians known by canceling war contracts. This was particularly inopportune at a time when Hungary was getting ready for a possible armed conflict with Romania. After France capitulated, Hitler turned his attention to the east, specifically, Yugoslavia and Romania. However, by the summer of 1940, he had already committed the German army to a grandiose campaign against the Soviet Union. Romania was not about to wait for a German *Blitzkrieg:* its government accepted German "friendship," the price of which was Romania's loss of Bessarabia and the parts of Transylvania acquired in 1919.

Hungary and Romania were encouraged by Hitler to attempt to work out their differences. They failed, so Hitler settled the dispute. The Second Vienna Award was passed on August 30, 1940. It split Transylvania in two, with one part encompassing 43,000 square kilometers for Hungary (including the north as well as the territory occupied by Székelys, who were ethnic Hungarians), and another part for Romania. Naturally, neither party was satisfied with the deal. The Hungarians considered the award to be a meager reward, while the Romanians thought it a dire punishment. About one million Romanians were stranded in the new Hungarian territory, and about 400,000 Hungarians were left in Romania.

Mutual dependence and prudence might have resulted in some sort of understanding between Hungarians and Romanians. Instead, mutual hatred, stoked by Hitler and the local little hitlers, stood in the way of peace between the two peoples. Hungarian local authorities and the newly installed gendarmerie harassed the Romanian population. Even more tragic was the fate of Jews in Transylvania. The great majority of them had sympathized with Hungary while they were under Romanian rule and greeted an annexation by Hungary with joy. But the Hungarians did not greet them with the same feeling. Jews immediately became subject to Article 4 of the law of 1939, which called for limitations on "public and economic activities of Jews." Jews were discriminated against in all walks of life in Hungary. The measure of discrimination was not as severe then as it was in Romania where Jews had to endure forced labor in the swamps of the

Lower Danube, where hundreds of thousands were killed or crippled. However, during the spring of 1944, the Transylvanian Jews, even those who had declared themselves ethnic Hungarians under Romanian rule, were deported to German death camps.

The success of revisionism erased possible misgivings in the Hungarian public. Most considered it a given that Hungary should offer Germany economic advantages, that the Volksbund should acquire a privileged status, and that fascist propaganda gain ground in the country. Teleki was now willing to grant amnesty to Szálasi. He was also forced to receive the Arrow Cross leader as the head of the largest opposition party in parliament. Teleki had to swallow the bitter pill of having his government join the Tripartite Pact between Germany, Italy, and Japan on November 20, 1940.

All these events notwithstanding, Teleki did not abandon his independent course. Though he was aware of the possibility that Hitler intended to make Yugoslavia his next victim, he signed a treaty of friendship and non-agression with Hungary's southern neighbor in December 1940. When in the spring of 1941 Hitler made up his mind to attack Yugoslavia, he could not permit Hungary to obstruct the movement of his troops on their way to the south. Germany, therefore, made an offer to Horthy for another territorial revision should Hungary be willing to join in the next military campaign. Horthy was inclined to accept the German offer even if it meant the breach of the Yugoslav treaty of friendship. However, Teleki stood firm against this adventure. For him, a gentleman's honor was at stake, and he was also convinced that Hungary must stay out of any war involving Hitler's Germany. Moreover, he knew that the Western Allies would not sit idly by if Yugoslavia were attacked. But Teleki was powerless to prevent Horthy's decision to side with the Germans, and in the early dawn of April 3, 1941, Teleki committed suicide. In his farewell letter to Horthy he proclaimed: "Your Grace! We have become perfidious—out of cowardice . . . we have sided with the villains . . . I did not hold you back; I am guilty." Teleki's death was a misfortune, but it could not arrest the course of events.

Teleki's post went to a dispirited professional diplomat, László Bárdossy, his minister of foreign affairs. The new government joined the Germans in their attack on Yugoslavia. As a reward, Hitler gave Hungary some more territories, which finally tied Hungary to Germany for good. Not long afterward, Bárdossy announced plans for the introduction of a third anti-Jewish law. In August, the new law was ratified by parliament: it prohibited intermarriage between Jews and Christians and severely punished extramarital sexual relations between Jews and non-Jews. A virtual ghetto in Budapest was already being set up.

By June, it became apparent that Germany was getting ready to march against the Soviet Union. On June 13, the Slovak puppet government announced that it was ready to participate in a war against the Soviet state. A week later, Romania made a similar announcement. The invasion was launched at dawn on June 22, 1941 without a declaration of war. Four days later Hungary joined the fateful conflict.

The gradual shift to the right that followed Bethlen's fall a decade earlier followed its own laws of motion. Since the premiership of Gyula Gömbös, Hungary had been inching closer and closer to Germany and Italy, the country was getting mired ever deeper in its fixed course and was getting nearer and nearer to the war being instigated by the two radical powers. It was also becoming increasingly fascist in character. Several of Hungary's governments attempted to forestall this process but their initial successes gave way to coercion, or the so-called geopolitical need for compromise. The course led to the Darányi government's Györ program, Imrédy's attempt at introducing a totalitarian government and Teleki's approval of the fascist Tripartite Pact.

Why Hungary was unable to avoid the shift to the right and participation in the war might be explained by the pressure exerted by Germany's enormous military and economic potential and ruthless aggressiveness. But "geopolitical determinism" would be an easy and smug answer. There were other small countries in the region such as Czechoslovakia and Yugoslavia that accepted the risk and the accompanying misery of being occupied. Perhaps Hungary's previously flexible "shuttlecock policy" was not yet depleted even at the time of Teleki's suicide. However, the fixed course that Hungary had to follow between the two world wars was not determined by Germany's overwhelming power and agressiveness. Rather, it was a consequence of the Treaty of Trianon. Hungary, maimed and humiliated, was unable to avoid the shift to the right and had little choice but to fight back with a major power's backing in order to obtain the revision of the peace treaty. Hungary responded to its neighbors' nationalism with a nationalism of its own, especially since they did not secure the rights of Hungarian minorities as pledged in the peace treaty.

In order to achieve the aims of revisionism, there should have been alternatives as to both allies and the means. Hungary sided with Nazi

Germany because the country's ruling elite, among whom officers and politicians of German descent gained undue influence, worshipped right-wing ideals and felt drawn to some sort of authoritarian rule, staking the country's fate on Germany's victory in the war.

Economy and Society

Three factors determined Hungary's economic development between the two world wars. One was the defeat in the First World War, which depleted Hungary's resources. The subsequent two revolutions and the counterrevolution only compounded the losses in manpower and materiel. The second factor was the disintegration of the Monarchy's joint market coupled with Hungary's dismemberment. The losses included 64 percent of mineral energy resources, 80 percent of iron ore and iron production, 88 percent of the forests, 20 percent of paper production capacity, and all the salt mines. More serious was the fact that natural economic units and established market districts were disrupted and most of the usual transport routes were blocked. Autarkic economic policies dominated in the successor states stifling what before the war had been dynamic development in the entire region.

A third factor was the decline and stagnation of the world economy, which prevailed throughout the interwar years. Since most of the warring countries went deeply into debt to cover expenses, large-scale investments and reorganizations were held back. The uncertain boom of the 1920s was checked by the Great Depression: only another war could provide for a somewhat artificial take-off. Under these conditions, defeated and bankrupt Hungary was in an especially bad situation. It took until 1929 for economic output to surpass the prewar level just by a few percentage points, and the few good years after 1938 ended in the defeat and destruction of 1944.

The system of landownership and agricultural production hardly changed during the interwar years. The land reform of 1920 affected only a small fraction of the massive structure of landed estates. Almost one-third of the country's arable land was made up of estates controling over six hundred hectares of land each. In contrast, holdings of less than three hectares comprised 10 percent of small holdings and only 26 percent of farms belonged to productive units of ten to thirty hectares each. In addition to this distorted pattern of landholding, agriculture suffered severely for the lack of capital. Peasants were especially hard hit by their inability to obtain loans under favorable

TABLE 4.1
Hungarian Landholding Patterns in 1935

Size of Holding (Hectares)	Number of Holdings	Percentage	Total Area (Hectares)	Percentage of Total Area
0–6.5	1,389,254	85.0	1,992,700	19.3
6.6–65	233,089	14.2	3,356,390	32.6
66–130	5,712	0.4	516,130	5.0
131–650	5,202	0.3	1,362,050	13.2
650+	1,070	0.1	2,954,390	29.9
Total	1,634,407	100.0	10,180,660	100.0

terms. This had the effect of leaving outdated production methods and structures unchanged. With the diminishing size of external markets, Hungarian agriculture faced a chronic crisis. Temporary relief was achieved by the contribution of Hungary to food supplies for remilitarizing Germany. For the food Germany paid relatively low prices and, of course, Hungary eventually paid dearly for its deliveries.

Developments were more dynamic in industry and transportation. While before World War I the leading branch of industry was food processing, now it was textiles. After the break up of the monarchy, this was the branch of industry that could take best advantage of tariff protection and autarkic efforts. The number of machines (though most of them were acquired second-hand from Western industries) grew manyfold in one and one-half decades. The number of workers in the textile industry increased by a factor of five, and the value of their output was six times larger than before. Yet, this late boom in industrialization was a sign of weakness, not strength. Nevertheless, there were two branches of industry that were considered modern since the turn of the century. These were the chemical industry (producing pharmaceuticals that reached world standards) and electronics. The groundwork was laid for Hungary's electronics industry for decades to come. Hungarian radios and light bulbs were known all around the world. In 1920, electricity production in the new Hungary reached 276 million kws, and by 1938, it surpassed one billion kws. The energy level used by factories increased by 100 percent over the 1913 level during the following twenty-five years. The total production of factories, however, did not increase in corresponding measures. The 1938 production level surpassed its 1913 level by only 28 percent.

There was notable progress in transportation. Hungary's railway network ranked the country seventh among European nations. The wide use of an electric locomotive, invented by Kálmán Kandó, and the introduction of electric trains and diesel engines showed the qualitative improvements.

Nevertheless, economic growth was, on the whole, slow. Even during the peak level before the outbreak of the Second World War, Hungary's national income was only 10 percent higher than before the First World War. Yearly growth remained below 1.5 percent, way below the 2.5 percent of the previous period. The increase of 0.8 percent in per capita income was less than half represented by the 1.7 percent increase before World War I. Only in 1938 did per capita income reach the earlier level. Nor was there much change in the structure of employment. Before 1913, 57 percent of the workers worked in agriculture, and 21 percent were industrial employees. In 1938, the ratio was still 50 percent and 25 percent respectively. The number of civil servants and professionals increased only by a few percentage points. Such slight changes were not sufficient to change Hungary from a largely agricultural to an industrialized country.

Hungary's population in 1941 reached 9,316,000. Of these, 92 percent were ethnic Hungarians, while 8 percent were composed of minorities, mostly Germans and Slovaks. Two-thirds of the population professed to belong to the Roman Catholic church, over one-fourth belonged to various Protestant denominations, and the proportion of Jews was around 5 percent. Most of the Jews lived in Budapest where they made up nearly 20 percent of the population. The most significant demographic change in Hungary between the wars consisted of accelerating urbanization. This may be explained by the fact that most urbanized regions remained within the new post-Trianon borders. The proportion of urban residents increased from 19 percent in 1919 to 30 percent in 1920 and to 35 percent in 1941.

The capital's residential areas spread out over the hills and southern lowlands of Buda, while Pest was expanding northward into a new Lipótváros. Nearly 12.5 percent of the total population of Hungary was concentrated in the capital, and with the suburbs, which comprise present-day Greater Budapest, the proportion was closer to 18 percent. Economic life, political forums, major cultural institutions, and workshops were all thriving in the capital city. The loss of the important larger cities such as Kolozsvár (Cluj), Nagyvárad (Oradea Mare), Arad, to Romania and Kassa (Kosice) to Czechoslovakia was sorely felt, particularly, since in the new states they began to decline. On the other hand, a few rural economic centers and medium-sized towns which contained universities (such as Debrecen, Szeged, Pécs, Györ, and Miskolc) were beginning to grow.

The stratification of the population is shown by Table 4.2. It

TABLE 4.2
Hungary's Social Stratification, 1930 (in Percent)

Industrial workers	23.5
Agricultural workers	19.2
Servants (in homes)	2.3
Poor peasants (0.5–5 ha. land)	16.3
Smallholders (3–16 ha. land)	13.4
Landowners (16–30 ha. land)	3.4
Artisans	6.3
Dealers, shopkeepers	2.3
Petty bourgoisie	8.6
Officials, free professionals, employees	6.2
Landlords	0.2
Bourgeoisie	0.9
Pensioners	3.4
Renters	2.2
Other professionals	1.6
Others	7.2
Total workers	45.0
Total peasants	32.0
Total population	8,688,300

mirrors statistical categories based on occupation and source of income. Hence, it can provide only an indication of the true distribution of jobs. Missing are important historical factors, such as social origins and religion, status and prestige, traditions and education, social environment, and geographic areas. Historically, Hungarian society was divided both horizontally and vertically. At the top of the social pyramid one found the one thousand families of landed aristocrats. At the beginning of the current century, they were joined by several hundred families of the financial bourgeoisie. Below them was a mixed middle class, which included the traditionalists of noble background. Some of these were landlords, but for the most part they were civil servants of the déclassé gentry. Prominent in the so-called gentry-oriented (historical) middle class were high-ranking civil servants and military officers. The majority of the middle class, however, were neither traditional nor historical. They were simply bourgeois. They were backed by a sizable wealth- and business-network and by a stratum of educated professionals. This middle class consisted of immigrant and assimilated Germans, Greeks, Serbs, and, foremost, Jews.

The distribution of the party bourgeoisie was similar. Here the traditional craftsmen and old-family burgher-merchants, though more numerous, were economically weaker. A smaller but increasingly more powerful economic group was made up of assimilated Germans and Jews. It is evident, then, that the upper- and middle-classes' stratification was not only vertical, based on social status and wealth, but also split into groups according to family background, prestige, and values. On one side was the so-called traditional, or national, society and, on the other, the strictly middle-class structure. A great deal of mobility existed within each structure, with members of the national group more commonly moving down and members of the bourgeoisie usually moving up.

In the interwar years the old social structure did not fully disintegrate. Its most important structural elements continued to exist, each symbiotically locked into its traditional patterns with the others, but not in organic unity with the new classes shaped by the capitalist system. The dualistic structure was characteristic of Eastern European social developments and was quite apparent in Hungary. The framework of social exclusivity and the traditions of a feudal mentality never entirely disappeared.

While the status of the traditional nobility and the petty bourgeoisie had declined, that of the assimilated middle class improved. As a result, social conflicts took on a nationalistic hue with an anti-Semitic tint. The nobility, including the gentry, continued to play a leading role in Hungarian affairs, not only because the large landed estates remained intact (and the system safeguarded their dominant position) but also because all ranks of the nobility, regardless of social and economic differences, shared a common tradition and values. In this social-psychological sense they were to a large extent homogeneous. For that reason, a large portion of the rising administrative and intellectual stratum came from or joined with the gentry-oriented middle classes.

The separation of the two social structures was also evident in the case of the lower classes. No organic social mobility had ever come about among the agricultural laborers, the poor peasants, and the urban workers. Skilled labor consisted mostly of foreign immigrants or were recruited from among local craftsmen. Poor peasants streaming into the cities were stuck in construction or seasonal work. They also became policemen, gendarmes, office servants, or delivery men in order to obtain a foothold in the city. These semiproletarians were drawn more to the traditional "national" side and became one of the props of the system. The lower classes fused mostly through intermarriage and, after the mid-1920s, by way of their influx into industry.

The central line in the vertical stratification of Hungarian society also ran between the upper/middle classes and the lower classes, the two parallel structures coming into sharp conflict. As a result, internal politics revolved not only around the social sphere but also around the "bourgeois" and the "national" spheres. The ideology and propaganda resulting from these conflicts reinforced anti-Semitism.

Anti-Semitism in Eastern Europe was founded on three types of motivation of which the ancient, religiously rooted hatred of Jews was not especially strong and did not exhibit fanatic features. Much stronger was a popular anti-Semitism, a distorted popular struggle against capitalist rentiers and village usurers. The disproportionate representation of Jews in financial enterprise may have provided a certain basis for such ill will. This type of "class struggle" anti-Semitism found support among unskilled and unorganized workers, miners, and the village poor. But this type of popular anti-Jewish sentiment would never on its own have given rise to fascism.

Hungarian anti-Semitism received its strength and massive support from the déclassé lower-middle-class militants and racists. Its mouthpieces and leaders were extreme rightist civil servants, intellectuals, craftsmen, and shopkeepers who looked to some kind of conservative-initiated redistribution of Jewish wealth and/or the ouster of Jewish professionals from their jobs. Even these factors would have been insufficient by themselves to establish and sustain a potent anti-Semitic movement if, by a quirk of history, Hitler's Germany had not been next door to Hungary. While anti-Jewish racism did have a base in Hungary, it was the direct support of German Nazism which elevated it and gave it power as an ordering principle, as a crystallizing point for internal politics. This was the force that promoted the brutal persecution of Jews.

Deportations and racist terror claimed the lives of over half a million Hungarian Jews. This was a loss not only for Jewry but also for Hungary. The country lost many first-class experts in various fields, diligent workers, fine merchants, and professionals, not to mention international prestige and national self-respect. After the war, Hungary was left with a number of pressing social problems and with hundreds of thousands of victims, Jews and Gypsies, soldiers and civilians.

Cultural Life

Hungary's intellectual life during the interwar period was marked by the defeat of left-wing movements and the crisis of left-wing ideas. This was a worldwide phenomenon, one which was especially conspicuous in Hungary. Even before World War I, conservatism and nationalism—or to put it in milder terms, gentry traditionalism imbued with powerful national sentiments—were living forces promoted by literature, the arts, and the humanities. Yet the intellectual character of Hungary at the *fin de siècle* was determined more by modernism, which combined the national idea with radical democracy. Prominent influences were Endre Ady and the circle around the literary journal *Nyugat* (The West), Béla Bartók and the New Hungarian Music Society, and avant-gardism. Social science was bred on the traditions of German philosophy of culture. György Lukács and his circle flourished. The urban bourgeois drama of Sándor Bródy and Ferenc Molnár, the *art nouveau* of Kossák and others, and the metropolitan music theater of Ferenc Lehár and Imre Kálmán were in great vogue.

In the 1920s, however, urban culture saw a period of decay. The *Nyugat* circle began to disintegrate and even its great figures such as Zsigmond Móricz, Mihály Babits, and Dezsö Kosztolányi were compelled to make minor compromises with the prevailing atmosphere. Still, they produced their greatest masterpieces during the interwar period, in protest against the country's continuing drift toward fascism. Besides them, a younger generation of the *Nyugat* "silver age" came to maturity, and they had much in common with Attila József, the first genuine working-class Hungarian poet, as well as with Sándor Márai. Márai was the last novelist of stature among the liberal-humanist bourgeoisie. The attitudes and tastes of the wider public were, however, basically determined by conservative intellectual currents consonant with the prevailing Christian-national course.

The dominant cultural trend of the period was characterized more by Ferenc Herczeg in literature, Gyula Szekfű in the humanities, and Dezső Szabó, the fountainhead of populist literature and racist politics. It was during the age of the Dual Monarchy that Herczeg first became famous for his light novels about traditional topics, which flattered the complacency and popularized the mentality of the "gentle" middle class. In the interwar years Herczeg became the poet laureate of official culture who was able ex officio to raise the burning national and social issues of the age in a manner attuned to dominant ideology. In his wake, the historical novel became a fashionable genre; its underlying themes were gloom and tragedy.

The historian Gyula Szekfű exerted great influence on the intellectuals of the period. Early in his career Szekfű was a member of the Austro-Hungarist circle in Vienna. As such, he was critical of the legalistic attitude and the traditional, futile controversies that raged around constitutional law. After the revolutions, however, he placed the blame for Hungary's decline on liberalism, capitalism, and the

Jews as the main representatives of both ideologies. Szekfű saw the key to renewal in conservative, Christian spiritual reform, which he traced back to an idealized István Széchenyi. Later in his life, Szekfű became a conservative antifascist and a member of the anti-Nazi resistance and allied himself with democratic forces in the country.

Dezső Szabó identified liberalism and assimilationism as the sources of decay, but he considered the peasantry, instead of the Christian middle class, as the leading force of a possible Hungarian renaissance. In his major work, *Az elsodort falu* (The Village that was Swept Away), he suggested that the torpid Hungarian middle class, corrupted by the mentalities of the assimilated Germans and Jews, could be saved from ultimate doom only by the primordial force of the peasantry. Szabó's truculent personality, his intransigence masked as courage, and his generally disputatious stance offered an attractive example for young intellectuals in search of a solution to Hungary's problems.

Two intellectual and political currents originated with Dezső Szabó, one expanding on the concept of race, the other being Hungarian populism with a refined sense of social issues. The former led to the emergence of the "Hungarist" and Arrow Cross movements. The latter adopted anti-Semitism and social demagogy from Dezső Szabó. All right-wing parties promoted some form of anti-Semitism in their political programs; the fascists were distinguished only by their brutality. However, the ideas of the members of the Arrow Cross movement had no place for Szabó's anti-German sentiments. This current left no lingering mark on Hungarian culture.

Much more important were the works of the populist writers, who left a deep impression on Hungarian public thinking. One of their intellectual leaders, Gyula Illyés, was a member of the socialist left early in his career. This was a heritage that Illyés preserved even when his ideas turned toward efforts to raise the "people" to the level of the rest of the nation. His cautious but persistent antifascism and anticommunism raised him to the ranks of the authentic leaders of the nation in the dark decades when the country's political leaders were in the service of external powers. Together with Péter Veres, a writer of peasant origin, and the sociologist Ferenc Erdei, Illyés served as a bridge between the populists and the political left. In March 1937, they initiated the March Front, an organization combining left-wing democratic ideals with national traditions. Later a group of men from this movement established the National Peasant party, while others launched the resistance front in cooperation with the local communists.

László Németh, a major European thinker, writer, and essayist, was the key cultural figure among the populists. He defined the role of the Hungarian nation in Eastern Europe. He also eloquently propounded a populist view of the relationship between being Hungarian and being European. Confident about the possibility of creating a Hungarian version of socialism, Németh proclaimed the program of the "third road." In his novels and dramas he dealt with and illuminated questions of human fate. Although the essays he wrote in the 1930s and during the Second World War showed a drift to the right, he believed that the assimilation of Germans and Jews into Hungarian society was the cause of its decline. Nevertheless, Németh marked himself off from the populist writers who allied themselves with rightist extremism. Some of his post-1945 writings may be considered a form of self-criticism.

István Bibó was the most important theorist and political scientist among the members of the March Front. He correctly identified Hungary's distorted social structure and the adverse fate of the small nations of Eastern Europe as the cause of the region's misery. As a solution, he recommended the establishment of a democratic society, the abandonment of the remnants of feudalism and chauvinism, and work for mutual understanding and peaceful coexistence with neighboring states.

In other cultural areas some decline set in. In music, Bartók and Zoltán Kodály were considered supreme authorities among connoisseurs. The middle class, however, usually preferred Gypsy songs or light music and operettas. High musical culture was represented by Kodály's educational methods, the excellent company he assembled in the National Opera Company, and the Budapest Philharmonic Orchestra. Notable painters and scupltors did exist, but the dominant tastes of the age proved to be an insurmountable obstacle for the creative genius of the artists of the avant-garde and for postmodernists. In addition to the dramas of Ferenc Herczeg and Ferenc Molnár, important plays were written by Zsigmond Móricz and László Németh.

Large-scale emigration of intellectuals contributed to cultural decay. Because of political persecution or blighted prospects dozens of excellent artists and intellectuals left the country. Mathematics and physics suffered the greatest loss. It is probably no exaggeration to say that Hungary might have become a scientific power had János (John von) Neumann, a founder of game theory, Leo Szilárd, the nuclear physicist, Jenő (Eugene) Wigner, 1963 Nobel Prize recipient for physics, and Ede (Edward) Teller not gone abroad. Another blow was the emigration of György Lukács and the Sunday Circle. Giants of European intellectual life such as sociologist Karl Mannheim, art theorist Arnold Hauser, and art historian Charles Tolnay came from their ranks. Bauhaus masters László Moholy-Nagy and Marcell Breuer, Karl Polányi, the anthropologist and economist, and Oszkár Jászi, the sociologist, also left Hungary. Ferenc Molnár became a world-famous name in drama, while Sándor Korda dominated cinema. Béla Bartók's emigration to the United States was an especially grievous loss. He was unable to come to terms with the emerging fascism in Hungary and went to live in New York, where he died in 1945. In addition, hundreds of doctors, engineers, and other intellectuals felt compelled to flee the country or were destroyed in Nazi death camps (or, later, in communist concentration camps). It required a particularly rich or particularly wasteful country to give up so much knowledge, feeling, and value as Hungary did in that half century.

The gap that had earlier developed between high culture and mass culture did not narrow in the interwar period in spite of the fact that the governing circles placed a high priority on promoting folk costumes, dances, and songs which allegedly emphasized "Hungarian character." The divisions were reflected in the places frequented by various social strata: casinos and the opera house by the aristocrats; coffee houses and theaters by the middle class; inns and brothels by the rest of the people. The old divisions continued to survive. Yet there were three new areas of culture that were intended for the masses where at least a modicum of intercourse among the separate worlds was achieved. The first of these was the cinema, which began at the turn of the century and rapidly attracted a mixed audience. As early as the 1910s, Hungarian filmmakers produced some remarkable movies. The majority of the 150–160 films made in the interwar years were career stories, modern folk tales, operettas, and comedies of mediocre quality. However, some enduring works testify to the artistry, sensitivity, and innovation of Eastern European cinema during this period.

Radio was another important source of information and amusement. Regular broadcasts were launched in the mid-1920s, and by the Second World War, the radio network reached into most areas of the country. Like the cinema, radio also addressed all social strata, sometimes educating, at other times bamboozling them. Sports, especially European football, was the third area of shared cultural interest. Within just one or two decades, the popularity of football surpassed that of former favorites such as wrestling, gymnastics, and water polo. Towns, districts, factories, and political groups all had their own teams. Football became not only a means of amusement but also a theater of social and political conflict.

Participation in the Second World War

Although the Hungarian government sent a token army of about 45,000 men to the Russian front immediately after the declaration of war, the country did not experience the full weight of the war for a relatively long time. After suffering serious casualties, even this small Hungarian army was withdrawn at the end of 1941. The Hungarian leaders wished to confine the country's participation in the war to supplying foodstuffs and raw materials to the German war machine. However, this was far less than what the Germans demanded. They wanted from the Horthy and the Bárdossy governments a more effective armed contribution to the war effort, similar to the one provided by Romania during the fighting of October 1941. For the time being, internal calm was not disturbed even by the fact that consumer goods were more scarce than before. Britain declared war on Hungary and Hungary—rather rashly—reciprocated, and even declared war on the United States. However, there were already signs of an emerging resistance movement originating on the left. Antifascist and antiwar demonstrations took place but were not able to arouse the general public. Wartime economic prosperity continued while Hungary remained free from attack by the Allies. Soon, there was cause for anxiety; Hungary's military and political leaders, responding to German pressure, decided to send 200,000 Hungarian troops to the eastern front.

As it turned out, this was a most unfortunate decision. The Second Hungarian Army was not prepared to cope with the Russian winter or the requirements of fighting a mobile war against modern heavy artillery and armored troops. Originally, the Hungarian soldiers were to be used mainly for the maintenance of security and public order in the occupied territories, but the German high command soon sent them to a endangered segment of the front along the Don River. The Battle of Stalingrad was soon on, claiming enormous casualties from the aggressors by the autumn of 1942. By the end of the year, the Soviet army encircled the Germans, who suffered such a serious defeat that it proved decisive for the outcome of the war. At the same time, on January 12, 1943, a Soviet attack was launched against the Hungarian-held segment of the front at Voronezh. Within a week, the powerful Soviet forces almost completely annihilated the Second

Hungarian Army. About 50,000 Hungarian soldiers were killed or froze to death in the course of the fighting and the withdrawal; 70,000 were taken prisoner or disappeared. In addition, tens of thousands of unarmed Jews were used for mine clearing and the building of fortifications in the infamous "labor service" established specifically for them, and most of them died. The army was smashed and its remnants fled in disarray.

This was a disastrous defeat. The army was poorly equipped, it was unprepared for the fighting, and its commanding officers proved to be irresponsible. But the fact that the bulk of the Hungarian people had no sympathy for the war played its role in this disaster. Neither the simple soldier and the family he left behind nor the industrial workers considered the war to be in the national interest. Long before the tragedy along the Don River, their morale was undermined by the war, which produced no new marching songs, myths, or acts of heroism. Bitterness was especially strong toward the German high command, which used Hungarian soldiers together with other minor allies as cannon fodder and rear guards in the fighting.

The defeat had a sobering effect on the Hungarian people. By this time, the government was no longer headed by Bárdossy, but by Miklós Kállay, a former member of the circle of István Bethlen. Horthy had more trust in Kállay than in his predecessor. Kállay tried to maintain the status of Hungary as a German satellite while secretly preparing to withdraw the country from the war. At the time, this plan appeared feasible, since it counted on a British landing in the Balkans. Had it come, Hungary would have surrendered to the Western Allies and might have avoided Soviet occupation. Kállay intended to take Hungary out of the war and even expected tacit consent from the Germans. This strategy, however, proved to be an utter failure.

After the invasion of Italy in July and August 1943, followed by Italy's surrender, the British communicated their terms to the Hungarian government through secret diplomatic channels. They demanded unconditional surrender, the abandoning of the German alliance, and complete withdrawal of Hungarian troops from Soviet territory. Kállay believed that if these conditions were formally accepted, their actual performance could be postponed until the appearance of Allied forces in Hungary. But passively waiting for the opportunity was a totally unrealistic solution. First, the German spies who had succeeded in penetrating Hungary's political and military organizations informed Berlin about all these moves. Hitler had developed a growing mistrust of Hungary's policies. Second, the rapid advance of the

Soviet army in early 1944 made it almost certain that it would be the first to reach Eastern Europe.

In January 1944, the British warned the Hungarian government not to wait until the Soviet army invaded the country and not to commit the blunder—the crime—of continuing armed resistance against the Red Army. Such rash acts would certainly result in the complete destruction of Hungary's armed forces, while politically it would place the country in the same category as the Germans. Kállay, however, did not take this warning seriously. He insisted that the British and Americans would not oppose Hungary's resisting the Soviet offensive by military force. In this he was wrong, just as he was wrong in believing that the Germans were passive and patient spectators of the various Hungarian attempts at arranging a separate peace.

On March 19, 1944, without encountering any serious resistance, German troops occupied Hungary, their reluctant satellite.

Hungary Under German Occupation

The economic and military resources of the occupied country as well as its administration now came under German control. The Germans were assisted by a newly appointed government headed by Döme Sztójay, a notoriously pro-German former diplomat. Mass arrest and internment of anti-German politicians, leaders of the opposition, and the left were immediately undertaken. In May, the deportation of the 600,000 Jews in the country began and was accomplished within three months. The operation started with the complete isolation of Jews in ghettoes and the confiscation of their property. Then, beginning in the returned territories in the north and Transylvania followed by the central areas of the country, they were systematically deported from Hungary to the extermination camps. Only the Jews of Budapest were saved from deportation, though fascist thugs took victims there by the thousands as well. The losses suffered by Hungarian Jewry, including those who performed "labor service" at the front, came to 564,307 people killed. This was 75 percent of the Jewish citizenry of Hungary. Only about 120,000 Jews returned from the Nazi death camps, and about the same number survived in Budapest.

A question arises: Was it only the Germans or was it also the Hungarian government and society that were responsible for this genocide? It is relatively easy to assess the responsibility of the Hungarian government. Research has shown that, were it not for the effective assistance of the Hungarian government authorities, administration, railways, and especially the gendarmery that provided armed escorts, the German war machinery, already crippled, would have been unable to arrange for the mass deportations. The case of society at large is somewhat different, for a great range in attitudes toward the deportations existed. Apart from the racist minority filled with malicious joy over the forcible removal—which they actively aided—of half a million fellow Hungarian citizens, the vast majority remained passive, indifferent, or fearful. At the same time, several thousand people sympathized with the Jews and took great risks to save some of them. These included aristocrats and peasants, clerics and workers, institutions and groups of resistance fighters. Indeed, as the war was coming to an end, the defense of the Jews in hiding or those who were suffering in the Budapest ghetto became ever more vigorous.

In the summer of 1944 Romania ended its participation in the war on Germany's side. Soviet troops were standing on Hungary's borders. Regent Horthy decided at last to take radical steps to disengage Hungary from the war. At the end of September, he sent emissaries to Moscow with the task of negotiating an armistice. The talks were successful. Horthy, confident of the loyalty of his army, proclaimed the armistice and Hungary's withdrawal from the war on October 15. However, the Germans responded to Horthy's coup with a coup of their own. On the evening of the same day, German paratroopers occupied the royal castle in Buda and took Horthy with his family and close advisers as prisoners. Power was ceded to the Arrow Cross party and political leadership went to Ferenc Szálasi. This was one of the most tragic days in Hungarian history; it was followed by a five-month reign of terror by the Arrow Cross party.

Why did all this happen? What was the reason for the failure of the attempt to get Hungary out of the war in October 1944? Why did the bulk of the army refuse to obey the beloved supreme war lord and the civil servants His Highness, the Regent? A whole range of books and studies have sought the answer to these questions. The numerical superiority of the German occupying army does not fully explain the outcome. Romania managed to leave the war under circumstances that were not much more favorable. The Slovak national uprising succeeded in becoming involved in the endgame as well.

It was mainly on account of the territorial acquisitions granted by Germany and Italy that Hungary's special situation emerged. Whereas the neighboring countries suffered serious losses in lives and territories and had been òccupied by the Germans earlier than Hungary, Hungary's revisionist claims were largely satisfied, and further economic benefits accrued to the country from its alliance with Germany. The majority of the population, although not enthusiastic supporters of the war, were not filled with a passionate hatred of the Germans as were the Czechs, Poles, or Serbs.

In all probability, the satisfaction rendered to offended Hungarian nationalism was the reason behind the commitment of the bulk of Hungarian society to the side of Germany. It was this commitment that caused even political realists to hesitate in exploiting favorable historical circumstances for changing the course of Hungary. When Pál Teleki definitely decided to rebuff German claims, it was already too late. Miklós Kállay continued his shuttlecock policies too long: eventually, he lost the confidence of both the Germans and of the British and Americans. Horthy himself waited too long before openly opposing the Germans and attempting to leave the war. When he did, he blundered. Of the political elite, even the more realistic-minded were dazzled by the success of the territorial revisions. The top ranks of the staff officials and the majority of the officer corps, among whom pro-German individuals and men of German descent were increasingly numerous, had an implicit trust in the eventual triumph of the Third Reich. During the war, the conservative and chauvinist leaders often argued that defeat in the war would reduce the country to destitution and decades of serfdom. It was to be a self-fulfilling prophecy.

At the end of September 1944, the first Soviet troops entered Hungarian territory. They made a rapid advance as far as the line of the Danube River and Budapest. At the capital city, however, the Germans and the Hungarian Arrow Cross put up a stubborn resistance. Fierce tank battles were fought in Transdanubia around Lake Balaton, and the siege of Budapest lasted for six weeks. The Germans blew up all the bridges connecting Pest and Buda and dismantled and carried away most of the factories of Budapest. Their retreat, similar to their one-year reign in Hungary, was accompanied by great bloodshed. All things moving and movable—men and animals, foodstuff and machines, locomotives and works of art, the gold of the Hungarian treasury—were carried away to Germany.

It took over half a year for the fighting to end in Hungary. By April 1945, it was over. The tanks, cannons, and bombers left behind great devastation; there was little but ruined cities and ruined human lives.

On December 21, 1944, a Provisional Assembly convened in the city of Debrecen, and a provisional government was set up by representatives of democratic parties. On March 17, the government issued a radical land reform decree and announced a program for the reconstruction of Hungary.

Epilogue

In April 1945, a new era began in the history of Hungary. For a long time it was called an age of liberation. April 4 was celebrated for forty years as the day of liberation. Today, this is questioned by public opinion and most political parties. The historian who is not only *narrator rarum gestarum* but also lived through these events is of the opinion that Hungary was indeed liberated in April 1945. It was a liberation from the rule of Germans, Hungarian Arrow Cross men, and the *ancien régime*. However, the tree of liberty did not grow out of this liberation. Oppression was followed by oppression, dictatorship by dictatorship, devastation by devastation.

It is not easy for democracy and freedom to take firm root in this battered region of Europe.

1945 TO THE PRESENT, JOSEPH HELD

After October 1944 the Hungarian state had practically ceased to exist. The central government collapsed; the country was ruled by the Germans and their Hungarian Arrow Cross allies. The upper echelons of the civil service had disappeared. The economy of the country was also in complete ruins. Most factory buildings were damaged; their stocks and machinery had been carried away. What was left was seized by the Soviet army following in the Germans' wake. The housing stock of the population suffered greatly. Most bridges, even those across small streams, were destroyed. The animal stock of the peasants fell victim to the war. Even their carriages and wagons were confiscated by the retreating Germans. Transportation came to a complete halt; railroad tracks were uprooted or damaged and roads were destroyed. The question "Would there ever again be a country called Hungary?" was indeed apt.

Yet, all was not lost. On December 21, 1944, a provisional government was formed in the city of Debrecen by a coalition of embryonic political parties united in the Hungarian National Independence Front. These included the Hungarian Communist party, the Independent Smallholders and Agricultural Workers' party, the Social Democratic party, the National Peasant party, and the Civic Democratic party.

Even before the formation of the provisional government, the Communists began to organize. On November 30, 1944, the "Muscovites" (Hungarian communists who spent years in exile in the Soviet Union) gathered with local party members in the city of Szeged and declared their readiness to cooperate with "democratic forces" in rebuilding the country. The most important Muscovites were Mátyás Rákosi, Ernő Gerő, József Révai, Mihály Farkas, Zoltán Vas, and Imre Nagy. The Smallholders were led by Béla Vargha (a Roman Catholic priest), Ferenc Nagy, Zoltán Tildy (a Calvinist minister), and Béla Kovács. Later Dezső Sulyok, Zoltán Pfeiffer, and Kálmán Saláta joined the leadership. The principal Social Democrats were Károly Peyer (who had spent the last few months of the war in a German concentration camp), Anna Kéthly, and Ferenc Szeder. All were deputies in the prewar Hungarian parliament. Árpád Szakasits, editor in chief of the party's daily, *Népszava* (People's Voice), also belonged to the party's élite. Two other leaders, Illés Mónus and Lajos Kabók, were killed by the Nazis.

The fourth participant in the provisional government was the National Peasant party. Established by left-wing populist intellectuals in 1939, the party attracted few members. After the war, many crypto-communists joined the National Peasants. Consequently, the party often acted as a surrogate of the Communists in the countryside, where the latter had little support. The most important leader was Ferenc Erdei. Others included Imre Kovács and Ferenc Farkas.

The fifty party of the National Independence Front was the Civic Democrats, with its few members from among the urban middle classes. Their program was simple: to restore public order and rebuild Hungary. The leaders included Géza Teleki (an alcoholic aristocrat, who had been a member of the resistance), Géza Supka (a writer), and Ernö Bródy. Their party had never played a significant role in Hungary.

In the last months of the Second World War the Soviet army was arbiter of life and death in Hungary. For the first two years after the war, Stalin hesitated to include Hungary in the Soviet empire.[1] But he had ample means at his disposal to ensure a friendly Hungary. There were hundreds of thousands of Hungarian prisoners of war in the Soviet Union, and their return depended upon the behavior of the Hungarians at home. The amount of Hungarian reparations was not determined immediately, so Stalin could increase his demands as he pleased. He pressured the provisional government for the conclusion of trade agreements and the establishment of joint Soviet-Hungarian companies. These companies dominated air transport, shipping, and bauxite and oil production. Long before Soviet political control over Hungary was established, the Soviet Union had already achieved a stranglehold upon the economy of the country.[2]

The noncommunist Hungarian politicians expected that, after the conclusion of the peace treaties, the Red Army would be withdrawn from Hungary. They believed that it would be possible to create a democratic Hungarian society in the shadow of Stalin's Soviet Russia. However, they immediately detected danger signals: these came from the organization of the political police under the control of Mátyás Rákosi.

The political police was created in 1945 by Gábor Péter. He was a member of the illegal Hungarian Communist party during the war. Headquarters were established in 60 Andrássy-ut in Budapest, the original headquarters of the Arrow Cross party. The political police recruited criminals, former members of the Arrow Cross, and *lumpen* proletarians. All personnel were subject to strict control by the Hungarian Communist party. As events were to show the personnel of the political police—and its successors, the ÁVO and ÁVH—did not care about laws or human rights or even elementary rules of decency.

The first task of the provisional government was to sign an armistice with the Allied powers. This was accomplished in January 1945. The agreement included a symbolic declaration of war on Germany, the recognition of Hungary's 1937 borders, and the acceptance of the principle of reparations. An Allied Control Commission was also created, headed by Soviet Marshal Kliment Y. Voroshilov.[3]

The first phase of the reorganization of Hungarian politics and society was to be concluded by free elections in the second half of 1945. Questions were, however, raised by the noncommunist parties in the provisional government.[4] (One of these concerned land reform introduced under the sponsorship of the Communist party. The reform was long overdue, yet it was designed so that it could gain support for the Communists in the rural areas.)

Being aware of the dangers represented by the activities of the political police the Smallholder leaders wanted the presence of international observers during the elections. Mátyás Rákosi did not object; however, he argued that the municipal elections should be held before the national vote. The Communist leader convinced the Social Democrats to run on a joint ticket in Budapest. The expectation was that the "workers' parties" would gain a majority in these urban areas and this would have a decisive influence in the national elections.

The municipal elections took place on October 7, 1945. The Small-holders received 51 percent of the vote thereby gaining an absolute majority.[5] During the campaign there were several violent clashes between supporters of the Communists and Social Democrats and supporters of the Smallholders. This did not bode well for the national vote.

National elections took place on November 4, 1945. Ninety-two percent of the nation's 5,100,000 eligible voters went to the polls. The Smallholders received 57 percent of all the votes cast, an even greater margin than in Budapest. The Communists gained 17 percent. The Social Democrats, who ran on a separate ticket this time, outpolled the Communists by 0.5 percent. The Peasant party gained 6.8 percent, and the rest of the votes were distributed among the weak candidates of the Civic Democrats. The reporter for the *Washington Post* noted that this was a clean election.[6]

Normally, the Smallholders should have formed a majority government. But their inexperienced leaders were afraid of taking full responsibility for the political reorganization of the country. Consequently, a coalition government was created once again in which the ministerial posts were to be distributed according to the strength of each participating party. This, however, was not to be the case.

Zoltán Tildy became prime minister; Mátyás Rákosi was named minister of state; Árpád Szakasits became assistant prime minister. There were great disputes over the person's party affiliation who was to head the ministry of the interior. At first, it seemed that the Smallholders would prevail, but they eventually consented to the appointment of the Communist Imre Nagy. Ferenc Nagy was named president of the parliament.

The difficulties which the government faced were overwhelming. The Soviet Union pressed for reparations; inflation seemed uncontrollable, and the treasury was empty. Taxation was out of the question. By the fall of 1945 80 percent of the former civil servants were back at their jobs but the government was unable to pay their salaries. The food situation was simply catastrophic. In Budapest even the soup kitchens had to be closed. Rákosi demanded the nationalization of large firms and drastic action against black marketers and profiteers. Economic experts, on the other hand, urged the government to purchase food abroad. They also proposed the reduction of Soviet troops who had to be fed by the Hungarians. Rákosi rejected such advice. He proposed that the government appeal to the Soviet Union for help and, at the same time, create a Supreme Economic Council. His arguments prevailed.

The Council was set up in December 1945. It became the dominant economic institution as the major distributor of foodstuffs, energy and other commodities. Its activities were determined by the Communists, especially by the Muscovite Zoltán Vas. Stalin also consented to provide food relief for Hungary in January 1946.

During 1946 it became increasingly obvious that the Smallholder leaders were unable to stand up to the pressure of the Communists and their allies. The Social Democrats in fact offered greater resistance to Rákosi. Thus, the Communist *apparat* (especially their newspapers) began a vicious campaign of vilification against some Social Democratic leaders. István Ries, the Social Democratic minister of justice, was singled out. He was accused of being soft on "reactionaries." Ries threatened to resign and Rákosi backed off. Nonetheless, the attacks continued against Social Democratic trade union leaders and youth associations, which competed in urban areas with the Communists.

Szakasits and his supporters were willing to make concessions to Rákosi. However, another faction led by Peyer, Kéthly, and Szeder were not intimidated. Neither faction could defeat the other; the struggle revealed deep divisions within the Social Democrats and Rákosi was soon able to exploit these differences.

In December 1946, parliament began working on a new constitution. Hungary was a kingdom without a king and theoretically a governor had executive power in the name of the king. Tildy made a motion for the establishment of a republic and it was enthusiastically received. A few deputies, however, questioned the wisdom of this move as long as Soviet troops were stationed in Hungary. They proposed that the vote should be postponed until the withdrawal of the Red Army. Parliament could then exercise its sovereign power in deciding the form of the new Hungarian state. Parliament voted for the republic nevertheless, but the discussions had an unexpected consequence. Marshal Voroshilov ordered the NKVD (the Soviet secret police) to arrest Géza Pálffy and Iván Lajos—the two parliamentary deputies who spoke against the immediate vote. Parliament then elected Tildy president of the republic and Ferenc Nagy prime minister.

The new government had to begin preparations for the peace negotiations. A series of debates took place: some Smallholders proposed that Hungary ask for ethnic borders in order to include three million Hungarians who had been separated from Hungary by the Trianon treaty. József Révai, the ideological chief of the *Magyar Kommunista Párt* (Hungarian Communist Party or MKP) answered these proposals. He followed Stalin's line in approving the Trianon borders. He stated that doing otherwise would be considered chauvinistic. He warned that the proposal for ethnic borders could provoke the surrounding states to begin the mass expulsion of the Hungarian population, as Czechoslovakia was already doing. József Darvas supported Révai on behalf of the Peasant party.

These debates were important because Révai clearly reflected the Soviet position. In building his empire, Stalin insisted on "international solidarity." This was nothing more than the subordination of national interests to those of Stalin's empire. One can see in these moves that Hungary was to be included in this empire.

At this point important changes occurred in the Ferenc Nagy government. Rákosi was dissatisfied with the minister of the interior, Communist Imre Nagy, and replaced him with László Rajk. Rajk was not a Muscovite. He joined the illegal Hungarian Communist party in the early 1930s and volunteered to fight in the Spanish Civil War. He ended up in a French detention camp and, in 1941, he volunteered for work in Germany. He then escaped and returned to Hungary where he continued his underground activities. In 1944 he was working with Géza Losonczy, Ferenc Donáth, and Gyula Kállai when they were discovered. Rajk was arrested. His brother, who was a member of the Arrow Cross "cabinet" after October 15, 1944, saved his life. Rajk was a convinced Marxist and an anti-Semite, for which he earned the special respect of Communists who had formerly been Arrow Cross members.

In the summer of 1946, new disputes arose over the redistribution of civil service positions. The Smallholders wanted these to be distributed according to the electoral strength of the various parties, but the Communists and Social Democrats objected and were joined by the Peasant party. When Ferenc Nagy did not give in, Rákosi convinced Szakasits and Erdei that their parties form a leftist bloc. They would coordinate the activities of their parliamentary deputies. Rákosi succeeded in drawing the trade unions into the bloc. At the same time, Communist thugs attacked municipal officials in rural districts and threw them out of their offices bodily. Rákosi announced that this was the "expression of indignation of the people." In response, however, Communists were driven out of several municipalities in Szabolcs county and Ferenc Nagy threatened to call on the people for self-defense. The Soviet head of the Allied Control Commission was now pressuring the government to be more accommodating to the Communists. First, a note was sent to the prime minister complaining that Hungary had failed to fulfill its reparations obligations. Since these obligations had not yet been defined, anything could be demanded by Stalin. When a newspaper article described the acts of Communist thugs in the countryside, Stalin protested what he considered the slow transfer of German goods to Soviet jurisdiction. Another note complained about the provisioning of Soviet troops in Hungary and threatened that if improvements were not forthcoming, the troops would acquire their food directly from the population. Still another note complained that the Hungarians were not complying with Soviet-Hungarian trade agreements and announced the cessation of Soviet raw material deliveries.

In tandem with these moves Rákosi ordered a campaign against the so-called right wing of the Smallholders party. He demanded the expulsion of right wing deputies from parliament. At the refusal of the Smallholder leaders the Communists organized mass demonstrations in Budapest. In March nearly 300,000 demonstrators gathered in Budapest, and they were addressed by Rákosi himself. The Smallholder leadership caved in. It expelled twenty-two parliamentary deputies from the party. Ferenc Nagy stated later that the party did not want to bring on civil war. But this was a specious argument.

In order to iron out their differences, a Hungarian government delegation visited Moscow and met Stalin and other members of his government. They were cordially received and left with the impression that they had gained Stalin's trust. This was, of course, an illusion. Back at home, Rákosi now succeeded in introducing regulations that gave the political police a free hand in arresting "enemies of the state."

By the summer of 1946 the entire police apparatus was under the control of László Rajk, who reported directly to Rákosi, not to the prime minister. The police openly participated in campaigns against the opponents of the leftist bloc. In the rural districts the campaigns were particularly vicious. The political committee of the Smallholders, the governing body of their party, finally issued a demand for the immediate distribution of civil service positions, including commanding posts of the police. They announced the end of the coalition government unless their demand was met within eight days. In response, Rajk began an "investigation" of an alleged conspiracy to overthrow the republic. He soon presented the vague outlines of such a "conspiracy" accusing the Smallholders of harboring criminals among their ranks. Tildy and Ferenc Nagy were aghast. If the charges were true, some of the most vocal opponents of the Communists in parliament would have to face criminal proceedings. They could not believe that Rajk would lie in such an important matter. Therefore they agreed to an investigation of the alleged conspiracy.

In the meantime the economic situation was worsening. In desperation a Hungarian delegation, including Ferenc Nagy and Rákosi, traveled to Washington, London, and Paris asking for help. They received promises for the return of Hungarian goods and the gold belonging to the Hungarian treasury that had been carried away by the retreating Nazis. But by the time the delegation returned to Budapest, it faced another crisis.

Historians generally consider that the Stalinist show trials began in Hungary with the Rajk case in 1949. However, in 1946 and 1947 Rajk himself conducted a show trial of the so-called Hungarian Community. The Soviet NKVD cooperated in this trial as in all subsequent trials.

György Pálffy-Österreicher, head of the political division of the army's police, allegedly discovered the "conspiracy." As we now know he acted upon instructions received from General Sviridov, the new head of the Allied Control Commission. Pálffy's thugs arrested Bálint Arany (chairman of the Smallholders' election committee), István Szentmiklósy (a former major of the Hungarian general staff and a member of the anti-German resistance), Béla Demeter (a member of the Hungarian peace delegation), and Károly Kis and János Héder (both Smallholder parliamentary deputies). Domonkos Szentiványi, one of the signers of the armistice, was also arrested. In January 1947, the communist daily, *Szabad Nép* (Free People), announced the "discovery" of an even wider conspiracy of Smallholder deputies, including Kálmán Saláta, Pál Jackó, and others. It named the Smallholder minister of reconstruction, László Mistéth, as a member of the "conspiracy."

On January 12, Rajk claimed that the conspirators planned the overthrow of the government. He stated that Arany and Saláta were the leaders. Two days later he added the names of six other deputies under arrest. Ferenc Nagy gave in once again. Mistéth was removed from his ministerial post and Nagy appointed a committee to examine the case of the accused deputies. In addition, the political committee of the Smallholders party removed all members who joined the party after 1945 from all executive positions and ordered a general review of the membership.

On January 16, 1947, Tildy and Ferenc Nagy agreed to the arrest of all the accused Smallholder deputies even before their parliamentary immunity was lifted. Only Dezső Sulyok had the courage to protest.

It seems that by 1947 Stalin had decided that all Eastern European states would be included in the Soviet empire.[7] The so-called conspiracy of the Hungarian Community was part of this process. The case, therefore, had a broader significance than the subsequent show trial of László Rajk. Similar cases were manufactured with the NKVD's help in Romania, Bulgaria and Poland. The general secretary of the Hungarian Smallholders party, Béla Kovács, was arrested by the NKVD in January 1947. By the end of February, twenty-three Smallholder parliamentary deputies were expelled from their party and were arrested. The leaders of the Social Democrats and the National Peasant party cooperated in this process.

The pressure, however, did not let up. In March the entire leadership of the Budapest organization of the Smallholders was removed and József Bognár, a cryptocommunist, was appointed mayor of Budapest. By then the struggle for power was over and Mátyás Rákosi and his Muscovite collaborators were rulers of Hungary in all but name. Soon Ferenc Nagy himself was attacked as being responsible for his party's harboring "criminal elements." Nagy tried to offer concessions if only the Communists stopped the campaign but he was too late. In May 1947, he left for Switzerland for a brief vacation. While there, he received a personal call from Rákosi that he was under investigation for alleged activities against the republic. Nagy agreed to resign on condition that his four-year-old son be permitted to join him in exile. His condition was accepted. On June 2, 1947, Ferenc Nagy resigned his premiership and several other important Smallholder leaders followed his example. New parliamentary elections were held in August. Although the vote had no significance whatsoever, the Communists were not leaving anything to chance. Communist party members received absentee ballots (the so-called blue slips) and thousands of them roamed the countryside on election day casting their ballots at every conceivable election booth.[8] Trucks for their transportation were once again provided by the Red Army. The Peasant party also participated in this sham and only the Social Democrats refused to be part of the deception. The results were predictable. Yet, the MKP received only 22 percent of the total vote nationwide, and the Smallholders became a minority party with 15 percent. The Social Democrats gained 11 percent and the National Peasant party 7 percent. Two opposition parties led by disgruntled former Smallholders received a total of 38 percent of the vote. Nevertheless, the MKP became the largest single party. Rákosi could now "legally" take power.

The new government signed the Paris peace treaty accepting the 1937 borders of Hungary. This, however, did not result in the withdrawal of Soviet troops. These troops were to stay "temporarily" in Hungary ostensibly to secure communications with other forces stationed in Austria. In reality they were to secure communist control of Hungary.

After the elections the opposition parties were banned. In March 1948 Rákosi forced a fusion between the Social Democratic and Communist organizations. The new party was called *Magyar Dolgozók Pártja* (Hungarian Workers Party or MDP). The takeover was therefore completed, and the Stalinist phase of Hungarian history began.

The takeover did not end the terror. The State Security Office or ÁVO emerged as a separate organization in 1946, under the supervision of the minister of the interior. In 1949 it was removed from the interior ministry and placed under the control of the head of the cabinet, at that time Rákosi. For all practical purposes it was the Hungarian branch of the Soviet NKVD. The ÁVO (later renamed the State Security Division or ÁVH) became a huge apparatus. It controlled the border guard troops and other special units. But its major task remained the discovery and destruction of opposition to communist rule. The tentacles of the organization reached into every sphere of life. Its most important sections conducted surveillance of potential opponents of the regime. Separate offices were maintained for the surveillance of foreigners. Other offices dealt with religious institutions, mass organizations, and the army. Divisions were also responsible for discipline in the workplace and kept an eye on party officials. Therefore, the ÁVO-ÁVH was the real executive organ in Hungary. The reports of the security offices were sent to Rákosi, while a copy was transmitted to the NKVD. Rákosi's permission was necessary only for the arrest of high party officials. The arrest orders were then signed by Gábor Péter (and after *his* arrest, by his successor, Mihály Farkas).

In 1948 the new target was the Roman Catholic church. Catholic bishops were singled out, especially Cardinal József Mindszenti, whose views were sharply critical of the communists. Bishop József Grösz came next. They were arrested, tried and coerced under torture into making false confessions. They were sentenced to life imprisonment. Religious orders were then dissolved and their houses were confiscated. Nuns serving in hospitals as nurses were removed. Many priests were arrested and sent to labor camps. The ÁVO organized the so-called peace priests who were communists disguised as servants of God. In a new wave of terror, Mindszenti's successor, Bishop Meszlényi, the bishop of Csanád, Endre Havas, and other church leaders were arrested. Church properties were confiscated, their schools turned over to local party officials.[9] An office for the supervision of all religious activities was created which interfered with the daily practices of the churches, even demanding copies of sermons delivered at masses. The Calvinist and Lutheran churches were treated with more consideration and, in turn, they often cooperated with the communists.

On August 3, 1948, Rajk was suddenly removed from his post at the interior ministry and appointed minister of foreign affairs. By then Rákosi had already received instructions from Stalin for a show trial intended to prove that Rajk conspired with Yugoslavia's Tito for the overthrow of socialist governments in Eastern Europe. He was arrested on June 8, 1949. Belkin, an NKVD general, was Rajk's principal interrogator. Rajk and several other high-level communist officials were tried on September 22, 1949. They were subjected to terrifying tortures and confessed to every charge. According to Rajk's "testimony," he was recruited by the OSS (the precursor to the CIA) and the French secret service while he served in Spain. Then he was to have conspired with Tito against the Hungarian People's Democracy, planning to murder "Stalin's best pupil," Mátyás Rákosi. Rajk, Pálffy-Österreicher, and others were executed on October 15. Other show trials followed, including those that charged Western businessmen with conspiring against the socialist state.

On August 20, 1949, parliament voted in a new constitution based on the Stalinist Soviet constitution of 1936. The document named the Communist party as the leading force in the process of building socialism in Hungary. A new set of laws was also enacted "in defense of the republic" which gave the ÁVO a virtually free hand against suspected political opposition.

This was the essence of the system imposed on Hungary. One cannot really speak of the violations of "socialist legality," as later apologists of the system have attempted to do; this dictatorship recognized no legality except its own. Regulations were introduced by the dictator, in this case Mátyás Rákosi. This was real Soviet-style socialism.

Following his master's example Rákosi developed his own personality cult. He was, indeed, the "best pupil of comrade Stalin," as he liked to be called. No other Eastern European communist leader was trusted more by the Soviet dictator, and no other leader groveled so willing to execute and overfulfill Stalin's orders.

Rákosi was a quick-thinking, cynical man. For him ideology served only one purpose, namely, to grab and hold onto power. He had no redeeming qualities. Ernő Gerő, his number two, was an economist. He was no less ruthless than Rákosi. He was the most feared NKVD operative in the Spanish Civil War, responsible for the murder of scores of people, the so-called Trotskyists. He was cold and distant, a modern version of a medieval inquisitor. József Révai aspired to the role of the Hungarian Zhdanov (the ideological guru of Soviet-style communism). His major task was the Sovietization—and Russification—of Hungarian culture. He wanted to create a "new socialist man," one fully committed to the goals of the Soviet empire. Mihály Farkas, the fourth member of the Muscovites' circle, was the most primitive-minded of them all. His brutality and sadism were matched only by his cringing servility toward Rákosi. None of these men considered themselves Hungarian. They did speak the Hungarian language but that was by accident of birth. They were truly devoted citizens of the Soviet Union. Their rule in Hungary was always based on brute force alone. Between 1949 and 1953, over 750,000 people out of a population of 10 million came under investigation for suspicion of political deviance. Of these, 150,000 ended up in prison or in concentration camps. Four thousand of them were former members of the Social Democratic party, and about the same number belonged to the Hungarian Workers party. About 2,000 were executed on trumped-up charges, and thousands were maimed by the brutal investigators. Not even the highest party officials escaped. Sándor Zöld, Rajk's successor in the interior ministry, was berated by Rákosi for having the wrong type of friends. Fearing arrest, Zöld killed his wife and children and committed suicide. János Kádár, György Marosán, and countless others were thrown into jail. Ferenc Donáth, the head of Rákosi's secretariat, was arrested and tortured. The list of those who suffered in this insane system is too long to mention here. Yet even such a list would not fully reveal the horrors of Rákosi's rule in Hungary. Stalin needed Rákosi, and Rákosi needed terror to subdue the people in the service of the Soviet empire.

In 1949 the Hungarian educational system was reorganized in the service of creating a "new socialist man." From kindergarten to the universities, Marxism became the "guiding light" for the education of young people. Compulsory study of the Russian language, together with the study of the falsified history of the Soviet Communist party, were introduced. The Marxism taught in the schools, however, often changed with the changing party line. These changes were explained by the vulgar application of dialectics.

With all this, confusion became a matter of everyday life. Yet one must point out for the sake of objectivity that education was made widely available to large segments of the population. Illiteracy all but disappeared. Engineering and technological subjects received high priority, along with Marxist economics. The teaching of Hungarian history was, on the other hand, de-emphasized, and sociology and psychology were practically excluded from the curriculum. The children of the former middle classes were excluded from the universities, while offspring of party officials received preference in admissions, regardless of their talents. This was affirmative action, Stalinist style.

It was party politics rather than education that set the new tone for Hungarian society. The newspapers and radio stations spewed forth a steady stream of primitive anti-Western propaganda. Most newspapers were copies of *Pravda* and other Soviet journals. The Hungarian News Agency (MTI) simply commented on reports of TASS, the Soviet news organization. The party daily was compulsory reading for every working man. Each morning industrial workers were required to attend a half-hour "seminar" where the *apparatchiks* commented on articles published that day. No questions were tolerated. Listening to the broadcasts of Radio Free Europe or the BBC could land one in jail or in a labor camp.

Between 1949 and 1953 Hungarian "literature" consisted mainly of anti-Western propaganda. The activities of Révai resulted in a complete paralysis of nonpolitical writings. What was published was called "socialist realism," portraying mostly happy workers who, in alliance with the peasantry and the intellectuals, were building socialism. Many Soviet books were translated into Hungarian, mostly of the "socialist realist" variety. The Russian classics were neglected, but thousands of copies of Lenin's and Stalin's "works" were distributed to libraries and party offices.

The power struggle and a cultural coup were therefore won by the communists, but the ruthlessness of the party leaders and their openly Russianizing policies left the people cynical and demoralized. Although the propaganda *apparat* churned out tons of posters and other material consisting of rosy pictures of the victorious proletariat building socialism, the Hungarian people's perception of reality was something else.

During 1949–50 the peasantry were forced into Soviet-style collectives. Their land, equipment, and animals were declared to be property of the collectives. The first five-year plan, introduced in 1950, intended to create a "country of steel and iron" out of Hungary. But the plan demanded the constant raising of work norms accompanied by a hidden but obvious lowering of wages. The nationalization of factories, all private firms, and banks and the centralization of all investment funds gave complete control over the economy to the communist leaders. When things did not improve, they were held responsible for the failures. Hungary's increased industrial capacity, together with those of the other Soviet colonies in Eastern Europe, was serving Stalin's grandiose military plans. The emphasis was therefore placed on heavy industry. Consumer industry and agriculture were neglected. (Later Imre Nagy was to point out the failures of the First Five-Year Plan.) Hungarian statistics were doctored: they showed a phenomenal growth of 258 percent for industry between 1949 and 1953. Heavy industrial production allegedly increased by 288 percent. But much of this was wishful thinking. As Imre Nagy remarked in 1955, production increases came about in a haphazard way, and technological improvements were neglected. There was indeed an increase in production, especially since the country started almost from a zero base after the war, but per capita productivity remained stagnant. The stress on heavy industry was wrong: chemical and electrical industries were neglected at a time when these could have been fueling the continuous industrial revolution in the West.

The burdens on society were further increased by an emphasis on military preparedness. The size of the Hungarian army was increased to 210,000 soldiers by 1952. The ÁVO had control over another 140,000 men. Therefore, 350,000 soldiers or about 3.5 percent of the total population were constantly kept under arms. In 1953 military expenditures came to 7.4 billion forints, or 16.7 percent of the total state budget.

Only by maintaining a constant level of terror could such a system survive. As a result there was a continual emphasis on vigilance against wreckers, saboteurs, and other enemies of the state. The atmosphere of suspicion was pervasive. At the same time cynicism penetrated every level of society, especially members of the Hungarian Workers party. But the party, quite capable of creating fear, was unable to create respect for itself. Similarly, there was no respect for laws. Morality changed: stealing, cheating, and petty pilfering were no longer considered wrong. "The factory is yours," the simple worker said; "take home as much of it as you can." The situation was no different in the rural areas.

There was a huge and widening discrepancy between ideology and reality. Living standards plummeted at a time when the party preached prosperity. The party elite led a luxurious life, however, which was noticed by the population.

Rákosi and the other Muscovites could not have cared less about the mood of the population. They had power and the ultimate force, the Red Army in Hungary. But society was changing; rapid industrialization and its accompanying education created a more complex social structure whose cohesiveness could not be maintained indefinitely by terror alone. Such a society needed a minimum of consensus about its goals. Such a consensus did not exist even in the Communist party, whose 800,000 members were mostly opportunists. Marxist ideology was so far removed from reality that it no longer held the party together. Competing factions soon emerged; the party became the "opium of the people," and its members no longer believed in its slogans and promises. By 1953 it became obvious that the very nature and policies of the party and its ideology served nothing but Soviet imperialism. The pitiless servility and self-criticism it demanded were rooted in human weakness and dishonor.

When Stalin died, he was replaced by a collective leadership dominated by Malenkov and Khrushchev. The new leaders soon expressed dissatisfaction with the Hungarian situation. In a stormy meeting in Moscow they collectively berated Rákosi and ordered the reorganization of the leadership of the Hungarian Worker's party. Consequently, Imre Nagy became prime minister, but Rákosi retained the position of first secretary of the Hungarian Workers party. Révai and Farkas were removed from the political committee. It seemed to all but Rákosi that his policies were repudiated. But the "best pupil of Stalin" did not give up that easily. He was convinced that, given time, the new Soviet leaders would recognize his indispensability.

The new prime minister, Imre Nagy, was also a faithful Muscovite. He was not interested in airing the guilty secrets of Rákosi's rule. The major difference between him and his predecessor was that Nagy did not want power for its own sake. He wanted to use his new authority to better the lives of Hungarians. He believed that good relations with Moscow could be maintained without the exploitation of Hungary. He was perhaps naive, but he was a sincere, honest man of good will.

Imre Nagy proclaimed that the forced industrialization of Hungary could no longer be maintained. He hoped that the regime of socialism could gain public support if living standards were improved quickly. He knew he could count on at least some of the Soviet leaders for support.

But the Soviet leadership was divided. Some members supported Nagy, others still favored Rákosi. The Hungarian party *apparat*, fearful for its privileges, stood solidly behind Rákosi. Nagy failed to obtain majority support in the Central Committee of the Hungarian party. The government, tied to the party *apparat* by thousands of threads, followed the new prime minister only reluctantly.

In June 1953 the new course proposed by Imre Nagy was reluctantly accepted by parliament. Nagy wanted to reduce support for heavy industry and ordered increased support for the consumer goods industry instead. He permitted the dissolution of collectives if their membership so desired. He closed the concentration camps and ordered the rehabilitation of the unjustly accused. But Nagy was stymied everywhere. The subcommittee of the political committee charged with supervising economic development was headed by Ernő Gerő. Rákosi was the chairman of another subcommittee charged with the rehabilitation of the unjustly accused. These men did everything to sabotage Nagy's instructions.

In the meantime, the country breathed a sigh of relief. Collective farms dissolved themselves, their members taking with them their tools and animals. Soon the peasants produced more foodstuffs than before. The end of the persecution of better-off peasants, the so-called *kulaks*, created a more relaxed atmosphere in the villages. The service industry began to recover from the paralysis of state-imposed restrictions. But the ministry of heavy industry stymied Nagy's plans for reduced investments.

In May 1954 the third congress of the Hungarian Workers party was held. Rákosi was the keynote speaker. He used the occasion to deliver a vicious attack against Imre Nagy's policies. Nagy, in order to counter the *apparat,* began to organize a Patriotic People's Front. He thought that this mass organization would bring the people in touch with the party. He proclaimed that the party alone could not build socialism. He formulated the thesis—later expropriated by his executioner, János Kádár—that "those who are not against us are with us."

In January 1955 the long-simmering feud within the Soviet Politburo over policy in Hungary came to the fore. At this time a Hungarian government delegation was visiting Moscow and had to listen to criticism by every member of this august body. In February Imre Nagy suffered a mild heart attack. While he was recuperating, Rákosi made his move. On April 14, 1955, the political committee of the Hungarian Workers party relieved Imre Nagy of all his party functions and expelled him from the Central Committee.

Rákosi had won a pyrrhic victory. He was no longer able to regain unlimited power, since the Soviet leaders would not permit him to restore the terror. Yet he partially reestablished previous economic policies and threatened the peasants with recollectivization.

As a consequence of Nagy's previous policies former party members who had disappeared began to reappear. János Kádár, Géza Losonczy, Sándor Haraszti, Ferenc Donáth, Gyula Kállai, Szilárd Ujhelyi, István Szirmai, and Béla Szász, to mention only a few, were walking the streets of Budapest once again and spoke to their friends about the horrors to which they had been subjected. The people, especially Hungary's young, committed writers listened to their stories with feelings of betrayal. Then the question was raised: "What happened to those who disappeared forever? Why did they have to die?" By the summer of 1956 everyone in Hungary knew that the victims of the show trials were innocent of the crimes of which they were accused. Everyone remembered the announcements of Rákosi as he "discovered" ever newer "conspiracies" against socialism. All knew that he personally "unmasked Rajk and his gang." The party's propagandists desperately tried to place the blame on Gábor Péter, former head of the ÁVO-ÁVH, now himself in jail. Rákosi continued to argue for himself but to no avail. There was a general feeling of revulsion toward this vile dictator.

During 1955, the Austrian State Treaty was signed, and Soviet troops were withdrawn from that fortunate country. Soon there was a meeting of the diplomats of the great powers in Geneva, and they agreed upon the toning down of cold war propaganda. The Soviet leaders then decided to patch up their feud with Yugoslavia and Tito's price was to end Rákosi's rule in Hungary.

The Hungarian Workers party was now in shambles. Party members no longer believed their leaders. On the other hand, the Muscovites and their protegées still tried to hold onto power. Khrushchev and Bulganin finally "went to Canossa" and visited Tito in Belgrade. Yet Rákosi continued to refuse to apologize to the Yugoslavs and refused to release Yugoslav nationals who were jailed in the wake of the Rajk trial.

On May 11, 1955, the leaders of the Eastern European satellites were called to Warsaw where they signed the Warsaw Pact treaty. This encouraged Rákosi, since the agreement's purpose was the legalization of Soviet occupation in each Eastern European state.

In June 1956 the Soviet leaders finally gave in to Tito and removed Rákosi from the Hungarian party and government. He retired to the Soviet Union where he lived for the rest of his life. However, the Soviet leaders installed Ernő Gerő as Rákosi's successor, and he was closely identified with Rákosi's repudiated policies. This should not have surprised anyone: after all, Rákosi was not against the Soviet Union; on the contrary, the Soviet leaders counted on Gerő to keep Hungary toeing the Soviet line.

Then in early October Poland erupted. This left a lasting impression on Hungarians who always considered the Poles as their friends.

On October 6 the Hungarian Workers party reburied a posthumously rehabilitated László Rajk. Two hundred thousand people silently marched by his coffin. On October 23 university students and workers demonstrated on the streets of Budapest, demanding reform. They toppled Stalin's giant statue and demanded that their reform proposal be aired by Budapest radio. The ÁVO-ÁVH opened fire on the demonstrators. The revolution was on.

The Hungarian revolution—ten days that shook the Kremlin—is one of the most written-about events of our times. Its chronology is well established. The shooting was initiated by the security organs. At the same time the Soviet forces that were "temporarily stationed in Hungary" were already moving on Budapest. It is not clear if these troops were responding to a request of the Gerő-led government or, more likely, to orders from Moscow. In any case, their intervention was halfhearted and proved to be a mistake. The Soviet tanks and armored vehicles were fired on by the revolutionaries, causing severe casualties. Arms arrived to them through the Hungarian army, whose soldiers were ordered to disperse the demonstration. Workers in the armament factories around Budapest also delivered arms and participated in the fighting themselves. The fighting continued sporadically until October 25. On that day a huge crowd gathered in front of parliament, asking for Imre Nagy to address them. They were fired on by hidden ÁVH troops from across the square. Hundreds were killed and hundreds more wounded. The next day revolutionaries, seeking revenge, besieged the headquarters of the Hungarian Workers party and forced the defending ÁVH troops to surrender. In turn, these were all shot and killed. Given the enormity of the crimes committed by the ÁVO-ÁVH, there were remarkably few incidents of this sort during the revolution.

By October 28 the Hungarian revolutionaries were victorious. The Soviet government withdrew its troops from Budapest and began negotiations for the complete withdrawal of the Red Army from Hungary. A government headed by Imre Nagy was formed; he was trusted by most of the population to lead the country toward democracy. His government included János Kádár and Pál Maléter.

On November 1, however, some prominent communists, including János Kádár and Ferenc Münnich, disappeared. They left Budapest in Soviet vehicles. By then fresh Soviet divisions crossed the Hungarian borders. Two days later, 200,000 Soviet soldiers and 2,000 heavy tanks and fighting vehicles were in Hungary. On November 4, while a Hungarian government delegation was negotiating with Soviet representatives about the troop withdrawal, they were treacherously arrested by NKVD operatives led by General Serov.[10] A concerted attack was made on Budapest and other centers of revolutionary activity. By then, in desperation, the Nagy government declared the country's withdrawal from the Warsaw Pact and asked for help from the United Nations.

The Soviet attack was swift and was executed with overwhelming force. It was aided indirectly by the preoccupation of Western powers with the Suez crisis. The Imre Nagy government eventually fled to asylum in the Yugoslav embassy, trusting in Tito's sympathy for Hungary's independent course.

However, Imre Nagy was mistaken: Tito's Yugoslavia betrayed the Hungarians. Most people's democracies were in full support of the Soviet invasion of Hungary, and China gave its enthusiastic approval. In three weeks time Nagy and his entourage were forced to leave the Yugoslav embassy and were promptly arrested by NKVD troops. They were deported to Romania. For more than a year Hungary's legal prime minister was held prisoner in a foreign country. On June 16, 1958, after a short trial, he and several members of his government were executed. They were secretly buried in unmarked graves. In the aftermath of the revolution, 200,000 Hungarians fled to the West.

János Kádár was named prime minister by the Soviet government. His betrayal of Imre Nagy and the brutal revenge that the former ÁVH troops exacted from the population in his name made him the most hated communist in Hungary. Kádár's counterrevolutionary terror lasted well into the early 1960s. The atrocities and judicial murders were no less brutal and vicious than those in Rákosi's time.

By the mid-1960s, however, it was obvious that the reorganized Communist party, now renamed the Hungarian Socialist Workers party (MSZMP) attracted only the most cynical opportunists. Marxist-Leninist ideology was but a fig leaf in which few believed. By 1968 the regime grew desperate for legitimacy. It introduced a set of economic reforms (NEM) intended to stimulate the economy. These reforms were based on modified plans originally introduced by Imre Nagy in his first premiership in 1954. They established the rights of individual peasant proprietors to cultivate a private plot of land as part of their share in their collectives. They were permitted to sell their products on the open market at uncontrolled prices. This way the peasantry's unmitigated hatred for the collectives—reestablished in 1959–61—was somewhat eased. The prices of essential consumer goods (such as bread, sugar, flour, and meat) were still subsidized and regulated. The state retained its monopoly on foreign trade, but controls over internal trade were relaxed.

The reforms brought about unprecedented economic activity. They also brought a certain measure of prosperity for Hungary. The stores soon filled up with long-missed consumer goods, and the population began to recover from the misery to which it had been subjected since 1947. Commerce with the Soviet Union and the people's democracies, which brought in automobiles and other industrial products such as freezers and television sets, began to expand. Hungarians were increasingly permitted to visit relatives and friends abroad, and a trickle of former refugees, now citizens of their adopted countries, began visiting Hungary. The press was permitted to criticize lower party officials for misusing their power. But there were also taboos that could not be touched: no one was permitted to question Soviet-Hungarian relations, and the revolution of 1956 could be discussed only in derogatory terms. This was Kádár's albatross until the end of his life.

In August 1968 Hungary participated in the suppression of the Prague Spring which seemed to confirm the Kádár line, namely, that no independent course was possible for the Eastern European Soviet satellites. In time, however, Kádár took a further step; he co-opted many Hungarian intellectuals if they were willing to abide by his rules. These rules were determined by subjects that were supported, others that were tolerated and again others that were forbidden. Those who refused to cooperate had to keep silent. But the Kádár regime needed experts in technical fields and had to support talented individuals in these areas regardless of their political opinions. Thus Kádár adopted the slogan, originally coined by Imre Nagy, that "those who are not against us are with us." Nevertheless, this was not a regime moving toward some form of semidemocracy. Kádár remained an old-fashioned dictator whose word was final.

In spite of all this, Hungarians began slowly to prosper. The country was becoming, as the popular saying went, "the happiest barrack in the socialist camp." Kádár was gradually accepted as the architect of a better life. This was the basis of his *Ausgleich* (compromise); as long as life continued to improve and forbidden subjects were left alone, his system was accepted. The populations of other Eastern European socialist countries watched the Hungarian developments with envy. Soon Western reporters were singing the praise of Kádár and asserting that he could win even in a free election. This assertion was never tested.

In 1972 there was a slowdown in the reform process. Further reforms were stopped or were even reversed. It seems that Kádár went too far. There were complaints by hardliners that the peasants were too greedy and that they earned more than industrial workers in whose name socialism was being built. Instead of paying more to workers, Kádár decided to tighten the screws on the peasants. The new policy, however, backfired. Food production slowed down, and there were empty shelves in the stores. Consequently, Kádár hastily reversed course. But the oil crisis of 1973 hit Hungary hard. Although the Soviet Union continued to supply Hungary with oil and natural gas at somewhat below world-market prices, the subsequent reordering of the world market created great difficulties. The opening to the West that Kádár attempted faced grave difficulties. Hungary's industry was not modern enough to compete. The volume of exports declined while production costs continued to increase. Yet Hungary was able to obtain loans from Western banks, and these loans eventually reached twenty billion U.S. dollars. Kádár's greatest mistake was that he did not insist on using the loans for the modernization of Hungary's industry. Instead, the loans were used for subsidizing products that otherwise could not be sold, especially for products delivered to the Soviet Union. Therefore Hungary's loans were actually helping the Brezhnev leadership postpone *their* economic reform program. The repayment and interest charges on the Western loans soon became a real burden for Hungary. Kádár tried to hide the fact from the population, but by the mid-1980s the cat was out of the bag; Kádár's compromise began to unravel.

The ascendance of Mikhail Gorbachev to power signaled a real turning point in the history of the Soviet empire. The Eastern European communist leaders learned soon enough that they could no longer count on Soviet tanks nor could they call in the KGB to help out in case of difficulties. At the same time intellectuals were emboldened to demand greater freedom of expression, and dissent increased. Suddenly history became a very important subject. Its practitioners—both amateurs and professionals—increasingly resorted to underground publications to inform their readers about an alternative to "official" Marxist-Leninist history. This was particularly damaging in Kádár's Hungary, where the true history of the 1956 revolution remained a sore point in the nation's memory. The Marxist-Leninist interpretation of history, long questioned, lost its last vestiges of credibility.

János Kádár was getting old. He was sickly, and his hands and voice were shaky. Yet he continued to cling to power. Perhaps he believed that he alone knew how to deal with the "Soviet comrades." But the younger members of his party's central committee were becoming restless and eventually concluded that Kádár had to be removed.

In March 1988 at a meeting of the political committee of the Hungarian Socialist Workers party, János Kádár was relieved of his post as first secretary and was named to the newly created and largely meaningless office of president of the party. The Kádár era was over. Károly Grósz, a gray *apparatchik,* became his successor, and Rezső Nyers, Imre Pozsgay, and others took the reins of the party into their hands.

However, the party created by Kádár could not survive his demise. Dissenting voices could be heard even at the highest levels of the party. Imre Pozsgay broke with his colleagues first. On the basis of a study concluded by members of the Hungarian Academy of Sciences he proclaimed that the 1956 "events" represented a popular uprising against abuses by the party leaders. Suddenly he was not alone, and the hardliners were in a minority. In May 1989 Kádár was completely removed from the leadership and retired. In June Imre Nagy, Kádár's true victim and his martyr followers, executed in the wake of the 1956 revolution, were reburied in the presence of hundreds of thousands of mourners. On the day Imre Nagy's rehabilitation was announced, Kádár died. By then he was a lonely man who was not hated but considered irrelevant in Hungary by all the population except a few hardliners.

Miklós Németh, a young member of the party's political committee, formed a new government with dynamic young supporters. Németh soon declared the complete separation of the government from the party. The new minister of education, Ferenc Glatz, a historian, abolished the compulsory teaching of the Russian language and Marxism in the schools. Gyula Horn, the minister of foreign affairs, began to forge an independent foreign policy for the Hungarian state. In the summer of 1989, President George Bush visited Hungary and delivered a rousing speech at the Economics University (formerly named for Karl Marx).

In October the last congress of the Hungarian Socialist Workers party was held. It was dominated by the reformers who beat back several attempts by the hardliners who demanded "administrative measures" to restore the party to power. In the end the party declared itself dissolved. Two successors emerged, one led by the reformers

who took the name Hungarian Socialist party, and the old MSZMP.
Both parties proved irrelevant in the new order. By then a multiparty
system was well developed in Hungary.

In the first free elections held since 1945, in June 1990, a new party
called Hungarian Democratic Forum emerged as the strongest with
24 percent of the total votes. Its closest rival, the Association of Free
Democrats, gained 21 percent. The revived Smallholders party and a
new Christian Democratic party gained 11 percent and 7 percent
respectively. The Socialist party received 11 percent, and the most
dynamic party, the Alliance of Young Democrats, received 10 percent
of the votes.

The Németh government had already committed itself to the
democratic reorganization of Hungarian society. It opened the border with Austria to a flood of East German refugees. This indirectly contributed to the collapse of the Honecker regime in East
Germany. Soon Czechoslovakia followed with its "Velvet Revolution," and the Eastern European segment of the Soviet empire was no
more.

In July 1990 the freely elected Hungarian parliament approved the
formation of a coalition government headed by József Antall from the
Hungarian Democratic Forum. Negotiations with the Soviet government were already under way for the complete removal of Soviet
troops from Hungary. An agreement signed in March 1990 stipulated
that all Soviet personnel and military equipment must leave the country by July 1991. The process is well under way at the time of this
writing.

The Warsaw Pact was dissolved in March 1991. The Antall government is rapidly moving toward the establishment of an economic
system based on the private ownership of property. The last vestiges
of communist rule are being removed; the media are now completely
free and often attack the government with great enthusiasm.

Hungarian democracy could be an achieved fact within a very
short time. If the problems of the economy created by nearly four
decades of mismanagement can be solved, Hungary should enter a
new era of prosperity the likes of which it has not experienced for at
least a century. This may all end in a debacle, however; in the first
few months of 1991, old "values" emerged in Hungary, among them
nationalism, anti-Semitism, and impatience with dissenting opinions.
Unless strong efforts are made to avoid the pitfalls represented by
such trends, Hungary may find itself in a precarious position once
again.

NOTES

1. W. Averell Harriman, American ambassador to the Soviet Union, believed that Stalin had three alternative solutions for the Eastern European states: (1) recognize Western interests in the region in the name of extending the alliance with the Western powers, (2) establish a Soviet security region, thus excluding the West, and (3) control Eastern Europe and, as a corollary, influence West European countries through the local communist parties. The last two of these alternatives presupposed tight controls over Eastern Europe. Stalin would never yield Poland to the West; on the other hand, he expected to bargain over Hungary and Czechoslovakia and was surprised that the West did not do so.

2. This seems to be a contradiction of the generally assumed toleration of a multiparty system, which emerged in Hungary in 1945 under the tutelage of the Soviet authorities. However, the contradiction is only apparent when one considers that economic dominance does not presuppose political control, although eventually the two tend to catch up with one another.

3. The policies of the Allies toward Hungary were not entirely clear. On the one hand, they recognized the sovereignty of the provisional government; on the other, the Commission restricted Hungary's sovereignty.

4. This concerned the activities of the Communist-led political police. For example, the police arrested the noncommunist leaders in the village of Gyömrő and murdered twenty-six of them. In Kaposvár, the local leaders of the Smallholders were all arrested. In Kecskemét, the local police chief, Bánó, blackmailed the wives and daughters of noncommunist politicians to grant sexual favors to him and his henchmen. When parliamentary deputies demanded investigations of these cases, Erdei, the minister of the interior, simply refused.

5. Smallholders received 259,000 votes; the joint Communist–Social Democratic ticket gained 249,000. The Civic Democrats garnered 22,000, while the National Peasant party received 11,000. A new party, the Hungarian Radicals, were given 5,000 votes.

6. This was, of course, not entirely true, because the Red Army provided all sorts of support for the Communists, including paper for their press and trucks and loudspeakers for their election propaganda.

7. It seems that Stalin would have been willing to trade Hungary for Poland, but Western pressure for such a move never materialized.

8. See the report by György Gyarmati, "Ne legyenek az elvtársak túlzottan törvénytisztelők" (Comrades, do not respect the laws too much) in *Rubicon* (Budapest), no. 2, 1990, 7, in which the instructions given to Communist party workers are described.

9. Before World War II much of elementary education was in the hands of churches. The Roman Catholic church alone maintained over four thou-

sand schools. The Calvinists and Lutherans also ran some schools, but their numbers were smaller. At the time in question all these schools were taken over by the state.

10. Sándor Erdei, who was a member of the Hungarian delegation at these negotiations, reported that both the Hungarian and Soviet delegations were arrested by KGB troops under the personal command of General Serov. If this turns out to be true, then it may point to a split within the ranks of the Soviet Politburo: Zsolt Csalog, *Doku 56* (Budapest, 1990), 14.

6 Poland: 1918–1990

Andrzej Korbonski

A historian or political scientist asked to discuss political, economic, and social developments in a single country over several decades must first choose an approach likely to produce some interesting results. Selecting such an analytical framework is not easy: it becomes very difficult indeed when the country to be studied happens to be Poland—a state in Eastern Europe that in the past seventy-odd years has gone through several dramatic changes; that thus far has defied easy generalizations and classifications; and that even today continues to be a locus of sharp and growing contrasts and paradoxes.

The choice of an approach is largely determined by the issues one seeks to examine. In this particular case, the major issue concerns the ability of the Polish state to fulfill a nation's traditional objectives: retaining its independence and national identity, maintaining a political system capable of satisfying the population's basic needs and aspirations, and establishing an economic system able to provide the country's citizens with reasonable subsistence—during the seventy-one-year period from the regaining of independence in November 1918 to the emancipation from communist rule in 1989. In order to examine the issues at hand, one must analyze such variables as Poland's changing political structure; its leadership; its socioeconomic and cultural traditions, patterns, tendencies, and beliefs; and its foreign relations, not only with its immediate neighbors but also with other states in Europe and beyond.

The framework should also make allowance for the fact that Poland in the period 1918–1990 did not represent a country changing slowly; far from it. In fact, during those years there were four sharply distinct phases: interwar Poland, 1918–1939; Poland under German and Soviet occupation during World War II, 1939–1945; Communist Poland, 1945–1989; and postcommunist Poland, after 1989.

The approach that appears best suited for analyzing the seven decades of modern Polish history is the so-called developmental approach, based on the pioneering work of Gabriel Almond.[1] The key assumption behind this approach is that throughout history, all societies have to go through a process of political and socioeconomic development and that at some point or points they are bound to face and solve at least four developmental "requirements" or "challenges": nation-building, state-building, political participation, and economic distribution. Also, all societies passing through this process have to manage and resolve crises resulting from a lack of congruence between the developmental criteria listed above. The most frequently found challenges are those of identity, penetration, participation, distribution, and legitimacy.

For example, a society that has succeeded in accomplishing the tasks of nation- and state-building must sooner or later create channels and outlets for popular participation so that the populace can freely articulate its authentic demands and grievances. Similarly, unless the state can ensure its people a reasonably decent standard of living, the people can reciprocate by denying the state political legitimacy.

Any political system may be seen as consisting of various, mostly institutional, elements, all of which are subject to change. Samuel Huntington[2] distinguishes five major systemic components—culture, structure, groups, leadership, and policies—and postulates that the process of political development is, in the final analysis, strongly influenced by the interplay between these components—their type and rate of change.

I propose to analyze Polish history since 1918 by focusing on the five developmental challenges or crises identified by Almond, and on the five systemic components outlined by Huntington.

Poland, 1918–1939

November 11, 1918, was considered during the interwar period as Poland's birthday: a national holiday, marking Armistice Day, which saw the end of hostilities in World War I, and the proclamation of the country's independence after a one-hundred-twenty-eight-year absence from the map of Europe. On that day, formal political authority in Poland was assumed by Jozef Pilsudski, soon to be recognized as a *pater patriae*, but at that time simply a former leader of the so-called Polish legions—auxiliary troops fighting alongside the Austrian and German forces against Russia—who returned to Warsaw only the previous day after being interned by the Germans for disobedience.

As was the case with most of the other newly-formed states in Eastern Europe, except for its name, Poland in November 1918 had hardly any of the wherewithal that one associates with independence. To begin with, it really had no state territory it could claim to control: the various parts which in time were merged into a single country were still ruled by two of the former partitioning powers, Austria and Germany. The country had no well-defined national boundaries; it would take several years to fix and legalize them. Poland had neither an army nor a police force; it had neither its own parliamentary bodies nor a government in the conventional sense of the word. It had no judiciary and no legal system of its own, nor did it possess a civil service.

The various tasks and challenges facing the new state appeared daunting and their solution doubtful. However, at that particular juncture, the Polish people were fortunate to have a number of outstanding political leaders. These, despite the obstacles, were determined to see their longstanding dream of a free and independent country come to fruition. That even they could not successfully accomplish all their objectives was only partly their fault: as we will examine, both the domestic and international environment in the interwar period made success virtually impossible.

Developmental Issues

Nation-Building

Historically, Poland had never been a nation state comparable to France, Spain, or England. Quite the opposite: for centuries, a Polish minority managed to control a large non-Polish majority composed of Ukrainians, Belorussians, Ruthenians, Lithuanians, and Jews, among others. The only example of successful nation-building was confined to the ruling elites when the Polish aristocracy and nobility Polonized its Lithuanian and Ukrainian counterparts. Until its demise as a result of the Third Partition in 1795, Poland was very much a multinational state.

It is not surprising, therefore, that the question of nation-building occupied the attention of Polish leaders prior to the regaining of independence. For some of them, the only Poland they could envisage was that of the second half of the eighteenth century, prior to the partitions. This state reached far to the East into what later became the Russian empire, occupied in 1918 by military forces of various hues: the Austrian, German, White Russian, and Red armies, Ukrainian nationalist forces, and others. It was expected that sooner or later the foreign invaders would leave the territory that most Poles considered rightfully theirs, and which they expected ultimately to become part of the new, reborn Poland. There were some unresolved questions regarding the method of incorporation—full integration versus federation or confederation—but there is little doubt that the idea of a "Great Poland," stretching from the Baltic to the Black Sea, appealed to a significant number of Poles. They were eager to assert Poland's great power status after its lengthy absence from Europe.

The other scenario was that of "Little Poland," limited essentially to the areas inhabited by a Polish ethnic majority, including the former German territories in the western part of Galicia, which had belonged to Austria prior to 1918, and the former Congress Kingdom of Poland around Warsaw, once the core of the Russian partition. The proponents of this solution accused their opponents of harboring imperialistic ambitions. This particular conflict added another dimension to the highly divisive atmosphere which characterized the early stages of the country's independent existence. In the final analysis neither side won: following the Polish-Soviet War of 1919–1921 and the Treaty of Riga that terminated it, Poland's border with the Soviet Union extended considerably beyond the eastern limit of the Polish ethnic settlement but remained well west of the 1795 Polish-Russian frontier, and still further west than the line of the First Partition of 1773.

Although neither side could claim victory, Poland between 1918 and 1939 remained a multinational state with a Polish majority accounting for roughly two-thirds of the population. Of the remaining one-third, the largest segment was represented by the Ukrainians, concentrated in the southeastern part of the country, followed by the Germans in the western provinces, and the Belorussians and Lithuanians in the northeast. The official policy toward the minorities was hostile from the start and there is no evidence that the rulers of the reborn Poland ever seriously contemplated a policy of nation-building that would try and persuade the minorities to adopt voluntarily Polish national identity. Instead, with very few exceptions, the official policy of "pacification," especially in eastern and southeastern Poland, was characterized by a widespread use of violence intended to enforce a Polonization of reluctant Ukrainians and Belorussians. As a result, by 1939 the degree of hostility between the Polish majority and the various minorities was higher than it had been twenty years earlier.

Reprehensible as it was, the policy of repression could be justified on several grounds. In most cases the multinational nature of the Eastern European states, characterized by the presence of large national minorities, was the outcome of decisions reached at the end of World War I by Allied leaders, namely, Wilson and Lloyd George who, despite their laudable intentions, knew little if anything about the linguistic, ethnic, and cultural complexities of the region. The idea of national self-determination, so strongly associated with Wilson, was a powerful magnet exerting tremendous attraction for the peoples of Eastern Europe, yet it soon became obvious that strict adherence to the principle of national independence would result in an excessive fragmentation and proliferation of states with little chance of survival. Hence, a compromise proved necessary and the outcome was the emergence of such multinational states as Poland, Czechoslovakia, Romania and Yugoslavia, each containing several minorities resentful of their status and hostile to the ruling majority.

In the Polish case, it was the Ukrainians who appeared most hostile and unwilling to accept some *modus vivendi* throughout the entire interwar period: the failure to create an independent Ukraine after World War I increased their nationalistic animus. The Lithuanians, although numerically insignificant, never forgave the Poles for the seizure of their historical capital of Wilno (Vilnius) and regularly rejected offers of rapprochement. The Germans, who until 1933 remained reasonably loyal to the Polish state, following Hitler's takeover turned increasingly against Poland, becoming a Nazi fifth column on the eve of World War II.

There remained one other ethnic group in Poland that deserves special attention: the Jews. An integral part of Polish society since the thirteenth century, by 1939 the roughly three and one-half million Jews accounted for about ten percent of the country's population, representing the largest concentration of Jews in the world outside the USSR. An overwhelming majority was urban: about one-third of the population of Warsaw, Lodz, Krakow, and Wilno was Jewish, with the rest of the Jewish population inhabiting the many *shtetls* of central and eastern Poland.

In light of the sheer size of the Jewish population, it was not really surprising that anti-Semitism was very much part of the Polish political culture. The slowly growing Polish bourgeoisie competed with its Jewish counterpart for scarce positions in the professions, trade, and academe, and the same was true for university students seeking access to institutions of higher learning. The Polish peasants looked at the Jews with distrust as usurers and exploiters. Polish anti-Semitism was exacerbated by two additional factors: the role of the Catholic church and the character of Poland's domestic politics. There is no doubt that the church, which between the wars enjoyed a highly privileged status, was a major source of anti-Semitism. In the political arena, the Polish right viewed the Jews either as the natural allies of communism or as inimical to Polish national aspirations. There was a grain of truth to these accusations: Jews formed a majority of the membership of the Polish Communist party until its forcible dissolution by Stalin in 1938, and there was considerable evidence showing that the Jews were actively opposed to Poland's independence in 1918. It was also believed that it was they who persuaded the League of Nations to impose on Poland the so-called "Minority Treaties" that were greatly resented by the Poles, who saw them as an unnecessary humiliation. In those circumstances any idea of a Polish-Jewish reconciliation appeared highly unrealistic.

Faced with major obstacles on the road to creating a sense of Polish national identity, one might have expected the political leaders to have no problems with the purely ethnic Polish population, but this was not the case. Here the difficulty lay with the eighteenth-century partitions which, as mentioned earlier, left the Polish population divided between Austria, Germany, and Russia for more than one hundred and twenty years. It was only natural for the respective populations to acquire certain psychological characteristics from their rulers, and to take advantage of the existing sociopolitical systems to develop certain behavior patterns of their own. Thus, the western Poles saw themselves as the most modern, the best organized, and the hardest working and looked at their brethren to the east and the south with considerable contempt. These, in turn, viewed their western neighbors as having lost their Polish national identity and being well on the road to becoming Germanized. As a result, the westerners were seen as not fit to share in the governance of the resurrected

Poland and they were widely discriminated against because of that perception.

On the eve of World War II, it was quite obvious that if there had been any progress at all on the road to generating a sense of a Polish national consciousness, it had been very limited. The most visible achievement was the forging of a national identity among the three segments of the ethnic Polish population, which until 1918 had lived under foreign domination. There may also have been some marginal improvement in Polish-Jewish relations but that was viewed by some as ephemeral, leaving the task of nation-building in Poland essentially unresolved.

State-Building

In most cases the process of state-building parallels that of nation-building, and both processes are usually discussed together as a single phenomenon. In the Polish case, however, I believe that it makes sense to separate the two processes and to treat them as basically separate.

If nation-building in Poland was impossible, building a state in Poland after independence in 1918 proved to be somewhat easier. State-building itself has been defined as the construction of an institutional framework capable of making authoritative allocations of values and able to extract obedience from its citizens. A state should be able to rule or to govern, ensure the maintenance of law and order, protect its subjects against foreign enemies, and provide them with a reasonable standard of well-being. In return, the state should expect overall public compliance with its policies without resorting to coercive measures.

The process of state-building in Poland between the wars, although less difficult than that of nation-building, remained far from complete. In addition to securing national frontiers, the principal task faced by the country's new rulers was somehow to glue together the three disparate regions resulting from the partitions, each of them sharply distinct from the others.

Of the three partitioning powers, imperial Germany came closest to being a modern state. It had a well-developed governmental structure, including a judiciary; its efficient and incorruptible bureaucracy was a model for the entire world. Its economic system was predominantly based on the competitive market principle, yet the public sector also retained a large share of control in heavy industry and utilities;

and finally, Germany from the second half of the nineteenth century came close to being a modern welfare state, providing many benefits to its citizens. They were also granted a relatively modern and democratic parliamentary electoral law, certainly more advanced and comprehensive than in Britain, France, and even the United States. It must be noted here that while the Polish population enjoyed the various benefits provided by the German state, it was as a rule discouraged from entering German civil and military service.

The contrast between Germany and the other two partitioning powers was striking, especially with respect to tsarist Russia. Prior to the revolution of 1905, Russia was an autocratic state with the tsar exercising absolute authority in every conceivable respect. Even after the revolution and the laying of rudimentary foundations for a constitutional monarchy, not much progress was achieved until the outbreak of the Bolshevik revolution in November 1917. The governmental structure was that of a typical autocratic state: the bureaucracy and the judiciary represented a personal fiefdom of the tsar, and were corrupt and insensitive to people's needs and interests. The economic system was dominated by governmental and private monopolies, and by foreign capital. The Habsburg empire fell somewhere in between: it had a well-developed institutional governmental framework which allowed considerable democracy to its citizens, more so even than in Germany; and its civil service tried to emulate the German one albeit with only limited success. Its economic system, although more highly developed than that of Russia, was still considerably behind that of Germany. Significantly both the Habsburg empire and Russia imposed no obstacles on the entry of the Poles into their respective civil or military service, with the result that a rather large number availed themselves of that opportunity.

It is not surprising then that the Austrian Poles were most actively involved in the process of state-building, followed by the Russian Poles, with those coming from the former German provinces being represented only at the margin. The Austrian Poles had considerable work experience: under the Dual Monarchy they occupied many important governmental positions and had had to solve a variety of problems they would again encounter in independent Poland. This gave birth to a bureaucratic culture that made the inhabitants of what was formerly Galicia almost indispensable in the new Poland. The officials who acquired their spurs under the tsars may have been just as capable but were not yet initiated into bureaucratic culture and, if anything, tended toward corruption and general *Schlamperei* (disorder).

This short account helps to explain why the process of state-building proceeded so slowly and why, on the eve of World War II, there were still sharp institutional differences among the three main parts of the country. In 1939 in western Poland there were still local government institutions inherited *in toto* from the kingdom of Prussia; there were still sharp regional differences in the legal and tax systems; and identical school grades in different Polish provinces meant entirely different things. Yet institutional and legal integration had progressed. In many respects, great advances in the codification of laws had been made. It simply meant that twenty years was not long enough to accomplish so many goals, especially at a time when the country's sheer physical existence and long-term survival were threatened by its neighbors to the east and west and by the national minorities at home.

Political Participation

At least two of the three partitioning powers—the Habsburg empire and Germany—had had in place for some time rather liberal and democratic electoral systems that provided for a significant degree of political participation for their Polish citizens. In Russia, the first elections to the popular assembly, the Duma, were held in 1905, which meant that the Russian Poles had considerably less exposure to electoral politics than their brethren across the partition lines, and especially those in Austria-Hungary.

The Poles in Galicia had been deeply involved in both state and local politics. Together with the other nationalities, such as the Czechs, Slovenes, Croats, and Ruthenes, they were able to send an impressive national delegation to the Viennese Reichsrat, to guard Polish national interests at both the executive and legislative levels. Not surprisingly, the first Polish political parties were organized in Galicia in order to mobilize support for Polish-born deputies. The situation in the German provinces was different: although they enjoyed a liberal franchise, relatively few Poles were selected as candidates for the Reichstag so that Polish voters had no choice but to cast most of their ballots for non-Poles. Several Poles were actually elected to the Russian Duma in 1910. Thus, the political elite—at least a core—in newly independent Poland had enough parliamentary experience to move the new political system toward constitutional democracy providing sufficient outlet for authentic political participation.

This initially strong commitment to representative institutions was helped by a longstanding attachment to the principle of popular representation. Polish historians and constitutional lawyers have made much of the presence of elected bodies in Poland long before their appearance elsewhere in continental Europe. To be sure, the system which ultimately became known as the "republic of the nobles" was highly restricted, representing less than five percent of the population. However, within the category of gentry, everyone had the right to vote regardless of wealth or national origin, and this emphasis on—albeit limited—equality survived to modern times.

Reflecting widespread popular enthusiasm, the first parliamentary elections in independent Poland were held in 1919 while large parts of the country were either still occupied by foreign troops or were subject to impending plebiscites that were to determine their ultimate fate. The impressively democratic constitution, guaranteeing political participation at various levels, was passed in March 1921, and it appeared that in contrast to the lack of success in nation- and state-building, Poland was well on the way to becoming a secure and self-confident democracy. This was not to be. By 1926, progress toward further democratization came to a halt, to be followed by a period of uneasy stagnation until the early 1930s, when a rapid retreat from democracy was manifested by the passage in April 1935 of a new constitution, some of the articles of which soon became an international laughingstock.

Among the various reasons for the collapse of democracy in Poland, the most important were the declining influence of Western European democracies and the rise of Nazi Germany and fascist Italy, the escalation of the national minorities conflict, and the deteriorating economic situation in the wake of the Great Depression.

There is little doubt that the World War I victory of the Western democracies—Britain, France, and the United States—and their presiding over the birth of three new Eastern European states (Czechoslovakia, Poland, and Yugoslavia) and substantial changes in the three others (Bulgaria, Hungary, and Romania)—meant that most of the new states almost became by definition democratic entities, if only to curry favor with their conqueror benefactors. But when the United States turned isolationist and both Britain and France lost interest in the region, the various countries—including Poland—no longer had much incentive to emulate their Western creators. If anything, they began to turn their attention to Germany and Italy. The rise of Nazism undoubtedly contributed to the rise of German hostility toward Poland and it also added fuel to Ukrainian irredentism (kindled by Berlin). There is also little doubt that the economic crisis of the early 1930s led to much greater centralization of governmental decision making at the expense of fledgling representative institutions.

Twenty years after regaining its independence, Poland appeared to be less rather than more democratic: the exemplary liberal franchise was replaced in 1935 by a highly restrictive electoral law that imposed obstacles on the voters, establishing a definite pattern of discrimination against national minorities and political opponents of the increasingly authoritarian regime.

Economic Conditions and Policies

Poland in the interwar period was a predominantly agricultural country. About two-thirds of its population depended on farming as a source of income. Agriculture accounted for the largest share of gross national product. Industry was underdeveloped and depended to a large extent on agriculture for its raw materials. The predominance of farming was the result of a long process of economic, social, and historical development and in this, as in many other respects, Poland was no different from most of the other Eastern European countries.

The overwhelming economic problem that cast its shadow over all aspects of life in interwar Poland was the poverty of the peasantry. The low productivity of the farming sector led to low real income, a paltry capacity to save, and a commensurate lack of capital. Low productivity and low real income meant low buying power and small aggregate demand, which reduced any incentives to invest and resulted in lack of capital. The low productivity of Polish agriculture was due to the relative scarcity of both land and capital. Employment in Polish farming was so high in relation to available land and capital that the marginal productivity of labor was close to zero. This meant that a large part of the agricultural population contributed little or nothing to output and could have been removed without reducing the level of production.

The term *employment* was therefore misleading and Poland, in fact, provided an almost classical example of rural or "structural" unemployment. Before 1914 the pressure exerted by hidden farm unemployment was largely relieved by emigration to the United States, Canada, and Brazil. After World War I, however, this outlet was sharply curtailed. The only way to increase productivity in Polish agriculture was to provide employment opportunities for the surplus population in industry and other nonfarm sectors. The main drawback was again scarcity of capital, attributable to low inducement to invest. This arose from the low purchasing power of the large majority of the population, reflected in the low demand for manufactured goods and services. Such conditions did not attract foreign capital, and the government was very much afraid of stimulating inflation—at least until the mid-1930s—and had few disposable funds available.

Agricultural productivity tended also to be affected by the size and form of production units. In Poland in 1921, less than one percent of all holdings accounted for nearly one-half of the total area in agriculture, meaning that the farming sector consisted predominantly of small, inefficient family farms. This alone created a climate favoring land reform. Right from the start the reform was regarded as an act of social justice and not as an economic measure. This view was held particularly by the upper and middle classes who considered the "peasant question" as having been one of the main causes of Poland's downfall in the eighteenth century. Another reason why there was no serious opposition to land reform per se was the Bolshevik revolution and its impact on Russian agriculture as well as the general radicalization of Polish society after the war. The fear of a serious peasant revolt, comparable to that in Russia after November 1917, was due not only to physical proximity but also to many similarities in agrarian structure and peasant-to-land ratio.

On balance, the accomplishments of the Land Reform Acts of 1920 and 1925 proved to be less than impressive. The reforms did not really cure the highly unequal land ownership structure, nor did they provide full employment for those whose livelihood depended on farming. Especially with respect to the amount of distributed land, Poland did not compare favorably with other Eastern European states. In a sense this was not surprising since, as stated earlier, the motives behind the land reform were political, social, and national rather than economic.

At the time of regaining its independence, Poland's industry reflected the pattern of industrialization followed by the partitioning powers. The greatest concentration of heavy industry—coal and metallurgy—was in Upper Silesia, part of Germany until 1921. Elsewhere in western Poland there was some light industry (principally food processing) taking advantage of the relatively productive agriculture of the region. Galicia, formerly part of the Habsburg empire, was least industrialized except for the beginnings of an oil industry in its eastern sector. In the former Congress Kingdom, the fairly developed manufacturing industry (engineering, textiles) around Warsaw and Lodz was the outcome of Western European capital moving into the Russian empire toward the end of the nineteenth century.

Ironically, independence hurt Polish industry. To begin with, industry in the former Russian part, that had for many decades thrived on the ever-expanding Russian market for its products, was suddenly cut off from its market after 1917 and was never able to find a substitute. The same was true to a lesser degree for industry in the rest of the country: a small and (after 1918) ever-shrinking Polish domestic market could not fill the gap left by the disappearance of the much larger German and Austrian markets. The expanding post–World War I regimen of customs barriers, trade quotas, and other commercial restrictions hit the newly created countries much harder than more established states.

The result was that in the 1920s the principal indexes of Polish industrial production showed a significant drop when contrasted with the pre-independence period. This had several important political implications. First, industrial stagnation and/or decline contributed to rising unemployment, further reducing the already meager purchasing power of the population and increasing budgetary expenditure, already straining under a heavy defense burden. Decline in aggregate demand further diminished the already weak incentives to invest, especially among foreigners. Worried about both political and economic instability, foreign capital not only showed no inclination to invest in Poland but, in fact, many foreign firms decided to sell their Polish assets for fear of bankruptcy. Adding to its budgetary woes, the Polish government had little option but to buy out the foreign owners and thus preserve at least a modicum of industrial employment—at the cost of enlarging the public sector, already looked upon with suspicion by the West.

As suggested earlier, Poland suffered a good deal from the Great Depression and took longer than most other European countries to recover from it. However, the recovery was also accompanied by the adoption of a new economic policy that represented a sharp break from the traditional laissez-faire, deflationist measures which took a heavy toll during the crisis. Beginning in the mid-1930s Poland embarked on an ambitious, expansionist industrial policy that turned out to be highly successful if somewhat late.

Considering the initially low level of development compounded by the legacy of partitions, the damage caused by World War I, the outright indifference if not hostility of the Western powers which, having put Poland on the map at Versailles, declined to provide it with economic support, and the effects of the worldwide crisis, Poland's economic achievements during the interwar period were far from negligible.

To be sure, from the point of view of the peasant majority, the situation in agriculture looked hopeless and the prospects for improvement appeared poor. The agrarian problem could have been solved, theoretically, in a number of ways: through an increase in the availability of land, emigration, or industrialization. The first two options did not offer much promise, at least in the short run. Industrial growth was clearly a possibility as illustrated by the decision to establish the Central Industrial Region, situated in a part of Poland suffering from the highest level of rural underemployment. The Region was a great success. But for the outbreak of war in 1939, it might have served as a model for similar regional development projects in other depressed areas.

What factors were responsible for the success or failure of these policies or, to put it differently, for the ability or inability of Poland's decision makers to deal adequately with the different developmental challenges? A consideration of the five systemic variables listed at the outset may prove helpful in explaining the policy outcomes.

Systemic Issues

Culture

Culture as a systemic variable is defined by Huntington as embracing "the values, attitudes, orientations, myths, and beliefs relevant to politics and dominant in society,"[3] including mass perceptions as well as political ideologies. In the Polish context, it is also useful to distinguish between elite and mass political culture.

It may be taken for granted that Poland's traditional socioeconomic structure, which for all practical purposes did not undergo substantial changes until the eve of World War I, gave birth to a host of rather perverse and unique ideas, beliefs, and complexes that determined nearly all phases of the life of the country. One tangible and perhaps the most significant result of the psychological confusion was the emergence of a peculiar group of people who in a very short time managed to acquire a monopoly on political, social, and economic power. This amorphous group, acknowledging no superior and stretching across all the traditional social classes, was the intelligentsia. Having its roots in the aristocracy and the gentry, the intelligentsia believed that it was destined to rule the Polish nation because it alone had the necessary prerequisites for leadership. It was not really interested in mobilizing the support of workers and peasants, both of whom it considered inferior.

The *political* culture of the Polish ruling class was hardly to be equated with a *civic* culture, which is generally recognized as a necessary condition for democracy. At the same time, as shown by the experience of World War II, the Polish intelligentsia was aghast at the thought of a totalitarian state. What did it believe in? It seems that the Polish rulers between the wars had no clear idea of the system to be adopted. Any system, save full democracy or complete dictatorship, was acceptable to them as long as they were able to preserve their status. The Polish political system between the wars was a good testimony to their beliefs.

One could also assume that after more than a century of captivity, the elite political culture was bound to be characterized by fierce nationalism, even chauvinism. Paradoxically, this was not quite the case. One of the most interesting and least publicized aspects of Polish elite attitude and behavior at the turn of the century was its willingness to accept foreign rule and to discount the possibility of Poland's independence. Only a relative minority still believed in achieving independence; the majority appeared satisfied with the status quo and, whenever possible, reaffirmed its loyalty to the Habsburgs, Hohenzollerns, or Romanovs.

If anything, the rise in nationalism followed the regaining of independence and was at least partly stimulated by the hostility to the new Polish state expressed by national minorities. Interestingly enough, although the Polish ruling class did not support the Jews, it was not openly anti-Semitic. That epithet better suited the workers and peasants who tended to accept racial stereotypes and prejudices, which, in turn, added fuel to existing religious, cultural, and class animosities, making coexistence unattainable. Although some progress was made in reducing prejudice, on the eve of World War II anti-Semitism in Poland still remained a force to be reckoned with.

Another mass behavioral feature was a deeply-rooted mistrust and dislike of authority which hindered the process of state-building. Although these anti-authoritarian attitudes went back several centuries, they acquired their modern expression during the partition period. Centuries of resistance to foreign domination left marks on the Polish psyche that twenty-one years of independence did little to eradicate.

The final cultural component affecting political processes in interwar Poland was a strong attachment to the Roman Catholic church. While space limitations preclude a full discussion of church-state relations between the wars, the church did enjoy a privileged status in Poland, and during that time there was no separation between church and state. Catholic bishops and clergy remained strongly loyal to successive regimes and proved most helpful to them not only in the process of nation- and state-building but also in keeping the peasants quiet and defusing their demands for radical land reform.

Structure

The concept of "structure" in this context includes "formal organizations through which the society makes authoritative decisions, such as political parties, legislatures, executives and bureaucracies."[4]

Poland between the wars displayed the standard spectrum of political parties, ranging from the extreme left to extreme right. The extreme left was occupied briefly by the Polish Communist party, formally established in 1918 and outlawed by the government a year later. After that, and until its unexpected and still not fully explained forcible dissolution and the execution of its top leaders by Stalin in 1938, the party barely managed to survive.

In light of what happened in Poland after 1945, it is necessary to emphasize the marginal importance of communism in Poland prior to World War II. Not only was the party numerically weak but throughout its twenty-year existence it managed to attract mostly ethnic and national minorities (such as Ukrainians, Belorussians and Jews) which, ipso facto, made it anathema to the Polish majority. The 1919–1921 Polish-Soviet war showed very clearly the hostility of Polish workers and peasants toward the Bolsheviks, who were not only Russians, but also reviled religion. The well-publicized introduction of agricultural collectivization in the USSR severely antagonized the Polish peasants and the Moscow purges in the second half of the 1930s alienated the intelligentsia, some of whose members had flirted with communism in the wake of the Great Depression. Finally, the destruction of the party by Stalin for all practical purposes removed the communists from the Polish political arena for the next several years.

Moving to the right, the Social Democratic party (the "PPS") never quite fulfilled the expectations of its leaders and followers. Its natural base of support, a growing industrial working class, was small. Together with the other socialist parties, the Polish party had to wage a war on two fronts: against the Communists on the left, who accused the PPS of splitting the unity of the working class, and against the centrist and right-wing parties who claimed there was not much difference between the Social Democrats and the Communists. Despite these difficulties, the PPS never wavered in its acceptance of democratic principles and, throughout the period under discussion, managed to poll about 15 to 20 percent of the popular vote in general elections and considerably more in local and city races.

The center of the political spectrum was occupied by several peasant parties. One of the peculiarities of the Eastern European political landscape was the fact that despite the peasantry accounting for a substantial majority of the population of all countries, except in Czechoslovakia no peasant party ever achieved an electoral victory that would allow it to form a government that could push through a radical land reform.

The reasons for this are complex, but it is clear that in addition to being notoriously hard to mobilize and organize, the Eastern European peasants—including the Poles—were essentially outside the political and socioeconomic pale. Before World War II there was a huge chasm between the cities and the countryside. In the absence of an even modest infrastructure, including transportation and communication, and with widespread illiteracy, there were in fact two Polands: the urban one which in some respects resembled parts of Western Europe, and the rural one which, some would claim, had hardly changed from the time of the partitions.

All this was largely responsible for the lack of electoral successes on the part of the peasant parties, burdened also by sharp regional and class distinctions inherited from the partitions. For example, as mentioned earlier, the farmers from western Poland were less interested in land reform and more in improved infrastructure. The peasants from Galicia and the Congress Kingdom were split between subsistence-level poor peasants and the middle-level and rich farmers. As a result they were represented by two distinct peasant parties protecting their particular interests. Were they to vote together, the peasants would most likely have managed to achieve an electoral majority, but this never happened. The peasant parties produced some outstanding Polish political leaders of the interwar period but their overall input into political decision making was slight.

The right side of the spectrum was occupied by a variety of conservative and nationalist parties. Here, it is necessary to dispel a myth that has refused to disappear from any discussion of interwar Polish politics: the supposed existence of extremist right wing, Nazi-like parties in Poland. Unlike the Iron Guard in Romania, the Arrow Cross in Hungary, the Ustaši in Croatia, or the Hlinka Guards in Slovakia—all of which ended up collaborating with the Nazis during World War II—the Polish right wing groupings did not deserve to be called parties: they were really part of the lunatic fringe to be found in any polity. What is perhaps even more telling is the fact that many of their leaders fought in the anti-German resistance movement.

The main occupant of the right was the National Democratic

party. It had its roots among the Polish intelligentsia in the Russian partition and considered Germany to be Poland's greatest enemy. It was strongly nationalistic in economic and social issues, and also anti-Semitic. After independence its influence spread westward and on the eve of World War II its main base of support was in western Poland. It was probably the single strongest Polish party although, like the peasant parties, it never scored a decisive election victory.

Curiously enough, despite the powerful position of the Catholic church, Poland never developed a denominational party comparable to the German *Zentrum* that had served as an instrument protecting the church's interests. There were some attempts to create parties such as the Christian Labor party or a Christian Democratic party, but they were never very successful.

At this stage one has to mention a rather peculiar Polish political invention, initially known as the "Non-Party Bloc for Cooperation with the Government" and later as the "Camp of National Unity." Both organizations were intended to provide parliamentary support for the regime of Marshal Pilsudski and, after his death, to force the passage of a new authoritarian constitution to perpetuate the rule of the Pilsudski clique. Neither of the two had much of a political program, except to stay in power, although the ideological declaration of the Camp of National Unity contained some vague references to Italian fascist and German Nazi slogans.

To complete the picture, national and ethnic minorities also formed several parties to protect their interests. Many had Jewish origins and membership, ranging from the Bund on the left to various Zionist and religious parties on the right. The Ukrainians were also divided between the extreme left, represented by the Communist party of Western Ukraine, and the extreme right, split among several nationalist and chauvinist parties. The Germans until the arrival of the Nazis also displayed a whole plethora of political organizations but after 1933 nearly all of them merged into a strongly pro-Nazi front. Most of the minority parties were strongly anti-Polish and worked actively toward the demise of the Polish state.

The remaining structures can be discussed only briefly. The constitution of March 1921 put the legislative branch well ahead of the others. What some called the parliamentary dictatorship was first curtailed following the military coup of May 1926, and then eliminated entirely in the April 1935 constitution which established an executive hegemony, making the two legislative chambers virtual rubber stamps.

The executive branch represented a typical example of a weak coalition government which until 1935 played the game of musical chairs with some regularity. The electoral system based on proportional representation prevented a single party from ever achieving a majority in the Polish Sejm (lower chamber), so that between 1919 and 1935 all governments were coalition governments lasting on the average only a few months. Only in the mid-1930s, with the country drifting toward authoritarianism, did the new Camp of National Unity government manage to stay in power for three years.

In the bureaucracy the legacy of the partitions also played an important role. As we saw earlier, only in Habsburg-ruled Galicia were Poles given an opportunity to enter the *Kaiserliche-und-Königliche* civil service, and they did so with a vengeance. Their counterparts in the Russian part of Poland also had some access to government jobs but usually outside their own homeland, in the other parts of the empire. Finally, the inhabitants of western Poland were precluded from government service, which was the domain of the Prussian *Junkers* (landed gentry or nobility) and members of the German middle class.

This strongly suggests that throughout the interwar period the character, procedures, and ethic of the Polish bureaucracy were clearly determined by the former members of the Viennese civil service. Although not as efficient as its German counterpart, the Habsburg bureaucracy was relatively free of corruption and performed rather well. In time, the civil service became a refuge for the sons of the Polish upper and middle classes who considered government service as rightfully theirs.

Groups

Groups can be seen as "the social and economic formations, formal and informal, which participate in politics and make demands on the political structures."[5] In this respect the Polish record in the interwar period was less impressive than that of the other Eastern European countries. The notion of pluralism, however broadly defined, had never been an integral part of Polish political culture.

One of the reasons for this could be found in the low level of socioeconomic development; industry was almost nonexistent and there was a resulting lack of class and economic differentiation. The behavior of labor unions is a case in point. For the most part the unions acted not as authentic articulators of workers' interests, engaging in collective bargaining with employers, but mainly as tools of the owners, trying to limit labor unrest. But whatever their alignment, in the presence of high unemployment, the authority and prestige of the unions remained weak throughout the period.

Two other groups, however, deserve considerable attention: the Catholic church and the Polish military. In contrast to the post–World War II period, the church between the wars preferred to maintain a low profile and operate from behind the scenes, and only now and then would it actively involve itself in politics. Its position was so strong that it could behave passively: it occupied the leading position among religious organizations; it exerted considerable influence on the social, educational, and cultural milieux, and occasionally also on foreign and domestic politics. For all practical purposes there was little separation between the Polish church and the Polish state. The church was happy to repay the state for the benefits: it strongly supported its nation- and state-building policies and, especially in the 1930s, openly favored the creeping authoritarianism over democracy.

Did the Polish military in the interwar period behave or act forcefully or decisively like a pressure group, articulating and protecting its own interests? The answer is both yes and no. A good case can be made that, at least until 1926, the military did not act like a pressure group; that between 1926 and 1935 it behaved very much like a typical interest group; and that after 1935 it was transformed into a ruling oligarchy.

In the early years of Poland's independent existence, the military could not be called an interest group since it lacked corporate identity, agreement on its fundamental interests, and a strong leadership capable of articulating these concerns. This changed with the May 1926 coup. First, despite some violence between factions within the military, the armed forces emerged from the coup more united and integrated than before. Moreover, the existing imbalance between the civilian and military elites was redressed in favor of the latter: while the civilians were still formally in charge of the government, after 1926 the military acquired easy access to policymakers and began to act like a conventional interest group, putting pressure on various political structures. Its ability to gain access and to make its demands known was aided by the fact that the policymakers, though formally civilian, were increasingly being recruited from among high-ranking military officers. Conflicts of interest began to merge into common or congruent interests. By the mid-1930s the issue of a potential military-civilian conflict became academic as the military began to monopolize decision making in nearly all spheres of public life. It had achieved its corporate identity, it appeared strongly united, and it had found a new strongman who inherited the mantle of leadership from Marshal Pilsudski.

Leadership

It is probably no exaggeration to say that interwar Poland had not been blessed with great political leaders—"the individuals in political institutions and groups who exercise more influence than others on the allocation of values."[6]

The most important among them was Marshal Jozef Pilsudski (1867–1935) who clearly dominated politics, especially in the period immediately following independence and after the May 1926 coup (which he led). Whether he deserved the accolade of "great" or "charismatic" is subject to discussion, but there is consensus among scholars that he was truly popular, mostly by virtue of his role in regaining Polish independence and his victory in the Polish-Soviet war.

It may be said, generally, that he embodied both the positive and negative traits of the traditional Polish landed gentry. He was strongly nationalistic, rather indifferent to democratic values, a strong believer in elitism (particularly in an elite military corps), fiercely loyal to his supporters, and basically unconcerned with economic and social issues, as illustrated by his contempt for parliamentary and party politics. Nonetheless, he was a person of authority, and perhaps that strong authority was exactly what Poland in the mid-1920s needed most of all. His successors, mostly weak cronies of the Marshal, were never able to produce the kind of popular support he enjoyed.

Civilian leaders were able to exert direct influence only until the coup of 1926 but even during that period their authority tended to be overshadowed by the ever-present figure of Pilsudski. Part of the difficulty faced by such well-known peasant party leaders as Wincenty Witos (1874–1945) and Maciej Rataj (1884–1940) or the Socialist party leader Ignacy Daszynski (1866–1936) was that they acquired their political skills in the Habsburg parliament and exercised their leadership during the period of legislative supremacy. Once that gave way to authoritarianism some of them, like Witos, were first arrested and then exiled by Pilsudski. Others were simply sent back into private life.

The one leader who could directly challenge Pilsudski was Roman Dmowski (1864–1939), the founder of the National Democratic party and intellectually the most sophisticated Polish politician of the interwar period. He represented Poland's interests at Versailles, and there is little doubt that the territorial gains Poland managed to extract from Germany were largely due to Dmowski's perseverance and his close contacts with the French. Later, however, Dmowski was pushed aside by Pilsudski, lived abroad for several years, and returned to Poland shortly before his death in 1939.

Although Dmowski himself never achieved power, his ideas proved much longer lasting and influential than their author. Ironically, his pro-Russian, anti-German stance was found most attractive by the Polish Communist party which, though it openly denounced Dmowski, adopted many of his ideas both implicitly and explicitly as part of its post-1945 platform.

Policies

The two mega- or macropolicies that absorbed most of the energy and resources of the new Polish state were the creation of a national consciousness and identity and the establishment of a state capable of protecting its independence and territorial integrity. Both represented a synthesis or an aggregate of various initiatives and endeavors, linked by the need for a common source of leadership and administration. Nation-building involved the creation of a national political culture which would be acceptable to and internalized by at least some of the minorities. This required the construction of a modern educational system that, together with other institutions, would carry the burden of Polish socialization.

With regard to the process of state-building, the creation of an administrative state with recognized boundaries was only part of the story. The state and its institutions had to be protected from enemies foreign and domestic. Because of the prevailing international tension characteristic of the entire interwar period, this proved to be very costly, especially for a poor country such as Poland. As a result, high defense expenditures absorbed many of the state's resources that would otherwise have been earmarked for the general welfare.

Insofar as economic policies were concerned, initially it was agriculture and land reform that attracted most attention. Once these problems were laid to rest, at least temporarily, other priorities came into play. One of them was an attempt quickly to eradicate the rather deep economic differences between the three post-partition regions. The continuing existence of such differences had deleterious political effects, delaying nation- and state-building, perpetuating local and regional particularism, and tearing apart the none-too-strong fabric of Polish society. The process of working out the differences proved difficult and expensive. On the eve of the German attack many of the differences continued to fester. Most had to wait for the war and the Communist takeover, both of which greatly contributed to a general leveling from the top, which largely patched over the problems without actually solving them.

Until the mid-1930s, the economic policy of the Polish government was couched in classical terms which emphasized the stability of the currency above all. The price paid for this policy proved enormous and both the deflationary bias and the obsession with maintaining the stability of the zloty were responsible for severe impoverishment of the country, especially when the price level of both agricultural and manufactured goods fell considerably below that in other European countries. The last few years before the war were characterized by a dramatic turnaround in government policy: the government embraced Keynesian economics and launched an expansionist investment policy which yielded spectacular results. While the period in question was too short to offset the failure of the previous fifteen years, it did augur a bright future.

The image of Poland on the eve of World War II is that of a country which after a rocky start (which lasted the first fifteen years or so of its independent existence) appeared to have found its bearings and was poised for dynamic growth, especially in the socioeconomic sphere. Faced with a convergence of crises and challenges typical of a developing country, Poland was unable to manage all of them successfully, and yet it did survive the worst and emerged in the mid-1930s in a rather optimistic cast of mind. One may go so far as to assert that had the country been spared the ravages of World War II, in another decade or so it would have crossed the threshold of development and joined such Eastern European countries as Czechoslovakia and Hungary which had moved into the category of developed states.

Of the challenges mentioned at the beginning of the chapter, the questioning of the system's legitimacy seemed most serious during the interwar period. In light of the multinational character of the country, one-third of the population was bound to deny the legitimacy of the Polish republic. However, a good case can be made that within the ethnic Polish population an overwhelming majority accepted the regime as legitimate. To be sure, in the 1920s the military and police had to be called upon to stem violent workers' strikes, and in the mid-1930s there was a rather unique peasant strike that demonstrated the growing alienation of the peasantry from the increasingly nondemocratic system. However, the ultimate test of the government's popular acceptance came with the outbreak of war in September 1939. The Polish population responded to the call to arms even when it soon became clear that Poland would be quickly defeated by Germany with Soviet support.

The simultaneous presence of other challenges aggravated the already difficult situation. Nonetheless, taking into account the legacy of the partitions and considering its lack of experience in crisis management, its limited economic resources, and the absence of any moral and material support from the West, the Polish state in the period between the two world wars did as well as could be expected, if not better.

The War: 1939–1945

There is no doubt that in World War II Poland suffered a massive amount of human and physical destruction. The country lost about one-fifth of its population; the material damage wrought to its cities, its industries, and its infrastructure was incalculable. On top of that, as a result of decisions beyond its control, Poland was moved physically westward, losing about 40 percent of its territory in the east and being partially compensated for it by being given former German lands in the west.

Critical as the changes were, they were ultimately overshadowed by the dramatic changes in the European configuration of forces whereby the old international order, exemplified by the 1938 Munich conference, attended by Britain, France, Germany, and Italy, was replaced by a bipolar system controlled by the United States and the Soviet Union. Without having anything to say about it, Poland together with the other Eastern European states found itself being forcibly pushed into the Soviet sphere of influence.

The German Occupation

Following its quick victory in September 1939, Germany announced its territorial and administrative reorganization of that part of Poland given to it as part of the Ribbentrop-Molotov treaty. Berlin formally incorporated into the German Reich lands that had belonged to Germany from the time of the eighteenth-century partitions until Versailles, as well as areas which at no time in history had been German. The remainder of German-occupied Poland was made into something called the *Generalgouvernement* headed by a governor, Hans Frank, one of Hitler's close confidants and a legal authority in the Nazi party.

The *Generalgouvernement* was viewed as a kind of Polish national home, a colony to be exploited in every conceivable way by the German occupiers. As agreed between Berlin and Moscow, any trace of the "monstrous offspring of Versailles"[7] was to be eradicated. As part of this campaign, the capital of the *Generalgouvernement* was to be Krakow rather than Warsaw. All artistic and cultural activities were to be severely circumscribed. Since the Polish people were viewed by their German masters as fit only for the most menial tasks, all Polish high schools and institutions of higher learning were closed for the duration of the occupation. The ban extended also to political activities but, as in the case of the previously listed restrictions, it proved to be largely ephemeral.

Within a relatively short time the traditional prewar political parties began to operate underground, to be followed by the creation of an underground parliament and even an executive branch. The civilian resistance structures were from the very beginning paralleled by military resistance organizations both of which became later known as the Polish "underground state." Despite displaying a high degree of pluralism, the "secret state" was fiercely loyal to the Polish government-in-exile in London and strongly opposed to the Soviet Union and its Polish agents.

In late 1941 Moscow apparently decided to resurrect the Polish Communist party, which Stalin had virtually destroyed three years earlier. However, instead of its historical name of *Komunistyczna Partia Polski* (Polish Communist party), the new formation was called the Polish Workers party (*Polska Partia Robotnicza*), presumably to make it more appealing to prospective recruits. At least until the arrival of the Red Army in central Poland in the summer of 1944 the new party failed to attract many members and played only a marginal role in underground politics.

In the summer of 1944, when Soviet forces entered the area inhabited by ethnic Poles, Moscow created something called the Polish Committee of National Liberation. The committee issued a manifesto to the Polish people on July 22, in the city of Chelm, proclaiming the establishment of a new political and socioeconomic order. Even though the language of the manifesto was carefully drawn and devoid of revolutionary and radical statements and slogans, its meaning was clear, suggesting that communist rule in Poland was just around the corner. In a desperate move, fighting for its very survival, the exile government in London ordered its military resistance organization, known as *Armia Krajowa* (Home Army) to launch an uprising in Warsaw in order to liberate it from the Germans and to prepare it as a base for the return of the exile government.

The insurrection that began on August 1, 1944 lasted longer than expected, but it ended in the destruction of Warsaw, the death of one-fourth of the city's population, and the capture of the best and the brightest resistance fighters in German prisoner-of-war camps. The end of the Warsaw Uprising marked, for all practical purposes, the end of organized anti-German resistance in Poland, paving the way for the Communist takeover.

The Soviet Occupation

Unlike their German antecedents, the Soviet occupiers did not bother with such niceties as a Polish national home. They transferred a small area of northeastern Poland around Wilno (Vilnius) to Lithuania—redressing, as they and the Lithuanians would have it, a historic injustice. In the fall of 1939 the Soviets staged phony elections in the remaining parts of Poland, quickly renamed Western Ukraine and Western Belorussia, and, not surprisingly, the elected assemblies joyfully voted to merge their lands with the Soviet Ukraine and Soviet Belorussia, respectively. This provided a model for what was to transpire in the Baltic republics some nine months later. Between the spring of 1940 and the summer of 1941, the Soviet authorities deported about one and a half million inhabitants of eastern Poland to labor camps in central Asia and Siberia. As with the case of the Soviet secret police murder at Katyn of more than ten thousand Polish officers captured by the Red Army during its invasion of Poland in September 1939, the reasons behind the deportations remain obscure.

Following the German attack in June 1941 and the quick advance to the east, the Germans, for reasons best known to themselves, incorporated the area of eastern Galicia around Lwow, which prior to 1918 belonged to Austria and between 1918 and 1939 to Poland, into the *Generalgouvernement*. This, for the next two years, marked the end of territorial changes begun by the Ribbentrop-Molotov treaty, which some historians call the Fourth Partition of Poland.

During their occupation of eastern Poland in 1941–1943, the German authorities did not consider it as part of Poland. Whenever they were forced to do so, they preferred to deal with the local nationalities—the Ukrainians, Belorussians, and Lithuanians—whom they considered more pliant and willing to collaborate than the Poles, who attempted to assert their rights in the territories by supporting armed resistance against the Germans. However, it was generally assumed that the Riga Peace Treaty of 1921, which fixed the Polish-Soviet frontier between the wars, was dead. It was to be replaced by a combination of the Ribbentrop-Molotov Line and the so-called Curzon Line, which the British Foreign Secretary suggested at the height of the Polish-Soviet war in 1920. The final border line between Poland and the USSR as well as the compensation Poland was to receive for the loss of its territory to the Soviet Union were to be worked out later by the Big Three.

Poland and the Great Powers

Following the debacle of September 1939, the Polish government crossed the border into Romania in the hope of moving to France and continuing the anti-German struggle. It expected help from Britain and France, which had not only provided the famous guarantee to Poland only a few months earlier in April 1939, but had also assumed additional treaty obligations to the Warsaw government. However, that government was forced to resign and was replaced by a new government-in-exile, headed by General Wladyslaw Sikorski (1881–1943), a well-known prewar political and military leader and a staunch opponent of the Pilsudski regime. The government, which moved to England after the French defeat in June 1940, was ultimately recognized by Britain and the United States as the legitimate government of Poland.

Between 1939 and 1941, the Sikorski government enjoyed great popularity in England as the only British ally. The day after the German invasion of the Soviet Union, things began to change in a dramatic fashion against Poland's favor. The process of selling Poland to the USSR took roughly four years and culminated in July 1945 in the transfer of diplomatic recognition from the exile government in London to the communist-dominated government in Warsaw.

Even though Poland emerged as the victim, according to Winston Churchill, the resolution of the various Polish issues at the Yalta conference took up more time than any other issue discussed by the Big Three.[8]

The two main questions that proved particularly time-consuming were the future Polish borders and the composition of the government. Although there was a basic consensus regarding Poland's eastern boundary with the Soviet Union, the future delineation of the Polish-German frontier along the Oder-Neisse line was only tentatively agreed upon at Potsdam, pending the signing of a peace treaty. On paper Poland appeared a clear winner: it gave up territories that were not only economically backward but also largely inhabited by minorities hostile to an independent Poland, and it gained areas that were economically considerably ahead of even the advanced provinces of Poland. To be sure, the "Recovered Provinces" were inhabited by hostile Germans but Poland received carte blanche at Potsdam to deport them to the west. This freed housing and jobs for the Poles who as part of a Soviet-Polish agreement were repatriated to Poland from western Ukraine and western Belorussia. Thus, despite the calamitous human and material destruction caused by the war, the territorial decisions managed to introduce an element of optimism with regard to the country's future.

Poland Under Communist Rule: 1945–1989

As a result of the havoc and dislocation caused by the war, Poland in the spring of 1945 resembled a country which once again was forced to embark on the painful process of political and economic development. In this respect there were some striking similarities between the Poland of November 1918 and that of May 1945.

Developmental Issues

Nation-Building

The one developmental challenge that postwar Poland was spared, in contrast to several other Eastern European countries, was that of nation-building. While the process in Poland had not been successfully achieved in the interwar period and the problem of hostile national minorities prevented the establishment of full national integration, the country emerged from the disasters of World War II as a nearly homogeneous nation-state. The Nazi mass genocide of the Jews, the expulsion of the Germans from the newly acquired territories in the west, and the annexation of Poland's eastern provinces by the Soviet Union resulted in Poland becoming ethnically and religiously quite homogeneous, probably for the first time in its long history.

There is no doubt that this had a considerable impact on postwar developments. The major beneficiaries appeared to be the country's new communist rulers, who did not have to deal with the kinds of ethnic and national conflicts that characterized political processes in Yugoslavia, Czechoslovakia, Romania, and even Bulgaria, all of which carried a heavy burden of substantial minorities from the pre-communist period.

The process of national integration was further strengthened by the mass dislocations and migrations during and immediately after the war, all of which went a long way toward reducing the strong regional antagonisms that had characterized prewar Poland. As pointed out earlier, these were the result of differences caused by more than 120 years of Russian, German, and Austrian rule.

It was only toward the end of communist rule in the late 1980s that it became evident that the rosy picture of an ethnically pure Poland was not quite true. As part of the negotiations between Poland and West Germany, it turned out that despite official Polish assurances that there were no more ethnic Germans left in Poland, several hundred thousand were suddenly discovered to be living in Silesia. Most of them left for the Federal Republic during the 1980s, and as of 1990 it was estimated that no more than 250,000 mostly elderly Germans were still residing in Poland.

This rather embarrassing disclosure had its roots in the policies of the Communists of the late 1940s who, after sending most of the Germans westward, proclaimed those who remained to be "autochthons" or simply Germanized Poles; it took these Germans more than forty years to assert their true national identity.

A similar policy, with minor variations, was applied to other minorities, and here again, it took four decades and the downfall of the communist regime for the truth to come out. The present government of Poland has formally acknowledged the existence of national minorities and some initial, rather modest, measures have been introduced to provide some visible recognition to national pluralism. Still, as compared to the pre-1939 period, there is no real minority problem in Poland.

State-Building

After the war the process of state-building can be identified with the Communist seizure of power that took place in the period 1944–1948. The takeover in Poland did not differ significantly from that in some of the other Eastern European countries and, as aptly described by Zbigniew Brzezinski, it represented a synthesis of certain socioeconomic reforms and a fairly substantial degree of Soviet-sponsored terror and violence.[9]

There were two features of the Communist takeover of Poland whose impact still affects political developments in that country today, more than forty-five years after the fact. The first was a comprehensive land reform begun in 1944, which initially succeeded in politically neutralizing the peasants (who at that time still represented about two-thirds of the country's population); over time, the land reforms worked to strengthen the peasant class, which subsequently became a major thorn in the Communists' side.

The other special feature was the issue of Poland's border with East Germany along the Oder-Neisse line and the incorporation and settlement of the former German provinces of Pomerania, Silesia, and East Prussia, with which the new Communist rulers strongly identified themselves. The need to uphold the incorporation of the newly acquired areas, the status of which remained uncertain until most recently, united both friends and foes of the Communist regime and also made the process of state-building somewhat easier, since the incoming Communists presented themselves as defenders of Poland's national interest and integrity.

It may be said that the process of Stalinization (1948–1953) that followed the seizure of power was simply a continuation of the process of state-building whereby the Communists tried to penetrate Polish society and to establish total control over it. Here again, the various stages and methods in the gradual imposition of Soviet political, economic, and societal models followed the customary path and did not differ greatly from the policies pursued by other countries in the region.

However, as in the case of the takeover process, there were some interesting deviations from the model that were to have major repercussions. One of these was the relative absence of the high degree of terror and mass violence that accompanied the Sovietization process in Bulgaria, Czechoslovakia, and Hungary. While all resistance to Stalinization was brutally suppressed, the various purges of the party and society at large claimed relatively few victims. An overwhelming majority of those who suffered persecution and imprisonment survived and reappeared after Stalin's death and played a major role in the country's affairs in the late 1950s and afterward.

The first major challenge to the legitimacy of the system took place in 1956. The failure of the Communist party fully to penetrate Polish society—a major contributory factor in the crisis—represented a deepening of the socioeconomic crisis within the country, the growing gap between the rulers and the ruled—the peasants, the workers, and the intelligentsia, and the availability of alternative leadership. It so happened that Poland and Hungary were much more affected by the above factors than was the rest of Eastern Europe. Both went through major upheavals in the fall of 1956: a bloody revolt in Hungary and a bloodless changeover in Poland. The latter brought Wladyslaw Gomulka to power and was accompanied by a series of political and economic changes, among which the collapse of agricultural collectivization and emancipation of the Catholic church were by far the most significant. Gomulka, one of the chief engineers of the postwar Communist takeover, had fallen victim to the Stalinist purges and his elevation to the leadership represented a major break with the past. Although the double crisis of penetration and legitimacy did not last long, it was clear that Poland's politics would never be the same and that the sharp challenge to the seemingly impregnable system would continue to echo.

The next twenty-five years witnessed a generally unsuccessful attempt at what may be called "system maintenance," "consolidation," or "business as usual." The regime's efforts to acquire legitimacy failed on several occasions, most signally in March 1968 when university students and intellectuals rose up in protest against increasingly restrictive government censorship and cultural policies. In December 1970, workers on the Baltic coast rioted in protest against a drastic increase in retail prices and succeeded in bringing down the Gomulka regime. In June 1976, a similar, ill-considered price increase caused rioting in several industrial cities. All these represented major crises of legitimacy and penetration, which simply laid the basis for what was to follow in the 1980s.

Political Participation

The crisis of participation did not occur in Poland until the mid-1950s. Beginning with the October 1956 upheaval, the Polish regime attempted to expand the scope of popular participation at various levels but progress was rather modest. It may be argued that the crises of December 1970 and June 1976 represented not only crises of legitimacy and penetration but also a crisis of participation. In this respect they illustrated rather well the syndrome of mass politicization leading first to social frustration and ultimately to political instability, in the absence of channels for meaningful participation.[10]

It may be argued, however, that in Poland throughout most of the postwar period, the frustration, anomie, and alienation from the system were related more closely to the questions of economic welfare than to participation. In other words, economic demands tended to take precedence over political desiderata. While both factors probably merged in the first systemic crisis of October 1956, there is little doubt that economic grievances were primarily responsible for the challenges to the communist regime in December 1970 and June 1976.

A good case can be made for asserting that the worst crisis of participation in the postwar period occurred in the summer of 1980. It culminated in the formation of "Solidarity" (*Solidarnozc*) and, ultimately, the collapse of Communist rule some ten years later. The difference between the previous crises and the one in 1980 was the fact that neither in 1970 nor in 1976 was there a resultant radical change in the relationship between the rulers and the ruled. To be sure, the Workers Defense Committee (known by its Polish acronym, KOR) was organized in the summer of 1976 to assist and represent the repressed workers, yet even KOR could not do much. It was not until the birth of Solidarity, the "independent and self-governing" labor union, recognized as such by the regime, that the Polish masses finally gained an authentic voice to articulate their interests and participate as an equal in negotiations with the Communist regime. For the first time in the history of international communism the Leninist conception of the ruling party, based on its hegemony and total monopoly of power, was successfully challenged. From then on it was only a matter of time before the entire communist system would give way to the opposition.

The Solidarity trade union managed to operate alongside the government for about eighteen months (August 1980–December 1981) but, following the imposition of martial law, it was eventually outlawed. However, as the economic situation in Poland continued deteriorating and when in 1988 two separate waves of strikes threatened the stability of the country, Solidarity was revived and persuaded to intervene with the striking workers. The price of the successful intervention was the government's agreement to initiate the so-called round table negotiations between the Communist regime and the opposition. The talks began in February 1989 and ended with a joint declaration published in April of that year.

Although there were several important aspects of the Round Table declaration, undoubtedly one of the crucial ones was the decision to introduce a new electoral law to govern the parliamentary elections scheduled for June 1989. The law made it clear that the elections, for the first time since the communist takeover of Eastern Europe, would allocate in advance a rather significant percentage of seats in the Sejm to the anticommunist opposition. Today, following the elections held in East Germany, Hungary, and Czechoslovakia, in which the local communists were invariably soundly beaten, the Polish electoral model may hardly appear revolutionary: one must remember, however, that at the time it was approved, all of the above countries were still ruled rather tightly by their respective communist parties, and that the Polish electoral experiment, tame as it may appear today, clearly served as a trigger to the reforms in the other states.

The importance attached to the new electoral law reflected the anger and frustration with the long passivity of the Sejm, which had failed dismally as an outlet for popular participation. In the early postwar period, the incoming Communists tried to make an allowance for the strong Polish attachment to the idea of political participation. They staged a popular referendum in 1946, where one of the questions dealt with the abolition of the Senate, and then in January 1947, held parliamentary elections. Although it has now been officially admitted that the results of both were rigged, the Sejm elected in 1947 contained some opposition deputies. In 1952 a new Stalinist constitution was approved for Poland which, despite some amendments and revisions, continues to be valid at the time of writing. The record of the past thirty-odd years shows that of all the various institutions in Poland, the Sejm's performance was most disappointing. Each time there was a crisis in the country, the leaders of the Sejm promised to assume the leadership in the liberalization process, and yet they failed every time, including even the Solidarity period when the parliament faithfully obeyed the government.

Therefore, it is not surprising that the new electoral law and the subsequent elections caused much excitement in Poland. The Polish electorate, prevented for more than fifty years from participating in a meaningful way in political decision making, was now given its chance. As will be shown below, it took advantage of it with a vengeance.

Economic Conditions and Policies

The communist takeover was accompanied in Poland as elsewhere in Eastern Europe by two sets of radical reforms—land reform and the nationalization of industry. Land reform was long overdue and warmly welcomed by the peasants. The nationalization of industry was clearly more controversial than land reform, but in this case the internal opposition was weak. With Jewish factory owners victims of the Holocaust and foreign capitalists absent, homegrown capitalists were simply not strong enough to put up a fight. Thus, one may argue that both reforms enjoyed considerable support among both the government and the masses, a rather unique event in the history of postwar Poland.

The importation of the Stalinist model into Poland was followed, as in the rest of the region, by the imposition of agricultural collectivization and central planning in the nonfarm sectors. Poland fell considerably short of fulfilling the so-called Six-Year Plan (1949–1955) designed to lay the foundations for socialism. Perhaps it was this failure that persuaded Gomulka, who returned to power in October 1956, to allow the mass dissolution of collective farms and to consider, for the first time in the Soviet bloc, the possibility of major economic reforms.

Despite the seemingly propitious proreform atmosphere, none of the optimistic plans were fulfilled. The private farm sector, ostensibly free, in fact enjoyed less autonomy than the cooperative sector in Hungary: although the land was again in private hands, the entire agricultural infrastructure remained under state control, leaving private farmers essentially impotent and totally dependent on the often arbitrary and capricious policies of the government. To a large extent, this situation has continued until today.

Although the worst excesses of central planning were modified after 1956, no real economic reform took place. It soon became obvious that whatever he was, Gomulka was not an economic reformer, and the decade of the 1960s provided an excellent illustration of his limitations. While other countries in Eastern Europe—Czechoslovakia, East Germany, and Hungary—took Poland's example and embarked on economic reform, Gomulka stuck to a traditional, largely orthodox path. As a result Poland's economy stagnated and slow growth finally forced Gomulka to implement some reforms. The infamous reform of retail prices in December 1970 was part and parcel of that decision.

The replacement of Gomulka by Edward Gierek in December 1970 seemed to inaugurate a new era in Polish history. For the first few years these predictions appeared to be largely validated. The country's stagnating economy entered a period of rapid growth, stimulated mostly by massive injections of Western credits and technology, and simultaneously, the Polish peasants, finally freed of the heavy burden of compulsory farm deliveries, responded by sharply expanding their output.

The most important achievement of the Gierek regime was the

development of a new model for Poland's economic development. This was based on an extensive modernization of the country's industrial structure with the aid of the West. Although the new strategy proved highly successful in stimulating rapid economic growth, it also overheated the economy and added to already existing inflationary pressure. Shortages began to occur when the price level of key foodstuffs remained frozen following the rollback of January 1971. Gierek finally decided to raise these prices in June 1976. Although on its economic merits the decision was eminently rational, its implementation and timing were disastrous. This suggested that the Polish leadership was ignorant of popular attitudes, a rather striking fact in view of its earlier concern to gain legitimacy and acceptance.

By rapidly expanding Poland's economic relations with the West, Gierek quickly succeeded in making Poland one of the fastest-growing countries in the world in the first half of the 1970s. The apparent success of this policy, however, had several negative consequences. It made economic reform less pressing: the importation of Western know-how and technology was seen as a substitute for reform. Second, the improvement in living standards welcomed by the Polish masses not only delayed political reforms but also tightened Communist controls on society. Finally, the ultimate cost of economic improvement proved prohibitive as Poland's balance of payments deficit and hard currency debt at the end of the 1970s soared to unprecedented heights.

Whether it saw itself as such when it emerged at the end of August 1980, Solidarity was above all a political movement. But what about its economic ideas? One could easily imagine that since the new movement arose at least partly in protest against the deteriorating economic situation, its leaders would, sooner or later, turn their attention to reforming the faltering economy, but there was a strong possibility that amidst the euphoria generated by the largely unexpected victory of the workers, little time would be devoted to economic reforms. The example of Czechoslovakia in the spring of 1968 was a case in point: Dubček and others were so busy attending to political matters that the Czechoslovak economic reforms, after a highly promising start in the mid-1960s, were simply ignored by the political leaders. That this was likely to be repeated in Poland was well illustrated by a highly publicized 1980 interview with Lech Walesa and his associates who, when asked about their attitude toward economic reforms, showed little interest in them and disclaimed responsibility for their initiation and progress.[11]

This lukewarm stance vis-à-vis economic reforms proved to be characteristic of Solidarity's marginal interest in drastically reforming the economy. Only toward the end of 1981 was there some revival of concern for economic improvement, but by that time it was simply too late. Its rather cavalier attitude toward the worsening economic situation hurt Solidarity and tarnished its image. On the eve of the imposition of martial law in December 1981, "a curse on both your houses" best expressed the disenchantment of the Polish population with both the government's and Solidarity's neglect of the economy.

Although the military junta was too preoccupied with running the country to give much thought to economic reforms, some of its policies helped improve the economic situation. This involved a series of drastic price reforms in the direction of greater rationalization of the retail price structure. In the past, all attempts at reforming prices had ended with the new prices rolled back as a result of popular protests. This time, protected by martial law, prices were adjusted upward without much public reaction.

Agriculture also prospered under martial law and contributed significantly to an improvement in the balance of payments. There is little doubt that the increase in farm output was helped by the attitude of the military regime which, initially at least, appeared sympathetic to peasant concerns. The policy of Western economic sanctions against Poland also helped to reduce imports, thus benefiting the overall balance of trade.

All these were short-term improvements and did not affect the core of the economic system. Beginning in the mid-1980s, the economy once again entered a downward spiral, causing new mass dissatisfaction. A series of political concessions granted by the Communist regime did not help. Various policies—aimed at reducing inflation, introducing a market mechanism, and raising living standards—came to nothing. The same applied to another highly publicized attempt at economic reform, this time based on the apparently successful Hungarian New Economic Mechanism. Popular anger was escalating and, as mentioned earlier, on two separate occasions—in the spring and late summer of 1988—culminated in a series of strikes in some of the key industrial areas of the country. The result was the round table negotiations.

The greatest interest in Poland and abroad was focused on the "political table," which tended to overshadow all the other "tables" or negotiations. The economic talks brought together top specialists from the Communist party and Solidarity who produced a statement that did not fully satisfy either side. It may be hypothesized that faced with a catastrophic and worsening economic situation, the negotiators were primarily concerned with short-term solutions and stopping galloping inflation.

The introduction of a new, totally unprecedented economic model had to await the elections of June 1989 and the resulting formation of the first noncommunist government in forty-four years. Then and only then did it prove possible for the new rulers to overcome the resistance of the former communist oligarchy and its *apparat* and to push through parliament the highly ambitious model of the new economic system.

Now we will examine the above developments through the prism of the five systemic variables, defined at the outset of the chapter.

Systemic Issues

Culture [12]

Looking back at the post–World War II period, perhaps the most striking aspect of the cultural scene in Poland is the remarkable persistence of what may be termed "traditional" values, despite the massive socialization and indoctrination campaigns conducted by successive communist regimes. At the risk of oversimplification, the most relevant of these appear to be the basic distrust and disobedience of governmental authority, an emphasis on egalitarian values and equality, fervent nationalism, and attachment to certain historical institutions and structures.

Over the years Polish Communist leaders must have often been frustrated by their inability to lay foundations for a new political and social system, eyeing with envy the situation in other Eastern European countries where the obedient masses seemingly accepted and became reconciled to the new order. (It was Stalin who was quoted as saying during World War II that imposing communism on Poland was bound to be difficult and unproductive.)

There is no doubt that the deeply rooted mistrust and dislike of authority were largely responsible for the failure of the communist system to penetrate Polish society. It was suggested above that although antiauthoritarian attitudes go back several centuries, they acquired their modern expression during the partitions period, further reinforced by six years of German and Soviet occupation during World War II. The fact remains that throughout the entire postwar period the average Pole most likely considered the Communist regime to be essentially illegitimate and forcibly imposed from the outside.

Whether one chooses to call it attachment to freedom, rugged individualism, lack of discipline, or simply a proclivity to anarchy, the Polish people steadfastly refused to accept the communist system as legitimate. This was as true for the educated classes—traditionally the bastion of independent thought and action—as for the peasants and workers, assumed until recently to be much more malleable and obedient.[13]

The second cultural variable to influence the popular attitude toward communism was nationalism, traditionally a powerful force in Polish politics. Successive party leaders tried, with some measure of success, to utilize nationalist feelings for their own purposes by appearing as defenders of the country's national interests (as in the case of the Oder-Neisse line) or its ethnic purity (as in the case of the virulent anti-Semitic campaign of March 1968). On the other hand, the Communist party was unable to eradicate the traditional anti-Russian feeling that has permeated Polish society for generations and that attaches an indelible stigma to anything entering Poland from the East. With the West German threat to Polish western frontiers gone and few Jews remaining in the country, the Communist leadership was in no position to mobilize nationalist sentiments against real or imaginary enemies, unless it were the Soviet Union.

The final cultural component affecting the political process in the postwar period was the continued attachment to certain traditional political and social institutions, laws, and customs, be it family farms, the state constitution, or the Catholic church. Here a word should be said about the presumed religiosity of the Polish people. Conventional wisdom has long maintained that the Poles are strongly religious. This view is based on mostly anecdotal or impressionistic evidence, such as crowded churches, a homogeneous population, and a striking increase in the numerical strength of the clergy. If, indeed, the church is still popular in Poland today, it is much less because of its religious or spiritual role, and more because of its function as the bastion of independence from communist control. In the past the church enjoyed its greatest popularity at the height of communist persecution and lost support when church-state relations improved.

Structure

In many respects, the Polish Communist party did not differ greatly from its counterparts in the other satellite countries. Its membership until the 1980s accounted for roughly seven percent of the population and in terms of social composition, it typified a highly bureaucratized structure with the plurality of its membership being government officials and other white-collar workers.

Throughout its entire history the situation within the party must have given little cause for joy to its leaders. The near-permanent dissatisfaction with the system's performance, especially in the economic sphere, meant that the party, the self-proclaimed vanguard of Polish society with the task of leading the country to a better future, had not only failed to generate mass support for its policies but also had allowed a serious challenge to the system's legitimacy to develop almost overnight.

The fact that the Polish military seized power in December 1981 speaks for itself and testifies to the near collapse of the ruling party. Apparently, shortly after the imposition of martial law there was some discussion about dissolving the Polish Workers party and replacing it with a new party, purged of both the conservative and revisionist wings, for which there was a precedent in Hungary following the revolt of 1956.

What were the reasons for the malaise of the Polish party? Perhaps the major one was its failure to penetrate and become an integral part of Polish society. Throughout most of its history, quantity rather than quality was the chief determinant of recruitment into the party. Moreover, successive leaders never quite managed to define the proper role for the ruling party, except by making sure that even in the late 1980s *nomenklatura* still played a decisive role. As a result, decision making in general was left to those who tended to avoid the solution of the real problems confronting Polish society. Periodic calls for the reestablishment of "links with the masses" fell on deaf ears and the chasm between the ruling oligarchy and the masses continued to widen. This was clearly one of the major reasons for the series of blunders committed by successive Communist regimes.

Little need be said about the remaining Polish political parties—the United Peasant party and the Democratic party—which for all practical purposes amounted to little more than links from the ruling party to the peasants and white-collar workers. At times the parties acted as a kind of pressure group, but their influence on decision making was marginal, and they served mostly as window dressing.

Both the party and government bureaucracies resembled the traditional communist stereotypes, characterized by inherent conservatism, fear and distrust of innovations and reforms, and determination to defend the status quo. In particular, the party *apparat* tended to be opportunistic and careerist and its level of intellectual and professional sophistication left much to be desired. One of the major reasons why Poland lagged far behind its neighbors in implementing economic reforms was the resistance of the bureaucracy which successfully delayed and even sabotaged proposed reforms.

With respect to the legislative branch, as was pointed out earlier, early promises of greater parliamentary involvement in, and influence on, the political life of Poland never materialized. At regular intervals, party leaders kept promising to make the Sejm a focal point in the discussion of economic and social issues by granting it a greater role in consultations and decision making. However, little changed and the infrequent and brief plenary sessions of the Sejm continued mainly to serve the ritualistic purpose of rubber-stamping governmental decrees.

The political structures in Poland in the postwar period tended generally to conform to the Soviet model. As such, they often acted as a major obstacle on the road to modernization and development, and periodic attempts to transform them in the direction of greater efficiency usually failed in the face of bureaucratic opposition.

Groups

To a large extent, the growth of functionally specific interest or pressure groups in Poland followed the same path as elsewhere in Eastern Europe and was a by-product of rapid industrialization and increasing complexity and differentiation of the sociopolitical system. This ultimately forced the ruling Communist elite to seek advice from experts in various fields. Interestingly enough, in Poland, in contrast to some of the other states in the region, only relatively few groups were institutionalized and brought into the decision-making process. Most of the groups never developed a corporatist élan or image of their own, and seemed content with playing the role of traditional "transmission belts" between the rulers and the people.

The most prominent of these were the official labor unions that, even during relatively liberal periods, never quite abandoned their role of obedient tools of the party. Throughout, their record of defending workers' interests was most dismal and the fact that they played no part in the three major confrontations between the workers and the regime in December 1970, June 1976, and July–August 1980, speaks for itself. Hence, it is hardly surprising that the chief demand of the workers striking on the Baltic coast in the summer of 1980 was the establishment of an independent trade union that would articulate workers' interests in an authentic fashion. It is also not surprising that demands for restoration of the outlawed Solidarity continued to be articulated by the opposition throughout the 1980s until the request was granted in 1989 as part of the Round Table agreement.

In addition to Solidarity two other groups must be considered: the Catholic church and the military. The status and prestige of the church, high to begin with during most of the period after the war, received a powerful boost in 1978 with the election of a Polish pope, John Paul II. The pope paid a long-delayed pontifical visit to his native land in the summer of 1979—the first of three such sojourns—which was an overwhelming success for the church and represented a crucial step in the gradual increase in political opposition, culminating in the birth of Solidarity a year or so later.

No longer threatened by the Communist regime, the church in the 1980s moved away from defending its own institutional interests toward broader involvement in the country's political life. This was most likely due to the growing realization by the church that its ties with the Communist authorities since the early 1970s were resulting in an erosion of support among many segments of Polish society. It may also be possible that the growing church militancy represents a shift caused by the entry of a new generation of clergy into leading positions within the hierarchy. The old generation, personified by Cardinal Wyszynski, was primarily concerned with survival in the face of Stalinist pressures; later, these leaders became interested mostly in the preservation of the status quo which guaranteed the church a privileged and unique position in the system.

The younger clergymen at different levels of the hierarchy were becoming impatient with their elders' benign neglect of major political and social issues plaguing the country. Judging from its pronouncements at the various Vatican councils, the Polish church enjoys a rather conservative reputation abroad, which initially could have been justified by its situation at home. Nevertheless, some of the reforms decreed by the councils may have had an impact on the younger clergy who gradually became politically and socially more conscious than in the past. The next logical step was greater engagement in political activities.

There are some interesting comparisons and contrasts between the Polish military between the wars and in the post–World War II period. Just as in the interwar period one could distinguish three separate periods during which the military played various roles in the political system, one could say the same for the postwar period. The Polish army after 1945 had to take part in the formation of the state and, in the process, it became an obedient tool of the Polish Communist party. At the height of Stalinism its top leadership was heavily dominated by Soviet military officers, sent by the Kremlin to ensure absolute obedience and loyalty.

The first break in this pro-Moscow stance, which had made the military highly unpopular among the Polish people, came in October 1956. At that time the new leader, Gomulka, insisted on the departure of Soviet officers, including Marshal Constantin Rokossovsky, whom Stalin had dispatched in 1949 to take charge of the Polish armed forces. Throughout the Gomulka regime (1956–1970), the military tried hard to erase its unpopular image and, although partly success-ful, it still tended to identify itself rather closely with the communist establishment.

Another change in the status of the armed forces came as a result of Polish military participation in the Baltic coast riots. In hindsight, it is clear that neither the high command nor the rank and file of the military were comfortable with their new role as a police force, ordered to shoot at the striking workers. There is evidence that the then minister of defense, General Wojciech Jaruzelski, decided that the Polish army would never again be used to suppress the workers. Judging from the behavior of the military in June 1976, July–August 1980, and even December 1981, Jaruzelski kept his word.

It may be said that the military acted as a typical pressure group in the 1970s, although perhaps a better description of its role would be that of a veto group, suggesting that no important decision could be taken by the Communist party without consulting the military lead-ers. In the 1980s the military and the government were one-and-the-same, even after the suspension of martial law. In sharp contrast to the behavior of the military in the 1930s, which basically favored authoritarianism, the behavior of the military in the 1970s and 1980s essentially supported the idea of greater freedom and democracy. Certainly, in both 1988 and 1989, when the fate of democracy was at stake, the military under Jaruzelski was in a perfect position to turn things around and stop the process of democratization, yet chose not to intervene.

Leadership

As was the case with interwar Poland, the country was ruled between 1945 and 1989 by various individuals, none of whom fared well in retrospect.

Despite some attempts to exonerate and rehabilitate him, Boleslaw Bierut (1892–1956), who ruled Poland during the Stalinist period, must go down in history as essentially a mediocre leader. His major achievement was that he managed somehow to spare the country from the worst excesses of the mass political terror practiced in Bulgaria, Czechoslovakia, and Hungary. While this accomplishment was not unimportant, it was largely offset by his crude policy toward the peasants, the intelligentsia, and the remnants of the anticommunist opposition. Bierut's successor, Edward Ochab (1906–1989) personally picked by Nikita Khrushchev, was an interim leader whose tenure lasted barely six months. His greatest achievement, in turn, was to pave the way for Gomulka's return to power.

Wladyslaw Gomulka (1905–1982), who headed the Polish Communist party for roughly twenty years (1943–1948 and 1956–1970) was not a run-of-the-mill leader. For a brief period (1956–1957) he was the only legitimate national leader in postwar Polish history, at least until 1989. He was also a man of some principles, as illustrated by his behavior in the early postwar period when his convictions almost cost him his life. Yet, in hindsight, he was also a person of rather limited ability and narrow horizons, whose principles and convictions frequently turned into sheer obstinacy and irrational attachment to discredited concepts. There is a good chance that he will be remembered chiefly as the leader who took almost fifteen years to squander the great reservoir of credit and confidence granted him by the Polish people in October 1956, and who ended up as a bitter and humiliated man.

By all counts, Gomulka's successor, Edward Gierek (b. 1913), appeared to be a man for all seasons. Unencumbered by ideological baggage from the past, untainted by participation in the factional struggles between the "Muscovites" and the "natives," he possessed an impressive wartime resistance record in France. He was experienced as a party bureaucrat and famed for his efficient administration of Silesia, economically the most important Polish province. He seemed an ideal choice to lead the country from inertia and stagnation—inherited from Gomulka—toward a better future. In a few years, however, the laboriously constructed image of the pragmatic modernizer and efficient administrator became tarnished, and he lost credibility overnight.

Gierek's ouster in September 1980 was inevitable in light of the events in July and August 1980 and the creation of Solidarity. However, his replacement by Stanislaw Kania (b. 1927) simply reflected a dearth of suitable candidates. Kania, who was first secretary of the Central Committee from September 1980 until October 1981, was an experienced bureaucrat. He had been in charge at various times of the military, police, and church affairs. As it happened, he did reasonably well in negotiations with both Solidarity and his own critics within the party. His ouster was a surprise: it is possible that Kania was viewed as being too soft by the Kremlin, which wanted the Polish crisis terminated and was looking for someone willing to take extraordinary measures to do so.

Although Jaruzelski (b. 1923) was probably Moscow's choice, he also enjoyed considerable popularity as the first truly professional soldier commanding Poland's armed forces. He was known to be opposed to the use of the military for internal policing functions and his imposition of martial law in December 1981 can be interpreted as the result of a sincere belief that he and the military were saving Poland from catastrophe—either in the form of a bloody confrontation with an invading Red Army or in the shape of an equally bloody civil war.

During the period of martial law, Jaruzelski was likely the most hated person in Poland. However, as János Kádár of Hungary before him, Jaruzelski took advantage of his powerful position as party chief, prime minister and minister of defense, to start slowly rebuilding bridges to the Polish masses. Following the suspension of martial law, he freed most of the leaders of the anticommunist opposition, proclaimed a comprehensive amnesty, and ultimately agreed to the round table negotiations with Solidarity. It was Jaruzelski who on several occasions managed to cut through stalemated positions and thus saved the negotiations from collapse. There is little doubt that his contribution to the emergence of a democratic society in Poland has been invaluable.

Policies

In many cases, the different Polish governments after 1945 had an easier time than their prewar predecessors in initiating and implementing various policies. The Communist regimes in the post–World War II period did not have to worry about conducting a nation-building policy, as forces and factors beyond their control were responsible for the emergence of an ethnically quasi-homogeneous Poland.

The policy of state-building took a considerable time to be put through and it may be argued that although successful in its initial stages, it ultimately failed to firmly establish a communist political system in Poland. All anticommunist opposition was eliminated in the few years following the takeover but for various reasons the Polish population refused to accept the system. As suggested previously, failure by the system to provide adequate outlets and channels for political participation alienated many important segments of Polish society.

Over the years, most of the attention of successive governments was focused on the economy. Following a rapid recovery from the ravages of the war, the Communist regime was ordered by the Kremlin to start implementing the Stalinist economic model of collectivization and industrialization. That policy did succeed in laying the foundations for future economic growth and in transforming Poland from a rather backward, agrarian country into a mixed economy. The cost of the transformation was staggering. Yet even the Communists' staunchest critics must admit that considerable progress was made, telescoping several decades of development into a few years. For example, millions of young peasants were enticed into migrating to the cities and, partly as a result, the perennial deep gap between the cities and the countryside was narrowed significantly. Finally, the rapid pace of development generated a large demand for skilled labor, which became translated into high vertical mobility with young peasants and workers gaining access to higher education and joining the ranks of a new intelligentsia.

Unfortunately, Communist policymakers erroneously assumed that this policy could be continued indefinitely. As it turned out, these results began diminishing sooner than anyone had expected and the existing political and economic system was simply not prepared to deal with a declining rate of growth, reduced mobility, and slowly creeping stagnation. The Communist rulers tried to stem the tide of growing discontent, but they failed, and in the course of the 1980s they had to admit, albeit tacitly, that the communist system as a whole had outlived its usefulness and would have to be replaced by some other system.

Poland Since 1989

There was a good deal of uncertainty in Poland in April 1989, following the conclusion of the round table negotiations between the Communist government and the opposition, led by Solidarity. Although both sides fully realized that their agreement represented a historic watershed and that Poland's history would be indelibly altered, in the short run the shape of things to come was unclear.

The Communist ruling elite was well aware of the fact that it was taking a risk, yet the new electoral law that guaranteed the Communist party and its allies 65 percent of the seats in the Sejm seemed to ensure continuing Communist hegemony, despite the other constitutional changes, which included the rebirth of the Senate and of the office of the president of the republic. While the elections to the Senate were to be free and open to all parties, the Communists assumed that they would do reasonably well, even though they might not gain an absolute majority.

The results of the June 1989 elections astonished everyone. They resulted in a staggering victory for Solidarity and a blistering defeat for the ruling Communist party. It was only a matter of time before the long-standing Communist allies—the United Peasant party and the Democratic party—changed sides and joined Lech Walesa and Solidarity in establishing a parliamentary majority which left the Communists no choice but to agree to relinquish power for the first time in Poland since 1945. A new government took office in September 1989, headed by Tadeusz Mazowiecki, a veteran Solidarity activist. His cabinet was composed mostly of Solidarity members and also representatives of the two smaller parties. Communist party members headed the ministries of defense and of interior, in addition to two less important ministerial posts. In due course, also as part of the bargain, General Jaruzelski was elected president of Poland by an electoral assembly.

Many questions remain unanswered about the events of the spring and summer of 1989, and this is not the place to try to answer them. They are part and parcel of the whole series of astonishing and totally unexpected developments that seem to have been triggered by the Polish experiences, and which affected nearly all Eastern European states that until December 1989 were still ruled by the communists.

The ensuing year witnessed a number of critical changes in Poland's economic and political environment. First, there was the introduction on January 1, 1990, of a new economic model intended to introduce a competitive, free-market economic system. As of the time of this writing (May 1991) the results of this revolutionary measure appear mixed; everyone agrees, however, that more time is needed before conclusive results become available.

Another equally important policy is focused on the eradication of the forty-five-year legacy of communist rule. It means the introduction of the policy of privatization aimed at eliminating state ownership of the economy and at introducing private ownership, both foreign and domestic. It also includes the gradual replacement of communist *no-*

menklatura officials by individuals not tainted by affiliation with the former regime. Both policies have been only partly successful and are likely to take a long time: so far there have been few cases of successful privatization and the lack of qualified personnel makes the ouster of communist *apparatchiki* a rather slow process.

The country has witnessed a tremendous proliferation of political parties, clubs, and organizations of various hues: pluralism has arrived in Poland with a vengeance. As an example, as of July 1990 there were five peasant parties, two communist parties (which since January 1990 have been operating under the name of "Social Democrats"), and a slew of others. The Mazowiecki government made some changes in its composition, ousting the communist ministers of defense and interior and replacing them with Solidarity members. There was more and more talk about speeding up the parliamentary elections to be held prior to May 3, 1991, which had been set as the day for the approval of a new democratic constitution, on the two-hundredth anniversary of Poland's first democratic constitution of May 3, 1791.

The first truly free presidential election in Poland since 1922 took place in November 1990. In addition to Solidarity leader Walesa and Prime Minister Mazowiecki, four other candidates representing the political spectrum from left to right vied for the office. Surprisingly, although Walesa led the field with 40 percent of the popular vote, the second highest total of 23 percent was received by Stanislaw Tyminski, a political unknown from Canada, who succeeded in outpolling the incumbent Mazowiecki. In the runoff election at the beginning of December, Walesa swamped Tyminski by a margin of 3:1, thus becoming the first president of Poland elected by the people rather than by an electoral assembly.

This brief summary of events since June 1989 suggests that much has been accomplished in a short period of time. Looking ahead, there is no doubt that if there is a dark cloud on the bright Polish horizon, it is the economic situation. Even though the early results of the new policy seem to be positive, they are inconclusive and one cannot exclude the possibility that economic improvement could be too slow and meager to satisfy the impatient population, willing to grant the government a considerable measure of support on the condition that the dismal economic situation would change for the better. The worst-case scenario would include rioting workers once again forcing the government to resign, possibly to be replaced by a military junta similar to that of December 1981.

Is this a probable scenario? It is hard to say. The recent strikes by railroad workers and the blockades of highway and government offices by irate peasants, both settled at the last minute by the personal intervention of Walesa, do not augur too well for the future. Moreover, in the background looms a potentially destructive conflict within the leadership of Solidarity which could disrupt the fragile fabric of the new Polish democracy. In the absence of a common communist enemy, such a conflict was probably inevitable and is likely to result in a division of Solidarity into right and left factions that ultimately will become parties. As long as the process of political differentiation proceeds peacefully, it will be for the best and will reinforce the fledgling democracy. The lingering fear is that if the conflict takes a long time to be resolved and if the economic situation does not show visible improvement, the amazing achievements since 1989 will come to nothing.

NOTES

1. Gabriel A. Almond and G. Bingham Powell, Jr., *Comparative Politics* (Boston: Little, Brown, 1966), 35–7 and 306–10.

2. Samuel P. Huntington, "The Change to Change: Modernization, Development, and Politics," *Comparative Politics* (April 1971),2(3):320.

3. *Ibid.,* 316.

4. *Ibid.*

5. *Ibid.*

6. *Ibid.*

7. This is one translation of the phrase "urodlivye detishche Versalskogo dogovora," used by Foreign Commissar Molotov in his address to the Supreme Soviet on October 31, 1939. *Isvestia* (Moscow), November 1, 1939. Other options include "misshapen monster," or "monstrous bastard."

8. Winston S. Churchill, *Triumph and Tragedy* (Boston: Houghton Mifflin, 1953), 365.

9. Zbigniew Brzezinski, *The Soviet Bloc,* revised and enlarged ed. (Cambridge: Harvard University Press, 1967), 8–9.

10. Samuel P. Huntington, *Political Order in Changing Societies* (New Haven and London: Yale University Press, 1968), 55.

11. "Plan rozmowy ukladamy wspolnie," *Polityka* (Warsaw), no. 44, September 1, 1980.

12. An earlier discussion of this and the other systemic variables appeared in my "Poland" in Teresa Rakowska-Harmstone, ed., *Communism in Eastern Europe,* 2nd ed. (Bloomington: Indiana University Press, 1984), 63ff.

13. "Poland," 63.

7 The Multiple Legacies of History: Romania in the Year 1990

Trond Gilberg

Introduction

During the fateful autumn of 1989, Romania joined the rest of Eastern Europe in casting off the yoke of communist rule. That rule was particularly onerous and irrational in the case of Romania, and it was therefore only fitting that the process of its dismantling also be violent and sweeping in its manifestations. The speed with which the Romanian revolution was accomplished surprised many observers in the West. The thoroughness of the cleaning of Ceauşescu's Augean stables seemed to belie the seemingly monolithic and all-encompassing system established by the clan that ruled the country with an iron fist for a quarter of a century. The chaos, political back stabbing, and veto group activity now characterizing the Romanian scene stand in sharp contrast to the euphoria of togetherness, sacrifice, hope, and faith of the heady days in December when the dictatorship was brought to its knees. But these contrasting images of Romania are mutually intelligible in the context of history, political culture, and the structures of political power as well as the processes of exercising it. To understand the present in Romania, one must examine the past. To predict the future requires a journey into earlier decades in Romanian political history.

The Flawed Democracy: Romania at the Time of World War I

As Romania emerged in stages from Ottoman domination in the nineteenth century, it developed a political system with the trappings of a pluralistic political democracy, but without the traditions, values, or attitudes necessary to make such a system functional. Emerging from the corrupt, inefficient, and tyrannical rule of the Ottoman Turks and the Phanariot Greeks, the Romanians set about the task of constructing a political system that would reflect their new freedom. The trappings of parliamentarism were adopted; there were elections, a structure of representation based on those elections, and a mechanism for rotating political elites in and out of office. A number of political parties emerged, and a lively process of interest-group formation began. The press was unfettered and argued the views and programs of the various parties with gusto.[1] Outwardly, then, independent Romania resembled other political systems that had emerged from foreign rule and autocracy. But behind the facade there were many flaws that carried the potential for systemic disintegration or subversion by those who wished to destroy it. This would later produce rule by the monarch, by military dictatorship, by the Iron Guard, and, finally, by a fascist autocracy which lasted until the establishment of another authoritarian regime, that of the Communist party. It behooves us to examine the origins of disintegration and the potential for their reappearance in Romania in the present.

The Lack of Noblesse Oblige

The Romanian people had always known that foreign rule was rapacious, with little regard for the welfare of the peasants and their families. Any notion that their own leaders would be more solicitous of the average person was soon dispelled by the *boyars* and other notables who emerged on the scene after independence. These individuals fashioned a political structure to fit their needs and their quest for aggrandizement. They utilized the political order to enhance their own interests while blocking others. The corrupt practices that developed as a result expanded the gap between ruler and ruled and established the image that politics is a dirty game not worthy of one's time, respect, or even consideration if one wishes to remain an honest man. The responsibility of high position, which the French so aptly term *noblesse oblige,* never developed; instead, mutual distrust characterized the relationship between those inside the political power structure and those outside. Political power was traded, bought, and sold. Resources were squandered, and autocratic methods of policy implementation developed. The ruling elite behaved like locusts upon the land, using people and other precious resources to its own advantage. In such a political climate the formal trappings of pluralistic democracy mattered little. In fact, the difference between these formal structures and procedures and the reality of political life created much cynicism among the masses. Thus, when the time was right, "men on horseback" obtained the support of many among the masses who had become thoroughly disenchanted and cynical of the *Scheindemokratie* (mock democracy) that was Romania before World War I.[2]

The lack of noblesse oblige was evident in many of the policies produced by the elites of the country, regardless of political color or ideology. During the 1920s, for example, elections were regularly "stolen" by the incumbents or "bought" by elements of the opposition. Either way, the policies that emerged were uniformly exploitative of the vast majority of the people, be they workers or peasants. The highly touted land reform of 1921 was flawed in its structure, so that the peasantry remained steeped in poverty as a result of the financial burdens of land redistribution.[3]

This level of poverty was readily discernible during the 1920s and 1930s if one carefully examined the official statistics. Life expectancy was low, infant mortality high, rural overpopulation resulted in low productivity per acre, and agricultural practices diminished the quality of the soil. Most of the peasantry remained illiterate and possessed only a very limited vision beyond the edge of their respective villages. In the cities the proletariat survived in miserable conditions; much of this proletariat was, in fact, a class of "peasant-workers" whose vision and attitudes remained that of the countryside, even if members of this class lived in the cities and performed industrial tasks.[4]

The higher strata of society, made up of absentee landlords and the urban high bourgeoisie, lived in relative luxury, exhibiting little concern for the unfortunate masses in the cities or on the land. This life of conspicuous consumption and even debauchery was deeply offensive to the masses and showed the chasm between the haves and the have-nots—a graphic example of a dramatic absence of noblesse oblige.[5]

Authoritarianism Among the Masses

The Romanian people had no experience with democratic forms and processes when they had these thrust upon them with the advent of independence. They did have experience of authoritarian (and at times brutal) rule, because much of Romanian history exhibited these characteristics. The man and woman in the street or in the village had only known power from above; their only participation in it was the avoidance of its manifestations such as the tax collector, the gendarme, and the army recruiter. There was no reason to expect such historical experiences to produce citizens suited to pluralist democracy. A functioning pluralist system must operate on the basis of compromise, of give and take, of acceptance of the rights and needs of others. Furthermore, the principle of the "loyal opposition" must be accepted; it is not treason to question the existing leadership or the programs of other participants, but rather a necessary process of decision making. Finally, democracies operate on the assumption that politics is a variable-sum game, not a zero-sum affliction. The peasants and workers of Romania, on the other hand, knew from experience that the latter game prevailed, in which they got the zero and "the others" the sum.

Authoritarianism and intolerance of other political participants were further enhanced by widespread anti-Semitism and various other religious and ethnic hatreds. While most of the Romanians were Eastern Orthodox, the Hungarians and Germans were Protestants or Catholics. The history of Romania showed that the Hungarians and Germans had been politically, economically, and educationally privileged for a considerable period of time; this caused resentment of these groups. All groups despised the Gypsies and discriminated against this sizeable element of the population. All these factors combined produced a high level of actual or potential intolerance and a considerable amount of hidden or overt authoritarianism.[6]

This authoritarianism manifested itself in various ways, and through a number of groups and movements. The Legion of the Archangel Michael gathered considerable support. It emphasized Orthodox religious belief and commitment, coupled with fervent rejection of the "sinful" ways of the city and many of the political leaders of the country. These were seen as selfish, uncaring, and bent upon personal enrichment, without the requisite concern for the people. As is so often the case, this movement utilized existing and proper grievances to establish its own following in which basic intolerance of others and of divergent views was justified in the name of a worthwhile cause. The same can be said about the Iron Guard movement, which combined within it the most authoritarian tendencies of the peasantry, the intolerance of the religious true believer, and the jealousies and hatreds of the urban *lumpenproletariat*. Together, these movements (and others like them) propelled Romania into regal dictatorship and, ultimately, the rule of fascist terror.[7]

An Exploitative and Inefficient Economic System

Political deficiencies can at times be overcome by superior economic performance. An economically satisfied peasantry is not likely to produce jacqueries, and a well-to-do working class probably will not man barricades in the streets. But the Romanian economic system was underdeveloped and inefficient in the extreme, producing great riches for the few and poverty, famine, high infant mortality and low life expectancy for the many. Much of the land was held by absentee landlords and the church; little was farmed by the family farmer. Production was extensive, based on relatively low yield on large estates, rather than intensive production per acre. Millions of peasants lived in abject poverty and in subjugation to the landlord. The forces of law and order, representing the political system, were utilized to perpetuate, even strengthen, this exploitative system. The confluence of political and economic power was exercised upon the miserable masses, further widening the chasm between ruler and ruled.[8] Under these circumstances one can surely understand the elemental anger and desperation that developed among the peasants and also the jacquerie that resulted from it in 1907.

The inequities of the system have been described in considerable detail by a number of authors, one of whom was R. W. Seton Watson. Professor Watson's study showed the political ramifications of such a system:

> The revolt broke out with remarkable suddenness on 15 March 1907 near Botosani, and soon spread all over Moldavia. In the first instance there was plundering of Jewish houses, but it soon assumed a definitely agrarian, rather than anti-semite, character and was directed against the large tenant farmers and absentee landlords. The troops were called out and engaged with the rioters near Jassy itself, but as the movement spread southwards they were outnumbered near Vaslui, and had to beat a retreat. The political situation was obscure, owing to the sudden death of the foreign minister, General Lahovary, on the first day of the outbreak, and owing to dissensions between the premier and Take Ionescu. Finding himself unequal to the task of restoring order, Cantacuzene resigned on 25 March, and the king summoned the Liberals under Sturdza, with Ionel Bratianu in charge of the Interior, and with Haret and Stelian as ministers of Education and Justice. Peter Carp spoke in the Chamber in favour of strong measures of repression, and

two days later the new minister of War, General Averescu—a staff officer of high promise, trained in the Italian school—proclaimed a state of siege in Bucarest itself. Still the disorders continued. Bands of peasants invaded Galat, demanding the division of the great estates, and 4000 others from Teleorman began to march upon the capital. There was a fresh crop of pogroms, and wholesale systematic destruction of property. The Brancoveanu estates in Oltenia, those of Stirbei, Pherekyde, Florescu and Arion suffered especially severely. The revolt spread westwards into Wallachia and then up into the mountains. There were signs of anarchist organisation, subversive manifestos passed from hand to hand, and rumours of King Charles's death were put abroad. By the beginning of April 120,000 troops were under arms, the banks were everywhere guarded, a cordon was drawn around Bucarest itself, and the parliamentary session was closed, after Sturdza had made an appeal for urgent legislation and had shaken hands dramatically with Take Ionescu as leader of the Opposition, on the floor of the House. A royal proclamation promised the abolition of middlemen on the state lands, an uniform system of valuation, the restriction of agricultural leases to a maximum of 8000 acres and the extension of small holdings.[9]

The system had developed no mechanism to deal with such public outrage, and it responded predictably, by violent suppression. But the great uprising of 1907 showed that even a quiescent people will rise up when conditions have become intolerable and the spark of anger is present. That lesson was forgotten and forcefully restored at another time.[10]

A Penchant for Direct and Dramatic Solutions

In a political culture such as the one discussed above, "direct" solutions to problems of all kinds found a fertile ground among the masses and many societal elites alike. (Direct solutions, I take it, propose easy and sweeping remedies for complex problems; "getting rid of the Jews" would, presumably, improve economic conditions for everyone else, while "throwing out the bastard politicians" in favor of a strongman would produce order and justice.) Direct solutions by definition cannot solve problems that are soluble only in part; instead, such an approach is likely to reduce the likelihood of *any* success at problem-solving, and will most likely establish a whole new set of crises, equally insoluble. The main point here is that this penchant made parliamentary democracy very difficult to maintain while it set the stage for various authoritarian movements and caudillos who proclaimed their ability to deal with the situation dramatically and forcefully. Patience, piecemeal approaches, and the willingness to accept less than everything are crucial ingredients in all functioning pluralistic democracies. These were sorely missing in Romania around World War I.[11]

The reasons for this crucial deficiency were many and varied, but the behavior of the political elite itself certainly represented one of the most important. Political parties were concerned with narrow goals and the maximization of power and influence for the short run; a grand vision for the larger society was sorely missing. The capture and maintenance of power was considered a game, in which coalitions were made and unmade with astonishing rapidity. As described by one of the foremost of modern Romanian historians:

> The stability of the government and, in general, the consolidation of the political power of the bourgeoisie did not exclude the fragmentation and regrouping of the political forces in Romania in the years 1922–1928. A powerful regrouping of the political organizations of the bourgeoisie occurred through the merger of the Transylvanian National Party, whose main leaders were I. Maniu and Alexandru Vaida-Voevod, with the Peasants' Party, whose leader was Ion Mihalache, (thus) establishing the National Peasants' Party (October 1926), the most important opposition party to the liberal government. . . . Parallel to the union and dismantling of various parties in (this system of) bourgeois democracy, there appeared in these years in the political life of Romania also organizations of the extreme right, for example, "The Christian League of National Defense," a fascist organization, which, by the assistance of internal reaction and external fascist circles, developed rapidly. Not one of these parties succeeded in the years 1922–1928 in creating a mass base, because their programs represented control over the people and the strangulation of rights and freedoms of democracy.[12]

A Legacy of Corrupt Bureaucracies and Public Schlamperei

Most serious students of Romanian history point to the pervasive corruption of public officials, be they Ottoman, Phanariot Greek, or Romanian. This was, indeed, a prevailing characteristic of bureaucratic behavior, in part reflective of the lack of noblesse oblige discussed above. But it also represented something more widespread in the Romanian population, namely, a tendency to treat public goods, public trust, even public property with little regard, at times merely as an extension of personal interest. It is certainly understandable that people who lived with abuses of that public trust every day should despise the greedy representatives thereof, and that the concept of a public domain would suffer from such conditions. Civic pride, focused on the national level, was missing; instead, Romanians tended to focus on the immediate community of family, friends, perhaps the village and the local church. National symbols served as guides to action only in opposition to another nation, or another religion.

This tendency was vividly illustrated by the events at Alba Iulia in 1918, in which Transylvania was joined to Moldavia and Wallachia to establish (or reestablish, as some would have it) "Greater Romania" or "Historic Romania." There was indeed a genuine feeling of national fulfillment at that time, in part because of enthusiasm for the nation as such, and partly because of a common sense of animosity against Magyar rule. But this dramatic event failed to bridge the many gaps and fissures of Romanian society and polity. In a few months after Alba Iulia, the squabbling of the politicians had resumed, and the haves treated the have-nots as another nation, to be exploited, and not as part of a "greater Romania." Thus, a lasting civic spirit again failed to develop, with disastrous consequences.[13]

The Legacies Become Realities: Romania Between Corrupt Democracy and Communist Rule

The characteristics of the Romanian political and socioeconomic order discussed above combined during the 1920s and 1930s to render the political system impotent, thereby paving the way for other forms and other systems. By the time these tendencies had played themselves out, Romania was no longer a democracy, however flawed, but rather a full-fledged and brutal dictatorship that could only be unseated by other, more brutal, more efficient, authoritarians.

The corruption of the politicians and bureaucrats, and their obvious lack of public virtue, produced powerful feelings of resentment in the population. This resentment focused both upon the individuals responsible and the system per se; after all, it was argued, a system that produced such flawed leaders must itself be flawed. This kind of reasoning, combined with the tendencies toward authoritarianism and sectarian hatreds discussed above, paved the way for numerous movements and leaders who claimed to speak for the downtrodden masses, representing their interests as well as the interests of the nation itself. Indeed, these groups claimed to fuse all elements of society together into one powerful nation, united under God and the leader for the benefit of the whole as well as all of the parts. This was an expression of the idea of the general will, so eloquently enunciated by Rousseau and his disciples; the only difference was the crudity with which the self-proclaimed leaders of the people shouted their messages to the Romanian masses.[14]

The populist message had a powerful appeal for the peasants, because it made a complex entity (the political system) into an understandable whole (the ruler and the nation united). Furthermore, many of the populist messages combined God and nation—a powerful argument with the deeply religious Romanian masses. This message was further enhanced by the fact that Orthodoxy traditionally subordinated itself to secular authority in political matters; populist leaders could therefore argue that they were the representatives of God in the general population, and the religious hierarchy would find such an argument acceptable. The populists also made it clear that the people and the leader must unite against the squabbling politicians and the various middlemen who could be expected to enrich themselves at the expense of the simple peasants. The peasant workers, recent immigrants to the city who felt and thought like peasants despite doing industrial work, could also support the populists. The populist argument "made" the nation and the people one, just as the village and the people were one. This was clearly a most powerful argument.[15]

The populist program also appealed directly to the peasants, with a nationalistic ideology which stressed "Romanianness" over the alien elements of the other ethnic groups. It also emphasized traditional rural and peasant themes in politics, arts, and literature, and the notion of the pastoral good life which stood in sharp contrast to the alien and sinful ways of the city. The city was the home of many foreign elements, such as Jews and Armenians, whose life-style, religion, and values clashed visibly with those of the predominantly rural Romanians. There has always been a powerful attachment to the fields, forests, and mountains in the Romanian psyche, while the culture of the city was perceived as the realm of foreigners, sinners, and infidels. The populists played upon this predilection with great skill and determination.

The populists, while professing to speak for the people, also represented authoritarianism. The overt disdain in which the populist leaders held the squabbling and rapacious politicians fitted in with the actual behavior of these individuals and groups and helped solidify the images already in existence. This powerful interaction was one of the most important factors in the successes of the populists and their organizations.[16]

286 · TROND GILBERG

The various movements that represented Romanian populism had a number of these characteristics in common; other aspects were specific to each group. Gradually, the Legionnaire movement and the Iron Guard became the most important of these groups, and they came to dominate much of political and cultural life in interwar Romania, particularly in the 1930s. The populist message, coupled with overt and covert terms and the skillful exploitation of mass tendencies towards violence, frightened and cowed most of those who stood for alternative methods of rule. In a few cases, prominent individuals objected to these trends and attempted to persuade their fellow citizens that the path upon which Romania found itself would be disastrous. The renowned academic Professor Nicolae Iorga strongly criticized the rise of fascism and extremism in Romanian life. See, for example, Alexandru Porteanu in *Istoria Romaniei*:

> Romanian cultural figures, on the whole, advocated a democratic path; many figures of literature, science, and the arts (Sadoveanu, Arghezi, Rebreanu, Iorga, Enescu, Parhon, Titulescu, Traian Savulescu and others) fought systematically for the principles of democracy, progress, and peace. Only the lesser intellectuals, subordinated to the pressures of internal and external reaction, became exponents of these views in cultural and scientific life, but suffered an immediate rebuff of the public.[17]

Iorga became one of the main opponents of authoritarian rule in the troubled decade of the 1930s. He paid for this with his life; members of the Iron Guard murdered him.[18]

While the authoritarians and populists shared a disdain for the existing political system and a commitment to its destruction, their programs differed considerably. Significant elements of the populist groups were dedicated to an agrarian society, but the fascists looked to the corporatist notions of Mussolini and Hitler for their inspiration. The king had his own political ambitions, as he exhibited by his coup in 1938.

The royal dictatorship contained elements of old-fashioned conservatism and paternalism, mixed up with populist and fascist notions; this admixture dealt the fledgling democracy of Romania a mortal blow before the onset of World War II.[19]

By contrast, the extremists of the left were insignificant in the political system of the interwar period. There were small groups of anarchists and syndicalists, as could be expected in a political culture strongly influenced by other Latin European countries, but these coteries of true believers amounted to very little in the context of the political order and the major developmental trends. The same can be said for the Communist party, despite the valiant (and hollow) efforts by communist historians and rulers to "prove" otherwise. The communists of Romania were mostly Jewish or Bulgarian; they had a few pockets of mass support, such as in the railway workers' organizations, but little else; their stance on issues of great importance, such as nationalism, religion, and the question of "greater Romania" in territorial terms only inspired disdain and outright rejection by most of the population, particularly the peasantry. This lack of mass support continued to haunt the communists until the fall of the Ceauşescus. Their constant talk about the "organic unity" of the leader and the people was nothing but fabricated nonsense. But the authoritarian nature of rule from above, exemplified by Romanian communism, was a natural outgrowth of the endemic political attitudes discussed previously.[20]

A direct outgrowth of the notion of unity between the leader and the people, without intermediaries, was the tendency toward mass rule, occasional pogroms, and eventual systematic political terror. The masses, living under harsh political and socioeconomic conditions, with the experience of power exercised directly upon them, could easily be mobilized for direct action against real or perceived enemies. Direct action fitted well into the collective psyche of the illiterate peasants who had little understanding of, or patience with, political procedures and the niceties of rules and regulations. The enemy was there for all to see: the bureaucrat, the city-dweller, the "foreigner," the member of a different religion, the cosmopolitan, the money lender. Increasingly, such direct action (or its threat) became a major factor in the political life of Romania. Insofar as the monarch could assume the role of the leader of the nation, he was able to achieve full personal power. But even that was not sufficient in interwar Romania; there developed a need for a new form of populist authoritarianism, the curious hybrid of nationalist and internationalist ideology then embodied by fascism.[21]

Much in the ideology of fascism appealed to the instincts of certain elements in the Romanian population and the political elite. The emphasis on direct action, hailed by the populists and their followers, was part and parcel of the ideology of fascism. There were also considerable similarities between the two ideologies in the themes of a simple life, the decadence of the cities, the need for personal sacrifice for the collective good, and the almost mystical connection between man and nature, the tiller and the soil. Both systems emphasized the idea that there must be a strong leader, an individual with vision, courage, and the ability to sacrifice personal and parochial interests for the good of the nation. Fascism also allowed for political representation of major economic interests: the landlords, the peasants, and the emerging class of large industrialists could all expect access to power in this system in a way they could not under other representative schemes. Thus there was a rare confluence of mass and selective elite interests in the form of fascist ideology, soon put into practice.[22]

Directly linked to the rise of native populism and fascism in interwar Romania was the increasingly important tendency toward emphasizing the rule of the strong man, which soon became preoccupation with the rule of a great man. The great man theory of leadership, which reached its height under Hitler and German Nazism, found echoes elsewhere: Pilsudski in Poland, Admiral Horthy in Hungary, and Stalin himself all subscribed to this notion, as did the intellectual progenitor of fascism, Mussolini. Later in Romanian history, the peak (or abyss, depending upon one's view) of such personality cults developed around Nicolae and Elena Ceauşescu.[23]

Personalized rule means more than just the power of the leader to rule alone; it also means that this leader has the opportunity to choose lieutenants on the basis of personal preference and acquaintance. Skill, representation of group interests, or ethnic and religious heterogeneity are considered irrelevant, if not directly harmful. This becomes rule by coterie, clan, tribe, or family. It establishes the internal cohesion of a group of leaders because they all depend upon personal relationships (and their relationships with the leader) for power and prestige; there is no fallback position based upon education, occupational skills, or the support of intermediate groups. Such a system also widens the distance between ruler and ruled, since there is only one mechanism for advancement (personal acquaintance or nepotism) as opposed to the multiple avenues of more pluralistic systems. You are either in, completely, or out, completely. The leaders of such systems may appear unchallengeable, because of the loyalty of the praetorian guard around them, but once that layer has been penetrated, they may fall quickly, because there are few, if any, intermediate layers between them and the masses themselves, and hence no separate sources or bases of support. Personalized rule of this kind tends to become absolute, unfettered by rules, regulations, or countervailing power. Power and procedure are dictated by the leader. The interwar history of Romania exhibited many of these characteristics, particularly in the 1930s and during the years of fascist dictatorship. And it seems to hold true that absolute power corrupts absolutely;

this is the key to the continuation and intensification of the corruption that had so characterized Romanian political life from the beginning of independence.[24]

As the trends toward populism and fascism unfolded in the political realm, similar tendencies manifested themselves elsewhere. There was a powerful tendency to reject cultural developments that could be perceived as critical of, or detrimental to, the interests of the people. Leveling criticism in the artistic field emphasized the importance of "art for the people," while decrying "elitist" art. Populist themes in literature vied with some of the most avant-garde ideas found in the cities, notably Bucharest and Iasi.

The populist trend in politics and in culture also produced suspicion of interest groups and other structures that allegedly focused upon "parts of the whole" rather than the interests of "all of the people." Again, the trend was towards direct solutions and answers. This was the background to the tragic murder of Iorga as he spoke out against the dangerous tendencies of fascism, especially the excesses of the Iron Guard.[25]

While the tendencies toward leveling, personalized rule, and direct action continued in much of Romanian society, the political parties, pressure groups, and other representatives of the existing political order continued to indulge in corruption, political horse trading, the buying and selling of elections, and the general misbehavior that was charged against them by the populists, royalists, and fascists. The representatives of the established political order could not produce a common ethos for the Romanian people. They also failed to form coalitions and thus ended up with parochial goals and a badly fragmented political system. Stalemate and cynical compromise resulted. In the end, populist and fascist ideas prevailed because they appeared to offer a reasonably effective alternative to the mess that was Romanian pluralism.[26]

Romanian Communism and the Legacy of History

When the Romanian Communist party (RCP) came to power in 1944 (assuming complete control in 1947) the political rhetoric of the new order emphasized the symbiotic unity of the party and the people. This unity was nowhere established under communism in Eastern Europe, but Romania experienced a more profound division than the other countries of the region. This was due, in large measure, to the lack of civic responsibility that existed (or developed) in the minds of the ruling RCP elite. This was so for the Ana Pauker and Gheorghe Gheorghiu-Dej leaderships, but the real height of such attitudes and policies came under the long and oppressive rule of Nicolae Ceaşescu and his clan. The Ceauşescus and Petrescus represented the epitome of nepotism, personal greed, and disregard for the population. During twenty-five years of clan rule, this rapacious clique gradually amassed riches by systematically despoiling the national resources of Romania. Money, art, and other treasures that really belonged to the nation became the personal property of the ruler and his family and coterie. Draconian economic laws milked the working class and the peasantry, allowing the general secretary to boost his credit rating abroad while many went hungry in a country that was once the breadbasket of Europe. And all the while, Ceauşescu speeches stressed the "organic ties" between himself and the people. The cruel irony of the discrepancy between words and deeds was not lost on the Romanian people.

An example of this rhetoric can be found in Ceauşescu's speech to the fourteenth party congress, which took place in November 1989, just over a month before his fall:

> From this great democratic platform for communists, I address all delegates and invited guests a warm communist and revolutionary greeting, with the best wishes for the work of the congress! . . . Let me also take this opportunity to send a warm revolutionary greeting to the members of the party, to all working people, without regard to nationality, to our entire people, which, in full unity, assures the success of socialism, lifting the level of civilization and happiness, ensuring the independence and sovereignty of Romania! . . . (strong, prolonged applause, long shouts of "reelect Ceausescu at the fourteenth congress! Ceausescu and the people! Ceausescu—Romanian Communist Party!"). . . . The fourteenth congress of the Romanian Communist Party represents an epochal event in the thousand year history, and especially in the modern history, of Romania, in the workers'-revolutionary movement of our party, in the entire socioeconomic development (designed to) lift our fatherland to new levels of progress and civilization, to complete with success the establishment of the multilaterally developed socialist society and begin the golden era of mankind—communism![27]

This statement differed from countless others made over the years only in detail, not in substance. It reflected a mixture of self-deception, conviction, and perhaps dissimulation on the part of the dictator himself. Politically, however, such statements became less and less believable as the experiences of daily life worsened month by month and year by year for the average man and woman. In the end, the masses had nothing but scorn for such hollow rhetoric.· When a catalyst emerged, the masses moved.[28]

As the Ceauşescu regime matured in its ideological schizophrenia, its lack of noblesse oblige turned to outright contempt for the people. As the economic crisis deepened throughout the 1970s and 1980s, the general secretary refused to accept the blame, even though it was clear to almost everyone else that the fault clearly lay with irrational economic policies conceived at the highest level. Instead, the Ceauşescus blamed bureaucrats, managers, and, ultimately, the workers and peasants for the economic catastrophe of the country. In the end, Nicolae and Elena both talked about the extent to which the people were not worthy of their leadership. Even at their trial, this theme was part of their defense. Rarely has the world seen such a display of political and personal arrogance and irrationality. It created a pervasive climate of fear and cynicism, which will remain as one of the main legacies of this nefarious dictatorship.[29]

The arrogance of the top leadership was matched by the attitudes and behaviors of the regional and local party bosses and bureaucrats. This was of course traditional in Romania in any case, but these behavior patterns were exacerbated by the nature and style of the Ceauşescus themselves as they ruled imperiously over the people, rather than with them.

The arrogance and cynicism displayed by the ruling clique have been vividly described by Ion Pacepa, former head of Romanian intelligence, in his book *Red Horizons*. While some of his statements may be overdramatized, it is now clear that they were correct in their basic message. Furthermore, we can verify these attitudes by examining Nicolae Ceauşescu's own statements on numerous occasions, in which he spoke in a self-congratulatory manner while blaming all others, including the public, for the plight of Romania:

> In the period discussed there were mistakes and illegalities, detrimental to the principles at the root of socialism, and it is necessary for our party to liquidate all these manifestations of negative work and to take firm measures, go on new paths so that we can find better formulas, corresponding to the realities and needs of the Romanian people, in order to assure the success of socialism. . . .
>
> Only in this fashion, acting as real revolutionary communists, can we assure the firm measures (necessary) to assure the (realization of) the party program and the victory of socialism and communism in Romania![30]

Today, after the demise of the Ceauşescus and much of their entourage, remnants of such attitudes remain among those who helped lead the revolution and now profess their own symbiotic relationship with the people. There are many instances of heavy-handed rule, which outrage the population. This, in turn, leads to demonstrations and counterdemonstrations, where demands are constantly raised for greater accountability and more concern for the needs and wishes of the people. Distrust and hatred of political power have developed over a long period of time in Romania. Such attitudes will also be a long time in disappearing.

The attitudes discussed above have been vividly expressed by Ion Iliescu, the self-appointed leader of the Front for National Salvation, which was established after the overthrow of the Ceauşescu regime in December 1989. On numerous occasions, Iliescu has criticized opposition groups and demonstrators as "hooligans" (or other pejorative terms).[31] The campaign leading up to the elections of May 20, 1990 was marred by many cases of intimidation of opposition groups as well as the use of terror and coercion to persuade the masses to vote in the "correct" manner:

> As we approach the moment of elections—the first free elections in Romania in half a century, there are isolated but persistent tendencies to artificially accentuate (within the scope of the electorate) political tensions, tensions which are inherent in the processes of change generated by the revolution.
>
> Contests and competitive dialogues are probable in the days and weeks (ahead), but nothing justifies attempts to erode the revolution and put in jeopardy the democratic climate necessary for the manifestations and execution of the rights and liberties of the citizenry.
>
> From this point of view, the demonstrations at University Square are not of a nature to contribute to the stabilization of civil life. (They) disturb normal traffic day and night in the central parts of the capital and, through their effects, also in two or three other cities, inconveniencing a large number of citizens.
>
> More aggravating is the fact that these are, through their manifestations, an undemocratic substitution for the popular vote freely expressed, representing instead the will and interests of a few minority groups, which utilize the mechanism of the pressure of the street, thus contradicting not only the adopted electoral laws but also the fundamental principles of the state of laws for which we struggled in the revolution.[32]

The similarities with some of Nicolae Ceauşescu's statements are striking. The new leadership of Romania, elected by popular vote in

May 1990, represents the old tendencies of authoritarianism, populism, and one-man leadership. It shows no inclination toward pluralism and respect for diversity so necessary for a real, functioning, democracy. This gives some credence to those who consider the new leader representative of Ceauşescuism without terror and irrationality. It is more fitting to say that the new Romanian leader appears to function in the spirit of traditional Romanian political history. This is indeed a serious (and dangerous) legacy.

It should come as no surprise that the authoritarian attitudes characteristic among the mass public, so profound in the period up to communist rule, were further strengthened by the nature of that rule. This was especially so during the Ceauşescu era, when the authoritarian and populist nature of the regime became more and more marked as the years progressed (at least until the early 1980s, when Ceauşescu himself began to distrust the masses both implicitly and expressly). For example, during the celebration of the centennial of Romanian independence, which began in the mid-1970s and lasted for several years, the themes of "people's culture," "people's art," and "people's literature" were prominent, with thousands of workers and peasants participating in celebrations, song fests, and poetry competitions. At the same time, the "elitist" culture of the intellectuals and professional artists was decried. This anti-intellectualism extended to anyone who might conceivably stand for alternative views on politics, arts, and society.[33]

The clearest example of this authoritarianism, however, was the increasing incidence of chauvinism (anti-Hungarian sentiment and anti-Semitism) in the Romanian population, particularly during the 1970s and 1980s. These were long-standing albeit restrained attitudes among ethnic Romanians, but they were fueled by the strident rhetoric of the Ceauşescus, who sought to establish a form of political legitimacy on the basis of such chauvinism. The symbiotic relationship between mass attitudes and political rhetoric strengthened this authoritarianism, and remains in the new political order that has emerged in post-Ceauşescu Romania.[34]

Authoritarianism was also an important part of the workplace during the communist era. Again, this was partly a reflection of traditional values and attitudes; in part, it stemmed from the management structure of *Edinonachalie* (one man rule) which was so central to communist leaders themselves, schooled in the forms of political socialization of Pauker, Gheorghiu-Dej, and the Ceauşescus. But such views could only be effective if they were accepted by the masses of workers and peasants in Romania. This was indeed the case. These views produced a quiescent population that accepted much greater hardships than any other (with the possible exception of Albania) until the elemental conflagration of December 1989.[35]

Authoritarianism provided a receptive audience for parts of the Ceauşescu message during the 1970s and 1980s. Significant elements in the peasant population shared the disdain, fear, and jealousy felt by Nicolae and Elena Ceauşescu and their clan for urbanites, intellectuals, and artists. These attitudes were also a prominent part of the ethos of the working class; most of the urban proletariat was, in reality, composed of peasants in workers' clothing, the so-called peasant-workers, whose attitudes, values, goals, and aspirations reflected the outlook of the village. In fact, it is possible to see the rise of Ceauşescuism as the triumph (albeit temporary) of the peasantry over the city and urbanity as a life-style. Hence, the peasants in the city and in the countryside accepted the messages of Ceauşescu about the arrogance of the intelligentsia, the perfidy of regional and local leaders (but not the leader himself, who wished to be considered "above politics") and the real Romania, the masses of the factory and the farms.

While Nicolae Ceauşescu created a chasm between himself and the masses through his irrational economic policies, he also constructed some bridges across this abyss. One of these was the concept of the common enemy. In addition to the urban intelligentsia the enemy also included Jews, Hungarians, other ethnic minorities and, indirectly, all those in the societal elites who stood for diversity and the acceptance of the rights of others. As time passed, mass anti-Semitism became more virulent, and the attacks on ethnic Hungarians (and, occasionally, Germans) intensified. The tone of the press and of these elements of the "intelligentsia" who made a living as court poets and sycophantic defenders and promulgators of the Ceauşescu era became more and more assertive. This trend was only modified by the important instance of interethnic solidarity that started the revolution in Timişoara. Events since have shown that the old animosities were only temporarily papered over because of the existence of a greater enemy, Ceauşescuism itself.

The similarities between elements of Ceauşescuism and mass attitudes did not represent a real, positive confluence of values and goals. Ceauşescuism, in one manifestation or another, was resented by most citizens of Romania, regardless of ethnic origin or occupation. This became clear in December 1989. The rule of Ceauşescu was not noblesse oblige, but unenlightened despotism. At some point, the negative connotations of this destroyed him and his entourage. But other aspects remain as a dangerous and ugly legacy for the Romania of the future.

Mass authoritarianism is alive and well in post-revolutionary Romania. In fact, it may be argued that this is, indeed, the *main* political phenomenon of the country at the present time, and it may remain so for a number of years to come. True, there is a great deal of political activity in contemporary Romania; over eighty political parties participated in the recent elections. There are also constant demonstrations, sit-ins, and much speechmaking. But the style of this participatory system is distinctly confrontational, with occasionally violent demonstrations, clashes with police, the shouting down of the other side, and the storming of buildings. The interim regime of the Front for National Salvation utilized the advantages of incumbency to restrict access to the mass media for others, thereby seriously hampering the process of campaigning. And the vote itself was a powerful manifestation of mass authoritarianism; an enormous majority of the population selected Ion Iliescu, a former aide to Nicolae Ceauşescu who fell out of favor and became associated with reform communism, Romanian style, and a group of leaders with strong ties to communism and certain aspects of the Ceauşescu regime. Some of these election results may have been inflated through fraud and intimidation, but there can be little doubt that a substantial part of this majority reflects the Romanian masses' outlook, attitudes, and values. This was indeed a democratic manifestation of mass authoritarianism.[36]

Authoritarian values also continue in the workplace. One of the main reasons for the overwhelming support for the Iliescu regime was the conviction among the masses that the Front would sponsor economic reform but would implement it slowly, thereby presumably reducing the dangers of mass unemployment, plant closings, and other serious dislocations. There is considerable argument among economists and political scientists that this piecemeal approach to reform is inadequate and will fall short of the needs of the economy. But mass attitudes favoring the slow approach also reflect a basic egalitarianism that has developed in much of the proletariat and the peasantry, and, above all, it reflects the prevailing attitude toward work, which emphasizes security over productivity and conformity over hustle and entrepreneurship. Romanian entrepreneurship is characterized by *bakshish* (bribery) and other forms of corruption in the workplace. There is little evidence that this is changing under the new system.[37]

Perhaps the most disturbing element of this mass authoritarianism is the rising incidence of anti-Semitism and violence directed against minorities, especially the ethnic Hungarians. During the Ceauşescu regime, such discrimination took political and economic (as well as cultural) forms, while actual physical violence was less common, primarily because of the pervasive nature of the police state itself. Now, the tables have been turned; the national leadership is ostensibly opposed to any form of discrimination and is on record as advocating equal rights for all, but its inability to enforce its own program has given authoritarian elements the opportunity to exercise their fears and hatred through confrontation and violence. The ethnic riots in parts of Transylvania in the winter and spring of 1990 are dreaded manifestations of this attitude. While the open confrontations seem to have died down, there are many cases of discrimination on a daily basis. And the impressive showing of the party representing ethnic Hungarians in the recent elections is a sign of solidarity among this group, representing further polarization of the political order.[38]

The Deepening of Economic Deprivation Under Communism

The legacy of economic underdevelopment left by the precommunist order became an important element in the socioeconomic system that emerged under communist auspices. The rapid industrialization of the country represented a form of modernization insofar as it introduced new methods of production, new machinery, and different organizational forms. But it did not produce modern economic cultural attitudes; the Romanian working class continued to be characterized by low productivity, excessive egalitarianism, corruption, and an emphasis on time spent at work rather than on goods and services produced. This was in many ways a continuation of the traditional economic culture of old Romania. Its legacy is there for all to see as the new regime (whatever it may eventually turn out to be) tries to effect the difficult transition from extreme centralization to something resembling an open-market economy.

The legacy of deprivation is coupled with the pervasive existence of corruption, graft, and personal self-interest in economic matters. For a very long time, goods and services could only be obtained in "unauthorized" ways. Only bakshish could make bureaucrats and planners perform, and bribes were extracted at every turn. Thus a new economic order based upon different methods and different value systems will be difficult to establish. There is a real danger that corruption will continue; that new bosses will behave in old ways;

and that the public trust that must be established will lag behind other developments. This, in turn, will reduce the legitimacy of any new system. In the end, the lack of public trust may undo any chance for the political order to survive, and new crises will develop in an ever-widening cycle of instability.[39]

The final characteristic of the economic system is the run-down infrastructure of industry and agriculture and the savage exploitation of the environment carried out by the Ceauşescus. The severe damage done to natural resources cannot be remedied overnight, and problems will continue to build while the process of repair continues. The prewar legacy of economic underdevelopment and the Ceauşescu legacy of exploitation stand to haunt Romania for quite some time.[40]

The legacies of an unproductive economic culture cannot be undone quickly. Economic productivity continues to lag, because much of the system is in flux in organizational and managerial terms, and because the attitudes of workers and peasants cannot be changed quickly and dramatically. For this to happen, a considerable period of time must elapse. In the meantime, the system must survive and improve its performance. This is a very tall order.

Infrastructural problems are also soluble only over time. The deterioration of factories, farms, transportation facilities, and rolling stock continues because of widespread uncertainty about the future economic system. Massive amounts of capital and an influx of expertise from the West are needed for improvements in this sphere. Unfortunately, most of the West's attention so far has been focused further north, in Poland, Hungary, and, to some extent, Czechoslovakia (while Germany takes care of eastern Germany through the process of unification). Unless Romania can improve its political performance and its reputation, prospects for massive Western aid and investment remain bleak.[41]

The populist traditions of the prewar political culture in Romania became an important part of the communist order, particularly under Nicolae Ceauşescu and his clan. As discussed in a number of scholarly works,[42] Ceauşescu was particularly eager to emphasize the notion that he ruled the people directly, unencumbered by bureaucratic layers and cumbersome procedures. The general secretary would periodically travel to industrial towns and agricultural regions, engage in dialogue with the workers and peasants, accepting their complaints about the bosses and their mistakes. Such meetings would always end with "spontaneous" mass demonstrations displaying the affection of young and old alike for the leader. The general secretary could then use these occasions as mechanisms for control over the bureaucracy "in the name of the people" and unleash popular praise or blame for specific *apparatchiki*. At the same time, Ceauşescu could claim credit for his own commitment to popular rule and the rule of the masses.[43]

As the years of increasingly personalized rule passed, the general secretary became more and more insistent upon his role as *Conducator* (Leader). He was the greatest planner, the most profound philosopher, the deepest thinker, the most brilliant writer, and the supreme nationalist of all Romanians. Under these circumstances there was no need for any intermediate structure or procedures for decision making. In the end, the dictator and his wife met the firing squad claiming that they were misunderstood and unjustly maligned. The two dictators firmly believed that the problems of Romania were ultimately ascribable to the failures of the people, not the leadership.[44]

It should come as no surprise that elements of these attitudes remain in the leadership and the masses alike. Many members of the government are former communists. They are not dedicated to the idea of Western-style democracy, which emphasizes "unity in diversity" and decision making as a process of bargaining and compromise. Basic authoritarianism remains acceptable to many in the population. But even those who advocate real democracy have problems understanding the piecemeal nature of decision making and implementation in pluralistic democracies. These groups and individuals want their entire political program implemented, and they want it now. This is simply not possible anywhere, and certainly not in a country whose physical and spiritual resources are in short supply after decades of systematic and irrational exploitation. Until the new democrats learn this, they will be part of the problem, not the solution.[45]

The legacies of autocracy, direct solutions, and Ceauşescuism create powerful roadblocks to the development of pluralism and a civil society. The network of organizations outside party control in Romania was negligible. There were few overt dissenters. There was little opportunity for various strata in society to exercise semiautonomous judgment on various issues and no opportunity for them to add to the decision making process. Instead, the clan ruled by its own methods, its own procedures. The Securitate (secret police) network spread throughout all layers of society, draping a blanket of fear, suspicion, and paranoia over the entire population. Under these circumstances, independent political stands became dangerous and devolved into ritualistic ratification of the policies devised by the Ceauşescus, no matter how irrational.[46]

Such a system of rule provided no checks and balances, no mechanism or pattern that could take over if the central system itself failed. Thus when the revolution of December 1989 swept the Ceauşescu clan and much of its infrastructure away, an enormous political vacuum developed. Into that vacuum sprang a large number of groups, associations, political parties, and movements of all kinds. These are structures with no traditions of political activity; above all, they have no experience with the notions of compromise so crucial for political pluralism. Groups that sprang up on the new Romanian political scene developed full-fledged political and socioeconomic programs of a maximalist nature, in which few of the demands are negotiable. This is predictable in a system that allows for free and unfettered participation for the first time. But it is also a dangerous development in which the many new participants tend to block each other as they jockey for center stage in the political arena. They acquired a veto function that stalemated the decision-making and implementation processes, even after the elections of May 1990. The Romanian political scene continues to be characterized by these phenomena, coupled with frequent mass protests of various groups claiming to be unjustly excluded from the political order.

Perhaps even more important than these problems are the deficiencies associated with the lack of a civic culture. By civic culture, I mean one in which the citizenry is used to some aspect of regular political participation and established procedures and processes for such participation, even if individuals do not regularly avail themselves of such mechanisms. Furthermore, the citizenry must believe that political participation is meaningful and effective; and that others, with different values and goals, have an equal right to participate. There needs to be acceptance of the idea that public matters are important and that their pursuit is worthwhile in personal and ethical terms. Finally, in a civic culture substantial numbers of individuals must have "administrative efficacy," meaning that they expect the representatives of established political structures to act responsibly, fairly, and in pursuit of goals and values that are widely shared by the population.

Most political systems fall short in one or more of these ingredients of civic culture, but contemporary Romania falls short in all of them, to varying degrees. If an ethical political culture does not develop it seems likely that the Romanian masses will grow tired of the experiment in democracy now under way and will instead turn to new forms of authoritarian or one-man rule. Romania may represent the most difficult case of transition to a functional democracy in all Eastern Europe.

Whither Romania?

What are Romania's prospects? The many legacies of history produce a cloudy picture for the immediate, even the intermediate, future of the country.

The problems of Romania in 1990 will continue, perhaps even be exacerbated, during the next few years. The May 1990 elections clarified the political picture somewhat, but it is possible that the changes and fissures in society, now so visible, will be reproduced in the political order as a fragmented people exercises its first full set of political rights after the elections. In that case, there must be further willingness in the political elites to develop procedures for compromise. But this new approach must be established in such a way that the general public is satisfied; it cannot be perceived as another set of corrupt dealings. Given the political culture and traditions of Romania, that may be difficult.

The generally deplorable state of the Romanian economy will worsen before it can be significantly improved. This is also true for the social and health services, which are in desperate shape. Measures must be undertaken to avoid winter food shortages. Fuels and raw materials must be provided for the run-down industrial plants, and modernization must begin. All these are races against time and the impatience of a population that did not undertake a revolution in order to go hungry or die from lack of medical care.

Given the traditions of autocracy and the penchant for one-man rule in Romanian history as well as the worsening socioeconomic crisis of the moment, there is a real chance that the future of this afflicted country will be more authoritarianism, albeit in a noncommunist form. This is likely to happen if inadequate attention is paid to the establishment of proper procedures and to the provision of civic education in the schools and the general public. The future of Romania clearly hangs in the balance.

We should expect that, for a considerable period of time, authoritarian tendencies and behaviors will coexist with new democratic forms and actions. Old attitudes and values will vie with the new. It is clear that an arbiter must be found to mediate between the various participants, to regulate their behavior and (hopefully) to provide the needed impetus for democratic development. This arbiter and protector of democracy is likely to be the armed forces, especially the younger officers, who are relatively untainted by Ceaușescuism. Should this come to pass, there is hope for a new Romania.

A systematic analysis of Romanian history and the legacies of the communist era (particularly the Ceauşescu period) produces an essentially negative assessment of the prospects for this unfortunate country in political, socioeconomic, and cultural development. But it should be noted that Romania's past is not all negative (although the impact of communism may indeed be considered almost wholly detrimental to Romania's future development). For Romania to join the family of democratic European states or those on the path to democracy, the positive inheritance of the past must be emphasized and nurtured in the years to come. Only enlightened and inspired political leadership can do this.

Romanian history is a living monument to the survivability of a nation in the face of overwhelming odds. After centuries of Turkish rule and extended periods of rule by other external actors, the Romanian nation survives with its own language, culture, and symbols. Furthermore, the national culture overcame the onslaught of communist orthodoxy and the curious blend of chauvinism and internationalism that made up the basic ingredients of Ceauşescuism.

Historically, the Romanian village was a system of interlocking relationships among families and socioeconomic strata that exhibited much unity and a basic sense of decency in interpersonal relations. Indeed, this kind of solidarity produced a form of civic-mindedness at the local level, in which the more fortunate attempted to act responsibly and compassionately toward others. This stands in sharp contrast to the lack of such relationships between the localities and the national leaders of the country. Future leaders of Romania must harken back to this positive legacy and begin to use it for the development of a *national* civil (and civic) culture of mutual trust and responsibility.

During the centuries of exploitative foreign rule and rule by their own elite, the Romanian people achieved amazing successes in literature, arts, and some areas of the sciences, despite the odds. Names like Caragiale, Enescu, Iorga, and Arghezi are part of the heritage of international (especially European) culture. An entrepreneurial tradition in the Romanian people was corrupted during the centuries of economic construction and development. If unlocked, it might be the catalyst for the transformation of collectivist Romania into a competitive system of free enterprise. Again, enlightened leadership and a mass civic consciousness are the only factors that can bring this about. This revolution will have to begin in the homes of a ravaged and dispirited people.

Romania has always been a vibrant place full of creative people, despite its well-documented shortcomings. During the last two de-

302 • TROND GILBERG

cades of the Ceauşescu regime, and particularly in the 1980s, the
spreading tentacles of the Securitate and the fear that descended upon
the people threatened to extinguish this vibrancy and creativity altogether. Those of us who visited Romania regularly in the last decade
of the "Ceauşescu epoch" can testify to the frightening vision of
dispirited masses trudging along dark and dingy streets in search of
food and basic necessities, fearful of any contact with outsiders,
apparently cowed by the power of the regime and its security police.
The revolution itself and the enthusiasm with which many Romanians
threw themselves into the political fray afterward show that such
activism still exists despite the legacies of the dictatorship of the
Ceauşescus. Directing this creativity is difficult, but it must be accomplished. That is a sine qua non for Romanian democracy.

NOTES

1. See V. Andrei Otetea in *Istoria Poporului Roman* (Bucharest: Editura Stiintifica, 1970), 308–315; see also A. Deac in *ibid.*, 349–65.

2. A number of books have been written on the rise of Romanian author-itarianism between the two world wars. See, for example, Alexander F. Webster, *The Romanian Legionary Movement: The Carl Beck Papers No. 502* (Pittsburgh: Center for Russian and East European Studies, 1986); Mihai Fatu and Ion Spalatelu, *Garda de Fier: Organizatie de Tip Fascist* (Bucharest: Editura Politica, 1980). One of the classics is still Stephen Fischer-Galati, *Twentieth Century Rumania* (New York: Columbia University Press, 1970).

3. This reform was partly triggered by the great peasant revolt of 1907; for an account of this event, see A. Otetea et al., *Marea Rascoala a Taranilor Din 1907* (Bucharest: Editura Academiei Republicii Socialiste Romania, 1967), especially ch. 9, 787–847. See also Miron Constantinescu et. al., *Istoria Romaniei* (Bucharest: Editura Didactica si Pedagogica, 1969), especially Ion Oprea, "Romania in Primii ani Dupa Razboi," 451–62.

4. See, for example, Trond Gilberg, "Political Socialization in Romania," in Daniel N. Nelson, ed., *Romania in the 1980s* (Boulder: Westview Press, 1981), ch. 5, 142–74.

5. See Ion Oprea, "Perioada Crizei Economice Dintre Anii 1929–1933," in Constantinescu et al., *Istoria Romaniei*, 477–500.

6. Romanian academics have toiled mightly to revise the history of these troubled relationships; see, for example, Stefan Pascu, *A History of Transyl-vania* (Detroit: Wayne State University Press, 1982); see also L. Banyai, *Pe Fagasul Traditiilor Fratesti* (Bucharest: Institutul de Studii Istorice si Social-Politice de pe Linga C.C. al P.C.R., 1971). For a more realistic discussion, see

John F. Cadzon et al., *Transylvania: The Roots of Conflict* (Kent, Ohio: Kent State University Press, 1983).

7. Fatu and Spalatelu, *Garda de Fier;* see also Alexander E. Rommett, *Romanian Nationalism: The Legionary Movement* (Chicago: Loyola University Press, 1974), which is an apologist's story of these movements. An interesting account of the position of many Romanian academics and politicians on the Iron Guard and other fascist movements is Vasile Netea, *Nicolae Iorga* (Bucharest: Meridiane Publishing House, 1971), especially ch. 5, 97–123.

8. Otetea, *Marea Rascoala a Taranilor Din 1907*, especially ch. 2, 31–155.

9. R. W. Seton-Watson, *A History of the Roumanians: From Roman Times to the Completion of Unity* (Cambridge: Cambridge University Press, 1934), 386–87.

10. Similar sparks had ignited conflagrations in the past; see, for example, Joseph Held, "The Horea-Cloşca Revolt of 1784–85: Some Observations," in Cadzon et al., *Transylvania: The Roots of Ethnic Conflict,* 93–108.

11. Seton-Watson, *A History of the Roumanians,* ch. 17, 521–55.

12. Oprea, "Epoca Contemporana," in Constantinescu et al., *Istoria Romaniei,* 472.

13. Even a great historian such as Constantin Giurescu papers over these conflicts and discusses the greatness of the new Romanian state; see Constantin C. Giurescu, *The Making of the Romanian Unitary State* (Bucharest: Meridiane, 1971), especially 143–63.

14. Fatu and Spalatelu, *Garda de Fier,* especially ch. 6, 67–89.

15. *Ibid.*

16. Oprea in Constantinescu, *Istoria Romaniei,* especially 477–526.

17. *Istoria Romaniei,* 537.

18. E.g., Fatu and Spalatelu, *Garda de Fier* (pictorial supplement); see also 269–301.

19. A. Deac, "Romania in Fata Pericolului Fascist (1933–1939)," in Otetea, ed., *Istoria Poporului Roman,* 365–78.

20. Much of the official literature of the communist era is dedicated to a description of the progressive nature of the communist movement and its organizations and the mass support accorded it before World War II. See, for example, Constantinescu, *Istoria Romaniei,* especially the chapters "Revolutia Populara," 545–76; and "Orinduire Socialista," 526–615. See also Otetea, *Istoria Poporului Roman,* ch. 4, 406–29, and ch. 5, 429–41. On the alleged mass support for communism, see, for example, *Din Istoria Luptelor Greviste Ale Proletariatului Din Romania* (Bucharest: Institutul de Studii Istorice si Social-Politice de pe Linga c.c. al. P.C.R., 1970). Much better and more objective are Ghita Ionescu, *Communism in Rumania, 1944–1962* (London: Oxford University Press, 1964); and John Michael Montias, *Economic Development in Communist Rumania* (Cambridge, Mass.: MIT Press, 1967).

21. Fatu and Spalateu, *Garda de Fier.*

22. *Ibid.*, especially ch. 5, 6, and 7, 56–100.

23. This view of political power was expressed in great detail by Corneliu Zeleu Codreanu, e.g., in his *Pentru Legionari* (Sibiu: Editura "Totul Pentru Tara," 1936).

24. See, for example, Stephen Fischer-Galati, *The Socialist Republic of Rumania* (Baltimore: Johns Hopkins University Press, 1969), ch. 1, 3–29.

25. E.g., Nicolae Iorga, *Memorii*, vol. 7 *Sinuciderea Partidelor, 1932–8* (Bucharest, 1939). See also D. M. Pippidi, ed., *Nicolae Iorga: L'homme et l'oeuvre* (Bucharest: Editiora de L'Academie de la Republique Socialiste de Roumanie, 1972), especially the chapter by Nicolae Banescu, 391–405.

26. These problems are well illustrated in Iorga's memoirs, where vol. 7 is appropriately entitled "The Suicide of the Parties" (see note 25).

27. *Scinteia*, November 21, 1989.

28. Much has been written on the dramatic events of December 1989. For a contemporary account, see the *New York Times*, December 25, 26, 27, 28, and 29, 1989.

29. This cynicism was vividly displayed by Ion Iliescu in the middle of June 1990, as he called upon the miners of the Jui Valley to "defend the revolution," while they were actually used to intimidate the legitimate press and organizations of the opposition.

30. *Scinteia*, November 21, 1989.

31. See Dan Ionescu, "Violence and Calumny in the Election Campaign," *Radio Free Europe*, Report on Eastern Europe (May 25 1990), 1(1):39.

32. *Adevarul*, May 6, 1990.

33. This was evident in Ceauşescu's closing remarks at the fourteenth RCP congress in November 1989; see *Scinteia*, November 25, 1989.

34. See, for example, the statement about Ion Iliescu in *Romania Libera*, January 14, 1990.

35. Such attitudes of submission are still important; see, for exaple, the election results of May 20, 1990, which elected Ion Iliescu and his followers to national leadership by a very wide margin, described in the *New York Times*, May 21 and 22, 1990.

36. *Ibid.*

37. See, for example, Josif Pop on agricultural organization, *Adevarul*, January 5, 1990.

38. The violence in certain areas of Transylvania, notably Tirgu Mures, was reported by *Süddeutsche Zeitung*, March 23, 1990.

39. The authoritarianism of Iliescu is well documented. See his statements about the electoral campaign, discussed by Dan Ionescu, "Violence and Calumny in the Election Campaign," *Radio Free Europe*, vol. 1, no. 21 (May 25, 1990).

40. E.g., articles on the heavily polluted city of Copsa Mica; see *Tribuna* (Sibiu), February 4, 1990.

41. It was reported that the Common Market would suspend economic

aid to Romania because of the regime's violence against the opposition; see the *New York Times*, June 15 and 16, 1990.

42. E.g., Mary Ellen Fischer, "Idol or Leader? The Origins and Future of the Ceausescu Cult," in Daniel N. Nelson, ed., *Romania in the 1980s*, ch. 4, 117–42.

43. E.g., Trond Gilberg, *Nationalism and Communism in Romania: The Rise and Fall of Ceausescu's Personal Dictatorship* (Boulder: Westview Press, 1990), especially ch. 6, 111–37.

44. Much has been written on this. For detailed accounts see the *New York Times*, December 22, 23, 24, 26, and 27, 1990.

45. For a discussion of the opposition's demands, see Victor Roman in an interview with *Die Welt*, May 8, 1990.

46. This fear has been resurrected owing to recent violence by the Iliescu government. I refer to live reports and interviews on "CBS Evening News," Sunday, June 17, 1990.

8 The Yugoslav Phenomenon

Dimitrije Djordjevic

The history of multinational Yugoslavia, which appeared on the historical stage in 1918, includes the origins of the movement for unity, its realization in the infant state tottering during the interwar period, its death in World War II, and its resurrection and survival since. For more than seventy years the maverick Yugoslav state has searched for a viable solution, torn between unifying and disruptive trends.

Nec tecum nec sine te (Neither with you, nor without you) characterizes Yugoslav unity. Bound by South Slavic ethnicity but separated by particular national affiliations, joined by a common language but distinguished by its dialects, united by the need for survival but divided by history, alphabets, religions, and cultures, the Yugoslav phenomenon has been supported and challenged in the past and present by both common and divergent interests of peoples irrevocably mixed, linked as well as opposed to each other.

Over more than a century several Yugoslavias have succeeded each other. Four of them can be distinguished, each with a markedly different character. The first Yugoslavia originated in the vision of nineteenth-century intellectuals and politicians, mainly in Croatia. The second Yugoslavia was bound together by centralism and unitarism through the Serbian mortar injected into the country's shaky foundations after 1918. The third Yugoslavia emerged from the shock of genocide and fratricidal strife of World War II and was molded into a federation, dominated by a highly centralized communist regime. The fourth Yugoslavia is emerging in the post Tito era, resonating with divergent national and/or democratic trends, which in turn are encouraged by recent sweeping changes in Eastern Europe.

The Origins of Yugoslavism: Realities and Dreams

For centuries Yugoslavs lived divided under foreign rule. Civilizations which crisscrossed the Balkans left their imprint on national characters. Geography initially separated them: migrations caused by wars, invasions, and population movements between the mountains and plains caused an intermingling of peripheral parts of Yugoslav peoples to the degree that no historian or demographer can establish a dividing national line among them.

During the nineteenth century, the Yugoslavs developed in three distinct zones—under the Habsburg empire, the Ottoman empire, and in the gradually emancipated Serbian and Montenegrin states. The Slovenes were divided by Austria into six administrative units. By the terms of the 1867 dualistic Austro-Hungarian compromise, Civil Croatia and Slavonia were allotted to Hungary, Dalmatia stayed with Austria, and Bosnia and Herzegovina were under a separate administration after 1878. Serbia and Montenegro embraced only some of their conationals living in the neighboring empires. In the south, Macedonia was subject to the crumbling Ottoman administration and pressures from neighboring Balkan states.

Modern Yugoslav nationalism, which emerged during the nineteenth century, expressed above all the struggle by the peoples of the region to achieve their own specific national integration and the recognition of political rights.[1] Methods to realize these goals varied, as did their timing. Pressured by Germanization, the Slovenes turned to "natural" instead of "historical" rights and found their *Volkgeist* in a linguistic and cultural renaissance. Repelled by the complex structure of the Habsburg monarchy, the Croats fought for national identity through demands to unify the historic Triune Kingdom of Croatia-Slavonia-Dalmatia, torn between the factions of the Zagreb-Budapest-Vienna triangle. Serbia, engaged in state building and inspired by its achieved emancipation, sought to play the role of a Serbian Piedmont, unifying all the Serbs. On this road the fragile state was to confront two surrounding empires and the Anglo-Russian and Austro-Russian rivalries surrounding the Eastern Question.

The idea of Yugoslav unity, based on the common South Slavic ethnicity and linguistic community of the Serbs and Croats, originated as an instrument for particular national integration and emancipation. While the different national renaissances followed different paths, Yugoslavism emerged as a national-political ideology, a supernational movement to support and guarantee individual efforts in the struggle for emancipation. The most deeply rooted national identification cannot easily be changed, but a political ideology can be questioned or amended. The tension between the two helps explain the ups and downs in the development of the movement for Yugoslav unity. It manifested the weakness and strength of Yugoslavism: challenged in crisis, it recovered and revived, due to common needs.

Yugoslavism from its formative stage advocated the idea of one Yugoslav nation. *Narodno jedinstvo* (national oneness) was to unite Serbs, Croats, and Slovenes as three branches of a unique tree. The nation was identified with the Serbo-Croat language. German, Czech, Slovak, and Yugoslav scholars referred to the linguistic nationhood of Serbs and Croats. Reference to history was not pertinent: the Yugoslavs were not a "historical nation," a powerful emblem in the legitimistic Europe of the time. Historical rights were to be replaced by natural rights based on the ethnic-linguistic entity.

Growing nationalism in the nineteenth century developed two strategies: to break up multinational states in favor of one nation in one state, or to unite a nation previously divided among national states. The 1848 revolution in the Habsburg monarchy, and the later Italian and German unifications, offered inspiration and guidance. The promoters of Yugoslavism extolled the creed *U slozi jedinstvo* (Unity in Harmony).

Promoters of genuine Yugoslavism were recruited among the intellectual elite and the idealistic youth, both open to the rational and progressive ideas of their epoch. The Illyrian movement, which originated in Croatia in the 1830s, extolled Yugoslav cultural unity in order to support both Croatian national integration and South Slav unity. The Serbs were reluctant to replace their name, already upheld by their rising statehood, with the rather ambiguous Illyrian one. From historical experience, Serbian politics gave priority to the Ottoman Balkans, including Bosnia and Herzegovina, attempting to break the encircling chain at its weakest link.

The Yugoslav question had to face both Central European and

Balkan realities. The Yugoslavs faced the choice of being in or out of the Habsburg monarchy—that is, either in a tripartite reorganization within the empire or an outside entity built around emancipated Serbia, the promoter of Balkan self-determination. The first option required a federal restructuring of the Central European empire, which would become an attractive center for the rest of the Yugoslavs. The second option presumed a revolutionary dissolution of Austria-Hungary. Dualism stamped the Yugoslav ideology: either the cultural supremacy of Zagreb within the empire or the political superiority of Belgrade in an independent nation: a choice between evolution or revolution.

At the time, only a dreamer could foresee the dissolution of the Habsburg monarchy. The great promoter of Yugoslavism Bishop Josip Juraj Strossmayer favored a federalized empire, in which Croatia would be the Yugoslav center. The dualistic issue provoked suspicions on both sides, reinforced by the Catholic-Orthodox schism. Serbia saw in the Habsburg monarchy the main foe of any form of national emancipation in the Balkans. The Austro-Hungarian occupation of Bosnia and Herzegovina in 1878 contributed to the discord over what belonged to whom in the era of growing nationalism on both sides at the end of the century.

The idea of Yugoslav unity was revived at the dawn of the twentieth century, stimulated by the general trend for national emancipation in southeastern Europe. A new generation originated the "new course," which resulted in a coalition of Croatian and Serbian political parties in Croatia in 1905. It became the precursor of future Yugoslav unification.

Democracy, introduced in Serbia after 1903, unleashed dynamic national energies, challenging both Ottoman and Habsburg rulers. In an Orwellian vision, the Serbian historian Stojan Novaković predicted in 1911 the formation of a unified Yugoslav state from Ohrid to Maribor and from Split to Subotica.[2] Despite the movement for unity, many unresolved problems regarding unification remained unanswered on the eve of World War I.

The Untuned Yugoslav Music: World War I

Unification of the Yugoslavs in 1918 was made possible as a result of World War I. This unification was influenced by the character of the war, the policy of the Entente with regard to the Habsburg monarchy and the Eastern Question, the role that Serbia played in the camp of the victorious Allies, the activity of the Yugoslav Committee, and the military results on the battlefield.

For the Yugoslavs, drafted into armies on both sides, World War I was a fratricidal and religious war. After the 1914 assassination of Francis Ferdinand in Sarajevo, anti-Serbian demonstrations erupted in the Habsburg monarchy. During the war Serbian societies, journals, and the Cyrillic alphabet were suppressed, prisoners were taken and high-treason trials conducted. In some units of the XV corps (Sarajevo), the XVI corps (Dubrovnik), and the XIII corps (Zagreb) of the *Balkanstreit Armee* assigned to invade Serbia in 1914, 50 percent were Croats and from 20 to 25 percent Serbs.[3]

Orthodox, Roman Catholic, and Muslim religious affiliations and their clergy contributed to the dispute. The Serbian Orthodox church, traditionally linked to the state, was "fighting more for the Serbian kingdom than for the kingdom of God." The Roman Catholic church ardently supported the Apostolic Majesty in Vienna. Pope Pius X preached that a final settlement with Serbia had to end "the corroding disease which will, in due time, jeopardize the vital nerve of the Monarchy." After joining the Central Powers, the Sultan in Istanbul proclaimed a *Jihad* (holy war) against the infidels, including Serbia and Montenegro. Muslims in Bosnia and Albania were incited to fight for the Austrian imperial eagle, together with pan-Islamic Turks in Macedonia.

Supporters of Yugoslav unification, fighting on the side of the Entente, all emphasized the wish of "our people" to unite. It is almost impossible to gauge how much the population at large supported the idea of unification during the war. Pressured from all sides, drafted in embattled armies, influenced by their local priests, and isolated from the pro-Yugoslav activity abroad, the population was waiting for the military outcome of the world conflict. The Serbian soldier, who fought for the survival of his own army and state, had no choice but to continue the battle to its conclusion. Among the "Habsburg Yugoslavs" opinions gradually changed during the war. In 1914, according to Supilo, with the exception of the young generation, the majority of Croats were hesitant. The mood was turning in favor of unification as the war approached its end. In August 1918 General Stjepan Sarkotić, the last imperial governor of Bosnia, estimated that 100 percent of Dalmatia favored Yugoslav unification, and about 60 percent of Croatia, Slavonia, Bosnia, and Herzegovina approved unification. It can be assumed that Sarkotić referred to the non-Serbian population, as the Serbs in the Monarchy were assumed to favor unification with Serbia. The majority of Slovenes, squeezed between Austria and Italy, expressed similar feelings.[4]

There were only two revolutionary outbursts among the Yugoslavs in the Monarchy during the war—the February 1918 mutiny in the Austro-Hungarian navy in Boka Kotorska and the May 1918 rebellion of a Slovene regiment in Judenburg. Antiwar and anti-Habsburg feelings were more often expressed by defection to the Russians on the eastern front. The Green Cadre was made up of defectors who fled to the forests at the very end of the war.

Somewhat different reactions occurred in the south. After the Bulgarian authorities began recruiting in occupied territories, an armed uprising erupted in February 1917 at Toplica, in southern Serbia. After an initial success, the insurgents were smashed by the regular Bulgarian army. The result was a massacre of some twenty thousand people.

Two divisions of volunteers were organized in Russia in 1916 and 1917. They were composed predominantly of Serbs, as the Croats were mostly alienated by the command going to Serbian officers. Other volunteers joined the Yugoslav division on the Salonika front, recruited among ethnic Yugoslavs coming mainly from the United States.

Yugoslav unification as well as that of the other Eastern Europeans depended on the outcome of the war in which the destiny of the Yugoslavs was attached to the cause of the Entente. Because of the Balkan–Central European character of Yugoslav unification, it was contingent on the policy of the Allies regarding the future structure of Europe, the postwar balance of power, and the resolution of the Eastern Question.

Yugoslav unification presumed the dissolution of the Habsburg monarchy, an idea the Allies opposed almost to the end of the war. The 1917 Bolshevik revolution contributed to their fears of a vacuum in Central Europe. One possible solution was the federalization of the Habsburg monarchy, with autonomy granted to its peoples (with the exception of an independent Poland). In this scheme Serbia was to be restored and rewarded by access to the Adriatic via Bosnia and Herzegovina. Yugoslav unification was also seriously challenged by the 1915 London pact concluded between the Allies and Italy and the early 1917 negotiations for a separate peace with Austria-Hungary.

The approach to the formation of Yugoslavia was further influenced by traditional Anglo-Russian rivalry in the Eastern Question.

The Catholic Croats and Slovenes were considered part of Central Europe, and the Orthodox Serbs and Montenegrins categorized in the pro-Russian Balkans. British diplomats looked upon Serbia as an outpost of Russia. Yugoslavia, with a Serbian core, would support Russian predominance in the Adriatic and the Balkans.

The gradual British acceptance of Yugoslavia came after the 1917 Russian revolution which eliminated the Russian factor. The western Yugoslavs, culturally and economically more advanced, were to rein in Serbian expansionism. The "western variant" was to overcome the "Balkan variant," and the new country was to become a barrier to any revived German *Drang nach Osten* in the future.

On the other side, Russia did not favor the unification of Serbia and Montenegro with the "Habsburg Yugoslavs." Traditional Russian policy divided the Balkans along Catholic-Orthodox religious lines. St. Petersburg worried that Catholic Yugoslavs would pollute the Serbian Orthodox wine and enforce the influence of the Vatican. Finally, Italy also opposed the formation of a strong Slavic state on the other side of the Adriatic as a rising competitor in *mare nostro*. The international climate was not favorable to the formation of Yugoslavia. The skies cleared only at the end of the war.

Both the Serbian government and the Yugoslav Committee in London fought for unification, although they disagreed about how to accomplish it. The question was: is Serbia the liberator or a partner in liberation? The Serbian government looked toward an extended Serbia in which the united Yugoslavs would obtain their national freedom (on the Italian and German pattern). On the other hand, the representatives of Yugoslavs from the Habsburg monarchy favored dualism (the Austro-Hungarian pattern).

On their way toward unity the Serbian government and the Yugoslav Committee faced monumental difficulties. In 1914 the Serbian army of 350,000 men, supported by 35,000 Montenegrin troops, engaged in a desperate struggle to repel the Austro-Hungarian invasion in two victorious battles during which the country's survival hung by a thread.[5] In 1915 the Allies pressured the government to cede parts of Macedonia to Bulgaria, and negotiated with Italy and Romania by offering parts of Yugoslav territory. The pro-German Greek monarch refused to support Serbia. Casualties in the campaign were heavy and typhoid fever ravaged the country.

The 1915 invasion of surrounded Serbia marked the breaking point; its decimated army withdrew across Albania to the Adriatic, to be rehabilitated by the Allies and sent to the newly opened Salonika front. The "Easterners" and "Westerners" among the Allied strategists argued about the value of the Salonika front, which was essential for the continued participation of Serbia in the war and for its financial and military survival.

Enticed by initial victories in 1914 and expecting a brief war, the Serbian government formulated the country's war aims. In September Prime Minister Nikola Pašić instructed his representatives abroad to plead for Yugoslav unification as a guarantee of future stability in the Adriatic and the Mediterranean. A group of distinguished scholars and intellectuals was assigned to study and elaborate the unification program. On December 7 the parliament, convened in the city of Niš, issued a declaration that officially proclaimed the liberation of Serbs, Croats, and Slovenes as Serbia's war aim.[6]

In 1915 the Yugoslav Committee was established in London as a political action group of Yugoslav émigré-politicians from the Habsburg monarchy to promote Yugoslav unification among the western Allies. The committee gradually became an independent body and a counterpart to the Serbian government. The committee faced numerous obstacles: the Allies were opposed to the dissolution of the Habsburg monarchy; Italy challenged the unification as it pursued advantages obtained in the London pact; the Pašić government refused to share authority and leadership in unification, keeping them for Serbia. The émigré composition of the committee was another handicap. Pressured by the war's realities, in May 1917 the South Slav representatives in the Reichsrat in Vienna demanded autonomy in a federalized monarchy, under Habsburg rule.

Frictions between the Serbian government and the Yugoslav Committee contributed to the Allies' impression of "anarchistic trends" among the South Slavs and the questionable viability of their union. Military developments, the February revolution in Russia, and the American entry into the war imposed an agreement on the Yugoslavs. It was reached in Corfu between the representatives of the two bodies on July 20, 1917. The declaration called for the formation of a democratic, constitutional kingdom of Serbs, Croats, and Slovenes under the Karadjordjević dynasty. Cultural and religious rights were to be guaranteed by a constituent assembly, which would determine the internal state organization after the war.[7] National autonomy—not a federation—was debated at Corfu. Despite ambiguities, the declaration became the Magna Carta of future unification.

Two factors arose to fill the vacuum created by the collapse of the Habsburg monarchy at the end of the war. On October 29, 1918, the secession of Croatia and Dalmatia was proclaimed and a government was announced representing the South Slavs of the former Monarchy. This introduced a new option of dualism with Serbia, whose troops were returning from the south, after the victorious breakup of the Salonika front. A dualistic agreement was reached in Geneva in November 1918, with both sides retaining authority over their respective territories.

The agreement was unworkable for several reasons. Regent Alexander and the Serbian government refused to accept it; the Italians proceeded to implement the London pact; the chaotic situation in formerly Habsburg territories challenged the establishment of new Yugoslav authorities. The Serbian army became the main guarantor of the integrity of Yugoslav territory, as Lloyd George had suggested to Pašić.[8] Montenegro, influenced by Serbia, and the majority of Bosnia and Herzegovina, decided in favor of union with Serbia. Representatives of the National Council in Zagreb rushed to Belgrade, where on December 1, 1918, in the presence of Regent Alexander, the unification of the new Kingdom of Serbs, Croats, and Slovenes was proclaimed. The unification was accomplished, but the way it was done left many unresolved questions that would pose problems in the future.

Unitarism Versus Federalism: The Tottering Union

For the first time in history in 1918 the Yugoslavs woke up in the same country. No serious resistance opposed the unification. Emotions ran high over the victory, the end of the war, and hopes for a better future. The Serbian soldier was welcomed as a liberator in large parts of Bosnia as well as in Dalmatia and Slovenia. He offered the option to switch to the victors in the war. Yugoslav nationalists were enthusiastic. The previously subject nations were expected to become the ruling ones, to the disappointment of the now-destitute pro-Habsburg aristocracy and bureaucracy.

The new state emerged as a fait accompli before its formal recognition in Versailles. Yugoslav representatives at the Paris peace conference faced two major problems: to gain international recognition and to get approval of the requested frontiers. A legally awkward situation appeared during the first phase of peace negotiations. While the Yugoslavs addressed the conference in the name of their united kingdom and referred to the principle of national self-determination, the official conference protocols listed them as the "Delegation of Serbia." The United States was the first country to recognize the new state (on February 2, 1919), followed by Britain and France at the beginning of June.

More difficult was the question of new frontiers, over which the Yugoslavs had pending disputes with six bordering states, Greece being the only exception.[9] The toughest confrontation was with Italy over the application of the 1915 London pact; Italy had the advantage of membership in the exclusive council of four leaders of the great powers while the Yugoslavs profited from the support of President Woodrow Wilson. The result was a deadlock to be resolved later in Rapallo in 1920. The Italo-Yugoslav frontier conflict poisoned their relationship and became one of the major destabilizing factors in the Balkans during the interwar period.

Despite such challenges, the Kingdom of Serbs, Croats, and Slovenes emerged as one of the major war beneficiaries in Eastern Europe. The 1919–1920 peace treaties concluded with Austria and Hungary ratifying the partition of the Habsburg monarchy and recognizing the sovereignty of successor states, included the "full independence of the Serb-Croat-Slovene state."

The new state had first to cross the rocky road strewn with the effects of the war, the chaotic economic situation, and the diversity of inherited social and political systems. One-third of Serbia's population, military and civilian, perished in the war, which destroyed one-half of the national wealth. The Yugoslavs in the Habsburg monarchy suffered heavy losses on the Italian and Russian fronts. One-fifth of their prewar wealth was wiped out. The new kingdom inherited six different customs areas, five currencies, four railway networks, and three types of banking systems.[10] Slovenia and Croatia were cut off from former Austro-Hungarian markets. Misery and poverty fueled social discontent incited by the Bolshevik revolution.

In a country where the peasantry made up an overwhelming majority, the variety of agrarian systems and the character of land tenure was among the major problems. Small peasant property ownership prevailed in Serbia and Montenegro; a variety of land ownership, including large landed estates, characterized the former Habsburg territory; in Bosnia and Macedonia the remains of the Ottoman feudal system survived.

Establishment of a common currency, unification of legislation, and agrarian reform were among the major duties of the central government. Centered in Belgrade—which claimed major Serbian sacrifices in the war—legislative decisions provoked discontent in the other parts of the country. Agrarian reform was aimed at appeasing the revolutionary zeal of the peasantry, eliminating foreign aristocracy, and rewarding war veterans. Although it was hampered by bureaucracy and mismanagement as well as by the lack of available land to satisfy peasant needs, one of every four peasant families obtained land and the old feudal system was abolished. In 1931 the average landholding was 4.2 hectares (10.4 acres) of arable and 8.5 hectares (21 acres) of cultivated land. The dwarf peasant holding was not economically competitive and, according to Oscar Jászy, only delayed the revolution to come in Eastern Europe.

The kingdom of Serbs, Croats, and Slovenes did not acknowledge the fact of its multinational character. Rather, it was based on the idea of national unitarism, expressed in a political union of major South Slavic ethnic groups, among which Serbs were the most numerous (39 percent), followed by Croats (24 percent), and Slovenes (8.5 percent). The rest included large ethnic minorities of Germans, Magyars, and Albanians as well as Macedonians and Bosnian Muslims, making the country a microcosm of the Balkans. The extension of frontiers was based on the nineteenth century concept that acquisition of territory and population makes a great state. Confident that they could control or assimilate the 16.67 percent of non-Slavic minorities, the authorities in Belgrade refused to exchange reciprocal neighboring populations, as stipulated in the peace treaties of other Balkan states. Deprived of their national rights, the dissatisfied minorities turned into destabilizing factors, feeding both the extreme political right and left, encouraged and supported by revisionist European powers.

The main problem that the country faced during the interwar period was the lack of consensus between the two major national groups, the Serbs and the Croats. This resulted in the collision between unitarism on the one side and dualism and federalism on the other.

The Serbs transferred into the new state the tradition of a centralized, unitarian statehood that they had applied during the nineteenth century development of their nationally homogenous state. Democracy and parliamentarism were to be the counterweights to centralism, as they had been in Serbia from 1903 to 1914.

The 1918 unification was to a large extent the result of Serbia's role in the war. Its army jumped into the vacuum created by the dissolution of the Habsburg monarchy. History has never known a dynasty to abdicate, an army to dissolve, or a state establishment to vanish after victory was won. Dualism, federalism, and autonomism were for good reason regarded in Belgrade with suspicion as forerunners of separatism and secession—the diseases that had corroded and caused the collapse of the former Habsburg monarchy. The result was that a Serbian-designed unitary Yugoslavia was too big to tackle: Serbian authorities lacked the expertise and capacity to carry out their predominant role.

From the times of Count Metternich, Alexander Bach, and Khuen-Héderváry, centralism had been anathema to Croatia. Historical state rights were not recognized in the new Yugoslav state. Torn between the yearning for independence on the one hand, and at least an approved national autonomy on the other, Croatian politics turned to the old methods of boycott and obstruction, copied from the previous Hungarian opposition to Vienna. The Serbian dynasty was for the majority of Croats a Balkan substitute for the Habsburgs. Belgrade was looked upon as a distant center of alienated authority, as Budapest or Vienna had been regarded in the past. Slovenians would have prefered autonomy but complied with unitarism under pressure from Italian and Austrian revanchists. Muslim leaders in Bosnia found in Yugoslavism a shield against absorption by Serbs and Croats.

Political developments during the interwar period went through three phases: shaky democracy and parliamentarism (1919–1929); the authoritarian regime of King Alexander (1929–1934); and the quasi-parliamentarian, restrained authoritarianism under the regency of the minor King Peter II (1934–1941).

From the very beginning parliamentarism was challenged by the activities of ethnic, regional, and religious political parties with colliding ideas over centralism, autonomism, and federalism. In general the Serbian parties favored unitarism, with strong support by Serbs from Croatia as well as by some previous protagonists of Yugoslavism among Croats and Slovenes. The issues of monarchism or republicanism, centralism with or without national-historic autonomy, loose or strong federation with the right of secession, were all hotly debated in the constituent assembly that was preparing the new country's constitution.

The main challenge to unitarism came from Croatia, where the population at large finally obtained male suffrage in 1919 and dynamically entered politics. The Croatian Peasant party emerged as a populist mass movement in the fight for national recognition. It found in Stjepan Radić a charismatic and popular leader, a demagogue and a realist, a Croatian nationalist and an internationalist, an anti-Yugoslav and a pro-Yugoslav proponent, a republican who yielded to the king, and a man who conquered the soul of his countrymen.[11]

The rise of the Croatian Peasant party was similar to the Radical party, which in the 1880s mobilized the peasantry in Serbia. There was a tragic intransigence on both sides. When Radić went abroad, where he publicly questioned unification, the government in Belgrade responded with repression and Zagreb reacted with boycott and obstruction. This proved to be a mistake: the boycott eliminated the Croatian opposition in the Constituent Assembly. The communists were already contained (due to their radical revolutionary activity in 1920). The Serbian Radical party, headed by Nikola Pašić and supported by the Democratic party and the Muslims, was able to carry out the 1921 Vidovdan constitution that confirmed the Serbian-cemented unitarism.

The 1921 constitution, a replica of the 1903 Serbian constitution, provided a parliamentary democracy in a unitary state. It was challenged from the very beginning by requests for revision. A political merry-go-round resulted in a succession of twenty-three governments from 1918 to 1928. Coalition cabinets reflected the changing policy of their members. However, during the entire interwar period only one government was headed by a non-Serb prime minister, and all the main portfolios were distributed among Serbs.[12] The core of the army's upper ranks was recruited from former Serbian military commanders.

Bitter interparty conflicts centered around unitarism and federalism, in which allies and archenemies switched sides on the political chessboard. Serbian Radicals and Democrats parted company, the first impeding and the latter attempting to reach a Yugoslav understanding. After being arrested for denouncing the monarchy and for joining the Peasant International in Moscow, Stjepan Radić dropped republicanism and briefly joined his archenemy, Nikola Pašić, in the Radical government of 1925–1926. Svetozar Pribičević, the main advocate of centralism among Serbs in Croatia, switched sides from Serbian Radicals to Democrats in 1924–1925, finally allying himself with Radić, his nemesis, in 1927. Mutual distrust dominated relations between Croatian and Serbian parties, with King Alexander meddling behind the scene in domestic political squabbles.

In 1928 the parliament became the arena of mutual recriminations, insults, and threats. This culminated in the assassination of the brothers Stjepan and Pavel Radić by a fanatical Montenegrin deputy. At that moment Yugoslavia's continued existence was in question. The reaction in Croatia was understandably strong. At first King Alexander tried unsuccessfully to rally all the embattled political parties behind the Slovene leader, Mrs. Anton Korošec. On the other hand, the king rejected the proposal of Radić's successor, Vlatko Maček, to reorganize the country into a federation. On January 6, 1929, the king suspended the constitution and stepped in with his personal rule, supported by the army.

The royal coup recalled the nineteenth-century regimes of Balkan monarchs and paralleled the authoritarian rule introduced in Eastern Europe during the 1930s. It resulted from the malfunction of democratic institutions and the explosion of national passions.

The 1929 royal coup did not face instant resistance. Few considered the regime to be permanent. Business hoped for more economic stability and an efficient bureaucracy. The public at large was tired of political squabbles. The country's name was changed to Yugoslavia to confirm the assumed oneness of its people. Political parties were suppressed, the administration was centralized in nine *banovine* (provinces), a unified penal code was introduced, and school curricula were standardized.

The unitarism concept failed in the long run. Unable to quell the Croatian opposition, it actually intensified it. More than ever before, Croats opposed centralism. Although the king enjoyed in Serbia the prestige of being the army commander during the war, the Serbs lost the democratic freedoms they had fought for decades before.

The 1931 constitution granted by the king provided a quasi-parliamentarian system subordinated to the monarch. The bogus parliament and the new official Yugoslav National party met fierce opposition from former Croatian as well as Serbian political parties. The whole system relied on the king's authority. It suffered a heavy blow when King Alexander was assassinated in Marseilles in 1934 by Ustaši and Macedonian terrorists, sheltered by Mussolini's Italy.

Yugoslavia had inherited the prewar rivalry between Austria-Hungary and Italy over the Adriatic as well as the Serbian confrontation with Bulgaria over Macedonia. Surrounded by revisionists—Italy, Austria, Hungary and Bulgaria—and refusing to recognize the Soviet regime, isolated Yugoslavia sought political support from the war victors. Under King Alexander Yugoslav foreign policy continued the traditional Serbian allegiance to France. Encouraged by France, the Little Entente was formed in 1921 between Yugoslavia, Czechoslovakia, and Romania to prevent the restoration of the Habsburg dynasty in Hungary. It became a part of the cordon sanitaire structured by

France as a buffer zone between Eastern Europe and the Soviet Union. Active in the League of Nations, the Little Entente established a close mutual political, economic, and cultural collaboration in the early 1930s.

In the south, the Balkan Pact was created in 1934 between Yugoslavia, Greece, Romania, and Turkey to contain Bulgaria, in response to Mussolini's policy of aligning with Austria, Hungary, Bulgaria, and Albania. It was the last attempt to organize the "Grand Western Alliance," including Eastern Europe and Soviet Russia, to confront the rising threat of Nazi Germany.

Both architects of the antifascist polity of containment, the French Foreign Minister Louis Barthou and King Alexander, were its first victims. The Great Depression, the impotence of the League of Nations, and above all the rise of Adolf Hitler, together with the Anglo-French flirtation with Mussolini, were among the fatal blows inflicted on the Little Entente and the Balkan Pact. Frightened and disoriented, isolated and abandoned, their members tried individually to save their skins. In the late 1930s, both alliances died natural deaths.

Sharp ideological polarization between the extreme right and left ruled the domestic Yugoslav political stage. On the right three types of factions appeared: unitary Yugoslav, particular ethnic, and explicit fascist.[13] The first two were recruited mainly among the nationalistic youth: they used violence against their internal adversaries but opposed Italian fascist aggression against Yugoslavia.

The most dangerous and militant were two explicitly fascist groups, recruited among ultranationalists in Croatia and Macedonia, respectively, both of which turned to terrorism and obtained support from Mussolini's Italy. Among the first were the Ustaši, who were Croatian nationalists, espoused fascism, anti-Serbianism, and anti-Semitism, and advocated armed struggle for Croatian independence. Their leader, Ante Pavelić, found shelter in Italy and, according to some estimates, had attracted some forty thousand Croatian followers by the eve of World War II.

The Internal Macedonian Revolutionary Organization (IMRO) split after World War I into two wings. The first demanded the annexation of Macedonia to Bulgaria. During the 1920s it played an important role in Bulgarian domestic politics and organized terrorist groups to perpetrate sabotage in Yugoslavia. The other wing favored communism and a Balkan Federation, to include Macedonia. (The Fascist party in Serbia, founded in 1935, showed poorly in the elections, failing to obtain a single seat in the parliament; after colliding with the authoritarian regime it was banned in 1940.)

On the other side of the political spectrum—on the extreme left—was the Yugoslav Communist party (CPY). After an astounding show of strength in the 1920 elections, the party hoped for a social revolution. Terrorist acts committed by "Red Justice" provoked the party's suppression in 1921 and pushed it underground. Pressured at home, corroded by factions, the CPY became fully subordinate to the Comintern in Moscow, which in its turn became subservient to Stalin. From 1924 the Bolshevization of all European communist parties transformed them into an obedient "quasi-religious, quasi-military instrument of Soviet foreign policy," as Adam Ulam has written. They regarded Yugoslavia as a "product of Versailles" and an "agent of French imperialism." According to them, Yugoslavia was to be dismantled. Serbia, the core of Yugoslavia, became the main target. The Resolution on Yugoslavia, adopted at the Fifth Congress of the Comintern in 1924, instructed the CPY to break up the country into independent republics of Croatia, Macedonia, and Slovenia. Montenegro was added soon thereafter.

A disciplined member of the Comintern, the CPY called until 1928 for the dissolution of Yugoslavia into independent states joined in a communist Balkan Federation. During that time the CPY collaborated with the Ustaši and the IMRO on the intended destruction of Yugoslavia.

From 1935 on, frightened by the rise of Nazi Germany, the Comintern changed its tactics, supporting the formation of antifascist popular fronts. The CPY obediently followed the switch, from the dissolution to the federalization of Yugoslavia. The party suffered from both persecution at home and Stalin's purges in the late 1930s. In 1937, in the midst of the purges, Josip Broz Tito (then in exile in Moscow) was appointed secretary general of the party. The role he played in eliminating competitors has been recently discussed in Yugoslav historiography, but he made a wise move in coming back to the country, away from the waspish center in Moscow. It enabled him to reorganize the party and appoint a new leadership of his own choice, one which was personally attached to him.

The zigzagging policy of Moscow, which in 1939 abruptly signed the non-aggression pact with Hitler, embarrassed the CPY and forced it to switch from resistance to the Nazis during the Czechoslovak crisis to the condemnation of Western "capitalistic warmongers." The party was in trouble: from 120,000 in 1919 the membership dropped below 3,000 during the period from 1925 to 1928. It reached a low point of 1,000 members in 1939 and slowly recovered to 12,000 members in 1941.[14]

"The strong man," Alexander, was replaced at the helm of the country by the regency of the minor King Peter II. The first regent, Prince Paul, a British-educated gentleman, was an art connoisseur who established the art museum in Belgrade and introduced golf to the country. But he was unfamiliar with the passions dominating domestic politics.[15] He was suspected by Serbs of being pro-Croatian, and by the Croats of being pro-Serbian. The country was tired of authoritarianism, while at the same time the storm was approaching from abroad. Serbian and Croatian opposition parties formed a United Opposition, challenging the rightist government of Milan Stojadinović (1935–1938), which was supported by Slovenian Populists and Bosnian Muslims. The rightist government tried to benefit from German economic penetration in the Balkans and to find a political counterbalance to Hitler in Mussolini's Italy. The 1937 rapprochement with Italy and the 1938 reconciliation with Bulgaria finally buried the already moribund Little Entente and the Balkan Pact.

By annexing Austria and dismantling Czechoslovakia, Hitler opened the door to the Danubian and Balkan region. To confront the foreign danger, a Serbo-Croatian consensus became the only option for the country's survival. Unable to reach it, Stojadinović had to accede to the demands of the Cvetković-Maček government. Maček switched from the opposition to the government's side in order to obtain Croatian autonomy. In August 1939 a self-governing *banovina* (province) of Croatia was approved. It included Croatia, Slavonia, and Dalmatia as well as parts of Bosnia and Herzegovina, with a population of 4.4 million, which included 866,000 Orthodox Serbs and 164,000 Muslims.

As usually happens with compromises, neither side was satisfied. It became the first step toward federalism, but was too little too late: the Croats and the Serbs thought that not enough or too much was conceded, while other nationalities expected similar treatment. In the meantime, a war that would involve both sides was imminent.

The post–World War II Communist-inspired historiography is extremely critical of interwar Yugoslavia, contrasting it unfavorably to the revolutionary restructured country. This criticism has some justification, but it is also biased. The critics of interwar Yugoslavia overlook the difficulties which the infant country had to meet during the twenty years of domestic and international turmoil. At the time there was no European labor market to absorb Yugoslav *Gastarbeiter* (guest workers) nor was there an International Monetary Fund to rescue domestic economies from collapse. Interwar Yugoslavia can be credited with postwar reconstruction, agrarian reform, a unified free market, and a gradual (though insufficient) industrialization. Foreign policy aimed to protect the country's integrity and independence. The war debt was repaid by 1926 and the dinar stabilized in 1927. In the mid-1920s the trade balance was positive. During the Great Depression, which hit the country severely, the government tried to protect the peasants with a tax moratorium, a Chartered Agricultural Bank to provide favorable credits, and encouragement for peasant cooperatives. Heavy investments were made to integrate the railway network, to improve transportation and to equip the army. Central authorities introduced protective tariffs and invited foreign investments. Progress was made in schooling and housing. All this took place while the population increased dramatically: from twelve million in 1921 to sixteen million in 1941.

The country remained predominantly agrarian, with peasants making up 75 percent of the population in 1941. Industry doubled the number of enterprises and workers, but Yugoslavia remained an exporter of agricultural products and raw materials and an importer of industrially manufactured goods. Despite loud recriminations about "Serbian exploitation," the north was economically and industrially ahead of the south throughout the interwar period.

Death and Resurrection: World War II

Although Mussolini's invasion of Albania, the Soviet dismemberment of Romania, and the Italo-Greek campaign brought the war to the Balkans, the die was cast in late 1940 when Hitler decided to attack the Soviet Union. For the forthcoming eastern front he required the security of reinforcement in the Balkans. By March 1941, with the exception of Greece, Yugoslavia was completely surrounded by hostile fascist powers and their satellites. Isolated, demoralized and unable to obtain effective military support from the British, Prince Paul decided to yield to the heavy pressure from Berlin. On March 25, 1941, he joined Yugoslavia to the Tripartite Pact.

The response was an uproar in Belgrade, and on March 27, a military coup overthrew the regency, proclaimed the minor king to be an adult, and established a coalition government including representatives of major political parties. The putsch was organized and conducted by Serbian army officers, encouraged by the British Intelligence Service.[16] It was enthusiastically greeted in traditionally anti-German

Serbia, but provoked reservations in Croatia over the future of the autonomy obtained by the former government in 1939.

The new coalition government tried to appease Berlin via Italian mediation and asked the Soviets for support, but to no avail. Stalin's response was vague, while an infuriated Hitler ordered a "merciless, lightning attack" on Yugoslavia. On April 6 air raids turned Belgrade into flames and ruins, the encircled army was forced to capitulate in twelve days, and the king with his government fled the country in panic, heading for London.

The dismemberment of Yugoslavia followed the invasion. On April 10 the Independent State of Croatia was proclaimed—a puppet fascist state including Croatia, Bosnia, and Herzegovina under the *Poglavnik* Ante Pavelić and his Ustaši cohorts. Slovenia was partitioned between Germany and Italy. Italy also obtained the Dalmatian littoral and control over Montenegro, while Kosovo was joined to Albania. Bulgaria was rewarded with Macedonia, and Hungary got large parts of Vojvodina. What was left of pre-1912 Serbia was placed under German military occupation. A puppet government under General Milan Nedić, formed in the summer of 1941 under tight German control, took care of the administration.

Between 1941 and 1945 the Yugoslavs experienced, besides the invasion and occupation, a national, religious, and ideological civil war that caused suffering greatly in excess of that in World War I. The collapse of the state establishment unleashed submerged passions and hatreds, paving the way for revolutionary outbursts. An array of "final solutions" was offered, coupled with brutalities inherited from the past. As Stevan Pavlovitch has written, extreme Croatian nationalism attempted to Croatize the fascist state by totalitarian terror, while the Serbian insurgents, for self-defense and survival, were repaying atrocity with atrocity whenever they had a chance. Roman Catholic, Orthodox, and Muslim alike, in the ethnically mixed regions of Yugoslavia, were locked in a vicious struggle, forced to turn to the foreign conquerors for protection.[17]

Even after fifty years it is impossible to establish the exact number of victims who fell prey to the occupiers, the civil war, and genocide. The official postwar number of 1.7 million seems exaggerated, and recent research has reduced it to 1.1 million.[18] Whatever the figure is, it is a fact that more Yugoslavs died at the hands of their countrymen than in battle with foreign enemies.

The worst atrocities were committed against the Serbs and the Jews in the fascist Independent State of Croatia (NDH), in which one-third of the Serbian population was to be exterminated, one-third deported and one-third converted to Roman Catholicism.[19] Brutalities against the Serbs included throwing their bodies into mountain caves. The savagery shocked even the Nazis, who advertised the "final solution." The Jasenovac concentration camp became one of the most atrocious death camps in Europe. The totalitarian state also frustrated the Croatian population, initially warmed by long yearned-for statehood but eventually alienated by its terror. The Croatian Peasant party leader, Vlatko Maček, who stayed in the country, refused to collaborate with the Ustaši. The Catholic priesthood supported Catholic-Croatian nationalism and anticommunism but disliked the totalitarian character of the Ustaši state.

The first organized resistance originated in Serbia, incited by its revolutionary tradition, direct German occupation, and the flood of horrified refugees pouring into the country. The first to start the resistance was Colonel (later General) Dragoljub-Draža Mihailović, who tried to assemble what was left of the former defeated army. He soon faced another resistance group under Tito and the communists, who entered the battle in July 1941 after Hitler's "treacherous" attack on Soviet Russia.

Both the četniks, as the Mihailović "Yugoslav Army in the Fatherland" became known, and Tito's "National Liberation Army" or "Partisans," were antifascist resistance movements, but they differed in ideology, politics, and strategy. These differences resulted in bitter confrontation and civil war during the occupation.

Mihailović was a pro-Western Serbian monarchist, an anticommunist and antifascist, fighting for an improved postwar democratic order in which the Serbs would keep their central role. Tito was a communist who joined the social revolution to the national revolution, from which a Soviet-style Yugoslavia, based on proletarian brotherhood and unity, would emerge.

After a brief collaboration, both movements, looking to future postwar issues, clashed in a way that foreshadowed the forthcoming cold war. Aware that overt resistance would be tantamount to national suicide and invite merciless German reprisals, Mihailović espoused "existentialist realism,"[20] postponing the general uprising to the end of the war when the Allies would land in the Balkans. In the meantime, while conducting local attacks against the Nazis, he tried to get rid of his communist opponents, accommodated the Italians, and facilitated German antipartisan offensives. Entrenched in his native Serbia, Mihailović, often unsuccessfully, tried to impose his authority over a rather loose organization. This policy, though it reduced casualties, failed in the end. The Germans put a bounty on both Mihailović and Tito, and, for good reason, mistrusted the *četniks* until the end of the war. Mihailović also lost the support of the British. His Yugoslav resistance was narrowed down to the Serbian resistance. The Yugoslav government-in-exile, into which Mihailović was co-opted until 1944, was not of great help, being torn by Serbo-Croatian squabbles and losing credibility among the western Allies.

On the opposite side, Tito and the Partisans applied the strategy of "revolutionary existentialism" in which the end justifies the means, regardless of human sacrifice. Seasoned, disciplined communists, experienced in underground activity, composed the core of the movement. The CPY also adapted to the realities of war. Expecting a Soviet victory and the beginning of world revolution, the CPY initially directed the resistance in 1941 and early 1942 toward establishment of a Soviet-style republic in Serbia and the elimination of the "class enemy" in Montenegro. Forced to leave Serbia and cautioned by Moscow, with which regular radio contact was established, Tito stressed the national-liberation character of the Partisan movement. Recruiting Serbian survivors of the genocide in the NDH and offering the alternative of brotherhood and unity to a population locked in internecine strife, he enlarged the ranks of his army. Promises of a new classless society, with social and economic equality, attracted the impoverished peasantry.

However, the road to victory was rocky. In April 1943, worried about rumors of an Allied landing in the Balkans, Tito proposed a truce with the Germans to enable him to get rid of the *četniks*[21] and even to oppose an Anglo-American landing in Yugoslavia. He was saved from further embarrassment by Hitler's refusal to deal with "bandits," but the Germans allowed Tito to defeat Mihailović in Montenegro.

Both Tito and Mihailović tried to enforce their own politics, defying the advice of their respective Soviet and British patrons. They both rejected the strategy of unifying their forces in an anti-Hitler coalition. Mihailović refused to continue with overt resistance, required by the British. Stalin could not understand why Tito was unable to collaborate with the *četniks,* when Stalin himself was allied with the arch anticommunist Winston Churchill. In Yugoslavia the proletarian divisions, with their red-star emblems, embarrassed the Soviets who, dissolving the Comintern, renounced world revolution in order to placate the Allies. Tito reversed his instructions from Moscow: instead of a popular front formed from above, he created one from below, symbolically including dissidents of the former middle-class leftist parties.

Tito politically outmaneuvered Mihailović. With raw pragmatism he grabbed the hand extended by the British, who supported an active resistance. The 1943 capitulation of Italy enabled the Partisans to obtain the armament of a disintegrating army and marked the turning point in the civil war. Mihailović's efforts to shelter American pilots who were shot down by the Germans in Serbia came too late.[22] The die was cast: Tito and his Partisans were victorious.

Federalism Under Communist Centralism

If Yugoslavia was to survive, federalism became the only option. Monarchists, republicans, nationalists, and communists were all aware of the failure of unitary Yugoslavism. The main difference among them was their notion of how the federation would be structured: in three Serbo-Croatian-Slovenian parts or with additional Montene-grin, Bosnian-Herzegovinian, and Macedonian federal units. The distinction expressed the collision between the two concepts: Strong Serbia–Strong Yugoslavia or Weak Serbia–Strong Yugoslavia. The first was backed by monarchists and Serbian nationalists; the second was promoted by the communists and all the rest of the nationalities and minorities in the multinational country.

The communist-led resistance came through the war with an organized army and gradually introduced revolutionary authorities in regions as they were liberated. The birth of the new Yugoslavia was announced in November 1943 when the Antifascist Council of National Liberation (AVNOJ) declared itself to be the supreme legislative body. It proclaimed the federalization of the country, prohibited the return of King Peter II, and elected a National Committee, under Marshal Tito, as the country's government.

The Partisans' victory was legalized by the agreement reached in May 1944 between Tito and the newly appointed prime-minister-in-exile in London, Ivan Šubašić. The agreement was further approved in Moscow and at the Yalta conference in 1945. In the meantime the Red Army, on its way to Hungary, effectively contributed to the liberation of Belgrade and the installation of the new regime.

The federalism proclaimed in 1943 was based on the principle of a symmetry of Yugoslav nations regardless of their numerical strength. It expressed a combination of historic experience and the heritage taken over from the prewar Comintern policy. It was essentially a

Soviet model adapted to Yugoslav patriotism. The spirit of national balance and compromise was taken from the defunct Habsburg monarchy. The prewar Serbian central role was to be abolished by separating Montenegro from Serbia, by carving out two autonomous provinces from the Serbian republic, and by establishing a Macedonian republic. The Muslim nationality in Bosnia (later specifically recognized by the communists) was to keep equilibrium between the Serbs and Croats in that new republic, placed as it was in the middle of Yugoslavia. Equal partnership of nations and national minorities was to guarantee unity in the new mini-Soviet state of Yugoslavia.

The Yugoslav federalism inaugurated in 1943 required two prerequisites: one real, the other assumed. While the prewar unitarism was backed by Serbian centralism, the new federalism was cemented by a highly centralized Yugoslav communist party which appropriated a dominant, uncontrolled ruling monopoly. Yugoslavia became a centralized communist-governed country in which federal issues were determined by the inner party elite, with Marshal Tito as the supreme arbiter. Yugoslav federalism was not democratic: it was a sui generis communist-dominated Marxist unitarism. When the party was subjected to the process of decentralization and democratization, the country's federal structure came under question.

The architects of Yugoslav federalism relied on the Marxist assumption that nationalism is the product of a bourgeois society. Once the bougeoisie was eliminated, proletarian Yugoslavism would overcome national separatism. However, ambiguous "dialectic contradictions" soon emerged. Following the Leninist example, the right of each people to self-determination and secession was acknowledged in the preamble of the AVNOJ Declaration of 1943 but was followed by Article 1, which proclaimed the "indisputable will of all Yugoslav peoples to unify." The right of secession, characteristic of a confederation, was rejected by the people's "declared will" to join into a federation. This ambiguity, repeated in further Yugoslav constitutions, would hound the post-Tito Yugoslavia facing revived nationalism. As in the multinational Soviet Union, secession was theoretically approved, but the methods of applying it were not specified and in practice were denied.

Stalinism Versus Stalinism

The new communist-shaped Yugoslavia faced advantages and disadvantages during the period immediately following the war. When the country was liberated from foreign invaders, the population was weary of war. The proclaimed brotherhood and unity and promises for a better world based on social equality—all these counted among the advantages. The devastation of the war, the inexperience in erecting a fundamentally changed state establishment, the enormous task of securing the results of the victorious revolution and stabilizing the new regime—these counted among the disadvantages.

The dictatorship of the proletariat was to be either voluntarily accepted or coercively imposed. On the one hand, the slogan of "people's democracy" and the facade of the Popular Front were aimed to attract the population at large. On the other hand, enemies and opponents of all colors—former Nazi collaborators as well as middle class liberals and democrats—were to be eliminated in order to secure the political monopoly of the CPY. According to Tito, the secret police (OZNA) had "to strike terror into the bones of those who do not like this kind of Yugoslavia."[23] Harassment of noncommunist politicians, farcical trials such as those which preceeded the execution of Mihailović and the incarceration of Bishop Stepinac, and labor camps for real or alleged enemies, created an atmosphere of fear, which successfully broke the opposition.

With an officially proclaimed wartime army of 800,000 fighters, the Yugoslavs would hold the record for European resistance, but with 300,000 alleged collaborators, they would also hold the record for cooperating with the enemy. The "ghastly mistake" made by the British in returning thousands of anticommunist refugees from Austria to Tito's Partisans resulted in the refugees' mass execution.

For ideological and practical reasons the CPY leadership turned to Moscow, copying the Stalinist model. The 1946 Yugoslav constitution was a replica of the 1936 Soviet constitution; the Yugoslav army and police were molded after the Soviet pattern, relying on Soviet advisers. The first five-year plan, inaugurated in 1947, copied the Soviet type of heavily centralized economy. Radical agrarian reform distributed the property of the church and the large estates to the landless peasantry and rewarded war veterans. The richer peasant, the *kulak,* was eliminated by the policy of compulsory grain deliveries, which sent thousands to prison, unable to fulfill the delivery targets.

The Yugoslav-Soviet honeymoon ended abruptly in 1948, like the relationship of two lovers who change their minds after the marriage. The dramatic clash between Stalinism and Titoism has been thoroughly studied in modern historiography, although some details are not yet fully revealed.[24] The split was the result of domestic national

Yugoslav policy and global Soviet policy in Eastern Europe and the acceleration of the cold war. It was not a question of ideology, although this was later introduced as a contributing factor, but a collision between two states and two personalities, Stalin's and Tito's, over larger political issues.

The historic rift was caused by Russian imperialistic policies inherited by the Soviets, and the Yugoslav drive for independence, manifested in previous wars and revolutions. Resistance during the war produced national communism: basking in the sun of victory, Yugoslav communists strove to be masters in their own home. Tito not only emerged as the uncontested leader of the revolution and the architect of victory but revealed ambitions that went beyond his country's boundaries.

Tito's aggressive foreign policy, inaugurated in 1945 through 1948, placed Yugoslavia in the international spotlight. His conflict with Italy over Trieste almost provoked a war between the superpowers, as did his support offered to the communists in the Greek civil war. Projects for the Balkan federation proposed a political restructuring of southeastern Europe. At the 1947 meeting of the Cominform, the Yugoslavs criticized Western European communist parties for missing revolutionary opportunities at the end of the war. Tito was warmly greeted during his visits to Eastern European countries as a young and vital national communist, a potential viceroy in an eventually emerging polycentric Soviet empire.

Tito's "unpredictable behavior," as Stalin put it at Potsdam, contradicted the Soviet dictator's policy of *Gleichschaltung* in the East European countries, which were to be satellites of the Soviet empire. National communism, exemplified by Tito's Yugoslavia and Gomulka's Poland, challenged the strategy of the "Muscovites" in Eastern Europe. Busily consolidating authority in his own backyard from 1945 to 1948, Stalin tried to avoid an overt military confrontation with the West, which held a monopoly on the atomic bomb. Yugoslavia's shooting down of American planes in the Trieste affair and Tito's involvement in the Greek civil war as well as the premature alliance concluded with Bulgaria risked involving the Soviets in a confrontation beyond their direct control.

The Stalin-Tito clash focused on two basic issues. The domestic issue centered on who would govern Yugoslavia: Stalin or Tito. The Eastern European issue presented the choice between polycentric national communism or Soviet monocentrism. The June 28, 1948, resolution of the Cominform, which ostracized Yugoslav communists, was to resolve the ambiguity.

In the conflict that followed, Stalin made two mistakes: the first resulted from his unwarranted confidence that he could defeat Tito; the second was in providing the CPY with his own system of party purges. The CPY was no longer the obedient Comintern party. The most dedicated Marxists, the prewar revolutionaries, had perished during the war. The new party that emerged from the war had 141,000 members in 1945 and 468,000 in 1948. They were recruited mainly among peasant fighters and among those who, for various reasons, ideological as well as opportunistic, joined the victors. In 1948 only half of the party membership had a basic education.[25] For them Stalin was a distant god, while Tito was their own.

Stalinism in Yugoslavia was eradicated by Stalinist methods. More than 50,000 party members, caught in the dilemma between the two idols, were mercilessly tortured and massacred in the same manner as medieval heretics.

The Yugoslav-Soviet break was of historical significance. It was the first rupture in the communist world centered in Moscow and the first step toward the polycentrism which forecast, in the long run, the collapse of the Soviet empire in Eastern Europe.

The Yugoslav Experiment

The break with the Soviet Union paved the way for a Yugoslav "road to socialism." It required a Marxist theoretical explanation about why it happened, as well as the restructuring of domestic and foreign policies. It had to justify the break in the eyes of the Yugoslav communists and of the international communist movement and had to formulate the specific character of Yugoslav socialism. In foreign policy it had to provide survival and protection from the tremendous pressure applied against the country by the Soviet bloc. The result was the emergence of two doctrines: self-management in the domestic economy and nonalignment in foreign politics.

Yugoslav Marxists accused Stalinism of Marxist-Leninist deviations: instead of socialism it had turned into state capitalism with a bureaucratized, centralized, omnipotent state that subjugated the working class. When they discovered that the Moscow key did not fit the Yugoslav lock, leading Yugoslav communists Milovan Djilas, Eduard Kardelj, and Boris Kidrič turned back to Marx as well as to a plethora of studies of socialist theories that had mushroomed earlier in the Marxist movement.[26] The slogan "factories to the workers" was to transform state property into social property in Yugoslavia.

The planning of production was to be replaced by the planning of investments. Tito, at first hesitant to embark on this course, eventually understood its powerful political ramifications.

Self-management, introduced in 1950, first in economic and then into political and social institutions, became the cornerstone of the Yugoslav system. It allowed the regime to safeguard its allegiance to Marxism and to offer an alternative model to Stalinist Eastern Europe. It influenced eventual economic reforms in Eastern Europe and China and attracted the interest of scholars and political scientists around the world.

Economic decentralization and economic pluralism meant liberalization from a rigid, state-dominated economy. It tried to provide incentives in a socialist system combined with a free market, in a book which could have been authored by Karl Marx, Adam Smith, and Antonio Gramsci. Socialism was to be achieved by Marxist ideology and capitalistic money, both coupled with Yugoslav improvisations.

During the 1960s and early 1970s the economic system proved successful: life became prosperous not only for the communist elite but also for the middle social segments, especially in comparison with the rest of Eastern Europe. In the late 1970s a higher standard of living was stimulated by heavy borrowing from abroad. However, the realities soon became apparent: the Yugoslavs were spending more than they earned. They were living on borrowed time.

The rapid pace of industrialization brought mass relocation from rural to urban centers and radically changed the social structure of the country. The population actively engaged in agriculture dropped from 67.2 percent in 1948 to 19.9 percent in 1981. In a wise move, in order to alleviate pressures on industry, the frontiers were opened, providing the opportunity for *Gastarbeiter* to work abroad. The economy profited from their income that was partially returned to the country but lost their productivity at home.

With a passion for innovation and enamored with their discovery, Yugoslav policymakers, with Kardelj as the main architect, continued escalating self-management in constant experimental changes of the federal system, the party, and the economy. Since World War II Yugoslavia has changed its official name three times,[27] inaugurated four constitutions (1946, 1953, 1963, 1974), amended them four times (1967, 1968, 1971, 1988), and applied a succession of economic reforms in the 1960s, 1970s and the late 1980s.

Initially, self-management stimulated the development of small- and middle-sized industrial enterprises. It also provided the opportunity for producers to participate in the decision-making process. However, its application in growing industrial complexes threatened to atomize their efficiency. The Yugoslav railway system, divided into eight republican and provincial systems and further subdivided among 365 basic associations of self-managing "associated labor" units, is one illustration.

Economic decentralization—the pluralism of economic interests— did not extend to political pluralism. Theoretically, self-management anticipated the withering away of the state bureaucracy. Practically, it produced a huge, pervasive, self-managing bureaucracy. The militarization of Yugoslavia for defense reasons, the burden imposed on the domestic economy by military expenses, and the disproportionate rise of Tito's personal cult were among the side effects of the break with the USSR. Accusations against alleged "foreign enemies and agents, counterrevolutionaries, cominformists, reactionaries, nationalists, pseudoliberals," justified the crushing of whatever opposition arose. Self-management was to be surveilled by the party.

However, the process of decentralization necessarily produced liberalization and therefore backlashed on the party. It preserved its Leninist character, based on democratic centralism, but changed its social composition in favor of professional politicians and *aparatchiks,* military officers, technocrats—all self-confident and self-conscious members who rubber-stamped decisions made by Tito and the top party elite.[28]

In 1952 the CPY redefined its role in order to comply with the principle of self-management and renamed itself the League of Yugoslav Communists (LCY). The party renounced interference in day-to-day decision making, keeping for itself the task of "political and ideological education of masses." At the same time Tito confirmed the leading role of the party, which was to keep growing. Behind the facade, the political monopoly was preserved, together with the *nomenklatura* for "certain key positions of power." According to Milovan Djilas, who quit the party in 1954 and paid for it dearly with years in prison, the party "remained the ruling caste as a modified version of Soviet autocracy."

While keeping the power secured by political monopoly, the party could not escape the effects of decentralization. The spectacular fall in 1966 of the vice-president and mighty minister of interior, Alexander Ranković, was a result of an inner party struggle for power, but it contributed to further decentralization and liberalization of the country.

Winds of liberalism started blowing, challenging the policy of the

LCY. The first harbingers of the changing times appeared among intellectuals, writers, philosophers, and students. They were followed by philosophers grouped around the journal *Praxis*. The short-lived student movement in 1968 revealed the trend among the young generation for a "socialism with a human face," and demonstrated that political initiatives could emerge from below.

In the early 1970s the semiliberal movement in Croatia, imbued with nationalistic overtones, and the mildly liberal regime in Serbia were characteristic of the new generation of communist reformers ready to take over leadership of the country. Both movements were crushed by Tito, who turned back to the old boys and the army.

Although the old order was restored, it could not stop further political decentralization. Yugoslavia was gradually moving from a federation toward a loose confederation. This was confirmed by the 1974 constitution (with 406 articles, the world's lengthiest constitution) which recognized the sovereign status of the republics, elevated the two provinces of the Serbian republic—Kosovo and Vojvodina—to near-equal federal partners, granted to all of the republics and provinces the right to veto decisions taken at the federal level, and prevented any revision of the constitution in the future. Wandering between state centralism and self-managing decentralism, the 1974 constitution established a polycentric centralism, which resulted in the dysfunction of the whole system. It confirmed the regionalism of the country and stimulated economic disunity among republics. As Milovan Djilas put it, the 1974 constitution feudalized Yugoslavia into eight little party-states with eight small competing economies. The party, "the ring to bind them all," the main device of federal unity, split into confederated parties. The only remaining link was the myth of Tito, the supreme arbiter and leader, who secured communist unity.

Expelled by Stalin and his Eastern European satellites from the Cominform in 1948, Yugoslavia faced in foreign policy a dangerous isolation from both East and West. The 1948–49 radical collectivization of land failed to soften Stalin and had to be abandoned. Pressed from all sides, yet showing a remarkable flexibility and ingenuity and inspired by his war experiences, Tito cautiously moved toward the West, which was glad to remove the Soviets from the Adriatic to the Danube and to corrode the Soviet empire in Eastern Europe with Yugoslav heresy.

Both sides were to pay the price. From 1951 to 1960 the United States extended to Yugoslavia $2.7 billion worth of military and economic assistance on a nonrepayable basis—more than Turkey and Greece received at that time. The 1951 United States–Yugoslav Mutual Defense Assistance Agreement, terminated in 1957, equipped and modernized the armed forces and saved the country from economic collapse. The price Tito paid was the withdrawal of his support to the Greek communists, a compromise with Italy over Trieste, and, as a strategic necessity, the rapprochement with former foes Greece and Turkey in 1953–54.

The incongruity between Yugoslav communism and Western democracies made Tito balance on a tight rope. Khrushchev's de-Stalinization and the apology in 1955 for the 1948 break alleviated the danger of direct Soviet intervention. However, Soviet-Yugoslav relations were beyond repair and turned into a game of hide-and-seek. The Soviet specter was constantly on the horizon, especially during the 1956 Hungarian revolution, when Tito approved the Soviet intervention, and in 1968 when he disapproved the Brezhnev doctrine's application in Czechoslovakia.

Eager to safeguard the dominant CPY rule in Yugoslavia and the nation's integrity in the East-West confrontation, Tito reentered the international arena through the back door. In the 1950s he turned toward the Third World, which was to catapult the rejected communist leader of Eastern Europe into one of the main leaders of the new rising nations in Asia and Africa. Coexistence, resort to the United Nations, anticolonialism, and anti-imperialism were attractive to the frustrated young states that emerged from the postwar decolonization process.

Tito's policy was not exactly new: prewar and postwar Soviet policy exploited national liberation movements to advance world communism and Soviet imperialism. The novelty was that Tito did not rely on Asian and African communists, already polarized between the USSR and China, but asked support from socialists and nationalists. Profiles of the nonaligned movement's founding fathers show the diversity of its members. They included Tito (the national communist), Nasser (the militant Arab nationalist), Nehru (India's pensive and sophisticated Brahmin), and Haile Selassie (the feudal Ethiopian emperor). The movement was composed of a colorful group which rose from twenty-five members attending the first conference in 1961 in Belgrade to over one hundred in the late 1980s.

One advantage to the movement was the number of votes it had in the U.N. General Assembly. The disadvantage was the disunity in the movement itself, whose members were involved in mutual wars, estranged by historical, regional, political, and economic differences. In due time some of them leaned toward one of the two superpowers. The nonaligned countries knew more about what they did not want than what they did want.

Despite inner controversies, nonalignment served Yugoslav interests during the crucial 1950s and 1960s. It enabled Yugoslavia, its only European member, to assume a significant role in the Third World and in international diplomacy. Tito bolstered his ego by joining politics with pleasure and hunting lions and tigers in Asia and Africa. His sybaritic taste for luxury contributed to his personal cult in the country and to prestige abroad. On one of the trips to African countries in 1961, which lasted two and a half months, Tito's yacht, transformed into a floating mansion, was escorted by three battleships and one supply ship, carrying tuxedos for 1,400 members of the crew as well as gold and jewels to present to African leaders.[29]

Yugoslav nonalignment, having served its purpose in the 1960s, is being reevaluated in the post-Tito era. Critics point to Tito's neglect of Europe and to his unconditional support of the Arab cause. The result was a foreign policy heavily weighted toward countries that could not provide Yugoslavia with economic advantages. Tito's recognition of the German Democratic Republic in 1967 led to the break with the Federal Republic of Germany, one of Yugoslavia's major economic partners. His unconditional support of Nasser in the 1967 war and the breaking of diplomatic relations with Israel made Yugoslavia, according to a foreign journalist, "the last Arab state that will restore relations with Israel."

Nonalignment served Yugoslavia during the period of isolation imposed by Soviet Russia. But the thawing of the cold war and the economic and political integration of Europe have made it counterproductive economically and obsolete politically. New realities imposed on Yugoslavia point the way, not out of Europe, but into Europe, with the possibility of great gains.

Yugoslavism at the Crossroads

When the main actor leaves the stage the entire drama of his regime comes into question. The alleged last words of King Alexander—"take care of Yugoslavia"—were to be mocked when war broke out. "Tito After Tito" was the slogan extolled when Tito died in 1980. To preserve continuity the 1974 constitution had confirmed Tito's presidency not only during his life but for an "unlimited time," and two laws were enacted in 1977 and 1984 to protect Tito's name and achievement from reevaluation. Tito himself signed the first law.

Like Lenin and Stalin, Tito did not designate a successor. Instead, a collective presidency of the state and the party, rotating annually, was introduced. The octopus leadership was designed to control and check itself in the competition for power over the state and party hierarchy.

By the mid-1960s Tito's main achievements belonged to history. The aging man, who convulsively grasped for power, was surrounded by sycophants, corrupt members of the inner circle of the new ruling elite who fought for the ear of the supreme leader. Court intrigues and marital scandals characterized the last decade of his life. From 1972 Tito was relieved from daily decision making, but until his last days he remained the indisputable arbiter in domestic politics. The Comintern agent who opposed Stalin and got Khrushchev's apology, the communist revisionist who clashed with Mao Zedong and was acclaimed by Mao's successors, the politician who duped Churchill and was honored by the Court of St. James's, the revolutionary who shot down American planes and was welcomed in the White House, the dictator who ruled over his maverick Yugoslavs for thirty-five years, lived in the luxurious seclusion of Brioni, leaving to his country the heritage of transformation from the agricultural to the industrial epoch, together with an embarrassing collection of villas, palaces, yachts, and cars he enjoyed during his lifetime.[30]

Within forty years Yugoslavia was transformed from an agrarian into an industrially developing country in which the gross national product increased by a factor of six, the working class rose from one million to seven million, and the rising tempo of urbanization radically changed the country's social structure. Although limited, the infrastructure for the private sector took root. Illiteracy was significantly reduced and education was expanded, while scholarly institutions, academies of science, and universities mushroomed.

Keeping the country together and leading it into the industrial epoch came at a cost: the loss of democracy and freedom. The seeds of de-Titoization were already planted during Tito's lifetime and resulted from failure of the economic and political system, which provoked the resurgence of particular nationalisms.

The Yugoslav system of self-management took on more responsibility than it was able to handle. The workers' income got priority over productivity. Social demagoguery, characteristic of the rest of Eastern Europe, brought privileged idleness and stimulated the trend to an easy life without hard work.

From the 1970s the balance between spending and earning was restored by heavy borrowing from abroad. Easy money was spent easily: more than half of the twenty billion U.S. dollars obtained through foreign loans went to subsidize consumption or was wasted on projects providing no real return.

The Feni smelting plant in Macedonia serves as an illustration. A technical marvel, built at a cost of $300 million, with pink marble stairways and floors, it processed ore too low in nickel content to make production profitable.

Regionalism and local politicians' ambition to leave monuments to posterity contributed to economic bankruptcy. "By the end of the 1970s," said the vice president of the federal government, the Slovenian Živko Pregl, "Yugoslavia was placed in a situation where it had to earn its own living. It took all the 1980s to realize that we are in crisis."[31] The result was a spiraling inflation which hit 2,500 percent per year in the late 1980s, with an unemployment rate of 16 percent.

Economic stabilization, attempted in the early 1980s, required determination and unity, both of which were lacking. In the final analysis, it became obvious that an unsound political system could not provide a sound economy. Titoism was basically a residue of Stalinism, applied in a milder form, but dedicated to the unchallenged monopoly on power by the Communist party.

But the absence of Soviet pressure and the open frontiers that fostered a developing intercourse with Western Europe allowed the liberalization of the country's intellectual and cultural life. Progressive economic decentralization and national regionalization challenged party unity on local, republican, and federal levels. While previous integral Yugoslavism and centralism had neglected the parts for the supposed benefit of the whole, communist Yugoslavism sacrificed the whole for the alleged benefit of its parts. The fear of unitarism and centralism became the excuse for promoting particular nationalisms.

It is a paradox that until 1971 Yugoslav population censuses registered those who declared themselves "Yugoslavs" as "nationality not designated." The 1981 census registered only 5.4 percent self-declared Yugoslavs in a population of twenty-two million.

In order to preserve their dominant rule and respective privileges, communists turned away from the party to their individual republics for support and became promoters of regionalism and provincialism. Nationalism proved to be stronger than communism. The result was that the ruling League of Yugoslav Communists gradually turned into nationalistic Leagues of Communists.

The destabilization of Yugoslavia started in the south and moved northward. In the multinational Yugoslav structure only two ethnic groups are territorially almost homogenous: the Albanians in the Serbian province of Kosovo and the Slovenes in the Slovenian Republic.

The Serbo-Albanian confrontation has deep historical roots, with one side then the other dominating. During centuries of Ottoman rule Muslim Albanians were favored over Christian Serbs. The situation was reversed when the Serbs incorporated Kosovo into Yugoslavia during the interwar period. The situation changed again when Mussolini joined the region to Great Albania under his dominance, chasing out the Serbs. After the war both Serbs and Albanians were victims of the wavering policy of the communist regime. The Serbian émigrés were forbidden to return, while Albanians in Kosovo were subject to a carrot-and-stick policy. Tito's plan for a communist Balkan Federation including Albania ended when Enver Hoxha took the Soviet side in 1948. The tough policy of Alexander Ranković kept the Kosovo Albanians under centralist control. His fall in 1966 and the loosening of the federal system, confirmed by the 1974 constitution, made the province of Kosovo virtually independent of the Serbian republic. This created a backlash in Serbia, which was eager to restore authority over its own territory on an equal footing with the other Yugoslav federal republics.

The problem of Kosovo is two-sided. On the one hand, Albanians in Kosovo had recognized national rights, education in the Albanian language, an Academy of Sciences, a university, pedagogical schools, and cultural institutions. The province obtained the lion's share of the Yugoslav Federal Fund for Nondeveloped Regions, and its representatives participated in the highest levels of government, including taking their turn at the country's revolving presidency. On the other hand, Kosovo still remained the poorest part of the country. The reasons were inherited poverty, nepotism and corruption in the local bureaucracy, wasted investments, and above all, the Albanian demographic explosion, unique in Europe. From 733,000 in 1948, the Albanian population in Kosovo grew to 1,730,000 in 1981. In the meantime the Serbian population in Kosovo dropped from 27.9 percent in 1953 to 14.9 in 1981, further declining to 10 percent in 1987. The exodus of Serbs from Kosovo, partially due to economic factors, was also caused by the pressure, physical as well as psychological, from the overwhelming Albanian majority. The Albanians, trained in their own language, with a hyperproduction of jobless intelligentsia, became noncompetitive in the Yugoslav market and became trapped in their own ghetto.[32] The frustrated Serbian minority turned for help and support to Belgrade. The mounting economic crisis in the entire country would only contribute to the problem.

The tinderbox exploded in 1981 with massive Albanian demonstrations in Kosovo and continued to scorch the country. They caused provincial, republican, and federal ramifications. The approval of an Albanian request for its own Kosovo republic would impose a restructuring of three federal republics—Serbia, Montenegro, and Macedonia—in which Albanians now live.[33] The Kosovo republic would result in an "ethnically pure" Albanian state, leaving the remaining Serbian minority to the mercy of the majority as well as producing a nucleus for the eventual merging of two Albanian states into one Great Albania.

In 1989 the Albanian movement triggered a national populist reaction in Serbia to protect conationals in Kosovo. In June 1989 approximately one million Serbs gathered in Kosovo to mark the six hundredth anniversary of the 1389 battle in which their medieval state was defeated by the Ottomans. This gathering also helped fuel resentments against the "symmetric federation" imposed on Serbs in postwar Yugoslavia. The mass movement in Serbia, channeled and exploited by Serbian communist reformers, toppled the corrupted leadership in Vojvodina, Kosovo, and Montenegro. The fear of a resurgent Serbia provoked a chain reaction in the northern Yugoslav republics, Slovenia and Croatia. History reappeared: the Croats revived apprehensions about a strong Serbia; the Serbs remembered the genocide suffered in Croatia during the war.

It is said that "an empty stomach burns a hole in the flag." The mounting economic crisis contributed to the rise of recriminations about who was the winner and who the loser aboard the common sinking ship. With the cold war fading and in the absence of foreign pressures, the Yugoslavs turned against each other. Political centrism was supported only by the leadership.

The Yugoslavs are still prisoners of their own history. Instead of looking forward, they have turned to the past. Centuries-old recriminations—the religious, social, cultural, and economic dualism between the north and the south—have resurfaced. Ideological monopoly has been replaced by particular nationalistic monopolies. Pressured by winds blowing from Eastern Europe, the LCY renounced its political monopoly, aware that "pluralism of social interests," previously extolled as a substitute for democracy, could not replace political pluralism.

The divided reformers faced a difficult challenge. The long-overdue economic reform, inaugurated in December 1989, is the only way to get out of the economic crisis: to stop inflation, to make the currency convertible, and to promote a free market open to foreign investment. But as in the rest of Eastern Europe, the process requires heavy sacrifice and belt tightening.

Political pluralism in a multinational society has inevitably produced national, ethnic, and regional parties, questioning their reasons for unity. The claustrophobic Slovenians—the most prosperous, diligent, and efficient, but also the most privileged—turn their backs on the rest of the country. The Croats have revived the historic yearning for statehood, frustrated by the failure of their fascist state in World War II. Rejecting the "symmetric federation" that split the nation, the national movement in Serbia has spilled over the republic's frontiers, embracing the whole Serbian nation, sacrificing traditional democratic trends for the sake of national unity. Ostracized by their Balkan neighbors, the Macedonians are hounded by the memory of prewar Serbian dominance and obsessed by the never-realized dream of national unity. The Muslims in Bosnia have found themselves squeezed between mounting Serbian and Croatian nationalism and Islamic fundamentalism. The Montenegrins have again started asking who they are: Montenegrins or Serbs or both?

It is always easier to be an emotional nationalist than a rational democrat. The Yugoslav phenomenon raises the questions, is a multinational state viable at all, and is a centralized authority indispensable for such a state to survive?

Compared with the rest of Eastern Europe, Yugoslavia enjoys some advantages. Decentralization and liberalization as well as the rapprochement with Western Europe happened earlier than in other Eastern European states, but national squabbles hampered democratization. Instead of becoming a unifying national factor, the wave of democratization had in Yugoslavia, as in the Soviet Union, an opposite effect.

The Yugoslav phenomenon is again coming to a crossroads. From unitarism, centralism, and federalism it is shifting toward a confederation and/or a dissolution: from a union to a disunion. It is a movement that contradicts the modern integrating trends in Europe.

The political spectrum in Yugoslavia is polarized, in a way familiar in Eastern Europe, between the national populists, communist reformers (renamed Social Democrats) and liberals. The pendulum is generally moving from the left to the right. The national populists exploit national euphoria and repressed nationalistic feelings. The communists try to survive by turning toward social democracy and adapting to new democratic trends. The liberals try to revive nineteenth-century economic and political creeds.

Indeed, the Yugoslav phenomenon is specific, reflecting old national and religious differences—the Roman Catholic north against the Orthodox south. In Serbia communists are exploiting national populism and, with the support of the Orthodox church, are requesting the unification of all Serbs living both within and outside the republic. In Slovenia and Croatia a landslide victory of the anticommunist center right, supported by the Catholic church, demands independent statehood. While Serbia favors a federation, Croatia and Slovenia ask for a confederation keeping the door open for secession. Moving toward economic and political integration, Europe is not ready to integrate its eastern parts and opposes the dissolution of Yugoslavia.

In such a euphoric and ambiguous situation historical icons and ghosts from the past have revived among the Albanians in Kosovo, the Serbs in Croatia, and the Croatians and Slovenes in Yugoslavia. It is obvious that the country must start from scratch and choose among five alternatives: federation, confederation, asymmetric union (federation south–confederation north), civil war coupled with an army intervention, or dissolution.

As of May 1991, the time of this writing, the future of the country seemed to depend on the ability of the newly elected leadership of the Yugoslav republics to reach a compromise through democratic dialogue. The regrettable alternative would be civil war with the army's intervention, which would be the end of the country.

The unity of the Yugoslavs is a *mariage de raison*. In case of a divorce all partners will lose. Too many economic, social, and other ties have been established during some seventy years of living together. Yugoslavia is a community of antagonistic nations joined together because any other arrangement would be worse. Separation would create either several insignificant small states or mini-Yugoslavias challenged by their own irredentism, reminiscent of the old Habsburg empire.

The Yugoslavs must remember that tolerance and democracy are required for equal peoples to share responsibility for the welfare of their multinational community in an integrated Europe. They must remember the lesson of history: either hang together or hang separately. History may very well teach them that sacrifices for the common good are worth the effort.

NOTES

1. Ivo Banac, *The National Question in Yugoslavia: Origins, History, Politics* (Ithaca: Cornell University Press, 1988), 70–115. Also Dimitrije Djordjevic, ed., *The Creation of Yugoslavia, 1914–1918*, (Santa Barbara: CLIO Press, 1980), 1–17.

2. Stojan Novaković, "Nakon sto godina—May 15, 2011," reprinted in Radovan Samardžić, *Pisci srpske istorije* (Beograd: Prosveta, 1976) 1: 342–52.

3. Vladimir Dedijer, Ivan Božić, Sima Ćirković, and Milorad Ekmečić, *History of Yugoslavia* (New York: McGraw Hill, 1974), 480.

4. Milorad Ekmečić, *Stvaranje Jugoslavije, 1790–1918*, 2 vols. (Beograd: Prosveta, 1989), 2: 829–32.

5. Dimitrije Djordjevic, "Vojvoda Putnik, The Serbian High Command and Strategy in World War I," in Bela Kiraly and Nandor Dreiszinger, eds., *East Central European Society in World War I* (Boulder: East European Monographs, 1985), 569–89.

6. Milorad Ekmečić, *Ratni ciljevi Srbije 1914* (Beograd: Srpska književna zadruga, 1973), 80–112. Also Dragoslav Janković, *Srbija i jugoslovensko pitanje, 1914–1915* (Beograd: Institut za savremenu istoriju, 1973), 469–74.

7. Dragoslav Janković, *Jugoslovensko pitanje i Krfska deklaracija, 1917* (Beograd: Savremena administracija, 1967), 189–207.

8. Alex Dragnich, *Serbia, Nikola Pašić, and Yugoslavia* (New Brunswick: Rutgers University Press, 1974), 131.

9. Ivo Lederer, *Yugoslavia at the Paris Peace Conference: A Study in Frontiermaking* (New Haven: Yale University Press, 1963). Also Andrej Mitrović, *Jugoslavija na konferenciji mira, 1919–1920* (Beograd: Zavod za isdavanje udžbenika SRS, 1969).

10. John Lampe, "Unifying the Yugoslav Economy, 1918–1921: Misery and Early Understandings," in Djordjevic, ed., *The Creation of Yugoslavia*, 139–52.

11. Banac, *The National Question in Yugoslavia*, 226–48.

12. Wayne Vucinich, ed., *Contemporary Yugoslavia: Twenty Years of Socialist Experiment* (Berkeley: University of California Press, 1969), 10–11.

13. Peter Sugar, ed., *Native Fascism in the Successor States, 1918–1945* (Santa Barbara: ABC Clio Press, 1971), 125–43.

14. Ivan Avakumović, *History of the Communist Party of Yugoslavia* (Aberdeen: Aberdeen University Press, 1964), 1:72.

15. Neil Balfour and Sally Mackey, *Paul of Yugoslavia: Britain's Malignant Friend* (London: Hamish-Hamilton, 1980).

16. David A. T. Stafford, "SOE and British Involvement in the Belgrade Coup d'Etat of March 1941," *Slavic Review* (1977), 36(3):399–419.

17. Stevan K. Pavlowitch, *Yugoslavia* (London: Ernest Benn Ltd., 1971), 114.

18. Bogoljub Kočović, *Žrtve Drugog svetskog rata u Jugoslaviji* (London: Veritas Foundation Press, 1985), annex 33, 182.

19. Fred Singleton, *A Short History of the Yugoslav Peoples* (London: Cambridge University Press, 1985), 177.

20. Veselin Djuretić, *Saveznici i jugoslovenska ratna drama*, 2 vols. (Beograd: Srpska akademija nauka i umetnosti, 1985).

21. Mišo Leković, *Martovski pregovori, 1943* (Beograd: Narodna knjiga, 1985). The first to write about these negotiations was Walter Roberts, *Tito, Mihailovic, and the Allies: 1941–1945* (New Brunswick: Rutgers University Press, 1973).

22. See introductory essay by David Martin, ed., *Patriot or Traitor: The Case of General Mihailovich* (Stanford: Hoover Archival Documentation, 1978), 3–40.

23. Dennison Rusinow, *The Yugoslav Experiment, 1948–1974* (Stanford: Stanford University Press, 1977), 15.

24. In the era of glasnost Soviet archives became more accessible. See I. Ia. Gibianskii, *Sovietskii Soiuz i Novaia Iugoslavia, 1941–1947* (Moscow: Nauka, 1987).

25. Among them were 231,032 peasants and 145,226 workers. Paul Shoup, "The League of Communists of Yugoslavia," in Steven Fischer-Galati, ed., *The Communist Parties in Eastern Europe* (New York: Columbia University Press, 1979), 360.

26. Milorad Ekmečić pointed to the influences of Consiglio di gestione, the Assemblea and the Consiglio d'administrazione introduced by Mussolini in the Republica of Saló at the end of the war, NIN (Belgrade), no. 2037 (January 14, 1990).

27. Demokratska Federativna Jugoslavia (DFJ), Federativna Narodna Republika Jugoslavia (FNRJ), Socijalistička Federativna Republika Jugoslavia (SFRJ).

28. For changes in party structures, see Rusinow, *The Yugoslav Experiment*, 144–45.

29. Slavoljub Djukic, *Čovek u svome vremenu: Razgovori sa Dobricom Ćosićem*, 2d ed. (Beograd: Filip Višnjic, 1989), 107–45.

30. The annual cost to maintain Tito's "blue train" and the palaces and villas placed at his disposal was $750,000 in 1990.

31. *Wall Street Journal*, February 20, 1990.

32. In 1981 Priština University enrolled 51,000 students, while the province had 178,000 employees and 67,000 unemployed in the public sector. Stevan Pavlowitch, *The Improbable Survivor: Yugoslavia and Its Problems, 1918–1988* (London: Hurst, 1988), 85.

33. There are 377,000 Albanians in Macedonia, 72,000 in the rest of Serbia outside Kosovo, and 37,000 in Montenegro. *Statistički godišnjak Jugoslavije* (Beograd: Savremena administracija, 1986), 451.

9 Germany and Eastern Europe

Melvin Croan

By virtue of its geographic position alone, Germany must face East as well as West. Its pivotal position in Europe has always been fraught with danger, for Germany itself as well as for its neighbors. Historically, a weak and fragmented Germany, without the protection of natural physical barriers, invited repeated foreign incursion and served as a major arena of international conflict. A united and powerful Germany, in turn, provoked hostile foreign coalitions and served as a prime source of international instability. Whether united or divided, powerful or weak, Germany's position as *Land der Mitte* (the country in the middle) typically posed a crucial question of self-identification. Did Germany belong to the West or to the East? To both or to neither?

The Europe of the twenty-first century may know neither East nor West as these concepts have been previously understood. That is, of course, the larger promise of the unification of Germany that occurred in 1990, a promise which, if realized, will sharply differentiate this second German national unification of modern times from the first, wrought by "blood and iron" in 1871. However that may turn out, Germany has certainly played a major role in the troubled history of Eastern Europe in the twentieth century. Indeed, no other country except the Soviet Union has played a greater role in this century. And, arguably, Soviet influence need not have dominated for so long had it not been for World War II, unleashed by Nazi Germany, and its consequences.

The Second World War brought Germany's military defeat and unconditional surrender; it also resulted in the expulsion of millions of *Volksdeutsche* (ethnic Germans) from their ancestral homes in Eastern Europe and from major portions of prewar Germany, i.e., East Prussia and the territories east of the Oder-Neisse line that were to demarcate Poland's postwar western frontier. Finally, in the immediate aftermath of World War II, the developing cold war witnessed the division of a territorially diminished Reich into two antipathetic successor states, the Federal Republic of Germany (FRG) in the west and the German Democratic Republic (GDR) in the east.

Germany's cold war division between East and West fashioned its relationship to Eastern Europe along new lines. The GDR came to function not only as a glacis against the West but also as the lynchpin of the system of Soviet client states in the East. For its part, the FRG served not only as a barrier against further Soviet expansion westward but also increasingly as a bridge to the East. However, West Germany's *Ostpolitik* (i.e., policy toward Eastern Europe as a whole, including the Soviet Union) was always inextricably intertwined with and in large measure subordinate to its *Deutschlandpolitik* (i.e., policies toward East Germany and concerns over the host of problems attendant upon Germany's national division). Circumstances changed dramatically with the unexpected collapse of East Germany's communist regime in 1989–90. By paving the way for the unification of the two postwar German states or, more accurately, the self-liquidation of the GDR through voluntary accession to the FRG, the East German debacle also served to open fresh vistas of active involvement in Eastern Europe on the part of a resurgent united Germany.

The prospects for Germany's post–cold war relationship with its eastern neighbors will be touched upon at the end of this chapter. Most of the treatment that follows will, however, be devoted to an examination of the more than four-decades-long history of East Germany as a separate German state and, in its time, a vital component of communist Eastern Europe. Since GDR foreign policy and, indeed, East German domestic politics were always inseparably linked to the larger "German Problem" of the post–World War II period, *Ostpolitik* (including *Deutschlandpolitik*) will also have to be considered, as a necessary counterpoint to our treatment of East German developments. The whole post–World War II experience of Germany's enforced national division, involving a Soviet foothold within East Germany, made for a set of highly distinctive German relationships to Eastern Europe. To appreciate the extent to which this was the case necessitates a preliminary glance back at the broad outlines of Germany's encounters with Eastern Europe over the ages.

Some Historical Considerations

Germany's historic ties to the East contain many tangled strands. For centuries Eastern Europe offered a field of colonization for German settlers. On occasion it also became the object of German political expansion. Of both phenomena, Nazi war aims and occupation policies in Eastern Europe represent only the most recent and most brutal manifestations. Yet the history of contact between the Germans and their Slavic and other eastern neighbors is far from being only a story of unrelieved conflict. Before the rise of nationalism as a political force, the German-Slav relationship was essentially amicable. It sustained cooperation in a wide variety of human endeavors and, indeed, produced significant cross-cultural fertilization. Even in subsequent periods of nationalist hostility, there always persisted residual elements of mutual attraction between the Germans and the Slavs.

As a major case in point, German-Russian attitudes have run a wide gamut of contradictory emotions. There is the traditional German fear of Russia, often coupled with contempt—a feeling which, incidentally, has been reciprocated in full measure by the Russians with regard to Germany. Yet, despite this deeply rooted and frequently expressed mutual revulsion, each society has periodically found itself rediscovering traits to admire in the other.

There is, of course, an age-old tradition of political enmity between the Germans and the Russians. Its roots run back to the thirteenth-century clash between Alexander Nevsky and the Teutonic Knights, and its full fury was never more apparent than in the bitterness of Russo-German conflict during World War II. Yet there is also the recurrent historical experience of mutually advantageous political coalition. The latter tradition has come to be symbolized by Tauroggen, when in 1812 the Prussian General York joined forces with Tsar Alexander I against Napoleon, and by Rapallo, when in 1922 Weimar Germany and Bolshevik Russia concluded a treaty expressive of their common antipathy to the Versailles settlement in Europe. The same tradition of political coalition was also manifest in Bismarck's successive treaties of alliance with imperial Russia in the late nineteenth century as well as in the short-lived, rapacious Nazi-Soviet pact in 1939 (in both cases, at the expense of another Slavic nation, Poland). All told, the chronicle of traditional German-Russian relations and attitudes entails, as one noted historian has put it, "a love-hate relationship perhaps unique in history." [1]

With respect to Eastern Europe, traditional German attitudes have ranged from acceptance of and even admiration for the cultural diversity of its peoples to condescension and worse, to ethnic animosity, at times on grounds of ostensible "racial" incompatibility. Of the former, the eighteenth-century writer Johann Gottfried von Herder may be cited as a prime example; of the latter, Nazi ideologues and a host of pan-Germanist, racialist, and imperialist publicists who preceded the Nazis but did not survive them. Karl Marx offers a case of highly idiosyncratic attitudes which nonetheless enjoyed great influence. Dubbed by one biographer "the Red Prussian," Marx regarded the Czechs as doomed to ethnic extinction and treated the national aspirations of the Poles with something akin to contempt. Marxism's assignment of nationalism to the superstructure and concomitant dismissal of nationalist aspirations as false consciousness facilitated the "national nihilism" manifested by Rosa Luxemburg with respect to the quest for Polish independence. It also went a long way toward shaping the manipulative treatment of nationalism for tactical purposes practiced by Lenin, Stalin, and other Soviet leaders, to the great misfortune of the peoples subject to their revolutionary ministrations and, ultimately, at the expense of the Soviet Union itself.

As concerns practical policy, the two major nineteenth-century Germanic powers, Austria and Prussia, differed greatly in approach. The Habsburg realms were multinational; accordingly, Austria tolerated ethnic diversity as long as the different nationalities showed themselves *kaisertreu* (loyal to the Emperor). Prussia, by contrast, sought to Germanize its ethnic minorities with policies that bore down heavily, especially upon the Poles under first Prussian, then, after 1871, imperial German rule. In the course of World War I, which found imperial Germany allied with Austria-Hungary, the notion of *Mitteleuropa* gained wide currency. As propounded by various patriotic figures, Friedrich Naumann the most notable among them, this geopolitical concept provided a rationale for imperial Germany's expansionist schemes, albeit one that was thought to appeal to the economic self-interest of all the inhabitants of the vast continental tracts to be placed under German political domination and hence at the disposal of Germany's organizational skill and managerial talents. Imperial Germany's real motives became only too apparent in the predatory treaty of Brest-Litovsk dictated by the German high command to a prostrate Soviet Russia as the price of peace. This "forgotten peace" of March 1918 set an ominous precedent that was to be applied against Germany in the onerous treaty of Versailles, concluded the following year.

Under the Versailles system, the Weimar republic, Germany's first experiment in constitutional democracy, pursued an *Ostpolitik* at once hostile to Poland but somewhat friendlier to the Soviet Union. Its objectives included rectification of the 1919 German-Polish border so as to recover upper Silesia, the Polish corridor, and Danzig for Germany. Toward this end, good relations with Soviet Russia might, it was thought, prove useful; they were deemed essential in order for Germany to balance the West. At the hands of the Weimar republic's long-term foreign minister, Gustav Stresemann, *Schaukelpolitik* (i.e., see-saw diplomacy between East and West) was carried out with consummate skill; it proved considerably more successful than the *Ostpolitik* directed against Poland which failed conspicuously to bring any territorial revision in Germany's favor. In contrast to its preoccupation with Poland and the Soviet Union, Weimar Germany paid relatively little attention to the other states of Eastern Europe.

All this changed with the Nazi accession to power in 1933. Relations with the Soviet Union stagnated and then deteriorated until the surprise reversal that resulted in the infamous Hitler-Stalin pact of 1939; with Poland, ironically, relations initially improved with the conclusion of the 1934 German-Polish nonaggression treaty. But all such diplomatic niceties were nothing more than cynical ploys in Hitler's plans, which aimed, as a contemporary British scholar noted, at nothing less than "full political, economic, and military control of the whole space between Germany and Russia."[2] The *Anschluss* (annexation) of Austria in March 1938 was followed by the dismemberment of Czechoslovakia in the wake of the 1938 Munich agreement, the West's futile attempt to "appease" Hitler's appetite for expansion. When Nazi Germany struck against Poland on September 1, 1939, Britain and France, capable no longer of deluding themselves about the reality of German aggression, declared war. Hitler's geopolitical objectives had always included the acquisition of *Lebensraum* (living space) in the East. Accordingly, he launched a massive invasion of the Soviet Union, his erstwhile ally, on June 22, 1941.

The aggressive designs of Nazi Germany were animated by a fanatical racist ideology of Hitler's own concoction, which led directly to a program of colonization, subjugation, and extermination throughout the whole of Eastern Europe and further east in the large expanses of

Soviet territory that fell under German occupation. It should never be forgotten that the whole panoply of the Nazi SS state, the murderous totalitarian machine that Hitler fully intended to reimport back into Germany after the war,[3] first came into full-blown existence in the occupied East. Those who suffered the untold horrors of the Nazi yoke demanded retribution. Theirs was the animus that sustained the massive expulsion of the *Volksdeutsche* and accompanied the territorial truncation and internal partition of the Reich itself.

Small wonder, then, that Germany's military defeat and unconditional surrender in the Second World War should have seemed to mark the end of any German role in Eastern Europe. In 1945 no one could have foreseen the emergence four years later of two separate German successor states, the FRG and the GDR, much less anticipated the novel roles each was destined to play vis-à-vis the East. And if anyone had been so prescient, who would have dared predict German unification in 1990 and, with it, the rapidly changing horizons of European international relations? Europe has obviously come a very long way in a very short time from the cold war, to the onset and impact of which our discussion of Germany and Eastern Europe now turns.

Cold War and National Division (1945–1949)

In January 1948, more than a full year before the establishment of the Federal Republic of Germany in the Western zones of occupation and the transformation of the Soviet zone into the German Democratic Republic, Stalin reportedly predicted that "the West will make Western Germany their own, and we shall turn Eastern Germany into our own state."[4] Had the Soviet dictator cared to elaborate on his terse prediction, he might well have repeated a remark which he made to confidants even before the end of World War II, when he pronounced with accustomed pedantry that "whoever occupies a territory also imposes on it his own social system. Everyone imposes his own social system as far as his army can reach. It cannot be otherwise."[5] This pronouncement, so expressive both of the activist impulse that once characterized Soviet communist ideology and of Stalin's own high regard for the uses of political power and the perquisites of physical possession, proved to be nothing less than a self-fulfilling prophecy.

To be sure, the imposition of control over merely one truncated portion of a divided Germany by no means exhausted the ambitions of the Soviet leadership. Stalin, for one, began by playing for quite different and potentially much higher stakes; stakes well beyond the immediate reach of his armies. In addition to his determination to exploit Germany by exacting a maximum of reparations (from current production as well as through the sequestration of physical plants) and his concern lest the defeated enemy should someday again threaten Soviet security, Stalin was also intent upon influencing the whole of Germany's future political development. To his mind, this could only mean the social and political transformation of the entire country under direct Soviet aegis. Just how Stalin proposed to accomplish all these objectives in a situation rendered more complex by the active involvement of the Western powers was altogether another matter. He would throw himself into the fray and then take stock.

As things turned out, the logic which Stalin himself had enunciated took its course and resolved many of the contradictions inherent in his own initial aims and policies. The very same logic contributed to, if it did not actually precipitate, the dissolution of the Grand Alliance of World War II and the start of the cold war between the Soviet Union and the West. More particularly, it rapidly circumvented the restraints seemingly interposed by the agreements reached at the 1945 Potsdam summit conference to govern Germany as a single entity on the basis of common Allied policies. This became evident in the distinctive nature of the collectivist measures carried out in the Soviet zone under the guise of fulfilling the goals of demilitarization, denazification, and democratization that had been decreed but not precisely defined at Potsdam. (The machinery actually set up by the Potsdam agreement proved powerless to prevent this, for it sanctioned the exercise of "supreme authority" in Germany by individual Allied military commanders, each within his own zone of occupation, and, in addition, established the veto principle in the quadripartite Allied Control Council.) As might have been expected, the Soviet occupation authorities proceeded to implement the Potsdam accords in line with what they considered to be elemental requirements of Marxist doctrine. Almost at once they began to strike at the supposed socioeconomic roots of "German militarism and Fascism" through an extensive land reform (autumn of 1945), nationalization of banking and heavy industry (July 1945–March 1946), expropriation of the holdings of leading Nazis and war criminals, and the like.

These Soviet measures may have seemed moderate in themselves, but behind the initial social and economic changes was the latent dynamic of full Sovietization. In pace and timing, the imposition of the Soviet system on East Germany was inextricably bound up with the diplomacy of competition and conflict between East and West over Germany as a whole. One Soviet action, however, stands out in retrospect as crucial to both aspects of the subsequent story. The forcible Soviet intervention in Germany's newly revived political life which brought about an organizational fusion between the Communist party (KPD) and the Social Democratic party (SPD) not only ruptured an embryonic nationwide party system; it was responsible for much more besides.

In fact, the founding of the Socialist Unity party (SED) in April 1946, in the Soviet zone alone, marked a threefold turning point in postwar German affairs. First, it signified open and deliberate Soviet support for German communism and thus anticipated the eventual emergence of the Soviet zone as a full-fledged "people's democracy." Second, it heralded a change in the relationship between the Germans and the military authorities who governed them, a change in the West as well as the East. By provoking the Western powers into a common cause with German politicians—at the time with the Social Democrats under Kurt Schumacher in the Western zones and West Berlin, who opposed the forced merger with the communists and determined to resist it—this development inaugurated the broader cooperation that made possible the creation of the Federal Republic. Finally, and as an inevitable consequence, it brought a change in the atmosphere of relations among the occupying powers themselves; a change that, along with disputes over Soviet reparations demands and Western disgust with Soviet high-handedness elsewhere in Eastern Europe, destroyed the last vestiges of the wartime alliance against Germany. By mid-1946 the antagonistic competition between East and West known as the cold war had unmistakably focused upon Germany as the major strategic prize.

With that in mind, the Soviet authorities took an increasingly active role in the political life of their zone of military occupation. As early as the summer of 1945 the Soviet Military Administration (SMA) had already licensed four political parties, the Christian Democratic Union (CDU) and the Liberal Democratic party (LDP) as well as the SPD and the KPD. From the outset, however, these parties were directed to work together in a "United Front of Antifascist Democratic Parties," a bloc that was subjected to the strictest Soviet supervision. Not only did Soviet political officers exert direct pressure to bring about the 1946 KDP-SPD organizational merger into the SED, the SMA also repeatedly intervened in the internal affairs of both the CDU and the LDP to remove leaders critical of occupation policies.

In point of fact, the "antifascist democratic order" over which the SMA presided always presupposed a dominant position for the communists. No amount of democratic verbiage could long disguise this underlying reality. The SED's privileged position was quite apparent in the first Soviet zone elections, held in the autumn of 1946. Though competitively conducted, which is more than can be said for any subsequent East German election until 1990, the SED was given a number of advantages, including material resources with which to campaign and a place on the ballot for certain "mass organizations" which, though still in their infancy, were already under SED control.

Despite massive SMA assistance, the SED failed to win the overwhelming victory at the polls that it had anticipated. Together with an SED-dominated peasant mass organization, the party was barely able to eke out a slim majority. The elections to the *Land* (state) parliaments of October 1946 actually marked a decline of popular support for the SED by comparison with the results of the local elections one month earlier. In Berlin, where Four-Power supervision enabled the SPD to participate as an independent force, the SED received slightly less than 20 percent of the popular vote.

These electoral disappointments did not diminish the Soviet determination to secure the SED's dominant position in the political arena. On the contrary, the SED's questionable popularity rendered the task that much more urgent. To achieve the desired end—without as yet openly renouncing avowed commitments to parliamentary democracy—nothing was better suited than the practice of including representatives of all the parties of the Antifascist Democratic Bloc in the Soviet zone's state governments. Given the distribution of the popular vote, the SED could claim for itself the post of minister-president in four of the five Soviet zone *Länder* and obtain most of the states' ministries of interior, education, and economic affairs. At the same time, the party could also invoke the bloc's common "antifascist democratic" platform to forestall general political controversy and stifle specific criticism of the SED itself. Inasmuch as basic policy decisions remained the exclusive prerogative of the Soviet Military Administration, with which the SED enjoyed a uniquely intimate relationship, the chances for genuine parliamentary government were fatally compromised from the start.

The process of consolidating communist dominance, already implicit in these arrangements, was greatly accelerated by the continued deterioration of East-West relations. If Stalin had ever seriously counted on a free hand throughout the whole of postwar Germany, his calculations were upset at a relatively early date. By 1946 American policy not only stood in direct opposition to Soviet ambitions but also began to bid for the support of German public opinion and prepared to sponsor the economic revival and political reconstruction of the western portions of the country. Although initially limited to the bizonal framework agreed upon by the United States and Great Britain, Western policy generated its own forward momentum, which, in turn, stiffened Soviet intransigence. The announcement of the Marshall Plan for the economic recovery of Europe in June 1947 and the subsequent decision to extend its provisions to Germany found their echo in the establishment of the Cominform (September 1947) and Moscow's enunciation of the doctrine of the division of the postwar world into two implacably hostile camps. Following the abortive London meeting of the four-power Council of Foreign Ministers in December 1947, France reluctantly consented to align its previously independent German policy with that of the United States and Great Britain. In the face of vehement Soviet protests and despite the dangerous challenge presented by the Soviet blockade of the western sectors of Berlin, the Western powers successfully carried through the major reform of German currency in June 1948 to which the Soviet Union so strenuously objected. There followed in September 1948 the convocation of a Parliamentary Council in Bonn to draft a constitution (or "Basic Law," as it was to be called) for the Federal Republic of Germany, which was formally established on May 23, 1949.

Long before these developments reached their culmination on the western side, their reverberations registered on political life inside the Soviet zone. As early as 1946 the SED's top functionaries were speaking openly about the transitory character of the Soviet zone's "antifascist democratic order." The following year they proclaimed the idea more insistently and coupled it with an assertion of the SED's claim to play the "leading role" during the "transition." Such claims obviously enjoyed the Soviet occupation authorities' full endorsement. By 1948 the two "bourgeois" parties, the CDU and the LDP, had been reduced to complete political impotence. While both parties continued their separate organizational existence, neither one enjoyed a shred of real political independence. Their role had become that of Leninist-style transmission belts to sectors of the population deemed relatively inaccessible to direct penetration by the SED. Precisely the same function was envisaged for two wholly new and essentially artificial parties that appeared on the scene in the summer of 1948. Created by Soviet fiat, both these organizations, the National Democratic party (NDP) for reconstructed nationalists and pliable ex-Nazis and the Democratic Peasants party (DBP) for farmers, were promptly staffed with veteran communist functionaries.

The unmistakable dominance over the entire arena of zonal politics achieved by the SED by no means tells the whole story of the Sovietization of East Germany that accompanied initial cold war competition over Germany as a whole. Another important facet, the systematic transformation of the SED into a "party of the new type," i.e., a genuinely Leninist party, purged of Social Democrats, will be discussed below. Suffice it to note here the development of centralized zonal administrative structures as levers of communist control and agencies of Sovietization. Foremost among these was the German Economic Commission (DWK). Established in the summer of 1947 to coordinate the activities of the numerous centralized administrative bodies that the SMA had set up two years earlier, the DWK soon acquired vastly expanded economic powers and administrative responsibilities. With the introduction of coordinated economic planning for the Soviet zone as a whole in 1948, the DWK's powers came completely to overshadow those of the *Länder*. From the start communist cadres staffed the DWK secretariat, and key positions in its organizational network went to members of the SED. Thus, well before the formal establishment of the German Democratic Republic, the SED was not only in possession of a centralized economic administration but also in charge of a quasi-governmental apparatus covering the entire Soviet zone.

The delay in proclaiming a separate East German state can be chalked up to the Soviet desire to present this event as an unavoidable reaction to the policies of West German "separatists" and their Anglo-Saxon "imperialist" patrons that had led to the establishment of the Federal Republic. In this way Stalin and his German henchmen sought to present themselves as steadfast champions of German national unity. But all the prodigious propaganda campaigns along these lines could not disguise the Soviet authorities' own preparations for the division of Germany into two states that occurred in 1949. In fact, one major effort of mass mobilization in the Soviet zone, the *Volkskongress* (People's Congress) movement served both to beat the drums for national unity, Soviet-style, and prepare the way for a separate communist state in East Germany. In a series of steps beginning as early as March 1948, the People's Congress furnished the necessary constitutional groundwork and provided a pseudoparliamentary facade for what was to follow. By May 1949 these preparations had run their appointed course. It remained only for the *Volksrat* (People's Council), an offspring of the parent People's Congress, to transform itself, at the appropriate moment, into a *Volkskammer* (provisional East German legislature). This occurred on October 7, 1949, the day of the official proclamation of the German Democratic Republic. In a congratulatory telegram to the veteran German communist leader Wilhelm Pieck, installed as the first (and to be the only) president of the GDR, Stalin hailed the founding of the new state as a "turning point in the history of Europe." If Europe seemed to take scant notice at the time, the world was to become much more attentive in future years.

Crises and Consolidation (1949–1961)

By itself, the formal establishment of the German Democratic Republic brought no particularly noticeable change to domestic East German political life. To be sure, the SMA became the Soviet Control Commission (SKK), a cosmetic change that was accompanied by a pointed reassertion of the Soviet occupation authorities' rights and responsibilities in Germany. For the East German population, the new state appeared a disingenuous construct, at once artificial and transitory. For some years after its inception, the GDR failed to obtain diplomatic recognition, except from the Soviet Union and other communist states; indeed, East Germany was not to overcome its status as an international pariah for well over two decades after its establishment.

Meanwhile, domestic Sovietization proceeded at a pace seemingly incessant and yet also carefully contrived so as to conform to the needs of Soviet policy toward Germany as a whole. First introduced in 1948, Soviet-style central economic planning became more comprehensive with the announcement in 1950 of East Germany's First Five-Year Plan (1951–55). This development was accompanied by such familiar accoutrements as harrassment of the shrinking private sector of the economy, abolition of free collective bargaining, introduction of administratively determined work quotas, and the deliberate fostering of an atmosphere of terror, featuring a frenzied witch hunt for "spies," "agents," and "wreckers." (In early 1950 a Ministry for State Security, the infamous *Stasi*, was instituted.) At the very same time, however, an incongruous pseudonationalist appeal was mounted in the direction of West Germany. The assignment fell to the National Front of Democratic Germany, an organization founded simultaneously with the establishment of the GDR, as an earnest token of the new state's ostensible commitment to national unity.

To master such conflicting imperatives presupposed the thorough-going Leninization of the SED. The 1948 Stalin-Tito split provided a major fillip on the road to a full-fledged Leninist "party of the new type." The SED's key administrative positions were already in the hands of Communists; in 1948 the party's rank and file membership was subjected to a mass purge. In January 1949 the principle of parity between Communists and Social Democrats at all levels of party organization was officially discarded; the following year proclamation of "democratic centralism" as the SED's organizing principle led to a revamping of the party's administrative structure to render it a virtual carbon copy of the CPSU (Communist Party of the Soviet Union). Walter Ulbricht, a veteran Stalinist subaltern who had been Moscow's key functionary in Germany since April 1945, emerged in July 1950 as party general secretary. Under his ministrations the party purges became more extensive, resulting in the ouster of some 150,000 rank and file members on grounds of various ideological failings, especially "social democratism." The purge also reached up into the SED's top echelons where individual German Communist leaders of long standing fell victim to the "revelations" and "lessons" of the Stalinist show trials under way elsewhere in Eastern Europe at the time.

Following the outbreak of the Korean War (1950–51), the United States determined that the policy of Western containment of the Soviet Union in Europe now required a German military contribution. As plans for the European Defense Community (EDC) with West German participation neared completion, Stalin went on the diplomatic offensive. In a series of notes (March–July 1952), Moscow proposed the reunification and neutralization of Germany which, it stipulated, might be allowed limited armed forces of its own. The West rejected the offer, in part because of the inflexibility of Chancellor Konrad Adenauer who regarded the Soviet overture as a dangerous snare. In subsequent years in the FRG the West's rejection of Stalin's offer gave rise to considerable recrimination about a possibly "missed opportunity" to reunify Germany. At the time the diplomatic miscarriage led directly to a concerted Stalinist onslaught against East German society.

The Second SED Party Conference, meeting in July 1952, announced a drive to "construct socialism" in the GDR. To implement this new dispensation, Ulbricht called for the strengthening of state power, a major governmental reorganization (including the abolition of the East German *Länder*), agricultural collectivization, liquidation of remaining private holdings in industry and commerce, an ideological offensive against religion, and open remilitarization (which had actually been begun earlier under the cover of the formation of the "people's police in barracks"). To counter resistance against these measures, the leadership was prepared, in the name of "sharpened class struggle," to launch a reign of terror against the entire population.

The "construction of socialism" proved utterly disastrous. The class warfare unleashed by the SED accelerated large scale flight to the West by some of the most productive sectors of East German society. (Although the East German border with West Germany had been effectively sealed off in May 1952, the escape hatch to West Berlin still remained open.) For its part, the regime simply did not have the financial wherewithal to achieve the prodigious investment in heavy industry and all the other mammoth administrative and socioeconomic projects envisaged by its Stalinist program. As a result, Ulbricht made the fateful (and near fatal) decision to "construct socialism" on the backs of the East German industrial workers by deliberately depressing their wages through a steep increase in official work quotas. No doubt Stalin would have approved, but after the Soviet dictator's death in March 1953, the Kremlin epigones were of a different mind.

The result was the East German uprising of June 17, 1953, the first of several major upheavals to shake the very foundations of communist rule in Eastern Europe in the post-Stalin period. In the East German case, the revolt was sparked by East Berlin construction workers. They took to the streets to protest the heightened work quotas to which the regime continued to cling at a time when the SED had been compelled by Stalin's successors in the Kremlin to renounce the forced "construction of socialism" program and publicly apologize for all its ill-advised excesses. Confronted by the lightning spread of the protest in Berlin to the rest of East Germany and its almost instantaneous transformation into a political revolt, the SED regime all but disintegrated. Communist rule was saved only by the massive deployment of Soviet tanks and the imposition of martial law.

It is now fairly well established that immediately before the June 1953 uprising, Moscow was preparing Ulbricht's downfall. The East German leader's Stalinist record was a less pressing consideration than the obvious political utility of sacrificing him as a scapegoat for the economic disasters of Stalin's own policies in East Germany, which Ulbricht had put into effect. After the June uprising, however, Moscow was no longer willing to risk tinkering with the top leadership of the SED. Ulbricht was allowed to move against his inner-party opponents, the Zaisser-Herrnstadt group. Members of this group had been in contact with Lavrenti Beria, the Soviet secret police chief who was himself arrested and executed in 1953 and whom both Ulbricht and Khrushchev were subsequently to charge with willingness to sacrifice the GDR and its "socialist achievements" in exchange for a negotiated settlement with the West on Germany as a whole.

Subsequent political recrimination about the event aside, the June uprising marked a decisive turning point with respect to Ulbricht's position and also in other crucial respects as well. Its naked exposure of the total bankruptcy of the East German communist experiment must have come as a rude awakening to the entire Soviet leadership and convinced the Kremlin of the inadvisability of entering into serious diplomatic negotiations with the West concerning Germany from such a position of palpable Soviet weakness. This, in turn, must surely have obliterated whatever initial differences of opinion on the German question may have existed among Stalin's immediate successors.

To have been thus constrained to leave Ulbricht in charge of the East German domestic scene almost guaranteed that the "New Course," now recommended by the Kremlin for Eastern Europe as a whole, would experience great difficulty in gaining popular support in the GDR. In part to shore up the badly damaged prestige of the SED regime, the Soviet Union made a number of demonstrative gestures to the GDR. These included the termination of reparations as of January 1, 1954, a substantial reduction of occupation costs, and the return to East Germany of thirty-three enterprises that were being operated as extraterritorial Soviet enterprises (SAGs). In May 1955 the GDR was invited to be a signatory of the treaty creating the Warsaw Treaty Organization (the Warsaw Pact); in January 1956, with the formal establishment of East German armed forces, the GDR became a full-fledged member of the Soviet bloc's military alliance system. The previous September (1955) had witnessed the nominal bestowal of "full sovereignty" upon the GDR by the Soviet Union. As with West Germany, only more so, the retrocession of sovereignty to East Germany was contingent upon its phased integration into the cold war camp of its superpower patron. While the process served to deepen Germany's division between East and West, it could not by itself fully secure the internal foundations of communist rule in the GDR.

The next challenge to East German political stability and to Ulbricht's personal power came in 1956. It occurred in the wake of Khrushchev's initial anti-Stalin campaign, inaugurated by the Soviet leader's bombshell of a secret speech on the crimes of Stalin delivered to the Twentieth CPSU Congress (February 1956). Manifesting remarkable tactical agility, Ulbricht immediately sought to disassociate himself from the late Soviet dictator and to preside over the requisite de-Stalinization of the GDR, precisely in order to limit its inroads. However, intellectual ferment grew nonetheless and soon threatened to get out of hand. Individual spirits clamored for greater freedom for philosophical inquiry and artistic creativity; some economists and administrative specialists criticized the priorities and practices of Stalinist central planning. By late autumn 1956 student unrest enveloped East Germany's universities and technical schools. All this conjured up shades of the events that were transpiring at the time in Poland and Hungary. Not only Ulbricht but the entire top SED leadership together with party and security cadres throughout the land were horrified and probably not a little scared. But their deliverance was assured once the Kremlin decided to crush the Hungarian revolution. At that juncture the Ulbricht regime struck back; free speech was quickly choked off, and some prominent intellectuals were arrested and put on trial. In early 1957 they received stiff jail sentences for having had the temerity to venture too far from the Stalinist "dogmatism" that Ulbricht himself had ostensibly rejected only a year before. Those thus punished included the philosopher Wolfgang Harich and a handful of like-minded party intellectuals, journalists, writers, and editors.

The charges that were brought against the members of the "Harich group" expressed the regime's own deep-seated anxieties; the prosecution accused them of having conspired to "restore capitalism" in East Germany so as to liquidate the GDR as a separate German state. Harich's oppositional platform had actually been revisionist-Marxist rather than restorationist-capitalist in character, but it had also postulated the need for major changes in the GDR to facilitate German reunification. That the reunified Germany desired by the GDR's revisionist intellectuals of 1956 was envisaged in democratic collectivist (read: left Social Democratic) terms scarcely rendered their vision more palatable to the GDR's communist rulers; on the contrary, they had good reason to fear that the proposed reforms would undermine the entire East German edifice. In 1956 and for more than three decades thereafter, nothing demonstrated the Leninist mettle of the SED's top leaders more than their obsession with the retention in undiluted form of their own political power as *die Hauptfrage* (the "main question"), to employ their own jargon.

Such concentration on considerations of raw power guaranteed that the elite infighting that did erupt in 1956 would be kept secret until it was resolved. Only in February 1958, with the announcement of the purge of the so-called Schirdewan-Wollweber-Oelssner group was it revealed that Ulbricht had had powerful opponents at the very apex of the SED organizational structure. Why had they failed to best Walter Ulbricht, a veteran Stalinist utterly devoid of personal popularity? For one thing, Ulbricht's critics lacked a moral issue of the sort which existed, say, in Hungary at the time. (Not without reason did Ulbricht think it fitting during this period to stress that East Germany had been spared the travesties of the Rajk and comparable show trials and had avoided a blood purge of the communist faithful.) The fact that Ulbricht himself had presided over the rehabilitation of individuals who were still alive served to enchain the most likely leaders of the party opposition, notably Dahlem and Ackermann, to Ulbricht's own cause. More important yet, deprived of a moral issue, none of the newer "factionalists" dared associate himself with the discontents of the SED rank and file, much less with popular disaffection. To have done so, they instinctively recognized, would have jeopardized the very survival of the SED regime itself and thus their own chances for power. As a result of such well-advised concealment within the SED central *apparat,* the regime's revisionist intellectual critics of 1956 were denied access to the leaders of the party opposition and found themselves politically disarmed from the start. This, in turn, enabled Ulbricht to control domestic unrest thereby rendering a major service to the Kremlin by sparing Moscow another upheaval in East Germany at the very time when it had to deal with the Polish October and the Hungarian revolution. Small wonder that for all of his avowed anti-Stalinism, Khrushchev experienced little difficulty in continuing to support Stalin's longtime German henchman.

His mandate thus renewed, Ulbricht set about fashioning something of a tentative modus vivendi between the SED regime and the East German population. By the late fifties this was being pursued under the rubric, *"ökonomische Hauptaufgabe,"* literally, "the economic main task," if not quite "the primacy of economics." This phrase was to be invoked in subsequent decades both by the Ulbricht leadership and its successors under Honecker, but in each instance with a slightly different twist. What was originally involved entailed a modest improvement in the standard of living through the belated termination of rationing, greater availability of foodstuffs and consumer goods, a more equitable price structure, a better system of distribution, and the like. Although popular attitudes remained difficult to gauge, there were certain indications of an incipient social consolidation: in 1959 the number of refugees to the West fell to below 150,000, the lowest annual level since 1950.

It would probably have been asking too much to expect the SED leadership to rest content with a few encouraging social indicators. In any event, the Ulbricht regime remained acutely conscious of its competitive struggle with West Germany for the allegiance of its own subjects; it also harbored an ideological commitment (fully shared by its Soviet patrons) to the continued "socialist transformation" of East German society. These contradictory imperatives were in full evidence in the wake of the Fifth SED Party Congress (July 1958) at which Ulbricht promised that the GDR would "catch up with and overtake" West Germany economically by 1961. Presumably this was to be accomplished in the course of a new Seven-Year Plan (1959–65) whose crowning achievement was to be, according to Ulbricht, the final "victory of socialism" in the GDR.

The party went on the ideological offensive in other ways as well. At the Fifth SED Party Congress, Ulbricht himself enunciated the "Ten Commandments of Socialist Morality." This was the harbinger of a renewed campaign to win away hearts and minds from the churches, among other things through a wide variety of secular sacraments (e.g., baby-naming ceremonies, youth dedication, socialist marriage, and socialist burial). High culture—art, music, and literature—was henceforth to be brought much closer to the masses and, naturally, infused with positive socialist content. Such was the notorious "Bitterfeld Road" of cultural revolution begun in 1959 under the slogan "Grab a Pen, Mate. Our Socialist National Culture needs you!"

These developments were paralleled by the gradual but unrelenting expropriation of the trade and service sectors of the economy still remaining in private hands. In part this was accomplished through fostering the growth of semistate enterprises modeled on Chinese experience. With respect to agriculture, however, expropriation was sudden, rapid, and brutal. Although Soviet-style agricultural collectivization had been introduced in the GDR in the early fifties, its appeal remained limited so that by the end of 1958 only about one-third of the GDR's arable land had been collectivized. In July 1959 the SED reiterated its solemn commitment to "freedom of choice" in the countryside, only to embark on the forcible collectivization of agriculture a few months later. Party shock troops augmented by secret police detachments descended on villages and individual farmhouses. Within a matter of three months (January–March, 1960) about a half million peasants had been impressed into agricultural collectives. By the end of the year private land holdings had been virtually eliminated.

Not surprisingly, such domestic upheavals served to call into question the domestic stabilization of the GDR to which the Ulbricht regime purported to aspire. Of course, its domestic aspirations were always inextricably intertwined with the unresolved national question, i.e., Germany's division, a latent crisis that erupted anew in November 1958 when the Soviet Union issued an ultimatum to the West demanding a change in the status of West Berlin.

Just what may have animated Khrushchev need not concern us here. Suffice it only to note that the ensuing period of some twenty months of East-West tension over Berlin took a serious toll on East Germany. Together with the SED regime's renewed offensive against society, the Berlin crisis also worked against prospects for anything like a durable sociopolitical consolidation of the GDR. Of this, the marked increase of refugees to the West (almost 200,000 in 1960, an even higher monthly rate by mid-1961) was apt testimony. This human outpouring, in turn, put added pressure on Khrushchev—with much of the additional pressure being actively generated by Ulbricht—to solve the Berlin issue one way or another. Although Ulbricht may well have favored an even more radical course of action, he had no choice but to settle for the Kremlin's decision to seal off West Berlin. On the night of August 13, 1961, in a skillfully executed quasi-military operation under the direction of Erich Honecker, the infamous Berlin Wall was thrown up. Officially designated an "antifascist defense wall," this hideous barrier (at first only barbed wire, then massive concrete blocks, later outfitted with military watchtowers and other lethal control devices) was the sine qua non of all subsequent East German political development even as its being torn down twenty-eight years later signaled the beginning of the end of the GDR itself.

Behind the Wall: Ulbricht's Last Decade (1961–1971)

In certain ways, the 1960s (or, more precisely, the decade 1961–1971, Ulbricht's last in office) was a period of undeniable progress in East Germany; in other more important respects it turned out to be a time of disappointment both to key sectors of society and for the Ulbricht regime itself. In the first instance, once the erection of the Wall blocked the escape route to the West, the new-found stability of the domestic labor market coupled with an overhaul and partial devolution of authority within the GDR's command economy enabled East Germany to enjoy a period of sustained growth, heralded at the time by some observers as an "economic miracle in red."[7] On the other hand, domestic liberalization proved both limited and short-lived while the regime's increasingly grandiose socioeconomic schemes fell far short of the intended mark. Last but not least, Ulbricht's evident aspiration to raise the GDR from the abject status of a Soviet satellite to that of a junior, if not quite full, partner of the Soviet Union came, in the end, to grief.

These developments could scarcely have been foretold in the months immediately following the erection of the Berlin Wall. Flushed then with an excess of ideological zeal, communist functionaries set out to settle scores with the domestic "class enemy," among other things, ironically, by compelling industrial workers to produce more for the same pay and by badgering peasants to adjust to the requirements of their newly collectivized existence on pain of criminal prosecution for sabotage. The SED also determined to liquidate once and for all pernicious influences emanating from the West. Toward that end, squads of young toughs were dispatched against households whose television antennae were positioned to receive programs from West Germany. Concerning East-West relations, East German spokesmen, including Ulbricht himself, continued to make bellicose noises about the necessity for further measures, including a separate Soviet-GDR peace treaty, to force the West out of Berlin entirely.

For his part, Khrushchev turned out to be of a less belligerent disposition, especially after the Cuban missile crisis of October 1962. Appearing at the Sixth SED Party Congress (January 1963), the Soviet leader lectured the East German Communists to the effect that with the erection of the Berlin Wall they had achieved the requisite domestic security and that it was now incumbent upon the GDR to demonstrate its viability by improving its economic performance. For this, the SED had already begun to prepare as early as mid-1962 when it began to sponsor a series of specific measures designed to modernize the economy and increase its productive capacity. These changes culminated in a more general economic overhaul, initially called the "New Economic System of Planning and Management" (NES), which was unveiled in January 1963 at the Sixth SED Congress.

Owing much to discussions then taking place in the Soviet Union, the NES never really sought to do away with central planning; rather it attempted to combine planning with some limited market practices. The NES postulated an overhaul of the entire pricing system to take realistic account of the actual value of capital equipment and of the economic costs of all production processes. The original reform blueprint also envisaged the devolution of decision-making authority and an unprecedented reliance on various material incentives. Indeed, the NES seemed initially to sanction an extraordinary degree of independence both for individual enterprises (VEBs) and for industrial combines (VVBs); the latter were officially dubbed "socialist concerns" and each of their managers received the previously unthinkable designation of "General Director." Yet, although precise regulations governing the rights, duties, and responsibilities of the VVBs and the VEBs were drawn up, they were never promulgated. In fact, at the end of 1965, the "General Directors" of "socialist concerns" had to forfeit many of the decision-making prerogatives that had only so recently been bestowed upon them. The VVBs lost their financial autonomy and were once again subordinated to their respective industrial ministries. The National Economic Council, which originally had been charged with providing general economic coordination under NES, was abolished at the same time. Its functions reverted to the State Planning Commission.

At the Eleventh SED Plenum in December 1965, Ulbricht announced a "second stage of the New Economic System." By that he meant the introduction of restrictive practices aimed at maintaining and strengthening central direction and control of the economy. Thus, when the Seventh SED Party Congress, meeting in April 1967, rechristened the NES the "Economic System of Socialism" (ESS), more was involved than merely a name change. As the economic discussions at the Seventh Congress repeatedly stressed, the accent henceforth was to be upon "mastering the scientific-technical revolution." In other words, the primary purpose was now to streamline central planning and economic administration by utilizing cybernetics, information theory, input-output and systems analysis, and the like. The goal was still to improve economic performance but now essentially from the top down and in a manner that had little if anything to do with any prior intimation of decentralization.

Despite the obvious retrenchment entailed in the transition from the NES to the ESS with its growing emphasis on the "scientific-technical revolution," the GDR's economic performance during the 1960s was genuinely impressive. The annual growth rate of the GDR gross national product, which had fallen to 3.7 percent in 1961 and 3.3 percent in 1962, attained the following levels in subsequent years: 4.2 percent (1963), 7.4 percent (1964), 9.5 percent (1965), 5.5 percent (1966), 8.3 percent (1967), 7.1 percent (1968). Between 1964 and 1968 industrial production increased at an average annual rate in excess of 6 percent. Agricultural production which in the wake of the brutal collectivization of 1960 registered a negative growth rate of −1.5 percent for 1961 and −2.3 percent for 1962 experienced a dramatic recovery, recording the following annual percentage increases: 12.3 percent (1963), 13.0 percent (1964), 11.5 percent (1965), 10.6 percent (1966), 6.1 percent (1967), 6.5 percent (1968).[8] Improbable though this would have seemed only a short while before, the GDR had come to attain a level of productive output that rendered it something of a major economic power, ranking at the time ninth or tenth among the world's industrial giants. The standard of living rose accordingly, contributing to the process of reconciliation between the population and the regime.

The great premium that had come to be accorded to economic expertise, administrative skill, and scientific talent served to open up new avenues of social mobility, increasingly stamping the GDR as a "career-oriented society." Bowing to some practical imperatives of the new economic orientation, the political use of terror was de-emphasized. While the dreaded secret police remained an omnipresent reality, the regime came to rely on other compliance mechanisms such as those provided by its network of institutionalized social controls. Within the party itself, no less than within other administrative structures, unprecedented opportunities were opened up for career advancement on the basis of individual talent rather than political toadyism.

All these developments prompted some Western observers to conclude that the GDR had changed in fundamental ways; in place of what had once been a totalitarian political system, it was argued, there had emerged a system of "consultative authoritarianism."[9] Evidence to support this interpretation was sought in the rise of an ostensible East German managerial-technocratic "counter-elite," juxtaposed to the old guard of party functionaries around Ulbricht. In fact, a new breed of able, well-trained, younger specialists with a high degree of competence in their individual fields was being co-opted into the top echelons of the SED. One need only recall the sudden prominence attained in the mid-1960s by such previous political unknowns as Gunther Mittag, Werner Jarowinsky, Georg Ewald, Gunther Klieber, Walter Halbritter, and, perhaps most symbolically of all, Erich Apel, the reputed mastermind of the NES until his suicide in late 1965. These new men at the apex had their counterparts on lower rungs of the party and state bureaucratic ladder, especially in the field of economic administration. Yet these specialists never constituted a self-conscious managerial-technocratic faction, much less a concerted force for liberalization. Indeed, no politically relevant cleavage between "red" and "expert" ever really developed in the GDR. If, in its haste to introduce the first NES reforms, the SED seemed to neglect the "leading role of the party," the oversight was quickly remedied.

Developments in Czechoslovakia—the 1968 Prague Spring followed by Soviet-led invasion, in which GDR troops participated—promoted a forceful reassertion of the primacy of the party by the SED. Actually, in the crucial sphere of domestic cultural policy, ideological guidance and political supervision had never really been relaxed. Even during the somewhat permissive hiatus of the years 1963–65, the party's cultural watchdogs always remained on the alert. At an international literary conference, held at Liblice near Prague in May 1963, they fought hard to oppose the "rehabilitation" of Franz Kafka whose protagonists the SED was subsequently to count among the "intellectual forerunners of counterrevolution" in Czechoslovakia. At home, they banned unpalatable foreign authors, including Solzhenitsyn, and pounced upon a wide variety of heterodox expression. In effect, the party declared war on East Germany's best-known intellectual figures and hounded individuals as diverse as the writer Stefan Heym, the philosopher Robert Havemann, and the balladeer Wolf Biermann. Behind the Wall, under the party's ministrations, East German cultural life was being drained of most of its intellectual vitality.

After the events of 1968 in Czechoslovakia—with the obvious intention of countering any lingering appeal of Prague's "socialism with a human face" but with other much grander objectives in mind—Ulbricht directed his ideologists to elaborate a distinctive East German vision of socialism, present and future. Under this dispensation, there was unveiled a pretentious normative construct, officially termed the "Developed Social System of Socialism" or, in a related version, the "Socialist Human Community." Premised on a distrust of individualism and a fear of pluralism, the official concept amounted to a blueprint for a tightly integrated grid of social subsystems tied to the "economic system of socialism" with the entire monolith motored by advanced techniques of social control operated by the party as the repository of political authority and ideological truth. All this may now seem preposterous—it was even ridiculed as totally unrealistic and by implication even slightly mad only a few years later by Ulbricht's own successors—but at the time it was treated with the utmost reverence and extensively discussed, always with requisite solemnity.

At stake, of course, was no mere abstruse theoretical issue but rather a highly practical policy matter. In the immediate aftermath of the suppression of Czechoslovakia's experiment in freedom, Ulbricht strove to enhance the GDR's influence on the affairs of the socialist bloc in Europe and sought as well a decisive role in shaping Soviet foreign policy toward Europe, particularly as concerned the German question (i.e., toward West Germany and concerning Berlin). This was the deeper meaning of all the theoretical ruminations designed to elevate the GDR (not the USSR) as *the* model of "socialist development," i.e., a paragon of economic efficiency and political stability, and the authoritative guide to all future social progress.

Such presumption was also Ulbricht's undoing. A Kremlin that was prepared to invoke the so-called Brezhnev Doctrine to bring a deviant Czechoslovakia to heel was certainly in no mood to countenance the power of veto over any aspect of its foreign policy in the hands of a self-righteously orthodox East Germany. When by 1970 Moscow had taken up the diplomacy of détente with respect to Germany (including Berlin), only to witness Ulbricht's attempts to stall and even sabotage its diplomatic exertions, the East German leader had become dispensable and his days in office were clearly numbered. On May 3, 1971, on the eve of the Eighth SED Party Congress at which he had been scheduled to deliver yet another major discourse detailing the GDR's idiosyncratic vision of socialism, Ulbricht resigned as SED first secretary. His was a quiet exit—the low-keyed termination of a decade in which Ulbricht had served not only as party boss but also as head of state (chairman of the State Council) and military chieftan (chairman of the National Defense Council), presided over the growth of a cult of his own personality yet also sought to strike the pose of a rather shy and retiring *Landesvater* (father of his country), and even managed to earn some grudging respect in the West.[10] When he stepped down, Ulbricht said he was doing so because the years were beginning to take their toll. Actually, Ulbricht fell victim not so much to his own old age as, in a real sense, to Soviet détente and Bonn's *Ostpolitik*.

The Challenge of West German Ostpolitik

For a number of years after its creation in 1949, the Federal Republic had no policy toward the East worthy of the name. Toward the West, West German policy was internationalist, forward-looking, and not only affirmative but also, on occasion, even creative. Toward the East, by contrast, West Germany's goals seemed narrowly nationalistic, pronouncements that passed for policy predominantly negative, and basic attitudes rigid and unimaginative. The root cause of this state of affairs was, of course, Germany's division into East and West. As a result, *Ostpolitik* was initially treated as a function of *Deutschlandpolitik*. This continued to be the case right up to the restoration of German national unity in 1990, although well before then the linkage between the two realms of policy had undergone considerable loosening, subject to shifting priorities and previously unthinkable twists.

At the outset, under Chancellor Adenauer (1949–1963), certain basic principles seemed set in stone. They followed from West Germany's very raison d'être, enshrined in the Federal Republic's Basic Law, which stipulated that as the one and only post–World War II German political system that enjoyed democratic legitimacy, West Germany had the right to speak for all Germans (i.e., the inhabitants of the GDR, or, as official West German usage long preferred, the Soviet Zone of Occupation). As a corollary of this basic proposition, Bonn's Hallstein Doctrine ruled out diplomatic relations with any country that recognized the GDR. An exception was made for the Soviet Union for fairly obvious reasons; even so Bonn's explanation of the exception sometimes seemed a bit contrived. In any case, the official ties with Moscow that were established in 1955 remained for many years no more than formally correct, and on more than one occasion they became politically embittered. When Yugoslavia extended diplomatic recognition to the GDR in 1957, Bonn promptly invoked the Hallstein Doctrine and broke off relations with Belgrade to discourage any other nations from following suit. Since all the Soviet satellites already had diplomatic relations with East Germany, West Germany refused to have anything whatsoever to do with them, at least at the governmental level. To make matters worse, by officially espousing Germany's claims to the territories lost as the result of World War II, Bonn readily invited suspicion of nurturing revisionist designs on Germany's eastern neighbors.

Paradoxically enough, the erection of the Berlin Wall in 1961, an event that seemed to cement Germany's division, also served to energize Bonn's previously lethargic *Ostpolitik* and direct it into constructive channels. Although signs of change were in the air during the final months of Adenauer's tenure, a significant departure from prior policy occurred only after he left the scene. Under Ludwig Erhard (1963–1966), Foreign Minister Gerhard Schröder devised a plan to isolate the GDR without budging in any way from Bonn's sacrosact doctrinal principles. This ambitious objective was to be pursued by entirely modest and ultimately inadequate means: East Germany was to be kept under strict quarantine while the Federal Republic extended its favor to the other East European countries, in the form of trade ties, economic credits, cultural relations—but not formal diplomatic relations unless and until they broke with East Germany. Not surprisingly, this appeared to the Kremlin to be a brazen flanking move designed not only to isolate the GDR but also to subvert Soviet hegemony in Eastern Europe as a whole. As a consequence, the Soviet–East German alignment grew tighter, scarcely the result Bonn had desired.

With the formation of the grand coalition (CDU-SPD) government in late 1966, West Germany inaugurated a new, more comprehensive, and much more positive *Ostpolitik,* intended to proffer assurances to the Soviet Union and incentives to the GDR as well as to Eastern Europe. In a nutshell, Bonn now offered to suspend the Hallstein Doctrine and establish full diplomatic relations with the communist governments of Eastern Europe. With respect to East Germany, it offered official negotiations at every level and on every subject, except on the GDR's formal diplomatic recognition as a separate state under international law. To the Soviet Union it proposed a mutual reduction of force agreement (an offer also made to the USSR's Eastern European allies, including the GDR) and negotiations between NATO and the Warsaw Pact for a reduction in the level of their respective armed forces then stationed in Germany. This seemingly attractive package also came to naught because the Kremlin deemed it a direct threat to the Soviet hold over Eastern Europe. In 1967 Romania accepted West Germany's overture, but at the time rebellious Romania was a thorn in Moscow's side; in 1968 reform-minded Czechoslovakia evinced considerable interest in a rapprochement with West Germany, something that must have heightened Soviet fears of the potential disintegration of its entire strategic position in Europe.

As long as the Soviet Union attached overriding importance to the maintenance of cohesion and discipline within the Eastern bloc, as exemplified by Moscow's brutal intervention to crush the Prague Spring, West German détentist overtures seemed doomed to failure. Only as other considerations (e.g., the dangerous deterioration of Sino-Soviet relations, the promise of Soviet access to Western technology and West German credits) entered into the Kremlin's calculations did the prospects for change improve. The advent of an SPD-led government, headed by Willy Brandt, in October 1969 occurred under precisely such changed circumstances. For his part, Chancellor Brandt was prepared to reorder the various components of Bonn's new *Ostpolitik* so as to give first priority to Soviet interests. The better to accommodate these interests, Brandt expressed a willingness to accept the territorial and political status quo in Europe (although *not* to forgo efforts to change the status quo in Germany to ameliorate the consequences of national division with a view to eventually overcoming it). In late 1969, West Germany signed the nuclear nonproliferation treaty, renouncing any claim to nuclear weapons; in December 1969 far-ranging talks between Brandt and Brezhnev commenced in Moscow; these negotiations culminated in the Soviet–West German Treaty of August 19, 1970, one of whose major provisions obligated both signatories to respect the territorial integrity of all states in Europe within existing frontiers, including the Oder-Neisse frontier and the border between the GDR and the FRG. The following December (1970) West Germany signed a treaty with Poland acknowledging that the Oder-Neisse line constituted Poland's western frontier.

To bring these diplomatic undertakings to fruition (in the first instance through ratification of the two treaties by the West German parliament), Brandt continued to insist, as he had from the start, upon a satisfactory Four Power agreement to settle the status of West Berlin and, by extension, a political détente (or as the chancellor liked to call it, "regulated coexistence") between the GDR and the FRG. Both these objectives were distinctly unpalatable to Ulbricht who, by setting himself against them, brought the GDR into open disalignment with the Soviet Union.

At stake, in Ulbricht's mind, was the security if not the very survival of the GDR. This required the utmost in sustained confrontation against the West in general and against West Germany in particular, at least as Ulbricht viewed things. Both before and immediately after the Wall, he had repeatedly called for a decisive showdown on Berlin so as to oust the West from the city entirely, only to have to settle for somewhat less. When certain Eastern European communist governments showed some interest in West Germany's offer of better trade relations, Ulbricht's spokesmen were quick to denounce Bonn's overtures as discriminatory to the GDR (which, under Schroder, they were meant to be) and also subversive of the entire socialist bloc (which was not necessarily the case). Confronted in late 1966 by the grand coalition government's new détente-oriented *Ostpolitik*, Ulbricht did not even bother to wait for the Kremlin to make up its mind about how to respond to Bonn's advances. East German spokesmen lost no time in denouncing them as dangerous as well as disingenuous. The GDR at once began a diplomatic offensive to counter West Germany's fresh approaches to the East. The goal of its frenetic activities was to construct an impregnable phalanx against the FRG through a series of bilateral treaties between the GDR and other East European states on the basis of the "Ulbricht Doctrine" (no diplomatic relations with the FRG without prior full West German recognition of the GDR "under international law": a mirror image of the Hallstein Doctrine).

Until 1969 Ulbricht's confrontational attitude toward West Germany enjoyed general Soviet support even though the Kremlin did not always see fit to endorse all the East German leader's hard-line gambits. The Soviet-GDR alignment seemed exceptionally close during 1968, both in the period of the Prague Spring and in the immediate aftermath of the Soviet-led invasion of Czechoslovakia. Judging by his pronouncements of the time, Ulbricht may even have persuaded himself that henceforth the GDR would play a major role in socialist bloc affairs in Europe and have the decisive voice in Soviet and Eastern European policy toward West Germany. If so, Ulbricht was quickly proved mistaken on both counts. Once the Kremlin opted to reciprocate Brandt's offer of rapprochement, Ulbricht had little choice but to give the appearance of going along, although he obviously did so with little relish.

This was the unpromising background for the two inter-German summit meetings that took place in 1970, in Erfurt (GDR) in March and in Kassel (FRG) in May. Both meetings amounted to little more than a rehash by each side of mutually exclusive positions. (Erfurt witnessed one dramatic incident in the spontaneous outburst of popular acclaim for Chancellor Brandt—validation, if any were needed, of the worst anxieties of the SED leadership.) Inter-German discussions were then suspended, pending progress in West German–Soviet negotiations. Conclusion of the August 1970 Soviet-FRG Treaty set the stage for the resumption of the inter-German dialogue. Ulbricht now opted for a policy of "preventive negotiations," i.e., a strategy of employing inter-German talks to sabotage Four Power negotiations on Berlin and, if possible, even the Soviet-FRG Treaty itself. With respect to the Berlin negotiations, Ulbricht lost no opportunity to assert the GDR's "legitimate interests and sovereign rights" and to reiterate its oft-repeated demand that West Berlin be treated as "an independent political entity," protestations that were made especially pointed when the East German authorities resorted to the dangerous tactic of harrassing traffic from West Germany to West Berlin, doing so now on their own initiative, in a last-ditch effort to undercut Soviet diplomacy.

In retrospect, it is clear that such efforts could never have prevailed. Rather than being a force to be reckoned with, Ulbricht had become a nuisance to be disposed of. In all probability, the decision to orchestrate an orderly succession of the SED leadership was taken by the Kremlin in March 1971. At the Twenty-fourth CPSU Congress which met that month in Moscow, Ulbricht had the temerity to invoke his personal acquaintance with Lenin, citing Lenin to the effect that "the Soviet comrades also had things to learn." Ulbricht also conspicuously failed to join other fraternal delegates to the Soviet party congress in the chorus of indictment of Maoist China. All told, this was behavior that must have looked to Brezhnev and his associates as a studied, if ill-considered, provocation. The succession was easily arranged, not only because Ulbricht's own lieutenants recognized more clearly than did he that in such matters the Kremlin was still master in East Berlin but also because these same lieutenants had their own growing doubts about Ulbricht's management of the East German domestic scene, especially with respect to economic affairs.

With Ulbricht out of the way as of May 1971, the Four Power agreement on Berlin was concluded with relative dispatch. The finished instrument was unveiled on September 3, 1971, some eighteen months after the start of negotiations but a mere four months after Ulbricht's political demise. It remained for his successor to urge his fellow SED epigones to develop "the courage to run risks." [11] By this Honecker meant: learn to live with the challenge of détente.

Détente and Delimitation (1970)

Ulbricht's fall from power signaled the abandonment of any further claim on behalf of the GDR as a model socialist society in favor of a reassertion of Soviet primacy in all things, including foreign policy toward the West. Under Honecker, East Germany not only echoed Moscow's espousal of détente but also resumed negotiations with the FRG, quietly dropping its prior insistence upon full diplomatic recognition by West Germany. In the process the GDR acceded to a "special relationship" with the FRG, thereby implicitly accepting a major provision of Bonn's new *Deutschlandpolitik*.

The *Grundlagenvertrag* (Basic Treaty), concluded in late 1972 between the FRG and the GDR, fell far short of de jure recognition of Germany's national division. Together with a package of related agreements, concluded both before and immediately afterward, the Basic Treaty provided for numerous ongoing contacts between the two sides in various fields and opened up East Germany to influence from the West in the form of restored lines of communication and a massive influx of visitors. By the second half of the 1970s visits to the GDR from West Germany climbed to more than three million annually, with an additional three million-plus visits on the part of West Berliners and some sixteen million individual transits through East German territory each year to and from West Berlin. Although this traffic was basically one way—East Germans were allowed to travel to the West only if they had passed retirement age or could demonstrate a family emergency—it was bound to have a dramatic impact. At the individual and family levels, reassociation between the two parts of Germany became a new social reality. East Germany's communist rulers now had to deal with the potentially disruptive domestic consequences of the rapprochement with West Germany brought on by détente.

The Honecker regime's answer took the form of a concerted effort at *Abgrenzung* (delimitation) designed to throw up a host of internal barriers, administrative as well as ideological and political, against possible Western inroads. Initially, restrictions on personal contacts with Westerners were imposed on an entire category of East Germans, a million or so people deemed to have access to official secrets. At the same time, a massive propaganda campaign was mounted to underscore the ostensibly unbridgeable differences between East Germany and West Germany. "Social democratism" came under heavy fire as did "revisionism," "theories of the convergence of social systems," and subsequently, "bourgeois nationalist conceptions," "ideological diversions," and other related bugaboos. At the practical level, what might be termed "preemptive delimitation" (e.g., the procurement of individual pledges to refrain from personal contacts with West Germans) was followed by "reactive delimitation" (e.g., the expulsion of individual representatives of the West German media and, for that matter, selected East German malcontents).

Delimitation vis-à-vis West Germany was from the start augmented by measures of integration with the socialist bloc as a whole and, with an even greater sense of urgency, on a bilateral basis with the Soviet Union, the latter officially referred to as a process of *Verflechtung* (literally, "intertwining"). Delimitation and integration gained strong expression in all the major normative documents of the early Honecker period. Thus the 1974 revision of the East German constitution dropped all references to national unity in favor of a designation of the GDR as "a socialist state of workers and peasants" and "an inseparable component of the socialist community of states."

The same formulations were contained in the 1975 Soviet–East German Friendship Treaty and in the new SED party program adopted in 1976. In the realm of practical policy, the Honecker regime eagerly cooperated with Moscow in forging a host of bilateral bonds, military, political, and economic, with a view to linking the Soviet Union and East Germany almost organically.[12] In discharging its "internationalist obligations," the GDR readily joined forces with the Soviet Union not only in Europe but also further afield, particularly from the mid-1970s in sub-Saharan Africa.

During the 1970s the GDR seemed to be reaping rewards for its energetic loyalty to the Soviet Union that went far beyond the ultimate guarantee Moscow continued to provide with respect to East Germany's internal security. Honecker's adjustment to East-West détente enabled the GDR to achieve a crucial goal that had always eluded Ulbricht: international recognition. East Germany's virtually universal diplomatic recognition went hand in hand with membership in the United Nations and full-fledged participation in its own right at such major international gatherings as the Conference on Security and Cooperation in Europe (CSCE) summit, held at Helsinki in 1975.

Although it was undoubtedly invaluable in so many other respects, the GDR's Soviet connection could not fully cushion East Germany against the global economic recession of the mid-1970s. An energy shortage, together with the worldwide rise in the price of raw materials, not to mention that of crude oil, dictated renewed domestic austerity. As a result, these years featured repeated campaigns devoted to reducing imports and conserving raw materials, while increasing the quantity and quality of production for export. Such fresh imperatives served to reemphasize the GDR's dependence on foreign trade and also to underscore the crucial importance of East Germany's economic relationship to West Germany.

Although trade with the FRG accounted for only about 15 percent of the GDR's total foreign trade, West Germany constituted the GDR's second-largest trade partner. GDR-FRG economic ties conferred great benefits upon East Germany. Thanks to West German insistence on treating inter-German trade as domestic German trade, the GDR enjoyed all the trade and tariff advantages of de facto association with the European Common Market. In addition, West Germany provided the GDR with barely disguised financial subsidies in the form of sizable interest-free credits on its trade clearing accounts, under arrangements known as the "swing." Finally, West Germany became an indispensable supplier not only of capital equipment and advanced technology but also of high-quality consumer goods, including luxury items of the sort that Honecker had come to rely upon in order to appease the East German population.

The GDR's dependence on West German economic support helped set the stage for the Honecker regime's slow and at first largely imperceptible conversion to the cause of inter-German détente.[13] By the late 1970s, the regime had gained considerable experience in handling relations with the Federal Republic; it had also grown confident of its ability to guard the domestic ramparts against any "subversive" influences that might emanate from West Germany. For its part, in pursuit of the humanitarian objectives of its *Deutschlandpolitik,* Bonn had foresworn any intention of destabilizing the GDR.

Two decades after the Wall the erstwhile cold civil war in Germany had been effectively transformed into an indigenous version of coexistence, often troubled but essentially peaceful and, on occasion, conspicuously cooperative. This much was evident when West German Chancellor Helmut Schmidt moved in tandem with Erich Honecker to preserve Germany as an "isle of détente" in the face of the deterioration of East-West relations that accompanied the Soviet invasion of Afghanistan (1979) and the protracted crisis in Poland ending in the imposition of martial law (1980–81). When subsequently the Kremlin pressured Honecker to take countermeasures against the FRG so as to punish West Germany for agreeing to NATO deployment of advanced intermediate-range nuclear forces (INF) on its territory, Honecker demurred and a novel miniconflict between East Berlin and Moscow ensued.[14] Honecker visibly chafed under the Kremlin's ministrations in the final years of Brezhnev's tenure in office and during the Andropov-Chernenko interregnum. Gorbachev's accession to power in March 1985 seemed to herald a change for the better. Little could Honecker have sensed at the time that the new Soviet leader's policies would contribute only a few years later to the overthrow of East Germany's "real existing socialism" and to the liquidation of the GDR itself.

"Real Existing Socialism" Under Honecker (1980–1989)

The GDR under Honecker managed to acquire something of a positive reputation as being perhaps rigid and repressive but also efficient and effective, an exemplar of Marxism-Leninism in practice, proof positive, as was sometimes said, that Germans could make anything work, even Soviet-style socialism. The truth was quite different. Although the GDR could boast of having made considerable progress against improbable initial odds, that was achieved thanks in real measure to East Germany's special relationship with West Germany. And, even more to the point, as the Honecker regime grew sclerotic, the GDR became only too susceptible to the stagnation and corruption that characterized the Soviet Union in the Brezhnev era and beyond.

As official doctrine, the SED's espousal of "real existing socialism" was nothing if not a deeply conservative reflex in defense of the status quo. As initially employed in 1972, however, the formulation was meant to counter not only ostensibly revisionist and/or utopian visions of socialism advanced by protagonists of Czechoslovakia's "springtime of freedom" (e.g., Robert Havemann) but also the grandiose socialist futurology that had been peddled by Ulbricht. Under Honecker, the emphasis shifted to the here and now, current production and distribution, the satisfaction rather than the deferral of consumer needs and wants. This was the spirit in which the Eighth SED Party Congress, meeting in June 1971 (a month after Ulbricht's fall from power and in his absence), reinstated economics as the *Hauptaufgabe*. It was also the sense in which the Honecker leadership preached "the indivisible unity of social and economic policy" enshrined in the SED's 1976 party program.

To be sure, one of Honecker's first moves on the economic front was against the GDR's minuscule private sector. In early 1972 most of the remaining independent enterprises and all the semistate-owned firms were taken over. This increased the state's share of industrial output from 82 percent to more than 99 percent, thereby completing the GDR's "socialist profile," obviously a crucial consideration with respect to *Abgrenzung*, the GDR's delimitation from West Germany that was then being pursued so strenuously. At the same time, however, wages and pensions were raised, a massive housing construction program inaugurated, investment in consumer goods production greatly increased, and the official commitment to relatively stable prices maintained. By the end of the 1970s, despite the disruption occasioned by the adverse international economic conditions of the decade's middle years, East Germany's standard of living had risen markedly.

Raising domestic living standards was always a key element in the formula for governing implicit in "real existing socialism." The core of the formula itself can be labeled "consumeristic authoritarianism," a designation that may well suggest a blatant contradiction in terms. Precisely as such, however, it captures better than any other terminology all the major contradictions inherent in the Honecker era. On the one hand, concerned lest it lose power as the result of any ill-considered political relaxation, the Honecker regime, virtually to the very end of its eighteen-year existence, continued to insist upon the utmost in political discipline and social control. On the other hand, the regime also sought to broaden its social base and to legitimize its authoritative rule by satisfying the popular demand for goods and services.

Achievement of this objective was to prove exceptionally difficult if only because of the growing appetite of the GDR consumer. For East Germans the standard of comparison of economic well-being was never with the Soviet Union, the other Soviet bloc countries, or even with Western industrial societies at random, but rather quite specifically with the other, increasingly affluent Germany, the FRG. Even though they may have been immured, East Germans always knew the score, often down to the smallest detail. This was thanks to contacts, personal as well as those provided by the media, that enabled East German society to keep in close touch with its Western counterpart. Comparisons and contrasts were also brought home thanks to the "Intershop" phenomenon, a kind of "white market" comprising an elaborate network of state stores blanketing the entire GDR and selling a whole range of western products for hard currency. With such official sanction, it was scarcely surprising that the DM-West (West German deutsch mark) circulated freely throughout the GDR. This, in turn, led to a situation in which certain goods and services (e.g., spare parts, specialty items, the services of various craftsmen and artisans) could only be obtained against payment in West German currency, something which served to generate the "DM-Nationalism" that was to propel the unification of East and West Germany in 1990.

By the early 1980s the SED leadership deemed it advisable to try to fashion the domestic strength with which to compete for the allegiance of the East German population by streamlining the GDR's command economy and emphasizing high technology. Under an organizational restructuring carried out in 1979–80, 132 new industrial *Kombinate*, each coordinating the production and research activities of between twenty and forty individual enterprises, received various administrative responsibilities and certain decision-making prerogatives. The rallying cry quickly became rationalization, intensification, mechanization, and automation, all within the framework of the overall Plan. By the mid-1980s—the Eleventh SED Party Congress in 1986 was in many ways the highpoint—the Honecker leadership championed advanced technology as the answer to all its economic dilemmas. A number of "key technologies," including microelectronics, robotics, computer-aided design, and computer-aided manufacturing, were looked to for a quick fix to such otherwise intractable domestic economic problems as an inadequate resource base, low capital productivity, a worsening labor shortage, and deficient managerial innovation.

As it turned out, even though the GDR did better than other communist states, East Germany simply lacked the wherewithal to excel in the high-tech arena. Its domestic research and development base was far too small and the bureaucratic constraints of its command economy far too great. Specialized input from the Soviet Union and the GDR's other East European Council of Mutual Economic Assistance (Comecon) partners was inadequate in amount and deficient in quality. Economic credits and technology transfer from West Germany did not come close to making up for these shortcomings. The fact that the FRG alone disposed of the necessary resources (and under the right circumstances might even be prevailed upon to undertake the requisite commitment) was seen as a standing reproach and, as far as the Honecker leadership was concerned, an unacceptable political challenge.[15]

At stake, of course, was the extent to which the West was to be allowed to penetrate into the GDR domestic arena. Despite Honecker's evident embrace of inter-German détente, there had to be limits. It was one thing for the East German leader to accept improvement of GDR-FRG relations at the official level or even for Honecker to travel to Bonn in September 1987 for a much-delayed state visit; it was quite another for him to countenance pressures for internal changes within East Germany wherever these might come from, be it from West Germany or, as soon became the case, from the Soviet Union in the person of Gorbachev.

The political society that crystallized under the twin lodestar of consumeristic authoritarianism and the drive for high tech was not without its own domestic critics. To the familiar methods of unrelenting surveillance and repeated police harrassment to which, for example, Robert Havemann continued to be subjected right up to his death, the regime now added a new technique—expatriation to the West, after the manner of the Soviet treatment of Solzhenitsyn. This was the fate meted out in the mid-1970s to almost two dozen prominent East German writers and artists, notably the irreverent troubador, Wold Biermann, who was stripped of GDR citizenship while away on an officially sanctioned performance tour in West Germany.

A comparable fate, only considerable worse, befell Rudolf Bahro. A previously obscure minor SED party functionary, Bahro had the effrontery to venture a devastating critique of the GDR's "real existing socialism" from a Marxist point of view and the nerve to have his damaging disquisition published in the West.[16] Bahro was promptly arrested and sentenced to eight years imprisonment on charges of espionage, only to be released in 1979 and dispatched directly to West Germany, apparently yet another case of *Menschenhandel* (the notorious East German practice of selling domestic political prisoners to the Federal Republic for hard currency).

Such practices, juxtaposed to the GDR's much-touted adherence to the 1975 Helsinki accords (including its provisions for the free flow of ideas, information, and people), generated no end of cynicism. One sarcastic saying, much in vogue at the time, held that rulers who locked in those who desired to leave but threw out others who wanted to stay had to be certifiably insane. In fact, the number of East Germans applying for permission to emigrate was quite substantial—an estimated 120,000 by the end of 1976. While almost all applications for legal exit were rejected in the 1970s, the situation changed in the early 1980s. As an East German trade-off in inter-German relations, with a major increase in financial credits from Bonn at stake, a record number of East Germans (approximately 40,000 during 1984) received authorization to emigrate to West Germany. Two years later travel restrictions on short-term visits to the West by GDR citizens were relaxed. Although the regime purported to derive satisfaction from the fact that only a relatively small number of individuals utilized the relaxed travel regulations to defect, it was in no mood to facilitate a wholesale westward movement of the East German population by granting permanent exit permits in anything like the requested numbers. (Applications for these permits reached a total of 500,000 by mid-decade.) On the contrary, the SED saw fit to launch a major new propaganda campaign aimed at discrediting emigration as morally unsound. Clearly, the whole matter of emigration policy posed an insoluble problem for the Honecker regime, as the events of 1989 were to prove quite conclusively.

Nor was the forcible expulsion of troublesome individuals any longer a viable solution to the problem posed by a novel outcropping of dissidence in the 1980s. Now, in addition to individual writers and artists of a critical bent of mind, there appeared on the scene groups—at first minuscule in number, mostly youthful in composition, and as often as not countercultural in coloration—with all the markings of an incipient dissident movement.

Peace and ecology as well as emigration were the basic issues: antimilitarism and environmental protection (or, increasingly, environmental restoration) as well as the right to free travel were the major demands, and the Evangelical (Protestant) church was a handy operational base and ready sanctuary—in fact, the one and only conceivable institutional support structure. This was so not only because the churches alone (Roman Catholic as well as Protestant) enjoyed organizational autonomy and thus always served as "islands of separateness" but also on account of the Evangelical church's own politicization. Until 1969 the Evangelical Church of Germany constituted a single association covering both East Germany and West Germany. Subsequent organizational partition impelled the search for a proper definition of the East German church's new role as, in its own description of itself, a "Church in Socialism." The very phrase implied both accommodation and affirmation. What balance to strike between the two became the subject of intense discussion within the church. By the late 1980s, there emerged a loose but determined group calling itself the *Kirche von unten* (church from below). It comprised younger clergy and laity who were critical of the restraint practiced by the ecclesiastical hierarchy, seeking instead a much more forceful stand by the church on a wide variety of political matters and social issues.

More than looking to the church, all those who chafed under the GDR's "real existing socialism" pinned their hopes on Gorbachev. How else to interpret the huzzas of "Gorby" sent up in June 1987 by the throngs of unruly youth, crowded together hard by the eastern face of the Berlin Wall the better to catch the sounds of a British rock concert being performed on the other side? Scarcely less awkward for the regime was the unwelcome participation by several hundred dissidents in the annual official commemoration of the murder of Rosa Luxemburg and Karl Liebknecht held in January 1988. In the spirit of glasnost, they unfurled banners proclaiming, "Freedom is always the freedom to think differently," one of Luxemburg's best known maxims but also an utterance of hers that Leninists have always considered thoroughly objectionable. Such specific incidents aside, by 1987–88 East German dissidents were taking considerable heart from the new leadership in the Kremlin, finding in Gorbachev's summons to perestroika welcome legitimation from an unexpected source for their own exertions on behalf of change in the GDR.

The East German ruling elite saw matters in an entirely different light. Glasnost, SED leaders remonstrated, could be quite pernicious—had not the reactionaries exploited the freedom of expression provided by the Weimar republic to undermine it and establish a fascist dictatorship? As for perestroika, why, one should wish the Soviet Union all the best, but the GDR had managed its own affairs so well that it had absolutely no need of any such restructuring. Or, as the veteran SED ideologist Kurt Hager put it in an April 1987 interview in the West German illustrated magazine *Der Stern,* in a statement that was then widely publicized in East Germany, "Just because your neighbor sets about repapering his house, doesn't mean you've got to do the same." [17]

Such smug self-satisfaction permeated the entire top leadership with the possible exception of Ernst Mielke who as boss of the Stasi presided over an organization conditioned to expect the worse.[18] On every possible ceremonial occasion, at the Eleventh SED Party Congress in April 1986, and on the fateful occasion of the GDR's fortieth anniversary celebration in October 1989, the leadership repeatedly boasted that East Germany enjoyed both a full measure of economic prosperity and unprecedented political stability.

At the 1986 party congress Honecker appeared to be in full control, vigorously exercising long-consolidated personal power.

No serious rival loomed on the horizon. Although already approaching his seventy-fourth birthday, Honecker appeared the picture of good health, his mental abilities seemed unimpaired, and his capacity for sustained hard work undiminished. Soon thereafter the projected date of the next SED party congress was moved up from 1991 to 1990. Far from providing an early occasion for Honecker to step aside in favor of a younger man, insiders purported to know that the change in scheduling was meant instead to facilitate another renewal of Honecker's mandate.

That, of course, was not to be. By autumn 1989 the GDR stood at the threshold of a revolutionary upheaval. Honecker did not even begin to comprehend the situation for what it was. To be sure, the GDR's veteran leader now confronted severe health problems, but he did not suffer from senility. Rather, his failure to grasp what was transpiring reflected certain ingrained traits of his political personality—stubbornness, narrow-mindedness, and, perhaps most of all, quite limited basic intelligence.[19]

The German Revolution of 1989

In his *Critique of Hegel's Philosophy of Right,* Karl Marx complained that German history knew the revolutions of other nations only in the form of restoration. However that may once have been, in 1989 East Germans proved Marx wrong—they did not experience the revolution of others as reaction; they made their own revolution. In the process, they also disproved Lenin's well-known dictum, "Without a revolutionary theory there can be no revolutionary movement."

In fact, although much dissident thought went into the upheaval that shook the GDR to its very Marxist-Leninist foundations, there was no single coherent revolutionary philosophy behind the popular insurgency that helped topple East Germany's old (indeed, gerontocratic) regime. Rather, a host of concrete demands generated by relatively few critical intellects suddenly acquired a mass following. The popular movement grew more assertive in direct proportion to the evident loss of confidence on the part of the GDR's disoriented communist rulers, in keeping with rather elemental revolutionary dynamics so well diagnosed by that incisive student of another ancien régime, Alexis de Tocqueville. In this particular instance the revolution was allowed to run its course without external interference of the sort that put down the June 1953 uprising, crushed the 1956 Hungarian revolution, and suppressed the 1968 Prague Spring. If anything, awareness of the dissonance between a reform-minded Kremlin and the stand-pat SED old guard, together with a growing perception that Moscow would not intervene to save the likes of Honecker, emboldened the insurgents while simultaneously disheartening the GDR's dumbfounded domestic masters. It is for future historians to determine whether Gorbachev was fully cognizant of the likely consequences of his stance, up to and including the possibility of the liquidation of the GDR and thus the end of Germany's national division, up until then the fulcrum of Soviet policy in Europe. In the event the Soviet leader manifested considerable diplomatic aplomb in accepting the inevitable.

The East German revolution transpired peacefully and ran its course rapidly. Not many months before, dissidents' grumbling—about the patently falsified results of the May 1989 local elections—had been swiftly stifled. This was an SED regime whose spokesmen were quick to welcome the bloody repression of Chinese prodemocracy demonstrators at Tiananmen Square. But they were entirely at a loss as to how to deal with Hungary's May 1989 decision to begin to dismantle its Iron Curtain to the West. During the ensuing summer and autumn months growing numbers of East Germans, at first hundreds, then thousands and tens of thousands, mostly young and highly skilled people, sought to leave the GDR for the West—via Hungary, Czechoslovakia, and Poland.

s,

Although the westward passage was greatly facilitated by Hungary's grant of official permission for GDR refugees to exit in early September, and by a comparable agreement involving the two German states, Czechoslovakia, and Poland at the beginning of October, the wound to the East German body politic was scarcely staunched. At home an increasing number of people began to call for change in open, public demonstrations. Citizens' groups such as New Forum, founded in mid-September, flourished and grew in membership to the consternation of the regime which declared all such activities illegal and "subversive."

Most observers now agree that the turning point in the 1989 East German revolution occurred on October 9 in Leipzig where plans to disperse a massive peaceful demonstration, if need be by force, were aborted. This transpired in the immediate aftermath of the official celebration of the GDR's fortieth anniversary (October 7). On hand for that commemorative occasion was Gorbachev, whose aloof demeanor toward Honecker was matched by the Soviet leader's scarcely unconsidered observation to the effect that "life punishes those who come too late," a remark that gained instantaneous currency. Just how bloodshed was averted on October 9 in Leipzig remains the subject of much speculation. At the time, however, one thing was crystal clear: the days in office of the ailing Eric Honecker were now numbered. On October 18, amidst continuing protest demonstrations, Honecker stepped down in favor of his longtime "crown prince," Egon Krenz.

Krenz's tenure in office proved short-lived but highly eventful. Ineffectual against incessant mass protests and powerless to hold back a fresh wave of emigration through Czechoslovakia, the GDR government and the SED Politburo suddenly resigned and, in a desperate gamble, on November 9 the GDR threw open its borders to the Federal Republic and West Berlin—the hated Berlin Wall was a political barrier no more; its physical dismantling was now only a matter of time.

The demise of the SED party dictatorship was also well under way. On December 1, the *Volkskammer* amended the GDR constitution to strike out any reference to the party's "leading role," its normative claim to a monopoly of power. The following week, a special party congress elected a new leader, the relatively youthful, reform-minded Gregory Gysi. As an earnest token of its avowed de-Leninization, the party's name was changed to Socialist Unity Party–Party of Democratic Socialism, soon to be officially shortened to the latter designation alone and thereafter to be familiarly known by the initials PDS.

In the fertile soil of the East German revolution many different political groupings took root. These included a host of citizens groups (e.g., New Forum, Democratic Awakening, Democracy Now) and rejuvenated and/or reconstructed political parties (e.g., the Christian Democratic Union [CDU], the Liberal Democratic Party [LDP], the Social Democratic Party [SDP, then SPD], among others). All such formations clamored for access to government power so that by early December the sometime ruling communists had to agree to roundtable negotiations to provide for free elections.

By the time of the December 1989 roundtable negotiations, the East German popular mood had, however, undergone a significant shift. Whereas earlier street demonstrations had proclaimed *"wir sind das Volk"* (we are the people), they now began to chant *"wir sind ein Volk"* (we are one people). Virtually overnight, German national unification had been pushed to the top of the agenda. The unification issue was rendered even more urgent on account of the continued (now unobstructed) movement of people from East to West Germany. As an immediate consequence, the East German elections originally scheduled for May 16, 1990, had to be moved up to March 8. The March 1990 elections produced a grand coalition government (Christian Democrats, Free Democrats, and Social Democrats) under the leadership of Lothar de Maiziere (CDU). It was the GDR's first—and its only—noncommunist government: for more than simply marking the consummation of the East German revolution of 1989, the March 1990 election was really a vote for the rapid unification of the GDR with the Federal Republic of Germany.

The Politics of Unification 1989–1990

In the course of the East German revolution Helmut Kohl came to consider himself the "Chancellor of German Unity." Initially, the very designation appeared to be pretentious self-promotion and an implausible fantasy to boot, considering that Kohl's own domestic political fortunes had been on the wane not so very long before. Never a great visionary, a grand strategist, or—unlike his foreign minister, Hans-Dietrich Genscher—previously occupied to excess by the "national question," Kohn nevertheless manifested the requisite determination and drive to realize his aspiration. Having seized the initiative, Kohl pressed relentlessly forward right up to the all-German elections of December 2, 1990, which returned him as the first chancellor of a newly united Germany.

The framework for the attainment of unification received the designation "two-plus-four," referring to parallel negotiations between the two German states and among the four sometime-occupying powers (the World War II Allies) who retained responsibility for "Germany as a whole." In fact, the driving force in both sets of negotiations was West Germany in the person of Helmut Kohl.

By late November 1989 in a major speech to the West German Bundestag, Kohl unveiled a ten-point program aimed at overcoming the division of Germany and Europe. The chancellor followed this up in early 1990 with meetings in Moscow with Gorbachev and in Bonn with the GDR's last communist prime minister, the reform-minded Hans Modrow. But having received from Moscow the green light on German unification (at that point still a conditional go-ahead), Kohl decided to make short shrift of various schemes for a "contractual community" through a *Vertragsgemeinschaft* (network of treaties) and "confederal structures" between the two Germanies, schemes with which he had originally toyed. In place of all such notions, he now determined to press forward to nothing less than complete political unification. To that end, following the March 1990 East German elections that effectively ratified Kohl's conception, the chancellor decided to hasten the introduction of monetary union. Contrary to the advice of almost all his expert advisors, Kohl insisted upon a currency union based essentially upon parity between the Western DM and the incomparably weaker East German Mark. In an agreement heralding the introduction of the West German market economy to the GDR, German monetary union went into effect on July 1, 1990.

The treaty governing the German currency union (or, monetary, economic, and social union, to give its full title) also affirmed the political unification of the two German states as a matter of immediate urgency and stipulated that it should take place on the basis of Article 23 of the West German Basic Law. This meant the GDR's direct accession to the Federal Republic in conjunction with the reconstitution of the five East German *Länder* that had been abolished in 1952. It signified the complete triumph of the West German constitutional and legal order and thus effectively ended the arguments, pro and con, that had raged in East Germany (and, to a lesser extent, in West Germany) about the preferability of achieving unification through the convocation of a new Constitutent Assembly (a possibility envisaged in Article 146 of Bonn's Basic Law).

With German domestic foundations firmly in place (the "two" having agreed on the modalities of becoming "one"), the international dimension (the "four") needed to be brought into line. By midsummer 1990 this essentially boiled down to the Soviet Union alone. From the start of international negotiations on German unification, Bonn had enjoyed the crucial support of the United States; Britain and France were less enthusiastic participants, but they weren't about to be seen as spoilers. Gorbachev had agreed to unification in February 1990, but Moscow's assent remained conditional upon finding a formula agreeable to the Soviet Union governing united Germany's future international status. In the ensuing months Soviet spokesmen floated various trial balloons: neutralization of Germany, German membership in both the North Atlantic Treaty Organization (NATO) and the Warsaw Pact, the abolition of both NATO and the Warsaw Pact, their melding into a single comprehensive European security system, and myriad variations on all the above. Much as Kohl had single-mindedly pursued his socioeconomic and political conceptions of German unity, so also did he insist that united Germany must be free to maintain its membership in NATO. This too was finally achieved at the congenial summit meeting between Kohl and Gorbachev that took place in the Soviet leader's hometown of Zheleznovodsk, near Stavropol, in the Caucasus in mid-July 1990.

Notable though Kohl's achievement undoubtedly was, it would be a great mistake to regard the Stavropol agreement as anything like a one-sided German triumph. On the contrary, Gorbachev's willingness to accord to united Germany full sovereignty and thus apparently complete freedom to choose whatever international alliance obligations it saw fit to maintain (i.e., to retain Germany's membership in NATO) entailed a price. First, Kohl agreed to prohibit the stationing of non-German alliance troops in eastern Germany, to limit the total size of united Germany's armed forces to 370,000, and to forsake the acquisition of nonconventional ABC—atomic, biological, and chemical—weapons. Moreover, the German chancellor also undertook to shoulder the entire financial burden of withdrawing Soviet forces from eastern Germany and rehousing them in the Soviet Union (a redeployment scheduled for completion no later than 1994). Finally, the agreement envisaged extensive German credits to the faltering Soviet economy, sums over and above Bonn's earlier commitment to assume financial responsibility for all the GDR's commercial obligations to the Soviet Union. All told, the 1990 Soviet-German entente, consummated against the background of a veritable explosion of Gorbamania inside Germany, disquieted some thoughtful Western observers. The London *Economist* coined the expression "Stavrapallo" to prompt its readers to ponder the similarities (and the differences) between the agreement at Stavropol of 1990 and the treaty of Rapallo of 1922.

Clearly, the differences far outweighed any similarities. Among the most important was the fact that the post-Stavropol Germany of 1990 still had to complete its political unification, a process destined to run well beyond the date designated as "the day of German unity," October 3, 1990, the day on which the GDR went out of existence.

Kohl's brand of unity, so distasteful to those East German political figures who had hoped to salvage something of value from GDR's four-decades-long collectivist experience, and so much resented by a whole host of critical German intellectuals, East as well as West, was nonetheless ratified by the East German population. In state elections held on October 14, 1990, Kohl's CDU won in four of the five freshly reconstituted eastern German *Länder*. The following month in Paris the thirty-four members of the CSCE gave their benediction to German unification in a summit that French President Mitterand euphorically termed an "anti-Versailles" conference, "without winners, without losers." In fact, almost everybody agreed that the November 1990 CSCE Paris summit could well be interpreted as marking the end of the cold war in Europe.

All these activities notwithstanding, the all-German elections of December 2, 1990, need not be considered merely a denouement. Rather, the elections constituted both a conclusion and a commencement. On the one hand, the electoral victory of the long-governing Bonn coalition of the Christian Democrats (CDU/CSU) and Free Democrats (FDP) put the final stamp of democratic legitimacy upon the unification program so successfully pursued by the Kohl-Genscher team. Viewed from a slightly different angle, the poor showing of the Social Democrats probably had less to do with the personal shortcomings of the SPD candidate, Oskar Lafontaine, than with the socialists' doubts and hesitations concerning unification, a major factor in the Social Democrats' unexpectedly poor showing in 1990 GDR elections, beginning in March. By the same token, the surprising failure of Greens to win a single seat in the Bundestag (having fallen below the requisite minimum of 5 percent of the popular vote) was attributable to that party's uncompromisingly negative attitude toward unification.

On the other hand, the December 1990 elections marked the beginning of the final phase of the political absorption of the ex-GDR and therefore also heralded the emergence of a new postunification Germany. Thanks to a "this time only" ruling of the Federal Constitutional Court allowing the 5 percent hurdle to apply separately to eastern Germany, the East's Greens, allied with Alliance '90, the remnants of the citizen's groups that had been so active at the outset of the 1989 revolution, managed to win eight seats in the Bundestag. For its part, the PDS, direct descendant of the once mighty ruling Communists, picked up seventeen seats. But to speak in Leninist parlance, both groups appeared to constitute "phenomena of the transition," doomed to vanish from parliament, probably with the very next national elections.

All this, it has been said, amounts to nothing other than an *Anschluss,* the outright annexation of East Germany by West Germany. This assessment has become grist for the mill of all those who bemoan the wholesale loss of distinctive (and many would argue, superior) East German values and mores. But it has also been a source of solace for those who want to believe that united Germany will be simply West Germany writ large, replete with the latter's economic prosperity, social stability, and democratic political order. In all likelihood, things will not work out quite so simply for postunification Germany. With the ex-GDR, the new, enlarged Federal Republic of Germany has taken on a host of severe socioeconomic problems and courted a series of possible threats to its carefully nurtured but still potentially fragile democratic political culture. This new Germany must simultaneously confront a range of novel foreign policy challenges and opportunities, not least with respect to its new-old neighbors, the now largely ex-communist countries of Eastern Europe.

United Germany and Eastern Europe

It is scarcely surprising that the countries of Eastern Europe should have experienced mixed feelings concerning Germany's unification. Their ambivalence was in a certain sense reciprocated by Germany in its uncertainty about specific foreign policy priorities bearing on the East and in its vague but nonetheless real malaise concerning the new Germany's role in the world.

For Germany's eastern neighbors historical recollection obviously weighed heavily. So did an uneasy premonition that united Germany's size and strength might lead to the eventual recovery of its former regional domination. Poland in particular was anxious about the possibility of territorial revisionism and only too cognizant of revived national consciousness on the part of the tiny remnant of the Silesian German ethnic minority in and around Wroclaw (formerly Breslau).

390 • MELVIN CROAN

Warsaw sought iron-clad guarantees of the inviolability of the Oder-Neisse boundary, at one point in early 1990 going so far as to broach the possibility of latching on to the "two-plus-four" process so as to turn the "four" into "five," the better to enable Poland to look after its own vital interests. That having come to nothing, Warsaw was understandably perturbed when, thanks largely to petty domestic political calculations, Kohl for a time hesitated to offer the Poles the reassurance they craved. A definitive German-Polish border treaty was finally signed in November, 1990, but Polish nervousness about the border issue has become pronounced and may never completely subside.

At the same time, many influential East European voices were heard to endorse the restoration of Germany's national unity. During 1990 Polish foreign minister Krzysztof Skubiszewski echoed his Hungarian counterpart Gyula Horn in recognizing Germany's right to national self-determination, a right which the valiant Polish political thinker Adam Michnik eloquently argued could not be denied the Germans if it were effectively to be claimed by other nations. In a similar vein, President Václav Havel acknowledged in early 1990 that Czechs had committed past injustices against Germans in connection with the forcible expulsion of the Sudeten Germans at the end of World War II. Although Havel's remarkable speech did not necessarily go down well with all segments of Czechoslovak public opinion, his conciliatory gesture was indicative of new attitudes throughout Eastern Europe.

Although the resurrection of a united Germany may have served to revive disagreeable historical memories and perhaps also to generate fresh political anxieties on the part of its eastern neighbors, the ex-communist countries clearly recognized their need for major outside assistance and substantial foreign investment during their transition to a market economy. Not surprisingly, they looked to Germany as the most promising source of such support. For its part, Germany proclaimed its desire to help, and in 1990 the Federal Republic provided state guarantees for German commercial loans to Poland and Hungary totaling nearly one billion DM. (In 1990 Chancellor Kohl told Hungarian leaders that Germany owed a special debt of gratitude to Hungary for having opened its borders the previous year; there was no reason to question either the chancellor's sincerity or the likelihood that it would lead to further financial generosity.)

Yet while a number of individual economic ventures were begun (e.g., the collaborative German-Czech venture involving Volkswagen and Skoda) and general German goodwill toward all the Eastern

European countries in the quest for the marketization of their economies was never in serious doubt, Germany's immediate ability to sustain a serious long-range policy of economic assistance was an entirely different matter. For the time being it appeared that Eastern Europe would have to fall in line behind other, larger, and more immediately pressing German financial commitments—to the Soviet Union to pay off the full (and still rising) price of unification and to the ex-GDR to counter rampant socioeconomic dislocation and repair the infrastructural and ecological devastation wrought by decades of communist neglect and mismanagement. Estimates of the total cost of setting things right in eastern Germany keep rising; even if the final amount falls short of the figure of one trillion DM over the next decade, now being bruited about, the total cost is certain to be astronomical.

Not only was the absorption of the GDR a matter of economic cost, it also entailed political and moral stakes. The issue of whether and how to bring individual members of East Germany's former communist leadership to justice on charges of corruption and criminal abuse of power remained to be resolved. After unification, Harry Tisch, the last boss of the official East German trade union organization, was put on trial. Honecker himself, though gravely ill, was subject to indictment, but he was put beyond the ready reach of the law thanks to the sanctuary afforded by his confinement in a Soviet military hospital. The question of what to do with the once ubiquitous Stasi, which continued to lead a shadowy afterlife, and with the East German secret police lists of agents and informers continued to be hotly debated. The debate itself repeatedly claimed new victims from among the ranking personages of the ex-GDR's freshly revived political life. Thus in December 1990 allegations that he had once served as a Stasi informer prompted de Meziere to resign his posts as a member of Kohl's cabinet and vice chairman of the national CDU. Another related controversy erupted as the result of uncovering apparently major financial irregularities involving the PDS's considerable wealth and extensive property holdings, which had been accumulated in the heyday of the communist dictatorship.

With respect to larger economic considerations, if Eastern European needs could not be readily met by united Germany, neither could they be entirely neglected. At the beginning of the 1990s no specter alarmed both policymakers and the general public more than that of massive immigration into Germany from a poverty-stricken East. Whether Germany could utilize its leverage within the European Community (EC) to obviate the danger remained open to doubt. That very query served also to raise the question of whether Germany would champion the "deepening" of the EC (i.e., the further integration among the present Western European members projected for 1992) or else endorse a "broadening" of the community (i.e., throwing it open to membership—or, at a minimum, associate membership—to the Eastern European states). It also conjured up other related vexatious issues such as the propriety of opening up the Federal Republic to visa-free access. This, in turn, touched an exposed raw nerve: the prevalence of antiforeign (and particularly anti-Polish) sentiments in Germany (and especially in the ex-GDR).

At bottom, then, united Germany confronted the perennial question of German national identity.[20] Basic concerns of identity confounded a thousand practical issues; e.g., whether to move the seat of German government to Berlin, united Germany's official capital, or keep it in Bonn. But could Germany afford to agonize afresh about its identity, and did it really need to do so? At the beginning of the 1990s leading German statesmen of a variety of political hues thought not. For them, the frequently reiterated goal of a "Europeanized Germany" was much more than mere rhetoric; it implied wholly new perspectives on power and wealth.

Over the longer term, if not necessarily in the short run, Germany seems destined to retain the enviable status of an economic powerhouse. It is sometimes suggested that international economic prowess constitutes a sublimation of the expansionist political drive or even its continuation by other means. If so, then vive la difference, for in that instance the future of Germany's role in Eastern Europe would surely prove to be much more constructive than it has been earlier in the course of this much tormented century.

NOTES

1. Walter Z. Laqueur, *Russia and Germany* (Boston: Little Brown, 1965), 13.

2. Hugh Seton-Watson, *Eastern Europe Between the Wars, 1918–1941* (New York: Harper Torchbook, 1967), 382.

3. Cf. Karl D. Bracher, *The German Dictatorship: The Origins, Structure, and Effects of National Socialism* (New York: Praeger, 1970).

4. Milovan Djilas, *Conversations with Stalin* (New York: Harcourt Brace, 1962), 153.

5. Ibid., 114.

6. Cf. the discussion in Adam B. Ulam, *Expansion and Coexistence,* 2d ed. (New York: Praeger, 1974), 661 ff.

7. See Joachim Nawrocki, *Das geplante Wunder* (Hamburg: Wegner, 1967) and Fritz Schenk, *Das rote Wirschaftswunder* (Stuttgart: Seewald, 1969).

8. For the source of these calculations, see Melvin Croan, "East Germany," in Adam Bromke and Teresa Rakowska-Harmstone, eds., *The Communist States in Disarray, 1965–1971* (Minneapolis: University of Minnesota Press, 1972).

9. Peter C. Ludz, *The Changing Party Elite in East Germany* (Cambridge: MIT Press, 1972).

10. Carola Stern, *Ulbricht: Eine politsche Biographie* (Cologne: Verlag für Politik und Wirtschaft, 1963).

11. Melvin Croan, *East Germany: The Soviet Connection* (Beverly Hills and London: Sage, 1976), 36.

12. Ibid., 44–52.

13. For a discussion of the process of conversion, see A. James McAdams, *East Germany and Détente* (New York: Cambridge University Press, 1985).

14. For a collection of relevant materials, see *East Berlin and Moscow: The Documentation of a Dispute,* compiled and introduced by Ronald D. Asmus, RFE Occasional Papers, no. 1 (Munich: Radio Free Europe, 1985).

15. For a discussion of the GDR and the high technology revolution, see William E. Griffith, "The German Democratic Republic," in William E. Griffith, ed., *Central and Eastern Europe: The Opening Curtain* (Boulder, Colo.: Westview, 1989), 316–17.

16. Rudolf Bahro, *Die Alernative: Zur Kritik des real existierenden Sozialismus* (Cologne and Frankfurt: Europäische Verlagsanstalt, 1977).

17. "Jedes Land wahlt seine Losung," *Der Stern* (Hamburg), April 9, 1987.

18. For a documentary collection of the East German secret police's truly remarkable situation reports for the period January–November 1989, see Armin Mitter and Stefan Wolle, eds., *Ich liebe euch doch alle!* (Berlin: Basis-Druck Verlagsgesellschaft, 1990).

19. A revealing picture of Honecker's total inability to come to terms with and even really to understand what happened to him and to the GDR in 1989–90 may be found in Reinhold Andert and Wolfgang Herzberg, *Der Sturz: Eric W. Honecker im Kreuzverhör* (Berlin and Weimar: Aufbau Verlag, 1990). See also the discussion in Joachim Nawrocki, "Ein langes Leben mit der Luge," *Die Zeit* (North American edition), January 11, 1991, and the pointed if obviously self-serving open letter to Honecker by Egon Krenz, "Die Karre steckt tief im Dreck," *Der Spiegel,* February 4, 1991.

20. For a stimulating recent treatment of the general issue stressing, perhaps excessively, the economic aspects, see Harold James, *A German Identity, 1770–1990* (New York: Routledge, 1989).

10 By Way of a Conclusion: Controlled and Uncontrolled Change in Eastern Europe

Iván Völgyes

The crumbling of communism was the biggest single newsmaker in 1988–89. Although the process appears to be an ongoing event that signals the end of communism everywhere on the globe, the concentration of change in Eastern Europe has made the most dramatic headlines of the decade. Indeed, it is astounding to contemplate the end of communism as a global ideological and political phenomenon, as the end of the Soviet empire in Europe, and as the disintegration of the Soviet communist empire within the USSR.

To diagnose the change and to observe its symptoms have been relatively easy tasks. The images of change appeared as powerful symbols on television screens across the globe; Walesa's raised "V," Dubček's hug to the people of Prague, the segment of the horrid Berlin Wall lifted out of the Brandenburg Gate, the candlelight ceremony in Budapest, Mladenov's abrupt announcement of the end of the Zhivkov era, and, finally, the bullet-riddled bodies of the Ceauşescus that signaled the mercifully quick termination of a reign that can best be compared to Hitler's in domestic brutality.

It all came easily in the region, far more easily than anyone would have guessed. And it occurred—with the exception of Romania—without bloodshed, without violence. Because it was so easy and so peaceful one can pointedly ask whether it could have been predicted or, alternatively, why it was not predicted by the august forecasters.

In Eastern Europe the communist political structure created and delimited only four types of political actors: (1) individuals; (2) institutions, or institutionalized groups; (3) organs of internal state power; and (4) organs of external—read, largely Soviet—coercive force. Controlled changes, or controlling change, therefore, presupposed the presence, ability, and willingness of any of these actors to act on behalf of a cause or policy. In the absence of these actors, or in the absence of their ability or willingness to act, change becomes uncontrolled.

The interesting point in Eastern Europe is that, in spite of the similarity of communist structures and socialization processes in the region during the last four-plus decades, in each of the states we examine, the actors all appear to be different, all appear to act differently, and all appear to have acted uncharacteristically without any plan with regard to controlling the processes of change. If we examine each of these states separately, the diversity becomes even sharper.

From the very beginning of the process Poland was blessed with an individual and an organization that could become the focus of change. Lech Walesa's charisma rested on the man's innate sincerity, and on his untainted image made all the more apparent because it contrasted favorably with the constant and openly acknowledged abuses of privilege detailed daily in the relatively open press. His leadership was not organizational, but inspirational and exemplary. Contrasted with Jaruzelski—the image of a dour, stern, unsmiling communist general, wearing the ever-present sunglasses—Walesa's image was populist and popular; one of us versus one of them.

Moreover, Solidarity was a real organization even underground, even in its embryonic existence. It had a nationwide network, local organizations, committed cadres who were willing to take up the cause the minute one of its members was arrested or disappeared from the scene. The parallel state that grew up along with the communist party state in Poland—parallel economy, parallel unions, parallel public information systems, and even parallel political leadership—was a guarantee that political change would mean a transfer of power from existing forms of state power to already extant organizational networks, either replacing the previous structures or supplanting and infusing them with new, radically different content.

State and external power in Poland did little to control developments; state power—as almost everywhere in the region—simply disappeared as a coercive force. At the same time, the external force (i.e., the Soviet Union) cooperated handsomely with the process of change by dealing with the issues that came to the fore as contentious problems without regard to their political context. Katyn, for example, was not dealt with as a state-to-state problem or an insult to the Soviet Union but rather as a dispute over a historical occurrence.

Consequently, Walesa and Solidarity as well as Gorbachev and company were able to exercise some control over the process of change. Jaruzelski and the communist leadership were left alone to deal with the disintegration of communist power. It was a task he could not accomplish. Yet by allowing the relegation of communist structures to the processes of "democratization" and accepting that "historical inevitablity," Jaruzelski may have made the greatest contribution to change in Eastern Europe.

In Hungary, the processes of change occurred totally differently. Here the attack on communism as a system came first from among the ranks of communist reformers themselves and from among the ranks of the few courageous, liberal dissidents. The role of Imre Pozsgay in the democratization of Hungary may have, indeed, diminished and time passed him by. The fact, however, is that Pozsgay and his circle were extremely influential in undermining the power of Kádár and his successors. And though the reform communists later could not become reformed enough to capture any real power, they were instrumental in creating the basis for a challenge to authority in the system.

Unlike Poland, institutional bases did not exist for a challenge to the system in Hungary. Nor were there institutions that could control change. Not even the local state security organs were unified as to the purpose and goals of the new administrative setup. The existence of parallel society and publicity—once again, unlike in Poland—did not assist in creating a parallel institutional state structure that could transform the state via the institutional route. The creation of parties that proceeded in Poland both by suffusing new directions into existing parties and by the transformation of a trade union into political power did not take place in Hungary. Here, the political parties grew out of a power vacuum that occurred as the Communist party disintegrated. As a result, most of the splintered Hungarian parties that emerged all lacked coherence or identity. They were still catch-all parties, collections of interests and visions, distinguishable only slightly from several other quite similar parties, organizations, or groups. These collective parties were not strong enough to control change. At best, they could influence it by the joint pressure of simply pushing for more power or simply a say-so in the future of Hungary.

Interestingly, state power emerged in Hungary as the greatest influence in controlling change. Prime Minister Németh and his government became experts at negotiating with their emerging challengers but by doing so undermined the "leading position" of the Communist party in the name of which they were supposed to rule. The Socialist party—the former communist holders of power—only bought time for itself to allow its largely peaceful divestiture from power. It attempted to secure a breathing space for most of its elite to fit in with the new Hungarian social structure. Yet its leaders had no idea of their own future when they began negotiations with their successors. In this sense, change was controlled by both a government representing a state power in search of a way out of the morass and an opposition that became more convinced daily that the days of communism were numbered.

The role of external force in controlling change also appears to have been the same as that played by the USSR in Poland. Gorbachev's decision to give up the external empire in Eastern Europe if only a decent, just, and acceptable way could be found, paved the way for success in changing to a different political system. Did Gorbachev then play an active role in Hungary, Poland, or even Czechoslovakia by signaling that a decisive but nonviolent system change would not threaten Soviet political interests? The term *active* may be too strong, but not entirely imprecise. The recognition that change was inevitable and that it would be better to give it a Soviet blessing was a considered policy even if it was born of necessity. The entire process of external controls of change appears in retrospect either to have been a deliberate gamble taken in order to achieve a benevolently neutral Eastern Europe or the inability and unwillingness of the Soviet leaders to deploy even the minimum necessary force required to maintain their empire. In the case of most Eastern European states— but especially with regard to Poland and Hungary—the costs of the second option appear to have been too high to contemplate. Consequently, the Soviet policy of disengagement from the region was a deliberate undertaking, intended to force change in the direction the Soviet leaders hoped it would go. They were not to be blamed that events soon transgressed the limits imagined by the Soviet elite.

In Czechoslovakia change appears to have come—at least partially— as a result of the recognition by the Czechoslovak political elite in opposition that the policies acceptable to, or even supported by, the Soviet Union were opposed to the domestic power holders' conception of style and substance of rule and vice versa. In contrast to Poland and Hungary, Czechoslovak elites initially appeared to be confident and were willing to employ force in order to keep communist rule. Yet the deployment of force against the students massed on Wenceslas Square backfired immediately when the people realized that the Soviet tanks that crushed their quest for freedom twenty-one years before were not going to roll against them. Did anybody tell them that that would be the case? Clearly not, but the simple truth is that they *knew* that the emperor had no clothes. The Czechs intrinsically, viscerally knew it in Prague, and the Germans knew it in Leipzig. The hesitation of the power elites, uncertain of Soviet support and fearful for their own future should Soviet support not come, acted as catalysts.

The men who came to power in Prague were hardened dreamers. Dubček's cherubic smile promised love, but Havel's determination to root out evil showed a moral force beyond love. Controlling change came easily at first; the intoxication of freedom pressured the institutions to accelerate the process of return to multiparty democracy. In the absence of external force—indeed, by its tacit support—internal force could not be used to control events. Havel was a man whom all could respect. His culture, his background, his style, his courage all contrasted favorably with everything the Czechoslovak communist regimes and their representatives stood for; Havel took charge and led the process of change, but he was smart enough to know that real change would be meaningful only if the institutions of democracy— parties, representation, normalized rotation—could be implanted and implanted quickly. Unlike elsewhere in the region, it was therefore with great alacrity that the suddenly unshackled Czechs and Slovaks began deliberately building institutions intended to control change.

The crumbling of power in the German Democratic Republic followed the same route. The sense, the conviction that Honecker and his followers no longer had Soviet tanks at their call, emboldened Germans to seek their own destiny and end a regime they all abhorred. The "Prussians," the "law-abiding Saxons" who believed their propaganda for forty years, changed practically overnight into Germans, pure and simple. Communism proved to be an even more hollow shell there than elsewhere as evidenced by the rapidity of change, which was strengthened by the eagerness to become part of a unified Germany.

Change in East Germany had to be controlled by both local institutions and individuals who were at the helm. Soviet power would not be utilized on the streets of Berlin, but would it be utilized in the defense of the Wall, or against American or West German troops? Nobody knew, and not even Gorbachev had the answer at the time. Thus the drama of crumbling communist power took place in the absence of any information as to the limit of Soviet tolerance. Yet, as the Soviets began to backtrack on all its threats, at first "definitely prohibiting" one thing, then allowing precisely the impossible to take place, the process accelerated. The Wall that was to be opened, but was to remain, suddenly disappeared. The leading role of the party that had to remain for eternity, suddenly was no longer important at all; all these were signs that no one in Moscow or East Berlin knew anything for sure anymore. Except for one thing: everyone sensed that the Soviets were going home if a way could be found of slowing down the process to avoid humiliating the USSR beyond its limits of endurance.

In the absence of individuals who could control the change and without institutions that could control the process as the once dreaded state power melted away in front of the eyes of people glued to TV sets watching the Stasi offices burn, the only force for controlling change had been external: the delicate minuet between Shevardnadze and Genscher, bowing as Kohl and Gorbachev glided across the slippery floor of diplomacy. It was this quadrille that controlled events, and most frequently it was the pressure from the Germans that seemed to dictate the direction. The Soviet duo shyly acquiesced. Surprisingly, Genscher was no longer the softy, the accommodationist. Realizing how fragile Soviet power really was, he now pushed relentlessly for greater speed toward German unification; hence, the rapid demise of the GDR as a separate entity within the Soviet orbit. He knew that only by the use of extreme military force would the USSR be able to stop the process and that the USSR, in fact, had enough trouble maintaining its domestic empire, let alone its external one.

Bulgaria has presented us with still another example, though no one knows how long that pattern will hold. Here, as in Hungary in May 1988, an *apparat* coup brought Peter Mladenov and the reform communists to power. Unlike in Hungary, however, masses of people began to push for change and the party began to retreat. Their dream ("We the reformers can save the country, communism, and ourselves") never really had any basis in reality. The Bulgarian communists were just as wrong in this assumption as was a Grosz or a Gysi.

The *people* already knew while the communist elites did not recognize it then, just as they do not realize it today. For even if the Communist party succeeded in creating a successor single-party system, its legitimacy would be just as precarious as those of the Mladenovs who have already disappeared from the stage of popular Bulgarian history.

At first glance, the case of Romania appears to be unique. The Stalinist power of the Ceauşescu gang was not backed by Soviet but by Romanian tanks, Romanian thugs, North Korean-trained Secus, and hapless cadres of the clan's own choosing. The process of change here was spontaneous. People suddenly had had enough. Romania did not explode; it imploded and took the house down with it. The collapse of authority was nearly total, with the bloodshed, the destruction clearly reminiscent of Hungary in 1956—without the presence of Soviet troops or, for that matter, of any external force. It was spontaneous also in the sense that it was not led by a Havel or a Walesa, by a Solidarity, or Free Democrats, by communist reformers or Jaruzelskis in national garb. If uncontrolled change took place anywhere, it was in Romania. It proved to be the maverick in the region once again. Sadly, it occurred and is still continuing to take place at the expense of the people of Romania.

In retrospect, some generalizations may be warranted as we examine the region we call Eastern Europe. As we have witnessed remarkable changes, many observers ask, "Why were experts or specialists unable to predict events?" Rightly, we may be asked if our skills or perceptive abilities have been duped by entrenched thinking or lack of imagination, by lack of knowledge, or, worse, by acceptance of something we thought "inevitable."

I believe that the changes in the region were the result of two coterminous trends. First, there was the disintegration of the Soviets' two empires, domestic and external. Accepted as the only realistic option to the total collapse of Soviet communist power and to the stagnation of a system that has run its course, Gorbachev and his government designed a plan to give limited autonomy to the constituent units. Unaware that surrender begins with the simple act of concession, the Soviet leaders thought that decompression could be attained by limited reforms.

In Eastern Europe—and to some extent even in the constituent Soviet republics—power crumbled as soon as the populace realized that Soviet tanks would not be used to prop up the local elites or to maintain the overextended and badly failing Soviet system. The objects of pseudolegitimacy—the party leadership, the party leader or the regime—appeared to have been devalued with incredible alacrity. As a consequence, the whole system fell apart.

This analysis, however, has to note a second element—namely, that none of these systems ever had any real legitimacy at all. The population simply considered the whole communist system, its objects as well as its rituals and symbols, as having been imposed upon them by an alien power. When they had an opportunity to discard them, they did so with as much speed as possible.

The speed and the extent of change has varied from state to state, according to culture and state-specific forms. In some states organs of transference—trade unions, parties, national fronts—quickly took up the slack and filled the power vacuum with elementary organizations and institutions that could be combined with substance later. Elsewhere, change depended on the amount of open and demonstrable popular support expressed spontaneously by people who had little to lose and everything to gain.

Many of the traditional political terms utilized in past debates are no longer applicable in the region. There are two reasons for this. First, many of these terms have been devalued during the last four decades. *People, democracy, progress, social forces,* and so forth have become catchphrases, Orwellian constructs devoid of comprehensible meaning. Leaders using such terms today in a context of totalitarian agendas immediately put the people of the region on guard. It is for this reason that other terms—long out of use in their purer contexts—such as *fatherland, God,* or *ethical values,* have great attraction for the population.

A second reason the devalued terms are no longer very useful is that Eastern Europe today no longer resembles the straight-jacketed model the communists so fervently tried to make it during the last forty years. Terms such as *class* are no longer useful as descriptive or analytical categories; related terms, such as *the working class, the peasantry,* or *the intelligentsia,* are equally useless. In these societies the cleavage between the rich and the poor, the elites and the masses, the bureaucracies and the lobbies, describe today's realities far more adequately.

In such circumstances, change as it has continued after its generally uncontrolled first phase, began to be controlled by those very forces that supported the change. The forces that began to push for open change began to control the spin: Solidarity, the communist reformers in Hungary, Havel and the National Front for Salvation just as much as Modrow and Gysi. They all desperately wanted to avoid the type of instability that has wrenched Romania recently.

It is far too early to predict the future shape of the region. The optimistic scenario holds that these states will become democratic entities with multiparty electoral systems, with checks and balances, and with stable, mixed, but market economies that will take their rightful place in the house of Europe. Indeed, there is a good chance that this could be achieved by most of these countries.

A more somber and reflective scenario, however, raises cautionary flags in the face of some of the events that are taking place. In most of these countries economic transformation will result in tremendous hardship for the vast majority of the population. In such circumstances sloganizing, demagoguery, labeling others as enemies, and seeking culprits for the sins of the past will bring to the fore a fragmentation in political culture for which a united Europe will have no use. Similarly, national, religious, and ethnic grievances and hatreds will be used and misused as groups, institutions, and individuals seek legitimation of power they otherwise could not attain. For such states that use these devices, once again Europe will have no space.

Allow me to close with a *caveat* for the gentle *lector* of these remarks. All too frequently in the past many of us in our profession have made compromises with the communist regimes of the region. Some out of misplaced conviction, some out of ignorance, some out of personal greed or the desire for *the* interview with *the* person, some out of ambition, some out of a sense of national glory or a social quest, but most of us, including me, out of an acceptance of the "inevitable." There was no hope of removing the Soviets and communism, we thought, short of a third world war.

While we were all perhaps children of realpolitik and practitioners of compromise, I think that we were wrong in lowering our ethical standards and making the compromises we—willingly or unwillingly—made with these regimes. The ethical rectitude of an uncompromising anticommunist in years past may not have been politically correct or the most popular tack to take, for such people were regarded as fossils when the whole world appeared to accept communism as a legitimate force.

An electrician from Gdansk, a playwright from Prague, and a

clergyman from Temesvár showed us all that a system that treated people as subjects and not as citizens never really had any basis of legitimacy. While one hopes that the people who have always held the ethical high ground will prove noble enough to avoid drenching their magnificent revolutions in the blood of vengeance, the people of the region should be able to find the West willing to accept with open arms those who could transform themselves in such a brief period from subjects to citizens.

Bibliography

The bibliography presented in the following pages does not purport to be a comprehensive list of sources relating to the history of Eastern Europe. Instead it represents those sources the contributors to this collection have relied on most heavily.

Ádám, Magda. *Magyarország és a Kisántánt a harmincas években* (Hungary and the Little Entente in the 1930s). Budapest: Akadémiai Kiadó, 1968.
——, Gyula Juházs, Lajos Kerekes, eds. *Magyarország és a második világháború: Titkos diplomáciai iratok a háború előzményeihez és történetéhez* (Hungary and the Second World War: Secret Diplomatic Papers to the Antecedents and History of the War). Budapest: Akadémiai Kiadó, 1959.
Adony, Ferenc. *A magyar katona a második világháborúban* (The Hungarian Soldier in the Second World War). Klagenfurt, 1954.
Anderle, Josef. "The First Republic, 1918–1938." In Hans Brisch and Ivan Volgyes, eds. *Czechoslovakia: The Heritage of Ages Past.* New York: Columbia University Press, 1979.
Apponyi, Albert. *Justice for Hungary: Review and Criticism of the Treaty of Trianon.* London: Longmans Green, 1928.
Arndt, Claus. *Die Vertraege von Moskau und Warschau: Politische, verfassungsrechtliche, und voelkerrechtliche Aspekte.* 3d ed. Bonn: Verlag Neue Gesellschaft, 1982.
Ascherson, Neal. *The Polish August.* New York: Viking, 1983.
Avakumovic, Ivan. *History of the Communist Party of Yugoslavia.* Aberdeen: University of Aberdeen, 1964.
Banac, Ivo. *With Stalin Against Tito: Cominformist Split in Yugoslav Communism.* Ithaca: Cornell University Press, 1988.
Bárány, George. "Hungary: From Aristocratic to Proletarian Nationalism."

In Péter F. Sugar and Ivo Lederer, eds. *Nationalism in Eastern Europe* Seattle: University of Washington Press, 1969.

Bender, Peter. *Deutsche Parallelen: Anmerkungen zu einer gemeinsamen Geschichte zweier getrennter Staaten.* Berlin: Siedler, 1989.

——. *Neue Ostpolitik: Vom Mauerbau zum Moskauer Vertrag.* Munich: Deutscher taschenbuchverlag, 1986.

Benes, Vaclav L. "Czechoslovak Democracy and Its Problems." In Victor S. Mamatey and Radomir Luža, eds. *A History of the Czechoslovak Republic, 1918–1948.* Princeton: Princeton University Press, 1973.

Berend, I. T. and György Ránki. *Magyarország gyáripara a második világháború előtt és a háború időszakában* (The Industry of Hungary Before and During World War II). Budapest: Akadémiai Kiadó, 1958.

——. *Magyarország a fasiszta Németország életterében* (Hungary in the Sphere of Interest of Fascist Germany). Budapest: Kossuth, 1960.

Berg, Hermann von. *Die DDR auf dem Weg in das Jahr 2000: Politik, Oekonomie, Ideologie: Plaedover fuer eine demokratische Erneuerugn.* Cologne: Bund, 1987.

Bethell, Nicholas. *Gomulka: His Poland and His Communism.* Harmondsworth, England: Pelican, 1962.

Bethlen, István. *Beszédei és irásai* (Speeches and Writings). 3 vols. Budapest, 1933.

Blumenwitz, Dieter. *Partnerschaft mit dem Osten.* Munich: Lurz, 1976.

Bohley, Baerbel, et al. *Und die Buerger melden sich zu Wort: 40 Jahre DDR.* Frankfurt: Buechergilde Gutenberg, 1989.

Borbándi, Gy. Molnár J. *Tanulmányok a magyar forradalomról* (Studies About the Hungarian Revolution). Munich: Aurora 1966.

Borsody, Stephen. *The Tragedy of Central Europe.* New York: Collier, 1962.

Braham, Randolph. *The Destruction of Hungarian Jewry.* 3 vols. New York, 1964.

Brisch, Hans and Ivan Volgyes, eds. *Czechoslovakia: The Heritage of Ages Past.* New York: Columbia University Press, 1979.

Brock, Peter. *The Slovak National Awakening.* Toronto: University of Toronto Press, 1970.

—— and H. Gordon Skilling, eds. *The Czech Renascence of the Nineteenth Century.* Toronto: University of Toronto Press, 1970.

Bromberg, Abraham, ed. *Poland: Genesis of a Revolution.* New York: Random House, 1983.

Bromke, Adam. *Poland's Politics: Idealism vs. Realism.* Cambridge: Harvard University Press, 1967.

Broszat, Martin. "Deutschland-Ungarn-Romanien: Entwicklung und Grundfaktoren nazionalsozialistischen Hegemonial- und Bündnispolitik." *Historische Zeitschrift* (1968), 206:45–96.

Brown, J. F. *Bulgaria Under Communist Rule.* New York: 1970.

Brzezinski, Zbigniew K. *The Soviet Bloc: Unity and Conflict.* Cambridge: Harvard University Press, 1967.

Burks, Richard V. *The Dynamics of Communism in Eastern Europe.* Princeton: Princeton University Press, 1961.

Campbell, F. Gregory. *Confrontation in Central Europe: Weimar Germany and Czechoslovakia.* Chicago: University of Chicago Press, 1975.

Childs, David, ed. *Honecker's Germany.* London and Boston: Allen and Unwin, 1985.

Childs, David. *The GDR: Moscow's German Ally.* 2d ed. Boston: Unwin Hyman, 1988.

——, Thomas A. Baylis, and Marilyn Rueschmeyer, eds. *East Germany in Contemporary Perspective.* London and New York: Routledge, 1989.

Clemens, Clay. *Reluctant Realists: The Christian Democrats and West German Ostpolitik.* Durham: Duke University Press, 1989.

Connor, Walter D. "East European Dissent," *Problems of Communism* (Jan./Feb. 1980) 29:1–17.

Crampton, R. J. *Bulgaria, 1878–1918: A History.* Boulder, Colo.: Westview, 1983.

Croan, Melvin. *East Germany: The Soviet Connection.* Beverly Hills: Sage, 1976.

Csalog, Zsolt. *Doku 56 Öt portré a forradalomról* (Documents 1956: Five Portraits from the Revolution). Budapest: Unio, 1990.

Dálnoki-Veress, Lajos. *Magyarország honvédelme a második világháború előtt és alatt* (The Defense of Hungary Before and During World War II). 3 vols. Munich: Látóhatár, 1974.

Davies, Norman. *God's Playground—A History of Poland,* 2 vols. New York: Columbia University Press, 1982.

Deák, Francis. *Hungary at the Paris Peace Conference.* New York: Columbia University Press, 1942.

Dedijer, Vladimir. *The Battle Stalin Lost: Memoirs of Yugoslavia, 1948–1953.* New York: Viking, 1971.

Dellin, L. A. D., ed. *Bulgaria.* New York: 1957.

Djilas, Milovan. *The Unperfect Society.* London: Methuen, 1969.

——. *Tito: The Story from Inside.* New York: Harcourt Brace Jovanovich, 1980.

Dreisziger, Nándor. *Hungary's Way to World War II.* Astor Park, Fla.: Danubian, 1968.

Dyba, Karel. "Rust, strukturalni zmeny a otevrenost ekonomiky." *Politicka ekonomie* (1989), 37(5):559–69.

——. *Reforming the Czechoslovak Economy: Past Experience and Present Dilemmas.* 1989.

—— and Tomas Jezek. "Czechoslovak Experience with Central Planning." Paper presented for the Conference on Socioeconomic Development and Planning in Budapest, 1989.

Dzambo, Jozo. "Bibliographie," in *Bulgarien* (1990), 739–77.

Ehmke, Horst, Karlheinz Koppe, and Herbert Wehner, eds. *Zwanzig Jahre Ostpolitik: Bilanz und Perspektiven.* Bonn: Neue Gesellschaft, 1986.

Ekmecic, Milorad. *Stvaranje Jugoslavije 1790–1918.* 2 vols. Belgrade: Rpsveta, 1989.

Erdey, Sándor. *A recski tábor foglyai* (The Prisoners of the Concentration Camp at Recsk). Budapest: Reform Kiadó, 1989.

Fejtő, Ferenc. *A népi demokráciák története* (History of the People's Democracies). 3d ed. Budapest-Paris: Seuil, 1990).

Fejtő, Francois. *Behind the Rape of Hungary.* New York: McKay, 1957.

Fenyő, Mario D. *Hitler, Horthy, and Hungary German-Hungarian Relations, 1941–1944.* New Haven: Yale University Press, 1972.

Fiszman, Joseph. *Revolution and Tradition in People's Poland.* Princeton: Princeton University Press, 1972.

Free Europe Committee. *The Revolt in Hungary: A Documentary Chronology of Events.* New York, 1956.

Freeze, Karen J. "The Young Progressives: The Czech Student Movement, 1887–1897." Unpublished Ph.D. Dissertation, Columbia University, 1974.

Fricke, Karl Wilhelm. *Die DDR–Staatssicherheit: Entwicklung, Strukturen, Aktionsfelder.* 2d ed. Cologne: Verlag Wissenschaft und Politik, 1984.

——. *Opposition und Widerstand in der DDR: ein politischer Report.* Cologne: Verlag Wissenschaft und Politik, 1984.

Galántai, József. "Trianon és a reviziós propaganda" (Trianon and the Revisionist Propaganda). In Erzsébet Andics, ed., *A magyar nacionalizmus kialakulása és története* (History and Development of Hungarian Nationalism). Budapest: Kossuth, 1968.

Garton Ash, Timothy. *"Und willst du nicht mein Bruder sein . . .": die DDR heute.* Reinbek bei Hamburg: Rowohlt, 1981.

Garver, Bruce M. *The Young Czech Party, 1874–1901, and the Emergence of a Multi-Party System.* New Haven: Yale University Press, 1978.

Gitelman, Zvi. "Power and Authority in Eastern Europe." In Chalmers Johnson, ed. *Change in Communist Systems.* Stanford: Stanford University Press, 1970.

Glaessner, Gert-Joachim. *Die andere deutsche Republik: Gesellschaft und Politik in der DDR.* Opladen: Westdeutscher Verlag, 1989.

——. *Die DDR in der Aera Honecker.* Opladen: Westdeutscher Verlag, 1988.

Golan, Golia. *The Czechoslovak Reform Movement: Communism in Crisis, 1962–1968.* Cambridge: Cambridge University Press, 1971.

Gömbös, Gyula. *Egy magyar vezérkeri tiszt biráló feljegyzései a forradalomról és ellenforradalomról* (Notes of a Hungarian Staff Officer About the Revolution and Counterrevolution). Budapest: Budapesti Hirlap, 1920.

Gosztonyi, Péter. *A kormányzó, Horthy Miklós* (Nicholas Horthy, the Regent). Budapest: Téka Kiadó, 1990.

——. *Föltámadott a tenger . . . 1956* (The Sea Has Risen . . . 1956). Budapest: Népszava Kiadó, 1990.

Griffith, William E. *The Ostpolitik of the Federal Republic of Germany.* Cambridge: MIT Press, 1978.

Grothusen, Klaus-Detler, ed. *Jugoslawien*. Sudosteuropa-Handbuch, Bd. 1. Gottingen: Vandenhoeck & Ruprecht, 1975.

——. *Bulgarien*. Gottingen: Vandenhoeck & Ruprecht, 1990.

Hahn, Walter F. *Between Westpolitik and Ostpolitik: Changing West German Security Views*. Beverly Hills: Sage, 1975.

Hajdú, Tibor. *Az 1918-as magyarországi polgári forradalom* (The Bourgeois Revolution of 1918 in Hungary). Budapest: Kossuth, 1968.

Hamsik, Dusan. *Writers Against Rulers*. New York: Random House, 1971.

Heinrich, Rolf. *Der vormundschaftliche Staat: vom Versagen des real existierenden Sozialismus*. Reinbek bei Hamburg: Rowohlt, 1989.

Heitlinger, Alena. *Women and State Socialism: Sex Inequality in the Soviet Union and Czechoslovakia*. Montreal: McGill–Queen's University Press, 1979.

Hodnett, Gray and P. J. Potichnyj. *The Ukraine and the Czechoslovak Crisis*. Camberra: Australian National University, 1970.

Hoensch, Jorg K. "The Slovak Republic, 1939–1945." In Victor S. Mamatey and Radomir Luža, eds. *A History of the Czechoslovak Republic, 1918–1948*. Princeton: Princeton University Press, 1973.

Hopter, J. B. *Yugoslavia in Crisis, 1934–1941*. New York: Columbia University Press, 1962.

Horthy, Miklós. *Titkos iratai* (Sector Papers). Budapest: Kossuth, 1965.

Horthy, Nicholas. *Memoires*. New York: Speller, 1957.

Horváth, Jenő. *Az országgyarapitás története* (History of the Rebuilding of the Country). Budapest: Magyar Külügyi Társaság, 1941.

Ignotus, Paul. *Hungary*. New York: Praeger, 1972.

Information Bulgaria: A Short Encyclopedia of the People's Republic of Bulgaria. Oxford: Oxford University Press, 1985.

James, Harold. *A German Identity, 1770–1990*. New York: Routledge, 1989.

Jancar, Barbara Wolfe. *Czechoslovakia and the Absolute Monarchy of Power: A Study of Political Power in a Communist System*. New York: Praeger, 1971.

Janos, Andrew. "The One-Party State and Social Mobilization: East Europe Between the Wars." In Samuel P. Huntington and Clement Moore, eds. *Authoritarian Politics in Modern Society*. New York: Basic Books, 1979.

Jelinek, Yeshayahu. *The Parish Republic: Hlinka's Slovak People's Party*. Boulder, Colo.: East European Monographs (distributed by Columbia University Press, New York), 1976.

——. *The Lust for Power: Nationalism, Slovakia, and the Communists, 1918–1948*. Boulder, Colo.: East European Monographs (distributed by Columbia University Press, New York), 1983.

Johnson, Owen V. *Slovakia, 1918–1938: Education and the Making of a Nation*. New York: Columbia University Press, 1985.

Josko, Anna. "The Slovak Resistance Movement." In Victor S. Mamatey and Radomir Luža, eds. *A History of the Czechoslovak Republic, 1918–1948*, 362–86. Princeton: Princeton University Press, 1973.

Juhász, Gyula. *Magyarország külpolitikája, 1919–1945* (Hungary Foreign Policy, 1919–1945). Budapest: Kossuth, 1975.

——. *A teleki kormány külpolitikája, 1939–1941* (The Foreign Policy of the Teleki Government, 1939–1941). Budapest: Akadémiai Kiadó, 1964.

Jungerth-Arnóthy, Mihály. *Moszkvai napló* (Moscow Diary). Budapest: Zrinyi, 1989.

Kállay, Nicholas. *Hungarian Premier.* New York: Columbia University Press, 1954.

Kanet, Roger E. and Maurice D. Simon, eds. *Background to Crisis: Policy and Politics in Gierek's Poland.* Boulder, Colo.: Westview, 1981.

Keithly, David M. *Breakthrough in the Ostpolitik: The 1971 Quadripartite Agreement.* Boulder, Colo.: Westview, 1986.

Kerekes, Lajos. *Allianz Hitler, Horthy, Mussolini.* Budapest: Akadémiai, 1965.

Kerner, Robert J. *Czechoslovakia.* Berkeley: University of California Press, 1949.

Kertész, Stephen D. *Diplomacy in a Whirlpool: Hungary Between Nazi Germany and Soviet Russia.* South Bend, Ind.: Notre Dame University Press, 1953.

——. *Between Russia and the West: Hungary and the Illusions of Peace Making.* (South Bend, Ind.: Notre Dame University Press, 1984.

Knabe, Hubertus, ed. *Aufbruch in eine andere DDR: Reformer und Oppositionelle zur Zukunft ihres Landes.* Reinbek bei Hamburg: Rowohlt, 1990.

Konrád, György and Iván Szelényi. *Az értelmiség útja az osztályhatalomhoz* (The Road of the Intelligentsia to Class Rule). Budapest: Gondolat, 1989.

Korbel, Josef. *The Communist Subversion of Czechoslovakia, 1938–1948: The Failure of Coexistence.* Princeton: Princeton University Press, 1959.

——. *Twentieth-Century Czechoslovakia: The Meanings of Its History.* New York: Columbia University Press, 1977.

Korbonski, Andrzej. "Bureaucracy and Interest Groups in Communist Societies: The Case of Czechoslovakia." *Studies in Comparative Communism* (January 1971), 4(1):57–79.

Košicky vládni program. Prague: Nakladatelstvi svoboda, 1974.

Krish, Henry. *The German Democratic Republic: The Search for Identity.* Boulder, Colo.: Westview, 1985.

Kroh, Ferdinand, ed. *Freiheit ist immer die Freiheit—die Andersdeneknden in der DDR.* Frankfurt: Ullstein, 1988.

Kulcsár, Kálmán. *A mai magyar társadalom* (Hungarian Society Today). Budapest: Kossuth, 1982.

Kulski, Wladislaw W. *Germany and Poland: From War to Peaceful Relations.* Syracuse: Syracuse University Press, 1976.

Kusin, Vladimir V. *The Intellectual Origins of the Prague Spring: The Development of Reformist Ideas in Czechoslovakia, 1956–1967.* Cambridge: Cambridge University Press, 1971.

——. *Political Grouping in the Czechoslovak Reform Movement.* New York: Columbia University Press, 1972.

——. "Husak's Czechoslovakia and Economic Stagnation." *Problems of Communism* (May/June 1982 [b]), 31:24–37.

Lackó, Miklós. *Nyilasok, nemzetiszolcialisták* (Arrow Cross Men, National Socialists). Budapest: Kossuth, 1966.

Lajtos, Árpád. *Emlékezés a második magyar hadseregre, 1942–1943* (Remembrances about the Second Hungarian Army, 1942–1943). Budapest: Zrinyi, 1989.

Lane, David and George Kolankiewicz, eds. *Social Groups in Polish Society*. New York: Columbia University Press, 1973.

Lederer, Ivo. *Yugoslavia at the Paris Peace Conference: A Study in Frontier Making*. New Haven: Yale University Press, 1963.

Leff, Carol Skalník. *National Conflict in Czechoslovakia: The Making and Remaking of a State, 1918–1987*. Princeton: Princeton University Press, 1988.

Lewis, Paul G. *Political Authority and Party Secretaries in Poland, 1975–1986*. Cambridge: Cambridge University Press, 1989.

Loebl, Eugen. *My Mind on Trial*. New York: Harcourt Brace Jovanovich, 1976.

Ludz, Peter Christian. *The Changing Party Elite in East Germany*. Cambridge: MIT Press, 1972.

——. *Die DDR zwischen Ost und West: Politische Analysen 1961–1976*. Munich: Beck, 1977.

Luža, Radomir. *The Transfer of the Sudeten Germans: A Study of Czech-German Relations, 1933–1962*. New York: New York University Press, 1964.

——. "Czechoslovakia Between Democracy and Communism." In Victor S. Mamatey and Radomir Luža, eds. *A History of the Czechoslovak Republic, 1918–1948*. Princeton: Princeton University Press, 1973.

Macartney, C. A. *Hungary and Her Successors: The Treaty of Trianon and Its Consequences, 1919–1937*. London: Oxford University Press, 1937.

——. *October 15: A History of Modern Hungary*. 2 vols., 2d ed. Edinburgh: Edinburgh University Press, 1961.

Mamatey, Victor S. "The Birth of Czechoslovakia: Union of Two Peoples." In Hans Brisch and Ivan Volgyes, eds. *Czechoslovakia, The Heritage of Ages Past: Essays in Memory of Josef Korbel*. New York: Columbia University Press, 1979.

——. "The Development of the Czechoslovak Democracy." In Victor S. Mamatey and Radomir Luža, eds., *A History of the Czechoslovak Republic, 1918–1948*. Princeton: Princeton University Press, 1973a.

——. "The Establishment of the Republic." In Victory S. Mamatey and Radomir Luza, eds., *A History of the Czechoslovak Republic, 1918–1948*. Princeton: Princeton University Press, 1973b.

——. and Radomir Luža, eds. *A History of the Czechoslovak Republic, 1918–1948*. Princeton: Princeton University Press, 1973.

Mastny, Vojtech. *The Czechs Under Nazi Rule: The Failure of National Resistance*. New York: Columbia University Press, 1971.

McAdams, A. James. *East Germany and Détente: Building Authority After the Wall.* Cambridge: Cambridge University Press, 1985.

McCardle, Arthur W. and A. Bruce Boenau, eds. *East Germany: A New German Nation Under Socialism?* Lanham, Md.: University Press of America, 1983.

McCauley, Martin. *East Germany: The Dilemmas of Division.* London: Institute for the Study of Conflict, 1980.

——. *Power and Authority in East Germany: The Socialist Unity Party (SED).* London: Institute for the Study of Conflict, 1981.

——. *The German Democratic Republic Since 1945.* New York: St. Martin's Press, 1983.

McIntyre, Robert J. *Bulgaria: Politics, Economics, and Society.* London, 1988.

Milosz, Czeslaw. *The Captive Mind.* New York: Knopf, 1953.

Mitter, Armin and Stefan Wolle, eds. *Ich liebe euch doch alle!: Befehle und Lagerberichte des MfS Januar–November 1989.* Berlin: BasisDruck Verlagsgesellschaft, 1990.

Myant, Martin. *The Czechoslovak Economy, 1948–1988.* Cambridge: Cambridge University Press, 1989.

Nagy, Ferenc. *The Struggle Behind the Iron Curtain.* New York: Macmillan, 1948.

Nagy, Imre. *On Communism.* New York: Praeger, 1952.

Nagy, Zsuzsa L. *A budapesti liberális ellenzék, 1919–1945* (The Liberal Opposition in Budapest, 1919–1945). Budapest: Akadémiai Kiadó, 1975.

Nagybaconi-Nagy, Vilmos. *Végzetes esztendők, 1938–1945* (Fateful Years, 1938–1945). Budapest: Gondolat, 1986.

Nagy-Talavéra, Nicholas M. *Green Shirts and Others: A History of Fascism in Hungary and Romania.* Stanford: Hoover Institution Press, 1970.

Nawrocki, Joachim. *Die Beziehungen zwischen den beiden Staaten in Deutschland: Entwicklungen, Moeglichkeiten, und Grenzen.* Berlin: Holzapfel, 1986.

Olivova, Vera. *The Doomed Democracy: Czechoslovakia in a Disrupted Europe, 1914–1938.* London: Sidgwick and Jackson, 1972.

Oren, Nissan. *Revolution Administered: Agrarianism and Communism in Bulgaria.* Baltimore: 1973.

Orton, Lawrence D. *A Reader's Guide to Bulgaria.* Washington: 1989.

Pavlowitch, Stevan. *Yugoslavia.* New York: Praeger, 1971.

——. *The Improbable Survivor: Yugoslavia and Its Problems.* London: Hurst, 1988.

Pelikan, Jiri. *The Czechoslovak Political Trials, 1950–1954.* Stanford: Stanford University Press, 1971.

Perman, Dagmar. *The Shaping of the Czechoslovak State: A Diplomatic History of the Boundaries of Czechoslovakia, 1914–1920.* Leiden: Brill, 1962.

Piekalkiewicz, Jaroslav. *Public Opinion Polling in Czechoslovakia, 1968–*

1969: Results and Analysis of Surveys Conducted During the Dubcek Era. New York: Praeger, 1972.

Pollman, Bernhard. *Daten zur Geschichte der Deutschen Demokratischen Republik.* Duesseldorf: Econ, 1984.

Pryor, Zora P. "Czechoslovak Economic Development in the Interwar Period." In Victor S. Mamatey and Radomir Luža, eds. *A History of the Czechoslovak Republic, 1918–1948.* Princeton: Princeton University Press, 1973.

Pundeff, M. V. "Bulgarian Nationalism." In Peter F. Sugar and Ivo J. Lederer, eds. *Nationalism in Eastern Europe.* Seattle: 1969.

Ramet, Pedro. "Christianity and National Heritage Among the Czechs and Slovaks." In Pedro Ramet, ed., *Religion and Nationalism in Soviet and East European Politics.* 2d ed., 264–85. Durham: Duke University Press, 1989.

Ránki, György. *1944 március 19: Magyarország német megszállása* (March 19, 1944: The Occupation of Hungary by the Germans). Budapest: Kossuth, 1968.

——. *Emlékiratok és valóság Magyarország második világháborús szerepéről* (Memoirs and Truth About the Role of Hungary in the Second World War). Budapest: Kossuth, 1964.

Rein, Gerhard, ed. *Die Opposition in der DDR.* Berlin: Wichern-Verlag, 1989.

Roberts, Walter. *Tito, Mihailovich, and the Allies: 1941–1945.* New Brunswick: Rutgers University Press, 1973.

Rothschild, Joseph. *East Central Europe Between the Two World Wars.* Seattle: University of Washington Press, 1974.

——. *Ethnopolitics: A Conceptual Framework.* New York: Columbia University Press, 1981.

Rubinstein, Alvin. *Yugoslavia and the Non-Aligned World.* Princeton: Princeton University Press, 1970.

Ruehle, Juergen and Gunter Holzweissig, eds. *13 August 1961: Die Mauer von Berlin.* Cologne: Edition Deutschland Archiv, 1981.

Rusinow, Dennison. *The Yugoslav Experiment, 1948–1974.* Stanford: Stanford University Press, 1977.

Sakmyster, Thomas L. *Hungary, the Great Powers, and the Danubian Crisis: 1936–1939.* Athens: University of Georgia Press, 1980.

Scharf, C. Bradley. *Politics and Change in East Germany: An Evaluation of Socialist Democracy.* Boulder: Westview; London: Pinter, 1984.

Schmid, Gunther. *Entscheidung in Bonn: die Entstehung der Ostund Deutschlandpolitik, 1969–1970.* Cologne: Verlag Wissenschaft und Politik, 1979.

Schneider, Eberhard. *The G.D.R.: The History, Politics, Economy, and Society of East Germany.* London: Hurst, 1978.

Schulz, Eberhard et al. *Die SED in Geschichte und Gegenwart.* Cologne: Edition Deutschland Archiv, 1987.

Scott, Hilda. *Does Socialism Liberate Women?* Boston: Beacon Press, 1974.

Seton-Watson, Hugh. *The East European Revolution*. New York: Praeger, 1956.

Shoup, Paul. *Communism and the Yugoslav National Question*. New York: Columbia University Press.

Skilling, H. Gordon. *Czechoslovakia's Interrupted Revolution*. Princeton: Princeton University Press, 1976.

———. *Charter 77 and Human Rights in Czechoslovakia*. Boston: Allen and Unwin, 1981.

———. "Independent Currents in Czechoslovakia." *Problems of Communism* (Jan./Feb. 1985), 34:32–49.

Spittmann, Ilse and Karl W. Fricke, eds. *17 Juni 1953: Arbeiteraufstand in der DDR*, 2d expanded ed. Cologne: Edition Deutschland Archiv, 1988.

Stanford, Gregory. *From Hitler to Ulbricht: The Communist Reconstruction of East Germany, 1945–46*. Princeton: Princeton University Press, 1983.

Staritz, Dietrich. *Die Gruendung der DDR: von der Sowjetischen Besatzungszone zum sozialistischen Staat*. Munich: Deutscher Taschenbuchverlag, 1984.

———. *Geschichte der DDR, 1949–1985*. Frankfurt: Suhrkamp, 1985.

"Statní úřad statisticka." *Statistická ročenka Československa*. Prague: Orbis, 1937.

Stehle, Hansjakob. *The Independent Satellite*. New York: Praeger, 1965.

Steiner, Eugene. *The Slovak Dilemma*. London: Cambridge University Press, 1973.

Stent, Angela. *From Embargo to Ostpolitik: The Political Economy of West German–Soviet Relations, 1955–1980*. Cambridge: Cambridge University Press, 1981.

Stevens, John N. *Czechoslovakia at the Crossroads: The Economic Dilemmas of Communism in Postwar Czechoslovakia*. Boulder: East European Monographs (distributed by Columbia University Press, New York), 1985.

Suda, Zdenek. *Zealots and Rebels: A History of the Ruling Communist Party of Czechoslovakia*. Stanford: Hoover Institution Press, 1980.

Szczepanski, Jan. *Polish Society*. New York: Random House, 1964.

Szporluk, Roman. "Tragedy, Triumph, and Tragedy: Czechoslovakia, 1938–1948." In Hans Brisch and Iván Völgyes, eds., *Czechoslovakia, The Heritage of Ages Past: Essays in Memory of Josef Korbel*. New York: Columbia University Press, 1979.

———. *The Political Thought of Thomas G. Masaryk*. New York: Columbia University Press, 1981.

Szuhay, Miklós. *Az állami beavatkozás és a magyar mezőgazdaság az 1930-as években* (State Intervention and Hungarian Agriculture in the 1930s). Budapest: Akadémiai Kiadó, 1962.

Taborsky, Edward. *Communism in Czechoslovakia, 1948–1960*. Princeton: Princeton University Press, 1961.

Teichova, Alice. *The Czechoslovak Economy, 1918–1980*. London: Routledge, 1988.

Teleki, Éva. *Nyilas uralom Magyarországon, 1944 október 16–1945 április 4*

(Arrow Cross Rule in Hungary, October 16, 1944 to April 4, 1945). Budapest: Kossuth, 1973.

Teleki, Pál. *The Evolution of Hungary and Its Place in European History.* New York: Macmillan, 1923.

Thomson, Samuel Harrison. *Czechoslovakia in European History,* 2d ed. Princeton: Princeton University Press, 1953.

Tilford, Roger, ed. *The Ostpolitik and Political Change in Germany.* Farnborough, Hants: Saxon House; Lexington, Mass.: Lexington Books, 1975.

Tilkovszky, Lóránt. *Pál Teleki: A Biographical Sketch, 1879–1941.* Budapest: Akadémiai Kiadó, 1974.

Tóbiás, Áron. *Nagy Imre in Memoriam: Megemlékezés egy miniszterelnökre* (Imre Nagy: Remembrances About a Prime Minister). Budapest: Szabad Tér Kiadó, 1989.

Turner, Henry Ashby. *The Two Germanies Since 1945.* New Haven: Yale University Press, 1987.

Ulc, Otto. "The Normalization of Post-Invasion Czechoslovakia," *Survey* (1979), vol. 24, no. 3.

UNESCO. *Literacy Statistics from Available Census Figures.* Paris: Education Clearing House, 1950.

Valenta, Jiri. *Soviet Intervention in Czechoslovakia, 1968: Anatomy of a Decision.* Baltimore: Johns Hopkins University Press, 1979.

Venohr, Wolfgang. *Die Roten Preussen: Vom wundersamen Aufstieg der DDR in Deutschland.* Erlangen: Straube, 1989.

Viczián, Antal. *Meghaltak a Donnál: Sebészként a háborúban* (They Died at the Don River: A Surgeon in the War). Szombathely: published by the author, 1989.

Völgyes, Iván. *Hungary in Revolution, 1918–1919.* Lincoln: Nebraska University Press, 1971.

Wadekin, Karl-Eugen. *Agrarian Policies in Communist Europe: A Critical Introduction.* The Hague/London: Allanheld, Osmun, 1982.

Weber, Hermann, ed. *DDR Dokumente zur Geschichte der Deutschen Demokratischen Republik, 1945–1985.* Munich: Deutscher Taschenbuchverlag, 1986.

——. *Die DDR, 1945–1986.* Munich: Oldenbourgh, 1988.

——. *Kleine geschichte der DDR,* 2d expanded ed. Cologne: Edition Deutschland Archiv, 1988.

Whetten, Lawrence L. *Germany East and West: Conflicts, Collaboration, and Confrontation.* New York: New York University Press, 1980.

Wiskemann, Elizabeth. *Czechs and Germans: A Study of the Struggle in the Historic Provinces of Bohemia and Moravia.* London: Oxford University Press, 1938.

——. *Czechs and Germans.* London: Oxford University Press, 1938.

——. *Germany's Eastern Neighbors.* London: Oxford University Press, 1956.

Wolchik, Sharon L. "Politics, Ideology, and Equality: The Status of Women in Eastern Europe." Unpublished Ph.D. dissertation, University of Michigan, 1978.

——. "The Status of Women in a Socialist Order: Czechoslovakia, 1948–1978." *Slavic Review* (December 1979), 38(4):583–603.

——. "Eastern Europe." In Jane Lovenduski and Jill Hills, eds., *The Politics of the Second Electorate: Women and Public Participation*. London: Routledge and Kegan Paul, 1981.

——. "Elite Strategy Toward Women in Czechoslovakia: Liberation or Mobilization?" *Studies in Comparative Communism* (Summer/Autumn 1981), 14(2&3):123–42.

——. "Regional Inequalities in Czechoslovakia." In Daniel J. Nelson, ed., *Communism and the Politics of Inequalities*. Lexington, Mass.: Lexington Books, 1983.

——. "The Scientific-Technological Revolution and the Role of Specialist Elites in Policy-making in Czechoslovakia." In Michael J. Sodaro and Sharon L. Wolchik, eds., *Domestic Policy in Eastern Europe in the 1980s: Trends and Prospects*. New York: St. Martin's Press, 1983.

——. "The Precommunist Legacy, Economic Development, Social Transformation, and Women's Roles in Eastern Europe." In Sharon L. Wolchik and Alfred G. Meyer, eds., *Women, State, and Party in Eastern Europe*. Durham: Duke University Press, 1985.

——. "Economic Performance and Political Change in Czechoslovakia." In Charles J. Bukowski and Mark A. Cichock, eds., *Prospects for Change in Socialist Systems: Challenges and Responses*. New York: Praeger, 1987.

——. *Czechoslovakia in Transition: Politics, Economics, and Society in the Post-Communist Period*. London: Pinter, 1991.

Wolchik, Sharon L. and Jane Curry. *Specialists and Professionals in the Policy Process in Czechoslovakia and Poland*. Report for the National Council for Soviet and East European Research, 1984.

Zinner, Paul. *Communist Strategy and Tactics in Czechoslovakia, 1918–1948*. New York: Praeger, 1963.

Zsigmond, László et al., eds. *Diplomáciai iratok Magyarország külpolitikájához, 1936–1945* (Diplomatic Documents About Hungary's Foreign Policy, 1936–1945). 4 vols. Budapest: Akadémiai Kiadó, 1962–1965.

Contributors

Melvin Croan is Chair of Soviet and East European Studies and Professor of History at the University of Wisconsin at Madison.

Dimitrije Djordjevic is Professor of History at the University of California at Santa Barbara.

Stephen Fischer-Galati is Distinguished Professor Emeritus of History at the University of Colorado at Boulder.

Trond Gilberg is Professor of Political Science and Director of the Soviet and East European Studies Center at Pennsylvania State University.

Péter Hanák is Division Director of the Institute for History at the Hungarian Academy of Sciences and Professor of History at Ötvös Kóránt University in Budapest.

Joseph Held is Associate Dean of the Faculty of Arts and Sciences at Rutgers University.

Andrzej Korbonski is Professor of Political Science at the University of California at Los Angeles.

Nicholas Pano is Associate Dean of the Faculty and Professor of History at Western Illinois University.

Marin Pundeff is Professor of History at California State University at Northridge.

Iván Völgyes is Professor of Political Science at the University of Nebraska at Lincoln.

Sharon Wolchik is the Director of Russian and East European Studies and Professor of Political Science at George Washington University.

Index